D0906062

The Struggle for Arab Independence

This book is about the making of the modern Middle East. The region, as we know it today, was shaped in the violent and tumultuous years of the first half of the twentieth century, when Britain and France seized and dismembered the Arab provinces of the Ottoman Empire, after its defeat in the First World War. That is when the successor states of Turkey, Syria, Lebanon, Jordan, Iraq and Israel were created – and when Arab Palestine was destroyed. The roots of many of the conflicts and crises which afflict the region today can be traced back to this period of wars, high drama and the cavalier re-drawing of maps.

Patrick Seale, a leading historian of the region, tells the story through the life of Riad el-Solh, a Lebanese politician who grew into the outstanding Arab statesman of his time. Until his assassination in 1951, he was at the forefront of the events and struggles which laid the foundation of the region today. He wrested Lebanon's independence from France and became the first prime minister of the post-independence era, with its many challenges and tragedies.

This book is a *tour de force*. Based on British and French archives, and on numerous interviews, it pieces together the history of the Arab struggle for independence through the lives of those most directly involved. It is an invaluable resource for students and researchers, and of compelling interest to anyone who wants to know more about the Middle East.

PATRICK SEALE was born in Northern Ireland and educated at Balliol College and St Antony's College, Oxford. He worked for Reuters news agency for six years and then spent a dozen years on the staff of *The Observer* as Middle East correspondent, Paris correspondent, and roving correspondent in Africa and the Indian subcontinent. He currently writes weekly syndicated articles for several newspapers and runs a consultancy on Middle East affairs.

His books include *The Struggle for Syria* (1965, new edn 1986, with an introduction by Albert Hourani); *French Revolution 1968* (1968, with Maureen McConville); *Philby, The Long Road to Moscow* (1973, with Maureen McConville); *The Hilton Assignment* (1973, with Maureen McConville); *Asad of Syria, The Struggle for the Middle East* (1988, 1989, 1990); *Abu Nidal: A Gun for Hire* (1992, 1993). He helped HRH Prince General Khaled bin Sultan bin Abdulaziz write *Desert Warrior* (1995), the Prince's memoir of the 1991 Gulf War to liberate Kuwait, in which he served as Joint Forces Commander.

1 – Riad el-Solh aged about 30, with his father, Rida el-Solh, in Beirut or possibly Sidon, *c.*1924. (By kind permission of Madame Leila Hamadi el-Solh.)

THE STRUGGLE
FOR ARAB PATRICK
INDEPENDENCE SEALE

RIAD EL-SOLH AND THE MAKERS OF THE
MODERN MIDDLE EAST

CAMBRIDGE UNIVERSITY PRESS
Cambridge, New York, Melbourne, Madrid, Cape Town, Singapore,
São Paulo, Delhi

Cambridge University Press
The Edinburgh Building, Cambridge CB2 8RU, UK

Published in the United States of America by Cambridge University Press,
New York

www.cambridge.org
Information on this title: www.cambridge.org/9780521191371

First published 2010

Printed in the United Kingdom at the University Press, Cambridge

A catalogue record for this publication is available from the British Library

ISBN   978-0-521-19137-1 hardback

To the Memory of Alia El-Solh

CONTENTS

MAPS

FOREWORD

I have long been fascinated by the life of Riad el-Solh, a leading pan-Arab statesman and the first prime minister of independent Lebanon. So, when Alia, the eldest of his five daughters – and my friend for many years, ever since we met at Oxford in the 1950s – urged me to write a book about him, I did not hesitate for long. To my great shock, Alia died suddenly on 26 April 2007, before I had finished writing. She was the initial inspiration for this work, which I have dedicated, with affection and sadness, to her memory.

I have approached the task less as a formal academic history than as an account by someone who has lived in, and written about, the Middle East for half a century. I wanted to show what it was like for that first generation of Arab nationalists to struggle for Arab independence – painfully, often desperately, always against great odds, yet with resolve and grit – in the face of implacable Western ambitions.

I hope this book will help uncover the roots of the many conflicts and crises which afflict the region today. These roots can be traced to the first half of the twentieth century, a period of violence, wars, massacres, high drama and the cavalier redrawing of maps. This was when the Turkish Republic emerged from the ruins of the defeated and dismembered Ottoman Empire; when Anglo-French colonial Mandates were imposed on the Empire's Arab provinces; when new states were brought to birth – the Syrian and Lebanese republics, and the kingdoms of Iraq and Jordan; when an ancient Arab society, Palestine, was destroyed and its inhabitants ruthlessly scattered; and when the Jewish state, given shape by firm British patronage between the world wars, emerged at the heart of the region, trouncing weaker – or secretly compliant – neighbours.

Riad el-Solh was actively involved in the history of this period, a history now largely forgotten by the general public, even in the region itself. His life was one of unceasing political exertion from an early age. He was deeply implicated in the events, discussions and struggles which laid the foundations of the modern Middle East. To understand what he attempted to do and what he managed to achieve – as well as where he failed – is to understand a great deal about the intractable challenges which still face the area. He wrested Lebanon's independence from the French and can, I believe, for reasons I spell out in this work, be considered the outstanding Arab politician of his time.

Riad el-Solh had a vision of an independent, united and democratic Middle East, a vision to which he devoted his entire life. As such, he provides an inspiring model for today's generation, for whom unity, democracy and real independence are more than ever out of reach.

In writing this book, I have greatly benefited from the advice, friendship and scholarship of Ahmad Beydoun, Walid al-Khalidi, Gérard D. Khoury, Henry Laurens, Nadine Méouchy, Roger Owen, Elisabeth Picard, Nadine Picaudou, Avi Shlaim, Raghid el-Solh and Ghassan Tuéni. I should add that I am deeply grateful to my friend Wafic Said because, without his mediation, the project might never have been launched.

For information about Riad el-Solh's early life and family background, I have depended on accounts by members of the extended Solh family, as well as others who knew him well and were still alive when I was doing my research. The story could not be garnered from Arab records, as they largely do not exist, remain closed or have been wilfully destroyed. I have, therefore, had to rely heavily on Ottoman sources, on secondary ones, on interviews, as well as on British and French diplomatic documents, which proved invaluable in revealing what the Powers were up to at the time. I could not have managed this task without the help of Alan Rush. With extraordinary skill and dedication, he helped me to locate in official archives the hundreds of documents I needed. Mustafa Külü helped me find material about the Solhs in the Ottoman archives, while Fadi Chaker scoured the newspaper collection of the American University of Beirut for all relevant material. In France, I owe a debt of gratitude to Constance Arminjon, Inès-Leila Dakhli, Sümbül Kaya, Fayza al-Qasem and Orass Zibawi; and in Oxford, to Deborah Usher of the Middle East Centre Archive

Rana Kabbani shaped the entire book with her brilliant editorial pen and was my most astute if ruthless critic. I have had the amazing luck over the past twenty-five years to enjoy her companionship and her many aesthetic gifts, which have reminded me, on a daily basis, of the grand Ottoman world described in the early part of this book, of which she must surely be the last great *khanum*.

ATLANTIC
OCEAN

R. Rhine

R. Seine

R. Danube

R. Loire

R. Garonne

R. Rhône

Vienna

Buda ● Pest

TRANSYLVANIA

HUNGARY

Venice

Genoa

BOSNIA Belgrade

HERZEGOVINA SERBIA

Sofia

R. Ebro

CORSICA

Rome

MONTENEGRO RUM

ALBANIA MACE

SPAIN

R. Tagus

Barcelona

Naples

Salonica

THESSALY

SARDINIA

Lepanto

R. Guadalquivir

M e d i t e r r a n e a n

SICILY

Algiers

Tangier

Bougie

Tunis

MALTA

Fez

Tripoli

Ottoman lands 1359

Conquests 1359–1451

Conquests 1451–1520

Conquests 1520–1566

Conquests 1566–1683

Territories restored to Safavid control 1603

0   300   600   900   1200   1500   1800   2100   2400 km

0   300   600   900   1200   1500 miles

1 – The expansion of the Ottoman Empire

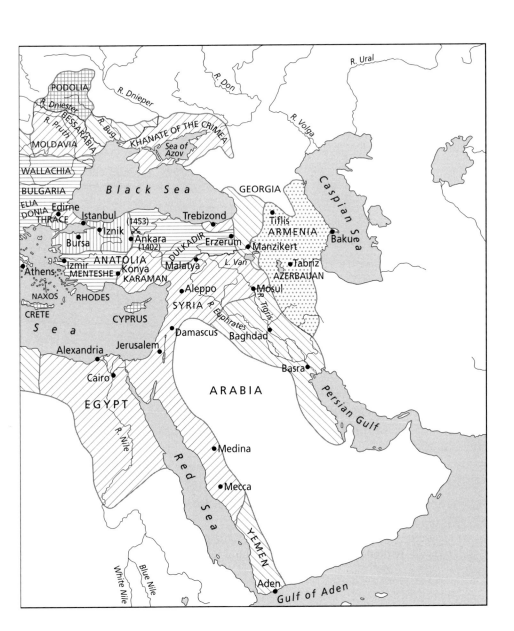

1 GRANDEE OF THE EMPIRE

The man who founded the Solh family's political fortunes – the ancestor who made them historically significant – was Ahmad Pasha, a nineteenth-century grandee of the Ottoman Empire. In Arabic, *sulh* means peacemaking, reconciliation, settlement. It seems probable that the Solhs acquired this name because of their role as peacemakers in a society where law courts were often lacking and the role of conciliator between conflicting parties was highly prized. Ahmad Pasha's grandfather was Khudr el-Solh, who, according to family lore, travelled to India in the eighteenth century to study alchemy. Although his quest for the philosopher's stone (meant to turn base metals into gold) was unsuccessful, it was early evidence of the family's adventurous spirit. Ahmad Pasha's father, Mahmud el-Solh, on the other hand, seems not to have left home at all, but lived the pleasantly quiet life of a landowning notable – until, that is, a quarrel with the local Ottoman governor landed him in jail. Wanting to save her son from the same wrath that had fallen on her husband, Mahmud el-Solh's wife decided to send the young Ahmad away to Istanbul.[1] There he learned Turkish and, on his return home some years later, was hired as a translator for the Ottoman army. Thus began his steady climb in the military and civilian bureaucracy of the Empire.

Ahmad was born in 1810 in Sidon, then the Mediterranean port of a mountainous hinterland, lying between the domains of the emirs of Mount Lebanon to the north and those of the Ottoman pashas of Sidon, Acre and Damascus to the south and east, and largely neglected by both. It was a poor, inward-looking rural society, dominated by

---

[1] Interview with Yusr el-Solh, Ahmad Pasha's granddaughter and last surviving grandchild, London, 10 January 2004.

landed families whose fortresses topped the peaks and controlled the approaches to the villages and estates that they owned, as well as to the caravan routes which wound their way from the coast to the interior. Like other leading families of South Lebanon – or Jabal 'Amil – the Solhs traced their origins to Arab tribes from the Yemen. Members of the Solh family believe that when their Andalusian forebears were expelled from Spain at the end of the fifteenth century, following the *Reconquista* of the Iberian Peninsula by the Catholic Kings, Isabella of Castile and Ferdinand of Aragon, these forebears planned to return to Yemen, from whence their distant ancestors had originally come. But they settled instead in Lebanon, on a hill in Sidon overlooking the Mediterranean. For generations after this, Solh houses were built, demolished and rebuilt on the same plot. The last of these is presently being restored as a museum to the memory of Riad el-Solh.

As Ahmad's ambitions grew, he moved to Beirut with his younger sibling, 'Abd al-Rahim. The latter entered the imperial Ottoman postal service, and worked in Damascus, Nablus, Jaffa, Beirut, Acre and Adana. In 1900 he served as director of posts and telegraphs in Kosovo.[2] Ahmad, on the other hand, started out as a soldier, fighting in many Ottoman wars, mainly in the Balkans, and rising to the rank of general. He later moved to the Ottoman civil administration, serving as *mutasarrif* or district governor of Acre, and later of Latakia. In this period of the 1880s, he was known as Ahmad Efendi.

In the last half of the nineteenth century, the Ottoman Empire was divided into some twenty-nine provinces (vilayet), each headed by a governor-general (vali), appointed by the Sublime Porte in Istanbul. Each vilayet was divided into a number of *sanjaq*, each headed by a *mutasarrif*, which in turn were subdivided into *cazas*, run by a *qa'im maqam*, or under-governor. Then came the *nahiye*, or groups of villages, headed by a director (*mudir*).

The Ottoman Empire was the most far-flung and pluralistic empire of its time. At the height of its fortunes in the sixteenth and

---

[2] For 'Abd al-Rahim el-Solh's career as recorded in the Ottoman archives, see BAO. SAIDd 71/93; 168/49; and BOA. DH. EUM 4şb 20/35; 6/17; and BOA. DH. EUM SSM 23/22. The Directorate of Ottoman Archives (*Başbakanlik Osmanli Arşivi*, or BOA) contains the Archives of the Ministry of Interior (*Dahiliye Nezareti*, or DH), which in turn are subdivided into *Sicill-i Avâl Idâresi Defteri* (SAID), subdivided again into a series of files or Defter (d). For an account of the SAID system, see Mehmet Ipşirli, 'The Sicill-i Ahvâl Commission and its Registers', in *Die Biographie in der Osmanischen Geschichte Quellen-Probleme-Methoden*, October 1993.

seventeenth centuries, *Pax Ottomanica* reigned over a vast area – from Algeria to Arabia, to Hungary and the Caucasus. But by the mid-nineteenth century, cracks had appeared in the five-hundred-year-old edifice. An early loss was the Tartar Khanate of Crimea, annexed by Russia in 1783. In the four decisive years from the Ottoman defeat by Russia in 1878 to the British occupation of Egypt in 1882, the Empire was to lose Serbia, Montenegro, Romania, Bosnia and Herzegovina, Cyprus, Tunisia and Egypt. Both the Romantic appeal and the actual success of the Greek nationalist movement encouraged other nationalities to plot to break away. In response to these important territorial losses, the Empire took the decision to tighten its grip over Asia Minor, and what was left of its Arab provinces.

Around mid-century, Ahmad Efendi consolidated his social position further by marrying the daughter of Hasan Taqi al-Din al-Hisni,[3] Mufti of Damascus in the late 1840s. The al-Hisni family were Husayni *ashraf*. They claimed descent from the Prophet Muhammad through his grandson Hasan. Such genealogy assured them considerable prestige in Damascus society. Moreover, Hasan Taqi al-Din al-Husni was a *naqib* of the *ashraf*, a leader who represented these descendants in dealings with the Ottoman authorities.

The Mufti's daughter bore Ahmad three sons. Kamil and Munah were born in the late 1840s; Rida was born either in 1861 or 1863 (the record is unclear).[4] From time to time, Ahmad would ride over the mountains from Beirut to Damascus to visit his wife's parents, to pay a courtesy call on the vali and on other notables in the Ottoman service there. It was an arduous journey of several days over rough tracks. A carriage road between the two cities – built with subscriptions from merchants and landowners in Damascus, Beirut and Aleppo – was begun in 1859, but not completed until 1863. A horse-drawn coach was then able to do the journey in thirteen hours, whereas the same journey by mules took four days. About a thousand mules would ply the route in both directions, bearing merchandise of all sorts.

---

[3] Linda Schatkowski-Schilcher, *Families in Politics: Damascene Factions and Estates of the 18th and 19th Centuries*, Stuttgart 1985, p. 206. Hasan Taqi al-Din al-Hisni's great-nephew, Shaykh Muhammad Taj al-Din al-Hasani, was later to serve a number of times as prime minister of Syria, and as head of state under the French Mandate between the two world wars.

[4] Rida el-Solh's date of birth is usually given as 1262 AH (corresponding to 1860–61), but a note (*teskere*) in his file in the Ottoman Ministry of Justice changes this to 1863.

(This was not unusual at the time, even in Western Europe. Mules and mule-trains accounted for more than two-thirds of all traffic on French roads until the mid-nineteenth century, as Graham Robb noted in his *The Discovery of France*, London 2007.) So dense was the traffic on the Damascus–Beirut road that construction of a railway was studied. But it was not until August 1895, after three years of construction work, that the 147-kilometre Beirut–Damascus line was finally opened, thereby cutting the journey to nine hours.

Ahmad's friend: the Emir 'Abd al-Qadir al-Jaza'iri

It may have been on one of his early visits to Damascus that Ahmad met and became friends with one of the most fascinating Arab personalities of the nineteenth century, the Emir 'Abd al-Qadir al-Jaza'iri.[5] This great revolutionary Algerian prince had, in 1855, settled in Damascus with his family and a large number of his retainers, exiled there by the French. He was to have a considerable influence on Ahmad's life. The emir was soldier and *sufi* at once. Born near Mascara in north-west Algeria in 1808, he was brought up in great piety by his father, Muhyi al-Din, Prince of Mascara and leader of the Sufi order of the *Qadiriyya*. 'Abd al-Qadir showed a precocious talent for philosophy and for Qur'anic exegesis, studying with local scholars and collecting books and manuscripts. But when French troops landed in Algeria in June 1830, seeking to subdue his whole country by force, he was the first to rally the population against these invaders. Proclaimed prince on his father's death in 1832, he declared a *jihad* against the French. By the mid-1830s, the young prince had managed to raise an army of 20,000 foot soldiers and 15,000 horse. By mobilising tribes, levying taxes, building forts, foundries, arms factories, flour mills and schools, he in fact created and directed a defensive Islamic state. With his lieutenants, he waged guerrilla war against the French army, trapping it in ambushes, harassing its heavy supply columns, and cutting it off from food and fodder. In the early years of battle, the courtesies of war were respected by both sides. Prisoners were decently treated and then exchanged. Truces were signed, with couriers carrying letters back and forth between 'Abd al-Qadir and the French generals opposing him.

[5] Bruno Etienne, *Abdelkader*, Paris 1994.

But, in 1841, France became determined to put an end to the Algerian rebellion once and for all. General Thomas Bugeaud was named governor-general of colonial Algeria. Dividing his huge army of 100,000 men into punitive columns which criss-crossed the country, he carried out a scorched-earth policy, burning whole towns and villages, destroying crops and herds, besieging and starving tribes to death, torturing people and cutting off ears. He ordered the killing of all boys over the age of 15. He shipped out in chains thousands of women and children to the Marquesas islands – desolate volcanic clusters in the South Pacific – where most of them were to die of exposure and hunger. Bugeaud's horrific brutality was much criticised, including in France. In 1847 he was finally recalled and replaced by one of the king's own sons, the duc d'Aumale.

Not wishing to inflict further suffering on his traumatised people, and having secured a promise from the newly appointed French duke that he would be free to leave Algeria for Alexandria, 'Abd al-Qadir surrendered on 23 December 1847. The French, however, immediately reneged on the pledge they had made to him. The emir's possessions, including his priceless beloved books and his entire manuscript library, were confiscated and sold for a pittance. He and his family, along with hundreds of his loyal retainers, were transported by force to France. There they were imprisoned in damp, gloomy fortresses at Toulon, Pau and Amboise, the latter a grim, freezing-cold chateau, flanked by two squat towers, built on a rock thrust up from the river Loire in central France. Amboise had been used as a deadly prison since the time of Henri IV. 'Abd al-Qadir was held there from November 1848 to December 1852. Scores of his immediate family and retainers died from the cold, their bodies buried in the grounds of the castle, where they remain to this day. The colonial party in France insisted on keeping 'Abd al-Qadir locked up. They argued suspiciously that if he were allowed to go to Egypt, as he had been promised by the king's son, he might become an instrument in British hands.

In December 1848, Louis-Napoleon Bonaparte, nephew of Napoleon I, was elected president of the French Republic, and in 1852 – after staging a *coup d'état* the previous year and crushing all resistance – he assumed the title of Napoleon III, thus inaugurating the Second Empire which was to last until 1870. Aware that the emir had been treated shabbily, and moved by pleas on his behalf by the comte de Paris as well as by other high-born French and British friends, the emperor decided to release him. He was brought to Paris and received by the emperor in his box at the opera during a performance of Rossini's *Moïse*. Suddenly lionised by French society, he was visited by scientists, prelates, princes and generals, admired for his learning, courtesy and noble bearing, showered with honours and invited to take the salute at a grand parade in the Tuileries gardens, mounted on a magnificent white horse, a gift from the emperor. The French imagined that they had thus wiped clean the slate of their cruelty and treachery.

On 21 December 1853, five years after agreeing to relinquish the fight in Algeria, 'Abd al-Qadir and his party finally embarked at Marseilles for the East. Their first stop was the imperial Ottoman capital, Istanbul. From there they moved to Bursa and, in November 1855, set sail for Beirut and travelled on to Damascus. The Ottoman and French governments had agreed between them that this ancient city would be the place of the emir's final exile. He and his party arrived there to a princely welcome on 6 December. Damascus was then a city of little more than 100,000 inhabitants, ruled by an elite of religious leaders – many of them heads of Sufi orders – by landed families and tribal chieftains. These latter, in the absence of a regular police force, maintained order in the various quarters of the city and offered protection against marauders of pilgrim caravans making their way to Mecca.

The emir's arrival with his large household caused a sensation. His reputation had preceded him, and he was immediately welcomed among the city's elite. After all, he was a hero of the struggle against European colonialism. He was a descendant of the Prophet, and the leader of the *Qadiriyya* Sufi order. Now on a French pension of 300,000 francs a year, he was also well-to-do. His Algerian guards soon provided security for his extended family in their various houses, farms and compounds. Over the years, the emir managed to arrange with the French and Ottoman authorities to bring to Syria several thousand more Algerians, veterans of his wars against the French, as well as their offspring. These he settled on land in outlying villages, as far south as Safad and the shores of Lake Tiberias. By the 1870s, Algerians in that region accounted for almost half the population.[6] The French authorities in Algeria were only too glad to be rid of them, so happily fell in with the plan.

---

[6] Elias Sanbar, *Figures du Palestinien*, Paris 2004, p. 67.

Ahmad el-Solh heard of 'Abd al-Qadir's arrival, and hurried to Damascus from Beirut to pay his respects and listen to his teachings. The emir had started holding forth on Islamic philosophy, theology and mysticism at Dar al-Hadith, a *madrasa* in the quarter of 'Asruniyya. What created the real bond, however, between the emir and Ahmad el-Solh, was their mutual concern, as charitable and high-minded Muslims, to save Christian lives during some tragic months in 1860. In the spring of that terrible year, mutual skirmishes and killings in the Lebanese mountains between Christians and Druze exploded into a savage war. There was looting, raping and dismembering – a huge loss of life and vast destruction of property.[7] Both sides were to blame for this insensate violence, which had its origins in the intercommunal clashes of the previous two decades. However, as well as strife between rival communities, it may also have been a struggle between two feudal systems to maintain control over the restive peasants. The Druze, better led and armed than the Christians, soon got the upper hand. When the mainly Christian Lebanese towns of Hasbaya, Rashaya and Zahleh fell to the Druze, they were sacked and burned. Thousands of terrified and destitute refugees began running for their lives, and many of them sought refuge in the Christian quarters of Damascus.

Although the Christians and Druze of Mount Lebanon ended their war with a peace treaty on 6 July, news of the atrocities and the influx of so many refugees heightened tensions in Damascus. Muslim hostility to the local Christian minority had been building up for several years, with political and economic resentments feeding a virulent strain of religious fanaticism. A widely held suspicion was that some Christians had become an advance party for European Powers, which were planning to invade, dominate and dismember the Ottoman Empire. Muslims had felt humiliated by the defeat of the Empire by Russia in the Crimean War of 1853–56, so the Russian consulate in Damascus was the first to be set on fire as the troubles escalated.

Resentment at the rapidly growing prosperity of local Christian merchants, who had been granted the right to trade with Europe on particularly favourable terms denied the rest of the mercantile class, may have played a part, as did the important financial support which foreign consuls gave to Christian schools, thereby creating

---

[7] Leila Tarazi Fawaz, *An Occasion for War: Civil Conflict in Lebanon and Damascus in 1860*, London 1994.

a better-educated elite among Christians than among their Muslim compatriots. But perhaps the greatest source of Muslim frustration was the new reform charter, the Imperial Rescript of 18 February 1856, or the *Hatt-i Humayun*, which decided the full equality of Ottoman subjects irrespective of religion. Promulgated by the Sultan under European pressure, it abrogated the legal edifice of the *ahl al-dhimma*, the subordinate but protected status that non-Muslims had always had under Muslim rule. This reform immediately robbed the majority Muslims of their traditional privileged status and their accompanying sense of social and political superiority.

Some foreign consuls had warned that war in Lebanon might easily spread to Damascus. Rightly fearing trouble as it turned out, the Emir 'Abd al-Qadir secured funds from the French, as well as permission from the Ottoman vali, to arm a thousand of his Algerians. But before this could be accomplished and when he was in a village many miles from Damascus, a fanatical mob burst into one of the Christian quarters of the city on 9 July and carried out an orgy of killing, burning and plundering which lasted eight gruesome days. When the awful news reached him, the emir rushed back to Damascus in time to save the Russian and Greek consuls from being murdered, together with some eleven thousand Christians, who crowded pitifully into his own compounds. Thousands were taken to safety in Beirut by his men. But thousands more (and estimates vary between five and ten thousand people) were slaughtered. Many Muslim families, including the Halabi, Hasibi, Tinawi, Nabulsi, 'Imadi, Shurbaji and 'Attar families, took Christians into their homes to save them from the rampaging mob. Such Muslims saved more than sixteen thousand Christians. They continued to feed and shelter the refugees for months afterwards.

'Abd al-Qadir al-Jaza'iri's humanitarian actions won the gratitude and plaudits of Europe. An emissary from Napoleon III was sent to confer on him the *grand cordon* of the Legion of Honour.

In Lebanon, Ahmad el-Solh, who had been in constant touch with the emir during the troubles, earned respect and fame for the aid he gave, both in his personal capacity and as Ottoman *mutasarrif* of Acre, to wave after wave of famished refugees as they made their desperate way to the coast. Other leading South Lebanon families, such as the 'Usayran and the Zayn, also gave shelter to fleeing Christians, establishing the basis for long-term good relations with the Christian community. Ahmad Efendi and the Emir 'Abd al-Qadir were also united in the need to clear the name of their religion, smeared by the ignoble crimes of the mob. Ahmad's good deeds – his protection of defenceless Christians in a time of war – were to become part of the moral heritage of his grandson, Riad el-Solh. Indeed, an understanding of Christian fears and a tolerance of Christian aspirations were to constitute remarkable features of Riad's political career.[8]

The 1860 crisis had a double – if contradictory – effect. In Damascus and the Syrian hinterland, the Ottoman authorities managed to take the situation in hand and actually head off foreign interference. Fu'ad Pasha, the able foreign minister of the Ottoman Empire (who shortly after the crisis was named grand vezir), arrived in the region with full powers to restore order. He hanged the governor of Damascus, 'Izzat Pasha, for dereliction of duty, together with fifty-six other officials and civilian offenders. Over a hundred Turkish officers and soldiers, who had been found to have taken part in the massacre of Christians, were shot.

In Mount Lebanon, however, the European Powers managed to dictate stiff terms by gunboat diplomacy, as it were. French opinion was agitating for the protection of Lebanese Christians, especially of the Maronites, traditional clients of France. Accordingly, French troops landed in Beirut in August 1860. The Sublime Porte was thus forced to accept a settlement, negotiated over several months, whereby Mount Lebanon became an autonomous Ottoman district, or *mutasarrifi-yya*, under the protection of the European Powers and governed by an Ottoman Christian. Dawud Efendi, an Armenian Catholic from Istanbul, was appointed governor. He was assisted by an administrative council, in which all religious communities were represented, but Christians (Maronite, Greek Orthodox and Greek Catholic) had the dominant voice.

The impact on Christians of the 1860 massacres was profound and prolonged. It helped breed a sentiment of Maronite particularism, which spread from Mount Lebanon to Maronite populations living outside the mountain. Independence from the Ottoman Empire – and the later establishment of Lebanese independence – became essential Christian political goals.

Ahmad Efendi el-Solh emerged enhanced from the 1860 crisis, and not only in Lebanon. Foreign consuls reported that he had given

---

[8] Interview with Alia el-Solh, Monte Carlo, 4–5 October 2004.

2 – Riad el-Solh aged 4, in 1898. (By kind permission of Madame Leila Hamadi el-Solh.)

3 – Riad el-Solh aged 8, in 1902, with his two sisters, Balqis and Alia. (By kind permission of Madame Leila Hamadi el-Solh.)

4 – Riad el-Solh aged 18, in 1912, as a law student in Istanbul. (By kind permission of Madame Leila Hamadi el-Solh.)

5 – Riad el-Solh aged 26, in 1920, with a group of young supporters of the Emir Faysal in Damascus. Riad el-Solh is third from the left in the back row. (By kind permission of Madame Leila Hamadi el-Solh.)

6 – The Emir 'Abd al-Qadir al-Jaza'iri, wearing the Grand Cordon of the Legion of Honour, conferred on him by Napoleon III for his role in saving Christian lives during the 1860 massacres in Damascus. It was then that he befriended Ahmad Pasha, Riad el-Solh's grandfather.

7 – The Emir Sa'id al-Jaza'iri at home in Damascus in 1935, under a portrait of his grandfather, the Emir 'Abd al-Qadir al-Jaza'iri.

8 – The first meeting of the Ottoman parliament on 18 March 1877.
Following the Ottoman defeat by Russia in 1877–78, Sultan Abdülhamit
dissolved the Assembly, suspended the Constitution and ruled as an autocrat
for the rest of his reign.

9 – Ahmet Mithat Pasha (1822–84), an enlightened grand vezir and Ottoman reformer, who, when governor of Syria, helped to rehabilitate Ahmad Pasha, Riad el-Solh's grandfather, and bring him back into government service. Mithat Pasha's fame aroused the suspicions of Sultan Abdülhamit, who banished him to Ta'if in Arabia, where he was murdered on 8 May 1884, probably on the Sultan's orders.

10 – Ahmad Abu-Khalil al-Qabbani (1836–1903), creator of the modern Arab musical theatre in both Syria and Egypt. (By kind permission of Dr Sabah Kabbani. Photo by Jules Lind, Beirut, *c.*1880.)

11 – The German Emperor Wilhelm II in Damascus in 1898. On his way from Jerusalem to Damascus, the emperor dined at Sidon with Ahmad Pasha, Riad el-Solh's grandfather. In order to cement its alliance with the Ottoman Empire, Germany gave great publicity to the emperor's tour of the Arab provinces, which was recorded by an Armenian photographer, Garabed Krikorian (1847–1920). (From the Otrakji family collection at www.creativesyria.com.)

12 – Salonica in the early twentieth century, where Rida el-Solh spent a year as *mutasarrif*, and where his son Ahmad was drowned. In 1908, Salonica was the base from which the Young Turks rose against Sultan Abdülhamit. (By kind permission of the Bibliothèque de Documentation Internationale Contemporaine, Paris.)

13 – The waterfront at Salonica in 1912, when the town fell to the Greeks. (By kind permission of the Bibliothèque de Documentation Internationale Contemporaine, Paris.)

14 – Ahmad 'Izzat Pasha al-'Abid, a powerful Syrian at the court of Sultan Abdülhamit, and the principal initiator of the Hijaz railway, linking Damascus to Medina. The imperial order to build the railway was issued on 2 May 1900. (By kind permission of Dr Sabah Kabbani.)

15 – Sultan Abdülhamit in his carriage, shortly before his deposition in April 1909.

16 – The Villa Allatini in Salonica, where the Young Turks confined the deposed Sultan Abdülhamit. The postcard, mailed from Salonica to New York City on 22 June 1912, reads: 'The ex-Sultan is closely guarded here and no one is allowed near the house. The guard is changed every month to avoid bribery.' Signed: Monte. (By kind permission of the Otrakji family at www.creativesyria.com.)

17 – Victims of the famine that killed half a million people in Lebanon in 1915. (By kind permission of Joseph G. Chami, *The Book of Syria: Photos from Syrian Life*, Damascus 2005.)

aid and protection to Christians in need. At the Sublime Porte, and especially at the office of the grand vezir – the real seat of Ottoman governance – there was gratitude to officials in the Arab provinces who had stood up to mob violence, thereby upholding somewhat the Empire's good name. Such brave behaviour was in marked contrast to that of the vali in Damascus, who, by criminal negligence or by collusion with the rioters, had allowed the slaughter to proceed.

Napoleon III's idea of an Arab kingdom

Ahmad Efendi's great esteem for the Emir 'Abd al-Qadir al-Jaza'iri and his cooperation with him during the crisis were later to get him into trouble. The emir had made such an electrifying impression in Paris that a lobby took shape – made up of French officers who had served in Algeria, together with financiers and businessmen – that believed that French strategic and commercial interests would be served if the emir were to play a leading political role in the Levant, perhaps at the head of an Arab kingdom. Needless to say, when word of such ideas reached the ear of the Sultan, they aroused the greatest suspicion as they were viewed as European plots designed to weaken Istanbul.

Britain and France were then much preoccupied with how to promote their rival ambitions in the Arab provinces. The French wanted Mount Lebanon (stronghold of their Maronite clients) to be made as separate from the rest of Syria as possible. Britain, always concerned with the security of land and sea routes to India, saw the 1860 crisis and its aftermath as its chance to restructure Ottoman administration in Syria, and put it under the firm control of European political agents. Napoleon III had his own big idea: he envisaged putting his friend, the Emir 'Abd al-Qadir, on the throne of an Arab kingdom, which would stretch from Syria to Mesopotamia to the Arabian Peninsula. This would serve as a buffer between Egypt and Ottoman Istanbul. Such a state, under French protection, would protect the Suez Canal project from Ottoman interference and give France control of the silk trade.[9] In the last decades of the nineteenth century, raw silk from Syria was needed for the French textile industry

---

[9] Marcel Emerit, 'La Crise syrienne et l'expansion économique française en 1860', in *Revue historique*, 207 (janvier–mars 1952), pp. 211–32.

at Lyon, which was facing shortages of supply. The emperor continued to entertain this geopolitical project until his downfall following the Franco-Prussian war of 1870.

The memory of the French emperor's blueprint lingered on in the Levant. The project of an Arab state headed by 'Abd al-Qadir was later taken up by the emir's Arab admirers, with Ahmad el-Solh at their head. Encouraged by his personal friendship with the emir, by his influential family connections in Damascus, and by his own excellent personal reputation, Ahmad Efendi took the lead of an Arab independence movement, centred on Beirut. One of his grandsons, 'Adil el-Solh (son of Munah) relates that, in the late 1870s, Ahmad spent a great deal of time in secret meetings trying to win support for such a project.[10] Along with some trusted associates, Ahmad returned to his home town of Sidon to consult with the heads of the main families of South Lebanon. He and his associates then journeyed to Damascus, to sound out the views of the city's notables and opinion-formers, before riding on to Dummar – then a cool, outlying village on the river Barada – where the emir and his family were spending the summer. Seeking the emir's views on the state of the Empire, they did not reveal their actual thinking to him. When he insisted they remain for three days as his guests, they must have felt sufficiently encouraged by his hospitality later to hold a secret conference in Damascus at which they agreed that the emir should be invited to assume the leadership of an independent Greater Syria. Ahmad was delegated to return to the emir's summer residence and put the proposal to him.

But these enthusiasts had misread the emir's mind. He was no longer the young man who, with blood and iron in the 1830s, had forged an Islamic state in Algeria to fight off the ferocious French. He now preferred to enjoy his status as an international celebrity, travelling to Paris for the Universal Exhibition of 1867, to Mecca for the pilgrimage, to Port Said – then a building-site emerging from the sands – to inspect work on the Canal at the invitation of his friend, Ferdinand de Lesseps.

Lesseps had canvassed international support for his visionary project of a waterway linking the Mediterranean to the Red Sea. In 1854 he had secured a concession to build the Suez Canal from

---

[10] Adil el-Solh, *Sutur min al-risala: tarikh haraka istiqlaliyya qamat fi al-mashriq al-'arabi sanat 1877*, Beirut 1966, pp. 91–102.

the Egyptian Khedive, Sa'id Pasha, but it took time to be ratified by the Ottoman Sultan, who feared that such a canal would serve to entrench Western interests in both Egypt and Arabia (as it no doubt was to do). Lesseps had, for seven years in the 1830s, served as French consul in Alexandria. He had been one of the Emir 'Abd al-Qadir's first French friends, even visiting him in 1848 in his prison at the fortress in Pau. 'Abd al-Qadir's spectacular arrival in Damascus in 1855, with the blessing of Napoleon III, suggested to Lesseps that the emir might help him win international support for his grand project, which, in fact, he did.

'Abd al-Qadir was there in 1869 for the formal inauguration of the Suez Canal, together with European princes, statesmen, admirals, ambassadors and the Empress Eugénie herself. Napoleon III sent a French frigate to carry the emir and his suite from Beirut to Port Said, to Suez and then back to Beirut.

When approached by Ahmad el-Solh in the 1870s, 'Abd al-Qadir had been more than fifteen years in exile in Syria. He was attached to the leafy luxuriance of his pleasant farms, to what remained of his family, to the renown which brought distinguished visitors to his door, to his voluminous correspondence, and to the ever-widening range of his disciples and friends. Above all, the ageing emir was more than ever immersed in theological studies and in Sufi mysticism. He wrote commentaries on Islamic texts, taught, composed poems and meditated. As he had earlier told a French official, 'My political career is over. I seek nothing further from men or from the glory of this world. I want to live henceforth in the sweet joys of my family, in prayer and in peace'.[11] In any event, he was careful not to burn his bridges with Istanbul by allowing himself to get involved in anything that might offend the Ottoman Sultan, whose guest he considered himself to be.

The fall and subsequent rise of Ahmad el-Solh

On 1 September 1876, Sultan Abdülhamit II came to the throne as the thirty-fourth sultan of the Ottoman dynasty.[12] On his accession at the age of 33, he was an unknown quantity. No one could tell if he would

---

[11] Etienne, *Abdelkader*, p. 299.
[12] François Georgeon, *Abdülhamid II*, Paris 2003.

be a liberal or a tyrant. But they were very soon to find out. Abdülhamit suspended the Constitution, dissolved parliament and took control of the army and the palace. He wrested effective power from the sprawling bureaucracy of the Sublime Porte, imposed centralisation on what had become an unruly Empire, and sacked and banished the visionary, reform-minded and highly effective Grand Vezir Midhat Pasha, who was a hero to so many for his enlightened liberalism. Abdülhamit also sought to contain the crisis over the loss of territory and the great diplomatic fall-out from Russia's devastating rout of Ottoman armies in the war of 1877–78.

The crushing defeat of the Ottomans aroused intense emotion in the Muslim world. A sense of insecurity began to pervade the Arab provinces. What would happen to them if the unthinkable were to occur and the Empire collapsed? Istanbul itself seemed on the verge of falling to Russian troops. The situation in Syria was no less lamentable. Thousands of men had perished at the front. The Ottoman treasury was empty and the Empire virtually bankrupt. A large slice of the state's revenues was controlled by the foreign administrators of the Ottoman Public Debt. Government employees, teachers, officers had to wait months for their salaries to be paid. When they were, they proved almost worthless because of spiralling inflation. Troops mutinied for lack of pay. Pleas for financial help from impoverished provincial capitals like Damascus fell on deaf ears in increasingly helpless Istanbul.

To the Sultan's alarm, a by-product of the economic and political crisis was a surge in Syrian national consciousness. It was at this difficult time that word of Ahmad el-Solh's secret attempts to create an Arab kingdom under the Emir 'Abd al-Qadir al-Jaza'iri reached Istanbul. Once the Ottoman authorities ascertained that the emir had actually rejected the idea outright, they pounced on Ahmad and his fellow plotters instead. Some were sent to jail, and others into exile. Ahmad was banished to Rhodes, then under Ottoman control. He was to remain there for several years.

The last quarter of the nineteenth century was a period of aggressive imperial expansion by rival European Powers anxious to divide between themselves the spoils of the enfeebled Ottoman Empire. The loss of vast Ottoman domains in Europe forced the Sultan to pay more attention to the increasingly restive Arab provinces. He was determined to bind them closer to Istanbul. With this in mind, he recruited young Syrians into his palace guard and appointed members of prominent Syrian families to important administrative posts in the Empire. They, in turn, accepted such posts in order to consolidate their social status as upper-class notables.

The Sultan then decided to recall the former grand vezir, Midhat Pasha, from his European exile and send him to Damascus as vali of that province. As a seasoned imperial administrator, who had occupied the highest positions in both Istanbul and the provinces, Midhat Pasha was very highly regarded. He immediately set about dispelling Syria's gloom by launching a large programme of essential public works, including the construction of a road from Homs to Tripoli. He opened exemplary schools, improved and extended the telegraph network, and reordered the province's messy finances. He also patronised the arts. It was under his enlightened protection that the first theatre in the Arab world was created by the gifted dramatist, Abu Khalil al-Qabbani. Midhat Pasha attended the premiere of the plays that were put on by Abu Khalil and his group, thus giving musical drama respectability and status in a conservative city that had traditionally frowned on artists, or worse.

Needing good men in the administration, Midhat Pasha eventually persuaded the Sultan to pardon Ahmad el-Solh and bring him home from exile in Rhodes. Midhat Pasha even went to dine at Ahmad's home in Beirut, a visit which sealed their friendship and their mutual regard. It was the Sultan's habit to distribute gifts, honours and administrative posts to disaffected public servants, and Ahmad el-Solh was duly appointed secretary-general (*mektupçu*) of the *sanjaq* of Beirut. This made him the right-hand man of the *mutasarrif*. In each governorate, two important functionaries, the *mektupçu*, in charge of official correspondence, and the *defterdar*, the chief financial officer, ran the place under the titular authority of the governor.

To press ahead with his reforms in the province of Damascus, Midhat Pasha wanted the Sultan to give him the same wide powers he had enjoyed as a governor of Ottoman provinces in Europe, but Sultan Abdülhamit would have none of it. His suspicions were aroused when the British ambassador in Istanbul, Sir Henry Layard, travelled to Damascus in November 1879 and held meetings with Midhat Pasha. Were the British conspiring to set up an Arab state with the Pasha at its head? Always suspicious of any sign of provincial autonomy, the Sultan was anxious to stamp out any hint of territorially based Syrian patriotism.

On three separate occasions in the early summer of 1880, revolutionary posters were pasted up on the streets of Beirut, calling on the people to revolt against the Turks. Informing London of the unusual event, the British Consul General John Dickson reported that the prevailing opinion was that Midhat Pasha himself was the author of the posters. Included in his dispatch was a memorandum from J. Abcarius, the consulate's dragoman, in which it was suggested that Midhat Pasha's motives may have been

> *intimidating the Porte and obtaining the unlimited power*
> *he had been seeking to procure . . . or to show to the*
> *European Powers, and especially to England, that a spirit*
> *of revolt has sprung up in Syria which adds immensely*
> *to the troubles of Turkey and . . . induce them to take up*
> *his cause and make something of him, either by detaching*
> *Syria and appointing him at its head or by placing him at*
> *the head of the Ministry in the Capital, where he thinks he*
> *can better carry out his plans of reformation.*

Dickson himself did not share the dragoman's assessment, believing that it was 'too dangerous an expedient' for Midhat Pasha to contemplate. He added, however: 'There is no doubt that for the last five years a secret society has existed in Syria . . . whose object . . . is to procure a sort of administrative autonomy for the Province, the Sultan being acknowledged as nominal Sovereign; and if this should be impossible, to make a strike for entire independence. These placards may have emanated from this Society.'[13]

Be that as it may, in 1880 the Sultan transferred the highly popular Midhat Pasha to Smyrna, and, within a year, had him arrested, tried, condemned to death and then banished for life. He was put in chains on board ship for Arabia, whence he was taken to the mountain fortress of Ta'if and locked up in appallingly harsh conditions, which the Sultan no doubt hoped would kill him. When they did not, he was murdered in prison in May 1884, almost certainly on the orders of the Sultan.

There was even a witch hunt against all those whose careers or talents Midhat Pasha had helped to promote. Abu Khalil al-Qabbani's

---

[13] J. Dickson to Secretary of State, 3 July 1988 (PRO F 195/1306 14475).

theatre was ransacked by a mob and burnt to the ground. He narrowly escaped with his life, leaving everything behind to flee with his family to Egypt, a penniless and dispirited dramatist of great courage and innovation. He was eventually to build another theatre in the Egyptian capital, on the site where the Cairo Opera House now stands.

A year earlier, the Emir 'Abd al-Qadir died in Damascus. He was buried in a great outpouring of grief from the multitude of his family, friends, retainers and admirers. Eighty years later, in 1963, escorted by 'Abd al-Aziz Bouteflika, then foreign minister of Algeria and later president, the emir's remains were repatriated to the country of his birth. He was reburied in Algiers – not in his native Mascara, where, shockingly enough, the Qadiriyya *zawiya* was razed immediately after Algeria's independence in 1962. In 2005, the mayor of Paris, Bernard Delanoë, named a street in the French capital after 'Abd al-Qadir al-Jaza'iri.

Ahmad el-Solh suffered the loss of both these friends, but survived to become a grand old man himself. It is said that when Hamdi Pasha, the Ottoman governor-general of Damascus in the 1880s, came to Beirut from Damascus, he would call on Ahmad el-Solh rather than the other way round, as protocol required. In 1891 Ahmad was promoted to the rank of pasha, in recognition of his importance. In that year, a collection of thirty-five poems in praise of him and his family was published in Lebanon. Compiled by a historian of South Lebanon, Muhammad Jabir al-Safa, several of the poems were by Shi'i poets from religious families of the south. One such poem, by Muhammad Hasan Jabir,[14] related how, on one occasion, Ahmad Pasha, disregarding the bullets that were flying about, rode into the thick of a battle to separate two cousins, 'Ali Bey al-As'ad, master of the fort of Tibnin, and Tamir Bey al-Husyan, master of the fort of Hunin, who were engaged in a tribal shoot-out. He managed to arrange a ceasefire, even a reconciliation. He was not only brave, but concerned for the well-being of the people in his charge. In an introduction to the volume of poems, Muhammad 'Ali Farhat recounted that when Ahmad Pasha was *mutasarrif* of Latakia, he gathered fifty promising children from the poor surrounding countryside, and sent them off to Istanbul to continue their education.

---

[14] Muhammad Hasan Jabir, 'Silaf al-afkar fi madih hadrat al-mukhtar', in Muhamad 'Ali Farhat (ed.), *Ahl al-Solh*, Beirut 1891.

In 1935 the memory of Ahmad Pasha was once again celebrated by the same historian of South Lebanon, Muhammad Jabir al-Safa, in an article in a short-lived newspaper, *al-'Uruba*. He related how Ahmad Pasha was in the habit of travelling south from Beirut each year to see that all was well on his estates. On one such visit, he found that the tobacco and cotton harvests had been excellent and that grain and cattle were plentiful. A local notable from Nabatiyeh, Amin Jibris, gave a feast in his honour. When Ahmad Pasha sat down to eat, his host spread a white cloth on the table in front of him and poured into it a heap of gold coins. Astonished by this bizarre display, the Pasha enquired what it could possibly mean. His host replied that it bore witness to the prosperity which the region was enjoying under Ahmad Pasha's peaceful protection!

In his lifetime, Ahmad Pasha witnessed immense changes, most of them for the better. In the early nineteenth century, Beirut had been little more than a village, huddled behind its walls. Its gates were locked each night to keep marauders out. Within half a century, a dramatic transformation had taken place.[15] From being closed in upon itself, Beirut became an open, inviting city. Ships from all over the world dropped anchor in its harbour. In 1830 the port was handling 30,000 tons of merchandise a year. By 1860 this had grown to 600,000 tons. The population soared from 19,000 in 1846 to 115,000 in 1893. By 1859, Beirut was linked by telegraph to the rest of the world, a connection which greatly assisted the development of international trade. Its markets overflowed with local produce, but also with goods imported from the hinterland and from Europe. Foreign merchants came to live in Beirut, followed by consuls to protect their commercial interests. New buildings sprang up – warehouses, Italianate villas, restaurants, hotels. The first bank in the Arab world opened its doors in Beirut, and the first newspaper was published there in 1858. In 1862 the Sultan bestowed upon the city some significant relics – three hairs said to be from the Prophet's beard.

The region's first institutions of higher learning were established in Beirut, namely the Syrian Protestant College in 1866 (later to be called the American University of Beirut) and, in 1875, the Jesuit College of Saint Joseph (later the University of Saint Joseph).

---

[15] Nicolas Ziadé, 'Beyrouth, des années soixante du XIXe siècle à 1908', in Zahida Darwiche Jabbour (ed.), *Les Villes cosmopolites arabes 1870–1930, Beyrouth, Alexandrie, Alep*, Beirut 2004, pp. 13–44.

Three years earlier, in 1872, a municipal council was created which set about laying drains, building roads in the centre of town and paving them (with a steam-roller bought from the United States for $3,000). A British company was hired to pipe water from the Kalb river, and by 1875 water had reached a few houses and public buildings, although most of the population still had to make do with public fountains. By 1888, Beirut streets were lit by butane gas – one of the rare Ottoman cities to enjoy such an amenity.

In 1887–88, the Porte recognised the importance of Beirut as a rising coastal metropolis by making it the capital of a new vilayet carved out of geographical Syria, and containing the five *sanjaq* of Latakia, Tripoli, Acre, Nablus and Beirut itself. The Sultan approved the idea so as to allow for tighter control from Istanbul and also to keep European influence in check. The French, in particular, were managing to make deeper inroads into the Levant through their religious orders and schools, which were educating and influencing generation after generation of local students.

The creation of the Beirut vilayet followed earlier amputations of Syria. In 1861, Mount Lebanon had, as we have seen, been granted a special status as an autonomous province under a Christian Ottoman governor, while a decade later, in 1872, Jerusalem was also detached from the vilayet of Syria to form another separate *mutasarrifiyya*, which depended directly on the Sublime Porte.

One of the social high points of Ahmad Pasha's life may well have been the evening in November 1898 when Kaiser Wilhelm II and his wife came to dine with him at Sidon. According to the family, particularly fine silver cutlery had to be hurriedly purchased for the occasion. The month-long visit to the Ottoman Empire by the German emperor was a spectacular diplomatic triumph for Sultan Abdülhamit. It demonstrated to the world that, even if Great Britain, France and Russia coveted his territory, he could still count on Germany's friendship. German officers served in the Ottoman army training cadets. German bankers were considering investment in Anatolian railways, including in the *Baghdadbahn* project, which was to link Istanbul to Baghdad.

The imperial visit began in Istanbul, where the sovereigns arrived on 18 October on board their yacht, the *Hohenzollern*. They were housed in a pavilion specially built for the purpose in the grounds of the Sultan's Yildiz palace. They were showered with gifts, visited the city on horseback and attended a gala reception given by the Sultan in their honour. A week later they sailed for Haifa on their way to Jerusalem, which the Kaiser entered riding a white horse, escorted by Ottoman dignitaries in full dress uniform. He visited the Dome of the Rock, the Greek Church and the Wailing Wall, and gave an audience to representatives of the various religious denominations. It was on their way back overland from Palestine to Syria that the imperial couple dined at Ahmad Pasha's table, before heading on to Damascus, where they were shown the Umayyad Mosque and Saladin's tomb.

Ahmad Pasha was a pious Sunni Muslim, an Arab notable, a dedicated official of the five-hundred-year-old Ottoman Empire – the greatest Muslim empire since the time of the Prophet and his immediate successors. But, in the last decade of his life, a dreadful notion began to circulate that the Ottoman Empire might collapse and be shared out between the European Powers. The fear of dismemberment was in everyone's mind. Who would then rule the Arab provinces? Arab notables like Ahmad Pasha were inevitably deeply concerned. Would they have to suffer the fate of Egypt, occupied by the British, or that of the North African territories under French colonial rule? As the centre of the Empire weakened, the periphery began to stir.

Ahmad Pasha died in Beirut in 1902, a patriarch covered in honours, known and respected not only in Lebanon and Istanbul, but also in Damascus, Jerusalem and throughout the Arab provinces. By the time of his death, he was both rich and influential, owning four villages in South Lebanon – Tul, Tamra, al-Sharqiyya and 'Arnun. Ahmad Pasha had also acquired a stretch of the Beirut coastline, at that time some considerable way out of town. Although no longer in Solh ownership, it is today in the most highly prized part of the city, stretching from the Carlton Hotel to the Beirut lighthouse. Protruding from the sea just off this stretch of coast are some distinctive rocks called Rawsheh (an Arabic rendering of the French *rocher*) known at the time as *sakhrat al-Sulh*, the rock of the Solhs.

Huge crowds followed Ahmad Pasha's coffin to the cemetery. It was one of the biggest funerals the city had ever seen. Among the many messages of condolence the family received was one from the notables of Jerusalem, who praised his 'Muslim morality and noble Islamic qualities'. Among the mourners was his grandson, Riad, then aged eight.

2 AN OTTOMAN CHILDHOOD

Of widely differing ages and characters, Riad el-Solh's parents were plainly incompatible. His father was a dry, irascible autocrat, his mother a wild romantic. As a result, they were often apart. Only rarely could Nazira bring herself to accompany Rida el-Solh to his posts in different parts of the Ottoman Empire. Although she bore her husband five children, none enjoyed the sort of motherly passion which she felt for her eldest son, Riad. She would often take off with him, to Upper Egypt or to the Greek islands, leaving the others behind. She wanted space to be herself, to read, to be alone with this preferred child of hers, in order to forget the frustrating predicament of being trapped in what she considered a loveless marriage. But despite her alienation, her husband Rida continued to dote on her. Indeed, she seems to have been his only weakness.

Rida el-Solh was born in Beirut, most probably in 1861, when the region was still living under the shadow of the Christian-Druze civil war. The youngest son of Ahmad Pasha, he was very different from Kamil and Munah, his two older brothers. They were both tall, physically attractive men, at ease in the world. Rida was small, stiff and strikingly ugly. Kamil became an Ottoman judge, serving in Libya and in the Balkans. Later, in Damascus, he presided over the Court of Appeal. Munah, a poet and a music-lover, stayed at home to manage the family estates, and died young.

Rida's temperament was austere and his presence forbidding. He was a pedant, a stickler for discipline, a born bureaucrat. He entered the Ottoman service at the age of 20 and left it twenty-eight years later. His long-serving secretary swore that, in all the years he worked with him, he had only seen him smile four times.[1]

---

[1] Interview with Alia el-Solh, Monte Carlo, 5–6 October 2004. I am indebted to her,

Rida el-Solh's career

From the middle of the nineteenth century to 1922, the Ottomans paid great attention to recording details of the careers of all government employees. The curricula vitae of 92,137 civil servants are in 201 files of the Turkish Ministry of Interior's archives. Rida's career can therefore be traced with reasonable accuracy. Named in the archives as Hasan Riza Sulh Efendi, every post he occupied, from 1880 to his retirement in 1913, is meticulously listed.[2] Thus we learn that, after completing his schooling in Beirut, where he was given a school-leaving certificate, or *şehadetname*, at 19 he went on to train in calligraphy and in writing at the *tahrirat kalem* in the port city of Latakia, on the north Syrian Mediterranean coast. Like architecture, calligraphy was an art which the Ottomans valued very highly and at which they excelled. The writing of official letters and reports – from the most remote provinces to the Sublime Porte – was the very nerve-system of the Empire, and constituted an important accomplishment.

and to a series of articles she wrote in 1965 for the Beirut newspaper, *Le Jour*, for many details of Riad's early life.

[2] The career of Hasan Rida Sulh Efendi, as recorded in DH.SAIDd 18/167; 18/168 and 80/489, was as follows:

    13 May 1880, Lazkiye (Latakia), *refik-i ula* in Tahrirat Kalemi.

    16 May 1883, Sayda (Shukayf), *Mudir* of the *nahiye* of Shukayf.

    28 January 1885, Lazkiye (Merkab), *Qa'im maqam* of the *caza* of Merkab.

    17 September 1888, Beirut (Safita), *Qa'im maqam* of the *caza* of Safita.

    14 September 1889, Beirut (Merc-i uyun), *Qa'im maqam* of the *caza* of Merç-i uyun.

    17 December 1890, Beirut (Safita), *Qa'im maqam* of the *caza* of Safita.

    6 June 1892, Beirut (Sur: Tyre), *Qa'im maqam* of the *caza* of Tyre.

    6 January 1896, Adana (Islahiye), *Qa'im maqam* of the *caza* of Islahiye.

    23 July 1898, Sayda (Sidon), *Qa'im maqam* of the *caza* of Sidon.

    9 October 1900, Baalbek, *Qa'im maqam* of the *caza* of Baalbek.

    12 May 1902, Najd, *Mutasarrif* in Najd.

    16 October 1902, Cebel-i Bereket, *Mutasarrif* of the *sanjaq* of Cebel-i Bereket (today's Osmaniye in southern Anatolia).

    21 November 1905, Karbala, *Mutasarrif* of the *sanjaq* of Karbala.

    31 January 1906, Bolu, *Mutasarrif* of the *sanjaq* of Bolu.

    11 April 1907, Preveza, *Mutasarrif* of the *sanjaq* of Preveza.

    On 10 November 1908, following the Young Turk revolution which forced the Sultan to restore the Constitution, Rida el-Solh was elected to the reconvened Ottoman parliament in Istanbul, the *Meclis-i Mebusan*, as a deputy for Beirut, and served until the parliament was dissolved on 18 January 1912. (See chapter 3.) On 14 February 1914, he retired from the service of the state on a pension of 1,666 k, according to a note in *Meclis-i Mebusan* records.

After completing his apprenticeship, Rida was appointed a *refik-i ula*, or first scribe, in the same government office in Latakia on 13 May 1880. He resigned from this post on 13 October 1881, before being appointed in May 1883, aged 22, as a *mudir* of a *nahiye*, or group of villages, in the district of Sidon. His salary was 450 *kuruş* (or piastres, one hundred of which were an Ottoman gold pound, then on a par with an English pound). One of Rida's achievements as *mudir* was to found an official Ottoman school at Nabatiyeh, not far from Sidon, as part of the Sublime Porte's attempts to modernise the Empire. With teachers brought in from Beirut and Tripoli, this was an advance on the traditional religious schools, or the *kuttab*, where teaching was limited to grammar, logic and Qur'anic exegesis.[3]

Rida el-Solh rose steadily, if unspectacularly, in the service of the Empire. He was the sort of strict, efficient and loyal provincial administrator that the Sultan appreciated. Over the fifteen years, 1885–1900, Rida had occupied eight posts as a *qa'im maqam*. These were in Marqab (a *caza* of the *sanjaq* of Latakia) at a salary of 1,250 *kuruş*; in Safita (in the mountains south of Aleppo) at a salary of 1,750 *kuruş*; in Marj 'Ayun (in South Lebanon) at no increase in salary; in Safita, once again, at the same salary; in Tyre (on the coast of South Lebanon) at the same salary; and in Islahiye (in southern Anatolia) at a salary of 2,500 *kuruş*. This impressive salary was then adjusted downwards to 2,250 *kuruş*, when he fell ill and returned to Beirut on 20 December 1897. On recovering, he was once again posted as *qa'im maqam* to the Sidon area, on a written order of the Sultan, dated 23 July 1898. This was followed on 9 October 1900 by a posting to Ba'albek in the Biqa' valley of Lebanon.

Then, again by written order of the Sultan, he was promoted and, between 1902 and 1907, occupied five posts as *mutasarrif*. His first job was to undertake a mission to Najd in north-central Arabia, where he spent five months, between May and October 1902, on a salary of 6,750 *kuruş*. He was sent to assess the significance of the Emir 'Abd al-'Aziz Ibn Sa'ud, who, earlier that year, had captured from his tribal enemies the old Saudi capital of Riyadh, and was in due course to found the Kingdom of Saudi Arabia.

Rida's next post was to govern the *sanjaq* of Cebel-i Bereket, the present-day Osmaniye in southern Anatolia, on a salary of 5,670

---

[3] Tamara Chalabi, *The Shi'is of Jabal 'Amil and the New Lebanon: Community and Nation State, 1918–1943*, New York and Basingstoke 2006, p. 30.

kuruş; then as *mutasarrif* of Karbala in Iraq, on a salary of 5,400 *kuruş*, where his native knowledge of Arabic led him to be preferred over another Ottoman candidate. However, when he fell ill again, and needed a surgical operation, he was sent home to convalesce on a basic salary (*mazaret maaşi*) and replaced. On recovering, he was sent as *mutasarrif* to Bolu, in Turkey's western Black Sea region, a region of lakes and pine forests approximately halfway between Istanbul and Ankara.

The Solh Family in Salonica

Although the Ottoman archives do not mention that Rida el-Solh served in Salonica, he is nevertheless believed to have exchanged posts with an incumbent district governor and worked in that city. According to oral evidence from his family (and from an old nanny who recalled their stay there), he appears to have served in Salonica as *mutasarrif* for at least a year in the early 1900s.

Salonica, then the second city of the Empire, contained a large and prosperous Jewish community, many of whose members were descendants of Spanish Jews who had fled to the Balkans at the end of the fifteenth century, when the Catholic Kings issued an edict compelling all Jews to convert to Catholicism or be expelled. About 50,000 were forcibly baptised and remained, becoming known as the *conversos*; they were to suffer greatly from then on, especially at the hands of the Inquisition. But 250,000 chose exile. Many fled to France, England and Holland, but most preferred the more welcoming and sunny cities of the Ottoman Empire. There, on the orders of Sultan Bayezid II, they were warmly received and well treated. About 20,000 chose Salonica, thereby giving a great boost to its trade, education and culture. These Spanish Sephardim were soon followed by waves of other persecuted Jews, from Sicily and Portugal, who brought with them new skills and techniques, among them weaving. By 1515, for example, the Jewish weavers of Salonica were supplying most of the cloth needed for Ottoman army uniforms. Throughout the sixteenth and seventeenth centuries, and as a result of growing anti-Semitism in Europe, new waves of Jewish refugees kept arriving from France, Poland and Hungary. Jews soon overtook Christians and Muslims in numbers.

Salonica's large Orthodox Jewish working class lived in deplorable conditions, but the prosperous Jewish bourgeoisie – lawyers, doctors, teachers, merchants of all sorts – tended to be French-educated 'assimilationists', products of the many schools of the *Alliance Israélite Universelle*. These lived very well. In 1854, the first modern industrial plant, a flour mill, was founded by a Jewish-Italian family, the Allatini, and in 1865, the Jewish-owned *El Lunar* was the first newspaper to be published in the city. However, the Dreyfus affair in France dealt Salonica's Francophile Jewish liberals a severe blow. A new ideological current – Zionism – set about winning recruits in a semi-covert way, especially among the poor.

In Salonica, Rida el-Solh discovered that although Jews were the most prominent local community, they were nevertheless made anxious by uncertainty, aggravated by the spread of revolutionary and Zionist ideas.[4] This was his first exposure to what, for him – and for his son Riad – was to grow into a lifelong preoccupation with the fate of Jews and Palestine Arabs.

The Jewish community of Salonica was in later years to suffer the grimmest of fates. A devastating fire in 1917 left some 54,000 people homeless, destroying thirty synagogues, the offices of the Chief Rabbinate, several Alliance schools and much else besides. It dealt the community a blow from which it never fully recovered. But much worse was to follow. Within days of the Germans entering Salonica on 9 April 1941, many Jewish properties were confiscated or sacked. In 1942, all Jewish men between the ages of 18 and 45 were taken off to labour camps, and in 1943 the rest of the Jewish population was packed into cattle cars and sent to Auschwitz and Birkenau. There, some 45,000 Salonica Jews, from this most fascinating of communities that had dominated the city's life for almost four hundred years, were gassed.[5]

After the Ottoman Empire's defeat in the Russo-Turkish war of 1877–78, its three Macedonian provinces were incorporated into a greater Bulgaria under the Treaty of San Stefano of March 1878.

---

[4] Albertos Nar, 'Social Organization and Activity of the Jewish Community in Thessaloniki', and Basil C. Gounaris, 'Thessaloniki, 1830–1912: History, Economy and Society', in I. K. Hassiotis (ed.), *Thessaloniki: History and Culture*, Athens 1997.
[5] Mark Mazower, *Salonica, City of Ghosts: Christians, Muslims and Jews*, London 2004.

However, the Treaty of Berlin, three months later, restored them to the Ottomans. In these provinces, Turks, Albanians, Greeks, Serbs, Bulgarians, Jews and Romany had lived side by side, not always in harmony. It was a territory that was fought over by Serbia, Bulgaria and Greece, and closely watched by Austro-Hungary and Russia, the two external powers most concerned with Balkan affairs. By the end of the nineteenth century, various revolutionary groups had started attacking trains, taking prisoners for ransom, setting fire to mosques and churches and putting whole villages to the sword.

In April 1903, rebels blew up a French ship in the port of Salonica, as well as gas pipelines, the railway station and the head-quarters of the Ottoman Bank. A few months later, in August, a force of some 25,000 men launched a general insurrection in the whole of Macedonia, causing a bloodbath. The aim of the insurgents was apparently to provoke Ottoman reprisals which, they hoped, would bring about the intervention of the European Powers. Unfortunately for the victims and fortunately for the Sultan, no one in Europe had yet thought to eject the Ottoman Empire from Macedonia.[6]

Nevertheless, restoring order proved to be immensely expensive. The three provinces ran huge deficits, so that soldiers and officials could not be paid. Austro-Hungary and Russia proposed that financial management should be entrusted to the Ottoman Bank, which would raise taxes and pay officials under the control of an international financial commission. This would have meant foreign tutelage – a fate that the Sultan Abdülhamit had always fought to avoid. He tried to play for time, but when the battleships of five nations assembled off Piraeus and prepared to sail for the Straits, he was forced to give way. The Macedonian question was front-page news in both Europe and America.

During Rida el-Solh's spell as *mutasarrif* in Salonica, an event occurred which was to scar his family's life – and have a huge impact on his son Riad's career. His wife Nazira and their five children had joined Rida at his post for the summer holidays. Riad, the eldest, was there, together with his two sisters, Balqis and Alia, and two brothers, Ahmad and Darwish. One day, Riad and Ahmad were playing on the beach. Greek boys were racing up and down, collecting driftwood to build barricades and waging mock battles with shrill cries. They were

---

[6] Georgeon, *Abdülhamid II*, pp. 366–73.

re-enacting the battle of Missolonghi of 1823, early in the Greek war of independence, in which the Greek hero, Botsaris, routed an Ottoman army of 4,000 Albanian Muslims.

Riad and his brother wanted to join in, but the Greek boys would not let them. 'You can't!' they cried. 'You are Arabs! You Arabs are slaves of the Turks!' Stung by the insult, Riad attacked the barricades the Greek boys had built. Wading out to sea, he threw the driftwood into deep water. His brother Ahmad followed but, unable to swim, was knocked off his feet by a wave and drowned. When the boy's body was brought home, Riad confronted his father. 'It's your fault,' he sobbed. 'You work for the Turks. That's why my brother died!'

Rida was grief-stricken at Ahmad's death. He is said to have taken to his bed for weeks. Cut to the quick by Riad's accusation, he later tried to reason with the boy. 'Try not to judge people too severely,' he told him. 'My own father tried to rise against the Turks, but they banished him to Rhodes. I've always tried to serve in Arab countries, to help improve conditions there. We shouldn't rebel until we're ready.' Ahmad was buried in Salonica. Much later, Riad visited the grave and promised his mother he would bring his brother's remains to Beirut for reburial, but he was never able to do so.

It was shortly afterwards that Sultan Abdülhamit asked to see Rida el-Solh. In his later years, the Sultan liked to bypass the bureaucracy of the Sublime Porte and communicate personally with his governors. They, in turn, were encouraged to report to him directly using a palace cipher. In any event, he invited Rida el-Solh to bring his eldest son with him, perhaps as a gesture of condolence for Ahmad's death. For much of his reign, the Sultan had immured himself in Yildiz palace, overlooking the Bosphorus. It was a great complex of buildings, to which he was always adding new pavilions, set in a large park surrounded by a high wall. The Sultan was prey to all sorts of morbid fears – fear of crowds, of conspiracies, of assassination. He trusted no one. In nearby barracks lived the members of the Imperial Guard – his personal line of defence – some 15,000 Albanian, Bosnian and Arab soldiers. Beneath Yildiz, new suburbs had sprung up to house officials, secretaries, courtiers and a small army of palace servants.

Physically, the Sultan and Rida were not all that dissimilar, although Rida was slightly smaller. Foreign visitors described the Sultan as below average in height, thin and slightly bent. His large head was balanced on a seemingly undernourished body. He had a high forehead above thick, strongly arched eyebrows, dark sunken eyes, a large hooked nose and a well-trimmed beard, which he dyed black. His voice could be caressing with visitors, but was strident and imperious with underlings. He had a prodigious memory, especially for faces. He preferred to live simply, in comfortable but not luxurious apartments.

We do not know what the Sultan and Rida said to each other, but, once the serious business was concluded, the child, Riad, was summoned to join them. The Sultan drew him close and attempted to lift him on to his knee, reaching at the same time to put down his coffee. With a brusque gesture, Riad overturned the tiny Turkish coffee cup over the imperial frock coat. A coffee stain appeared on the pommel of the Sultan's sword. Recounting the incident later to his children, and no doubt embroidering the story, Riad believed the stain was a harbinger of his later rebellion against both the Ottomans and the French.

After Salonica, and suffering once again from ill health, Rida el-Solh was assigned on 11 April 1907 to Preveza, a place of clement climate on the Ionian coast. Preveza was then a small Albanian port in a European province of the Empire, located on an inlet of the Ionian Sea in the vilayet of Yanya. When Rida was its *mutasarrif*, its population numbered 6,500, of whom about four-fifths were Christian Albanians and Greeks and one-fifth Muslims. Surrounded by dense olive groves, the town boasted hot springs celebrated for their therapeutic properties. The harbour was small and closed to large vessels by a sand bar, but numerous small craft plied the coast, carrying dairy products, hides, wool, olives and olive oil. Despite its idyllic surroundings, sea breezes and old-world charm, Preveza was no sleepy sinecure, because the *sanjaq* was simmering with violent tensions. Immediately to the north and east lay Macedonia, then erupting in nationalist rebellion. This was to be Rida's last post as an imperial administrator. Just a few years later, in 1912, Salonica and Perveza both fell to the Greeks.

Mother and son

Riad el-Solh's mother, Nazira Muftizada, was not an Arab. Her father was an Uzbek and her mother a Circassian, possibly one of the many Circassians who had settled in southern Syria from the late 1870s, and who had played an important role in the economy and in security arrangements. Considered a beauty, her colouring – fair, blonde and blue-eyed – came from her mother, while her slit eyes and wide, flat face were inherited from her father. Such startling racial mixtures were common to the Ottoman Empire. Ever since the end of the eighteenth century, Russia's aggressive expansion in the Black Sea, the Caucasus and central Asia had caused Muslim populations to flee for safety to the Empire. More than 2 million immigrants from the Balkans and Russia – nearly 10 per cent of the Empire's entire population – flooded in during the reign of Sultan Abdülhamit II (1876–1909). The fact that the Sultan himself had a Circassian mother whom he adored may have made him particularly sensitive to the fate of these displaced populations. He did everything possible to help the immigrants, creating entire villages – several of which were called *Hamidiye* in his honour. He built schools and mosques for them out of his own private purse. At the end of the nineteenth century, Sir William Ramsay, an English traveller, described such a place in eastern Anatolia, where the inhabitants belonged to seven different religions and spoke no fewer than fourteen languages.[7]

Nazira's mother, Farida – Riad's grandmother – was the daughter of the Emir Hadji Baslan, a Circassian prince who had fought the Russians and been defeated. Fleeing the Caucasus, he had first made his way to Egypt. It is said that the only survivors of the long and dangerous journey there were himself, his two daughters, Farida and Safwat, and his two Circassian slave-girls, Boran and Firyal. He was welcomed by the Khedive Ismaʿil, to whom, in gratitude, he presented Firyal as a gift. In due course, she was given to the Khedive's son, Prince Tawfiq. She gave birth to Fuʾad – later King Fuʾad the First of Egypt. Fuʾad's son, King Farouk, fathered a daughter, who was named Firyal after her Circassian great-grandmother.

After a stay of some months in Egypt, the Emir Hadji Baslan left for Istanbul, where, just before his own death, he entrusted his two daughters to the Sultan himself. They were eventually to marry two Uzbek brothers, Sharif and Amin Rahim Khan, victims like themselves of Russia's imperial expansion. Amin had commanded the army of Muhammad Rahim Kul, one of the last Khans of Khiva, capital of the Uzbek khanate of central Asia before it was overrun by Russian forces. He had been forced to flee when the small force he

[7] Sir William Mitchell Ramsay, *The Intermixture of Races in Asia Minor, Some of its Causes and Effects*, Proceedings of the British Academy, vol. VII, London 1917, quoted in Georgeon, *Abdülhamid II*, p. 320.

commanded was routed. A Cossack sliced open the crown of Amin's head with a sabre, and he would certainly not have survived had his elder brother, Sharif, not sealed the wound with honey, which the Mongols used as balm, binding it in place with strips of goat skin, and then strapping him to his own horse for the arduous journey. They had to travel through desert and steppe, over mountain and into valley, in order finally to reach Anatolia, where other Uzbek refugees had come before them.

Amin arrived in Turkey not only physically cured but spiritually changed as well. The long trek had transformed him: the intrepid fighter had turned mystic. Immersing himself in religion, he became the Mufti of the small town of Azringan in Anatolia, where his descendants took the name of Muftizada after his title. When he died, his wife, Farida, was left with two small children, a boy and a girl. Nazira, the girl, was then aged two.

Amin's brother, Sharif, was more worldly-wise. He had pushed on to Istanbul and entered the service of the palace, rising eventually to become a *defterdar*, a finance officer, travelling on missions to the Arab provinces of the Empire. He brought his widowed sister-in-law, Farida, his niece, Nazira, and her brother to live with him in Istanbul. In due course, he was appointed *defterdar* of the Beirut vilayet, then already more cosmopolitan and therefore a more useful listening post for the Ottomans than the inland and more inbred city of Damascus.

In Beirut, Sharif built a big house on the fashionable seafront at Minat al-Husn, on a plot opposite what is now the St Georges Hotel. It was here that his family, and the family of his dead brother Amin, set up house together. Meanwhile, his niece Nazira was growing into an accomplished young woman. After attending the school of the Prussian Sisters in Beirut, she completed her education at an Islamic institution, *Jam'iyat al-maqasid al-khayriyya*.[8] She knew Arabic and German as well as Turkish, and was passionately fond of music. A Jewish musician, Murad, taught her to play the *qanun* (the Arab zither), while Murad's niece, Laila, taught her to sing and dance. Anxious to cut a

---

[8] See an interview with Nazira Muftizada in *Awraq Lubnaniyya* (*Papiers Libanais*), ed. Yusuf Ibrahim Yazbek, part four, April 1955. Two *al-Maqasid* schools for boys were founded in Beirut and Sidon in July 1875, followed two months later by two schools for girls. These schools adopted the same curriculum and teaching methods as Christian mission schools. In 1882, the Ottoman government closed down *al-Maqasid* and brought its schools into the official system, but when standards fell drastically, the society was rehabilitated in 1908.

figure in Lebanese society, her ambitious uncle Sharif decided to marry her off to an Arab notable. His choice fell on Rida Efendi, the youngest son of Ahmad Pasha. She was 16, he was twice her age. Rida was serving as *qa'im maqam* of the *caza* of Tyre in South Lebanon.

Nazira did not actually see her husband before the marriage. According to the family story, when she did catch sight of him, she begged to be taken back home! Rida was physically unattractive, and besides she was smitten with Safwat Bey, a young and handsome Turkish officer of the Imperial Guard, who was visiting Beirut from Istanbul. Bewitched by his courtly manner, gold epaulettes and polished boots, she was hoping to marry him instead. Indeed, he had asked for her hand, but her uncle had other plans for her and turned him down. Sharif's interest was to use her to consolidate relations with the leading families of Beirut.

After their marriage, Rida and Nazira moved into the house of her uncle in Minat al-Husn, and it was there that Riad el-Solh was born on 17 August 1894. *Riad* is the plural of *rawd* which, in Arabic, means garden. In the nineteenth century, it was a name common only among Egyptian Copts, and was unknown elsewhere in the Arab world. Ahmad Pasha wanted his grandson to be named 'Ali Wasfi – 'Ali after the Imam 'Ali, revered by the Shi'a among whom the Solh family had lived in South Lebanon for generations, and Wasfi after one of his close friends. But Rida el-Solh preferred Riad. He wrote to his father to say that he would agree to 'Ali but begged him to grant him Riad. It was therefore agreed that the boy would be named 'Ali Riad. The 'Ali was soon dropped, however, and Riad stuck, becoming a name well known in the region. All other Riads in Lebanon were apparently born after Riad el-Solh.

Riad grew up in a household of women. His father, distant and intimidating, was often absent. He certainly did not fit into the world of legends which filled the lives of Riad's mother, Nazira; his grandmother, Farida; his paternal aunt, Zahiyya, who also lived with them; and his black nanny, Dada Tuffaha. Each of these women had tall tales to tell, harboured bitter grievances, and longed to get even with former oppressors. Passionate wars of liberation were fought and refought over the dinner table. Uzbek and Circassian dreams of revenge against the hated Russians were part of the texture of their daily life. His grandmother Farida sang him Circassian songs, taught him sabre dances, dressed him in Circassian costumes with rows of cartridge pouches across the chest and urged him to set out on the reconquest of the Circassian mountains. When she was angry she would curse him with the worst insult in her vocabulary, and call him a 'Wretched Muscovite!' At other times, she would let down her golden tresses, which reached down to her ankles, becoming streaked with grey as she grew older, and parade him round the house – she as the 'sovereign' and he as her pageboy, holding her fall of hair as if it were a train. These parades were always in honour of a single man – her father, the Emir Hadji Baslan. His back, she would tell Riad, had been straight as a lance. Because he never lowered his proud gaze, he did not know the colour of the ground. His cloak, in her account, was always threaded in gold and his tents full of perfumed women. At nightly feasts, he would sit Farida on his knee, hold her hands in his and happily beat time to the music. But one night, she would recount, their camp was overrun by Czarist cavalry, and their tents went up in flames. A band one hundred strong took to the road, but only five survived the long exodus from Georgia to Egypt. Although Riad el-Solh never learned any of the Circassian languages, he could still reproduce, parrot-fashion, the few phrases his grandmother had taught him. He was later to tell his daughter Alia that whenever he was acclaimed by a crowd or carried shoulder-high in triumph, these Circassian phrases would come to his mind, and he would hum them, s*otto voce*, to himself in a singsong.

Not to be outdone by her mother's tales, Nazira, daughter of the Uzbek commander Amin Rahim Khan, would sometimes pull up her skirts, roll down her stockings and bounce Riad up and down on her thighs, as if he were riding bareback like the horsemen of her native land. 'At full gallop!' she would cry. 'Boum! Another *mujik* bites the dust!' Amin, she told him, was a tiger hunter. He was known as the 'tiger of tigers' because he was said to tame tigers by fixing them with his burning eyes. 'Khiva would never have fallen to the Russians if my father had not been seriously wounded,' she would never tire of telling her son. Riad's aunt Zahiyya was almost as frightening as her brother Rida, and was known for her strong personality. She had been married briefly to a Shambur of Tripoli – a descendant, it was said, of the crusading comte de Chambord. She was rich and independent because, on his death, Shambur had left her all his land. She possessed an ancient key to a house in Cordoba, from where her Arab ancestors had been expelled. On her death, she left Riad all her possessions, including this key. Dada Tuffaha, Riad's adored nanny, also wanted to recover a lost homeland. Kidnapped by slavers somewhere in East Africa, she was given to the Sultan of Zanzibar. He, in turn, gave her to Ahmad Pasha, but she continued to pine for her roots for years afterwards. These, then, were the four women who presided over Riad's childhood and who, in a way, were to determine the colourful and dramatic nature of his political life.

Until well into his teens, Riad el-Solh knew little of the world outside, only the account these women gave of it. Cosseted by them, his was a protected and happy childhood. As he was schooled at home much of the time, they had a considerable influence over him. A zeal for liberation is certainly what they taught him. The legends with which they filled his imagination helped convince him that his mission was to become a liberator, to free the oppressed. He was little concerned with money or status, nor did he seem to feel fear. He was hardly brought face to face with reality, which may have been one reason why he was later able to defy both the Turks and the French in so courageous and carefree a manner.

Of these four women, his mother Nazira was, of course, the greatest single influence on him. Although four of her five children were to predecease her, she would not allow herself to be defeated by life, as her hopes were settled on Riad. She was his first teacher, giving him a taste for reading, for history, poetry and botany. At the age of 6, he knew how to dissect flowers and how to arrange them in families. He was hardly made to bother with multiplication tables, or with addition and subtraction, since his mother believed that numbers were a 'poison for the soul'. It was a weakness he was to retain throughout his life, and it may well have primed him to run cheerfully through a family fortune that had been carefully amassed over several generations.

Riad was not sent to school until late in his childhood, and even then only fitfully. When he was 9, his father decided that his vacation had lasted long enough, and engaged two tutors to call at the house and accompany the family on their travels. One was Husni al-Jundi, a Syrian Muslim, who taught him Arabic, history, geography, mathematics and science. The other was Joseph Khoury, a Lebanese Christian, who taught him French, as well as the basic elements of Turkish, Persian and Latin. It was certainly an ambitious curriculum for a child who had started to learn so late. Husni al-Jundi had a passion for rhetoric and for speechmaking. He liked to stand Riad in front of a tall mirror and give him a theme. 'Imagine', he would say, 'that an angry crowd has forced its way into the Governor's palace. What must the Governor do?'

'I know,' the boy would say, knitting his brow. 'He must display his own anger. He must defy the crowd to win its respect.'

'Good!' the tutor said. 'But that's not enough. After the display of anger, he must put the crowd at ease. He must change the mood. He must smile. He must make promises in highly coloured phrases, ending with a witticism or a sentimental memory, which he must pretend to recount for the first time.' Years later, in 1950, when Riad's daughter Alia watched her father making a speech in the Lebanese parliament, she realised that it was a touching re-enactment of the well-rehearsed scenarios with his tutor.

In 1905, Rida el-Solh enrolled Riad at the *kulliyah al-ʿuthmaniyya al-islamiyya* (Ottoman Islamic College). This was a famous institution founded in Beirut in 1895 by Shaykh Ahmad ʿAbbas al-Azhari. Students came to it from all over the region for instruction in religious sciences, in Arabic grammar and literature, in argument and logic. French was added later, as well as additional subjects borrowed from foreign schools. Many of the future members of Arab nationalist societies were its graduates. Rida wrote to his wife, who had carried her son off to Aswan in Upper Egypt, to tell her of his decision.

> *My dear Umm Riad,*
>
> *I've learned the reasons for your sadness and I've delayed sending your Riad to school. But I've decided that this cannot go on. The little fellow will go to the Ottoman school. It's an excellent school, as may be judged by the fact that the Jesuits take its students without a special exam. The headmaster is Shaykh Ahmad ʿAbbas, my old teacher at the national school. He will be father and mother to your Riad.*
>
> *Have no fear in this regard and remember that whenever you feel like seeing your son, he will be sent to you with a special emissary, who will leave him with you for a few days before bringing him back to school.*
>
> *The Shaykh will promise you that no one will be allowed to visit Riad or take him out of school, even on orders of his grandmother or his aunt.*
>
> *(Signed) Hasan Rida.*

Riad then had a short spell at the Lazarist school in 'Aintura in the Lebanese mountains – the first French institute of higher education in Lebanon, founded in 1734 – before spending some years at the Jesuit college of Saint-Joseph in Beirut, where he perfected his French and acquired a knowledge of Christianity. The story goes that one day in the school refectory, a pietà fell out of the prayer book of a fellow student, Charles Corm,[9] who happened to be sitting next to him. Riad picked it up, and was moved by the image of a mother in tears, gathering to herself the body of her son. He wanted to know more, and learned enough to win first prize in catechism! But he also rebelled against the ascetic Christian precepts that did not suit his temperament. The black-robed priests taught humility, abnegation, an avoidance of sensual joys and earthly glories. Riad, on the other hand, was desperate to seize life with both hands, and could not wait to get away.

The family house at Minat al-Husn was situated on the seaside promenade where women drove up and down in their carriages – open carriages for Christian women, and carriages with drawn curtains for their Muslim sisters. On Sundays, the Jesuits' students went for long walks, pausing for a rest on the rocks by the sea below the road. It was here that Nazira would often organise games and treats for Riad and his friends. Once she managed to assemble five or six barrel organs to play popular tunes. On another occasion, no fewer than eight Guignol boxes were lined up waiting to amuse the children, while her servants distributed snacks, easy to hide and quick to swallow. Riad never failed to slip away from the monitors for a couple of minutes, in order to embrace his mother and to request some new distraction for the following Sunday.

They remained very close throughout his life. As a grown man, he would kiss her hand and wait for her blessing every single day. He would ask her permission before he left the house, no matter how many times he did so. She would then put her hand on his shoulder and enquire whether he was walking out to the right or to the left. When he told her which direction he planned to take, she would stand behind the lattice (the *musharabiyya*) on the second floor of their house, and recite the *ayat al-kursi,* or the 'Throne Verse', from the Qur'an (Q. 2:255):

---

[9] Charles Corm (1895–1963) was to become the foremost proponent of Christian Lebanese identity. He founded the *Revue phénicienne*, and published three anthologies of poetry extolling the inspirational merits of Mount Lebanon.

There is no god but He, the Living, the Everlasting.
Slumber seizes Him not, nor sleep;
to Him belongs
all that is in the heavens and the earth.
Who is there that shall intercede with Him
Save by His leave?
He knows what lies before them
and what is after them,
and they comprehend not anything of His knowledge
save such as He wills.
His Throne comprises the heavens and the earth;
the preserving of them exhausts Him not;
He is the All-high, the All-glorious.

Nazira would slowly exhale so that her breath might carry the divine words in the direction of her son in order to protect him; she who was only seventeen years his senior. When she died early in 1951, Riad was not only devastated but convinced that his luck had run out. And no doubt it had, for he was assassinated three months later.

The early death or incapacity of his brothers and sisters meant that Riad el-Solh was brought up as if he were an only child. His sister Balqis, who was married to her cousin, Sami el-Solh, died at the age of 25. His sister Alia died a poignant death of consumption at the age of 18, leaving behind a collection of unpublished poems. His brother Darwish was severely disabled, having contracted meningitis as a child. All the family's hopes were thus centred on Riad. Having a mother who lavished attention on him, who boosted his self-confidence and pushed him forwards with love, was clearly of decisive importance to his development. As was the fact that he came from a family of government officials, of politicians, writers and poets. The Solhs produced no businessmen, doctors, engineers or architects. Springing from such a milieu, a career in public service was for him the obvious choice.

3 EDUCATION IN REVOLUTION

The Solh family arrived in Istanbul in the late summer of 1908, just a few weeks after the 23 July revolution brought an end to Sultan Abdülhamit's authoritarian rule. Riad was 14. For his parents, Rida el-Solh, a newly elected deputy for Beirut in the Ottoman parliament, and his wife Nazira, travelling to the imperial capital at a time of revolutionary mayhem must have been a source of some anxiety. The city was in a ferment of excitement, yet with an undeniable undercurrent of violence and insecurity too. The Sultan, whom Rida el-Solh had served all his working life, still lived behind the walls of Yildiz palace, but he had been stripped of much of his power by the young putschists, who were of uncertain origins and had new-fangled intentions. One of the declared aims of the Young Turk revolutionaries was to replace the Sultan's autocracy with a constitutional, parliamentary regime on the Western model.[1] To many, this sounded like a hazardous leap in the dark. Such a drastic transformation could not take place painlessly or overnight. Inevitably, there was a chaotic period of transition as the new system fought to establish itself, while the old refused to admit defeat but continued to plot and plan a monarchical restoration.

The city which the Solhs discovered in the early years of the twentieth century was a densely populated metropolis of nearly 900,000 inhabitants. Pera, its main thoroughfare – now called Istiklâl Ceddesi – was lined with hotels, theatres, fashionable shops, photographic studios and foreign embassies, all built in different architectural styles, ranging

---

[1] For the chronology of events in this chapter, I have relied on Aykut Kansu, *Politics in Post-Revolutionary Turkey, 1908–1913*, Leiden 2000; on Hasan Kayalı, *Arabs and Young Turks: Ottomanism, Arabism and Islamism in the Ottoman Empire, 1908–1918*, Berkeley 1997; and on Feroz Ahmad, *The Young Turks*, Oxford 1969.

from neoclassical to rococo to art nouveau.[2] But there was another Istanbul – overcrowded, foul-smelling and constantly ravaged by pitiless fires. There, peasants drawn to the capital from the countryside spent their miserable lives living off handouts or the charitable soup served in mosques. They were joined by destitute refugees from the Balkans and Russia.

Having grown up in Beirut, a port which had blossomed in the latter part of the nineteenth century into a lively and cosmopolitan metropolis, Rida el-Solh had already been exposed to Western ideas, to mission schools, to foreign merchants and consuls, who had contributed to the spectacular growth of the city's *entrepôt* trade. He was, therefore, far from being an uncritical observer of the Ottoman scene. Drawing on his direct experience of several imperial provinces, he was well aware how badly Ottoman governance had been allowed to deteriorate under Abdülhamit, and how stagnant and backward the Empire had become if compared to Europe. He must first have thought the revolution a promising development – that is, until events caused him to change his mind.

The Young Turks burst on the scene

The Young Turks were not, literally speaking, Turkish nationalists – or at least not yet. The secret society they had formed in Salonica and named the Committee of Union and Progress, or CUP (*ittihad ve terakki cemiyeti*) was not exclusively Turkish. In a book published in 1917, less than a decade after the revolution, the British historian R. W. Seton-Watson wrote that 'From the very first hardly one among its true leaders has been a pure-blooded Turk'.[3] Most Young Turks were Ottoman Muslims, including Albanians and Circassians, as well as Jews and *Donmehs* (Muslim converts from Judaism), Christian Bulgarians, Armenians and Greeks. The majority of their leaders were freemasons. Their revolution was the culmination of years of semi-secret agitation and planning, mainly in Paris and Cairo, aimed at curbing the Sultan's autocratic powers and preventing what the Young

---

[2] Georgeon, *Abdülhamid II*, p. 333.
[3] Robert Wilson Seton-Watson, *The Rise of Nationality in the Balkans*, London 1917, pp. 135–6, quoted in Zeine N. Zeine, *Arab-Turkish Relations and the Emergence of Arab Nationalism*, Beirut 1958, p. 77.

Turks feared would be the utter ruin of the Empire. Their watchwords were 'Freedom' and 'Constitution'.[4]

A decisive turning point was the defection to them of the Sultan's brother-in-law, the rich and prestigious Damad Mahmud Cellaleddin Pasha. His son, Prince Sabaheddin, was to become a principal organiser of the first Young Turk Congress in Paris in 1902. There were, at that time, two main currents in the Young Turk movement. One, led by Sabaheddin, campaigned for a radical remodelling of Ottoman society by means of decentralisation and private enterprise, and could more accurately be termed 'Young Ottomans'. The other, led by Ahmed Riza Bey, attracted ambitious military officers into its ranks and was more obviously Turkish nationalist in temper, and entirely impatient with Ottomanism. It was the main force behind the second Young Turk Congress of 1907. The main aim of this Congress was to forge a unified opposition to the Sultan's regime.[5] Such radicals advocated open rebellion against the Sultan to save the Empire from tyranny and 'from the venomous clutches of the greedy Powers'.[6] They were outraged that European Powers had come to dominate and exploit the Empire's economy. The Istanbul stock exchange was foreign-controlled, as were the leading shipping lines, insurance companies and import–export firms. The Ottoman Public Debt Administration and the Imperial Ottoman Bank were the main agents of foreign financial control. The hated Capitulations – reminiscent in name and scope of those imposed by the Catholic Kings on the defeated Muslims of al-Andalus – severely restricted Ottoman sovereignty. They granted wide privileges to Europeans, to their local protégés and to Christian communities protected by foreign consuls.

Revolutionary ideas had spread to the distant provinces of the Empire, carried there by officers, officials and dissident students whom Abdülhamit had sent into exile in droves – to the Hijaz, to Yemen, to eastern Anatolia and even to the Fezzan desert of Tripolitania (now in Libya), which served as the Sultan's 'Saharan Siberia'.[7] Troops throughout the Empire were in restive mood. The years immediately before the revolution had witnessed repeated army mutinies, often because

---

[4] For a scholarly assessment of the Young Turks, see Erik J. Zurcher, *Turkey: A Modern History*, London 1993.
[5] Kayalı, *Arabs and Young Turks*, p. 44.
[6] Zeine, *Arab-Turkish Relations*, p. 63.
[7] Georgeon, *Abdülhamid II*, p. 159.

soldiers had been sent to fight and die pointless deaths in bleak places, with even their pay withheld. On their return to Beirut from Yemen in 1907, more than a thousand soldiers went on the rampage, seizing the Ottoman governor, the treasurer and the local military commander, only agreeing to release them when they were finally handed their back pay. Ottoman army tradition pampered the officers but dealt harshly with the troops. In July 1908, the Empire had 50,000 officers and 250,000 men in arms – one officer for every five troopers. Many officers, who were favourites or relations of the Sultan, had been given their rank with little regard for their competence or for the actual needs of the military service.[8]

On coming to the throne in 1876 at the age of 33, Abdülhamit had been persuaded by Midhat Pasha, his capable grand vezir, to adopt a Constitution and convene a parliament. Midhat Pasha, twenty years older than his master and with a great deal of political experience, had advised the Sultan to allow provincial governors greater autonomy, and to build on the radical reforms first introduced by Sultan Abdülmecid I in 1839, and extended by him in 1856, which were famously known as the *Tanzimat*. These 'organisations' had attempted to reshape Ottoman institutions on the Western model – especially the relationship between the Sultan and the state bureaucracy – as well as to institute equality for all Ottoman subjects, without distinction of race or religion.

Abdülhamit had accepted Midhat Pasha's advice largely because he was faced, almost immediately, with the threat of a war with Russia. He may have imagined that, by adopting a Constitution and convening a parliament, he would win a place for himself among the enlightened monarchs of Europe, isolate the czar and avert a looming conflict. When an Ottoman parliament met on 18 March 1877, therefore, it seemed as if a new era was about to begin, in which the Empire would be ruled by a trio of forces, more or less in balance with one another – the Sultan, parliament and the bureaucracy of the Sublime Porte. But war with Russia could not be averted, and the catastrophic Ottoman defeat of 1877–78 quickly cured Abdülhamit of any further taste for democracy. He chose to see the debacle as conclusive proof of the failure of the *Tanzimat*. Throwing off the newly adopted restraints on his absolute power, he sent parliament packing on 14 February 1878, less than a year after it had first convened, and

[8] Muçafir, *Notes sur la Jeune Turquie*, Paris 1911, p. 26.

banished the more outspoken deputies from Istanbul. With the brief constitutional experiment crushed, the Sultan set about consolidating his personal rule through an army of spies and a palace bureaucracy loyal only to himself. Nevertheless, throughout the long remaining years of Abdülhamit's increasingly paranoid autocracy, the ideal of a constitutional regime lived on in men's minds.

On 23 July 1908, Young Turk leaders and their military allies rose in revolt at Monastir in the name of parliament and Constitution. Other cities soon came out in support. Stern telegrams were sent to the Sultan – the telegraph office at Salonica being run by Talaat Bey, a leading Young Turk – warning him that if the 1876 Constitution were not restored, the Third Army would march on the capital. Further telegrams carried the news to cities throughout the Empire. Since Abdülhamit was terrified of assassination, and had always in mind the fate suffered by Sultan Abdülaziz (his predecessor but one), who had been murdered in a coup by the army officers and civilian bureaucrats of the *Tanzimat* reforms, he gave his panic-stricken agreement to the return of the Young Turks to the capital. He also agreed to the restoration of the Constitution, which he had suspended more than thirty years earlier.

As soon as they took control of Istanbul, the Young Turks set about organising parliamentary elections. They vowed that Abdülhamit's absolutist state would be replaced by a constitutional parliamentary regime. Every subject of the Empire, whatever his ethnicity or religion, would be considered a 'first-class citizen', enjoying equal rights but also assuming equal obligations, such as a requirement to pay taxes and serve in the army. There were to be no more privileges for minority communities, for foreigners or other favoured persons. Their ideal was to create a modern, unified, multicultural and centralised state, strong enough to protect the Empire against the dangerous encroachments of European Powers. Throughout the Empire, the 1908 revolution was welcomed with immense enthusiasm. It opened the floodgates to a great explosion of rebellious self-assertion. In all the major cities, Muslims, Christians and Jews marched in celebration of the end of Ottoman tyranny. Political groupings sprang up, Muslim as well as Greek and Armenian; the first trades unions were formed, as were the first women's associations. Political prisoners were released and censorship lifted, while palace spies and informers found that they now had to run for cover. Many exiles, whom the Sultan had banished to remote provinces, made their joyful way home, adding to the manic atmosphere in the capital.

The most striking feature was the new-found sense of freedom. In Beirut, stevedores and gas company workers went on strike, while labourers on the Damascus–Hama railroad downed tools for the sake of higher wages and better working conditions.[9] Countless public political meetings were held, while vituperative debates were conducted in the columns of a raucous press. In just a few months, no fewer than 353 journals and newspapers were published,[10] with another thirty-five in Syria – of better quality and enjoying greater freedom than those that exist there today – and, in Beirut, nearly twice that number in the years before the First World War.[11]

Deputy in the Ottoman parliament

In his first year in Istanbul, Rida el-Solh was still a comparatively young man of 47,[12] although already in indifferent health. After twenty-eight years in Ottoman service, including five years as a *mutasarrif*, he had been pensioned off and had returned to Lebanon, only to be elected to the newly convened Ottoman parliament – *Meclis-i Mebusan* – as one of two deputies for Beirut. The other was a Shi'i notable, Kamil al-As'ad, head of the most prominent landowning political family in South Lebanon, whose home was at Taibeh and whose fortress was at Tibnin. The As'ads were Ottoman loyalists. Kamil Bey's father, Khalil Bey, had been *mutasarrif* of Nablus. The Solhs and the As'ads had lived side by side for generations, sometimes in amity, but more often in competition and animosity.

Like other members of Istanbul's elite, the Solh family set up house in the new residential quarter north of Taksim Square, then inhabited by Europeans and wealthy Turks, Levantine Arabs, Armenians, Greeks and Jews. In the early years of the century, this cosmopolitan, largely French-speaking community of pashas, beys, foreign diplomats,

---

[9] Kayalı, *Arabs and Young Turks*, p. 59.

[10] Ibid., p. 53.

[11] Rashid Khalidi, 'Abd al-Ghani al-'Uraisi and al-Mufid', in Marwan R. Buheiry (ed.), *Intellectual Life in the Arab East, 1890–1939*, Beirut 1981.

[12] Or 45, if the correction to his date of birth in the Ottoman archives is to be accepted. See chapter 1, note 4.

rich merchants, high officials and senior officers congregated in clubs and societies, attended French plays and enjoyed the new craze for cinema. But the revolution had introduced a sharp note of fear. No one could be sure any longer what the future might hold.

Next door to the Solhs lived 'Azmi Bey, later the Ottoman governor of Beirut during the First World War. The children of the two households struck up a friendship over the garden wall, with the spreading branches of a lemon tree providing a useful perch. The young Riad and Mamduha, 'Azmi Bey's teenage daughter, soon fell in love. Clandestine messages, scribbled on a sheet of paper and wrapped around a lemon, would be tossed over the wall and into the garden on the other side. Greatly daring, Riad would sometimes climb down and hide with his beloved under the stairs of her house. One day, 'Azmi Bey, who suffered from asthma, had a more serious attack than usual and called out for help. As he was then in the house, Riad raced to call for a doctor and the Bey's life was saved in time. The incident was to have some considerable later significance.[13]

Deputies to the first Ottoman parliament of 1877 had not been elected by popular suffrage, but had been nominated by administrative councils in the various provinces. However, under the 1908 electoral law, deputies were elected in a two-stage ballot. In the first ballot, all taxpaying male Ottoman citizens over the age of 25 elected secondary voters, who in turn elected parliamentary deputies, according to the number specified for each *sanjaq*. For Rida el-Solh, this electoral process was something with which he was entirely unfamiliar. It was a new world of political parties, public meetings, press campaigns, as well as the cut and thrust of parliamentary debate, which he may well have found unsettling.

A huge upheaval was under way in the senior ranks of the Ottoman bureaucracy. By mid-August some 3,000 Ottoman officials had been sacked, and within twenty months all ambassadors and provincial governors had been changed. Many of the people Rida had known, or with whom he had corresponded in his career, had been summarily dismissed.

A number of Arabs who had held prominent posts in and around Yildiz palace were now in difficulty. Najib Pasha Melhamah, a Maronite from Lebanon, who had been the unofficial head of the

---

[13] Interview with Alia el-Solh, Monte Carlo, 6 October 2004.

Sultan's secret police in charge of his personal safety, was caught by the revolutionaries carrying away secret documents and no less than 63,000 Ottoman pounds in cash. A Syrian, 'Izzat Pasha al-'Abid, had been the powerful second secretary at the Chancellery, the Sultan's close adviser and in charge of all Arabic correspondence.[14] With a good education in Arabic and French from the Lazarist Fathers in Lebanon, he had been called to the Sultan's service in 1895. Over the years, he had acquired considerable influence, chairing several palace committees. He was the main intermediary between the Sultan and the notables of the Arab provinces, including the great families of Damascus, to one of which he himself belonged. Inevitably, Rida el-Solh had had long dealings with him. But, when the Young Turks seized power, 'Izzat Pasha fled abroad. This was hardly a good omen for Arab deputies such as Rida, or indeed for those Arab officials who were still at their posts, many of whom were soon to be removed.

'Izzat Pasha is remembered today for the key role he played in the construction of the Hijaz railway – the 2,000-kilometre line which revolutionised the journey from Damascus to Medina. For centuries, the route through Syria had provided the essential link between Istanbul and the Holy Cities of Arabia. It was the route of choice for members of the Sultan's family, for senior Ottoman officials, for merchants and, above all, for pilgrims setting out on the annual hajj. Before the railway was built, pilgrims faced an arduous forty-day overland journey. They were often waylaid and robbed by marauding tribes. The Ottoman sultans, therefore, had had to expend considerable effort on the organisation and protection of the pilgrim caravan.[15] But the railway project was on an altogether different scale. In his youth in Damascus, 'Izzat Pasha had witnessed the hardship pilgrims endured in going to Mecca, and also the problems the authorities faced in transporting troops and supplies to the Hijaz. Later, he had studied and drawn lessons from the way the Russians had built the trans-Siberian railway. On his prompting, the Sultan issued an imperial order for the building of the railway on 2 May 1900.

It was 'Izzat Pasha's idea to finance the project by soliciting subscriptions from Muslims all over the world. The Sultan himself pledged £45,000 sterling. To this day, six large volumes in the Prime Minister's

---

[14] Georgeon, *Abdülhamid II*, pp. 364–5, 387.
[15] Elizabeth Sirriyeh, *Sufi Visionary of Ottoman Damascus: 'Abd al-Ghani al-Nabulsi, 1641–1731*, London 2005, p. 39.

Archive in Istanbul contain more than 20,000 names, attesting to the success of the donations campaign.[16] By providing a quicker, safer and cheaper means of travelling to the Hijaz, Sultan Abdülhamit was able to demonstrate his piety and his concern for the Holy Places. He gained political prestige by matching Europe's industrial achievements with a massive project of his own. By 1908 the railway had already reached Medina, where the station was opened on 1 September.[17] But by that time, the Young Turks had taken power and 'Izzat Pasha thought it best to make a hasty exit.

Ottoman Pashas, like himself, and other ancien régime dignitaries, detested the new and unfamiliar political landscape. These men had had no experience of political life other than manoeuvring for power and influence inside the bureaucracies of the Porte and the palace. Almost from the first day, they vowed to bring down the Young Turks' Unionist regime. Although they still dominated the Senate in the new parliament, the lower house was filled with the 'new men' – those Albanians, Arabs, Slavs, Armenians, Greeks and Jews who, though still professing loyalty to the Sultan and to the Islamic caliphate, were nevertheless impatient to make their voices heard in the suddenly expedient climate of freedom. Greeks and Armenians, for example, wanted their respective languages to be accepted as languages of the state.

Apart from Rida el-Solh, Arab deputies who came to Istanbul for the opening of parliament in 1908 included the Arab elder statesman, 'Abd al-Nafi' Bey al-Jabiri, deputy for Aleppo and son of the mufti of that city. Thirty years earlier, when still in his twenties, he had been a member of the first Ottoman parliament of 1877, only to be sent home when the Sultan suspended the Constitution. He was the only deputy of 1877 vintage to sit in the 1908 parliament, which gave him extraordinary weight and status.[18] He took the initiative to form an Arab parliamentary group, with the aim of obtaining proportional representation for Arabs both in the new parliament and in the state bureaucracy.[19] Many years after Jabiri's death, Riad el-Solh was to marry his daughter, Fayza, in 1930.

[16] James Nicholson, 'The Hejaz Railway', in *Journal of the Society for Asian Affairs*, 37(3) (November 2006), p. 322.
[17] For a detailed account see W. Ochsenwald, *The Hijaz Railway*, Charlottesville, VA, 1980.
[18] Kayalı, *Arabs and Young Turks*, p. 27.
[19] Ibid., p. 70.

Rida el-Solh's Arab colleagues included 'Abd al-Hamid al-Zahrawi, son of a religious family from Homs who, after travels to Cairo and Istanbul, had returned home when the Constitution was restored, and was elected deputy from Homs to the Ottoman parliament.[20] Other colleagues were three deputies from Damascus, all from prosperous families: Shafiq Mu'ayyad al-'Azm, Rushdi al-Sham'a and 'Abd al-Rahman al-Yusuf. However, at a by-election in Damascus in 1911, al-Yusuf, a newly rich Kurdish sheep-seller and landowner, was suspected – rightly as it turned out – of being pro-French and anti-Arab, and was defeated by Shukri al-'Asali, who then made his way to Istanbul to join the other Arab deputies.

In Istanbul, Rida el-Solh found a substantial Arab community, several thousand strong, consisting of students, officials, businessmen and officers. That September, several of these Arabs formed a society which they called the Arab-Ottoman Brotherhood (al-ikha' al-'arabi al-'uthmani), which welcomed the Arab deputies with great fanfare at a grand reception.[21]

But behind the façade of good cheer was a great deal of nervousness among the Arab deputies about what the Young Turk revolution might actually mean for them. At first they tended to be cautious, wanting to see which way the political wind was blowing. From the start, though, they felt abysmally under-represented. Out of a chamber of some 288 deputies, there were only 60 Arabs compared with about 147 ethnic Turks. Although the Arabs of the Empire were more numerous than the Turks, both their numbers and their influence in the Chamber were pointedly kept small. This was to become a permanent source of soreness. Of all the cabinet posts available, only that of the Ministry of the 'Awqaf (religious endowments) – which brought with it little political influence, if any – was reserved for them.

In those uncertain times, the main problem that the Arabs faced was that they had no recognised voice in Istanbul. This was gradually to change with the advent of a proper parliamentary system. Arabs were then able to take part, and for the first time, in the political life of the Ottoman capital. The Ottoman parliament, ironically enough, gave them a chance to air grievances particular to them as

---

[20] Ahmad Tarabein, 'Abd al-Hamid al-Zahrawi: The Career and Thought of an Arab Nationalist', in Rashid Khalidi et al. (eds), The Origins of Arab Nationalism, New York 1991.
[21] Kayalı, Arabs and Young Turks, p. 67.

Arabs, and to fight for specifically Arab causes. The main issues that preoccupied them were the following: that they were being denied fair access to senior posts; that the Arabic language – which had traditionally been esteemed if not revered by the Ottomans as the language of the Qur'an – was being supplanted by Turkish; and that the CUP leadership seemed lenient about Zionist settlement in Palestine, which it appeared secretly even to favour.

The first session of parliament was held on 17 December 1908.[22] All Istanbul was in movement that morning. Troops lined the streets, with every crossroads manned by cavalry and staff officers in brilliant uniforms. Festive crowds surged into the city across the bridges over the Golden Horn, while artisans put finishing touches to the decorations. A guard of honour waited in front of the parliament building in the shadow of Hagia Sophia. Riad and his mother Nazira were there, accompanied by some of their household retainers. There had been great excitement in the Solh household that morning as Rida, having dressed formally for the occasion, was driven to parliament.

After much hesitation, the Sultan decided to attend the opening ceremony. Arriving in the Royal Carriage at half past twelve, accompanied by his son, Prince Burhaneddin and the grand vezir, he was greeted by loyal crowds, singing and cheering. The Turkish flag over the parliament gave way to the imperial ensign. Wearing a simple military uniform, the Sultan sat on a dais facing some two hundred deputies in black stambulines and red fezzes – a sombre group, relieved by the white and green turbans of the religious dignitaries, and the blue uniforms of the dozen military deputies. To the far right sat the senators: marshals and generals in full dress uniform, together with ministers in gold embroidered jackets.

Ali Javed, First Secretary at the Chancellery, rose to read the imperial speech in which the Sultan declared that the Constitution was entirely his own work; that he had suspended it at the time on the advice of officials, who had judged the public not mature enough for it; but that now that education was widespread thanks to the schools that he had himself established, it was only natural that he should decide to reconvene parliament! One Turkish historian commented that this was 'surely the strangest defence an autocrat had ever offered for the

---

[22] Kansu, *Politics in Post-Revolutionary Turkey*, pp. 24–8; Georgeon, *Abdülhamid II*, pp. 415–16; *The Times*, 18 December 1908, 'Opening of Parliament by the Sultan: Scenes in Stambul'.

suppression of liberty'.[23] He concluded by affirming his 'absolute and unchangeable' intention to maintain constitutional life, whereupon the deputies applauded and swore an oath of loyalty to him and to the Constitution. This pronouncement was marked by a salute of one hundred guns. A great shout went up from the crowd as massed bands played the Constitutional Hymn. Snatches of the hymn drifted up to the Chamber and mingled with loud cheering, as the Sultan, followed by ministers, deputies and ambassadors, made his way out of the building.

A couple of weeks later, the Sultan entertained Rida and other deputies at a banquet in the Chalet Pavilion in the grounds of his palace at Yildiz.[24] He had himself seen to every detail of the event, chosen the menu, ordered the musicians to play patriotic tunes during the meal, and determined the arrangement of the tables in a great horseshoe, with a seat for himself at the very centre. He chose to appear in full dress uniform. The grand vezir sat on his right. On his left he had placed his old enemy, Ahmed Riza Bey, who had headed one of the Young Turk factions before the seizure of power and who, after a long exile in Paris, had just been elected president of the Chamber. Ahmed Riza Bey now chatted amiably with the Sultan, telling him how he had learned to cook while in exile in France, as he much preferred their Turkish food to French cuisine. Once again, Ali Javed read out the Sultan's speech, in which he repeated the pledges he had already made in parliament. It was greeted by prolonged applause and cries of 'Long Life to our Sovereign'. One of the deputies went so far as to climb on a chair and cry 'Welcome to our Sovereign! Welcome to our nation!' The Sultan rose in respect when Ahmed Riza Bey responded with great rhetorical flourish that the peoples of the East had not known such happiness since the advent of Islam thirteen centuries earlier. The banquet over, the deputies moved into the grand salon, where Ahmed Riza Bey presented them to the Sultan. Some kissed his hand, one deputy even attempted to kiss his feet. The Sultan, who nurtured a deep and glowering hatred for these upstart revolutionaries, managed nevertheless to declare himself delighted with the occasion. For their part, now that they felt they had curbed his power, the Young Turks no longer saw the old man as a threat and could just about bear to be chivalrous.

---

[23] Kansu, *Politics in Post-Revolutionary Turkey*, p. 26.
[24] Georgeon, *Abdülhamid II*, pp. 416–17.

Arab grievances

The young Riad el-Solh lived in Istanbul with his father and mother from the age of 14 to 19 – from 1908 to 1913 – a highly formative period. It was in those years that he acquired a proper political education. He read the furious diatribes in the press, followed the oratorical jousts in the Ottoman parliament, the rebellions, wars, conspiracies, murders, revolutions and counter-revolutions of those years. In sum, he witnessed the death throes of a great Empire. The conversations at his father's dinner table must have been an education in themselves. Most Arab deputies – Rida el-Solh included – had been elected under the banner of the Committee of Union and Progress, the CUP. But within a year, many had moved closer to the monarchist opposition.

The strains between the Arab deputies and the CUP stemmed from a whole raft of unspoken doubts and grievances. The Arab deputies never wholly trusted the Young Turk leadership, because of its origins in Salonica's masonic lodges, which, they suspected, were under Zionist influence. Rida, for one, had observed the dynamism of Jewish society at Salonica during his spell there a few years earlier, and had had a chance to observe at first hand the spread of Zionist ideas among its members.[25] Another widely shared Arab fear was that the CUP's policies of centralisation and democracy might undermine the established social, political and economic order in the Arab provinces. Like Rida himself, most Arab deputies belonged to prominent landowning or religious families who had long been the traditional intermediaries between the local population and the Ottoman authorities.[26]

Following the *Tanzimat* reforms of the nineteenth century, such notables had joined administrative councils, tribunals and other municipal bodies in order to retain a measure of local power and influence. In Syria, for example, the 'Azm and Mardam families, among others, had sought and obtained important Ottoman administrative posts to safeguard their upper-class status. But the CUP's ideas of social equality between citizens, and their centralising policy of direct rule from Istanbul, threatened to undermine the position and prestige of such regional bigwigs. Landlords in Damascus, Hama, Aleppo, Beirut and South Lebanon, some owning swathes of villages, feared the loss

[25] Interview with Alia el-Solh, Monte Carlo, 4–5 October 2004.
[26] See 'Ottoman Reform and the Politics of Notables' (ch. 3), in Albert Hourani, *The Emergence of the Modern Middle East*, London 1981.

of power over their peasantry. The patriarchs of myriad Christian sects, long accustomed to lording it over their flocks, also saw the CUP programme as a threat to their privileges. They feared the disintegration of the *millet* system which they had long enjoyed – which constituted self-governing, non-Muslim communities of the Empire, and which had made of them important political leaders in their own right, with entrenched vested interests.[27]

In the Empire at that time, the idea of 'nationality' in the nineteenth-century, Western European, Romantic sense of the word was still rare. The political identity of the Sultan's non-Muslim subjects was Ottoman (Osmanli), but their 'national' allegiance – if such a term could be applied at all – was to the religious *millet* to which they belonged.

The issue of the Arabic language

The major grievance which loomed large from 1909 onwards was the Arabs' growing conviction that they had become the victims of cultural and linguistic discrimination, and that their language was in danger of being replaced by Turkish in the educational system, the bureaucracy and the courts. The CUP had, in fact, tried (and failed) to enforce the use of Ottoman Turkish in all spheres of public life. This issue, more than any other, seems to have led some Arabs to feel that they should now agitate for autonomy within the Empire. It was inevitable that they should feel a certain cultural superiority over ethnic Turks, who were now seeking to make them feel inferior. After all, the Revelation to the Prophet Muhammad had been made in Arabic. Arabs had brought the Islamic faith to the world and, in the process, had created a great world civilisation indeed. The visceral association of the Arabic language with Islamic culture was the very basis of Arab identity, even for Arab Christians.[28] Islam was what had held the Empire together for many centuries, uniting disparate peoples in far-flung places. It had certainly been the cardinal element in Arab-Turkish relations for nearly four centuries, ever since Sultan Selim I conquered Egypt and Syria from the Mamluks in 1516–17. Whether

---

[27] Kayalı, *Arabs and Young Turks*, pp. 63, 82.
[28] Ibid., p. 38.

they were Turk or Arab, the Muslim subjects of the Sultan were 'brothers in the Faith' – in other words, they were Muslims before being either Turks or Arabs.[29] Following the 1908 revolution, it came as a great psychological shock to the Arabs to realise that, not only did these historically significant givens no longer hold true, but that they were being rapidly reversed.

These considerable grievances did not yet amount to an urge to secede. The thrust of Arab opinion in the early years of the Ottoman parliament was still very much in the direction of unity within the imperial framework. Men like Rida el-Solh and his Arab colleagues in the Ottoman parliament could not yet conceive of the Arabs breaking loose from the Empire. Still subscribing fully to the conventional Ottoman ideology of a multi-ethnic and multi-religious state, they had not yet conceptualised a territorially based 'Arab nation'. What they wanted was greater influence and recognition within a tried and tested imperial system.

The deposition of the Sultan

From the early days of the new parliament, ferocious verbal clashes took place in parliament between monarchist and CUP deputies, disputes which found an echo outside the Chamber in rumours of opposition plots foiled by police raids. When the feeble Grand Vezir Kamil Pasha started edging towards the monarchist camp, the Unionists demanded an immediate vote of no-confidence to bring him down. They replaced him with Hüseyyin Hilmi Pasha, a man who shared their own sentiments. Although Rida el-Solh and most of the other Arab deputies had been elected under the CUP banner, they decided to support Kamil Pasha – a first joint action by the Arab parliamentary bloc led by 'Abd al-Nafi' Pasha al-Jabiri.

In the event, this turned out to be ill-advised, since Kamil Pasha was overthrown by a vote of no-confidence on 13 February 1909. His mistake had been to offend the army, which was largely loyal to the CUP. Earlier that month, he had fired the Minister of War Ali Reza Pasha, apparently to punish him for refusing to send troops loyal to the CUP out of Istanbul and replace them with troops loyal to the

[29] Zeine, *Arab-Turkish Relations*, pp. 29, 36–7.

Sultan. The Sultan replaced him with Nazim Pasha, commander of the Second Army Corps at Edirne, an officer known for his hostility to CUP officers. But when, the next day, Hüseyyin Hilmi Pasha – the candidate favoured by the CUP – was named grand vezir, he immediately sacked Nazim Pasha and reappointed Ali Riza Pasha as minister of war. These rapid changes at the head of the ministry, together with troop movements and the assassination on 6 April of a monarchist editor, Hasan Fehmi Efendi, combined to create a stormy climate of civil discord. Tens of thousands of the Sultan's loyalists turned out to attend the editor's funeral.

The stage was set for a monarchical counter-revolution, starting on the night of 12–13 April 1909,[30] when thousands of soldiers of the Imperial Guard and other units mutinied, locking up their officers and swarming into the main square in front of parliament. Inflamed by agents provocateurs, they demanded the imposition of religious law, because – or so it was later alleged – they had been told that the CUP intended forcibly to convert all Muslims to Christianity! They seized the parliament building and the Ministry of War, where they shot and wounded the Minister of War Ali Riza Pasha. They murdered the Emir Muhammad Arslan Bey, the deputy for Latakia, whom they mistook for Hüseyyin Jahid, a prominent Unionist deputy for Istanbul (who had taken refuge in the Russian embassy). They also murdered Nazim Pasha, the minister of justice, whom they mistook for the president of the Chamber, Ahmed Riza Bey.

The crew of a destroyer seized their captain, carried him to the front of the palace, lynched him and hanged him from a tree in the palace grounds. All semblance of law and order broke down. Throughout the city, gangs of mutineers killed military cadets wherever they found them. CUP offices were stormed and ransacked. The printing presses of Unionist newspapers were destroyed and the type scattered in the streets. The Chamber was too frightened to assemble. It was later suggested that the coup had been planned by the palace and that each soldier had been given 5 lira for his pains. Fearing for their lives, CUP leaders went underground. Recovering his powers, the Sultan pardoned the mutineers, thus legitimising the coup. Hüseyyin Hilmi Pasha resigned and Tevfik Pasha was appointed grand vezir in his stead. It seemed as if the Sultan's absolutist regime had once

---

[30] Sometimes referred to in the old-style calendar as the '31st of March incident'.

again been restored. But this was counting without the army in the provinces.

As soon as news of the monarchist counter-coup reached Salonica, tens of thousands of demonstrators volunteered to fight the monarchist rebels. The CUP and its military allies sprang into action. Mahmud Shawkat Pasha, commander of the Third Army Corps, made immediate preparations to crush the counter-coup. He was an officer from a Baghdad family with Georgian roots, whose father had served as a provincial *mutasarrif*. He himself had risen to prominence in the service of the Empire.

By 16 April, two military trains carrying 15,000 soldiers under his command arrived at Çatalca, some 70 kilometres from Istanbul, where they were joined by more troops from Edirne. A combined force, including cavalry and artillery, then marched on Istanbul. It was now the monarchists' turn to run for cover. Several pashas and their families, as well as rich Greeks and Armenians who had applauded the monarchist restoration, escaped from the city by boat. Rebel soldiers fled to the interior on foot. In Istanbul, thousands of troops and students began to rally to the CUP. Fearing an attack on the palace, people living near Yildiz deserted their homes. Mahmud Shawkat Pasha sent an ultimatum to the government of Tevfik Pasha, giving it twenty-four hours to resign. In panic, the Sultan gave orders that, if CUP troops entered the capital, Ottoman warships in the Bosphorus should open fire on the German, Russian, Austrian and French embassies. He thought, perhaps, that such a desperate move would trigger an instant foreign intervention and save him. But his orders were ignored.

About a hundred CUP deputies, led by Ahmed Riza Bey, then gathered at Yeşilköy, where they decided to call a joint session of the Senate and the Chamber – a National Assembly, a *meclis-i milli* – to debate the deposition of the Sultan. On 24 April, troops from Salonica entered Istanbul and, after a struggle, captured the Ministry of War. Dozens of troops on both sides were wounded or killed in the battle for other government buildings of the Sublime Porte. Unionist forces then surrounded Yildiz, where some 4,000 of the Sultan's troops were still holding out. By this time, his Albanian porters, his servants, gardeners, cooks, the eunuchs of the harem, his private guards and palace employees had fled, leaving Yildiz almost deserted. Only the harem women remained. That night, the Bosphorus was black with boats carrying fleeing monarchists to the relative safety of the Asian shore.[31]

By the late afternoon of 25 April 1909, the Sultan had surrendered. Calling on the imperial guard to lay down its arms, he put himself in the hands of the military. A horrifying consequence of the attempted counter-coup was a massacre of Armenians – mainly in Adana – where some 17,000 were slaughtered between 14 and 16 April.[32] It was later alleged that the Sultan himself gave orders to kill Armenian as well as all other members of the local CUP. The governor of Adana, Javid Pasha, who had turned a blind eye to the killings, was later sentenced to death for this gross dereliction of duty. This was not, alas, the first or last massacre of Armenians. About a decade earlier, in the mid-1890s, anti-Armenian riots in eastern Anatolia – provoked by fanatical local notables, by some disreputable 'ulema, and by Kurdish tribal chieftains – led to the killing of an estimated 37,000 Armenians and made a further 300,000 destitute. On both occasions, the mob was inflamed by the fear of Armenian independence, which, it was thought, would mean suicide for the Muslims of eastern Anatolia. Hundreds of thousands of these people had already been driven from their lands by the defeat of 1877–78, and by the loss of territory in eastern Anatolia and the Balkans.[33] This may partially explain the critical context in which the unspeakable slaughter took place. These massacres, appalling as they were, were to be tragically dwarfed by the deportations and genocide which the Armenians would suffer in 1915.

In April 1909, the strongman of the hour was Mahmud Shawkat Pasha, commander of the Third Army Corps, who was now the most important person in the capital. The Sultan offered him the post of grand vezir but he declined, judging rightly that his army command gave him far more actual power. Declaring martial law, he appointed himself inspector-general of the first three Army Corps and launched a manhunt for opposition suspects, followed by a great wave of arrests. Some 5,000 prisoners were interned in camps along the Golden Horn. Members of the Sultan's personal staff were captured and the luckier ones sent into exile. Prince Sabaheddin, an early inspirer of the Young Turk movement who had then chosen to revert

---

[31] Kansu, *Politics in Post-Revolutionary Turkey*, p. 114; Georgeon, *Abdülhamid II*, p. 423.
[32] Kansu, *Politics in Post-Revolutionary Turkey*, p. 122.
[33] Georgeon, *Abdülhamid II*, pp. 283–93.

to monarchism, was arrested on his estate, but was allowed to leave the country on the intervention of the British and French ambassadors.

Sitting in joint session, the Senate and the Chamber then voted to remove Sultan Abdülhamit II from the throne and replace him with his brother, Mehmed Reşad. Shortly afterwards, on the night of 27 April, Abdülhamit and his household were escorted from the palace of Yildiz to a special train which carried them to Salonica, where they were interned in one of the finest residences of the city, the Villa Allatini, belonging to the wealthy industrialist Jewish family of that name. With crucial backing from the Third Army Corps, the CUP had managed to restore the constitutional regime after a bloody two-week interregnum.

As chief court-martial administrator, Mahmud Shawkat Pasha then brought to trial those involved in the 13 April counter-coup, including its vociferous spokesman, Derviş Vahdetti. Thirteen were found guilty and hanged in public in Istanbul on 3 May. Further executions followed on 12 and 17 July, and then again on 19 July. Sixty-four monarchists were put on board a ship and exiled to Rhodes. Many pashas, ex-ministers and magnates of the ancien régime were sentenced to prison terms, including some prominent Arabs, such as 'Izzat Pasha al-'Abid (in absentia) and the Melhamah brothers, Salim and Nasib. Several pashas were exiled to the islands of Limnos, Bodrum, Mytilene and Chios along the Aegean coast.

On 3 May 1909, Tevfik Pasha resigned and Hüseyyin Hilmi Pasha was once again appointed grand vezir. Two leading CUP members joined the cabinet that summer – Javid Bey as minister of finance and Talaat Bey as minister of interior. This was a turning point in CUP fortunes – the first time since the 1908 revolution that its leaders had managed to capture key posts.

On the defeat of the monarchical opposition, a new anti-CUP party was formed in November 1909, called the Moderate Liberals (mutedil hürriyetperveran firkasi). Its members were more like the Young Turks who had gathered in Paris before 1908, and included many non-Turks. The party's president was an Albanian, but Arab deputies played a prominent role in it. Among its founders were 'Abd al-Nafi' Pasha al-Jabiri, who became the party's vice-president, as well as Shafiq Mu'ayyad al-'Azm and Rushdi al-Sham'a. The party was fervently Ottomanist. From abroad, it was backed by the Paris-based Parti radical ottoman, formed in September 1909 and financed by

Prince Sabaheddin and by Şerif Pasha, who had served as the Sultan's ambassador to Stockholm.

At about the same time, Dr Riza Nur, another former monarchist, worked hard to persuade Arab deputies to join his own group in the Chamber. At first, 'Abd al-Hamid al-Zahrawi, a leader of the Arab deputies in parliament, declared that, in such a volatile climate of coup and counter-coup, they preferred to remain a politically passive Arab bloc – in principle, opposed to the CUP, but not wishing actually to join the Moderate Liberals or indeed anyone else. Later, however, some Arab deputies joined the Riza Nur group. The record does not show where Rida el-Solh chose to stand at this time.

The Arabs find their voice

From 1910 onwards, Arab deputies in the Ottoman parliament, Rida el-Solh among them, adopted a more forceful posture in defence of a whole range of Arab causes. When the Chamber debated the so-called 'Lynch affair' – a plan to merge a state-owned steamer company on the Euphrates with the British Lynch Company, which would have given the British a monopoly on river navigation – Arab deputies were fierce in attacking the plan, fearing that it would lead to an expansion of British influence in Mesopotamia. Among the most outspoken were Shafiq Mu'ayyad al-'Azm, deputy for Damascus, who was joined by Muhammad Shawkat ibn Rif'at Pasha, deputy for Divaniye, and by Lutfi Efendi, deputy for Dayr al-Zor. So violent was the debate in the Chamber that the sitting had to be adjourned.

The all-powerful Mahmud Shawkat Pasha appears to have weighed in on their side, since he chose to back the Germans, who favoured a postponement on the Lynch affair until their own negotiations for a railway concession linking Baghdad to Istanbul were successful. It was thus decided to leave the matter in abeyance pending a later decision by the Ottoman government.

In January 1910, Arab deputies were again in evidence, expressing their disapproval at the replacement of Hüseyyin Hilmi Pasha as grand vezir by Hakki Bey, the Ottoman ambassador in Rome, because they considered him too close to the CUP. 'Abd al-Nafi' Pasha and other members of the Moderate Liberals expressed their reservations clearly and with passion. Nevertheless, Hakki Bey took office, was promoted to the rank of Pasha and appointed Mahmud Shawkat Pasha minister of war (largely, it would appear, as a way of curtailing his immense influence). The CUP leaders, Talaat and Javid, retained their posts at Interior and Finance.

Another fierce debate of great interest to the Arab deputies concerned secret reports – known in Turkish as *jurnals* – addressed to the Sultan by his spies and informers, of which a great number were discovered at Yildiz palace when it was occupied by the army. The debate was opened on 9 May 1910 by Shafiq Mu'ayyad al-'Azm, who expressed indignation that some Unionist newspapers had accused him of having served as one of the Sultan's spies. He urged the government to publish the *jurnals* in order to clear his name, while at the same time hoping to incriminate others in the process.[34] The minister of finance, Javid Bey, rejected 'Azm's accusations, but his protest aroused a storm among the Arab deputies, with 'Azm demanding an official enquiry. One of the accused Unionist newspapers, *Tanin*, then went into battle, alleging that the courts had proof that 'Azm and another Arab deputy were guilty of espionage on the Sultan's behalf. It demanded that their election be annulled. *Tanin*'s racist proposal that only those secret reports written by Arab deputies should be published aroused such Arab fury that the president of the Chamber was forced to suspend the sitting. Rida el-Solh had a moment of keen apprehension. As a *mutasarrif* of many years' standing, he had sent numerous private reports to the Sultan from different posts, using the palace cipher, as Abdülhamit had personally encouraged his governors to do, in order to bypass his own bureaucracy of the Sublime Porte.

A month later, on 11 June 1910, Rida al-Solh won the attention of the Chamber, the occasion being the murder forty-eight hours earlier of Ahmed Samim Bey, editor of an opposition newspaper, *Sada-yi Millet*. His paper had been founded some months earlier by Pantoleon Cosmidis, the monarchist Greek deputy for Istanbul, who now accused the CUP of the killing.[35] Rida el-Solh demanded an urgent enquiry into allegations of CUP involvement. He was perturbed by a letter which Ahmed Samim Bey had written shortly before his murder, in which he claimed the Unionists had 'condemned him to death'. The case bore an alarming resemblance to the assassination

---

[34] Kansu, *Politics in Post-Revolutionary Turkey*, pp. 190–1.
[35] Ibid., pp. 192–3.

fourteen months earlier of yet another monarchist journalist, Hasan Fehmi Efendi, on 6 April 1909.

Stormy exchanges in the Chamber took place against a background of disturbances in Istanbul and the provinces. In the spring of 1910, the Albanians rose in revolt against a proposed census, which they feared was a prelude to taxation, military conscription and the imposition of the Turkish language. They were put down with great brutality. The humiliating and painful flogging of Albanian chiefs in front of their wives aroused particular bitterness.

Such was the fevered climate in September 1910, when Riad el-Solh, then aged 16, enrolled in the Istanbul Law School, *Mekteb-i Hükük*, an institution which the Sultan had created in 1878. He was a serious student and worked hard, but he could not help being swept up in student politics. Among his close friends was Sa'dallah al-Jabiri (younger brother of 'Abd al-Nafi' Bey), who was also studying in Istanbul, and was to go on to a brilliant career as a nationalist politician in Syria. Riad had by this time developed a passion for politics, not missing a word of the discussions among his father's colleagues and in the local press. The battle between the CUP and the opposition was of consuming interest, as was the ill-concealed, behind-the-scenes role of the army, led by the towering figure of Mahmud Shawkat Pasha. Riad was given blow-by-blow accounts of his father's interventions in the Chamber, which were rehearsed, analysed and dissected at home.

On 14 November 1910, the Ottoman parliament ended its summer recess and, at once, the opposition began to attack the Hakki cabinet, with Shafiq Mu'ayyad al-'Azm in the role of a prominent opposition spokesman. From abroad, Şerif Pasha launched furious diatribes against the CUP leaders, calling on the military to overthrow their 'evil regime'. Unionist stars like Talaat Bey and Javid Bey found themselves under sharp attack. As the CUP seemed to grow weaker by the day, many Arab deputies decided to identify themselves more closely with the opposition.

In Beirut and Damascus, former allies of the CUP now united around an Arabist platform and, in the columns of two leading newspapers, *al-Mufid* in Beirut and *al-Muqtabas* in Damascus,[36] expressed their support for the opposition. By the beginning of 1911, the Arab

---

[36] Kayalı, *Arabs and Young Turks*, p. 119.

deputies who had attracted most attention in the Chamber were 'Abd al-Hamid al-Zahrawi, Shafiq Mu'ayyad al-'Azm and Rida el-Solh, who were joined in February by Shukri al-'Asali (following his victory over 'Abd al-Rahman al-Yusuf). The four of them created a short-lived Arab party (*al-hizb al-'arabi*), which was little more than an informal parliamentary group of Arab deputies. Their demands were the well-rehearsed ones: full equality for Arabs; Arabic as the language of instruction in state schools; protection for dismissed Arab government employees, and insistence that Ottoman government officers sent to the Arab provinces should know Arabic.[37]

Shukri al-'Asali provoked a storm by claiming, in a hard-hitting speech in parliament on 5 April 1911, that Arabs were being excluded from senior posts in key ministries. In the angry debate that followed, Rida el-Solh defended him vigorously. In Damascus and Beirut, and among the large community of expatriate Syrians in Cairo, 'Asali's speech was hailed as a milestone of Arab self-assertion. But in Istanbul, the Turkish press accused him of perfidy, forcing him to reply that he had implied no disloyalty to the Sultan or to the Empire. The bond that linked Turks and Arabs together, he declared, was an eternal one (*ribat abadi*).

The debate over Zionism

Zionism was perhaps the major issue which, in the spring of 1911, set Arab deputies against the CUP.[38] Already highly suspicious of Zionist influence over the Young Turks, Arab deputies felt that the party was not giving the problem of expanding Zionist settlement in Palestine the urgent attention it deserved. From 1882, when the first Jewish agricultural settlement was founded in Palestine by the Lovers of Zion, the pace of immigration had quickened. By 1908, some 80,000 Jews, mainly from Russia and Central and Eastern Europe, had established some fifty Zionist colonies there. The Sultan had opposed this Zionist influx, fearing that the arrival of these Europeans would give the European Powers a further pretext to interfere, which it did.

---

[37] Semir Seikaly, 'Shukri al-'Asali: A Case Study of a Political Activist', in Khalidi *et al.* (eds), *The Origins of Arab Nationalism*, pp. 85–6.

[38] Kayalı, *Arabs and Young Turks*, pp. 102–5; Neville Mandel, *The Arabs and Zionism before World War I*, Berkeley 1976.

He had tried but failed to stem the flow of Jewish immigration to Palestine. By the time of the Young Turk revolution, Arab opinion was already fully alert to the dangers posed to their region by this new situation. Politicians, journalists and intellectuals in Cairo, Damascus and Beirut had expressed their strong hostility to these foreign immigrants, and to their carefully planned and steady purchase of Arab land. Palestinian Arabs had sent telegrams to the Ottoman parliament, pleading for a halt to this immigration. Alarming reports from Beirut and Jerusalem disclosed that some absentee landowners, among them 'Abd al-Rahman al-Yusuf, had no scruple about selling their estates to the Zionists, who were paying over the odds to obtain as much land as they could.

Before his by-election victory in Damascus in 1911, Shukri al-'Asali had served for two years as *qa'im maqam* in Nazareth, then in the Beirut vilayet. He had witnessed Zionist colonisation first hand, and arrived in Istanbul with a reputation as the best-informed and most determined opponent of the Zionist programme in Palestine. In a debate in the Chamber, he charged that three-quarters of Tiberias and one-quarter of Haifa had already been acquired by European Jews, and accused the CUP of indifference to the loss of these strategic sites. Talaat Bey, minister of interior, responded laconically that Jews were entitled to buy property anywhere in the Empire, except in the Hijaz, whereupon Rida el-Solh voiced indignation at this shortsighted laissez-faire policy. When Ubeydullah, a Turkish deputy for Aydin in Anatolia, accused the Arabs of being motivated by spite, Rida el-Solh – supported by 'Abd al-Hamid al-Zahrawi, deputy for Homs, Khalid al-Barazi, deputy for Hama, and 'Abd al-Mahdi, deputy for Karbala – sprang to his feet and threatened to walk out unless Ubeydullah retracted his words. 'We will leave this Chamber', Rida told him, 'so that you can heap yet more insults on Arabs!'[39]

On 16 May 1911, Ruhi al-Khalidi, the well-born, erudite deputy for Jerusalem, treated the Chamber to an extended lecture on Zionism. He spoke about the difference between Zionism and Semitism, the different origins of the Jews, the creation of the first colonies of Russian Jews in Jaffa, Herzl's and Mendelsohn's theories, and much else besides. He also read out telegrams from Ottoman Jewish leaders, who themselves had denounced Zionism as a threat to their own situation. He

[39] Kayalı, *Arabs and Young Turks*, p. 104.

was followed by Sa'id al-Husayni, who urged the government to take effective measures against massive Jewish land acquisition in Jerusalem. But Jafiz Ibrahim, an Albanian deputy, scoffed at the notion that 'a hundred thousand Jews who have come to Jerusalem will conquer Syria and Iraq'. Jews, he argued, were taking over the economy and not the land, as they had done in England itself. All of Salonica's trade was in their hands. Rida el-Solh interjected to remind him that, unlike European Jewish immigrants to Palestine, Salonica's Jews were not foreigners. But Jafiz Ibrahim dismissed this argument, pointing out that trade in Rida's home town, Beirut, was also in the hands of foreigners. Instead of resenting the presence of foreigners, the Arabs should try to hoist themselves up to their level, he declared patronisingly.

It was about this time that the Arab community in Istanbul was galvanised by a frontal assault on the CUP by none other than the Syrian thinker, Shaykh Rashid Rida, the leading Islamic modernist of his day. Rida el-Solh and the other Arab deputies were well acquainted with his writings and had met him on his visits to Istanbul. On 4 July 1911, the monarchist *Ṣahrah* newspaper published in translation a lengthy article by Rashid Rida which had originally appeared in his Cairo monthly, *al-Manar*. It was a devastating attack on the CUP, laying out in the open many Arab suspicions. Shaykh Rida charged that the leading members of the CUP were freemasons, whose lodges were under strong Zionist influence. They were working for the benefit of Zionism, and towards the exploitation of Syria and Palestine by Jewish capital. The aims of the Freemasons, he alleged, were the gradual elimination of Muslim law; the 'Turkification' of the Empire; and the substitution of Turkish for Arabic in the provinces. The article and the uproar it created marked the first public breach between Arab deputies and the CUP.

On the night of 10 July, yet another leading monarchist journalist, Zeki Bey, was shot dead, allegedly by Unionists. He had published translations of other articles from *al-Manar* about the supposedly nefarious activities of masonic lodges. This third murder of a journalist in two years caused consternation among the political elite of the capital. Meanwhile, all was not well between the CUP and its military saviour, Mahmud Shawkat Pasha, whom it suspected of wanting to install a military dictatorship. An undeclared power struggle broke out between them. Anxious for their careers, many CUP officers began to drift over to his side. Talaat Bey was forced to resign as minister of interior in February 1911, followed some weeks later by

Javid Bey and by the minister of education, Babanzade Ismail Hakki Bey. In quick succession, the CUP's most prominent members thus lost their cabinet seats.

During this period, there was an attempt to finish off the CUP altogether. One of the instigators was Colonel Sadik Bey, who, after having been one of the early leaders of the CUP, had come to believe that his friends had gone to extremes. He now tried to rally officers for a putsch on the grounds that masonic and anti-religious elements in the CUP posed a danger to Islam. He organised a dissident New Faction (*hizb-i cedid*) inside the CUP, which demanded the resignation of Hakki Pasha, the banishment of Talaat Bey, and the resignation from parliament of Hüseyyin Jahid, editor of the Unionist journal, *Tanin*. This was a clear attempt to destroy the CUP from within. There were strong suspicions that the British were backing the plot, since Gerald H. Fitzmaurice, First Dragoman at the British Embassy,[40] had been in touch with opposition deputies.

After heated debates, the CUP managed to persuade Mahmud Shawkat Pasha to sign an order banishing Colonel Sadik Bey to Salonica, but he was met there by a large number of officers 'who escorted him in triumph to his quarters'.[41] When, in May 1911, Colonel Sadik was made to resign from the army and was forcibly placed on the retired list, he defiantly returned to Istanbul. There he renewed his attempts to incite the military against the government. He formed a party, the Ottoman Union, applied for a licence to establish a political newspaper, and hoped to lure some fifty Unionist deputies to his cause.

The Hakki government was already under attack from Arabs, Albanians, Greeks, Bulgarians and Armenians. It was held responsible for the sharp rise in rents, as well as the increase in the price of food and coal. Fires blazing out of control in the city destroyed whole residential quarters, leaving tens of thousands homeless. This added to the tribulations of the government, and to people's discontent with it. In this unhappy atmosphere, everyone awaited the outcome of the CUP congress due to open in Salonica on the last day of September 1911. A shocking development then threw the whole political class into disarray, bringing home the folly of such squabbling and self-absorption.

---

[40] For an account of his life, see G.R. Berridge, *Gerald Fitzmaurice (1865–1930): Chief Dragoman of the British Embassy in Turkey*, Martinus Nijhoff Publishers, Leiden & Boston 2007.

[41] Kansu, *Politics in Post-Revolutionary Turkey*, p. 238.

The Italian attack on Libya

On 28 September 1911, the Italian chargé-d'affaires in Istanbul handed the Turkish government an ultimatum: in consequence of its failure to meet the demands of the Italian government, Italian troops would occupy Tripoli and Benghazi. The Ottoman government was given twenty-four hours to communicate the news to the garrisons concerned. It was at once clear that to concede defeat without a fight would open the way to a rapid dismemberment of the Empire. The following afternoon, Italy declared war on Turkey and the Hakki government resigned. But even this state of emergency in North Africa did not put a total end to the infighting at home.

On 4 October 1911, Sa'id Pasha, a statesman who by this time was both old and sick, managed with great difficulty to form a cabinet. Mahmud Shawkat Pasha remained in the now crucial post of minister of war. The CUP press welcomed the new cabinet, but the opposition was distinctly cool towards it. The Third Army Corps at Salonica and Monastir continued to back the CUP, but the rest of the army was divided. On the opening of the fourth session of parliament on 15 October, the Unionists won some 130 votes – which included those of about forty dissidents of the New Faction. The opposition won about a hundred votes. The balance of some thirty-five deputies included a number of Arabs whose allegiance to either camp was uncertain, and seven or eight members of the Armenian Revolutionary Party.

In order to win over the Arabs, the Unionists offered the vice-presidency of the Chamber to 'Abd al-Hamid al-Zahrawi. He accepted and was duly elected, but resigned when the opposition (a combination of the Moderate Liberals, Independents, Greeks, a few non-Unionist Armenians, and some Albanian, Serb and Bulgarian deputies) refused the offer of another vice-presidency for one of its members. On 20 October, Sa'id Pasha did win a vote of confidence, but his position remained rocky.

Such was the situation when, on 21 November 1911, a much-talked-about new opposition party, conservative and monarchist in nature, was formed under the name of Liberty and Entente (*hurriyet ve ittilaf firkasi*), more often known as the Entente Libérale. Among its founders were Damad Ferid Pasha, a well-known monarchist senator; the ex-colonel Sadik Bey, leader of the New Faction; Ismail Hakki Pasha, leader of the Moderate Liberals; and 'Abd al-Hamid al-Zahrawi, the Arab deputy from Homs.[42] Each of these men had a different political agenda. The one thing they had in common was a hatred of the CUP. Shukri al-'Asali sat on its administrative council. Shaykh Bashir al-Ghazzi, deputy for Aleppo, and Kamil al-As'ad, the Unionist Shi'ite deputy for Beirut, immediately defected to it. The Entente Libérale was thus able to muster about seventy deputies – monarchist Turks, Arabs from Syria and Iraq, Albanians, Greeks, Bulgarians and a few conservatives of the Armenian Social Democratic Hentchak Party. Minority nationalists such as these resented the CUP for its 'Turkification' policies and hoped they might overthrow it.

Opposite them, the Unionist camp comprised Turks, Jews, Serbs, Armenians from the revolutionary *Dashnaktsuthiun* who were opposed to their conservative brethren, as well as some maverick Arabs from Iraq, Yemen and Tripoli. The Unionists denounced their opponents as a public danger. There were the inevitable violent exchanges in parliament, with the two sides almost coming to blows. On one particularly noisy occasion, the president of the Chamber, unable to bear the din any longer, actually left the chair. On 19 December, the Unionist paper *Tanin* wrote provocatively that neither the insurgents in Macedonia, nor the Italians with whom Turkey was at war, were as harmful to the constitutional order as was the opposition!

Unable to cope any longer with the disorderly situation, Sa'id Pasha resigned, but the Sultan insisted he form a new government. 'Abd al-Nafi' Pasha, deputy for Aleppo, and Shafiq Mu'ayyad al-'Azm, deputy for Damascus, called on the Sultan on 31 December 1911 to ask him to reconsider his decision. But their intervention was to no avail. Sa'id Pasha did form a government, which was described as a colourless *cabinet d'affaires*. But so fierce were the continued clashes between Unionists and opposition that the parliamentary system as a whole seemed in danger of breaking down. It was evident that the opposition's aim was to destroy both the Committee of Union and Progress and the liberal democratic regime. In an atmosphere of gloom, made deeper still by the war in North Africa and by a rash of terrorist incidents in Macedonia, the Sultan informed the Senate on 15 January that he had decided to dissolve the Chamber. Preparations were then made for fresh elections.

---

[42] Ibid., p. 287.

Rida el-Solh did not stand in the 1912 elections. Was it uncertainty about which way to jump? Was it because of ill health? The CUP was powerful, but there was still a chance of a monarchist restoration. Many Arabs, as indeed most minorities, did not want to have to choose between the two camps, since they were fearful of making a wrong choice and suffering the consequences. Perhaps Rida had simply had enough of parliamentary battles, of the violence both inside and outside the Chamber, and wished to go home to Beirut. But, with his son Riad still at law school, the Solh family decided to remain in Istanbul for a little while longer.

At the elections, Independents won 150 seats, the CUP 107 seats, the Entente Libérale 21 and the Armenian Revolutionary Federation 3. The new parliament convened in Istanbul on 12 April 1912. But almost immediately, the opposition – seeing that their poor results at the elections ruled out any possibility of capturing power by parliamentary means – decided to attempt yet another *coup d'état*. The plan was to destabilise the government by fomenting a revolt in Albania and, at the same time, launching an army rebellion in Monastir in early May. The rebels hoped to kick the CUP out of politics altogether, to put their leaders on trial, even execute them. Faced with these increasingly violent threats, Mahmud Shawkat Pasha resigned as minister of war on 9 July, followed by the Grand Vezir Sa'id Pasha on 17 July. After a confused interregnum, a cabinet was formed on 21 July by Ghazi Ahmed Muhtar, but it had no majority in parliament and seemed exceedingly fragile. It did manage, however, to win a vote of confidence and, in a bid to extract support from the opposition, lifted the state of emergency and amnestied the rebels. Pressured by the opposition, the Sultan was persuaded to issue a decree dissolving the Chamber, whereupon the government immediately re-instituted a state of emergency and banned all political activity. On 2 September, the annual conference of the CUP defiantly opened in Istanbul, electing Prince Sa'id Hilmi Pasha of Egypt as party secretary-general.

The death blow of the Balkan Wars

Less than a month later, as Unionists and their opponents continued to feud, news reached Istanbul that the Bulgarian and Serbian armed forces had been put on a state of alert. War fever once again gripped the capital. Students demonstrated before the Sublime Porte with cries of 'Down with the government!' and 'We want war!' On 8 October, Montenegro declared war on the Ottoman Empire, and on 13 October, in a collective note, the Bulgarian, Serbian and Greek governments demanded that the Empire grant full autonomy to the Macedonian provinces under Belgian or Swiss governors – or face the consequences. Istanbul responded to the ultimatum on 15 October by severing diplomatic relations with all three countries, and by declaring war two days later on Bulgaria and Serbia. On that same day, Greece declared war on the Empire. The Balkan Wars, which would prove fatal for the Ottomans, had begun.

On 29 October, Kamil Pasha replaced Ghazi Ahmed Muhtar as grand vezir, to the great satisfaction of the opposition. But this satisfaction was to be short-lived. The next day came news of the rout of Ottoman armies in the battle of Lüleburgaz in Thrace. This was the signal for an Ottoman withdrawal on all fronts before the advancing Bulgarian, Montenegrin, Serbian and Greek forces. With only the Ottoman Eastern Army trying to man the Çatalca defence lines a mere 70 kilometres from Istanbul, the government called on the Great Powers to intervene to stop the conflict. The Powers replied that they would offer their mediation only if the Ottoman government agreed to place itself unreservedly in their hands. Istanbul accepted the offer on 4 November – in effect, agreeing to unconditional surrender. But the CUP and the army opposed such abject peace. When Kamil Pasha convened a meeting of generals, they expressed themselves in favour of further resistance.

Fighting therefore resumed. On 8 November the Greeks seized Salonica, inflicting a terrible psychological blow on the CUP, as they considered the city their home base. Just before Salonica fell, the former Sultan Abdülhamit, who had been exiled there, was transferred back to Istanbul and was locked up in the palace of Beylerbey on the Bosphorus. He was to die there on 10 February 1918.

On 12 November 1912, Kamil Pasha's cabinet sued for peace and talks started between plenipotentiaries. To silence its warmongering critics, the government began to round up CUP members on evidence of an anti-government plot. Talaat and Javid managed to escape, but about sixty others were arrested. Further arrests and sentences by court martial continued into December. On 5 December, an armistice was signed, and a peace conference opened in London on 16 December.

But furious arguments continued into the New Year over the future of Edirne – of huge symbolic value to the Turks, as it had once been the capital of the Empire – as well as over the fate of Crete, the Aegean islands and the boundaries of Albania. The Great Powers urged Turkey to leave to them the question of the Aegean islands, while gifting Edirne to the Bulgarians.

To confront the crisis, Kamil Pasha convened a Grand Council of the Empire, consisting of senators, senior ülema, the Council of State, the Ministry of Justice, the Ministry of the Navy and the Ministry of War. Meeting in closed session on 22 January 1913, this Council reached the conclusion that further resistance was hopeless, and issued a statement declaring that it put its trust 'in the sentiments of justice of the Great Powers'. This was an unconditional surrender to the demands of the rebellious Balkan states, which were backed by the Western Powers.

A bloody riposte was soon to follow. On 23 January 1913, a small company of mounted CUP officers rode into the Sublime Porte. Their arrival was the signal for a concerted rush by various groups of CUP members that had been waiting close by. Enver Bey and Jamal Bey entered the Porte and asked to see the grand vezir. They were followed by Talaat Bey and other CUP leaders. When Nazim Pasha, the minister of war, came out of the Council Chamber, he was at once shot dead by a member of the advancing group. His aide-de-camp was also killed, as was Nazif Bey, the grand vezir's aide-de-camp, but only after he himself had shot and killed Nazim Pasha's assassin. Enver Bey then entered the Council Chamber and informed Kamil Pasha that he must resign or swear to continue the war. Kamil Pasha chose to resign.

The CUP leaders then proceeded to the palace, where they secured the Sultan's assent to the appointment of Mahmud Shawkat Pasha as grand vezir. The new cabinet was formed the same day. Although not a totally Unionist cabinet, it signified, in theory at least, the restoration of the constitutional regime after a lapse of some six months. In practice, it marked the forceful emergence of three battle-hardened CUP politicians: Enver, minister of war from early 1914; Jamal, military governor of Istanbul and later minister of the navy; and Talaat, minister of interior and grand vezir from 1917. They immediately set about arresting their opponents. From then on, and until the collapse of the Ottoman Empire at the end of the First World War, affairs of state were largely in their hands.

Riad's political education

Riad el-Solh was profoundly affected by the deluge of violent and dramatic events which engulfed the years of his youth in Istanbul. All in all, it amounted to a remarkable education in the precariousness of political life and the brutality of political revenge. It was then that he learned that some noble ideals – such as the Young Turks' early opposition to tyranny and their commitment to constitutional government – tended to vanish in the actual exercise of power and the bloody struggle to retain it.

It was in Istanbul, too, that he acquired a fascination with parliamentary politics and procedures, evidence of which was later to appear when he became a deputy in the Lebanese parliament. It is often arrogantly supposed that Arab politicians of his generation learned their parliamentary skills from their European tutors during the interwar Mandates, or from observing French politicians of the Third Republic in the 1920s and 1930s. In fact, it was the Ottoman parliament that was their schoolroom. Riad had had the benefit of his father's daily account of what had taken place in that often riotous debating Chamber.

Like many Arabs of their time, both Rida and Riad el-Solh were influenced by the reformist ideas of Muhammad 'Abduh, and by the liberal Islam he proposed. They were also seduced by the ideas and discussions that took place in *al-muntada al-adabi*, a literary and political club founded in Istanbul in 1909. This club played a pioneering role in reviving Arab culture and helping to create a new sense of Arab historical identity.

Those years in Istanbul were also the time when Riad first became aware of the Zionist plan to colonise Palestine, and the danger this was beginning to pose not just to Palestinians but to the whole of the Arab region. The grounding in the subject which he acquired in his teens in Istanbul was to grow into an understanding of the problem which was a good deal more complex than that of most of his political contemporaries. It also led to a lifelong commitment to the Palestinian cause.

When, in 1949, Colonel Husni al-Za'im horrified Damascus with the first Syrian military *coup d'état* soon after the Palestine War, Riad el-Solh – then prime minister of Lebanon – reacted with ill-disguised disgust at this brutal army seizure of power. The roots of his hostility to military intervention in politics – a feeling that most Arabs now share – should perhaps be sought further back in his early experience of Mahmud Shawkat Pasha's repeated putsches of July 1908 and February 1909, and in the CUP's ruthless dispatch of their opponents in January 1913. From the very start of the Young Turk revolution, bayonets cast their long shadow over parliamentary government.[43]

Riad's years in Istanbul also provided him with a course of instruction in international politics. First Italy, then the Balkan states, like jackals snarling at the heels of an exhausted old lion, dared take great bites out of the body of the Empire. It was evident that the Ottoman state could no longer defend itself either against the major European Powers or even against such lesser states which it had previously controlled. It was disturbing for him to witness this once great Muslim empire, which his father and his grandfather had both served so long and so faithfully, dying of a thousand cuts – while the Western Powers looked on, rubbing their hands and greedily biding their time.

The shrinking of the Empire, and the growing anxiety about European designs over the Arab provinces, now impelled Rida el-Solh and his Arab colleagues to concentrate on mainly Arab grievances, Arab causes, Arab aspirations. They could begin to entertain the novel idea of Arab autonomy within a Turco-Arab state – in a word, to embrace the new notion of 'Arabism'. Their loyalties were painfully divided, as they wrestled with what has been called 'the explosive problem of cultural dualism between an Arab self and an Ottoman wrapping'.[44] It was not, however, until a few years later that the Great War shattered their Ottoman world beyond repair, pitching them ruthlessly from 'Arabism' to full-blown Arab nationalism.

---

[43] Ibid., p. 315.
[44] Muhammad Muslih, 'The Rise of Local Nationalism in the Arab East', in Khalidi *et al.* (eds), *The Origins of Arab Nationalism*, p. 177.

4 IN THE SHADOW OF THE GALLOWS

The Solh family beat a hasty retreat from Istanbul some time in the year 1913. They most probably left after the assassination on 24 June of Mahmud Shawkat Pasha, grand vezir and military champion of the Committee of Union and Progress. His killing unleashed a reign of terror against members of the Entente Libérale and monarchists. From that moment, the atmosphere in the capital was too disturbed and violent for anyone associated, however indirectly, with the opposition to feel safe.

Although Mahmud Shawkat Pasha had not seen eye to eye with the Unionist leaders, they now used his murder (which some even pinned on them) to crush their remaining opponents. With Istanbul under the harsh governorship of Jamal Pasha, prominent Liberals were hunted down, thrown into jail and court-martialled. Twelve, accused of plotting the killing, were hanged, and a further 350 were exiled to the Black Sea region. These executions and deportations eliminated the Entente Libérale as an organised opposition and foreshadowed the murderous measures which this same Jamal Pasha was to take against Arab nationalists when he became governor of Syria during the First World War, earning himself the epithet of al-Saffah, or the 'Slaughterer', for ever after.

The record shows that Rida el-Solh retired from government service on 14 February 1914, on a pension of 1,666 kuruş. Like several other former Arab deputies and notables, he had become identified with the opposition Entente Libérale. But that party was now broken, dispersed and outlawed. By no stretch of the imagination did it seem capable of ever returning to power. Instead, the CUP ruled supreme, led by the triumvirate of Enver, Talaat and Jamal. At the January 1914 elections, which the CUP held so as to legitimise its own power, there was no opposition whatsoever. For people like Rida and his friends, Istanbul had become an undemocratic, hostile, even dangerous place.

Some Arabs may have been slow to grasp the shift towards narrow Turkish nationalism that was taking place inside the Young Turk movement in the crucial year or two before the First World War. Arabs, and in particular those of the older generation, continued to entertain the forlorn hope that the clock could be turned back, and that some sort of a Turco-Arab partnership would be restored. This was not wholly unreasonable, as the Young Turks had gone to considerable pains to suggest that such a notion seemed credible. Since they feared that the Arabs might be tempted to follow the Balkan example and break loose from the Empire, they set about wooing them – even giving emphasis to Islam as the ideology that would bind Arabs and Turks together. This was an approach which found favour with eminent men like the Emir Shakib Arslan, who, as a disciple of Muhammad 'Abduh, remained committed to the continued existence of an Islamic empire. In any event, Muslim sensibilities had been sharpened by the loss of Libya to the Italians and the Western-backed revolt of the Balkan states, blows inflicted on the Ottoman Empire by what was perceived as 'Christian' Europe.

The CUP even took to softening its earlier 'Turkification' measures, which had attempted to make Turkish the dominant language of the Empire. For example, when Kamil el-Solh, Rida's eldest brother and an Ottoman judge of long standing, was transferred from Monastir to Damascus to take charge of the Appeal Court in that city, he was first summoned to Istanbul to be told by the minister of justice, Najm al-Din Mula Bey, that the language of his Court had henceforth to be Turkish.[1] Orders had even been given to change all Arabic street names to Turkish ones, neither measure going down well in this city that prided itself on its great Arabic literary heritage. To bring litigation, knowing Turkish had suddenly become mandatory.[2] These vexatious new measures – which would have been unthinkable before – naturally aroused intense Arab anger. Realising this by 1913, the Turks began reversing the policy. In an evident attempt to placate the Arabs, the use of Arabic was once again widely allowed in law courts, although not in the elite higher *sultaniye* schools. Turkish

---

[1] The memoirs of Dr 'Abd al-Rahman al-Shahbandar, *al-Thawra al-wataniyyah*, Damascus 1933, pp. 2–3, quoted in Zeine, *Arab-Turkish Relations*, pp. 84–5.
[2] Seikaly, 'Shukri al-'Asali', p. 85.

officials appointed to the Arab provinces were even required to know Arabic, and to sit an examination in the language before they could proceed to their posts.

The Young Turks also appeared ready to give ground on the contentious issue of decentralisation, making far-reaching promises of reform in the hope of winning back the Arabs' loyalty. Two other factors served to appease Arab opinion. One was the appointment as grand vezir of Sa'id Hilmi Pasha, member of Egypt's Khedival house – Muhammad 'Ali's grandson and an intellectual with modernist Islamic leanings. Although he had served as foreign minister in Mahmud Shawkat Pasha's cabinet, Sa'id Hilmi Pasha's traditional Ottoman upbringing seemed to presage a definite tilt towards those Ottoman-serving Arabs who had been disturbed by the Young Turks' new and brutal measures. The other was that many prominent Arabs were co-opted by offers of prestigious titles and appointments. Even before the 1914 elections, several of them were appointed senators, including Yusuf Sursock and Muhammad Bayhum from Beirut; 'Abd al-Hamid al-Zahrawi from Homs; Ahmad Kikhia from Aleppo; 'Abd al-Rahman al-Yusuf from Damascus; and Muhyi al-Din al-Kaylani from Baghdad. Two leading campaigners for reform, Shukri al-'Asali and 'Abd al-Wahab al-Inkilizi, were appointed provincial inspectors in Syria. In 1908, Shukri al-'Asali had hailed the Young Turk revolution as the dawn of a 'new state' (*dawla jadida*), in which unity and equality would flourish. By 1912 he had certainly changed his mind. His appointment as inspector was clearly intended to draw him back into the fold.[3]

The attraction of the secret societies

Whereas older Arabs like Rida el-Solh, who had invested a lifetime in Ottoman service, preferred to be reassured by such gestures, the same could not be said of younger men, who had grown increasingly doubtful of CUP intentions. Educated Arabs in their twenties and early thirties flocked instead to the many secret societies and parties which had been formed to protect Arab rights and defend Arab causes. Ironically, the blueprint had been set by the CUP itself, since it had begun as a secret society which had then seized power and imposed its rule on the

[3] Ibid., pp. 76, 84.

whole of the Empire. By the end of 1912, Arab secret societies were very much in fashion.

The most important of them was the ultra-secret *al-fatat* (or, to give it its full name, *al-jam'iyya al-'arabiyyah al-fatat*, the Young Arab Society), a Muslim Arab organisation which had been founded in Paris on 14 November 1909 by five Arab students. Its purpose was to obtain Arab autonomy within the framework of a bi-racial Ottoman Empire – Arab and Turk – on the lines of the Austro-Hungarian Empire. It also had the ambitious aim of raising the Arab *umma* to the level of the West. When, a year or so later, Riad el-Solh heard whisper of *al-fatat*'s existence, he wrote to Jamil Mardam in Damascus, who was said to be one of its founders, asking to be admitted. Indeed, he was to remain a member until the society was dissolved after the First World War. Riad had had an even earlier contact with another secret society, *al-qahtaniyya*, founded in Istanbul in 1909 by an officer of Egyptian background and Circassian origin, 'Aziz 'Ali al-Misri.

According to Solh family records, Riad went early in 1913 to swear an oath of allegiance to *al-qahtaniyya*, accompanied that day by an older man, Nuri al-Sa'id, who had come from Baghdad to the Ottoman capital on a scholarship to the military academy. The initiation ceremony was brief. After someone read out what was described as their 'patriotic file', the two companions were declared to be 'above suspicion' and were promptly enrolled in the society. They were given a badge and a password, and were taught secret ways of recognising their fellow members. Together, they then intoned the society's credo: 'Arabs! Sons of Qahtan! Bear witness that, when the time comes, we will set the world on fire!' Like other secret societies at the time, *al-qahtaniyya*'s programme was scarcely revolutionary. Its objective was merely to seek autonomy for the Arabs within the Empire, with the Sultan wearing a dual Turkish-Arab crown.

Riad was not impressed. 'How can we hold our head high if a foreign crown rules over us?' he asked, returning his badge to the society almost at once. He had been a member for all of ten minutes. 'Freedom', he told Nuri al-Sa'id, 'isn't a watermelon, to be bought in slices. It has to be all or nothing!'

'With ideas like yours', Nuri told him, 'you'll go to the gallows before you're eighteen.'

'I wonder what sort of a death you will have,' Riad retorted. 'The sweetest of deaths at the age of a hundred?'

Nuri al-Sa'id related this story to the Solh family when he came to pay his condolences in 1951 after Riad el-Solh's assassination. By this time, Nuri had long been the single most powerful politician in Iraq. Seven years later, he was to die a terrible death. When the 1958 revolution broke out, he tried to escape Baghdad disguised as a veiled woman, but was recognised and lynched by the mob.

Al-'ahd (the Covenant), al-fatat's military counterpart, had in fact grown out of al-qahtaniyya. Founded in Istanbul in October 1913 by the same 'Aziz 'Ali al-Misri, it had branches in Baghdad and Mosul, and may have recruited as many as 250 Arab officers into its ranks. Al-Misri, who had served with distinction in the Ottoman army, notably in Libya, remained an Ottomanist. But having quarrelled with Enver Pasha in the spring of 1914, he left Istanbul for Cairo, offended by the purge of more than 300 officers which Enver had carried out when he became minister of war. Once in Cairo, al-Misri is believed to have broached with a British official the idea of an independent Arab state under British tutelage. It was evident that, like so many others during this confusing transitional period, this officer was torn between painfully conflicting loyalties.[4]

Whereas al-fatat and al-'ahd were small secret conspiratorial societies, the Ottoman Administrative Decentralisation Party (hizb al-lamarkaziyyah al-'idariyyah al-'uthmani), founded in Cairo towards the end of 1912 with the full knowledge of the Turkish government, was a political party open to all Ottoman citizens, whether they were Arab or non-Arab, as long as they supported its aims.[5] Its members, however, did tend to be Syrian, Lebanese and Palestinian émigrés, who had flocked to Egypt in the climate of relative political stability which flourished briefly after 1882.

The rise of the reform movement

Worried by this mood of self-assertion – of incipient rebellion even – which appeared to be gaining ground in the Arab provinces, the Sublime Porte decided to allow Arab notables to draft their own proposals for local reform. Beirut seized the initiative, taking the lead of a movement

[4] Kayalı, Arabs and Young Turks, pp. 177–8, 186.
[5] Zeine, Arab-Turkish Relations, pp. 2–3.

which quickly spread to other places. In January 1913, a Beirut Reform Committee was formed by Christian and Muslim notables. Kamil el-Solh, Riad el-Solh's uncle, who had served as an Ottoman judge in Damascus, was a prominent founding member. Beirut was more than ready for such a development. Its extensive foreign trade had created a commercial middle class anxious to throw off irksome controls from Istanbul. The nascent working class was stronger in Beirut than in any other Arab city. The city could boast of a lively intellectual life, thanks to the profusion of schools – state, private and missionary – and to renowned institutions of higher learning. University printing presses had been instrumental in enabling Beirut to develop into a centre of book publishing in Arabic. An important example of what was printed was an encyclopaedia of modern knowledge, which was compiled by Butros al-Bustani (1819–83), and continued by his family after his death. Above all, the city owed its intellectual edge to an explosion of newspapers and magazines – including the daring *al-Mufid*, the organ of the secret *al-fatat* society co-founded and co-owned, with Fu'ad Hantas, by a remarkable young man in his early twenties, 'Abd al-Ghani al-'Uraysi.[6] Another prominent standard-bearer for the Arab cause was *al-Muqtabas*, owned and edited in Damascus by Muhammad Kurd 'Ali.

The revival of the Arabic language in modern books and publications contributed to a national awakening for the Arabs. In the intellectual ferment of the times, the dominant ideas were fear of Western domination, hostility to European Zionist takeover of land in Palestine, a passionate attachment to as well as a desire to reform Islam, and a growing conviction of the need for Arab independence from increasingly xenophobic Turkish control. These ideas merged with notions of patriotism, of freedom of expression and human rights, which were part of a universal legacy. These years aroused hopes of change among thinking men everywhere in the region, including in this eastern Mediterranean seaport.

The Beirut Reform Committee, composed of eighty-six members from all the 'millet councils', which represented every

---

[6] Rashid Khalidi, 'Ottomanism and Arabism', in Khalidi *et al.* (eds), *The Origins of Arab Nationalism*, p. 56; see also his essay on 'Abd al-Ghani al-'Uraisi and *al-Mufid*'. In the Beirut *vilayet*, which included most of the Mediterranean coast from north of Jaffa to north of Latakia, the number of state schools rose from 153 in 1886 to 359 in 1914.

religious denomination in the city, held its first meeting on 12 January 1913 under its two chairmen, Muhammad Bayhum and Yusuf Sursock. In an attempt to mediate between the impatient reformists and the reluctant Ottoman government, they drew up a reform programme which they hoped would satisfy both sides.

This reform programme was announced just days after the coup in Istanbul of 23 January 1913 which restored the CUP to power. Approved at the Committee's third meeting on 31 January, the programme consisted of fifteen articles, of which the first stated that the vilayet's external affairs, together with everything to do with the army, customs, taxes, post and telegraph, would remain in the hands of the Istanbul government. The vilayet's internal affairs would be the responsibility of a locally elected general council. If irreconcilable differences were to arise between the council and the Ottoman vali, the council would have the power to depose the vali by a two-thirds majority vote. Article Fourteen stated that Arabic was to be recognised as the official language of the vilayet.

Not surprisingly, the new rulers in Istanbul did not take kindly to such a bold initiative by the Beirut Reform Committee, which they saw as a challenge to their hard-won authority. They greatly disliked *al-Mufid* and the Arab national views of its contributors – who included by this time Rida el-Solh. Although the CUP did make concessions in the realm of which language would be used – Arabic or Turkish – any proposal which so much as hinted at a desire for separatism was deemed wholly unacceptable.

Shortly after the Unionist takeover that January, Hazim Pasha returned to Beirut as vali, replacing Edhem Pasha who had been appointed by the previous Entente Libérale administration. Determined to quash the reform programme, Hazim Pasha began by closing down two Beirut newspapers. As the Beirut correspondent of the Paris daily, *Le Temps*, reported on 12 March 1913, the vali summoned Shukri al-'Asali, the former Damascus deputy and a leading reformer, to offer him the post of *mutasarrif* in Latakia. 'We Arabs are not looking for lucrative posts', al-'Asali replied, 'but for serious reforms, implemented with the guarantee of the Ottoman Imperial government'.[7] But Hazim Pasha would not give way. He dissolved the Reform Committee, arrested its leaders and shut down its 'club' – arbitrary measures which

---

[7] Zeine, *Arab-Turkish Relations*, p. 95, n. 54.

backfired on him so badly and aroused such fierce protest, that he was soon obliged to release the leaders unconditionally. At the same time, the Turkish authorities in Damascus even closed down the local branch of the Ottoman Administrative Decentralisation Party.

The General Arab Congress of 1913

When the reform movement was silenced in Beirut, it became vocal in Paris. There, eight young Arabs – Muslims as well as Christians – invited delegations from all the Arab provinces to a general Arab Congress in the French capital. The secretary of the preparatory committee was 'Abd al-Ghani al-'Uraysi, the impassioned young editor of *al-Mufid*, who was by then in France studying journalism. The Congress met on 18 June 1913. It was the first time since the fall of the early Arab empires that delegates from every Arab province, as well as émigrés from Europe and the Americas, had gathered to discuss the predicament of their nation, and to plan for the future. Several delegates came from Beirut. Among them was Salim 'Ali Salam. He had served both as head of the Beirut Municipality and of the important educational foundation, *al-Maqasid*,[8] whose schools were instrumental in giving several generations of students an excellent education in Arabic. Other delegates came from the Administrative Decentralisation Party in Cairo, as well as from the Syrian community in France. 'Abd al-Hamid al-Zahrawi, representing the Decentralisation Party, presided over the sessions. His prestige was high, not only because he had made a name for himself as a deputy in the Ottoman parliament, but also because, in Istanbul, he had published an Arabic-language newspaper, *al-Hadara* (Civilisation), which was widely read throughout the Arab provinces.[9]

The proceedings revolved around the ideas of Arab rights within the Empire, hostility to European occupation and administrative decentralisation. There was no mention yet of secession from Istanbul.[10] On the contrary, every speaker stressed the general desire to maintain the integrity of the Empire, provided that the Turks recognised the Arabs

[8] Ziadé, 'Beyrouth', p. 64.
[9] Khalidi, 'Ottomanism and Arabism', p. 60.
[10] Kayalı, *Arabs and Young Turks*, pp. 135–8; Tarabein, 'Abd al-Hamid al-Zahrawi', p. 104.

as their partners, not their inferiors. The assassination in Istanbul of the Iraqi-born Mahmud Shawkat Pasha coincided with the closing day of the Arab Congress on 24 June and aroused great emotion there.

Having failed to prevent the Congress from being held, the CUP sent a delegation to Paris to negotiate with the delegates. After much debate, an agreement was signed in which several Arab demands were conceded, including administrative decentralisation, specific quotas for Arabs as valis, *mutasarrifs* and senators, the use of Arabic in the provincial administration and in schools at all levels, service in the military to be done locally, and so forth. A serious hitch then occurred. It was suddenly revealed by CUP spies that two Christian members of the Beirut delegation – Dr Ayyub Thabit and Khalil Zainiya – had held private meetings with French officials before coming to Paris.

The Unionist government in Istanbul seized on this revelation to discredit the Beirut reform movement by depicting it as a Christian conspiracy.[11] Muslim delegates, who had not been made aware of these meetings, found themselves compromised and embarrassed, and decided from then on to settle questions of reform directly with the Ottoman government. Three members of the Beirut delegation, namely Salim 'Ali Salam, Ahmad Mukhtar Bayhum and Ahmad Tabbara, stopped at Istanbul on their return journey and, at an audience with the Sultan Reşad, swore their loyalty to the Caliph and to the Ottoman state. Abd al-Hamid al-Zahrawi also went to Istanbul to negotiate with the CUP about putting the agreed reforms into effect. In a clear bid to win his loyalty, he was nominated to the Senate by Imperial Decree on 4 January 1914, together with six other Arabs. Al-Zahrawi chose to see his appointment as evidence of the CUP's good faith, but younger Arabs saw his acceptance of the post as a political sell-out. Unfortunately for al-Zahrawi, Istanbul was in no hurry to implement the reforms it had promised him. Dispirited by such delays, he left for Cairo, where he stayed for several months, before returning to Istanbul.[12]

Following the unsuccessful Arab Congress, the reform movement in Syria seemed to peter out. Certain notables, such as the Emir Shakib Arslan, 'Abd al-Rahman al-Yusuf, Muhammad Fawzi Pasha al-'Azm, and Shaykh As'ad al-Shuqairi, went so far as to declare their opposition to the Congress, contending that it was not representative of

---

[11] Kayalı, *Arabs and Young Turks*, p. 141.
[12] Tarabein, 'Abd al-Hamid al-Zahrawi', p. 109.

general opinion. In truth, there was a state of real confusion at the time. The vast majority of the older generation remained loyal Ottomanists, favouring the maintenance of Arab ties with the Empire. Others believed that the solution was a caliphate under the Khedive 'Abbas Hilmi of Egypt, or some other member of an Arab ruling house. Some felt that the greatest threat came from the racial and linguistic chauvinism of the Young Turks, while others believed that it was European imperial ambition that posed the gravest danger. Some feared an Ottoman collapse, others an Ottoman victory. Lebanese Maronites put their faith in France, while some Muslim notables inclined towards Britain. Merchants worried that the Porte would requisition food and fuel, impose higher taxes and raise forced loans in order to meet the cost of the disastrous Balkan wars. Many thought that Arab autonomy, though a commonly held objective, could only be secured with foreign help.

In all this disarray, a hard core of politicised young Arabs was coming to the view that full Arab independence, not autonomy, had to be the goal. By the end of 1913, it had become clear to many of them that the CUP would never grant any of the reforms that the Arabs had demanded. The idea of full Arab independence might never have taken root in these men's minds, had they not been propelled in that direction by the foolishly brutal and politically obtuse behaviour of the CUP.[13] Its suppression of the Beirut Reform Committee and the Damascus branch of the Decentralisation Party only incited *al-fatat* to channel its considerable energies into clandestine work by going underground. Beirut became the centre of its activities in late 1913, and a branch was opened in Damascus.[14] Its members had by this time got to know each other quite well, and had a greater understanding of the particular problems of each individual Arab province. They now began working towards their goal in the utmost secrecy.

The Solh family and the Great War

When war broke out between the European Powers in August 1914, few expected the conflict to spread to the Middle East. But on 2 August the Ottomans signed a secret treaty with Germany, largely meant to

---

[13] Khalidi, 'Ottomanism and Arabism', p. 43.
[14] Muslih, 'The Rise of Local Nationalism', p. 168.

protect their Empire from Russia, its traditional enemy. They then entered into negotiations with Britain and France to see whether a basis could be found for them to remain neutral in the war. Their principal condition was the abolition of the hated Capitulations, which had for centuries kept the Empire in thrall to European interests. When the Entente Powers – Great Britain, France and Russia – refused to give way on this matter, the Ottoman government unilaterally abrogated the Capitulations with effect from 1 October. Less than a month later, on 29 October, the Empire entered the war on the side of the Triple Alliance of Germany, Austro-Hungary and Italy. The result was to open a new front in the Middle East.

There were compelling reasons for the Ottomans to side with the Germans against the Triple Entente of Russia, Great Britain and France. Perhaps the most important of these was the German pledge to restore to the Empire, in the event of victory, the many territories it had lost in Europe, along with Cyprus and Egypt which the British had occupied. Having been trained by German officers for three decades, the Ottoman army was used to German ways and convinced of a German victory. Mahmud Shawkat Pasha, the hero who had crushed the 13 April counter-revolution, was the capable product of German military training. Enver Pasha, the minister of war, had served as Ottoman military attaché in Berlin.

The Ottoman army by this time was burning to avenge its defeat in the Balkan Wars. When the British government requisitioned two warships being built for the Turkish navy in British shipyards, Germany provided substitutes in the shape of the *Goeben* and the *Breslau*. These managed to dodge the British fleet and arrive in the Dardanelles. Although manned and commanded by Germans, they passed formally into Turkish ownership and, at the end of October 1914, joined other ships in bombarding Russian Black Sea ports. The Triple Entente promptly declared war on the Ottoman Empire.

A week later, a division of the British Indian Army which had concentrated at Bahrain in anticipation of hostilities, occupied Fao at the mouth of the Shatt al-Arab – the confluence of the Tigris and the Euphrates – and began a slow and difficult advance northwards in the face of fierce Turkish resistance. The British then suffered a grave setback in April 1916, when 10,000 troops of the Indian Expeditionary Force were surrounded and forced to surrender to the Turks at Kut al-'Amara in Iraq. It was not until early 1917 that the British were able to launch a fresh counteroffensive, which led to the capture of Baghdad in March.

The government of India had sent the expeditionary force to Iraq on London's behalf to secure the Persian Gulf against penetration by German agents. It was feared that the Germans might threaten Kuwait and bring Persia and its vital oilfields over to the German side, together with the Anglo-Persian Oil Company's recently built oil refinery at Abadan. If Persia were to fall to the enemy, Afghanistan and the route to British India would then become dangerously vulnerable to a German assault. In London and Delhi, it was urgently debated whether Basra, and perhaps even Baghdad itself, should be annexed to the British Empire.

The war presented Arab notables like the Solhs with a daunting dilemma. Which side were they to be on? Rida el-Solh had served the Empire as a district governor and a member of the Ottoman parliament and was now retired on an Ottoman pension. Like other military, civilian and religious dignitaries, he was a patrician member of the Ottoman ruling class. There was no contradiction in his own mind between his overlapping Ottoman, Muslim and Arab identities. Yet the Empire he had so faithfully served had changed radically. He had witnessed first hand how a group of ruthless men had seized power in Istanbul; how the opposition party, the Entente Libérale, to which he had belonged, had been smashed; how Arab proposals for reform, decentralisation and local autonomy had been arrogantly rejected out of hand; and how the great 'community of the faithful' – which the multi-ethnic Empire had always represented – was being replaced by narrow, even racist Turkish supremacy. Arabs were quickly being reduced to an inferior political and social status. Rida was well aware that his own son Riad was, like other young men, inclined to side with Arab rebels who, in secret societies, were beginning to dream of breaking loose from the Turks altogether. Yet was this enough to overturn the commitment of a lifetime? Did this once mighty Muslim Empire not continue to represent the only effective shield against Great Britain, France and Russia and their pressing threat to the entire Islamic world? The Empire was at war: was it not his duty to rush to its defence? For all its many faults, the CUP was the Imperial government now. Its defeat remained too awful to contemplate, since it would throw open the door to direct European hegemony, to the inevitable loss of territory and unpredictable violence and chaos.

It was not surprising, therefore, that Rida el-Solh and his many friends and colleagues in Beirut, Damascus, Aleppo, Jerusalem and other Arab cities, chose to stifle their doubts, suspend their demands for reform and declare their support to the now only nominally 'Ottoman' government. The irony, of course, was that Istanbul was too little concerned to pay them attention, as the outbreak of war had greatly reduced Arab political influence there. Always dismissive and suspicious of the Arabs, and ever doubtful of their loyalty, the inclination of the three CUP leaders, Talaat, Enver and Jamal, was further to muzzle Arab activists – especially those who had formerly pressed for reforms.

The CUP's anti-Arab stance, belligerent and short-sighted as it was, was not entirely without cause. Word had reached Istanbul that some Arab exiles in Cairo, who were associated with the Decentralisation Party, had made contact with British and French officials; also, that some leaders in Beirut had even raised with the British consul the possibility of extending 'Egyptian' (a risible euphemism for British) rule to Syria. Istanbul acted quickly and firmly. On 11 November 1914, in a bid to rally wavering Muslims to the Ottoman cause, the Sultan instructed the senior Islamic functionary of the Empire, the Shaykh al-Islam, to issue a fatwa declaring jihad against the Allies – thereby making it a religious obligation on all Muslims to rally to the defence of the Holy Places of the Hijaz and Jerusalem.

In December, Cemal Pasha (hereafter referred to as Jamal Pasha, according to the Arabic transliteration), minister of the navy, who as military governor of Istanbul had made himself notorious by hanging so many members of the Liberal opposition, was sent to Damascus as vali, at the head of the 100,000-strong Fourth Army. His mission was to crush all separatist dissent and impose the most severe order. It was decided that he would checkmate any attempted move on the Arab provinces by the British. He began by enforcing the use of Turkish for all official use. He transferred Arab troops – whom he considered untrustworthy – to distant and highly dangerous theatres of war, deliberately reducing them to cannon fodder. Almost immediately, in February 1915, he launched an attack with 25,000 Turkish troops against the Suez Canal, with the aim of rescuing Egypt from the British, who had by then deposed the Khedive 'Abbas Hilmi and tightened their iron grip on the country. Although the attack was repulsed by British and British Indian troops, aided by the heavy guns of British and French warships stationed in the Suez Canal – the Canal that the Sultan Abdülmecid II had

rightly believed would come to constitute a chink in Ottoman armour –
it brought home to the British the strategic importance of both Suez
and Palestine for the defence of Egypt. Jamal Pasha launched a second
attack in August 1916, but was once again beaten back.

In a bid to demonstrate that the Ottoman government had firm
allies in the provinces, he ordered the mobilisation of local forces he
could count on in support of his own Turkish troops – a Beduin force
led by the Emir 'Ali, son of the Sharif Husayn of Mecca; a Druze unit
led by the Emir Shakib Arslan; a Kurdish unit led by 'Abd al-Rahman
al-Yusuf; and an assortment of other units, each about three hundred
strong, provided by Bulgarian as well as Circassian and Libyan
Muslims.[15] Few of these units actually ended up taking part in the
fighting. They were more for local propaganda purposes.

The British, for their part, tried to stir up revolts in order to pin
down Ottoman forces. They attempted to persuade 'Aziz 'Ali al-Misri
to bring over to Britain's side disaffected Arab officers from the Turkish
army in Iraq. More significant to future events were the contacts which
the Sharif Husayn's son, the Emir 'Abdallah, made with the British
before the war. He wanted to know what Britain's attitude would be if
he revolted against the Turks.

These contacts were then renewed with much greater vigour
soon after the war began. British strategists calculated that the obvious
route for a military strike against Turkey lay through the Arab territories. It was therefore imperative to bring the Arabs over to the Allied
side. It was thought that the Sharif's descent from the Prophet and his
control of the Holy Places of Islam would give him great influence
with the Arab populations. This seemed especially urgent after the disaster of the Gallipoli operation. In February 1915, British and French
ships had attacked the Dardanelles to open the way for an assault on
Istanbul, but had been forced to withdraw after suffering heavy losses.
Troops were then landed at Gallipoli in April, but were also withdrawn
by the end of the year, when faced by determined Turkish resistance,
stiffened by the arrival of troops from Syria. By January 1916, the
Gallipoli operation had had to be abandoned. The diabolical idea then
took hold in London and Paris that, if the Arabs were made to rise in
revolt against the Turks at that most vulnerable moment, the Ottoman
Empire could be finally brought to its knees.

[15] Kayalı, *Arabs and Young Turks*, p. 189.

The Sharif Husayn of Mecca played his cards carefully. While exchanging secret messages with the British, he made sure he retained his links with Istanbul, which was counting on him to support the Ottoman cause. As a cynical camouflage gesture, he even sent the banner of the Prophet – which his Hashemite family had preserved for centuries – on a tour of the Arab provinces. Its arrival in Damascus on 1 January 1915 was welcomed by the biggest crowds the city had ever seen gathered.

Since the young Riad el-Solh spoke fluent Turkish, his comrades in *al-fatat* assigned him the task of spying on Jamal Pasha and his staff. Riad reported that the Turks had placed great hopes on the presence of the precious banner to rally the public to their side. Jamal Pasha had knelt and kissed the relic. 'No one', he told his aides, 'unless he is a shameless heretic, would dare desert our camp or even remain neutral!'[16]

In May 1915, the Sharif Husayn sent his second son, the Emir Faysal, then aged 30, to Syria from the Hijaz to call on Jamal Pasha at his headquarters in Damascus to ask for arms and money. Husayn had no great expectation that the Ottoman government would comply with his request. Indeed, he had intercepted documents that revealed Turkish plans to depose him. He therefore instructed Faysal to seize the opportunity of his visit to Damascus to make contact with the young Arab nationalists of *al-fatat*. In fact, Faysal was sent twice to Damascus with this very purpose in mind. Declining Jamal Pasha's invitation to stay at his headquarters, he put up instead at the house of his friends, Nasib and Fawzi al-Bakri, where he believed he would be safe from Turkish surveillance.

A dozen young rebels gathered there in great secrecy to meet with him. As they waited edgily for his arrival one evening, they were roasting chestnuts on an open fire, and leapt up in alarm, fearing a gunshot, when one of the chestnut husks burst with a loud pop! Each night, the Bakri brothers deliberately gave rowdy dinners on the ground floor of their house, in order to conceal the secret parleys taking place on the upper storey. At first, the young nationalists were wary of Faysal, fearing that his family's Islamic credentials would cause them to rally automatically to the Ottoman side. But they were soon reassured.

---

[16] Alia el-Solh, *Le Jour*, 29 August 1965.

Riad el-Solh later told his daughter Alia that, after one of these secret meetings, he was entrusted with a written message from Faysal to the notables of Sidon, Tyre and other towns and villages of South Lebanon. Leaving Damascus on his way south, he was stopped by a Turkish patrol. Drawing from his boot a small Circassian dagger – the precious gift of his mother – he sank the blade into the arm of the Turkish sergeant who tried to arrest him, and then ran for his life. He was soon seized and knocked senseless by a blow which drove his fez down over his head. This was providential, because stitched into its lining was Faysal's message to the notables. Regaining consciousness, Riad found himself bound and lying in a ditch. Managing to free one hand, he struggled to remove his fez, crush it flat and retrieve from the lining the incriminating piece of paper. He put it into his mouth, chewed it up and swallowed it. A cart appeared into which his jailers threw him, calling him an 'Arab dog', and showering him with kicks and blows from their rifle butts. A day later, he found himself sprained and bruised in a pitch-dark cell of the special prison that was established by Jamal Pasha in the Lebanese mountain village of Aley. This was the grim place where Arab dissidents were held, as they awaited trial before a military tribunal – Âliye Divan-i Harb-i Orfisi. Riad spent long months in this jail. From a cousin who managed to sneak him in some fresh clothes, he learned to his astonishment and distress that his old father, Rida el-Solh, was also locked up in another cell of the same prison.

Jamal Pasha's martyrs

In 1915–16, determined to smash any incipient Arab rebellion as ferociously as he had smashed the Liberals in Istanbul, Jamal Pasha rounded up hundreds of prominent Arabs – former Ottoman provincial administrators and deputies; landowners, newspaper editors, local notables of all sorts – who, he imagined, were disloyal to Istanbul in one way or another. He was convinced that they would turn into a dangerous fifth column in the event of an Allied landing on the Mediterranean coast.

Some of those held at Aley had simply been denounced by their personal or political enemies. Others had their names taken from documents found at French consulates in Beirut and Damascus, which the Ottoman authorities had broken into and occupied after the declaration of war. Due to the treachery of one dragoman, who pointed them out to the Turks, many documents were found at the Beirut consulate in a room behind a concealed door. The names on them were of Syrian and Lebanese men who had been in contact with the French. Some of them had done nothing more incriminating than sign a petition during the agitation for reforms which had taken place earlier. But this was evidence enough to persuade Jamal Pasha that Turkey was facing an imminent threat from a nationalist uprising which was being aided and abetted by foreign powers.

A few years earlier, on the Solh family's return to Beirut from Istanbul, Rida, often accompanied by his son Riad, had spent a good deal of time in South Lebanon conferring with local notables in Tyre, Sidon, Nabatiyyeh and Marj 'Ayun. They would anxiously debate what course the Arabs should follow in view of the hardening trend of Turkish politics. On one of these journeys, one of the men they met was 'Abd al-Karim al-Khalil, a young Shi'i Muslim of radical Arab nationalist views. They had known him in Istanbul, where he had helped found *al-muntada al-adabi*, an Arab literary club of nationalist temper. He had been educated in Beirut at the renowned *Shaykh 'Abbas al-Azhari* school (which Riad had also attended), and had then earned his degree in law in Istanbul. He had been at the First Arab Congress in Paris in 1913.[17] It was not long before word of his meetings in the Jabal 'Amil with Rida and Riad el-Solh came to the ear of the Turkish authorities.

Kamil al-As'ad, the leading notable of South Lebanon and, like Rida el-Solh, a former deputy in the Ottoman parliament, was the man who denounced them to the Turks. Writing to Shaykh As'ad al-Shuqayri, the Mufti of the Turkish Fourth Army and a well-known Ottoman loyalist, he alleged that, in league with the Allies, Rida el-Solh and 'Abd al-Karim al-Khalil were organising a seditious nationalist movement in Sidon.

Kamil al-As'ad was then undoubtedly the most powerful man in South Lebanon. In Istanbul, he had been a member of the opposition Entente Libérale, like Rida el-Solh himself. But once home in the Jabal 'Amil, he calculated that it was more prudent to side with the local Ottoman authorities. As head of the As'ad family – the leading Shi'i feudal clan of the Jabal 'Amil – ruling over a Shi'i population of some

---

[17] Chalabi, *The Shi'is of Jabal 'Amil*, pp. 37, 49, 50.

140,000 persons in the *cazas* of Sidon, Tyre and Marj 'Ayun, he was weighed down with responsibilities, which made him cunning. This extensive district was bordered by the Awali river to the north, Ra's al-Naqura to the south, Mount Lebanon and Huleh to the east, and the Mediterranean to the west.[18] He had always been in rivalry with the Solhs, either for personal or sectarian reasons, and he may well have considered that the intellectuals, bureaucrats, urbanites and local notables with whom Rida el-Solh and 'Abd al-Karim al-Khalil were now conferring in his fiefdom, were developing into a grave threat to his own traditional power base.

When news of the alleged sedition reached Jamal Pasha, he ordered the governor of Sidon to investigate the matter at once.[19] Rida el-Solh, 'Abd al-Karim al-Khalil and a score of others were rounded up and interned in Aley to await trial.[20] Jamal Pasha had already cast his blood-drenched net far wider than South Lebanon. He had begun by hanging a Maronite priest, Father Joseph Hayek, who was accused of collusion with France. This miserable beginning was followed by a series of trials and death sentences passed by the Aley court, and presided over by Jamal Pasha himself. Almost to a man, the condemned were friends or associates of the Solhs. Eleven Beirut leaders, ten of them Muslims, were executed on 21 August 1915, in the town's main square – later appropriately renamed Place des Martyrs. Jamal Pasha then ordered the arrest of Shukri al-'Asali and 'Abd al-Wahab al-Inkilizi, the two newly appointed Ottoman provincial inspectors. Their execution was followed by another round of hangings, on 6 May 1916, of twenty-one Arabs – seventeen Muslims and four Christians – almost all from prominent Syrian, Lebanese and Palestinian families. They included 'Abd al-Hamid al-Zahrawi, who was arrested in Istanbul and taken to Syria for trial; Shafiq Mu'ayyad al-'Azm, Rushdi al-Sham'a, Hafiz al-Sa'id, and the editor of the Arab nationalist newspaper *al-Mufid*, 'Abd al-Ghani al-'Uraysi, then barely 25 years old. The

---

[18] General Staff Intelligence, *General Report on Western Syria (Occupied Enemy Territory – West)*, chapter 18 on Sidon, Beirut, July 1919.

[19] Hilal el-Solh, *Tarikh rajul wa qadiyya 1894–1951*, Beirut 1994, p. 28, who gives as his authority for the allegation Muhammad Jaber Safa's history of South Lebanon, *Ta'rikh Jabal 'Amil*, pp. 210–19. Safa was himself interned at Aley at the time, but was acquitted and released. For a detailed account of the proceedings of the Aley military tribunal and of Kamil al-As'ad's denunciation of Rida el-Solh and Abd al-Karim al-Khalil, see 'Ali Zayn, *Min awraqi*, Beirut n.d., pp. 11–61.

[20] Safa, *Ta'rikh Jabal 'Amil*, pp. 210–19.

executions took place in Beirut and in al-Marja square in Damascus. Among the victims sentenced to death and hanged was Rida el-Solh's friend and South Lebanon contact, 'Abd al-Karim al-Khalil, who, like him, had been denounced by Kamil al-As'ad.

More hangings followed in both Syria and Lebanon. Seventy-one notables were condemned to death in absentia. A great many Syrians – 5,000 according to a contemporary account – were deported to remote parts of Anatolia and had their property confiscated, instantly reducing many prominent and wealthy families to utter penury. Turkish fear of an Arab rebellion had triggered these murderous outrages. At much the same time, it was just such a Turkish fear of a Russian-backed Armenian uprising which led to the deportation and massacre of hundreds of thousands of Armenians in 1915. Those survivors of this Armenian genocide who managed to reach cities in Syria brought the most gruesome tales of death by starvation and thirst, rape, torture, maiming and slaughter. The Syrians began to fear that they would be next.

The tremendous shock of Jamal Pasha al-Saffah's murderous rampage reverberated throughout the Arab provinces, shaking the very foundations of Syrian society. The dominant emotions were panic, horror and utter bewilderment about the future, as well as a growing desire for revenge. Overnight almost, virtually the entire leadership of the nascent Arab national movement was wiped out. From then on, any notion of Arab autonomy within a reformed and decentralised Empire became unthinkable. For many Arabs in Beirut and Damascus, the breach with the Turks was final.

The nationalist torch now passed to a younger generation, and particularly to those Arab officers who were still attached to the Ottoman armed forces. The brutish Jamal Pasha had managed to alienate the entire Arab world. There is no doubt that, single-handedly, he did the greatest damage possible to the Ottoman imperial cause. He smashed a nascent national movement, in which an older moderate generation still flirted with Ottomanism. His orgy of killings had the effect of uniting this movement around clear Arab national goals, awakening a new and determined spirit of revolt. After the hangings, Arab political independence became an absolute necessity – for sheer survival if for nothing else.[21]

---

[21] Zeine, *Arab-Turkish Relations*, p. 104.

How did Rida el-Solh and his son Riad escape death? One suggestion is that Rida's prestige and long service to the Empire saved them both, although this does not reveal why others of no less prestige and years of service went to their terrible deaths on the gallows. Another suggestion is that Rida's elder brother Kamil, a leading Ottoman judge, intervened with Enver Pasha, then minister of war, to persuade Jamal Pasha to sentence Rida and his son to exile rather than death;[22] whereas Yusr el-Solh, Ahmad Pasha's last surviving grandchild, and daughter of the same Kamil el-Solh, told this author that it was a Druze notable, Milhem Bey Hamadeh, who managed to save Rida and Riad, by pushing their names to the back of the queue of condemned men.[23] Others yet say that the charge of 'treason' against Rida remained unproven and that this was why he was sentenced to deportation rather than to death, along with his son Riad. It is believed that Jamal Pasha wanted to deport father and son to two different places, far apart from each other, but that a leading Beirut notable, Salim 'Ali Salam, pleaded successfully for them to be exiled together.[24]

Riad el-Solh's daughter Alia provided yet another, more colourful, explanation for their lucky escape from death. She related that, when news reached Rida's wife, Nazira, that both her husband and her adored son, Riad, were interned in Aley and were in danger of execution, she galloped her carriage in a frenzy to the house of the vali of Beirut, 'Azmi Pasha, who had been their neighbour in Istanbul before the war, to plead for their lives. In the *haremlik* of Azmi Pasha's house, she was received by Mamduha, the vali's daughter, the very same girl with whom Riad had flirted over the garden wall so many years before. Mamduha reminded her father that Riad el-Solh had saved his life by running for a doctor when he had had an almost fatal attack of asthma. This roused the vali – who was obviously a man of honour – and made him feel, in good Muslim tradition, that he was personally under obligation for his own life to Riad. He travelled overnight to Damascus, where he managed to convince Jamal Pasha to deport rather than execute father and son. Shackled like common prisoners,

[22] Hilal el-Solh, *Tarikh rajul wa qadiyya*, p. 29.
[23] Interview with Yusr el-Solh, London, 10 January 2004.
[24] Salim 'Ali Salam, *Mudhakkarat, 1868–1938*, Beirut 1982, p. 227, quoted in Ahmad Beydoun, 'Riad el-Solh et les élections législatives de 1943', in Gérard D. Khoury (ed.), *Sélim Takla, 1895–1945: Une contribution à l'indépendance du Liban*, Paris and Beirut 2004, p. 406.

they eventually set out on foot on the hard road to exile in Anatolia. It is said in the Solh family that Riad's ankles bore the blue marks of those biting iron chains for the rest of his life.[25]

Once their convoy reached Aleppo, Rida el-Solh insisted on a meeting with the governor of the city. He somehow managed to convince this former colleague in the Ottoman service to allow them to head for Smyrna (Izmir), rather than the far bleaker Anatolia.[26] It was in this picturesque Mediterranean city, populated largely by Greeks, with its bustling port and its crowded bazaars hung with carpets, that father and son spent the two years, 1916–18, under a lax form of dusk-to-dawn house arrest. Nazira, meanwhile, was left to fend for herself in the harsh conditions of wartime Beirut, with her daughter Alia, a sensitive girl of fragile health, and her mentally disabled son, Darwish.

Origins of the Arab Revolt

Shortly before being sent into exile, Rida and Riad el-Solh heard news of the uprising in the Hijaz against the Turks. The Sharif Husayn and his sons had declared war on Turkey and, on 5 June 1916, attacked Turkish garrisons at Jeddah, Mecca and Ta'if. The revolt was the culmination of eight months of secret negotiations between the Sharif Husayn and the British, in which they agreed on a military alliance. The British had decided to back the Sharif in part because they felt the need for an Islamic figure to counter the influence of the Sultan-Caliph in Istanbul. No doubt they hoped that Indian Muslims would rally to him. But it was famously left unclear what political and territorial arrangements would follow an Allied victory. Indeed, with hindsight one can say that this revolt against the Turks proved far more damaging to the Arab and Muslim cause than could have been imagined at the time by any local observer or participant, and may well have set the Arabs on their catastrophic political decline.

From 14 July 1915 to 10 March 1916, ten letters were exchanged between the Sharif Husayn and Sir Henry McMahon, the high commissioner in Cairo, who was acting for the British government.

---

[25] Alia el-Solh, *Le Jour*, 5 September 1965.
[26] Hilal el-Solh, *Tarikh rajul wa qadiyya*, p. 29.

The Sharif Husayn was spurred to reach an agreement with the British by Jamal Pasha's reign of terror in Beirut and Damascus, but also by his own strategic situation. The British and French blockade of the entire sea boundaries of the Ottoman Empire – designed to drive the population away from the Ottomans and towards them – had resulted in a great deal of suffering. The Sharif was at the mercy of the Royal Navy in the Red Sea. Indeed, Britain's blockade of his ports had already caused serious food shortages in the Hijaz. Members of *al-fatat*, as well as *al-'ahd* deserters from the Ottoman armies, had appealed to him to take the lead of an Arab insurrection. The Sharif's inducement to take up arms was his ambition to create an independent Arab state under his own Hashemite rule.

On 14 July 1915, he sent a letter to McMahon in which he asked Great Britain to 'approve the proclamation of an Arab Khalifate of Islam' in a vast area 'bounded on the north by Mersina and Adana . . . up to the border of Persia; on the east by the borders of Persia up to the Gulf of Basra; on the south by the Indian Ocean, with the exception of the position of Aden to remain as it is; on the west by the Red Sea [and] the Mediterranean Sea up to Mersina.' Sir Henry replied on 24 October 1915 that 'Great Britain is prepared to recognise and support the independence of the Arabs in all the regions within the limits demanded by the Sharif of Mecca'.

This broad pledge, however, was subject to a number of 'modifications', which Sir Henry went on to outline. First, 'The two districts of Mersina and Alexandretta and portions of Syria lying to the west of the districts of Damascus, Homs, Hama and Aleppo cannot be said to be purely Arab and should be excluded from the limits demanded.' Second, 'With regard to the vilayets of Baghdad and Basra, the Arabs will recognise that the established position and interests of Great Britain necessitate special administrative arrangements in order to secure these territories from foreign aggression'. Third, McMahon stipulated that the promise of independence could only be made 'for those regions lying within those frontiers wherein Great Britain is free to act without detriment to the interests of her ally, France'.[27] In other words – and although this was left deliberately vague – Lebanon, Iraq and south-eastern Anatolia were excluded from the area pledged to the

---

[27] J. C. Hurewitz, *Diplomacy in the Near and Middle East*, 2 vols, Princeton 1956, vol. II, pp. 14–15.

Sharif and, as Britain would later claim, Palestine too – even though Palestine lay well to the south of the Damascus, Homs, Hama, Aleppo line that had been clearly specified.

As the Turks were still very much in evidence in the Levant, the reaction of the local population to the Hijaz revolt was necessarily cautious and ambivalent. Few dared applaud, even in private. Under Turkish pressure, the leading 'ulema of Damascus even passed a death sentence on the Sharif Husayn for treason. Members of Arab elites throughout the Arab provinces had to think twice before embracing Arab nationalism – at least in public. The penalties were simply too severe. Indeed, when the Sharif first assumed the title of 'King of the Hijaz', and then, in November, promoted himself to 'King of the Arabs', an Ottoman military court in Damascus brought to trial several Syrians suspected of collusion with him, including Faris al-Khoury, the Christian deputy for Damascus, Tawfiq al-Halabi, editor of *al-Ra'i*, and the Bakri brothers, in absentia, who had hosted Faysal on his visits to Damascus, and who had prudently left the city when news reached them of the revolt.[28]

In exile in Smyrna, Rida and Riad el-Solh followed news of the war as best they could. It was there, in April 1917, that they learned that the United States had entered the war against the Ottoman Empire. It was in Smyrna too that they first heard word of the Balfour Declaration – whereby Britain pledged its 'best endeavours' to facilitate the 'establishment in Palestine of a National Home for the Jewish people' – a document published in both the British and Egyptian press on 9 November 1917. Rida, who had followed the Zionist colonisation of Palestine with anxiety, and had raised the issue in the Ottoman parliament, immediately understood that the Balfour Declaration was a devastating blow to Arab rights. The Zionists had managed to win the backing of Great Britain, the foremost imperial power of the day.

Arab exiles in Egypt, remnants of the ruling elite of the Arab provinces, who had escaped Jamal Pasha's butchery, sent angry protests to the British authorities. Caught between a beleaguered Ottoman Empire, aggressive European Powers and ambitious Zionists, the Arabs' situation seemed desperate.

The Sharif Husayn's forces, however, were making good progress, but the Turks still held Medina, where lay the terminus of the

---

[28] Kayalı, *Arabs and Young Turks*, pp. 198–9.

Hijaz railway. It was heavily guarded and defended by a Turkish force of about 25,000 men. Supplying its garrison, however, was proving enormously difficult, as the railway was under repeated hit-and-run attack by Faysal's tribal irregulars, advised by a handful of British officers, including Colonel T. E. Lawrence, an ardent imperialist. He had arrived in the Hijaz in mid-October 1916 as 'adviser' to Faysal and as liaison officer between him and the British. Most of the action of the Sharif's men, spurred on by the British, was to take place along the axis of the Hijaz railway, that vital link between cities of the region, which had been paid for by many devout Muslims worldwide, and had been such a source of pride to the Ottomans.

At that moment, however, the British fear was that the Turks might break out of Medina, recapture Mecca, and use the railway to move their garrison to reinforce the Turkish main army in Palestine and Syria. This might have meant the collapse of the British-backed 'Arab Revolt'. The British strategy was to bottle up the Turks in Medina, but not to threaten them so utterly as to make an attempted breakout seem their only salvation. 'We must not take Medina', Lawrence had written shrewdly. 'The Turk is harmless there. In prison in Egypt he would cost us food and guards'.[29]

By the end of 1916, the British had cleared the Sinai Peninsula and prepared for larger conquests. On 9 January 1917, they took Rafah on the borders of Palestine in a very stiff fight. They then aimed for Gaza, which they failed to take, despite two assaults in March and April, with the loss of 10,000 men, killed, wounded or taken prisoner. It was not until General Sir Edmund Allenby was appointed commander-in-chief in June that the Turks were outmanoeuvred and driven back. They thought Allenby would aim again for Gaza; instead he struck inland and seized Beersheba on 31 October, thereby piercing the Palestine front. Meanwhile, Arab forces had occupied 'Aqaba in July 1917. On 9 December, Jerusalem was taken. Allenby entered it on foot two days later, supposedly to show his respect for the Holy Places, and perhaps to strike a telling contrast with the ostentatious way that the German Emperor Wilhelm II had ridden into the city two decades earlier.

---

[29] Hugh Leach, 'Lawrence's Strategy and Tactics in the Arab Revolt', in *Journal of the Royal Society for Asian Affairs*, 36(3) (November 2006), pp. 337–41. For a withering view of T. E. Lawrence's unstable and imperialist personality, see Rana Kabbani, *Imperial Fictions*, London 1986 (new edn London 2008).

Then came another massive blow. Following the Russian Revolution and the Bolshevik decision to withdraw from the war and sign an armistice with Turkey in December 1917, word reached the Solhs in Smyrna of the secret Sykes–Picot agreement, which Britain, France and Czarist Russia had concluded in May 1916. Revealed to the world by the Bolsheviks, who discovered the document in the Czarist archives, it confirmed the Arabs' worst fears: Britain and France were planning to partition the Arab provinces between them. To demonstrate the perfidy of the Allies, the Turks sent the text of the Sykes–Picot agreement to the Emir Faysal, hoping to wean him away from the Allies with a separate peace. But it was too late, and he was already up to his neck in British plans for the area.

Britain wanted the provinces of Basra and Baghdad, while France wanted the Syrian coast, Cilicia and the province of Mosul. Somewhere between these two zones, and almost as an afterthought, some sort of vague Arab 'state' or 'federation' would be created in the Syrian interior, itself divided into British and French spheres of influence. Palestine would be put under international administration. This carve-up of the region bore no resemblance whatsoever to the large independent Arab kingdom which the Sharif Husayn had been mendaciously promised by the British, and which Arab nationalists dreamed of creating once they had thrown off CUP rule.

The decisive battles for the rest of Palestine which broke the Ottoman army began in September 1918. Just before the British assault, an Arab force, directed and supplied by T. E. Lawrence and other British officers, made a desert journey of some three weeks round the left flank of the Turkish Army, to attack the main railway junction behind Turkish lines. Allenby relied conveniently and increasingly on the Emir Faysal's irregulars to secure his eastern flank. Without them, he would have been operating in completely hostile territory. Conversely, the Turks found themselves fighting in adverse conditions. Anglo-Arab troops then struck north, driving the retreating Ottomans before them. Haifa fell on 23 September, Damascus on 1 October, Beirut on 8 October and Aleppo on 26 October. By the end of the month, the whole region was 'liberated'. However, its troubles were only beginning, as it turned out.

The Sublime Porte capitulated to the Allied Powers nearly two weeks before the German surrender. With Russia eliminated from the war, Britain remained the only Entente power with fighting forces in the Middle East. It therefore drew up, in the name of the Allies, the terms of the Ottoman armistice which was signed on 30 October 1918, after a week of negotiations, on board a British warship, HMS *Agamemnon*, in the port of Mudros in the northern Aegean island of Lemnos. Hostilities between the Allies and Turkey ceased from noon, local time, on 31 October 1918.[30] It was clear to all that Turkish rule over the Arabs was over. Istanbul itself was occupied by British, French and Italian troops. But the Arabs were robbed of the inheritance they had expected to receive for siding with the British. Rashly, they had instead helped bring the last great Muslim empire to its end.

Famine in Beirut and Mount Lebanon

Towards the end of the Great War, Rida and Riad el-Solh hurried home to scenes of great desolation. Rida was allowed to return directly to Beirut, but Jamal Pasha insisted that Riad be held in Damascus where the Turkish military authorities could keep an eye on him. He joined his father in Beirut a few months later, when Jamal Pasha was recalled to Istanbul on the eve of the Turkish debacle.[31] Indeed, just as the Levant suffered devastation, Turkey itself was not spared (as may best be understood from Irfan Orga's evocative and poignant description of Turkey's suffering during the First World War, as seen through the eyes of one Turkish family[32]).

 Rida and Riad found Lebanon in a most pitiful state. The mountains had been ravaged in 1915 by great swarms of locusts, which consumed every green thing in sight. Occupied by a Turkish division, Lebanon began to feel the pinch of hunger in 1916. All boys over the age of 15 lived in fear of *Safarbarlik*, the harsh, lengthy and violently enforced conscription into Turkish forces. Famine devastated the entire region. The Turkish government sent some grain for the relief of the population, but these supplies were seized and manipulated by corrupt *mutasarrifs*, *qa'im maqams* and others, who in many cases sold the grain at exorbitantly inflated prices. As the area produced little or no grain and none could be brought in from outside, the last years of the war were catastrophic. The Allied naval blockade of the Syrian

---

[30] Text of Armistice in Hurewitz, *Diplomacy*, vol. II, pp. 36–7.
[31] Hilal el-Solh, *Tarikh rajul wa qadiyya*, p. 31.
[32] Irfan Orga, *Portrait of a Turkish Family*, London 1950.

coast, the hoarding of grain by unscrupulous merchants and officials, the requisitioning of camels, mules and horses by the Turkish army, the absence of transport to bring food from the interior, the cutting down of trees to provide fuel for the locomotives, and the ruthless spread of cholera, all contributed to the dreadful misery that people suffered, as much as did the war itself. Nearly half a million people died of famine during those years, including hundreds in the streets of Beirut and other coastal towns in the last weeks of the war.[33] French observers reported the harrowing sight of children with swollen stomachs scrambling for a piece of orange peel, of skeletal women chewing on mouldy crusts of bread, of municipal carts doing the rounds each night to collect the corpses of those dead from starvation.[34]

Appalled at what they saw, Rida and his son Riad (now aged 24) were eager to play their part in the struggle for independence. During their enforced two-year exile, they had become impassioned Arab nationalists, although there was necessarily some difference still between father and son, no doubt due to age, work experience and personal temperament.

[33] Consul R. A. Fontana to Earl Curzon, Beirut, 21 December 1920 (FO 372/6453).
[34] Gérard D. Khoury, *La France et l'Orient arabe: Naissance du Liban moderne 1914–1920*, Paris 1993 (new edn 2009, with a preface by Henry Laurens), pp. 79–82.

18 – Sayyid Husayn bin 'Ali (1854–1931), last of the Hashemite rulers of the Hijaz. As Sharif and Emir of Mecca, 1908–17, he proclaimed the Arab Revolt against the Ottomans in 1916, and assumed the title of King of the Hijaz. In 1924, he was defeated and expelled from the Hijaz by 'Abd al 'Aziz al-Saud, creator of the Kingdom of Saudi Arabia. He died in Amman and was buried in Jerusalem.

19 – Maronite Patriarch Elias Hayek led a delegation of bishops to the 1919 Peace Conference, where he pressed for the enlargement of Mount Lebanon to its 1861 borders. (By kind permission of Ghassan Tuéni and *al-Nahar*.)

20 – The Emir Faysal at the 1919 Peace Conference in Paris. The photograph is thought to have been taken by the wife of US President Woodrow Wilson. (By kind permission of the Trustees of the Liddell Hart Centre for Military Archives, King's College London.)

21 – After serving as a general in the Ottoman army, Yusuf al-'Azma (1883–1920) joined the Arab Revolt and became the Emir Faysal's minister of defence. He was killed at the battle of Maysalun, 12 miles west of Damascus, on 24 July 1920, when his small force of volunteers was overwhelmed by the 80,000-strong French army of General Henri Gouraud. (By kind permission of Sami Moubayed at www.syrianhistory.com.)

22 – Winston Churchill, then colonial secretary, and his wife Clementine in Jerusalem in 1921, with the Hashemite Emir 'Abdallah bin Husayn, ruler of Transjordan. Backed and financed by the British, 'Abdallah soon established friendly relations with the Zionists in Palestine, who were bent on creating a Jewish state. (By kind permission of the Imperial War Museum.)

23 – The Emir Faysal is crowned King of Iraq in 1921. Left to right, Sir Percy Cox, British high commissioner; Kinahan Cornwallis; Tahsin Qadri, the king's aide-de-camp (Riad el-Solh's friend from Istanbul days, and later the influential Iraqi ambassador in Lebanon); King Faysal; Sir Aylmar Haldane, British commanding officer; Sayyid Husayn Afnan, secretary of the Council of Ministers. (By kind permission of the Middle East Archive of St Antony's College, Oxford. Photographer: Kerim)

24 – From 1919 to 1931, Beirut's main square was known as the Place des Martyrs, in memory of the nationalists hanged there by Jamal Pasha. It then reverted to its original name of Place des Canons, since it was there that the French expeditionary force, dispatched to Lebanon after the 1860 massacres, pitched camp with its heavy guns. The square was destroyed in the 1975–90 civil war. (By kind permission of Ghassan Tuéni, and the publisher of his book, *el-Bourj*, Dar al-Nahar.)

25 – Al-Marja square in Damascus in the late 1920s. The column was erected
to celebrate the establishment of telegraphic communications between
Syria and the holy cities of the Hijaz. (With kind permission of Amer Bader
Hassoun and the publisher of his *Book of Syria*, Damascus 2005.)

5   FAYSAL'S FALSE DAWN

With barely contained excitement, Rida el-Solh and his son Riad –
together with tens of thousands of others – charted the progress of
General Allenby's forces as they relentlessly drove Ottoman armies
northwards from Gaza in September–October 1918. Most Arab hopes
lay with the Emir Faysal and his troops, who, after more than two
years of hard fighting on the inland flank of the Allied forces, now
had victory in sight. After conquering Palestine, Damascus was their
goal. Before making his hurried exit from the city, Jamal Pasha had
handed over power to two Algerian princes, 'Abd al-Qadir II and
Sa'id, descendants of the great Emir 'Abd al-Qadir al-Jaza'iri. But the
two Algerians were promptly ousted when Arab and Allied troops
entered Damascus early on 1 October. A month later, the Emir Faysal
issued an order for their arrest when it was rumoured that they had
sought to set up an opposition party with French support. Sa'id was
arrested and 'Abd al-Qadir was shot by Faysal's troops as he sought
to flee.

   For the Arabs to think that this was their victory too, Colonel
T. E. Lawrence, the Emir Faysal's British 'adviser', asked General
Allenby to allow Arab troops to enter Damascus ahead of the main
British force. This they did at about 6 a.m., although they may have
been beaten to it by a troop of the 3rd Australian Light Horse, which,
riding in hot pursuit of Turkish troops as they fled towards Homs, sped
through the north-western quarters of the city just before dawn.[1]

   Rida and Riad were in the city when Faysal, having come up
by train from Dar'a, entered Damascus on 3 October to a delirious
welcome from its inhabitants. Mounted on an Arab thoroughbred,

---

[1] Khoury, *La France et l'Orient arabe*, pp. 118–19.

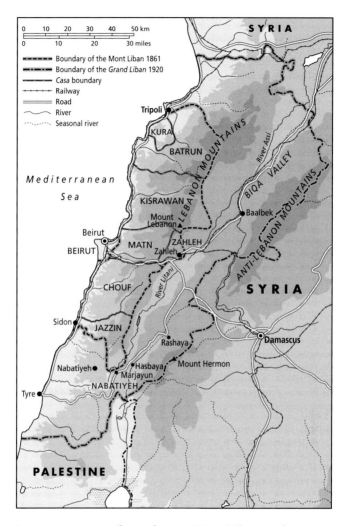

2 – The Ottoman *mutasarrifiyya* of 1861 (Mont Liban) and its expansion into Greater Lebanon (*Grand Liban*), as created by the French in 1920

flanked by Iraqi, Syrian and Hijazi officers of the Arab Revolt, and accompanied by Lawrence, the emir led a parade of 1,500 Arab horsemen through streets packed by jostling, cheering and dancing crowds, firing their guns and being sprinkled with rosewater by women from the upper storeys of houses. A little while later, in more sedate fashion, Allenby drove into the city in a grey convertible Rolls-Royce, followed by his headquarters staff. At the Great Mosque of the Umayyads, prayers were said in the name of the Sharif Husayn (who, defying British and French wishes, had adopted the title of 'King of the Arabs') and of his son and deputy in Syria, the Emir Faysal. It was a glorious moment for the history books. The Arab dream of independence seemed about to come true. But, unbeknown to the jubilant crowds, ominous clouds had already begun to gather.

Rida el-Solh joins Faysal's team

On that same day of 3 October, Allenby spelled out to Faysal in no uncertain terms the limits of his Arab authority. He could 'govern' inland Syria, but only with French advice and financial support. France, indeed, was to become Syria's 'protecting power'. Palestine, Mount Lebanon and the Syrian coast were to fall outside his area of responsibility. Faysal was shocked and outraged. He protested that Lawrence had promised him that the *whole* of Syria, with the sole exception of Palestine, would fall under his government. He categorically rejected the help of French advisers and liaison officers, although he showed himself ready, if it were deemed absolutely necessary, to accept British assistance.[2]

On 4 October, *Lisan al-'Arab*, the pro-Faysal newspaper in Damascus, announced the formation of a constitutional government for the whole of Syria. A score of horsemen galloped across the mountains to lend a hand to Faysal's followers in Beirut, where the Sharifian flag was raised over public buildings. Mumtaz Bey, the last of the Ottoman valis, had already turned over the city to 'Umar al-Da'uq, head of the municipality. But when French troops landed in Beirut on 7 October 1918, and took up positions in Mount Lebanon, Faysal's

---

[2] Vincent Cloarec, *La France et la question de Syrie, 1914–18*, Paris 1988, pp. 209–10.

horsemen were soon made unwelcome and were forced to beat their way back to Damascus.

Having liberated the whole area from the Turks, General Allenby had hoped to dispose of it without interference. But in view of the French troop landings and France's evident and pressing ambitions, he decided to divide the Levant into three 'neat' military zones: Palestine, administered by a British officer; Mount Lebanon and the Mediterranean coast from Acre to Alexandretta, administered by a French officer; and the Syrian interior and Transjordan, administered by the Emir Faysal, with British troops in occupation. A high point in the annals of Anglo-Arab entente occurred on 15 October, when Allenby and his staff drove to the seat of government in Damascus to be welcomed by General 'Ali Rida Pasha al-Rikabi, a former senior officer in the Ottoman army, whom Faysal, with Allenby's approval, had appointed military governor and chief administrator of the Syrian interior. The ceremony was attended by senior officers and officials, Muslim religious dignitaries, priests of the principal Christian communities, Druze notables and Jewish rabbis. French representatives were not invited, which suited both the British and the Arabs.

Allenby wanted to assert Britain's unfettered authority, while the Sharifians had become even more resolutely anti-French since their arrival in Damascus. The excited population of the city concluded naively that Britain was lending its support to the Arabs at a historic moment of their national rebirth. A new flag was raised over the Damascus municipality. Its colours were white (purity of deeds), black (as battles), green (as fields, to indicate prosperity), and red (with the blood of the enemy).[3]

In Damascus, the nationalist movement, which had been drastically thinned by Jamal Pasha's executions of 1915–16, was fast regaining heart and men. The defeat of the Ottoman Empire had not unduly disturbed the exercise of local power. In all the major cities, notables continued to rule as they had always done. For the most part, men who had been important in local affairs under the Ottomans remained influential in post-Ottoman Syria, where they or their sons continued to wield important political influence. In a region where the masses were still largely illiterate, urban leadership remained the basic

---

[3] As inspired by the 13th century Mesopotamian poet Safi al-Din al-Hilli.

building block of politics.[4] Faysal did rely on such notables, but a new force had arisen alongside them in the shape of the secret societies *al-fatat* and *al-'ahd*, which now came into their own and whose veterans occupied many of the key posts in Faysal's administration. They formed the political core of Faysal's Arab state. So powerful was this new force that, in its relations with Faysal, it was at times difficult to tell who was ruling whom.

Most of these men had risen against the Turks with one goal only: to win independence and unity for the Arab provinces. They were intensely worried about the possible implications of the Sykes–Picot agreement and the Balfour Declaration. The spectre of European rule and Zionist colonisation filled them with terror. But, for the moment at least, they continued to have faith in the undertakings Britain had given the Sharif Husayn in the years 1915–16. At this stage, they had only a partial grasp of the private Anglo-French bargaining over the spoils of the Ottoman Empire, and little understanding of the actual scope of Zionist ambitions.

On entering Damascus, Faysal sent messages to the cities and municipalities of Syria announcing the end of Ottoman rule, as well as his intention of forming an Arab government in Damascus, which he immediately set about doing. His chief administrator, 'Ali Rida Pasha al-Rikabi, aged 50, had deserted from the Ottomans to the British and then rallied to the Sharif. He was anti-French, a strong supporter of complete independence, a member of the Iraqi section of *al-'ahd* and, in the words of one snide British intelligence report, a 'past-master in Turkish methods of intrigue'.[5]

The team Rikabi assembled was impressive. Rida el-Solh was named minister of interior. Faysal is said to have summoned him with the words: 'You have two qualities I need. You are an honest man and you are not a Damascene!'[6] Rida became one of the emir's confidants in the difficult months that lay ahead. Through his father's appointment, Riad el-Solh therefore found himself at the very centre of affairs, on familiar terms with the men around the emir, some of whom he had already known in Istanbul. This might be considered his first real entry

[4] Philip S. Khoury, 'Syrian Urban Politics in Transition', in Albert Hourani, Philip S. Khoury and Mary C. Wilson (eds), *The Modern Middle East*, London 1993, p. 430.
[5] *Who's Who in Damascus*, July 1919. Compiled by General Staff Intelligence, Beirut; see also PRO FO 371/6454 Consul Palmer to Earl Curzon.
[6] Interview with Yusr el-Solh, London, 10 January 2004.

into politics. His view at that time was: 'Everything starts from today. Damascus is awakening from 800 years of slumber.'[7] Old enough to have had first-hand experience of the Ottoman world, yet young enough to throw all his energies into the new struggle for Arab independence, he was now ready to move out from under his father's wing and to come of age as a political figure in his own right.

The chief of staff of Faysal's Arab forces was Yasin Pasha al-Hashimi, aged 40, an officer from Baghdad with a reputation as an excellent soldier. He had commanded the 20th Turkish Division in Romania; subsequently the 8th Army Corps Artillery, and later the whole of the Corps itself. He had thrown in his lot with the Sharif when the Turkish collapse seemed inevitable. He, too, was a member of the Iraqi section of al-'ahd and was a believer in complete Arab independence. The British feared him as 'potentially dangerous'. Another Arab officer from Baghdad, who had also seen service in the Turkish army, was Nuri al-Sa'id, aged 35, whom Riad had known in Istanbul. He had won fame as one of the most capable officers of the Arab Revolt and had led Arab forces into Damascus on 1 October. British intelligence thought him 'trustworthy, with a penchant for British ways' – in other words, malleable to their ends.

Hashim al-Atasi, at 53, was an older nationalist from a patrician landed family of Homs, who was to serve as president of the Constituent Assembly and prime minister under Faysal, and later, in a long and distinguished political career, as president of the Syrian Republic.[8] Also close to Faysal as minister of finance was the lawyer Faris al-Khoury, aged 48, the son of a Greek Orthodox family from Hasbaya in Lebanon, who had been educated at the Syrian Protestant College in Beirut, had converted to Protestantism under the influence of British missionaries, knew English well, and had served as a dragoman for the British consulate in Damascus from 1899 to 1909. A skilful advocate and clever speaker, he was later to make a name for himself as prime minister of independent Syria, the only Christian ever to hold the post.

The 31-year-old Shukri al-Quwatli was a member of a highly prestigious Damascus family, a graduate of Istanbul University and a real patriot. As secretary to the vali of Damascus, 'Ala' al-Din al-Drubi,

---

[7] Interview with Alia el-Solh, Monte Carlo, 4–5 October 2004.
[8] Yusuf al-Hakim, *Suriyya wal 'ahd al faysali*, Beirut 1966, pp. 93, 144, 159, quoted by Beydoun, 'Riad el-Solh et les élections législatives de 1943', p. 404, n. 4.

he was appointed to reorganise the Damascus vilayet and then rose to become chief of the Arab government's intelligence department. Under the Turks, he narrowly escaped execution after being condemned to death by a Turkish court martial. To avoid divulging under torture information about al-'ahd, the secret society to which he belonged, he preferred to try to take his own life in prison by cutting the veins to his wrist. Before he could bleed to death, he was rescued by another inmate, Ahmad Qadri, who happened to be a doctor.[9] He was later to achieve great prominence in Syrian politics as a committed nationalist leader and the first democratically elected president of the Republic. He is considered the father of Syrian independence.

Faysal's minister of education was Sati' al-Husri, aged 40, from Aleppo, a graduate of Istanbul University and then a professor there, who had been sent to study educational methods in Europe before being appointed president of Istanbul's Academy of Education in 1916. After the armistice he returned to Syria, where he presided over the Ministry of Education and grew into a leading thinker and ideologue of Arab nationalism. When, having been expelled from Syria by the French, the Emir Faysal ascended the throne of Iraq in 1921, Sati' al-Husri accompanied him to Baghdad and threw himself into reshaping the educational system in that country. In Damascus, Faysal's chamberlain was Ihsan al-Jabiri, a former deputy for Aleppo in the Ottoman parliament, and for a time aide-de-camp to Sultan Abdülhamit. He was the brother of Riad's friend Sa'dallah al-Jabiri and was to become one of Riad's closest associates between the wars, when they joined forces to lobby the League of Nations in Geneva on behalf of the Arab cause. Faysal's Chief Secretary was Nasib al-Bakri, a keen Arab nationalist who, with his elder brother Fawzi, had hosted the emir on his earlier visits to Damascus, when it was still under Ottoman rule. They were the sons of 'Ata Bey al-Bakri, head of a landowning family claiming descent from the first Caliph, Abu Bakr.

Among Nasib's rivals for the ear of the emir was Dr 'Abd al-Rahman al-Shahbandar, a brilliant physician and political activist of 39, who had been a leading promoter of the Arab Congress in Paris in 1913. Having graduated in medicine from the Syrian Protestant College, and taught there for a while, he then ran his own

---

[9] PRO FO 371/6454. Quwatli was one of eleven signatories from al-'ahd to send a petition to the Foreign Office on 12 May 1921, appealing to Britain to assist Syrians against 'French oppression'.

clinic in Damascus, marrying the daughter of a rich landowner, 'Abd al-Qadir Mu'ayyad al-'Azm, member of the prominent 'Azm family of Damascus and Hama. His brother, Shafiq Mu'ayyad al-'Azm, had been hanged by the Turks as a nationalist during the war. Although under strict surveillance by Jamal Pasha, Shahbandar had managed to escape across the desert to Mesopotamia in 1916, and from there to Egypt, where he worked as a surgeon in a military hospital, edited a newspaper and founded a political party of Syrian exiles. While in Cairo he was in touch with British officials, which later earned him the unproven accusation of having had links with British intelligence. On returning to Syria, the suspicions of Nasib al-Bakri prevented him from becoming part of Faysal's inner circle once again. It was only in the summer of 1920, when Faysal was facing a final showdown with the French, that Shahbandar managed to prevail on the emir to appoint him foreign minister.

Also present in Damascus at that time was Riad's brother-in-law, Sami el-Solh, then aged 31. He was the son of 'Abd al-Rahim el-Solh, Ahmad Pasha's brother, and had married Riad's sister Balqis. After studying law in Istanbul and Paris, he returned to Syria in 1913, opened a lawyer's office, and was hired to look after the interests of the Baghdad railroad – the Istanbul-to-Baghdad rail link for which the Germans had won a concession in 1903. When war broke out in 1914, he was appointed military inspector of railways in southern Anatolia, but when he was suspected of harbouring sympathy for the Allies, he was recalled to Istanbul in 1916. Rehabilitated the following year, he was appointed director of the Hijaz railway in Damascus, a post he retained during the Allied occupation, when he was judged to have served the Allied cause.[10] His later career, which included a period as prime minister of Lebanon, was to be closely linked to that of his cousin Riad.

These, then, were some of the people whom Riad el-Solh frequented in Damascus in 1918–20. Not all were fervent Faysal supporters, but they were, on the whole, a distinguished body of men – educated, refined, resolute, of international outlook yet highly conscious of their Arabism. They had experienced in their formative years the collapse of the multi-ethnic, multi-religious Ottoman world under

---

[10] Archives du ministère des Affaires étrangères (MAE), Nantes, Fonds Beyrouth (Amb.), série B, carton 4 (dossier 55).

the assaults of Balkan nationalism, Young Turk chauvinism, European imperialism and the Great War. Their Arab nationalism was not a mere drawing-room affectation. It had been forged at the risk of their lives in secret societies, at the Aley military tribunal, in exile or in the shadow of the gallows, upon which so many of their friends had so gruesomely perished; also in literary clubs, universities and newspapers, where the glories of the Arabic language were being newly discovered in the intellectual ferment of the time. It was no accident that, under Faysal's brief rule, an Arab Library and a Museum of Arab Antiquities were opened in Damascus, as well as an Academy of the Arabic Language on 8 June 1919, presided over by Muhammad Kurd 'Ali, editor of the nationalist newspaper, *al-Muqtabas*.

Not everyone in Damascus was overjoyed at the arrival of the Emir Faysal. Some well-bred notables of the city found him and his Beduin tribesmen overbearing and uncouth. Having traditionally acted as intermediaries between the Ottoman authorities and the local population, they did not see why they should now submit to the rule of a prince from the far-off Hijaz, or to his motley, often squabbling, crew of Iraqi, Palestinian, Syrian and Lebanese officers, officials and hangers-on. Among the Muslim notables of Damascus, perhaps the most influential at that time was the 60-year-old Muhammad Fawzi Pasha al-'Azm, whom British intelligence described as 'wealthy, ambitious, unscrupulous and, at heart, pro-Turk'. Men like al-'Azm, whose ancestors had ruled Damascus since the eighteenth century, could not but regret the passing of the old order. Other prominent notables who did not wholly approve of Faysal's regime included 'Ata Bey al-Ayyubi, aged 45, whose patrician family claimed descent from Saladin (Salah al-Din al-Ayyubi). He had served as a provincial governor under the Turks. Then there was the cultured and affable Sami Pasha Mardam Bey, 50, heir to a property fortune in Damascus, whom Jamal Pasha had nominated as a member of the Ottoman parliament for that city.

Another influential notable was 'Abd al-Rahman al-Yusuf, aged 45, who was looked upon as head of the Kurdish community. He had managed to make himself the wealthiest landowner in Syria, acquiring large estates in the Biqa' valley and elsewhere. He decided he preferred Turkish or French rule to Faysal's haphazard administration. He had been Rida el-Solh's colleague in the Ottoman parliament and, as the Amir al-Hajj for most of his adult life, he had for many years led the pilgrimage caravan to Mecca. Personally acquainted with the ex-emperor of Austria and the ex-king of Bulgaria, he was socially ambitious. He had sent his sons to England to study at an agricultural college at Cirencester, so that they might return and run their lands in a modern and productive way.

Riad is named governor of Sidon

Once Faysal had established his government in Damascus, Riad was introduced to him, very probably by his father, Rida el-Solh. Riad must have impressed the emir, because he was sent late in 1918 to run Sidon, the town in South Lebanon where his family had come from, and where they still had estates, relatives and friends. On arrival, he was carried shoulder-high to the *Sérail*, the seat of government, which his own father had built when he was *qa'im maqam* there in 1898. The war had brought destruction and great hardship to Sidon, and a virtual standstill in commerce. Could normal life be restored? And under whose authority and within what national boundaries? It was a moment of huge uncertainty, with a real danger of a descent into chaos. There was an immense amount for the energetic young governor to do.

The town Riad was sent to govern had a population of about 18,000, made up of 13,000 Sunni Muslims, 3,500 Greek Catholics, and a sprinkling of Protestants, Maronites and Jews. In the surrounding villages lived some 25,000 Shi'i peasantry, whose acknowledged leader was Rashid 'Usayran, head of a landowning Shi'i family that traced its history in Sidon back to the late sixteenth century. The Qajar rulers of Iran had appointed the 'Usayrans Persian consuls in Sidon.[11] Rashid 'Usayran was locked in bitter rivalry with Kamil al-As'ad, overall boss of the Shi'i population of the Jabal 'Amil. Before the war, the town and its neighbouring villages had formed a fairly prosperous agricultural region, producing wheat, barley, maize, tobacco, figs, olive oil, silk cocoons and no fewer than 80 million oranges. Banking transactions, conducted by an agency of the Imperial Ottoman Bank and by the private bank of the Audi family (which continues to trade today), consisted mainly of payments made to landowners for the export of oranges, the cashing of remittances sent to their families by

[11] Chalabi, *The Shi'is of Jabal 'Amil*, p. 24.

Syrians in the Americas, and commercial transactions between Syria and Egypt.[12]

But before Riad could do much to restore Sidon's prosperity, he found himself suddenly out of a job. His daughter, Alia el-Solh, recounted that when General Henri Gouraud, a bearded, one-armed giant (he had lost the other arm to a shell-burst at Gallipoli), arrived at Sidon in 1919 at the head of French troops, the young governor rode out on a white horse to meet him. The two exchanged a few words from the saddle. Riad greeted the General with the words: 'We welcome you as passing guests, not as conquerors!' 'France has always stood for fraternity and equality,' the General is said to have replied. 'Especially liberty, mon général!' Riad retorted. The much-decorated Gouraud had spent most of his military career crushing French imperial subjects in Africa.[13] Latterly, however, he had won fame in 1918 by defeating the Germans on the Champagne battlefields of eastern France. 'A curious boy,' he remarked after the encounter with Riad. 'I've rarely seen such a bold look! A jailbird at twenty, a governor at twenty-four! He will go far! I'm reminded of Samori Touré.'[14] Gouraud was referring to the celebrated war chief of the Dioula, who had created a state on the eastern side of the upper Niger river, fighting the French for more than twenty years until he was captured by Gouraud himself at Guelemou, in the Ivory Coast, in 1898.

Under French pressure, the Sidon municipal council was dissolved, and Riad, to his intense disappointment, was forced to step down. His lifelong resolve to fight French rule in the Levant may be said to date from that moment. He resigned his post, when Colonel Feygerl, the local French military governor, took control of Sidon and the surrounding area. Having been thrown out of Sidon, Riad moved back to Damascus, where many of the important Arab politicians from the region were waiting with considerable anxiety to see what the French had in store for them. By this time, Riad was a combative nationalist, totally opposed to the French. A veteran of Ottoman jails and of *al-fatat*, he had matured in exile. With his quick intelligence and

---

[12] General Staff Intelligence, *General Report on Western Syria (Occupied Enemy Territory – West)*, chapter 18 on Sidon, Beirut, July 1919.

[13] Under the heading *Souvenirs d'un Africain*, General Gouraud wrote a series of books about his military exploits in West, central and sub-Saharan Africa. See, for example, *Mauritanie Adrar*, Paris 1945.

[14] Alia el-Solh, *Le Jour*, 3 October 1965.

vigorous personality, he was beginning to acquire the aura of a leader. His father, Rida, was no less of a nationalist, but he had less fiery enthusiasms than did Riad. Worn down by ill health and worries about the future, and no doubt depressed at the thought of having spent his life serving what was now a vanished Empire, Rida was more inclined to caution. As a senior official of Faysal's Arab state, he had the ear of the emir and understood better than his still untried son the acute problems with which the new regime had to cope.

The imperial interests of Britain and France

What Riad and others like him did not grasp, or perhaps did not wish to see, was that they were up against the world's two greatest imperial powers, who, at a vast sacrifice of men and treasure, had just fought and won the first 'total war' in history. Arab political aspirations were very low on their list of priorities, if they figured there at all. More than 10 million Europeans had died – almost a whole generation of young men. The pre-war system of international relations was shattered, as were European societies in their entirety. The Austro-Hungarian Empire, the German Empire and the Ottoman Empire were all gone for ever, while the empire of the czars had fallen to the Bolsheviks. France in particular had been devastated: it had lost a quarter of all men aged between 18 and 27, and had seen its northern industrial heartland destroyed. Fearing that Germany might rise again to seek revenge, it sought to cripple it with punitive reparations at the post-war Peace Conference. In the new emerging pattern of power in the Middle East and the Mediterranean, France and Britain, weakened by the war and confronted by the rising power of the United States, were concerned above all to protect their vital interests. When they spoke of 'independence' for the Arabs, what they really meant was their 'liberation' from Turkish hegemony, but certainly not freedom for them to run their own affairs. Although Britain and France tried to pay lip service to President Woodrow Wilson's principles of national self-determination, their real intention was to redraw the map of the Ottoman Empire's Arab provinces to suit themselves.

French interests in the regions which Allenby had conquered were substantial and of long standing. In the sixteenth century, the French king had wrested from the Ottoman sultan the right to protect all Europeans in the Empire. By the seventeenth century, other European Powers had secured similar privileges, which became known as the Capitulations. Since the Holy See had no diplomatic relations with the Sublime Porte, France took upon itself responsibility for the protection of all Latin clergy in the East, a 'right' which, by the mid-eighteenth century, it had expanded into a 'Catholic protectorate'. Under the Third Republic, this protectorate was further expanded to cover *all* Christians in the East, whatever their denomination. There was, of course, no juridical basis for such protectorates, but the Ottomans were by then too weak to challenge France.

France's military intervention in Mount Lebanon after the massacre of Christians in 1860 suddenly gave meaning to the notion of French protection, and confirmed the Maronites as France's principal clients. In 1861, as has already been mentioned, the European Powers obtained a privileged status for Mount Lebanon as an autonomous *mutasarrifiyya* under an Ottoman, non-Lebanese, Catholic governor. He was aided by a twelve-member Administrative Council, representing the six main religious communities of the Mountain. Lebanon's confessional diversity was thus given its first institutional form and, in many ways, became 'institutionalised' from then on, surviving more or less unchanged ever since, and perhaps creating some of the intractable problems the country is still facing today. French representatives established intimate ties with the local Christian clergy, the Maronite patriarch emerging as the central figure in France's client network. French influence was further expanded in the late nineteenth century by large investments in Ottoman roads, railways, ports and shipping companies; in utilities such as water, gas and electricity; in banks and other commercial enterprises; but also in a vast network of French-financed schools, hospitals and orphanages located in the main cities of the Empire, in Istanbul, Salonica, Smyrna, Beirut and Jerusalem. On the eve of the First World War, some 90,000 Ottoman children, either non-Muslims or the children of Muslim elites – provincial governors, administrators, officers and notables – were learning French and absorbing French ideas at French schools.[15] France and Britain were also heavily involved in the management of the Ottoman public debt.

The Capitulations had originally been treaties of commercial preference which the Porte had concluded with European Powers, but,

---

[15] Cloarec, *La France*, pp. 12–44.

under the protection and patronage of foreign consuls and ambassadors, these privileges were in due course extended to local Christian and Jewish families. Entire non-Muslim communities thus managed to secure immunity from Ottoman justice, as well as unfair relief from Ottoman taxes, which so burdened their co-citizens. For the Ottoman government, the Capitulations became the hated expression of Western domination. So, when war broke out, the Sublime Porte hastened to abolish the Capitulations on 1 October 1914. It also ended France's 'Catholic protectorate' and sent troops to occupy Mount Lebanon. One of France's war aims, therefore, was to recover the privileges, preferences and pre-war influence it had enjoyed in the Empire, an aim it shared with Britain. The more the Empire seemed threatened with dismemberment, the greater the determination of the European Powers became to hang on to advantages they had long enjoyed.

Syria lay at the heart of France's 'Eastern policy'. France's involvement in the region was so great that, throughout the war, the French authorities conceived of the possibility of turning the whole of Syria, from the Taurus mountains in the north to the frontier of Egypt in the south, into a vast *France du Levant*. On 29 December 1918, just before the start of the Peace Conference, French Foreign Minister Stéphane Pichon triumphantly outlined France's position to the National Assembly in Paris: 'We have inalienable rights in the Empire of the Turks. We have such rights in Syria, in Lebanon, in Cilicia, in Palestine. They are founded on historic titles and agreements . . . and on the aspirations and wishes of the populations who have long been our clients . . . We are firmly determined to have them recognised'.[16]

Therefore, as soon as France learned of the pledges Britain had made to the Sharif Husayn in the Husayn–McMahon correspondence, it went all out to weaken the impact of the Arab Revolt and secure its own hegemony over Syria. The British could not seriously object. They accepted that the French believed that Syria 'had been a recognised French interest since the days of Louis XIV – indeed, since the Crusades'.[17] Both powers, after all, saw the region as something to be divided up between them.

---

[16] Mahafzah, 'La France et le mouvement nationaliste arabe de 1914 à 1950', in *Relations internationales*, no. 19 (autumn 1979), p. 300, quoting P. Huvelin, *Que vaut la Syrie?* Paris 1921, pp. 4–6.

[17] Elizabeth Monroe, *Britain's Moment in the Middle East, 1914–71*, new rev. 2nd edn London 1981, p. 28.

Britain's interests were technically different from those of France, but were equally substantial and deep-rooted. Among them, none was more vital than controlling land, sea and air communications between the Mediterranean basin and the Indian Ocean.[18] British India – its trade and its huge reserve of military manpower – occupied an enormous place in British strategic thinking, continuing to do so through two world wars right up to Indian Independence in 1947.[19]

Two land and sea routes to India had to be controlled and protected: the Suez Canal route to the Red Sea and beyond, and the route from the Mediterranean across the north Syrian desert and down the Euphrates to the Persian Gulf, where Britain had established a preponderant position by means of treaties with local shaykhs. Indeed, as seen by London, all the way from the Suez Canal to the Persian Gulf was a vital British heartland.

A second crucial British interest, in which France also demanded a stake, was control of the output and disposal of Iranian and Iraqi oil, as well as protection for the Anglo-Iranian Oil Company's installations at Abadan. Britain landed a force at the entrance to the Shatt al-Arab in the first days of the war to prevent eastward penetration by German agents, but also because 25,000 tons of oil per month were by then being exported from the new oilfields in southern Iran, largely for use by the British Navy, which had converted from coal to oil in 1912. The crucial importance of oil was confirmed during the First World War. The battle of France in 1918 was waged by large military units being trucked back and forth from one sector of the front to another.

A third British interest was control of Palestine – as a buffer for the defence of the Suez Canal and Egypt, but also because Arthur Balfour, Britain's Foreign Secretary at the time, had pledged British support for 'the establishment in Palestine of a national home for the Jewish people'. London hoped that an Anglo-Jewish Palestine would weaken the French position on the borders of Egypt. There were other strong elements of self-interest, since Britain hoped that American Jews would influence the United States in favour of the Allied war effort, and that Russian Jews would keep Aleksandr Kerensky's provisional government in the fighting line against Germany. In the event, Kerensky was swept from power by the Bolsheviks after a mere four months.

---

[18] PRO FO 371/27308 Report on the Relations of France and Great Britain with the Arab World and with each other in the Eastern Mediterranean, 4 November 1940.
[19] Monroe, *Britain's Moment in the Middle East*, pp. 11–12.

The contradictory promises Britain made to the Arabs, the French and the Jews, respectively in 1915, 1916 and 1917, can be understood, but certainly not justified, by its burning desire to win the war against Germany and its allies. The repeated false pledges given to the Arabs in 1918, that their sovereign independence would be recognised once the Turks were defeated, were, needless to say, inexcusable. The Allies made a number of grossly hypocritical statements to soothe Arab fears. On 4 January 1918, the British government instructed Commander D. G. Hogarth of Britain's Arab Bureau in Cairo to deliver a message to King Husayn of the Hijaz, stressing that the Balfour Declaration did not conflict with earlier promises to the Arabs. 'So far as Palestine is concerned', the message read, 'we are determined that no people shall be subject to another'. Some months later, in June 1918, Britain's high commissioner in Egypt, Sir Reginald Wingate, declared in reply to a formal enquiry by seven Arab exiles in Cairo that it was the 'wish and desire' of the British government that the future government of regions liberated from the Turks 'should be based upon the principle of the consent of the governed'. Then, on 7 November, three days before the armistice which put an end to the Great War, the British and French governments, in what has been described as 'a crowning piece of insincerity',[20] declared that their only aim in offering support and assistance to the Arabs was to ensure 'the regular working of governments and administrations freely chosen by the populations themselves'.[21]

The wording of these assurances was evidently influenced by the new notions of national self-determination that had emerged during the war. But the truth was that France and Britain could not conceive of surrendering their extensive interests in the region to anyone – and certainly not to native governments. Suspecting that they were being duped, some Arabs started to regret that they had been hasty in rising up against the Ottoman Turks, if the alternative was to suffer European rule and Jewish colonisation. But it was to take the Arabs a very long time to realise just how immense were their illusions. Today, an increasingly large segment of Arab intellectual opinion, including a younger generation of Muslims worldwide, looks back on this period

---

[20] Ibid., p. 48.
[21] See Hurewitz, *Diplomacy*, vol. II, pp. 29–30, for the Hogarth Message, January 1918; the Declaration to the Seven, 16 June 1918; and the Anglo-French Declaration, 7 November 1918.

as one of catastrophe, and sees the break-up of the Ottoman Empire as the beginning of the Arabs' political misfortunes, which are nowhere near abating.

Faysal's doomed diplomacy

The Emir Faysal ruled in Damascus for 22 months, from 3 October 1918 to 25 July 1920 – the day the city fell to French forces after the massacre at Maysalun of Syria's practically unarmed force of brave defenders, headed by the heroic Minister of Defence Yusuf al-'Azma.

The verb 'ruled' is probably too strong to describe the uncertain authority that Faysal was allowed to exercise. In any event, he was away in Europe, pleading the Arab cause, for two long stretches, from December 1918 to April 1919 and then again from September 1919 to January 1920. In his absence, his young half-brother, the Emir Zayd, still in his twenties, the fourth son of the Sharif Husayn, struggled as best he could to keep a lid on the bitter frustration of the local population, as the truth gradually sank in that the Arabs were not going to be allowed to run their own affairs.

Faysal's real problem was that he was caught in a vice between the French, who were determined that Syria would be theirs, and his own nationalist allies, notably the veterans of *al-fatat* and *al-'ahd* in his administration, who were determined to assert absolute Arab independence, free from foreign control. Faysal's increasingly desperate attempts to find a compromise between these warring claims and counterclaims satisfied neither side. It was a most uncomfortable position to be in.

Alarmed by the proposed carve-up of the 'unified Arab state' which he believed had been promised to his father, Faysal went to London for the first time on 10 December 1918 to seek clarification of British intentions. He was then an inexperienced 33-year old and spoke no English. As a result, he was at the mercy of Colonel T. E. Lawrence, who had accompanied him as adviser and interpreter. His trip had been arranged by Lawrence and the Zionists without consulting the French, who were furious and received Faysal coldly when, sailing from Beirut, he landed at Marseilles on his way to England.

On arrival in London, Faysal learned that, some ten days earlier, on 1 December, the elderly French Prime Minister Georges

Clemenceau, *le père de la victoire*, had been given a great military and public reception in the British capital. It was the first visit there by the celebrated wartime leader, then aged 77, since the 11 November armistice. Although the city was still buzzing with the event, Faysal had no means of knowing what had passed between Clemenceau and Britain's Prime Minister Lloyd George when they met alone at the French embassy.

No written record was kept of that important meeting, but Maurice Hankey, secretary of the British War Cabinet, confided to his diary the account Lloyd George gave him shortly afterwards. Another, almost identical, version is contained in a memorandum on the Sykes–Picot agreement written by Lord Balfour himself, who reconstructed, eight months after the event, the conversation which had taken place at the French embassy, and which allegedly went something like this:

> CLEMENCEAU: *Well, what do we have to discuss?*
> LLOYD GEORGE: *Mesopotamia and Palestine.*
> CLEMENCEAU: *Tell me what you want.*
> LLOYD GEORGE: *I want Mosul.*
> CLEMENCEAU: *You shall have it. Anything else?*
> LLOYD GEORGE: *Yes, I want Jerusalem.*
> CLEMENCEAU: *You shall have it, but Pichon [France's foreign minister] will make difficulties over Mosul.*[22]

Although the French had done little fighting in the Middle East, they wanted a free hand in Syria. The problem they faced was that British forces were in military occupation of the whole of geographical Syria, including Lebanon and Palestine. Clemenceau's mind was focused on Germany, whose future was about to be settled at the Peace Conference. Germany was his obsession, as it had, single-handedly, very nearly defeated Britain, Russia and France. How could France make sure that a resurgent Germany would never again be fit to fight a war? As well as having led his country since the autumn of 1917 in the life-and-death struggle of the Great War, Clemenceau had also experienced France's defeat in the 1870–71 Franco-Prussian war. His

---

[22] Stephen Roskill, *Hankey, Man of Secrets*, 3 vols, London, 1972, vol. II, pp. 28–9. For Balfour's memorandum, see E. L. Woodward and Roham Butler (eds), *Documents on British Foreign Policy, 1919–39*, series 1, vol. 4, London 1952, document 242 of 11 August 1919, pp. 340–1.

overriding concern was to ensure France's security vis-à-vis its more powerful neighbour.

Aware that the Levant question was upsetting Anglo-French relations, he was looking for an agreement with Great Britain to strengthen his hand on the German question before the arrival of the stubbornly idealistic American President Woodrow Wilson, who liked to believe that a combination of providence and good planning had enabled the United States to escape Europe's murderous chaos. Clemenceau desperately needed a deal. He therefore gave up Mosul, as well as France's share of an international zone in Palestine, but in return secured Lloyd George's recognition of France's exclusive influence in Syria, an area which included Lebanon and extended north into the Turkish province of Cilicia. He also secured a stake in Mesopotamian and Persian oil, which had not featured in the Sykes–Picot accords. In seeking energy independence for France, Clemenceau laid the groundwork for the grand economic strategy of post-war French governments.[23] In the event, both he and Lloyd George got what they wanted. One can be quite certain that there was no reference in their beady-eyed discussions to 'the free choice of the populations concerned'.

Thus, Faysal arrived in London after Britain and France had already agreed on the carve-up of the region. On 11 December 1918, Lord Balfour, then Foreign Secretary, tried to reassure him about French intentions, but Lawrence, who had accompanied the emir, candidly explained to him that the British would certainly not make war on France on his behalf. If France insisted on pressing its claims, the British would simply give way. Faysal, he advised, should seek American support, and for that he had to conciliate the Zionists. T. E. Lawrence, as some recent research has shown, may by this time have been swayed by Zionist arguments. No doubt it was with this in mind that, later the same day, Faysal was persuaded to hold a second meeting with Dr Chaim Weizmann, the strong-willed Manchester-based chemist and Zionist leader who had been the principal architect of the Balfour Declaration. The French historian Henry Laurens has described the Balfour Declaration as 'the first official recognition, by a great power, of the existence of a Jewish people, and the beginning

---

[23] Henry Laurens, *La Question de Palestine*, vol. I, *1799–1922*, *L'Invention de la Terre Sainte*, Paris 1999, pp. 432–3.

of the confrontation between Jews and Arabs for the possession of Palestine'.[24]

Faysal had had an earlier meeting with the Zionist leader in June 1918, when Weizmann had suggested that a Jewish Palestine could lend valuable aid to an Arab kingdom, as it sought to extend northwards into Syria. He was well known for telling his interlocutors exactly what they wished to hear. His tireless efforts had won several prominent British politicians to the Zionist cause – including, ironically enough, the conventionally anti-Semitic Lord Balfour himself, as well as several influential journalists, such as C. P. Scott, editor of the *Manchester Guardian*, who had the ear of David Lloyd George.

In harnessing Britain to Zionist ambitions, Weizmann was highly successful. His political genius was to convince the British that Zionist goals in Palestine could be put to the service of Britain's world interests.[25] For Britain, the reckoning was to come later. Making good on the pledge of the Balfour Declaration was to saddle it with a host of painful problems, intractable to this day. In the words of one British observer, 'Measured by British interests alone, it was one of the greatest mistakes in our imperial history.'[26]

At their meeting, Faysal asked Weizmann for a clarification of Zionist aims. Brimming over with self-confidence in his dealings with the young emir, Weizmann told him that the Jews wanted Faysal and the Peace Conference to recognise the Jews' historic national rights in Palestine. Britain would be the tutelary power, he said, and agricultural reform would take land away from the effendis. Brisk economic development would allow for the settlement of 4–5 million Jews. The tracing of Palestine's frontiers and the future of religious endowments (*awqaf*) could be discussed later, *after* the peace settlement. The Jews, he pledged, would respect the Muslim Holy Places. Conceding that there was land enough in Palestine for the two peoples, Faysal agreed to support Jewish claims. But he preferred not to inform his father or his brother Zayd of this conversation.

A few days later, on 21 December, Lord Rothschild gave a dinner in his honour. 'I have heard from people who claim to be civilized', Faysal declared in an after-dinner speech, 'that the Jews want to turn our mosque in Jerusalem into a temple and chase out the peasants

---

[24] Ibid., p. 366.
[25] Ibid., p. 336.
[26] Monroe, *Britain's Moment in the Middle East*, p. 45.

from Palestine. For my part, I know that no true Jew could have such intentions . . . Dr Weizmann's ideal is our own'. Arabs and Jews should cooperate since 'they were united by ties of blood'.[27]

Pressing his advantage, Weizmann then arranged a further meeting with Faysal on 3 January 1919, when the emir was asked to put his signature to a text purporting to establish guidelines for relations between a future Arab state and a Palestine of indefinite status – but which the Zionist leader already conceived to be Jewish. According to the text, the constitution of Palestine was to provide the widest possible guarantees for the implementation of the Balfour Declaration. Large-scale Jewish immigration to Palestine was to be encouraged and assisted by all possible means. Faysal signed, adding in Arabic, however, a reservation in his own hand: if the Arabs failed to obtain their independence, his undertaking would be null and void. It was not clear whether Faysal was at all aware of what he was signing, or whether he was simply being manipulated.

Travelling to Paris, Faysal submitted a memorandum to the Supreme Council of the victorious powers at the Peace Conference, which he amplified in person on 6 January. 'The aim of the Arab nationalist movements', he declared in his memorandum,

> is to unite the Arabs eventually into one nation . . . [The Arabs] expect the Powers to think of them as one potential people, jealous of their language and liberty, and ask that no steps be taken inconsistent with the prospect of an eventual union of these areas under one sovereign government . . . In a word, we ask you not to force your whole civilization upon us, but to help us to pick out what serves us from your experience.[28]

The Zionist Organisation, in turn, put its case for a 'Jewish' Palestine in a detailed memorandum on 3 February, while the French, anxious to undermine Faysal's plea for independence, arranged for a Francophile Syrian Christian, Shukri Ghanem, to argue that France should be given a mandate over a united Syria. The case for a 'Lebanese' Lebanon was made by Dawud 'Ammun, the president of Mount

---

[27] Laurens, *La Question de Palestine*, vol. I, pp. 438–40.
[28] Text of the Emir Faysal's memorandum of 1 January 1920 to the Supreme Council, in Hurewitz, *Diplomacy*, vol. II, pp. 38–9.

Lebanon's Administrative Council, who called for the establishment of an independent Lebanese state within 'its historical and natural frontiers'.

As all these rival projects competed for the attention of the Powers, Faysal began to see that his optimism had been misplaced. Syria was to be divided up between Britain and France, and without the assent of its inhabitants. In a desperate bid to prevent this outcome, he called for an international enquiry into the wishes of the population. It was to be his only success – although even this was to turn against him and make his task more difficult.

The King–Crane Commission

On 20 March 1919, President Wilson proposed that an Inter-Allied Commission should visit Syria 'to elucidate the state of opinion and the soil to be worked on by any mandatory', and report its findings to the Peace Conference. Such 'a Commission of men with no previous contact with Syria', the president argued, would 'convince the world that the Conference had tried to do all it could to find the most scientific basis possible for a settlement'. His suggestion was adopted by the Supreme Council on 25 March 1919. France, however, refused to appoint representatives, while Britain, wishing to ensure its own freedom of action in Palestine, also withdrew. The American delegation, led by Dr Henry C. King and Mr Charles R. Crane, made preparations to leave by itself.

In late April 1919, Faysal returned to the Near East. His authority and credibility were still more or less intact, although local opinion had hardened in his absence because of persistent rumours of Zionist plans for Palestine and of an eventual French military occupation of Syria. Some Arabs began openly to regret the passing of the Ottoman regime, and accused Faysal of selling Palestine to the Jews for a handful of gold.[29] But when, in a speech on his return, Faysal asked for the nation's confidence, several notables rallied to his side. Rida el-Solh pledged his support, while his son Riad declared that he intended to enlist as a soldier in Faysal's army.[30]

---

[29] Laurens, *La Question de Palestine*, vol. I, p. 470.
[30] Eliezer Tauber, *The Formation of Modern Syria and Lebanon*, London 1995, p. 40.

It was, therefore, with great anger and apprehension that the Arabs learned that the Paris Peace Conference had decided to place the former Arab provinces of the Ottoman Empire under European Mandates. On 28 April, the Conference approved the Covenant of the League of Nations, and its celebrated Article 22, of which paragraph 4 reads as follows:

> *Certain communities formerly belonging to the Turkish*
> *Empire have reached a stage of development where their*
> *existence as independent nations can be provisionally*
> *recognised subject to the rendering of administrative advice*
> *and assistance by a Mandatory until such time as they*
> *are able to stand alone. The wishes of these communities*
> *must be a principal consideration in the selection of the*
> *Mandatory.*[31]

Devised as a supposed halfway house between national independence and European colonialism, the Mandates were conceived as a 'compromise' between Arab aspirations and the imperial interests of the Powers, although they were, in fact, no such thing. The mealy-mouthed reference to the 'wishes' of the local populations was no more than an empty gesture towards President Wilson's ideas of national self-determination, which had become the shining new principle of international relations, more honoured in the breach than the observance.

The King–Crane Commission arrived at Jaffa on 10 June 1919 and, over the next two months, carried out extensive enquiries in Palestine and Syria, visiting 36 towns, meeting the representatives of 1,500 villages and receiving no fewer than 1,863 petitions.[32] Just ten days after its arrival, the Commission sent a memorandum to President Wilson saying that Palestine was on the verge of an explosion, and that, whoever became the mandatory power, an army of 50,000 men would be needed to impose the Zionist programme by force against the will of the local population.

The arrival of the Commission, and the intense interest it aroused, led the Arabs to imagine naively that they could count on

---

[31] Text in Hurewitz, *Diplomacy*, vol. II, pp. 61–2. See also A. H. Hourani, *Syria and Lebanon: A Political Essay*, Oxford 1946, chs 9–13.

[32] See Khoury, *La France et l'Orient arabe*, p. 243, for details of the Commission's membership and of its feverish activities during its six weeks in the region.

American support. But, on 29 June, just four days after the King–Crane Commission reached Damascus and a day after the Versailles Treaty was signed, President Wilson sailed for the United States. The US Senate rejected the Versailles Treaty and the United States withdrew from the Peace Conference. Although he may not have realised it at the time, Faysal was gravely weakened by Wilson's departure.

The Solhs and the Syrian Congress

In Damascus, the activities of the King–Crane Commission created a current of radical opinion. It incited activists of *al-fatat* and *al-'ahd* to convene a General Syrian Congress in July 1919, with the aim of drafting and presenting their demands to the Commission. Delegates from Lebanon and Palestine joined their comrades from Syria. Also pressing for the holding of the Congress was the Arab Independence Party (*hizb al-'istiqlal al-'arabi*), formed four months earlier in February by *al-fatat*, which Riad promptly joined. Realising the importance of lobbying the King–Crane Commission, he took space in a local newspaper, *al-Ikha'*, to campaign for the application in Syria of President Wilson's celebrated 'fourteen points'.

Three members of the Solh family attended the General Syrian Congress and were actively involved in its work: Riad represented Sidon, his father represented Beirut (together with Jamil Bayhum, Salim 'Ali Salam, Shaykh Ahmad Rida, George Harfush and Farid Qassab),[33] while his cousin, 'Afif, represented Tyre.[34] At its first formal session on 2 July, the Congress adopted a resolution that left no doubt about the feelings of its members. They demanded 'complete political independence for Syria'; they refused to acknowledge 'any right claimed by the French Government in any part whatsoever of our Syrian country'; they refused to accept that France 'should assist

---

[33] See Hilal el-Solh, *Tarikh rajul wa qadiyya*, p. 42.

[34] 'Afif was the son of Kamil el-Solh, one of Ahmad Pasha's three sons. Kamil el-Solh had five children by two wives. His first wife, from the Syrian 'Attar family, had two children, Munif and Munifa. His second wife, from the Syrian Malki family, had three children, 'Afif, 'Afifa, and Yusr. 'Afif was born in Tripoli, Libya, where his father was serving as an Ottoman judge. He studied in Istanbul and was awarded a doctorate there. He was a handsome man, known for his refined elegance, and a former officer in the Ottoman army. He later became secretary-general (*amin al-sirr*) of the National Bloc (*al-kutla al-wataniyya*) in Damascus and a deputy in the Syrian parliament.

us or have a hand in our country under any circumstances and in any place'; and they opposed 'the pretensions of the Zionists to create a Jewish commonwealth in the southern part of Syria, known as Palestine'.[35]

The resolution which the Syrian Congress adopted was reiterated, in somewhat softer terms, by Faysal when he received the Commission the following day. There was a natural unity between Palestine and Syria, he explained. Separation could not be accepted. He added that he had been prepared, some months earlier, to accept a programme of controlled Jewish immigration into Palestine, but exaggerated Zionist claims and demands had terrified the Arabs, who now rejected any such influx. The conclusions of the King–Crane Commission confirmed the views of the General Syrian Congress and accelerated the political awakening of the region. 'We recommend', the Commission wrote, 'that the unity of Syria be preserved, in accordance with the earnest petition of the great majority of the people of Syria'. As for Lebanon, 'it would be better if she were a constituent member of the [Syrian] state, rather than entirely independent of it'. The Zionist claim to Palestine, 'based on an occupation of two thousand years ago, can hardly be seriously considered'.

The Commission recommended 'that only a greatly reduced Zionist program be attempted . . . and even that, only very gradually. This would have to mean that Jewish immigration should be definitely limited, and the project for making Palestine distinctly a Jewish commonwealth should be given up'. With considerable prescience, the Commission judged that implementing the extreme Zionist programme 'would intensify, with a fate-like certainty, the anti-Jewish feeling both in Palestine and in all other portions of the world which look to Palestine as "the Holy Land"'. It noted that 'The feeling of the Arabs of the East is particularly strong against the French. And there is grave reason to believe that the attempt to enforce a French Mandate would precipitate war between the Arabs and the French'.[36]

The Commission filed its report with the American delegation in Paris on 28 August, but another long month was to pass before it reached the White House on 27 September. Five days later, Wilson suffered a paralysing stroke and the report was shelved. Neither the

---

[35] Text in Hurewitz, *Diplomacy*, vol. II, pp. 62–3.
[36] Text of the King–Crane recommendations of 28 August 1919, in Hurewitz, *Diplomacy*, vol. II, pp. 66–74.

European Powers nor the United States gave it any further consideration. Faysal and the Solhs, who had devoted weeks of effort to working
with the Commission, were once again bitterly let down. They had
hoped for an American mandate, or at least for American assistance in
keeping the French and the Zionists at bay. The few British friends of
the Arabs were also disappointed, as they had hoped that the United
States would be able to curb the French appetite for the whole of
Syria.

With public opinion in Damascus inflamed against the Allies,
Faysal decided in the summer of 1919 to return to London in a last
attempt to influence the situation and restore his own authority,
which had by now been seriously undermined. He arrived in London,
via Marseilles, on 18 September, and, the very next day, saw Prime
Minister Lloyd George, Lord Curzon (who was soon to replace
Balfour as Foreign Secretary) and Field Marshal Lord Allenby at 10
Downing Street. But once again, as in the previous December, Faysal's
mission was undermined by an earlier development of which he knew
nothing. Overstretched in Ireland, India and Egypt, and wrestling
with army mutinies and other problems of post-war demobilisation,
Britain had taken the decision to withdraw its troops from Syria and
Cilicia with effect from 1 November 1919. They were to be replaced
by French troops in the western zone and by Arab troops in the Syrian
interior.

Faysal arrived in London on the day this Anglo-French agreement was announced. Lloyd George informed him of what had been
agreed with the French regarding troop withdrawals. It meant that
Britain was giving France full freedom of action in Syria, and was
breezily abandoning the Arabs to a colonial fate. Half the subsidy the
emir had been receiving from the British would henceforth be paid him
by the French, whose financial assistance he would now actively have
to request. Faysal could only protest, declaring this arrangement to be
contrary to the principles of the League of Nations, since it marked 'an
unjust return to a policy of imperial ambition'. He knew only too well
that many French politicians and officials considered the establishment
of a pan-Arab regime in the Syrian interior as a threat to France's interests, to be stopped by any means. Defiantly, he declared that he would
never agree to such a division of Syria.

When it was learned in Damascus that British troops were
leaving, there was popular pressure for mobilisation to fight the French.

A Committee of National Defence was formed by Shaykh Kamil al-Qassab and Dr 'Abd al-Rahman al-Shahbandar, with the aim of recruiting volunteers and collecting food, funds and weapons for guerrilla operations.[37] The chief of staff, Yasin Pasha al-Hashimi, agitated to raise a force of 12,000 men. The French promptly demanded his arrest, although the British were at first reluctant to comply. However, when armed bands dispatched by *al-fatat* and by Kamil al-Qassab's Defence Committee started mounting hit-and-run attacks against French forces in different parts of Syria, General Allenby ordered the Pasha's arrest on 22 November 1919. To make things worse, British subsidies to Faysal's Arab government were also suspended. This was a crippling blow to Faysal's status and authority.

At the same time, Arab nationalist opinion in Syria was following with excitement the progress of the Turkish nationalist revolt in Anatolia, led by General Mustafa Kemal, who was said to have raised a formidable army of 200,000 fighters. By midsummer 1919, Kemal had formed a nationalist association dedicated to the sovereignty and territorial integrity of Anatolia and eastern Thrace. There was talk in Syria of joining forces with the Kemalists, rather than succumbing to European dictation. It was rumoured that Mustafa Kemal had made contact with the Damascus government, and that the Emir Zayd had even sent him money to attack the French in Cilicia. In the heated atmosphere of the time, many Syrians still preferred to form an alliance with the Turks rather than accept what they saw as a profoundly unjust settlement duplicitously imposed on them by foreign Christians.

The Emir Faysal found himself utterly bereft of powerful friends. The British had dropped him, and the Americans had withdrawn their help. His choices were either to strike a deal with the French, or take the lead of an armed rebellion. But the latter was a foolhardy option in view of his depleted treasury and his puny army – 7,000 men, a few thousand horses and a few hundred transport vehicles, scattered between Damascus, Baalbek, Dar'a and Aleppo.[38] He understood that he could not run the risk of an armed conflict with France. He would have to come to terms.

---

[37] For a detailed account of the Committee of National Defence, see Tauber, *The Formation of Modern Syria and Lebanon*, pp. 68–78.
[38] Khoury, *La France et l'Orient arabe*, p. 282.

Destruction of the Faysal–Clemenceau agreement

Travelling from London, a deeply perturbed Faysal arrived in Paris on 19 October 1919 and met the French leader Georges Clemenceau two days later. They exchanged kind words. This French prime minister was personally opposed to French colonial expansion in the Levant. He did not like playing minority politics, based on religious and regional clients abroad. He was convinced that France should seek to forge a viable Arab policy, to replace the strategy it had pursued towards the now defunct Ottoman Empire. He was inclined to think that France should support the Arabs' national movement, now that it had helped liberate them from the Ottomans. The distinguished French orientalist Louis Massignon had confirmed to him that this was the best way to protect French interests in the Levant and North Africa, and his view coincided with Clemenceau's own.[39]

But Prime Minister Clemenceau needed to tread carefully, since his parliamentary majority included a small but shrill colonial party.[40] In fact, it was in order to silence such vociferous right-wing critics that, on 9 October 1919, he decided to send the colonial military hero, General Henri Gouraud, to replace François Georges-Picot as high commissioner in Beirut. Gouraud was given the highfaluting titles of commander-in-chief of the French Army of the Levant, as well as high commissioner in Syria, Lebanon and Cilicia. On 21 November, Gouraud landed in Beirut to be welcomed by Christians there with frenzied cheers. The warhorse he had ridden at the victory parade in Paris after the First World War had been shipped to Lebanon especially for the occasion. It now carried him through the excited throng to the Place des Canons. In Damascus, however, the mood was very different. News of his arrival brought furious demonstrators out on the streets. The Emir Zayd and the young officer Nuri al-Sa'id had the greatest difficulty keeping order in the angry city.

In Paris, meanwhile, Faysal engaged from mid-October to the end of December in lengthy and difficult negotiations with French

---

[39] For an account of Massignon's views on Arab nationalism and the policies of Britain and France in the Middle East in 1917–40, see 'L'Arabie et le problème arabe', in Louis Massignon, *Écrits mémorables*, Paris 2009, vol. 1, pp. 541–61.

[40] Ibid., p. 339, quoting A. M. Andrew and S. Kanya-Forstner, 'The French Colonial Party and French Colonial War Aims, 1914–1918', in *The Historical Journal*, 17(1) (1974), p. 106.

officials, notably with Philippe Berthelot, director of political and commercial affairs at the Foreign Ministry, who was being advised and assisted once again by Louis Massignon. These meetings ended with the conclusion of a provisional agreement on 6 January 1920, which both sides agreed to keep secret, so as to give Faysal a chance to sell it in Damascus. It was to be replaced in due course by a 'definitive and detailed agreement', which would be finalised and signed on the return of the emir to Paris, which was expected to happen within a matter of weeks. Under the provisional agreement,[41] the French government 'confirmed its recognition of the right of the Arabic-speaking peoples of all confessions, living on Syrian territory, to join together in order to govern themselves as an independent nation'. The emir, in turn, was made to recognise that the Syrian population had 'a great interest' in seeking the help of French advisers, instructors and technical agents, so as 'to realise their unity and organise the functioning of their nation'. A French financial adviser would supervise the preparation of the Syrian budget, and a public works adviser would oversee the railways. The French government would have 'complete priority' in the choice of firms working in Syria, and in the raising of 'loans' necessary for the welfare of the country. It would lend its aid in organising the gendarmerie, the police and the army. French diplomatic and consular officials would represent Syria abroad. Arabic would be Syria's official language, but French would be taught in a 'compulsory and privileged' fashion. The emir was also made to recognise 'the independence and integrity of Lebanon under the mandate of France'. Faysal thus made major concessions, striking the only deal allowed him in the circumstances imposed on him.

On his return to Damascus on 16 January, and as was only natural, the nationalists cried treason upon getting word of the terms on offer. So great was the hostility of the public to any compromise with France, that Faysal could not even admit that he had already signed a provisional agreement with Clemenceau. There could be no question now of his returning to Paris. There was no readiness whatsoever in Damascus to accept the dismemberment of Syria, the independence of Lebanon, a Jewish 'national home' in Palestine, or the imposition of any form of foreign tutelage. Members of *al-fatat* and *al-'ahd*, who dominated the emir's administration, now resorted

---

[41] Khoury, *La France et l'Orient arabe*, pp. 312–18, for a facsimile of the accord.

to everything in their power to prevent such an outcome. He believed that they were wrong, but he had no option but to bend to their will. Faysal then suffered another blow when it was learned that the amenable Clemenceau was retiring from politics and was withdrawing from public life to live in his remote native seaside province. Approaching his eightieth birthday, the veteran French leader had stood for the presidency of the French Republic, but had been defeated by Paul Deschanel. He resigned as prime minister and was replaced by Alexandre Millerand, a politician close to the colonial party and to its very active spokesman, Robert de Caix, then occupying the influential post of secretary-general of the French High Commission in Beirut.[42]

Caix's colonial policies were the very opposite of those that had been proposed by Berthelot and Massignon. Rather than lending support to the nationalist government in Damascus, Caix planned to undermine it by chopping Syria into a number of autonomous regions. French influence was to depend on client minorities – on the Christian Maronites of Mount Lebanon, and on Muslim schismatics such as the 'Alawis and the Druze. It was to be implacably hostile to the Sunni majority and its traditional, well-seasoned political elites. Syria, Caix fancifully theorised, was like a stained-glass window in which France would supply the lead beading, in order to hold the panes together. In another flight of patronising arrogance, he depicted it as 'soft and uncertain clay' that would be moulded by France. France, he argued, would create not one nation in Syria but an aggregate of dependent cantons, linked together only by a representative of France. Meanwhile, to give Lebanon more depth and weaken the internal cohesion of the Arab state in Damascus, it was essential to annex the Biqa' valley to Lebanon.[43] Robert de Caix's determined aim was to gut of all substance the provisional agreement of 6 January 1920, which Faysal had managed to reach with Clemenceau. Challenged by the French in Paris and by the nationalists at home, Faysal had been turned into a vulnerably isolated figure.

---

[42] A notorious propagandist and North Africa 'expert', Robert de Caix (1869–1970) was, from 1910 onwards, a moving force of the colonial party. For a detailed account of his career and an anthology of his political writings, see Gérard D. Khoury, *Une Tutelle coloniale: Le mandat français en Syrie et au Liban. Écrits politiques de Robert de Caix*, Paris 2006.

[43] Khoury, *La France et l'Orient arabe*, pp. 301–2.

The General Syrian Congress and the San Remo conference

It was in these circumstances that, in fiery and defiant mood, the nationalists reconvened the General Syrian Congress, under its president, Hashim al-Atasi, which three members of the Solh family – Rida, Riad and 'Afif – attended. Meeting in plenary session in Damascus, the Congress passed a historic resolution, which was promulgated the next day, 8 March 1920. It proclaimed the independence of Syria 'in its natural boundaries' – to include the Syrian interior as well as the coast; Palestine and the territory lying east of the Jordan; and Lebanon (although the latter was allowed autonomous status within the boundaries of the Ottoman *mutasarrifiyya*).

The Syrian Congress rejected the project of a national home for the Jews in Palestine and elected the Emir Faysal King of Syria.[44] Knowing that such a resolution would only incite the French to use force against him, Faysal tried hard to persuade the nationalists not to convene the Congress, or to refrain from declaring independence if they did convene it. But he was unable to sway them. The current of hostility to France had become too strong. Indeed, far from consecrating his power, his election as king only showed up his weakness.[45] Worse still, from Faysal's point of view, the Congress decided to remain in session for an indefinite period and demanded that Faysal and his government account to *it* for *their* actions.

The French reaction was immediate and muscular. French military reinforcements were rushed to the Levant. Prime Minister Alexandre Millerand instructed General Gouraud to inform Faysal that the French government would not recognise the right of the Syrian Congress in Damascus to determine the fate of the Arab territories, and that both he and the British government were obliged to declare the actions of the Congress 'null and void'. The 'Supreme Allied Council' – consisting of Lloyd George, Millerand and their colleagues – then decided to meet at San Remo on the Italian riviera on 24–25 April 1920, and invited Faysal to come to Europe to address it. But the Council's refusal to accept Syria's 8 March proclamation of independence made it impossible for Faysal to obtain a mandate from the Syrian Congress to attend. Still hoping against hope that

44 André Raymond, 'La Syrie du Royaume arabe à l'indépendance (1914–1946)', in André Raymond (ed.), *La Syrie d'aujourd'hui*, Paris 1980, p. 63.
45 Tauber, *The Formation of Modern Syria and Lebanon*, p. 45.

the provisional agreement he had reached with Clemenceau remained valid, he pleaded pitifully for a declaration from Paris recognising Syria's independence. But the new French government was in no mood to satisfy him. It was therefore in the absence of any Arab representative that the fate of the Arab territories was decided at San Remo by the Supreme Allied Council. Utterly ignoring the clearly expressed wishes of the local inhabitants, it gave France the Mandate over Syria and Lebanon, and Britain the Mandate over Iraq and Palestine.

These decisions sounded like a death knell in Damascus. They violated assurances given by the Allies in 1918, as well as earlier promises made to the Arabs, and raised terrible fears that Syria would suffer the same fate as had Morocco and Tunisia. Some hot-headed nationalists even demanded that Faysal declare war on France! In an attempt to calm opinion, he replaced 'Ali Rida Pasha al-Rikabi as prime minister with the more combative and popular Hashim al-Atasi. Diehard opponents of the French were brought into the government, notably the brave and handsome Yusuf al-'Azma as minister of war, and Dr 'Abd al-Rahman al-Shahbandar as foreign minister. Even so, a spontaneous rebellion did break out. Bands of irregulars, sometimes backed by Faysal's own officers, attacked and killed French troops in the north and south of the coastal zone. Those Christian villages in Mount Lebanon, which were considered French military strongholds, were attacked and pillaged. Shi'i guerrilla fighters from the Jabal 'Amil threatened Jewish colonies in Galilee. From General Gouraud's vantage point, the most galling development of all – which he would not let pass – was that, from February 1920 onwards, Faysal (or, more properly speaking, the committed patriots who were still propping him up) refused to allow the French to use the Rayak–Aleppo railway. This was essential for the reinforcement and supply of French troops fighting Mustafa Kemal's nationalists in Cilicia, where French garrisons were being besieged and defeated. Gouraud was therefore forced to send supplies and reinforcements to them by sea, which was expensive, slow and difficult.

By this time, Syrian opinion had turned decisively against Faysal, who was widely seen as too weak to handle the escalating crisis with France. In a bid to rally opinion to the emir – now only nominally king of Syria – Rida el-Solh, his minister of interior, proposed sending Faysal on a tour of the provinces, beginning with Aleppo. Riad and his friend Sa'dallah al-Jabiri were sent north to ask Sa'dallah's elder brother, the statesman Nafe' Pasha al-Jabiri, a leading Aleppo citizen and a former deputy in the Ottoman parliament, to put Faysal up in his mansion during his visit to Syria's 'second capital'. But Nafe' Pasha categorically refused to do so, thereby flouting the traditional Arab etiquette of hospitality. This had become a great political dispute. The 'king', he roared, should forget his title and act as a true leader of a revolution – at least until he was certain of the boundaries of his 'kingdom'. This once hardy Beduin, he charged, had been softened by the comforts of power. A revolutionary 'king', he added, was an anomaly as great as an elephant with wings!

During this spirited but dead-end exchange, Fayza, Nafe' Pasha's 6-year-old daughter, who had been sitting on her father's knee while the three men were arguing, sought to draw Riad into playing with her. But he pulled her hair instead to tease her, and she ran crying from the room. It was their first and only meeting, until, that is, she became his bride some ten years later.

If Rida el-Solh was dejected by Nafe' Pasha's adamant refusal to host Faysal, the visit to Aleppo had helped sharpen his son Riad's growing disillusion with the emir. On 22 June 1920, a group of young rebels, Riad among them, met at the Bakri house in old Damascus, where, in earlier times, they had plotted against the Turks. There they decided to take up arms against the French. From the meeting, Riad went to see his father at the Ministry of Interior.

'You must resign,' the son urged.

'And leave him on his own?' his father demanded.

'Yes! You handed him the throne far too hastily!'

After further discussion, Rida realised that, in view of the violent plans of the rebels, which included his own son, his position as minister of interior in Faysal's government was no longer tenable. Riad carried his father's letter of resignation to the like-minded Prime Minister Hashim al-Atasi, who, without so much as bothering to consult Faysal, accepted it at once.[46] Because of the heavy-handed political bungling of the Allies at San Remo, power in Damascus now passed to the more extreme nationalists. In Paris and in Beirut, the mood of the French authorities had also hardened even further and they were now intent on destroying by military force Faysal's Arab regime. A clash had become inevitable.

[46] Alia el-Solh, *Le Jour*, 26 September 1965.

Riad el-Solh's bold initiative

To an Arab nationalist like Riad, severing Lebanon from Syria, as the French were intent on doing, was a historical injustice to two communities which he felt had always belonged together. He found Faysal's readiness to recognise Lebanon's independence – albeit under French pressure – profoundly puzzling and short-sighted. Lebanon was Syria's outlet to the sea and to the wide world beyond, while Syria was Lebanon's gateway to the Arab hinterland. The mountain ranges rising above the Mediterranean coast and the cities, agricultural plains and deserts of the interior, all formed a single region inhabited by the same people, who spoke the same language, and had traded and inter-married over the centuries. Riad was, of course, well aware that the Christians of Lebanon – especially the Maronites among them – linked to Europe by generations of association, impregnated with French language and culture, fearful of the surrounding Muslim world, looked to Paris for protection. So much was obvious to anyone who had grown up in Beirut amongst Christian friends, and who had attended a French mission school as Riad el-Solh had done.

In February 1919, a Maronite member of Lebanon's Administrative Council, Dawud 'Ammun, had petitioned the Peace Conference for an independent, self-ruled Lebanon under French protection. The 'Lebanon' for which he pleaded was not just the traditional Mount Lebanon, but a country enlarged 'within its historic and geographical boundaries' to include Beirut as its capital, Tripoli and the north, Sidon and the south, and the Biqa' valley in the east. 'Ammun was one of many such petitioners, of whom the most influential was the Maronite patriarch, Monsignor Elias Boutros Hayek, a fervent French loyalist who, listing historical, political and linguistic reasons, campaigned for Lebanon's 'total independence vis-à-vis any Arab state which might be established in Syria'. Lebanon, he argued in his presumptuous address, was the main centre in the region of Western education and culture. It was quite different from Syria, he continued, 'where the nomadic element formed an important part of the population',[47] a reductive view that must have made the more urbane Damascenes and Aleppans laugh!

Such an extreme viewpoint begged a serious question: how to find common ground between anti-Arab Lebanese nationalists, who

---

[47] Khoury, *La France et l'Orient arabe*, p. 267.

saw their salvation in association with France, and Arab nationalists in Syria and among the Muslims of Lebanon, who were resolutely anti-French? It was a puzzle with which Riad el-Solh was to wrestle for much of his political life, and to which he, more than any other politician of his generation, was eventually to find a solution. Lebanese Christian sensitivities had indeed to be respected – they were a feature of the political landscape – but it was intolerable, he believed, that the French should use Lebanon as a base from which to pose a permanent colonial threat to an inland Arab government.

Early in July 1920, a month or so before his twenty-sixth birthday, Riad made a first stab at a solution to this complex problem. In Damascus, Faysal was coming under intensifying pressure from both the French and the nationalists. Gouraud's forces had been reinforced to enable him to overthrow the emir's government. A Senegalese brigade, withdrawn from the Rhine, was on its way to him, together with three Senegalese battalions from Thrace, five squadrons of Moroccan *spahis* from Istanbul, as well as a Madagascan artillery unit. Gouraud's instructions were to prepare military operations against Damascus because of the 'insolent and threatening attitude of Faysal's Sharifian government'.

It was then that Riad el-Solh devised an ambitious plan. If he could bring the Administrative Council of Mount Lebanon over to Faysal's side, this would demonstrate that even its Maronite members preferred an association with Syria to separatism under the French. France's role as 'protector' of the Christians, tirelessly invoked to justify its colonial presence, could then be exposed as unnecessary. It was Riad's first substantial political initiative and a direct challenge to French power.

With the help of two of his closest friends, 'Arif al-Na'mani, one of the wealthiest and most erudite French-educated notables among the Sunni Muslims, and Amin Arslan, a patrician Druze emir (both members, like himself, of the General Syrian Congress), Riad made secret contact with several members of the Administrative Council and, without alerting pro-French diehards like Dawud 'Ammun, persuaded seven of them to 'defect' from the French to Faysal. No doubt he was able to win them over because of their fears about the long-term consequences of French policy, and because he, Arslan and Na'mani were suave and brilliant interlocutors in French as well as in Arabic! These Christian Lebanese were prepared to come over to Faysal's side so long as he was ready to grant autonomy to a 'Greater Lebanon' within his Arab kingdom. Unlike some of their colleagues on the Council, they did not relish the prospect of total separation from Syria. They drafted a resolution outlining their views, which amounted to a readiness to move out of France's sphere of influence and into closer relations with Syria.[48]

Riad's plan was for the seven defectors – who surprisingly enough ended up including the Council's vice-president, Sa'dallah Hayek, brother of the staunchly pro-French Maronite patriarch himself – to travel to Damascus and pay allegiance to King Faysal. They would then sail for Europe via Haifa (they thought the French would not allow them to sail from Beirut) to declare their rejection of the French Mandate at the Paris Peace Conference and demand independence for Lebanon and economic integration with Syria. They were even prepared, if necessary, to take their case to the United States. 'Arif al-Na'mani, well known for his patriotism and his princely generosity, was ready to fund all their travel expenses – a move which the French would later use against him. In a report to Paris on 18 October 1921, Gouraud sneeringly claimed that members of the Administrative Council had been 'bought' with a first payment of 10,000 Egyptian pounds to be divided between them, and a promise of a further 30,000 pounds once they had assembled in Damascus. But the historian Zeine N. Zeine was later to record that Emir 'Adil Arslan, cousin of Amin Arslan, had in an interview categorically denied this French smear.[49] The whole episode provided an early example of Riad el-Solh's political daring, reflecting his lifelong efforts to conciliate the wavering Christians of Lebanon and rally them to the Arab nationalist cause.

The French were soon tipped off by one of their informers. On 10 July, the train carrying the delegation to Damascus was stopped by Senegalese troops at the mountain village of Sofar. Faysal had sent his chamberlain, Ihsan al-Jabiri, to meet the defectors and accompany them to Damascus. He arrived in time to relieve them of incriminating documents, including copies of the resolution demanding

---

[48] Tauber, *The Formation of Modern Syria and Lebanon*, pp. 60–3. The signatories of the resolution were Sa'dallah al-Hayek, Khalil 'Akki, Suleiman Kan'an, Elias Shu'ayri, Mahmud Jumblatt, Fu'ad 'Abd al-Malik and Muhammad Muhsin. See Alia el-Solh, *Le Jour*, 3 October 1965.

[49] Khoury, *La France et l'Orient arabe*, p. 375.

autonomy for Lebanon in association with Syria. The members of the delegation were arrested and, under torture, confessed. Riad, who was accompanying them, escaped arrest by hiding in a third-class carriage, where he guessed rightly that the snobbish French would not even bother to look!

On 12 July, Gouraud issued decree no. 273, dissolving the Administrative Council. And, on 19 July, the seven members of the delegation and their assistants were brought before a French court-martial, where they were accused of plotting against the occupying government, of receiving bribes and of treason against Lebanon. Sentenced to six to ten years of exile, heavy fines and deprivation of civil rights, they were transferred to the island of Arwad off the Syrian coast, and from there were shipped to Corsica. However, following pressure by French politicians and the public, several of them were allowed to return to Lebanon if they agreed to express regret for their actions. Those who refused to do so, like 'Arif al- Na'mani, had to remain in exile until the end of 1922.[50] Riad el-Solh's role in the affair was revealed at the trial.[51] By this time, he had fled to Damascus, where Arab political elites were gathering. But his stay there was soon disturbed by the French ultimatum to Faysal.

Faysal's final battle

While part of his force was tied down in Cilicia, General Gouraud had delayed moving against Damascus. He was reluctant to wage a two-front war. But once Robert de Caix managed to negotiate an armistice with Mustafa Kemal, the belligerent Gouraud was itching to impose by force a mandatory regime on Syria. On 9 July, a desperate Faysal announced that he intended to travel once more to Europe to put his case to the Peace Conference. But when Nuri al-Sa'id went to Beirut to make preparations for his journey, Gouraud informed him of the terms of the ultimatum which had been officially communicated to the Syrian government on 14 July. In it, Gouraud had made five demands which had to be accepted within four days: acquiescence to the French Mandate; the abolition of conscription and reduction of the Syrian

[50] Tauber, *The Formation of Modern Syria and Lebanon*, pp. 62–3.
[51] Centre des archives diplomatiques de Nantes (CADN), Fonds Beyrouth, carton 1583.

army to its 1919 level; the absolute right of French forces to use the Rayak–Aleppo railway and to occupy Aleppo; the introduction of a Syrian 'paper' currency tied to the franc, to be issued by the French-controlled Banque de Syrie et du Liban; and the punishment of all those considered guilty of hostile acts against France.

When these demands reached Damascus, they were met with popular outrage, sparking demonstrations. But the balance of power was clearly not in Syria's favour. Gouraud had deployed 80,000 men in the Biqa' valley alone, supported by tanks, artillery and aircraft. After a difficult moment of consideration, members of the Syrian government advised Faysal to accept Gouraud's ultimatum, the only exception being the courageous Yusuf al-'Azma, who continued to call for armed resistance. Faysal consulted Lord Allenby, who also advised acceptance of the ultimatum. Further communication took place with Gouraud, who consented to a delay until 21 July, so that the Syrian government could convey its official acceptance of the ultimatum and start fulfilling its demands.

On 20 July, Faysal accepted Gouraud's conditions, and set about complying with them. Army units were discharged. The General Syrian Congress was dismissed. When Kamil al-Qassab and a group of men from his Committee of National Defence angrily confronted the emir, he ordered them thrown into the citadel. Rioting broke out in Damascus, with the crowd calling for the traitor Faysal to be killed. A mob broke into the citadel, plundered the ancient armoury and freed al-Qassab. The young Emir Zayd, assisted by Yasin al-Hashimi and some still loyal troops, managed to put down the revolt, but the number of dead and wounded tragically ran into hundreds.

Despite his surrender to French demands, Faysal's telegram accepting the ultimatum failed to reach Gouraud in time. The French claimed the delay was due to the obstruction of nationalists in Damascus, or because rebels had cut down the telegraph poles between Damascus and the Biqa'. In any event, French troops resumed their advance. Further last-minute negotiations, conducted by Sati' al-Husri and French officers at the Lebanese mountain village of Aley, resulted in a further delay, but also in a fresh spate of French demands, most notably the installation of a French mission in Damascus to supervise the execution of the ultimatum, and to prepare the ground for the Mandate regime. Al-Husri returned to Damascus convinced that the French were determined to occupy the country, no matter what Faysal said or did. While Faysal had already shown himself ready to execute the original ultimatum, he knew that any further concessions on his part would provoke a civil war and sweep him immediately from power. This was the message he sent to Gouraud on 23 July.

By this time, however, French troops had reached Maysalun, some 30 kilometres from Damascus, where a tiny Syrian 'army' was encamped, numbering only 600 regular troops and 2,400 volunteers. These patriots, 'armed with old rifles, pistols, swords and even slings', had rushed to the front from Damascus.[52] The decisive clash took place on the morning of 24 July, when, in a few hours, the Syrian forces were defeated with great loss of life. Yusuf al-'Azma, the heroic minister of war, was killed as he sought, valiantly but impossibly, to stop the advance of the French army. To prevent further slaughter, Faysal declared Damascus an open city, thereby allowing French troops to enter Damascus on 25 July without encountering resistance. Within a few days, Syria had fallen under French military occupation.

Faysal withdrew to Kiswa, on the outskirts of Damascus, where he continued to entertain a somewhat demented hope of reaching an understanding with the French. Before leaving Damascus, he formed a cabinet under 'Ala' al-Din al-Drubi, a quiet personality with little popular influence, whom he imagined the French might accept. But, on 27 July, the emir was informed in no uncertain terms that the French insisted that he leave Syrian territory the very next day. With no choice but to comply, a bitter and crestfallen Faysal left the city by special train with his followers, reaching Dar'a on 28 July. The following month, he moved to Haifa, and from there to Europe. Such was the catastrophic end of his ill-conceived and ill-fated Arab kingdom.

A second train was reserved for those nationalist leaders who had no wish to stay on in a Damascus under French occupation. Riad el-Solh was on that second train, which went to Dar'a and then on to Haifa. On 9 August 1920, a French military court sitting in Damascus sentenced him and a score of others to death in absentia for their support of Faysal's regime. And on 29 October, another French military court sitting in Beirut sentenced Riad a second time in absentia, to five years in jail and a fine of 1,400,000 French francs. This time his 'crime' was attempting to mobilise members of Mount Lebanon's

---

[52] Tauber, *The Formation of Modern Syria and Lebanon*, p. 78.

Administrative Council against the French. He was charged with high treason for plotting against the state of *Grand Liban*. Gouraud called him '*l'auteur de la conspiration*'.[53] It was the start of a highly charged career as the leading freedom-fighter of his generation.

[53] Hilal el-Solh, *Tarikh rajul wa qadiyya*, p. 43.

6 FUGITIVE FROM THE FRENCH

In the summer of 1920, Riad el-Solh was a wanted man. He was on the run from French colonial 'justice' for the first – but not the last – time in his life. General Gouraud's troops had defeated the minute Syrian army, marched into Damascus, put an end to its Arab government and forced the Emir Faysal into exile on 27 July. On that same day, Riad and some seventy other nationalists left the city by train, before the French had had a chance to identify them and round them up. Disillusioned with Faysal and full of hate for their French oppressors, they travelled from Damascus to Dar'a, and from there to Haifa. There they spent some angry days pondering the collapse of their hopes for Arab unity and independence. What had gone wrong? Who was to blame? How could the injustice of the post-war Mandates now be undone?

When the group dispersed, some of its members went on to Cairo, others to Transjordan, and others yet returned home and lay low. This was the beginning of a three-way split in the nationalist movement. Some nationalists remained pro-Hashemite, especially after Faysal became king of Iraq, and his brother, 'Abdallah, emir of Transjordan. Others rallied around the Hashemites' enemy, 'Abd al-'Aziz ibn Sa'ud, Sultan of Najd in Arabia. A third group sought refuge in Egypt.

Riad made his way north to Beirut. He was 26, jobless, unmarried, with no prospects save those of an exiled would-be politician, and no objective save to continue the fight. Amazingly, and in spite of the grave setbacks suffered in Damascus, his self-confidence remained undented. His political daring and acumen had already allowed him to stand out from the crowd.

His mother longed for him to remain with her at the family home at Minet al-Husn, but both understood that his presence there would attract immediate and unwanted attention. So it was decided that, until the intentions of the French High Commission towards him became clearer, he would hide out at the house of his sister Balqis. Her husband Sami el-Solh was their first cousin. Sami had withdrawn from politics in order to enter the judiciary, where, in 1922, he became Chief Prosecutor (*Procureur Général*) at Greater Lebanon's Court of Justice.[1] But Riad's plan to hide at his house survived less than a week. Hurriedly returning home one day from the Palais de Justice, Sami brought Riad the alarming news that, on 9 August, he had been sentenced to death for high treason by a French military court in Damascus. A warrant for his arrest was about to be issued. If caught, he would certainly be put before a firing squad on the same day.

Riad's first thought was to jump into a car and flee to Palestine, only a short distance away and not under French jurisdiction. Liners calling at Haifa would enable him to sail away to safety in Europe. He decided to leave at once. As it happened, Balqis's children had a nanny, Umm Muhammad, whose son, Muhammad Khattar, owned a small transport company which ran taxis twice a day between Lebanon and Palestine. The man was summoned and a taxi booked. With the greatest reluctance, Riad agreed to put on a *milaya* – the gauzy black face veil worn by most women at the time. To be caught in such a disguise would have been deeply humiliating. But, as they drove out of the city, they passed the house of one of Riad's friends, Khayr al-Din Ahdab, who was also wanted by the French for his support of Faysal's government in Damascus. Ahdab's house was already surrounded by police. Riad realised the danger he himself was in, and calculated that it was clearly too late to cross the border by car.

Umm Muhammad then suggested hiding Riad at her house. This was at no. 11 (now no. 72) 'Umar ibn al-Khattab Street in Ras al-Nab'a, a densely populated working-class district of Beirut, crisscrossed by narrow lanes, where the police would not easily find him. He took shelter in a small laundry room at the bottom of her garden. A ladder was placed against the back wall to provide a means of quick escape if the police were to call at the front door. To meet with Umm Muhammad, Riad would sometimes scale a wall, then another one, and leap onto a patch of rough ground near the main road. But she

---

[1] Note on Sami el-Solh's career in MAE Fonds Beyrouth (Amb.), série B, carton 4 (dossier 55). French High Commissioner in Syria and Lebanon, February 1941, and Délégation de la France Combattante au Levant, Damascus, 17 August 1942.

became terrified that his irrepressible humour and his booming laugh would conspire to give him away, and came up with the idea that he should escape by sea.

'What about the police at the port?' he asked her.

'Well, you certainly won't be travelling on the *Khedive Ismail*!' she answered teasingly, referring to the great luxury Egyptian liner of the 1920s.

Instead, she made arrangements for him to sail to Palestine in a small fishing boat which was leaving the very next night from a small inlet near the mosque at 'Ain al-Mrayseh on the Beirut seafront (later cemented over to make way for an extension of the corniche). Riad's hideout was a dark, damp shack used by the mosque's doorkeeper. There he received word that both Khayr al-Din Ahdab and Amin Arslan planned to come along as well. But, hiding outside Beirut, they were having the greatest difficulty evading French police patrols on the roads into the city. Nevertheless, Riad was now obliged to wait for them.

Changing his woman's veil for a fisherman's black *sirwal* and head-wrap, Riad hunkered down in the dark for the wait. It was far too dim to read. Gaps in the flimsy walls of the shack had been sealed with planks and rag, so that no hint of light would give him away. He strained his ears for the sound of voices outside, but all he could hear were the waves lapping the shore and the muezzin's call to prayer from the nearby mosque. His own home at Minet al-Husn was just a few steps away. His mother and sister would be there, worrying about him and fretting. He had to wait another long and nerve-wracking week in the shack, but was at last delivered from the gloom by the arrival of a fisherman, 'Abdallah al-Mughrabi, who, without a word, proceeded to tie a rope around his waist, secured it firmly, and pushed him towards the edge of the parapet. Below was the glimmer of the sea.

'Step over the edge, and I'll do the rest!' Slowly he lowered Riad on to the shore. 'Wait for me behind that rock. If a patrol comes by, lie flat in the boat. You will find some sacks there to cover yourself.'

Riad's two companions arrived at last, and they set off. Exhausted and overwrought from their frightening journey, Khayr al-Din Ahdab and Amin Arslan dozed off in the hull. The helmsman hugged the coastline, and Riad trailed his hand in the water to keep awake.[2]

---

[2] Alia el-Solh, *Le Jour*, 7 November 1965, based on her father's recollections.

So began Riad's life in exile, which was to last three and a half years. It was not until January 1924 that he was allowed to return to Syria and Lebanon. These were years of despair and idleness, interspersed with bouts of serious work. From Palestine he went to Cairo, which was then the main centre for Arabs determined to continue the fight against the British and the French. From Cairo, some weeks later, he travelled to Rome to stay with childhood friends on the Via Appia Antica. It was there that he met the 17-year-old Count Galeazzo Ciano, who was to become Benito Mussolini's son-in-law and minister of foreign affairs.

One day in November 1920, Riad received a note from his father, together with a loose sheet of paper bearing the number 395. It was a copy of the sentence passed on Riad by a military court in Beirut on 29 October, condemning him in absentia to five years in jail, a fine of 1,400,000 francs and the loss of his civil rights. He was now an outlaw, adrift in the world, unable to go home. Letters from his mother, however, provided some relief, but even these were upsetting when she described excursions to the old family house at Sidon, where the orange trees were in blossom. 'Your brother', she wrote,

> cut himself a spear and, uttering fierce cries like a Zulu warrior, leaped around a lamb being grilled on a spit. Your sister Alia danced for us on her points, as she has learned to do at the Prussian College. But she is becoming more and more withdrawn, and it seems that she is writing poetry. Unfortunately, your cousins denounced her to your father – you know how strict he is – and he has confiscated all her writings. But let me go on about our picnic at Sidon. We were so happy.

But Riad could read no further. He was missing home and craving the warmth of human contact. He threw himself into a whirl of socialising, and when he had exhausted what Rome had to offer, he went off to Vienna, London, Jerusalem, Alexandria and Cairo. In Cairo, he met a mesmerising young woman, famous for her beauty and emancipation, with the name of Qut al-Qulub Demerdashi. She was the daughter of Demerdashi Pasha, a prominent politician and the head of a Sufi order. Unlike most other Muslim women of her time, she was allowed to attend her father's political meetings and to appear in public without a veil. More daringly still, she had even published some sulphurous novelettes in Paris. Riad was utterly bewitched and decided to marry her. He insisted that his family come at once to Cairo to arrange the matter, not thinking of the difficulty his father might face in making contact with a son under a sentence such as his. In the event, his mother Nazira came alone, and recognised at once that she faced a formidable rival. In her possessive eyes, she decided that the young lady was more than likely to make her son's life a misery. She immediately set about undermining the relationship. Torn between his adored mother and his beloved Qut al-Qulub, Riad began to hesitate. But this was outrage enough for the proud Egyptian beauty, who refused so much as to see him again. Much later, and to get even with his mother, she published another short novella, but this time with a woman named Nazira as the villain of the piece.

As he lost contact with his family, Riad began to run seriously short of funds. He sold his personal jewellery – the cufflinks, rings and studs that elegant young men were known to wear in those days – borrowed heavily from his friends, and soon fell into the hands of moneylenders. His father, whose own pension had vanished with the Ottoman Empire, tried to help him out from time to time – as may be seen, for example, from a letter dated 6 July 1923 from the Savings Bank of Alexandria, informing him of a transfer of 40,000 Egyptian piastres. But such gifts were never enough to settle Riad's escalating debts, which became a pattern of his financial life. Although always short of money, he remained a lavish spender. Later on, as he sold his land and spent his inheritance to fund his political campaigns, his casual attitude to money was to cause his family considerable anxiety.

With no money with which to cut a dashing figure in society, he began spending more and more time reading, building up the collection of books to which he would continue adding for the rest of his life. He made a habit of calling on the booksellers of Muski, in the older part of Cairo, with lists of books and manuscripts he was after, which he hoped would come onto the market from private sales. Reading widely, and making copious notes, he even decided to write a history of the Arabs. To fund the purchase of still more books for the project, he sold his gold watch. Finding lodgings in the quarter of the Muhammad 'Ali citadel, close to both the National Library and to the al-Azhar mosque, he settled down to work. A large number of notebooks, bound in moleskin and filled with his fine script in pencil, are still in his family's possession. But his project was never completed, nor was he a very rigorous historian. His airy inclination was to exaggerate past glories to make up for the painful humiliations of the present.[3]

As he approached the age of 30, this period of Riad's life was by no means entirely wasted in dissipation. In the summer of 1921, he attended the founding meeting in Geneva of the Syro-Palestinian Congress, a body with which he was to be intimately connected for the next several years. In November, anxious to understand the extent of Zionist ambitions, he travelled to London for a meeting with the Zionist leader, Dr Chaim Weizmann. This was followed, a month later, by an interview with Sir Herbert Samuel, the British high commissioner in Palestine. In Amman, he met the Emir 'Abdallah, third son of the Sharif Husayn, shortly after the British had carved out a fiefdom for him in Transjordan.

In Cairo, he befriended the leading writers, editors and political activists of the day. In Berlin and Paris, he made valuable contacts which he was later to put to good use for the Arab cause. Moving restlessly back and forth between Europe and the Middle East, he gained international experience. He was gradually learning to become a player in the big game, which would soon decide the future of the region.

Ironically enough, the homesick Riad could have returned home earlier than he actually did. On 23 November 1921, General Gouraud signed a General Order authorising the return to Syria of twenty-five persons, sentenced to death in absentia in August 1920, whose property had been confiscated. Riad was one of them.[4] In a speech in Damascus on 20 June 1921, Gouraud hinted at his intention to pardon them. They were invited to report to the local authorities, who had been instructed to confirm their identity and then inform them of the amnesty. Sentences passed on them would be formally annulled and they would be able to travel freely in Syria and Lebanon.[5]

But, as General Weygand, the French high commissioner and commander-in-chief, reported to the minister of war in Paris in January 1924, General Gouraud's General Order of 23 November 1921 had *deliberately not been made public*, and the individuals concerned had certainly not been informed. Learning of the amnesty by other means,

---

[3] Alia el-Solh, *Le Jour*, 10 October 1965.
[4] MAE Fonds Beyrouth, Mandat Syrie-Liban (dossier 17/1579), Service des renseignements, Beirut, 23 November 1921.
[5] Consul General Satow to Foreign Secretary, Beirut, 19 August 1921 (FO 371/6461).

a few of them, like Kamil al-As'ad, the Solh family's rival in South Lebanon who had spies in the French camp, had returned to Syria, recovered their property and been freed. But most of the others, like Riad, unaware of these French measures concerning them, continued to serve time abroad. He finally asked family and friends to intervene on his behalf with the French authorities. His cousin, Sami el-Solh, wrote to General Weygand in December 1923, requesting a pardon, while his father, in turn, gave guarantees for his son's behaviour. Weygand wrote to the minister of war in Paris:

> In the circumstances, I authorised Riad el-Solh's return to Syria and, in a service note number 12.717/I of 20 December 1923, I decided to implement the instructions regarding him in the General Order of 23 November 1921.
>
> I have the honour to attract your attention to the fact, however, that although Riad el-Solh benefits from General Gouraud's suspension of the sentence passed on him in Damascus in August 1920, he still remains subject to another sentence of five years in prison and a fine of 1,400,000 francs passed on him in October 1920 for the affair of the Lebanese Councillors.
>
> As a result, given that Riad el-Solh has made his submission and that his father has given all the moral guarantees I asked of him; given that he benefited from a pardon for the sentence of death passed on him; granted also that all the Lebanese Councillors (with the exception of Suleiman bey Kanaan, whose political activity still requires his distance from Syria) have had their sentences of banishment and fines lifted in application of the last paragraph of your letter No 26634-2/10 of 9 October 1923, I have the honour to ask that you suspend proceedings against Riad el-Solh with regard to the evidence against him cited in the sentence passed in absentia on 29 October 1920 by the military tribunal in Beirut.

The minister gave his consent and Riad returned at the end of 1923 to Haifa, where he obtained an amnesty from the French authorities. Armed with a safe-conduct signed by General Weygand himself, he returned to Beirut in early 1924 after an absence of three and a half years. A photograph of him at that time shows a slim, elegantly dressed young man of medium height, looking boldly out at the world, but with a humorous, quizzical expression, heightened by a lifelong habit of wearing his fez at an amusing rakish angle.

A great deal had happened while Riad was away. The whole political landscape of the region had changed beyond recognition. Britain and France had imposed their Mandates by force on the former Arab provinces of the Ottoman Empire. The Zionists, in spite of the hostility of the local Arab population, which was ten times more numerous than the new and small Jewish one, were racing to implement the British promise of the Balfour Declaration.

In July 1920, the same month in which French troops occupied Damascus and destroyed the Emir Faysal's Arab government, Britain faced a ferocious revolt in the lower Euphrates region of Iraq. Wanting to put an end to British occupation once and for all, Sunni and Shi'i Iraqis had prayed together in the months leading up to the revolt. The uprising was a seminal event in the forging of Iraqi nationalism and a rite of passage in the struggle for independence. Spreading north to the areas around Baghdad, the uprising at its peak had mobilised over 100,000 fighters, confronting Britain with the biggest and bloodiest challenge it had faced so far in the Muslim world. British troops did not regain control until February 1921, taking military casualties and at a cost of £40 million (an enormous sum at the time). At least 6,000 Iraqis and 500 British and colonial Indian troops were killed.[6]

Crushing an intifada of this magnitude, at a time of tight post-war budgets, caused Britain's newly appointed colonial secretary, Winston Churchill, to call a week-long conference in Cairo in March 1921, to determine what policy to pursue in the Arab world. His inclination was to create Arab client states, to be run by local leaders and policed by native armies, which could be counted on to protect British interests, without the need to endanger imperial troops or go to vast expenditure.

After being driven out of Syria by the French, the Emir Faysal had remained on good terms with the British, largely because of their

---

[6] For the Iraqi side of the conflict, see Pierre-Jean Luizard, *La Vie de l'Ayatollah Mahdî al-Khâlisi*, Paris 2005. This is a translation into French of Shaykh Muhammad al-Khalisi's *Batal al-Islam*, the life of his father, who was the leading Shi'i revolutionary *mujtahid* in Iraq at the time of the 1920 revolution.

'partnership' in his Arab Revolt. It was believed that he might still be amenable to British 'advice', and that paying him a subsidy would be far cheaper than assuming full responsibility for the Iraqi state. It was therefore decided to install him on the throne of Iraq in June, with the support of two fellow veterans of his Arab Revolt. Ja'far al-'Askari was made his defence minister, while Nuri al-Sa'id – 'Askari's brother-in-law – was appointed chief of staff of the new Iraqi army, and was to remain a key figure in the monarchical regime for the next thirty-seven years. The officer corps was made up of some 600 former Ottoman officers of Iraqi origin, almost all of them Sunni, who had followed Faysal to Baghdad. As British power remained preponderant in Iraq, Faysal became the 'sovereign of a state that was itself not sovereign'.[7] On Churchill's orders and using chemical weapons, repeated bombings of recalcitrant tribes by the newly formed RAF finally enforced 'order' and the collection of punitive taxes.

By the 1920s, Britain and France could no longer be seen to indulge in the naked, annexationist imperialism of the nineteenth century, judged increasingly unacceptable in the climate of the times. But their occupation and subjugation of Arab territories were nevertheless driven by nothing other than imperial self-interest, and should be seen as an extension of the centuries-old tradition of political and economic penetration of the Ottoman Empire. This had first occurred under cover of the Capitulations, and was then given a new lease of life following the Empire's bankruptcy in 1876, when Europe took over the administration of the Ottoman public debt.[8] The Mandates, at least for the British, did represent something of a new model of relations between the developed and the developing world, but a model still strongly coloured by old colonial attitudes.

The full-scale intifada which Britain faced in Iraq at the very start of its Mandate, may help explain why it chose to adopt a system of seemingly indirect rule. In contrast, the French, in clear violation of Article 22 of the League of Nations charter, decided to impose on Syria the more openly direct rule modelled on the protectorates they had established in Tunisia in 1881 and Morocco in 1912. Article 22 called on the mandatory power to prepare the populations in its charge

---

[7] Charles Tripp, *A History of Iraq*, Cambridge 2000, p. 49.
[8] Jean-David Mizrahi, 'La France et sa politique de mandat en Syrie et au Liban, 1920–1939', in Nadine Méouchy (ed.), *France, Syrie et Liban, 1928–1946: Les ambiguïtés et les dynamiques de la relation mandataire*, Damascus 2002, pp. 38–9.

for independence, by providing them with advice and assistance. The French set out to do the very opposite.

The creation of Greater Lebanon

To the horror of the Syrians, General Gouraud – advised by the insidious Robert de Caix, influential secretary-general at the High Commission – set about carving up their country on confessional and regional lines. The view in colonial circles in Paris was that the Levant should be turned into a broken-up mosaic of confessions and minorities. A policy of 'divide and rule' would be the best way to protect French strategic interests there. Arab aspirations for independence and unity were dismissed as so many sentiments stirred up by the British, with the aim of sabotaging the French. Indeed, throughout the interwar period, French officials en poste in the Levant, as well as their political masters in Paris, displayed a persistent Anglophobia. To cite but a single example among many: on 30 December 1920, when the French Senate was debating the subject of financial credits for Syria, Senator Dominique Delahaye thundered, somewhat out of context: 'Let England be warned not to arouse the hatred of France! . . . In the last century England took possession of the lands of the Egyptians. Now she has taken possession of the lands of the Ninevites and Babylonians. She has left for France a sort of little Pondicherry on the Mediterranean!' This was a reference to the south Indian enclave where the French East India Company had set up a trading post in 1673, and which was to remain under French rule until the 1950s.[9]

To counter strong Arab nationalist aspirations and ensure French supremacy, the area under French control was deliberately and systematically dismembered. This marked the triumph of the divisive policy of Robert de Caix, who argued that the 'nature' of Syrian society required a cantonal structure, in which France would play the role of arbiter between the different cantons – or 'coherent entities' – as he euphemistically took to calling them.

One of these so-called 'coherent entities' was Lebanon. The background to the creation of Greater Lebanon was to remain a

---

[9] Lord Hardinge (British ambassador in Paris) to the Foreign Secretary, Earl Curzon, 1 January 1921 (FO 371/6453).

subject of controversy for decades to come. As has been mentioned, the autonomous Ottoman province of Mount Lebanon, the *mutasarrifiyya*, was set up after the intervention of the Powers, in the wake of the horrific 1860 massacres of Christians. The extent of the province was loosely described in the *Réglement Organique* of 6 September 1864. But its boundaries remained unclear, as they had not been properly defined by the survey held in 1861. Moreover, because the province was too small to provide a livelihood for its inhabitants, who were largely engaged in agriculture, there was considerable emigration to adjoining vilayets. In the last two decades of the nineteenth century, some 20,000 Lebanese settled in these vilayets, especially in the *cazas* of Baalbek, Tyre, Sidon and Tripoli, as well as in the town of Beirut, which was not part of the autonomous province.

When, on 6 February 1919, the Emir Faysal stated his case before the Supreme Council at the Peace Conference, he did not mention any proposal for the enlargement of Lebanese territory. He expressed his willingness to accept the independence of Lebanon, adding, however, that in the interest of mutual development, some form of economic union with his Arab state in inland Syria was essential. He expressed the hope that the Lebanese would decide upon federal union with Syria of their own accord.

The following week, on 15 February, the case for an enlarged Lebanon – within 'its historical and natural frontiers' – was made before the Supreme Council by Dawud 'Ammun, president of Mount Lebanon's Administrative Council. 'The territories within the said frontiers are necessary to our existence', he argued.

> *Without them, neither commerce nor agriculture is possible for us and our populations are bound to emigrate; the mere closing of our frontiers by administrative measures would drive us to actual starvation, as happened during this war.*
>
> *Besides, the great majority of the populations living in these territories also ask to be attached to Lebanon. Their wishes are expressed in petitions addressed to the French Government. By giving them over to us, the Conference will perform a deed of justice and reparation, while acting in accordance with the principle of self-determination.*

> *We must say a few words about our relations*
> *with Syria. Between the two countries interests are closely*
> *connected. Syria requires our ports and mountains,*
> *we require her plains. Absolute separation would be*
> *detrimental to either, and yet Lebanon could unite with*
> *Syria, while retaining its distinct personality, only under*
> *the condition that Syria should profit by the same French*
> *collaboration.*

In other words, he was saying that Syria would have to accept French tutelage if it wanted a close link with Lebanon.

Under a secret agreement with the French government on 6 January 1920, Faysal recognised the independence of Lebanon under French Mandate. The boundaries were to be settled by the Peace Conference, taking into account the historic rights, economic interests and free wishes of the populations.

Meanwhile, the Administrative Council of Lebanon renewed its propaganda in favour of territorial expansion. When the Syrian Congress at Damascus – which proclaimed Faysal king of Syria in March 1919 – declared that the autonomy of Lebanon would be recognised only within its former limits, the Administrative Council protested to the French high commissioner. It subsequently issued a statement declaring that the Syrian Congress had no competence to discuss the affairs of independent Lebanon and asserting the absolute independence of the country in 'its historical and natural frontiers'.

Once the Mandate for Syria and Lebanon had been definitely allocated to France by the Supreme Council at San Remo in April 1920, the *Délégation Libanaise à la Conférence de la Paix* sent a memorandum to the Powers claiming the four *cazas* of Baalbek, Biqa‘, Hasbaya and Rashaya for Lebanon, on the grounds of historical boundaries, majority Christian populations and economic necessity. This was the background to the French government's decision in favour of the 'natural limits' of Lebanon. In August 1920, General Gouraud, high commissioner for Syria and Lebanon, made a speech in which he declared, in the name of his government, that the four *cazas* would thenceforth be united to Lebanon.

It was on this basis that he proclaimed the creation on 1 September 1920 of a separate Lebanese Republic within expanded frontiers – *l'État du Grand Liban*. This was formed by attaching to the autonomous Ottoman *mutasarrifiyya* (the old 'Mount Lebanon' of 1861), surrounding cities and regions, notably Sidon in the south and its Jabal 'Amil hinterland; Tripoli in the north and its hinterland of 'Akkar; the rich plain of the Biqa' in the east; and Beirut, which now became the capital of the new state. It was announced that this new state would extend from the Nahr al-Kabir to the Palestine frontier, and from the sea to the ridge of the Anti-Lebanon. Monsieur Millerand, the French prime minister and minister of foreign affairs, confirmed the decision in a published letter to the Maronite archbishop.

The economic viability of this 'Greater Lebanon' was thus ensured by giving it a Mediterranean frontage as well as a wheat-growing hinterland. The Maronites, France's main local clients, were guaranteed a politically preponderant position in it. The new state was thus conceived as a haven for Christians, but perhaps even more importantly for its French creators, it was a base from which France could control inland Syria and project power in the eastern Mediterranean. (In the same year, 1920, Sir Percy Cox, British high commissioner, created the modern state of Iraq; and just as France favoured the Maronites in Lebanon, so Britain in Iraq favoured the minority Sunni Arab community. Both arrangements were to be the source of much subsequent trouble.)

The areas which General Gouraud detached from Syria and added to Mount Lebanon were long to remain the subject of controversy. Muslim Arab nationalists wanted them returned to Syria, while Christian Lebanese separatists fought ferociously to retain them. These areas contained many Muslims, both Sunni and Shi'i, who now accounted for almost half the population of the new enlarged state. Although the Christians were still dominant, their majority had become a slender one.[10] When campaigning for a separate Greater Lebanon under French protection, fear of being overwhelmed by geographic Syria's Muslim majority had been uppermost in Christian minds.

Pursuing its policy of 'divide and rule', France then created an 'Autonomous territory of the Alawites' in northern Syria, administered by a French officer. In 1922, this 'Autonomous territory' was promoted to a 'state' under a French governor. In the south, a 'state' of Jabal Druze was also created in March 1921, while the Syrian interior was divided into the two separate 'states' of Damascus and Aleppo.

---

[10] The results of the Lebanese census of 1921 were as follows: Maronites 199,181; Sunni Muslims 124,786; Shi'i Muslims 104,947; Greek Orthodox 81,409; Druzes 43,633; Greek Catholics 42,462; Protestants 4,215; Miscellaneous 8,436.

These were only nominally under the rule of local governors. Haqqi Bey al-'Azm – in the case of Damascus – was appointed by the French, and was assisted by directors drawn from the rare families who were prepared to collaborate with the French.

In the north-west of Syria, the sanjaq of Alexandretta, which was of mixed Arab and Turkish population, was given an autonomous status, with special advantages granted the Turks following a Franco-Turkish agreement in 1921. At the same time, the French resettled large numbers of Armenian refugees, survivors of the Turkish massacres of 1915, in the main cities of Syria and Lebanon, while other non-Arab or non-Muslim populations – Assyrians, Chaldeans, Turks, Kurds, among others – were encouraged to settle in the Jazira region of north-east Syria.

This policy of extreme dismemberment, and advantage for the minorities at the expense of the majority, aroused such rancour among Arab nationalists, that in June 1922, in a transparent bid to disguise its monopoly of power, France grouped the 'governments' of Damascus, Aleppo and the Alawites into a 'Federation of the States of Syria'. In January 1924, the Alawites chose to withdraw from the Federation, which was officially dissolved at the end of that year. The Alawite state then recovered its full autonomy. The governments of Aleppo and Damascus were then merged to form the state of Syria.[11] To illustrate the restiveness of the local population, and the headache this caused in Paris, it is worth noting that yet further rearrangements to the Syrian map were made in 1922–25, 1925–36, 1936–39, 1939–42 and 1942.[12]

Armed with full political, legislative and military powers, the French high commissioner presided over this whole ramshackle edifice of 'states', 'autonomous territories' and powerless indigenous 'govern-ments'. His principal assistant was the High Commission's secretary-general – initially Robert de Caix – whose task was to coordinate the work of a dozen civilian directorates managing every aspect of life under the Mandate. At the system's core was the *Direction du service des renseignements*, an intelligence directorate staffed by officers of the *Services Spéciaux*, who, posted throughout the country, behaved like petty despots and aroused tremendous hostility and hatred.

The French Treasury funded the budget of both the High Commission and the Army of the Levant, whereas the various state

---

[11] Consul Satow to Foreign Secretary, 13 March 1921 (FO 371/7846).
[12] For the relevant High Commission decrees, see Mahafzah, 'La France et le mouve-ment nationaliste arabe de 1914 à 1950', pp. 301–2, n. 36.

budgets, artificially swollen by bureaucratic duplication and heavily in deficit, were funded by tax revenues from the local population and, in particular, by an agricultural tax. Customs revenues, which accounted for about 40 per cent of locally raised funds, were administered directly by the High Commission as so-called 'Common Interests', forming a complicated and deliberately obscure item, situated somewhere between the budgets of the High Commission and the Army on the one hand, and local state budgets on the other.[13]

The carving up of Syria weakened the economy badly, damaging both trade and industry. Damascus, in particular, lost a great deal of its financial and commercial importance. Before the war, Egypt, Palestine, the Hijaz, Transjordan, Mesopotamia, Cilicia and Anatolia imported 1.5 million Turkish pounds' worth of Syrian silks and textiles a year, the products of the country's ancient and principal industries, which employed more than 30,000 workers. But the barriers erected by Britain and France in their respective territories destroyed this trade. Syrian agricultural exports of grain, ghee, cotton, wool, apricot paste and nuts were much curtailed. With trade now limited to local needs, merchants' stocks went unsold, industry ground to a halt, unemployment spiralled, and destitution took hold.

Syrian émigrés in the Americas used to remit to their families some 300,000 Turkish pounds a year, but the situation in Syria became so grim that many families were forced to leave to join their relatives across the Atlantic, depriving the country of yet another source of funds. Damascus used to be the starting point of the 2,000-kilometre Hijaz railway, linking the Muslim world with Medina, and therefore with Mecca. Thousands of pilgrims from India, Persia, Turkey, Afghanistan and beyond would gather ceremoniously each year at Damascus for the journey to the Holy Cities, spending some 500,000 Turkish pounds in its markets to equip themselves for the hajj. But, as a result of the Anglo-French Mandates, Syria was left in control of a mere 150 kilometres of the railway line, the rest falling under the separate jurisdictions of Transjordan, Palestine and the Hijaz. These new customs barriers and transport difficulties led many pilgrims to alter this traditional itinerary, which had been the preferred one for centuries, and seek to reach Mecca via the Red Sea port of Jeddah instead.[14]

---

[13] Mizrahi, 'La France et sa politique de mandat', p. 44.

[14] Confidential report by Damascus branch of Banco di Roma to head office in Beirut on 21 March 1922, describing situation in 1921 (FO 371/9053).

Yet another Syrian grievance was the paper currency issued by the French-owned Banque de Syrie et du Liban. Since this was not backed by gold, it fluctuated wildly with the volatile French currency to which it was linked. The Turkish gold pound, in place of the now unreliable Syrian piastre, came to be considered the only firm basis of exchange. In such uncertain conditions, few businessmen were prepared to advance money, leading to a further paralysis of trade. Gold shot up in value, as the French were widely suspected – almost certainly correctly – of shipping large quantities of it out of the country to increase their own reserves at home. Consul Palmer even reported to London: 'It is alleged that gold is being bought on the quiet by [French] members of the Administration as a private speculation!'[15]

The situation in Lebanon was no better. A great many Lebanese had emigrated to the Americas before the war, and the wartime famine drove many more abroad, with the result that barely a third of the original population remained behind. As trade with the interior hit an all-time low, banks in Beirut became reluctant to grant credit. According to the British consul in Beirut, the French-controlled Beirut custom house was corrupt from top to bottom: French officers and officials were accused of receiving liberal presents in exchange for services rendered. One French officer was known to have left Aleppo 50,000 francs richer than when he arrived, after a mere three months' residence there!

A major cause of complaint lay in the nomination of French *conseillers* to every department of the local administration. No action could be taken without their approval. The French use of colonial Senegalese troops, under ferocious orders to be brutal and to break down doors and enter the harem areas of houses, was enraging, as was the contemptuous and high-handed French attitude towards the locals, even the elites amongst them. As the British consul reported, 'French officers have rendered themselves unpopular among ladies belonging to the higher native society at Beirut . . . The words *sale Syrienne* or *sale Syrien*, dropped by individual Frenchmen, are taken as a national insult.'[16] Even those few urban notables, like the 'Azms and the Yusufs, whom the French had succeeded in co-opting, came to realise that

---

[15] Consul Palmer to Foreign Secretary, Damascus, 3 May 1921 (FO 371/6454).
[16] Consul R. A. Fontana to the Foreign Secretary, Earl Curzon, 21 December 1920 (FO 372/6453).

they had enjoyed far more freedom and much greater respect under Ottoman rule.

Nevertheless, and despite their abominable behaviour, the French had a somewhat easier time in Syria and Lebanon in the very early 1920s – at least initially – than the British did in Iraq. This was no doubt due to the way they had plotted to dismember Syrian territory, as well as to the fact that most of the engaged nationalist leaders had left the country with the Emir Faysal.

But the real challenge to French rule was still to come, with the outbreak of the Great Syrian Revolution of 1925. In the meantime, resistance was sporadic. Battalions of *méharistes* – colonial troops mounted on camels – were sent to subdue the proudly defiant and constantly rebellious tribes of the eastern desert around Dayr al-Zor. In the Alawite territory, the single uprising by Shaykh Salih al-'Ali in October 1921 was put down. On the whole, the Alawites tended to accept French military administration, specifically designed to encourage an Alawite particularism, distinct from the rest of Sunni Syria. This divisive policy has had grave consequences, even to our own day.

At about the same time, French troops quelled uprisings in the Hawran, and occupied the Jabal Druze in the south of the country. The Kurdish notable, 'Abd al-Rahman al-Yusuf, who had rallied to the French and had joined a puppet administration in Damascus under 'Ala' al-Din al-Drubi, was assassinated in August 1920 for his pro-French and anti-nationalist leanings. The train on which he was travelling was attacked by an armed band from the Hawran when it reached the station at Khirbat al-Ghazala. Al-Drubi and a French liaison officer were also killed at the same time. The French punitively razed the entire village in retaliation for their killing. In the Aleppo region, a nationalist leader, Ibrahim Hananu, rose against the French in the last months of 1920 and the beginning of 1921. Pursued by French forces, he took refuge in Transjordan, but was handed back to the French by the British, put on trial and sentenced. He was eventually freed because of the great popular following he enjoyed.

When a Franco-Turkish armistice was signed in October 1921, the new boundary cut the former Ottoman vilayet of Halab (Aleppo) in two. Tariff barriers separated the city from its traditional commercial hinterland in southern and central Anatolia. Hananu might perhaps have preferred that Aleppo join Mustafa Kemal's newly emerging Turkey, rather than become part of a French-run protectorate. Indeed, had they been given the choice, some Aleppines might well have preferred such an association with Kemalist Turkey, or even citizenship in a state combining northern Syria with northern Iraq, rather than the humiliating position of subjection to a colonial mandate centred on Damascus. Indeed, it was not until the end of the 1920s that Aleppo came to a grudging acceptance of its fate as the new Syrian Arab Republic's second city, after its traditional urban rival, Damascus.[17]

On 27 June 1921, General Gouraud narrowly escaped assassination. He was heading for Quneitra on the Golan Heights in a convoy of four motor cars when four men on horseback, dressed as gendarmes, opened fire on his vehicle at close range. The General ducked, but not before three bullets passed through his clothing. His interpreter, Lieutenant Branet, was killed. The attackers were almost certainly Druze from the Emir 'Abdallah's principality in Transjordan, a fact which did little to improve Anglo-French relations. When Palmer, the British consul, called on Gouraud to congratulate him on his escape, he was kept waiting for half an hour, and then told that the General was too busy to see him.[18]

French reprisals were brutal against villages that were thought to shelter rebels. To placate the French, Winston Churchill, the colonial secretary, wrote to General Gouraud on 31 March 1921:

> *I am most anxious to give you effective security from raids and annoyance of all kinds. I have made an arrangement with Abdallah [of Transjordan] of an informal and temporary character whereby he is to use his whole influence to prevent any disturbances in the French zone ... His principal difficulty will be the Syrian exiles, who are roaming about in Transjordania homeless and hungry.*

Churchill, tellingly, received no reply to his over-solicitousness.

Therefore, on another occasion, when the French Foreign Ministry complained to London about a raid from Transjordan on the

---

[17] Peter Sluglett, 'Will the Real Nationalists Stand up? The Political Activities of the Notables of Aleppo, 1918–1946', in Méouchy (ed.), *France, Syrie et Liban*, pp. 282–4.

[18] Consul Palmer to Foreign Secretary, Damascus, 27 June 1921 (FO 371/6461) and 4 July 1921 (FO 371/6455).

Druze capital of Suweida, Lord Hardinge, the British ambassador to Paris, was instructed to reply curtly:

> As the French Government are aware, His Majesty's Government have felt bound by the statements made to the King of the Hedjaz in support of Arab Nationalist aspirations during the war and by such declarations of policy as the proclamation issued by Lord Allenby on the 9th November 1918, to do their utmost in Mesopotamia and in the Arab territories east of the Jordan falling within their mandatory zone to establish a form of government acceptable to the people. Having deliberately fostered the growth of Nationalist sentiments through the Shereefian channel as a weapon against the Turks, His Majesty's Government could not disregard these sentiments when the war was over.
>
> The French government ... have regarded themselves, in their relations with the Arab Nationalists and their Shereefian leaders, as under no such obligations as His Majesty's Government ... This divergence of view ... and of policy ... is ... the reason why the zone of Transjordania ... has become the refuge of a large number of Arabs exiled from Syria ... and bitterly anti-French in sentiment.[19]

By pretending that Britain's approach to Arab nationalism was different from that of the French, Hardinge was saying that France had brought its problems upon itself. But the British were being pompously obtuse in this. In the popularity stakes, they certainly did not fare much better than the French. Britain had betrayed the Arabs by abandoning the Emir Faysal, while backing the Zionist takeover of Palestine.

The politics of exile in Cairo

Such was the grim reality confronting Riad el-Solh and his fellow Arab exiles as they gathered dejectedly in Cairo in the early 1920s. All their hopes of national independence had turned to dust. Trusting in British

---

[19] FO 371/6461.

guarantees, and at great peril to themselves, the Arabs had joined forces with the Allies against the Ottomans. This short-sighted and foolish switch of allegiance had cost them dearly. Their leaders had been tortured in Jamal Pasha's fearsome citadel-prison in Damascus and in his jail cells at Aley. Hundreds had died by hanging or had suffered banishment and impoverishment. It was now clear that these terrible sacrifices had been made in vain. Arab troops who had fought side by side with the British in Sinai, Palestine and Syria, were rewarded by having their Arab lands dismembered and an Arab government in Damascus destroyed; by seeing French and British colonial rule imposed on them by force, and Palestine handed over to the Zionists. In Syria, the French had even adopted Jamal Pasha's cruel practice of death or banishment for nationalists. Most of the members of the Emir Faysal's two cabinets had, at one time or another, been arrested and hauled before military courts or convicted by these in absentia. Such French repression caused scores of Syrians to flee to Europe, to the Americas and to Egypt. In Cairo, the political climate seemed somewhat less oppressive than in other Arab capitals. Among the newcomers in the city, Riad el-Solh was not the only person under a sentence of death.

In Cairo, these exhausted men found an already well-established Syrian community, with its own businesses and newspapers, which opened its homes and clubs to them. But, this small mercy apart, their great dream of Arab freedom had turned into nightmare. Conversations in the city's political salons which Riad frequented were bitter. He found himself the youngest in a community of political exiles, of which the leading figures were ten, twenty, and sometimes thirty years his senior. These were men of substance and talent, who had won recognition in their various careers and were now down on their luck. For these older men – several of whom, like his own father, had been officials of the Ottoman Empire – the situation was particularly pathetic. They had already had to adapt to the collapse of the once great Empire; to the disruption of their eminent careers and the loss of their precious pensions. Now they had also to come to terms with the damaging dismemberment and division of their *patrie*, as well as to the diktats of new thuggish imperial masters. The institutions and symbols by which they had always defined themselves had been blotted out by force.[20]

---

[20] William L. Cleveland, *Islam Against the West: Shakib Arslan and the Campaign for Islamic Nationalism*, London and Austin, TX 1985, p. 47.

As ever in such situations, this émigré community was no united body. Rather, it was riven by ambitions, ideological disputes, rival allegiances and sharp personal antipathies. One of the most prestigious salons in Cairo was that of Michel Lutfallah, a leading light of Egypt's Syro-Lebanese community. He and his two brothers were the sons of Habib Pasha, an enterprising Greek Orthodox merchant and moneylender, who, having invested heavily in cotton plantations in the Nile valley, had watched himself become one of Egypt's richest landowners. The Egyptian government made him a pasha, while the Sharif Husayn of Mecca, whom he served as adviser and banker after the Young Turk revolution of 1908, had him dubbed *amir*.

Born in 1880, Michel Lutfallah inherited his father's considerable wealth, which he put to work in advancing his great political ambitions. In 1910, aged 30, he was elected to Egypt's first legislative assembly, as representative of the Syrian colony. He had been active in the Decentralisation Party until its dissolution in the First World War. He had then rallied the former 'decentralists' from among the Syrian community to found the Party of Syrian Unity (*hizb al-'ittihad al-suri*) in January 1919. A copy of the party statutes and a list of the twenty-one members of its central committee were sent to the French Foreign Ministry in Paris. Prince Lutfallah is rumoured to have secretly hoped that the French would consider him a candidate for the throne of Damascus, or, failing that, at least put him at the head of a Lebanese principality.

Lutfallah also rallied to the Hashemite camp, giving his support to the Sharif Husayn, just as his own father had done before him. Apart from ruling his Kingdom of the Hijaz, which he created at the time of the Arab Revolt in 1916, the Sharif had promoted himself 'King of the Arabs'. One of Michel Lutfallah's younger brothers, Habib Junior, had represented the Kingdom of the Hijaz at the Peace Conference and, in 1923, had set up an embassy for it in Rome – the first Arab embassy to open in Europe. Husayn's Kingdom only lasted until December 1925, when, having been abandoned by the British, it fell to Ibn Sa'ud's fighters. In the nine years of its existence, it had managed to win international recognition and, as an ally of the Entente Powers, had been one of the original members of the League of Nations. Husayn did not, however, ratify the Treaty of Versailles, claiming with justice that Arab rights had been violated by Article 22 of the League's charter which set up the Mandates.

One of Michel Lutfallah's main allies in Cairo was Dr 'Abd al-Rahman al-Shahbandar, a doctor of medicine, who had been trained by American missionaries at the Syrian Protestant College in Beirut. He had been an early supporter of the Young Turks, but, disappointed with their 'Turkification' policies, he had gone on to campaign for Arab equality with Turks. But, when he found himself in danger of being sent to the gallows, he fled to Cairo in 1916. There, during the war, he made friends with Hashemite representatives and with some British officials of the Arab Bureau, arousing the unfounded suspicion that he had been recruited as a British spy. When Syria was 'liberated' from the Turks, Shahbandar returned to Damascus, where the Emir Faysal made him his chief liaison officer with Allenby's forces. He then appointed him foreign minister in the final weeks of his Arab Kingdom, in order to placate hardline nationalists spoiling for a fight with the French, but to no avail. Following the battle of Maysalun, and shortly before he was condemned to death by the French, Shahbandar fled again from Damascus to Cairo, where he joined Lutfallah and others in their debates about what to do to continue the struggle.

Riad el-Solh was a frequent visitor at the Lutfallah mansion, where he became well acquainted with Prince Michel himself and with Dr Shahbandar. However, he was more attracted to the rival camp of the aristocratic politician, the Emir Shakib Arslan, who was to have a considerable influence over him. Of lesser wealth, but of older lineage and greater distinction than Lutfallah, Arslan was born in 1869 to a noble Druze family of Lebanon. He was a sophisticated thinker and political activist, whose intellectual gifts were noticed while he was still a schoolboy – first at a Maronite school in Beirut, where he learned French and Arabic; then at the *Sultaniye* state school, where he learned Turkish. He fell under the influence of the remarkable Shaykh Muhammad 'Abduh, the celebrated Egyptian Islamic reformer. This was during the years which 'Abduh spent in exile in Beirut, following the British occupation of Egypt in 1882.

From 1913 to 1918, the Emir Shakib Arslan had sat in the Ottoman parliament as a deputy for Mount Lebanon. He became a firm believer in Arab-Turkish unity, under the banner of pan-Islam. Also close to the Young Turks, he had approved Turkey's entry into the war on the side of the Germans, and had spent some time in Berlin. Michel Lutfallah, on the other hand, backed the Sharif Husayn, and preferred to court Britain and France.

Shakib Arslan was a lifelong enemy of British and French imperialism, and an anti-Hashemite by extension, believing – rightly, as it turned out – that the Sharif's 'Arab Revolt' had been nothing but a treacherous and costly mistake. Western threats to the Arabs, he argued, could be countered only by the rise of an Islamic power, grounded in a strong Islamic tradition – a view that has great resonance in today's Muslim world. Salvation lay in the regeneration of the Islamic world. The Islamic bond uniting Arabs and Turks was the sole effective barrier against the greed of European Powers, who had conspired to dismantle the Ottoman Empire and were now hungrily sharing out the spoils. The hated Mandate system was simply one more manifestation of such European perfidy.[21]

Shakib Arslan's main ally in Cairo was Ihsan al-Jabiri, born in 1882, who, after taking an advanced law degree from Paris, had had a noted career as an Ottoman official. His older brother Nafi' Pasha had served in both the first and second Ottoman parliaments, while his younger brother, Sa'dallah – Riad el-Solh's friend from their years in Istanbul – was to become a leading nationalist politician in Syria and a future prime minister. The Jabiris were the most sophisticated and politically powerful family in Aleppo at the time.[22] Ihsan's familiarity with Europe had led Faysal to make him head of his *diwan* in 1918 – his political chief of staff. He had also served as mayor of Aleppo, but, once the French occupied Syria, he too left for Cairo, and was sentenced to death in absentia. Ihsan al-Jabiri shared Shakib Arslan's view that an alliance with the Turks against Western imperialism was highly desirable, especially since Mustafa Kemal was then fighting the French in Cilicia in 1920–21, and had taken to supplying arms to the anti-French rebels in northern Syria.[23]

Another great Syrian figure in Cairo at that time was Shaykh Rashid Rida, born in 1865, who had become the disciple of Shaykh Muhammad 'Abduh and the devoted guardian of his ideas. In 1897, Rida left Syria for Cairo and, the following year, brought out the first number of his periodical, *al-Manar*, which he continued to publish

---

[21] Ibid., pp. 8 ff.
[22] For the Jabiri family and the Aleppo environment at the time, see Keith David Waterpaugh, *Being Modern in the Middle East: Revolution, Nationalism, Colonialism and the Arab Middle Class*, Princeton 2006.
[23] Philip S. Khoury, 'Factionalism Among Syrian Nationalists During the French Mandate', in *International Journal of Middle Eastern Studies*, 13 (1981), pp. 441–69.

more or less regularly until his death in 1935. It became the main organ publishing and explaining 'Abduh's ideas of Islamic reform.

Rashid Rida was not only a theologian. He was very much a political activist, who played a large part in Syria's political struggles, from the Young Turk revolution onwards. He had joined the Decentralisation Party before 1914, was involved in the difficult wartime negotiations with the British, and had chaired the General Syrian Congress which proclaimed Syrian independence in Damascus on 8 March 1920 – an epoch-making event in which Riad el-Solh had participated, together with his father and his cousin 'Afif.[24]

Rashid Rida was decidedly not in the Lutfallah–Shahbandar camp. He did not share their pro-Hashemite sympathies. But nor did he approve of the Arslan–Jabiri alliance. In fact, he was at loggerheads with Shakib Arslan on the question of Arab-Turkish relations. Whereas Arslan continued to champion the cause of unity between Arabs and Turks after the collapse of the Ottoman Empire, Rida was committed to their separation, holding the Ottomans responsible for the decadence of the world of Islam. The cause that he did come to champion was that of Arab pre-eminence in the greater Muslim world.

Yet another group of activists in Cairo at that time were members of the Arab Independence Party (*hizb al-'istiqlal al-'arabi*), which had been created as a political front for the secret society, *al-fatat*. Members of this party were situated, in terms of age, somewhere between Shakib Arslan's generation and that of Riad el-Solh. Among the leading Istiqlalists in Cairo were 'Adil Arslan, Shakib's young brother, and the patrician Damascene, Shukri al-Quwatli. 'Adil, born in 1882, had served the Ottoman state as *qa'im maqam* of the Shuf region of Lebanon in 1915–16, and then, when Faysal took over, was promoted *mutasarrif* of Mount Lebanon, a post he held until chased out by the French. Shukri al-Quwatli, born in 1886, had made his name as an early and committed nationalist and member of *al-'ahd*. He had joined Faysal's administration, but had gone to Cairo like so many others once Faysal was ousted.

Of all the rival groups in Cairo, Riad el-Solh was closest to the Istiqlalists. They were anti-British, anti-French, anti-Hashemite, outspokenly pan-Arab and totally devoted to the Arab nationalist and

---

[24] See the chapter on Rashid Rida in Albert Hourani, *Arabic Thought in the Liberal Age, 1798–1939*, Oxford 1962, pp. 222–44.

Palestinian causes.[25] These were sentiments he fully shared. He had, in fact, already joined the *Istiqlal* Party in Damascus. It was to be his link both to Shukri al-Quwatli and to Shakib Arslan, with whom he was later to work closely in Geneva.

The Syro-Palestinian Congress in Geneva

The idea of convening a great gathering of nationalists in Geneva was the brainchild of Prince Michel Lutfallah. The Party of Syrian Unity, which he had founded in 1919 and of which he was president, took the initiative of inviting to the meeting all the prominent supporters of Syrian independence and unity. He and his brother George, to their credit, met most of the costly expenses. Geneva was chosen as the venue, since the second General Assembly of the League of Nations was due to meet there from 5 September to 5 October, to discuss the question of the Mandates.

Between the wars, Geneva was the unrivalled forum of inter-national politics, where representatives of a dozen national causes came to put their case to the League – and none more assiduously, as the 1920s wore on, than did the Arabs. Lutfallah's idea was that his conference would unify the Syrian national movement, formulate a coherent stance against the Mandates, and inform the League of the severe injustice that was being done to the Arabs. It was inconceivable, he thought, that the League would justify the way the Mandates had been imposed.

The founding conference – known at first as the Syrian Congress, but referred to later as the Syro-Palestinian Congress – opened on 25 July 1921, with delegates attending from many parts of the world. It consisted of the first organised manifestation of Arab protest against the Mandates.[26] A strong contingent came from Cairo, including Prince Michel Lutfallah himself and Shaykh Rashid Rida, with Riad el-Solh as one of the representatives of the *Istiqlal*. The

[25] Khoury, 'Factionalism', p. 449.

[26] Philip S. Khoury, *Syria and the French Mandate: The Politics of Arab Nationalism, 1920–1945*, London and Princeton 1987, pp. 220–7; Marie-Renée Mouton, 'Le Congrès syro-palestinien de Genève (1921)', in *Relations internationales*, no. 19 (autumn 1979), pp. 313–28; Antoine Fleury, 'Le Mouvement national arabe à Genève durant l'entre-deux-guerres', in *Relations internationales*, no. 19 (autumn 1979), pp. 329–54; Cleveland, *Islam Against the West*, p. 49.

Emir Shakib Arslan and Shukri al-Quwatli travelled to the conference from Berlin, where they were at the time. A score of delegates came from Beirut and the Syrian interior, but their names were kept secret to protect them from the severe punishment which the French High Commission had threatened would be inflicted on anyone who was discovered attending. One delegate represented the exiled members of the former Administrative Council of Mount Lebanon, banished to Corsica for having agreed, on Riad el-Solh's prompting, to side with the Emir Faysal against France. Palestinians from Jerusalem and Egypt sent delegates, as did associations of Syrian exiles in New York, Boston, Chile and Argentina.

One of the first tasks of the delegates was to elect three of their number to leading positions on the executive committee of the Congress: Prince Michel Lutfallah was elected president; Shaykh Rashid Rida, vice-president; and the Emir Shakib Arslan, secretary-general. As foreign journalists flocked to Geneva to cover the League's General Assembly, Lutfallah seized the opportunity to summon and address a press conference.[27] He wanted the League, the Swiss and the world to know the 'truth about the Syrian question': the Mandate was contrary to the principles and pledges of the Allies; the Syrian people refused to accept it, and demanded the natural right to be consulted about their future; they wanted their independence under international guarantees.

French intelligence agents from the French embassy in Berne denounced the Geneva meeting as 'Anglo-Syrian intrigues against France', but Lutfallah dismissed such misplaced accusations: 'We want to preserve our traditional relations with France. But we reject all foreign domination. We do not want the French to be our masters.' Lutfallah invited several journalists to a lavish dinner at which he repeated this same message. He denied totally the rumours of a hidden British hand behind the Congress. Syrians had once believed in France's liberating mission, he said, but had found themselves subjected to a repressive colonial regime.

Other members at the Congress denounced France's military brutalities: the carpet bombing of rebellious villages, the death sentences passed in absentia, the martial law enforced by an occupation army of 80,000 men; and exposed the brutish mediocrity of French

---

[27] Mouton, 'Le Congrès syro-palestinien', for many of the details which follow.

officials sent to rule over Syrians, most of whom were far better educated and far more sophisticated than they.

The main preoccupation of the Jerusalem delegates was obviously the struggle against Zionism. They had come to Geneva from London, where, in talks with British officials, they had attempted to have the Balfour Declaration annulled – a declaration, in Count Bernadotte's memorable phrase, in which 'one nation promised a second nation, the country of a third'. They wanted the principle of a 'national home' for the Jews on their land cancelled completely. Indeed, it was at the request of the Palestinians that the name of the Congress was changed to the Syro-Palestinian Congress, to mark the gravity of what was actually taking place. But this did not win unanimous support, foreshadowing the schism of 1922, when Palestinian representatives withdrew in anger from the Congress, protesting that it was not paying enough attention to their increasingly urgent cause.

Despite its intense lobbying, the Congress was to suffer a bitter disappointment. The League's Council chose not to question the principle of the Mandates, nor to reverse any of the high-handed decisions taken at San Remo. Indeed, the Syrian, Lebanese and Palestinian delegations were not even allowed the chance to put their case to the Council! Following this setback, the Congress suspended its session from 9 to 20 September, and then held a closing session on 21 September, in which five resolutions were passed unanimously. These were:

1. Recognition of the independence and sovereignty of Syria, Lebanon and Palestine.
2. The right of these countries to unite under a civilian parliamentary government and to federate with other Arab states.
3. The immediate termination of the Mandates.
4. The evacuation of Anglo-French troops from Syria, Lebanon and Palestine.
5. The annulment of the Balfour Declaration.

These resolutions were then submitted to the League with a renewed request for 'an impartial enquiry to discover the real situation of the country and to ascertain that these final resolutions truly reflect the aspirations of the people'. The resolutions were clearly pan-Arab in tenor, indicating that the majority at the Congress had moved beyond the 'Greater Syrian' aspirations of Lutfallah's Syrian Union Party, and more towards the all-out Arab nationalism of the Istiqlalists and of Shukri al-Quwatli, to which Shakib Arslan had added a galvanisingly pan-Islamic tone. Mustafa Kemal's success that summer in driving the Greeks out of Anatolia won the admiration of the Arabs, reviving Arslan's hopes of an alliance with the as yet untried Kemalists, in order to drive the French out of Syria.

The Congress did not, however, manage to do much more than to paper over the profound differences between its leading members. The Western-educated and Christian Michel Lutfallah or the secular doctor 'Abd al-Rahman al-Shahbandar could not easily be reconciled with the Ottoman-educated and profoundly Islamic Shakib Arslan and Rashid Rida.

In Mecca, the Sharif Husayn had followed the debates among the Syrian exiles in Cairo, and knew very well whom among them he could count on as followers, and whom to consider opponents. When Michel Lutfallah's brother, George, came to Jiddah on 25 November 1921 to seek help for the Congress, Husayn gave a banquet in his honour, but regretted that he could not be of any assistance, since 'two members of the Congress, Shaykh Rashid Rida and Shakib Arslan, were inimical both to him personally and to the Hijaz'.[28]

In Palestine, Iraq and Lebanon, as men struggled to cope with the constraints of their respective Mandates, distinct national loyalties began to emerge. The Syrians, however, continued at a loss. The hiving off, by European plotting, of Lebanon and Palestine from the body of geographical Syria, and the division of the remaining rump into yet smaller 'states', left their national feeling with no clear focus. As a result, 'Syrian' nationalism turned outwards, and was replaced by a wider Arab nationalism. The overly optimistic idea took hold that a union with other Arab countries might be easier to achieve than the immediate reunification of Syria proper, and that it might even be the necessary first step towards that goal.[29]

The Congress completed its work by deciding to establish a Cairo-based executive committee (hailed as a step on the road to reviving Arab hopes), as well as a representative office in Geneva. This latter body became known as the Permanent Delegation of the Syro-Palestinian Congress to the League of Nations, and was directed by the

---

[28] Jiddah report by Major W. E. Marshall, British Agent and Consul, October–November 1921 (FO 371/6255).

[29] Hourani, *Arabic Thought in the Liberal Age*, p. 317.

Emir Shakib Arslan and Ihsan al-Jabiri, two men who were to become Riad el-Solh's closest colleagues in the years ahead.

The only journalist allowed to follow the proceedings of the Congress from inside the conference hall was a Swiss of Egyptian origin, Ali el-Ghaïaty. He was forced to flee Egypt in 1910, for publishing a collection of patriotic verse, which neither the British nor the Khedive had appreciated. He settled in Geneva and married the daughter of a Swiss State Counsellor, a move that helped establish him in Helvetian society. He became the editor of *La Tribune de Genève*, as well as the Geneva correspondent of *Correspondance d'Orient*, a bimonthly journal of the Syrian central committee in Paris. In these papers over the following years, he published the innumerable letters, messages, petitions, memoranda and telegrams which the executive committee of the Syro-Palestinian Congress addressed to the League – many of them signed by Shakib Arslan, Ihsan al-Jabiri and Riad el-Solh – as well as reports of the Mandates commission, and the speeches that were delivered at the Assembly of the League.

But this avalanche of protests and petitions produced no result whatsoever. France and Britain were not about to give way. In fact, in 1922, the League went so far as to endorse the very texts of the Mandates. For all its immense efforts, the Congress had attracted little international attention. These efforts seemed increasingly like a desperate attempt to reverse the outcome of a battle that had already been lost. As the Congress drew to its close, a Paris newspaper, *Le Temps*, published a short and dismissive item on 19 September, under the heading, 'A so-called Syrian delegation'. In the National Assembly, Prime Minister Aristide Briand declared in ringing tones that sympathy for France was growing in Syria, that France was a generous and pacifying nation, which was bringing reforms to loyal peoples. He derided the Geneva delegates as a bunch of rootless agitators and conspirators, in the pay of France's enemies.

Riad el-Solh travelled back to Cairo after the Congress. His finances were at an even lower point than usual, and he was homesick. Although not quite 30, he had made his mark in Geneva, and had managed to impress men who were far older and more experienced than he was. It was time to go home and ponder his next step.

In December 1923, and with considerable relief, he learned that his two pending sentences had finally been annulled. A few weeks later, in early 1924, he returned to Beirut for the first time in nearly four years, armed with a safe-conduct from the French High Commissioner General Weygand. Once there, he discovered, to his dismay, that his father, Rida, had been forced to give the French authorities assurances guaranteeing that his son would steer clear of politics. But this, for a man like Riad el-Solh, was a totally impossible constraint that he had no intention of respecting, whatever the consequences.

Riad's journalistic venture

Riad had often dreamed of owning a newspaper, which he felt was an essential tool in the struggle in which he was engaged. He liked to quip to his eldest daughter, Alia, that the press was like 'the wife of the government'; on her depended the peace of the home. If the wife was satisfied, peace would reign. If frustrated, all hell would break loose. 'The press has an advantage over us politicians', he would say. 'It can address a wide public with speed and regularity. The daily ritual of reading a newspaper can shape a man's mind in a way no politician can ever hope to do!'[30]

Once back in Lebanon in 1924, Riad quickly launched a newspaper that would give voice to Arab aspirations. His partner in the project was Khayr al-Din Ahdab, who was from a Sunni Muslim family, originally from Tripoli, but that had settled in Beirut. Ahdab's grandfather had served as an Ottoman judge. Khayr al-Din had studied mathematics at the Sorbonne, and had found work at the French High Commission on his return to Beirut. He had also been employed for a while on his uncle's estate in the Biqa' valley, where he met and married Olga Musallam, a Christian girl from a prominent Zahleh family. A young man in the big city, he was eager for political and social success, and may have thought that editing a newspaper would help him to achieve it. He was an out-and-out Arab nationalist, who was highly critical of Mount Lebanon's Maronite politicians, whose narrow particularism and anti-Arab prejudices contrasted with the tolerant coexistence of Muslims and Christians in Beirut and other Syrian coastal cities.

To launch the newspaper, Nazira, Riad's mother, sold a property she owned in Beirut, which allowed the two young men to rent a couple of rooms on the ground floor of a building behind the old

[30] Alia el-Solh, *Le Jour*, 28 November 1965.

French Lycée on the Damascus Road. The name they chose for their publication, al-'Ahd al-Jadid, meant 'The New Age' of freedom to which they aspired.

An agreement was drawn up between the two men. It stated that:

> The two parties will publish a political newspaper of four pages – three in Arabic, one in French – under the title al-'Ahd al-Jadid. They will be joint owners and will share expenditure and receipts equally.
>
> Khayr al-Din Ahdab will be named as the founder and responsible director of the newspaper, but this will not confer on him any advantage over his partner, Riad el-Solh who, if he so wishes, can at any moment also have his name appear on the masthead as co-founder and proprietor.
>
> All decisions regarding the newspaper (its administration, editorial content, printing, distribution; its contracts and agreements of any sort with third parties) will be by mutual consent.
>
> All items of expenditure and all receipts must be revealed to the other party and approved by it.
>
> The political line of the journal will be as defined in the first issue. Neither party has the right to modify or change it without the approval of the other.
>
> If the authorities close down the newspaper, or suspend its publication, and if the parties decide to publish another newspaper, or the same one under a different name, or in a different form, or to transfer its offices out of Beirut, this contract will apply to the new newspaper, wherever it is published and under whatever title.
>
> Neither party has the right to break away from the other in order to found another newspaper, or to associate with another proprietor, or to benefit in any way from the subscribers of al-'Ahd al-Jadid, except with the consent of the other.
>
> The present contract will be valid for seven years from the date of signature. When it expires, the parties have the right to renew it, modify it, or annul it.

> *The clauses of this contract are binding on both*
> *parties. In the event of any violation, the guilty party*
> *will pay the other a fine of one thousand gold pounds in*
> *compensation.*

As indicated, the partners agreed that Khayr al-Din's name alone would appear on the masthead and that he alone would sign editorials. Giving prominence to Riad's name would not, at this stage, have served their interests, as the High Commission's press office would simply not have allowed the newspaper's publication. Riad had had too many clashes with the French, and they considered him their bête noire. In the meantime, Nazira continued to foot the mounting bills. The staff consisted of Khayr al-Din Ahdab, editor-in-chief; Riad el-Solh, Arab affairs expert (and foreign correspondent when in exile or forced to flee abroad); Ahmad Dimashqiyeh, secretary and typographer; and Abu 'Ali Sarduq, doorkeeper and porter, who, every night, would carry the pages of type on his back to al-Ma'rad printing press, owned by Riad's friend, Michel Zakkur, who charged them knock-down prices, or would sometimes waive payment altogether.

Frequent interruptions or suspensions could not be avoided. Either the merchant supplying the newsprint would halt deliveries because he had not been paid, or Abu 'Ali would go on strike for his wages. The High Commission would sometimes stop publication for a few days or a few weeks. On one occasion, it decided that the sheet was altogether too revolutionary and closed it down completely, placing a seal on its office doors. But, somehow or other, the newspaper always managed to reappear. Number 475, for example (in the author's possession) appeared on Monday, 14 May 1928, in the fourth year of publication.

A single number of the paper cost one Syrian piastre; a year's subscription in Beirut cost one Turkish gold pound; for readers abroad, a subscription cost two pounds sterling. But raising money to keep things going was always a problem. The French *Sûreté Générale* (Police Intelligence department) in Beirut reported to Paris on 2 June 1927 that Rida el-Solh, Riad's father, had arrived in Beirut, and had called on several members of the 'Muslim Youth', notably the brothers Jabr, as well as 'Abd al-Rahman and Muhammad 'Ali Bayhum, to drum up subscriptions for *al-'Ahd al-Jadid*.

The newspaper was a forerunner of other journals which were to devote themselves to the cause of independence from France.

Al-Sha'b, founded in 1927 under the patronage of Jamil Mardam, was closely affiliated to the Syrian National Bloc. The more radical *al-Qabas*, founded a year later, was the successor of the famous nationalist newspaper, *al-Muqtabas*. It was published and edited by 'Adil Kurd 'Ali and Najib and Munir al-Rayyis.

The Great Syrian Revolution of 1925–26 was soon to provide *al-'Ahd al-Jadid* with the story of the decade. Stridently anti-French, it threw itself heart and soul into the struggle, inevitably suffering repeated closures. The Revolution propelled Riad onto the international stage, because he was soon abroad throwing all his energies into alerting international opinion to what was happening in Syria. The Revolution launched him as an international advocate of the Arab cause. He was quick to realise that the catastrophic defeat that the nationalists soon suffered called for a fundamental change of tactics. Instead of engaging in unequal combat with the French army in the Jabal Druze and in the villages around Damascus – a suicidal enterprise, as it turned out – it was wiser to seek to win French hearts and minds in the French capital itself. Only by persuading the French public of the errors of their government's Syrian policy would that policy ever change. It was in France – not in Syria – that the nationalists should now do battle.

The nationalists, Riad believed, should seek to put the French government in the dock of world opinion. This could best be done by lobbying the newly formed League of Nations in Geneva, and especially its Permanent Mandates Commission. Accordingly, from an office in Geneva in the second half of the 1920s, Riad el-Solh and his two older colleagues, the Emir Shakib Arslan and Ihsan al-Jabiri, were to bombard the League with a stream of petitions, letters and memoranda on the theme of Syrian independence. Riad's reputation as the standard-bearer of Arab nationalism was earned not only in Damascus, Aleppo and Beirut, but in the anterooms of the French National Assembly, in the newsrooms of French newspapers, and, above all, in the Geneva office lobbying the League of Nations. No Arab nationalist of his generation was as assiduous in promoting this cause in Europe. In the space of a mere three years, Riad el-Solh's status and reputation underwent a profound change. In 1924, outside the narrow circle of Arab exiles, he was still relatively unknown. By 1927, he had become a celebrity in the Arab world. He was now of increasing interest, not only to politicians and to the media, but also to the security services of France and other European countries.

7 THE GREAT SYRIAN REVOLUTION

The Revolt against the French of 1925–26, which the Syrians refer to as their 'Great Revolution', started in the Jabal Druze in the south of the country, before spreading to Damascus, Hama and areas further north. Although it was put down with great loss of life and massive destruction, it was to become an enduring landmark in Syria's struggle for independence. It created a nationalist epic as potent as that forged in Iraq by the uprising of 1920–21 against the British. By challenging the imperial pretensions of Britain and France, these popular insurrections were to have a major impact – felt to this very day – on the national identities of both Syria and Iraq.

The Druze of Syria were, and still are, a compact, warlike community, largely of Arab stock but with Kurdish and Persian elements. They practise an esoteric religion linked to a heterodox form of Shi'ism. As well as a belief in predestination and the transmigration of souls, the Druze are said to consider the Fatimid Caliph al-Hakim as the last divine incarnation in human form. Founded nearly a thousand years ago by Darazi, who was of Turco-Persian origin, this mysterious sect enjoyed relative isolation and independence in the mountains of southern Syria until modern times. Its members lived in small village communities under the control of local 'uqala, guardians of the faith, themselves subordinate to one or more emirs.[1] Today, Druze communities are to be found in Syria, Lebanon and Israel.

Druze power reached its zenith in the early seventeenth century, under the Emir Fakhr al-Din II (1585–1635), a figure of legendary status, who managed to bring most of Syria under his sway. When the

---

[1] See Philip K. Hitti, *The Origins of the Druze People and Religion, with Extracts from their Sacred Writings*, New York 1928.

Ottomans sent an army to subdue him, he sought refuge at the court of the Medici in Florence. In later times, during the civil war of 1860 in Mount Lebanon, the Druze community killed over ten thousand Christians in Zahleh, Dayr al-Qamar, Hasbaya and other Lebanese towns and villages, prompting a muscular European intervention.

On taking control of Syria in 1920, the French issued a so-called 'Druze Charter of Independence', and carved out a Druze mini-state, nominally ruled by a Druze governor, assisted by an elected council or *majlis*. But once French troops were garrisoned in the Druze capital of Suwayda, the whole community came under close French supervision. As governor, the French appointed Salim al-Atrash, a member of a family which had achieved local prominence. But the Atrash family were not all of one mind. There were important tensions within it. These were notably between Salim, who had been an Ottoman loyalist, and his more forceful and charismatic cousin Sultan, who – after his father had been hanged by the Turks – rallied to the Arab Revolt and became a committed supporter of the Hashemites, believing, naively as it turned out, in Britain's honourable intentions.

Sultan al-Atrash organised a local rebellion against the Turks in the Hawran and the Jabal Druze, in association with Nasib al-Bakri. When, therefore, the French occupied Syria, al-Atrash was not one to collaborate with them. He had no time for their phoney 'Druze Charter of Independence', which gave far too much away to the French themselves. When the Great Syrian Revolution broke out in 1925, he became a central figure around whom various insurgent leaders rallied.[2]

Most Syrians were wholly opposed to the Mandate, which they felt had established an illegal French presence in their country. France's colonial-style rule was bitterly resented, as was the annexation to Mount Lebanon of large slices of Syrian territory in order to create Greater Lebanon. But this was not all: the separation of Palestine from Syria, and Britain's unstinting support for the Zionist project, were further major grievances. The first objective of the nationalists, therefore, was Syrian unity in the widest sense – including elimination of the artificial frontiers drawn by the British and the French. They wished to expel France from Syria altogether. Men and women who held such

---

[2] Michael Provence, *The Great Syrian Revolt and the Rise of Arab Nationalism*, Austin, TX 2005, pp. 12, 189.

views were to be found throughout society, but most notably in the majority Sunni population.

When Lord Balfour visited Damascus on 8 April 1925, for example, he found ten thousand protestors gathered at the Umayyad Mosque. '*Yasqut wa'd Balfour!*' is the hostile slogan they shouted, 'Down with the Balfour Declaration!' This became the rallying cry of protestors from then onwards. Under French military escort, Balfour had to turn tail and flee to Beirut. Although they were obliged to protect him, the French were not unhappy at this angry display of anti-British feeling. But they fared no better. Indeed, in the loud regional chorus of hostility to France, the main dissenting voice was that of Lebanon's Maronite community, which chose to look to Paris for religious and cultural protection.

Unlike Syria, increasingly restive under French control, Lebanon enjoyed relative calm and prosperity in the early 1920s. In the summer of 1924, for example, almost fifteen thousand visitors from Egypt, Palestine and Iraq came to enjoy the cool air of Lebanon's mountain resorts. Iraqis came in unprecedented numbers, thanks to the newly opened trans-desert motor route. Parts of Beirut, torn down during the war by the Turkish vali 'Azmi Bey, were being rebuilt with French encouragement – and with cheap labour provided by destitute Armenian refugees.[3]

The Maronites were not the only ones to be pro-French. In several parts of Syria, French officials had managed to win over small numbers of persons – landowners, heads of tribal families, notables of various sorts – who came to rely on the mandatory power to prop up a social and economic order that continued to give them an elevated social status and a high income. Their great fear was that their place in society, and their material interests, would be threatened if pan-Arab 'extremists' were to triumph. In Damascus, Aleppo and Beirut – and also in the outlying 'statelets' which the French had created – some notables accepted positions in puppet governments formed under French tutelage. Any suggestion of confronting the French, let alone of armed revolt against them, filled these collaborators with genuine alarm. Many among the Druze, the Alawites and other minorities came to favour the French, unlike the Arab Sunni majority, which by this time was almost uniformly nationalist in temper.

---

[3] British Consulate, Beirut, to Foreign Office, July 1924 (FO 371/21914).

It was, therefore, quite unexpected that the revolt should break out in the Jabal Druze. To the French, it was a blow at least as painful as the one they suffered at much the same time in Morocco, where a rebel chieftain, 'Abd al-Krim, rose in rebellion in the Rif in the mid-1920s. He managed to hold out until May 1926, when he was forced to surrender after being besieged by Marshal Philippe Pétain, at the head of an army of a quarter of a million French, Spanish and colonial Moroccan troops. He was taken in chains to the French island of Réunion, where he remained until his escape in 1947.

The Syrian rebels were to pose an even greater challenge to France. The spark which ignited their revolt was the arrest in July 1922 of Adham Khanjar, a Lebanese Shi'i whom the French had accused of involvement in the attempt on the life of General Gouraud a year earlier. Khanjar was captured in Sultan al-Atrash's house, where he had taken refuge in the latter's absence. On hearing of the arrest, Sultan at once made his way to French military headquarters at Suwayda to claim the prisoner, as Druze hospitality demanded. When the French refused, Sultan and his men attacked the convoy, which they believed was transporting Khanjar to Damascus. (As it happened, he was being flown there by plane.) The French reacted by bombing Sultan's house from the air, and executing Khanjar on the spot. Sultan then attempted to raise the Druze in revolt, but his appeal was poorly followed, causing him to flee across the border to Transjordan. From there, he launched occasional raids against French territory. The French pressed the British to expel him. When he sensed that they were about to do so, Sultan thought it best to give himself up. He was pardoned in due course and allowed to return home.

When his cousin Salim al-Atrash died in September 1923, the French – ignoring local demands that a native governor be elected to succeed him – appointed a French officer, Captain Gabriel Carbillet, to the post, with the endorsement of an assembly of minor Druze shaykhs. Carbillet, who had served in French colonial West Africa, was an arrogant autocrat and impatient moderniser, who vaingloriously saw himself as the representative of revolutionary France. Not only did he set about building roads, irrigation ditches and schools in the wild mountains of the Jabal, but he also began attacking the ancient feudal structure of the Druze, giving peasants ownership rights on what was considered communal land. The Atrash chieftains were outraged.

They were not alone in taking offence. The Druze population as a whole was angered by Carbillet's methods – by his use of forced labour for public works, by the way French 'advisers' interfered in every aspect of Druze life, by the intimidating presence of the French garrison at Suwayda. The more long-sighted and politically aware among them even came to resent the creation of a separate Druze statelet, deliberately cut off from Damascus.

In the spring of 1925, the Atrash family sent a delegation to complain about Captain Carbillet's behaviour to General Maurice Sarrail, the new French high commissioner. They demanded the appointment of a native governor, as their treaty with France had specified. But Sarrail refused to dismiss Carbillet, merely sending him on temporary leave. On 11 July, and at Sarrail's invitation, three Atrash chiefs came to Damascus to discuss their grievances. It proved to be an ugly and dishonourable trap. He had them immediately arrested and deported to the grim French prison in Palmyra, where prisoners often contracted serious or even fatal illnesses. The British consul in Damascus, W. A. Smart, commented dryly that 'methods of deception such as these were often practised successfully by the Turkish rulers, but have not yet been generally associated by the native mind with European rulers'.[4]

This perfidious incident set the Jabal Druze on fire. There had been plenty of tinder lying about: resentment at the undermining of traditional Druze authority; the heavy-handed nature of French rule; the recourse to forced labour; the collapse of Syria's paper currency which had been pegged to the jittery French franc; runaway inflation that had destroyed people's incomes. In addition, a severe drought that year devastated harvests across southern Syria. Crops in the Hawran failed completely, causing whole villages to have to be abandoned. Water shortages in the Damascus plain were unprecedented. Parched, nomadic Beduin were forced to encroach on the cultivated areas east of Damascus, where their thirsty and famished herds of camels and flocks of sheep devoured what few crops remained. Then, to top it all, came a severe late frost which did further damage, especially to apricot trees, which had always provided valuable exports in the form of dried apricots and apricot paste. Together, these resentments and hardships fuelled the revolt.

Michael Provence, a historian of the Great Syrian Revolution, relates that, in the nineteenth century, migrants from the Druze mountains settled in the Hawran plain, which they managed to turn into

---

[4] W. A. Smart, Damascus, to Foreign Office, 12 July 1925 (FO 371/10850).

Syria's breadbasket with funding from Damascus merchants. The growing, financing and export of grain served to forge ties of trade and friendship between Druze farmers and Sunni merchants – the latter living mainly in the ancient Damascus quarter of Midan, located along the road south to the Jabal Druze. The main business of Midan was, in fact, the distribution and export of grain from the Hawran. Such commercial links had, for example, been put to good use when the Hawran supplied bread to the Emir Faysal's British-funded Arab army in the last few months of the First World War. In 1925, anti-French agitation was to course through the same channels. To quote Provence: 'The axis of the revolt was the grain trade'.[5]

In July 1925, Sultan's Druze tribesmen laid siege to the French garrison at Suwayda. A French relief column of 3,000 men under General Roger Michaud tried to break the siege, but was ambushed and routed, with heavy loss of life. The Druze captured 2,000 rifles – a spectacular coup which brought tribesmen flocking to Sultan's banner. His army soon grew to some ten thousand men, harrying and attacking the French wherever they could find them. Within a few weeks, the uprising had spread to the Ghuta, the area of dense and leafy fruit orchards in the Damascus oasis.

Incensed at having been caught off guard, the French overreacted, as they were prone to do. Villages suspected of harbouring rebels were set ablaze, and their inhabitants heavily fined, drafted into forced labour or simply shot. By late August 1925, Damascus nationalists had joined the Druze revolt, which they now vowed to bring to the capital. On the night of 23 August, handbills calling for an armed uprising were distributed all over the city, indicating that the daring notion had taken hold that France could be defeated and driven out.

> *To Arms! To Arms! Oh sons of the glorious Arabs! Let us seek death that we may win life . . .*
> *Syrians, remember your forefathers, your history, your heroes, your martyrs, your national honour.*
> *Remember that the hand of God is with you and that the will of the people is the will of God . . .*

---

[5] Provence, *The Great Syrian Revolt*, p. 13. See T. A. Spring Rice, Memorandum on the trouble in the Jabal Druze, 12 August 1925 (FO 371/10850).

> *We have drawn our swords and will not sheath them until our demands are met. The following are our demands:*
>
> *Complete independence of Arab Syria, one and indivisible, sea-coast and interior;*
>
> *Establishment of a Popular Government and the free election of a Constituent Assembly . . .;*
>
> *Evacuation of the foreign army of occupation and the creation of a national army to provide security;*
>
> *Application of the principles of the French Revolution and the Rights of Man.*
>
> *To arms! Let us write our demands in our blood, as our fathers did before us.*
>
> *To arms! God is with us.*
>
> *Long live independent Syria!*
>
> *Signed: Sultan al-Atrash*
>
> *Commander of the Syrian Revolutionary Armies.*[6]

Such was the challenge facing the new French High Commissioner General Maurice Sarrail.

Maurice Sarrail's ordeal

To understand the crisis which then unfolded, a word needs to be said about General Sarrail, a veteran soldier of enlightened views but short temper, who had distinguished himself in the early months of the First World War by commanding the French Third Army in the battle of the Marne. But this had not saved him from dismissal by General Joffre in July 1915, largely because of a deep-seated disagreement about war strategy which had divided French politicians and army chiefs at the time. 'Westerners' like Joffre – and indeed most of the French general staff – were convinced that Germany could be ground down and beaten by a war of attrition on the Western Front, and that military operations elsewhere were a wasteful sideshow.

---

[6] Provence, *The Great Syrian Revolt*, pp. 81–3. The declaration was published in translation in the French Communist newspaper, *L'Humanité*, on 9 September 1925.

'Easterners', in contrast – and Sarrail was one of them – believed that the war on the Western Front had become a costly stalemate, and that a breakthrough could be achieved by operations elsewhere. He argued that a military strike against the Balkans, or against the Arab provinces, would bring down Germany's Ottoman allies and, in due course, even Germany itself. Sarrail's plan was to land an expeditionary force at Salonica, on the Mediterranean coast of north-eastern Greece. This would assist Serbia's war effort, encourage Greece and Romania to join the Allies, and inflict a military defeat on Ottoman Bulgaria – thus severing the lines of communication between the Central Powers and the Ottoman Empire.

After much debate, Sarrail's military strategy was reluctantly adopted, and he was given command of a mixed French, British, Serbian, Italian and Russian force. But, intrinsically suspicious of French ambitions, British and Italian support for the campaign remained half-hearted, causing Sarrail to complain of having too few troops at his disposal and insufficient artillery. When he failed to achieve a decisive victory against Bulgaria, Sarrail was relieved of his command in December 1917 by Prime Minister Georges Clemenceau, a convinced 'Westerner'.[7] From then on, Sarrail harboured a sharp sense of grievance against the French government and its military chiefs.

General Sarrail was a freemason, an atheist and a left-winger. It was for these reasons that Prime Minister Edouard Herriot, himself a member of the Radical Party, decided to send him to Beirut as high commissioner in December 1924, to replace General Weygand, a Catholic right-wing monarchist, who was obsessively devoted to the Crusader notion of *La France du Levant*.[8] Weygand believed in Christianity as a 'civilizing mission' and in the benefits to France of its patronage of the Maronites.[9] 'Christian soldiers' such as Weygand were to be found throughout the Near East, in cavalry and infantry units; among French consuls, attachés and dragomen who had served in the region under the Ottomans; among clerics and businessmen, as well as in French trading families which had grown roots in the

---

[7] William Fortescue, *The Third Republic in France, 1870–1940*, London and New York 2000, pp. 125–6; General M. Sarrail, *Mon Commandement en Orient, 1916–1918*, Paris 1920, pp. 297–301.

[8] Pierre Fournié, 'Le Mandat à l'épreuve des passions françaises: L'affaire Sarrail (1925)', in Méouchy (ed.), *France, Syrie et Liban*, pp. 125–68.

[9] Ibid., pp. 133–4.

Levant over several generations. General Sarrail, however, sprang from a wholly different tradition. He was a religious rebel who held priests in contempt, and viewed the Beirut High Commission and the local French community as reactionaries, in thrall to the Jesuits and to their Maronite protégés.

The Great Syrian Revolution of 1925 was to provide an occasion for these two French camps – the clerical and the anticlerical – to do fierce battle. But the outcome could not be settled locally. It depended to a large extent on the political colouring of governments in Paris. And in Paris there was far more at stake than religion. Both during and immediately after the First World War, French politicians and their senior officials were divided between those who wanted to adopt an 'Arab policy' – that is to say, one which implied reaching out to Arab and Muslim opinion well beyond France's traditional Christian clients – and those who championed the altogether different and much narrower policy of giving priority to the Maronites, as well as to the cultural and religious activities of France's extensive network of schools and Christian orders.

Prime Minister Georges Clemenceau, himself anticlerical and anti-colonial, was strongly of the view that France should adopt a wide Arab policy. At the Paris Peace Conference, he was in much closer contact with the Emir Faysal than with the Maronite representatives. But, once the Right had won the legislative elections of 1919, Clemenceau chose to leave politics altogether, withdrawing to his simple house (without indoor plumbing) by the sea, far away from Paris. The field was thus taken over by the anti-Arab advocates, which resulted in the overthrow of Faysal's Arab kingdom in July 1920, the carving up of Syria into miserable mini-states, and the creation of Greater Lebanon on 1 September 1920. Catholic circles were delighted, since this 'Lebanese' policy somewhat made up for the loss of the Holy Land to Britain, and for the official renunciation at San Remo of France's 'religious protectorate' over all Oriental Christians.

When the Cartel of the Left won the French elections in May 1924, the pendulum swung back the other way once again. Anticlericalism became government policy. It was then that the new Prime Minister Edouard Herriot demanded the reinstatement in active service of General Sarrail – 'the only Republican general', as his supporters liked to refer to him. When Sarrail arrived in Beirut in early January 1925, Arab nationalists welcomed him exuberantly, fully expecting that he would grant political freedoms and promote Syrian unity. Syrian masonic lodges erected a triumphal arch in his honour, while the Beirut lodge put on a grand reception for him.

At the same time, he came under fierce attack from the right-wing press as an atheist and a freemason. The clerical camp went so far as to declare a 'holy war' against him. Jesuit missionaries were even rumoured to have asked for a minute's silence in their Lebanese schools in protest at his appointment. This clash of cultures, political and religious, raised the fundamental question of which France was to lead the Levant states to independence. Should the Mandate be entrusted to the sons of the Crusaders or to those of the French Revolution?[10]

Political developments in Paris encouraged Sarrail to put his liberal convictions into practice. Although Prime Minister Edouard Herriot was brought down by a financial crisis in April 1925, he was succeeded by Paul Painlevé, one of Sarrail's warmest supporters. Thus encouraged, Sarrail hastened to lift the state of emergency imposed on Syria in 1922, amnestied the last political prisoners, granted freedom of the press and of association and gave Syrians the right to form political parties in preparation for national elections. He even encouraged them to start a popular political movement which would justify and express their demand for Syrian unity.

In this far more liberal climate, and after some months of semi-clandestine gestation, a People's Party, led by Dr 'Abd al-Rahman al-Shahbandar, held a founding rally on 5 June 1925, attended by over a thousand people. Shahbandar himself had been recently released from jail, after serving eighteen months of a twenty-year sentence, merely for voicing opposition to the Mandate! Financed by Prince Michel Lutfallah, the People's Party was the first legal nationalist party to be formed under the French Mandate. It was immediately joined by leading patriots in Damascus, as well as by a strong contingent from Aleppo, including such prominent figures as Ibrahim Hananu, Ihsan al-Jabiri and 'Abd al-Rahman al-Kayali.

The party's declared goals were the independence and unity of Syria within its 'natural' borders – meaning the whole of Transjordan, Palestine, Syria, as well as those slices of Syrian territory which had been carved off and attached to Mount Lebanon. The British consul in Damascus reported to London that 'this movement towards unity, with

[10] Ibid., p. 140.

Damascus as the centre of a reunited Syria, excluding the 'Petit Liban', is strong and genuine. It is based on economic and administrative logic. It has behind it a venerable tradition with a powerful sentimental appeal to the Muslim masses'.[11] The nationalists, he added, wanted the French to heed 'the bitter cry of *cazas*, districts and villages torn, in spite of their protests, from their Mother Syria'.[12] The name of the new party, the consul remarked, was the same as that used by Mustafa Kemal's party in Turkey.[13]

All thoughts of campaigning for political elections, and of a peaceful political future, were, however, impetuously cast aside after the military successes of the Druze rebels. Thrilled to the core by these triumphs, Shahbandar immediately shifted his strategy from political mobilisation to armed rebellion.[14] Once he heard of the defeat of General Michaud's column, he entered into a secret alliance with Sultan al-Atrash, sending Nasib al-Bakri to exchange solemn oaths with him, in which they pledged to join in driving the French out of Syria.[15] Sultan's subsequent and eloquent call to arms was clearly the product of this collaboration.

When Nasib al-Bakri reported back from his meeting with Sultan, Shahbandar sent word to the Druze to march on Damascus. The attack on the city took place on 24 August 1925 by a combined force of Druze, Hawran and Beduin tribesmen – altogether about a thousand armed men. But they were spotted by a French aircraft, bombed from the air and put to flight by a cavalry charge of colonial Moroccan *spahis* under French command. The painful lesson was that, whatever their resolve, the Syrian rebels could simply not take on the French army in daylight and in open country. Their strategy had to be guerrilla warfare, waged at night.

The French strike back

On the night of 27 August, French security police raided the house in Damascus of 'Uthman al-Sharabati, where a secret meeting of the

---

[11] W. A. Smart, Damascus, to Foreign Office, 25 March 1925 (FO 371/10850).
[12] W. A. Smart, Damascus, to Foreign Office, 9 April 1925 (FO 371/10850).
[13] Ibid.
[14] Khoury, 'Factionalism', p. 455.
[15] Khoury, *Syria and the French Mandate*, p. 163.

People's Party was being held. Sharabati, Faris al-Khoury and Nazih Mu'ayyad al-'Azm were among those seized. Other important nationalists, including the journalist Najib al-Rayyes and the young and brilliant lawyer Fawzi al-Ghazzi, were arrested at their own homes. Fakhri al-Barudi had already been sent to jail. Jamil Mardam had to flee to Haifa; Shukri al-Quwatli to Amman and then to Cairo. Some of those captured were sent to the damp and awful citadel of Arwad, then a deprived and remote island off the Syrian coast. Dr Shahbandar and the two Bakri brothers, Nasib and Fawzi, managed to escape to the Jabal Druze, where, on 9 September 1925, Shahbandar proclaimed a general Syrian rebellion and the formation of a National Government. On 18 October, a band of some sixty insurgents, led by Hasan al-Kharrat, infiltrated Damascus. Other bands followed them and occupied the city without serious opposition. They seized the police station in the Shaghur quarter, and burned down part of the 'Azm palace. As these fierce rebels roamed the city, the police and gendarmes abandoned their weapons and fled from their posts.[16]

By this time, General Sarrail had had enough. He felt particularly betrayed by Shahbandar and the People's Party, whose formation he had actively encouraged. His liberal policy had backfired, shattering his hopes of a political settlement with the nationalists. Force, he bitterly concluded, was now his sole option.

Beginning on the night of 18 October, Damascus was shelled by French artillery and bombed and strafed by French planes for two full days, before a truce could be called at noon on the 20th. By this time, entire quarters had been flattened, and nearly fifteen hundred people killed. In a dispatch on 27 October, the special correspondent of *The Times* reported that

> *The whole area between the Hamadieh Bazaar and the Street Called Straight has been laid in ruins . . . The corrugated roof [of the latter] has been blown off for quite a hundred yards . . . shop after shop destroyed, either by tank machine-guns which riddled the iron shutters as they dashed through, or by shells, or by fire . . . The sweetmeat bazaar, al-Bzourieh, is seriously damaged and a shop, the famous 'Dalale' is completely destroyed . . . An irreparable*

---

[16] Provence, *The Great Syrian Revolt*, p. 103.

loss is the Palais Azm . . . Words fail to describe fittingly the
spectacle which the ancient and sacred city now presents.
Various authorities place the financial losses at between
one and two million Turkish gold pounds . . . None who
lived through those terrible days (October 18–20) will
ever forget the experience, particularly the two nights of
incessant shelling which, with the added horrors of fires
springing up on all sides, became veritable nights of terror.

A delegation of notables pleaded with the French Command to end the attack. Led by Sa'id al-Jaza'iri, grandson of the great Emir 'Abd al-Qadir, it included members of the 'Azm family, as well as a prominent religious figure, Shaykh Muhammad Taj-al-Din al-Hasani, Riad's maternal great uncle. This Damascus elite of the older generation had little enthusiasm for popular politics or armed revolt. Grain merchants, hard hit by the revolt, begged the rebels to leave the city before the French destroyed it altogether. The merchants had been unable to recover advances, estimated to total the huge sum of 300,000 Turkish gold pounds, which they had made to farmers in the Hawran and the Jabal Druze. This savage bombardment of Damascus ended any further rebel mobilisation in the city, and activists of Shahbandar's People's Party were forced to flee.

Shockwaves were felt abroad. The international outcry against France led to a political shakeup in Paris, where Sarrail became the target of a vicious press campaign. On the Left, he was vilified as an 'odious despot', accused of 'liquidating Syria'. The Right, on the other hand, predicted that his 'policy of treachery' would lead to the spread of insurrection to North Africa. His failings and failures were dragged into public view. The fall of the Painlevé government on 26 October 1925 removed the last obstacle to his recall. From his perspective, Sarrail had hoped to implement Georges Clemenceau's policy of an honourable bargain with Arab nationalism. But the Druze revolt, joined with undue haste by Dr Shahbandar's People's Party, had pulled the carpet out from under him. In Beirut, his clerical opponents rejoiced. So much so that there were even suggestions that Sarrail had been deliberately sabotaged by intelligence officials at the High Commission in Beirut.[17]

---

[17] Fournié, 'Le Mandat', p. 162.

A special correspondent of *Le Petit Parisien* managed to interview Sarrail on board the *Sphinx* in Alexandria harbour, as the disgraced high commissioner prepared to sail for France. 'What could I have done?' he exclaimed. 'Give the city over to the bandits? Attempt to fight them in the street? Blood would have flowed. Should I have appeared on a balcony and addressed the crowd? Or should I have done nothing and allowed Christians to be slaughtered as in 1860?'[18] Sarrail arrived back in Paris in deep trouble. Right-wing demonstrators took to marching past his house yelling, 'Assassin! To the gallows with him!' Sarrail died soon afterwards, in March 1928, going to his grave in an atmosphere of national indifference.

Riad el-Solh enters the scene

Riad was in Egypt when he heard that the Druze had risen against the French. He took the first boat bound for Haifa and, evading French surveillance, managed to enter Syrian territory and make contact with the leaders of the Revolution. Little is known of his exact movements at this dangerous time, except that he teamed up with a daring French woman journalist, Clara Candiani, whom he had met in France, and who had come to cover the uprising. Together, they made their way into rebel-held territory. At one time, or so the anecdote goes, they were even forced to bed down in the same tent in the Hawran, apparently separated from each other by a Qur'an and a sword!

Clara was to become a frequent visitor to the Middle East. Some years later, when the Revolution was no more than a painful memory, she described in a newspaper article how she had attended a gathering of nationalist leaders at the Orient Palace Hotel in Damascus. Fakhri al-Barudi had told jokes in French; Riad el-Solh had listened amiably to the animated conversation around him, occasionally drawing on his water pipe. The great Sa'dallah al-Jabiri had been there, as well as Jamil Mardam, Faris al-Khoury and Fawzi al-Ghazzi – erudite and well-bred young gentlemen. This was the anti-French elite; here, then, were the 'dangerous nationalists' she had heard so much about![19]

---

[18] *Le Petit Parisien*, 10 November 1925.
[19] *Al-Ma'rad*, Beirut.

When the Syrian Revolution broke out, its anxious supporters in Cairo decided that it was essential to mobilise international opinion in order to bring pressure to bear on France. The League of Nations had to be alerted to what was going on in Syria. Shaykh Rashid Rida decided to call for help from the Emir Shakib Arslan. After the surrender of the Ottoman Empire to the Allies in November 1918, Arslan had gone into exile, which was to last for the next twenty-eight years. He had been rendered rootless by the Ottoman defeat. He had wandered between Western Europe and the East – from Lausanne to Moscow, from Rome to Istanbul – holding firmly to his anti-imperial, pan-Islamic stance. He did not yet feel ready to commit himself to a purely Arab political movement. But Rashid Rida persuaded him at least to leave Mersin in Turkey, where he had set up house, and return urgently to Switzerland, to reactivate the Permanent Delegation of the Syro-Palestinian Congress. Arslan agreed, and within a very short time he was at work again, along with Ihsan al-Jabiri. They rented an office at 21 Glacis de Rive in Geneva, especially for the purpose.

Arslan then wrote to Riad el-Solh, enclosing some upsetting photographs, showing men and women fleeing from villages in flames, children crying in the ruins of their homes, and unburied bodies thrown about. 'Your place', Arslan said, 'is in Geneva at the League of Nations, not in the Jabal. There are plenty of men who can bear arms, but to thrash the French in eloquent and convincing language, only you can do.' Arslan explained to his young friend that his patriotism needed no further proof. He had been exiled, imprisoned, and had come close to death on the gallows. Surely that was enough! He added, with gentle teasing, that Riad must take care not to arouse the envy of their mutual friend, Ihsan al-Jabiri, who would have loved to have won his spurs in the same way.

Thus began Riad's stint as a political lobbyist. With Arslan and Jabiri, he worked in Geneva, on and off, for most of the next four years. He was busy writing, speaking in public, campaigning, building an international reputation, and bombarding the Permanent Mandates Commission with numerous memoranda and petitions. And this was by no means his only activity. Writing – often anonymously – for his newspaper in Beirut kept him busy too. He undertook numerous journeys to Palestine, Egypt, France and Belgium; he sought and was granted an audience with Pope Pius XI, and, when at the Vatican, he transmitted a special appeal from the Syrian revolutionaries to the

Pope, who promised to use his influence with the French Catholic Church in favour of peace.[20]

French intelligence tracked Riad's every move. While on a visit to Beirut, he was arrested by the French military authorities and charged with incitement of the Syrian Revolution. Under decree no. 274 of 27 June 1926, he was confined (*mise en résidence obligatoire et surveillée*) in the citadel of Arwad off the Syrian coast. But he managed to escape from the island a short while later, perhaps by bribing a guard. Then, travelling via Jerusalem and Cairo, he rejoined the Delegation in Geneva, where his derring-do arrival gave his colleagues fresh heart.

In July, while he manned the office in Geneva, his two colleagues, Shakib Arslan and Ihsan al-Jabiri, spent forty days in Paris, attempting to sway or at least soften French policy towards Syria. But they found French officials totally unresponsive, as the powerful French Right was in full cry against the Syrian rebels. On their return to Geneva, Arslan and Jabiri wrote a long report for the Permanent Mandates Commission of the League of Nations, in which they listed the reasons for the Revolution: direct French rule; the carving up of the country into mini-statelets; the annexing of parts of Syria to Lebanon against the wishes of its inhabitants. They described how 14,000 men had died in just fifteen months of fighting, quite apart from the countless casualties among women and children, and the destruction of 'historic cities and prosperous villages'. They appealed to the League to intervene to save Syria from ruin, calling for a commission of enquiry to be sent to the country.[21]

Working as a team, Shakib Arslan, Ihsan al-Jabiri and Riad el-Solh managed to place themselves at the forefront of the Arab cause, in the minds of both European leaders and of their Arab compatriots. No other individuals, from countries under European Mandate, are mentioned as frequently in the minutes of the Permanent Mandates Commission of the 1920s. By the sheer volume of their petitions, and the tenacity with which they pressed for appointments with officials, they forced the Syro-Palestinian Delegation to the attention of the Commission. Although they evidently gave priority to Syria proper during the years of the Great Revolution, they soon extended their

---

[20] Alia el-Solh, *Le Jour*, 17 October 1965.

[21] Petition of 11 September 1926 to the Permanent Mandates Commission. Archives SDN, Geneva, Commission Permanente des Mandats (CPM), 444–99, tome M, 1926, v. 423. See also Petitions of 10 and 19 November 1926, Archives SDN, Geneva, CPM, 500–48, tome 12, 1926–27, v. 424.

concern to cover 'southern Syria' – in other words, Palestine. Arslan, Jabiri and el-Solh thus became the first Arabs to present the Palestine case to the world at large.[22] But all their valiant efforts had no effect on French policy.

The collapse of the Revolution

General Sarrail was replaced as high commissioner in Beirut by Henry de Jouvenel des Ursins, a politician and journalist of liberal views, who had been editor of the newspaper *Le Matin*, and had married the writer Colette in 1912. During the First World War, she converted his St Malo estate into a hospital for the wounded. But in the 1920s they drifted apart. She became increasingly interested in the world of writing, theatre and painting, winning enormous fame with books like *La Vagabonde* and *Le Blé en herbe*. Their marriage ended in 1924, after she had had an affair with his son.

Henry de Jouvenel was the first civilian high commissioner of the Mandate. He arrived in Beirut in early December 1925, but remained at his post for only eight months. His policy was to seek to quell the insurrection by pardoning rank-and-file rebels, while drawing into negotiations those 'moderate' nationalists who had not been directly involved in the violence. However, the gap between what these nationalists demanded, and what France was prepared to offer, was too wide for him to be able to garner any greater success than his predecessors.

Before taking up his appointment, Jouvenel had invited the Emir Shakib Arslan to Paris for discussions. Arslan had accepted the invitation, but he made two serious mistakes. First, he assumed that he was empowered to negotiate on behalf of the entire Syro-Lebanese community, thereby bypassing both Dr Shahbandar in the Jabal Druze, and Prince Michel Lutfallah in Cairo. These highly suspicious men now saw Arslan as an enemy to be brought down. Arslan's second mistake was to make concessions that were not his to make. He agreed, for example, that France was entitled to create a *Grand Liban*, by adding to Mount Lebanon districts that had traditionally been part of Syria – a grave departure from nationalist dogma, which earned him the unfair charge of seeking to protect his own Lebanon power base before all else.

[22] Cleveland, *Islam Against the West*, pp. 52–4.

Arslan went even further. He accepted the principle of a thirty-year alliance between Syria and France; that foreign military advisers would be exclusively French; that French would be the (foreign) language taught in Syrian schools. In his defence, he truly believed that such concessions were necessary in order to obtain the independence of Syria and Lebanon from the grasping French, and he may well have been right. He was, therefore, startled and embarrassed when Jouvenel abruptly broke off the talks, without excuse or explanation, very probably after being worked upon by Arslan's nationalist rivals.[23]

On arrival in Beirut to take up his post, Henry de Jouvenel had given a pledge that rebels who surrendered by 6 January 1926 would escape execution – although not imprisonment. To a chorus of praise from the Christian press, he declared that he would wage war on those who wanted war, but would offer peace to those who wanted peace. On attending mass – something his predecessor Sarrail had rarely done, and then only with the greatest distaste – he was told from the altar steps that local Christian orders and religious educational establishments looked to France as their protector.

Jouvenel invited men he believed to be moderate – like Lutfi al-Haffar and Faris al-Khoury – to discuss peace terms. But he soon discovered that even they would not compromise on key items of the nationalist agenda. They wanted a general amnesty for the rebels; a united Syria which included the Alawite region as well as the territories that had been artificially attached to Lebanon; an Assembly to draft a new Constitution; real authority for the native government; and a timetable for the ending of the French mandate, such as the one the British had agreed in Iraq. They demanded, in effect, the departure of the French and the dismantling of Greater Lebanon. These demands were, of course, totally unacceptable to the government in Paris and to its French High Command.[24]

Rebel pressure continued throughout the winter of 1925 and into the spring of the following year. Guerrilla bands, which were estimated by the French as numbering some five thousand men, managed to gain control of much of the Ghuta, the verdant agricultural oasis around Damascus. The insurrection then spread to the Druze portions of Lebanon, where only a fierce French defence of Rashaya prevented

[23] Ibid., pp. 54–8.
[24] Provence, *The Great Syrian Revolt*, pp. 127–8.

the rebels from gaining control of large parts of the south and even threatening Beirut.

The French had to call in reinforcements and mount a counteroffensive with the aim of crushing the uprising with overwhelming force. Rebel-held villages were bombed savagely and daily, and only that way could they then be taken. Male villagers were killed and their family homes blown up. Villages that refused to pay fines – or were unable to do so – were burned down, causing their shocked and destitute inhabitants to flood into Damascus, upsetting and alarming its own inhabitants. French soldiers took brazenly to selling in the bazaars the loot they had plundered from people's homes. Male prisoners were publicly shot in al-Marja square. On one occasion, sixteen corpses were left on display for a whole day, traumatising the population and offending grossly against the Muslim practice of immediate burial for the dead. In May 1926, the French bombarded Damascus a second time to 'clear out' the rebels altogether.

In mid-September, General Maurice Gamelin, who had arrived with still more reinforcements, including brutish Foreign Legionnaires, marched on Suwayda on the 24th, and relieved the French garrison which had been holed up in the citadel. Any building that was still standing after their two months of bombardment was methodically set on fire. Ten thousand soldiers were deployed in rebel areas between the Jabal Druze and Damascus, and an equal number in and around all the major cities.

It took France more than a year to regain full control of the countryside around Damascus. To do so, it resorted to collective punishments, to wholesale executions, to house demolitions, to the use of tanks and armoured vehicles in urban areas, to population transfers from region to region, and to round-the-clock bombing of residential areas. In the words of Michael Provence, 'civilian populations were subjected to daily systematic aerial bombardment'.[25] Such were the appalling means used to 'pacify' a territory which the League of Nations had placed in France's care, with the declared aim of preparing it for national independence!

Attention had by this time shifted to a new front at Hama. Fawzi al-Qawuqji, a captain in the locally raised French forces, had mutinied along with his entire cavalry troop. Rallying a force of Beduin

---

[25] Ibid., pp. 26, 28.

fighters, he occupied the city and attacked French buildings there. His strategic plan was to divide French forces and wear them down, in order to compel France to abandon the Mandate. But the French hit back ruthlessly in Hama too. They bombed its venerable old commercial district, and ordered their colonial Senegalese troops to set fire to the houses of local nationalists, causing great damage and loss of life. Exactly as in Damascus, some Hama notables then struck a deal with the French, securing a pledge that the French bombing would cease as soon as Qawuqji and his Beduin troops departed the city.

In due course, the French managed to drive the Druze insurgents into the Hawran and, by 1927, had pushed them across the border into northern Transjordan. There, many of them – including Sultan al-Atrash and his family – settled in a miserable refugee camp at al-Azraq. Some families had already moved there during the fighting. But the Druze were soon compelled to move again. In the summer of 1927, Britain expelled them from al-Azraq to Wadi Sirhan, a barren and intemperate valley some 150 kilometres south-east of Amman, located in what had become the new Arabian sultanate of 'Abd al-'Aziz ibn Sa'ud. They were allowed in only after mediation on their behalf by members of the exiled Syro-Palestinian Congress. These proud and courageous patriots suffered there for a decade until 1937, living in inadequate tents and surviving on the charitable donations collected on their behalf by the Congress, from sympathisers in Syria and Lebanon and from Arab immigrants in the Americas.

Sultan al-Atrash was amnestied in April 1937. He returned to Syria and threw in his lot half-heartedly with the National Bloc, in the forlorn hope that his fortunes might revive, as had those of his former partner, Dr Shahbandar.[26] In the meantime, and during his absence in exile, his cousin, Hasan al-Atrash, had risen to become the paramount chief of the Jabal Druze.

The split in the nationalist camp

A French court-martial condemned the Emir Shakib Arslan to death in absentia for his role in the Revolution. Living in exile in Switzerland, he had become an authoritative commentator on Arab and Islamic affairs.

[26] Ibid.

The Syro-Palestinian Delegation, which he ran with Ihsan al-Jabiri and Riad el-Solh, became a focus for Arab hopes in the interwar years.[27] Arslan himself was a lifelong believer in Islamic unity. But, unable to return to either Syria or Lebanon until he was pardoned in 1937, he could not build a political base in his native land and was therefore denied a part in politics. Dr Shahbandar, the People's Party president, was also marginalised for several years. Making his way back to Cairo, he allied himself with Michel Lutfallah's faction within the Executive of the Syro-Palestinian Congress, adopting a pro-Hashemite position and preaching a doctrine of secular nationalism.

Nasib al-Bakri, who had been Sultan al-Atrash's closest Damascus ally during the Revolt, fared better. The rebel council he had formed, and which had consisted of former Ottoman officers and of men engaged in the Hawran grain trade, had been one of the most effective command centres of the Revolution.[28] Like so many others, he was sent into exile, but less than a year later, in March 1928, he was pardoned and his family's land was returned to him. In fact, he was the only prominent leader of the Revolt to be allowed back into Syria within that decade. It remains unclear why that was so. Perhaps the French simply considered him someone well-connected enough with whom they could deal.

Hundreds of former rebels fled to Haifa, Jaffa, Jerusalem and Cairo. Fawzi al-Qawuqji – who spent a decade under sentence of death – chose exile in Baghdad, where he helped train King Faysal's nascent Iraqi army. Journalists had been among the most active rebels, with Najib al-Rayyes foremost among them. He had fought in the Syrian revolt until 1927, then gone on to fight in Palestine in 1936 and in Iraq in 1941, each time alongside Fawzi al-Qawuqji. Most ordinary foot soldiers of the Revolt returned home, to try to rebuild their ruined farms and villages.

The cruel crushing of the Great Syrian Revolution, with heavy civilian casualties and massive destruction of property in Damascus, in Hama, in outlying villages and in the Jabal Druze, was a devastating

---

[27] Cleveland, *Islam Against the West*, p. 60.
[28] Provence, *The Great Syrian Revolt*, p. 145. Apart from Nasib al-Bakri himself, the council consisted of Muhammad 'Izz al-Din al-Halabi, 'Ali al-Atrash and Zayd al-'Amr (Druze from the south); Nazih Mu'ayyad al-'Azm, 'Abd al-Qadir Sukkar, Sa'id al-'As, Zaki al-Halabi, Zaki al-Drubi and the council secretary, Fa'iq al-'Asali (mostly from Damascus and Hama) (ibid., p. 133).

blow to Riad el-Solh, as it was to the nationalist camp as a whole. The military uprising had ended in costly failure – one further disaster to add to an already long list. This included the hanging by Jamal Pasha of the leaders of the early Arab nationalist movement; the Sykes–Picot agreement, which had dismembered the Arab provinces; the Balfour Declaration, which had given Palestine to the Zionists; the betrayal of the Arab Revolt by the British; the destruction of Faysal's Arab Kingdom by the French; and the imposition of the hated French and British Mandates.

The unhappy truth was that this Arab nationalist generation, which had come of age in the First World War with the destruction of the Ottoman Empire, had fared no better than that of its elders. Philip S. Khoury, in his history of the French Mandate in Syria, wrote:

> *The Great Revolt of 1925–27 was a major watershed in the history of modern Syria and in the national independence struggle against the French. In terms of its style, intensity, duration, scale and methods, it compared favourably with other resistance movements beginning to leave their mark on the countries of the Arab East after World War I, in particular the Egyptian Revolution of 1919, and later the Rebellion of 1936–39 in Palestine.*
>
> *The Great Revolt was popular insofar as its active participants were drawn from nearly all walks of life in Syria – urban and rural, Muslim and Christian, rich and poor. Its leadership formulated its aims and appeal in the new nationalist idiom of the times. And the Revolt itself let this new sentiment of nationalism spread faster, wider, and deeper than ever before, enabling it to become the dominant organizing principle of Syrian political life during the Mandate.*[29]

Nevertheless, and despite this sea change in political sentiment and national feeling, the immediate outcome of the Revolution proved catastrophic. France's defeat of the insurgency brought to the surface acrimonious splits in the nationalist camp itself, of which the public row between Shahbandar and Arslan was only the most spectacular.

---

[29] Philip S. Khoury, *Syria and the French Mandate*, pp. 166–7.

Shahbandar detested Arslan – a feeling that was entirely reciprocated. Shahbandar was a free-thinking secularist; he was also an impetuous man of action, who had led his People's Party to join forces with the Druze rebels, without really thinking through the political consequences. Arslan was a cautious intellectual and a reluctant revolutionary, who, far from embracing Arab nationalism, had for years – both before and after the First World War – defended the cause of an Arab alliance with the Ottomans, if only in the name of Islamic unity. Shahbandar went so far as to accuse Arslan – most libellously and unfairly – of the heinous crime of advising Jamal Pasha to execute Arab nationalists during the war, calling him a traitor and a Turkish agent. Arslan, in turn, and equally unfairly, accused Shahbandar of being a perfidious British agent and a Hashemite propagandist. And on it went.

The charge levied against Prince Michel Lutfallah, on the other hand, was that he had been willing to exploit the sacrifices of the Syrian martyrs for his own manipulative ends. He had been prepared, it was rumoured, to cooperate with the French in furthering his personal ambition for a principality in either Syria or Lebanon. He was rash enough to tell a correspondent of the Beirut newspaper, *al-Ma'rad*, that he was ready to accept the enlarged frontiers of Greater Lebanon – a clear betrayal of nationalist beliefs at the time. Indeed, and ironically as it turned out, the same Lutfallah had, in the autumn of 1927, tried to engineer Shakib Arslan's dismissal from the Delegation in Geneva, on the grounds that Arslan had exceeded his authority in discussions in Paris with Henry de Jouvenel in November 1925.

There was no doubt a deeper reason for these splits. Some of the men who had fought in the Great Syrian Revolution were now ready for a compromise with France. Striking examples were the brothers Nasib and Fawzi al-Bakri. They had certainly proved their fighting credentials, having participated in the rebel attack on Damascus in October 1925. But they were ready to reach an accommodation with France, despite the fact that they had no sympathy whatsoever for it.

Some Cairo-based diehards, on the other hand, like Shaykh Rashid Rida, editor of *al-Manar*, could not even conceive of such a compromise. Rida was said to have been deeply disturbed by reports of Michel Lutfallah's flirtation with France. One should bear in mind that these were men of the doctrinaire type, who were far from the front line. They themselves had not been made to suffer the damages, dangers or great physical ordeal of actual warfare.

On 19 October 1927, Rashid Rida and his friends[30] voted to depose Lutfallah from the presidency of the Executive Committee of the Syro-Palestinian Congress. Lutfallah struck back by summoning a meeting which quickly elected Dr Shahbandar to membership of the Congress. Thus two rival and squabbling groups suddenly claimed to represent the Executive Committee of the Syro-Palestinian Congress.[31] The bitter and self-defeating quarrel between the principal figures of Lutfallah, Arslan, Rashid Rida and Shahbandar had the effect of dividing Syrians in exile. It also robbed the Congress of any further effectiveness.

Riad seizes the opportunity

Riad el-Solh was certainly not ready to collaborate with the French, but nor was he a diehard rejectionist. He was totally opposed to French policy in the Levant, was committed to changing it, but he could not bring himself to be categorically hostile to France itself. After all, he was at home in French culture, he had lived in Paris and spoke and wrote French with stylish fluency. Personally laid-back and easy-going, he was certainly no xenophobe. This stance must have made his case persuasive with French opinion, and indeed helped give him a certain political immunity. The French did ban him from entering Syria and Lebanon from time to time, and, on occasion, hurried to lock him up. But this did not prevent him from travelling to France whenever he was freed. The French needed leading Arabs with whom they could thrash out matters, and eventually they were forced to consider him as a telling barometer of nationalist opinion.

On his many visits to Paris, Riad became quite an expert on French politics. He understood how important it was to influence the political decision-making process where it was taking place in European capitals. It is doubtful whether any other Arab politician of his generation forged such extensive contacts with French politicians and senior officials, or with influential journalists. Riad launched his

---

[30] As'ad Daghir, Khayr al-Din Zirkali and Jamal al-Husayni.
[31] Nevile Henderson, Acting High Commissioner in Palestine, to Sir Austen Chamberlain, 29 October 1927 (FO 371/12304).

attack from the very heart of the French Empire. It was the Radical Party that he wanted on his side – the secular, anticlerical movement which was the real backbone of the Third Republic. Formed on 21 June 1901 from a merger of electoral committees, sections of the League of Human Rights, masonic lodges and other groups, it was to dominate French political life for nearly half a century. And, although he gave the Radical Party his special attention, Riad did not neglect the Socialist and Communist Parties, which had parted company in 1920 at the Congress of Tours.

In the late 1920s, Riad el-Solh found himself in a unique position in the nationalist camp. Many of the men who had taken part in the Great Syrian Revolution had been killed in the fighting, had been condemned to death in absentia, or had been exiled for ten years or more, and were unable to return to Syria until the late 1930s. France's ferocious crushing of the Great Revolution removed them from the local political scene. Older leaders, such as the Emir Shakib Arslan and Dr Shahbandar, had suffered serious blows to their reputation because of their sustained and damaging mutual enmity. Arslan – twenty-five years Riad's senior, and banned from Syria and Lebanon from 1926 to 1937 – was now no longer a force to be reckoned with in Arab politics. Shahbandar, in turn, was hurt by criticism of his reckless strategy during the Revolution. After all, the battle of Maysalun in 1920, rousing and poignant and epically courageous as it had been, had shown clearly the futility of taking on France's mighty army. Yet the very same confrontational military strategy had been adopted in the Great Syrian Revolution of 1925–26, but on a far larger and more chaotic scale.

The eclipse of Arslan and Shahbandar created an opportunity for Riad el-Solh, which he now seized. He threw himself into frenetic activity on many fronts – in Paris with French politicians and journalists; in Geneva with Arslan himself and with Ihsan al-Jabiri; in Beirut with Khayr al-Din Ahdab and their joint newspaper, al-'Ahd al-Jadid; in sporadic negotiations with the Zionists; and in Syria and Lebanon with his friends in the nascent National Bloc. After the crushing of the Revolt, Riad became a pioneer of a new and more pragmatic nationalist strategy, which advocated engaging French opinion in dialogue, rather than fighting the French army in open military confrontation, which he knew could never be an equal contest for the largely unarmed and untrained Arabs.

The following gives some indication of his activities at that time. On 25 February 1927, he represented Syria in Brussels at a Conference of the League of Oppressed Peoples. As always, French intelligence kept a vigilant eye on him. In early March 1927, one of its officers in Beirut reported to Paris the remarks of a Lebanese politician, Ahmad Da'uq:

> We must admit that Riad el-Solh is rendering the greatest service. In the last two months, they [the Syro-Palestinian Congress] wanted to recall him to Cairo. But we wrote to friends begging them to keep him in Paris. He is so active that, single-handedly, he has organised an information and press service. He supplies information to Syrian and French newspapers. Read the articles in al-Ahrar! You will notice that this journal is well informed. Its news comes from Riad el-Solh![32]

From March to August 1927, Riad and Ihsan al-Jabiri spent six months in Paris attempting to influence French policy towards Syria. They were critical of France's 1926 report on Syria to the Permanent Mandates Commission of the League of Nations, which they rightly charged bore little relation to the gruesome facts on the ground. They spent a great deal of time and effort putting their case to whoever would give them a hearing and, on their return to Geneva, sent a detailed report on 1 September 1927 to Monsieur Villegas, president of the 8th General Assembly of the League, about the disastrous state of Franco-Syrian relations. This was followed, on 21 October 1927, by a letter to Sir Eric Drummond, secretary-general of the League, and by many more petitions in the same spirit, notably on 8 March and 8 June 1928.[33]

In May 1927, Riad also took the initiative to found an association in Paris of Arab students from Syria, Iraq, Palestine, Tunisia, Algeria and Morocco. The statutes were drawn up and a room reserved for the association at the Hôtel des Sociétés Savantes in the Latin Quarter. A few months earlier, in February 1927, he had had a hand in encouraging Syrian students at the University of Geneva to found

---

[32] MAE, Fonds Beyrouth, série B, carton 20, 3 March 1927.
[33] See Archives SDN, Geneva, CPM, 700–54, tome 16, 1928, v. 428, and Archives SDN, Geneva, CPM, 755–814, tome 17, 1928, v. 429.

their own 'Syrian-Arab Association', and to send an appeal to the new French high commissioner in Beirut, Henri Ponsot. A Swiss police report named the three members of the Association's committee as 'Adnan Atasi (born 1904), Nazim al-Qudsi (born 1905) and Mamduh 'Amiri (born 1906). 'These young men', the police report said, 'have come together to pursue a nationalist policy aiming at the creation of an Arab empire or confederation consisting of the Hijaz, Iraq and Syria, free from all Mandates or European protectorates . . . We will keep them under surveillance.'[34]

Riad's nationalist activities cost money and he was invariably short of it. French intelligence in Beirut noted that: 'Young Muslims report that Riad el-Solh has written to his parents and his friends asking for money. As his father can no longer send him any, he has intervened with the High Commissioner to seek permission for his return to Beirut.'[35] In June, it was the same story.

> *According to Muslim sources, Riad el-Solh, who is now in Paris and in financial difficulties, has written to the Jabr brothers asking for a loan of 40 Egyptian pounds, which was apparently sent to him. It will be recalled that some months ago, Riad asked for a loan of 30 Egyptian pounds which Kamal Jabr sent him when he was on a voyage in Palestine. The draft was found on him at his passage at [the frontier post of] Naqura.*[36]

In November, French intelligence reported that Riad el-Solh had recently made a statement to an Arabic newspaper in Paris, in which he said:

> *The Delegation has always been attached to the view, contained in its memorandum to the League of Nations of March 1927, that it was ready to accept any solution compatible with its national demands. We have managed to give the Syrian cause its true identity and to refute accusations levelled against it by its opponents. We have*

---

[34] Federal Archives, Berne, E2001 (D), S A 138, 21 April 1927.
[35] MAE, Fonds Beyrouth, série B, carton 20, 10 February 1927.
[36] MAE, Fonds Beyrouth, série B, carton 20, 17 June 1927, Service des renseignements, Damas Ville, Délégation française de l'État de Syrie, 14 November 1927.

*managed to destroy certain ambitions harmful to the
Syrian cause. We will pursue our efforts with French
public opinion, because we are convinced that the French
people view the Syrian question quite differently from their
government and would wish to create friendly relations
with an independent and unified Syria.*[37]

Here, then, was the cause to which Riad now devoted himself.

On his travels in France and Switzerland, he observed how people lived their political freedom. Switzerland in particular taught him a great deal and influenced him profoundly. He noted that several different ethnic groups, speaking different languages, lived together in apparent harmony. Lebanon was also such a mosaic. Could not the Swiss model be replicated there? What struck him was that freedom in Switzerland was not merely enjoyed by various communities, but by individuals too. Dominated by foreigners for centuries, the Arabs had had no opportunity to live in freedom. How were they to learn to live as free men? That was the great moral challenge that they faced. Later in his career, he was to be much afflicted by the thought that, even when they were free from foreign rule, the Arabs tended, all too often, to hand their hard-won freedom, all too casually, to repressive erstwhile liberators.[38]

[37] Ibid.
[38] Interview with Alia el-Solh, Monte Carlo, 4–5 October 2004.

8 A HERO'S RETURN

On a warm day in mid-May 1928, Rida el-Solh gave a lunch party at his home in Sidon in South Lebanon. A long table was laid under a trellis on the wide verandah. More than a dozen guests were expected. Word had reached Rida that the French authorities were about to allow his son Riad back home after a strictly imposed two-year exile. The lunch was held with the aim of preparing the ground for the political campaign that Riad was hoping to launch on his return.

Rida el-Solh was then in his late sixties and in poor health. Having suffered the double shock of the collapse of the Ottoman Empire and the imposition of the French and British Mandates, he felt that the Arabs now seemed destined to endure another long period of political servitude. Independence was more than ever a distant dream, with Syria the main victim of the artificial borders with which the imperialist powers had denatured the Arab map. Sidon, the Solhs' ancestral home, had always been part of the old Ottoman vilayet of Syria. The French, however, saw fit to attach it to Mount Lebanon in 1920 – together with Tripoli in the north and the Biqa' valley to the east – to create *Le Grand Liban*. Like other Arab nationalists, Rida wanted these territories returned to Syria. This was the burning issue that was to dominate Lebanese politics for many decades to come.

That day in early summer, Rida el-Solh had invited several prominent politicians, both Christian and Muslim, to his lunch party. Always vigilant where the Solhs were concerned, French intelligence had kept Paris well abreast of who had attended and what had been discussed. One of its agents reported that the guests had included three members of parliament – Emile Eddé, who was later to serve as president of the Lebanese Republic from 1936 to 1941; Subhi Haidar from Baalbek and Elie Saqqaf from Zahleh; two former members of parliament, Salim 'Ali Salam and 'Abdallah Abu Khatir; a Beirut municipal counsellor, George Khuri; and several other figures from Beirut and Sidon. Rida el-Solh's words of welcome had included a plea to his guests to bury their differences and strive for 'national union'.

Confessionalism, he said, had only done Lebanon harm. Sons of one country, Muslims and Christians should strive to live together in harmony. Salim 'Ali Salam, a prominent Sunni Muslim notable and an Arab nationalist, who had represented Beirut in the Ottoman parliament, thanked Rida for his 'beautiful words' and heaped lavish praise on his son, Riad, for his service to the Arab cause. Riad el-Solh, Salam said, had given the national movement real momentum. Every patriot was awaiting his return with great impatience.[1]

Although he had pleaded for an end to confessional disagreements, Rida el-Solh was well aware that the guests gathered around his lunch table held diametrically opposite, if not utterly incompatible, views. Whereas Lebanese Muslims wanted to throw off French control, terminate the Mandate and restore the 'unity' of Syria, Lebanese Christians – now constituting only a slight majority of the population – believed that they needed French protection against the religious 'fanatics' of the Syrian interior.[2] Emile Eddé, Rida's most important guest, was totally committed to *Le Grand Liban*, which had been created precisely to secure French influence and Maronite predominance. The Great Syrian Revolution of 1925–26 had brought home to Eddé, and to other Maronites, the vital strategic importance to Mount Lebanon of the Anti-Lebanon mountain range, as a physical barrier against any and all attack coming from inland Syria. Without the protection of towns such as Judaydah, Hasbaya and Rashaya, they believed, Druze rebels might well have invaded Mount Lebanon and set the whole region of the Shuf to the torch. It was hardly surprising, therefore, given this way of thinking, that the Maronites and their French patrons considered Riad el-Solh to be a dangerous agitator. As a champion of Syrian 'unity', he had grown to be more dangerous still because of the high-level links he had managed to forge in Paris.

French intelligence had carefully monitored Riad's movements on his journey home. Its agents had intercepted a letter about him,

[1] MAE, Nantes, Fonds Beyrouth (Amb.), série 199A4, carton 20, Service des renseignements, Beirut, 14 May 1928.
[2] Acting Consul General Norman Mayers to Austen Chamberlain, Beirut, 14 December 1925 (FO 871/10853).

dated 2 April 1928, which Nabih al-'Azma, a prominent Arab nation-alist living in Cairo, had written to Najib al-Rayyes, editor of the new Damascus nationalist newspaper, *al-Qabas*. Like many other nation-alists, Nabih al-'Azma had attended the Ottoman military school in Damascus, Maktab al-'idadiyya al-'askariyya, and then continued his studies in Istanbul. He had rallied to the Arab Revolt in 1916 and served in Faysal's administration. His letter gives a sense of the anxiety and dejection in nationalist ranks after the crushing of the Great Syrian Revolution. 'In a few days' time', he wrote,

> *our brother Riad el-Solh will be with you and will bring you all the news. Don't despair . . . Inside the country and outside it you have brothers and sisters who share your troubles. There are devoted men in our nation whom no force on earth can deprive of their rights . . . Unite with your nationalist brothers! Reactionaries and traitors will never triumph over sincere nationalists!*
>
> *Riad Bey will tell you everything. I request that you take all necessary measures to ensure his success. From the moment of his arrival, look after him and give him all your help.*
>
> *It is strength enough for a nation to have such a band of virtuous servants as 'Afif el-Solh, Muhammad al-Nahhas, Sa'dallah al-Jabiri, Ibrahim Hananu, Hashim al-Atasi, Fawzi al-Ghazzi, Faris al-Khoury, Ihsan al-Sharif, Bahjat al-Shihabi and many others. They will be the support of the legion of young people like yourself.*
>
> *Always keep in touch with Khayr al-Din Ahdab, owner of* al-'Ahd al-Jadid *in Beirut.*[3]

Riad arrived to an emotional welcome on Sunday, 20 May, a week after his father's lunch party. He had travelled from Palestine to Sidon via the border post at Naqura, but, to his parents' great disappointment, he could not be persuaded to stay home very long. Aged 33 and burst-ing with energy, he was eager to leave Sidon almost at once for Beirut and Damascus, to meet other nationalist allies. Getting the French

---

[3] MAE Fonds Beyrouth, série B, carton 20, Service des renseignements, Damas Ville, 5 April 1928.

to allow him back into Syria and Lebanon had not been easy: Henri Ponsot, the new high commissioner, had recommended to his superiors in Paris keeping the firebrand out altogether. In fact, on 3 April, he had instructed the French consuls in Jerusalem, Haifa and Jaffa 'to refuse a visa to the mandated territories to Riad el-Solh until further notice'. He testily explained his decision in a dispatch to the French foreign minister in Paris:

> You kindly informed me that Riad el-Solh had managed
> to renew his passport, and that he had undertaken not
> to return to Syria, but to travel only to Egypt. The truth
> is, however, that Riad el-Solh simply passed through
> Egypt, arriving in Haifa on 2 April, the city closest to
> our territory. He has lived there ever since. His friends
> have asked me repeatedly to allow him back but, without
> even waiting for the result of their interventions, he has
> informed all his extremist supporters in Damascus that he
> will soon be returning.
>
> Accordingly, I instructed our Consul to refuse him
> a visa. These facts should enlighten the Department as to
> the credit one can give to the undertakings of Riad el-Solh
> and his like.[4]

Henri Ponsot let Riad cool his heels in Haifa for several more weeks. It was not until 10 May that he wired the French consul in Haifa to say, 'You may issue a visa to Riad el-Solh'. On the same day, he signed a decree, no. 1144, annulling decree no. 274 of 27 June 1926, which had exiled Riad to the island of Arwad.[5] What finally persuaded Ponsot to relent was a pledge, given by Rida el-Solh, that his son would no longer engage in politics.

Needless to say, Riad was not about to consider his father's pledge to the French as binding on him. He was in confident mood, having made contacts in high places in Paris. He had successfully lobbied the Radical Socialist Party, securing from its executive committee a public statement declaring that 'The solution of the Syrian

---

[4] MAE, Nantes, Fonds Beyrouth (Amb.), série 199A4, carton 20, Haut-Commissair H. Ponsot à Ministre des Affaires Etrangères, Beirut, 13 April 1928.
[5] CADN, Fonds Beyrouth, carton 421, décision no. 1144, Haut-Commissaire, Beirut, 10 May 1928.

question can be found only in complete understanding with the Syrian nationalists . . . The Committee demands that satisfaction be given to the legitimate wishes of the Syrian people regarding unity and independence.' This important statement had been wired to the Syrian newspaper *al-Kashshaf* by its correspondent in Paris, and had been reprinted in several Beirut newspapers.[6] Riad knew that the local French high commissioner could not afford to get too far out of step with the political mood in the French capital. He was therefore determined to press his advantage as quickly and as vigorously as he could.

As ever, however, he lacked for funds. His many journeys, his prolonged stays in Paris, Geneva and Cairo, his need to entertain journalists and politicians, and his generosity to Arab students and to various impecunious friends, required a steady flow of cash. The Delegation of the Syro-Palestinian Congress was by now itself very short of money, and survived on increasingly irregular donations from its dwindling supporters in Cairo. The split in its ranks (especially the breach between the Emir Shakib Arslan on the one hand, and Prince Michel Lutfallah and Dr Shahbandar on the other) had had a disastrous impact on the Congress's image and finances.

Riad el-Solh himself earned nothing. He lived largely on credit, incurring substantial debts over the years, which his father had become unable to meet. Rida's attitude towards his remarkable and flamboyant son was a complex one: pride at his fame, anxiety over his spending habits, and perhaps even a certain unspoken resentment at having been elbowed off the political scene by Riad's more daring and radical political approach. In the meantime, the family land – the basis of their ever-decreasing fortune – was being steadily sold off. A family friend, Yusuf Yazbek, related that in 1928 he travelled to Tripoli with Riad, who there managed to sell an orange grove for 8,000 gold pounds, to keep some particularly pressing creditors at bay.[7]

From Henry de Jouvenel to Henri Ponsot

When Riad returned to the Levant in the spring of 1928, he found that France was still wrestling with the catastrophic aftermath of its

---

[6] MAE, Nantes, Fonds Beyrouth (Amb.), série 199A4, carton 20, revue de la presse, Beirut, 13 March 1928.
[7] Yusuf Yazbek, *Awraq Lubnaniyya*, 3 vols, Beirut 1955, 1956, 1957, vol. III, p. 552.

crushing of the Syrian revolt. The population was sullen, the cities flooded with impoverished refugees, trade severely disrupted and a great deal of property destroyed. Beirut, then the chief port of the Syrian interior, was a city of about 130,000 inhabitants, of whom 20,000 were Armenian survivors of the 1915 genocide, struggling valiantly and industriously to rebuild their shattered lives. This compared with a population of about 300,000 each for Damascus and Aleppo.

On the political front, France was caught between the irreconcilable claims of the Arab nationalists, who demanded 'Syrian unity', and the Lebanese nationalists, who insisted on preserving the territorial integrity of the French-created 'Greater Lebanon'. In these circumstances, it had proved impossible for High Commissioner Henry de Jouvenel to devise any form of government that would be acceptable to both.

On 26 April 1926, pending a choice by an elected assembly, he had thought to play safe by appointing a member of the old Ottoman aristocracy, His Highness Damad Ahmad Nami Bey, as head of the Syrian state. Born in Beirut in 1878, Ahmad Nami Bey was the son of a Circassian mother, and of Fakhri Bey, an aide-de-camp to the Khedive Ismail of Egypt. The title 'Damad' signified that he was a son-in-law of an Ottoman sultan. Indeed, he had married one of the daughters of the late Sultan Abdülmecid, who had conferred on him the title of 'Highness'. Reporting to London, the British consul general noted approvingly that the Damad 'has not been one of the crowd of office-seeking sycophants, who have been so prominent since the arrival of the French'.[8] But the Syrians failed to take warmly to him, and his insistence on surrounding himself with precious royal etiquette invited nothing but ridicule from a much-hardened population.

At the time of the Damad's appointment, French troops had recaptured from rebels the Druze capital of Suwayda. The implication, which Henry de Jouvenel tried to convey to a mostly sceptical public, was that France's military successes could also be read as a political turning point, the start of a new era. Anxious to put an end to the Revolution and restore normal political life, he had sought out moderate nationalists, with whom he thought France could reach some sort of an understanding. He formed a Syrian government on 5 May

---

[8] Consul General Satow to Austen Chamberlain, Beirut, 28 April 1926 (FO 371/11516 File 113809).

1926, which included three of them – Husni al-Barazi, a rich Homs landowner, as minister of interior, who was tasked with organising the forthcoming elections; the Christian lawyer, Faris al-Khoury, as minister of education; and Lutfi al-Haffar, vice-president of the Damascus Chamber of Commerce, as minister of public works. Jouvenel's strategy was to ensure the election of a Chamber that would draw up a Constitution and agree to a thirty-year treaty, which would preserve France's pre-eminent role in the country. To nationalist satisfaction, he went so far as to hint that he might even be prepared to settle the vexed question of 'Syrian unity' by returning to Syria some of the territories amputated from it when *Le Grand Liban* was created.

These ideas were, however, far too radical for General Gamelin, commander-in-chief of the Army of the Levant, and for his head of intelligence, Colonel Catroux, both of whom were still engaged in 'mopping up' with great brutality the remaining rebels in villages around Damascus. Their implacable view was that rebels and their nationalist supporters should be slaughtered, not negotiated with and rewarded. In the five years, 1920–25, the French army had lost 6,722 men in Syria, either killed or listed missing. It had incurred military expenditure of 2,500 million francs, an enormous sum, which, to unvarnished military men such as these, ruled out any possibility of political compromise.[9]

Much as General Sarrail's liberal policies had been sabotaged by his right-wing ultra-Catholic enemies, so Henry de Jouvenel was deliberately undermined by alarmist reports, sent to Paris by French army chiefs, who warned of the danger of a renewed outbreak of the insurrection. Ahmad Nami Bey, too, fell victim to France's military policies. When, in June, he was forced to reshuffle his government because of disagreements between nationalists and moderates, French security officers immediately arrested his three nationalist ministers – Husni al-Barazi, Faris al-Khoury and Lutfi al-Haffar – simply because they had wanted to send relief supplies to civilian victims of the Revolution. They were dispatched under military escort to Lebanon and imprisoned in the palace of Bayt al-Din. This French move made Ahmad Nami Bey even more deeply unpopular. Syria's nationalists had, in any event, never forgotten that he had agreed to serve as head of state during their Great Revolution.

[9] The Marquess of Crewe (Eric Phipps) to Sir Austen Chamberlain, Paris, 23 October and 7 November 1925, reporting on information given to the French Chamber of Deputies on 21 October and 5 November 1925 (FO 371/10851 File 114692).

One way or another, Henry de Jouvenel's rule in Syria was a failure. In Lebanon, he was only slightly more successful. Under his aegis, a new Constitution, adopted on 23 May 1926, provided for an elected president and an elected Representative Council, to which the government would be accountable. In June, a government was formed by Auguste Adib Pasha, a Maronite, while another Maronite, Shaykh Bishara al-Khoury, became minister of interior. On 1 September, the Republic of Lebanon was proclaimed, replacing the State of Greater Lebanon. The Representative Council was then promoted into a Chamber of Deputies, which proceeded to elect the Greek Orthodox politician Charles Dabbas as president of the Republic, a post he retained until 1932. By choosing him, the French hoped they could keep the rival Muslim and Maronite camps in some reasonable equilibrium.

The French-inspired 1926 Constitution was a far cry from the real independence that the nationalists demanded. Article 90 gave the French high commissioner control over foreign and defence policy. He was able to annul any legislation considered contrary to the Mandate, and could even, if he so wished, suspend the Constitution altogether. Article 9 stipulated that ministerial portfolios and public sector jobs would be filled on an 'equitable' confessional basis. This Article, in particular, entrenched sectarianism in Lebanon's public life. Some communities welcomed it, but the Lebanese have paid dearly for it to this very day.[10]

A dispirited Henry de Jouvenel resigned in the summer of 1926, and was replaced that October by Henri Ponsot, who went to considerable lengths to restore normal political life in Syria. An amnesty was declared and greater freedoms allowed. His Highness Damad Ahmad Nami Bey left office unregretted on 9 February 1928. Shaykh Taj al-Din al-Hasani then formed what the British consul in Damascus described as a 'completely subservient Ministry'.[11] Elections to a Constituent Assembly followed in April, which were won by nationalists in the towns and moderates in the countryside. The leading nationalist from Homs, Hashim al-Atasi, was elected president of the Chamber. Such, in brief, was the political situation that Riad el-Solh found on his return home in May 1928.

[10] Mizrahi, 'La France et sa politique de mandat', p. 47; George Corm, *Le Liban contemporain*, Paris 2005, pp. 91–2.
[11] Consul E. C. Hole to Sir Austen Chamberlain, Damascus, 23 February 1928 (FO 371/13074).

Riad and the Syrian National Bloc

A year earlier, in 1927, prominent nationalists from Damascus, Aleppo, Beirut and other cities of Syria and Lebanon, had started to make contact with one another in order to explore the possibility of engaging in a dialogue with the French. After the trauma of the Syrian revolt, they had come ruefully to recognise that military confrontation with France had not managed to advance their cause, but had, on the contrary, set it back most painfully. It was time to consider whether some other way forward could be found. When France indicated that it wished to regularise its presence in Syria by means of a bilateral treaty, some nationalists began to think that this might, after all, be one way to arrive at the long-desired ultimate goal of independence.

Riad had already pioneered a strategy of lobbying French politicians in Paris and appealing directly to French public opinion. Nationalists such as himself had felt enormous sympathy for the revolt and had hailed its fallen martyrs as their heroes, but they had not actually taken up arms themselves. They may even have had doubts about the wisdom – or indeed the feasibility – of trying to expel the French by force. In this, they stood in sharp contrast to men like Sultan al-Atrash, Dr Shahbandar and Nasib al-Bakri, who had been the standard-bearers of armed revolt. They were also very different from professional soldiers like Fawzi al-Qawuqji, from Druze and Hawrani tribesmen who had a traditional aptitude for warfare, or from Midan and Shaghur merchants and Ghuta villagers, who had borne the brunt of the fighting, given logistical support to the rebels, and had had to suffer France's brutal retaliation on their persons, homes and livelihood.

Those nationalist leaders who now looked for ways to engage with the French could not, in any sense, be decried as collaborators. Mostly from well-to-do, landowning families, they were members of Syria's traditional ruling elite, sons of the Ottoman Arab establishment. The crushing of the Revolution and the exile of its leaders had brought them to the fore as possible interlocutors with France. Several of them had attended Maktab 'Anbar, the prestigious Civil Preparatory School, which occupied a grand Damascene house of many ornate courtyards, which came to serve as a school for Syria's interwar elite.[12] Such men,

---

[12] Michael Provence, *The Great Syrian Revolt*, p. 39.

who had completed their education in Istanbul or Paris, were not prepared to submit to French dictation, but they were prepared to talk
to France. However, they were not to be confused on any level with
the handful of notables who, from the very beginning, had calculat-
edly thrown in their lot with the French Mandate. These included
'Abd al-Rahman al-Yusuf, Taj al-Din al-Hasani and Subhi Barakat in
Damascus; the Mudarris family in Aleppo; the Kinj family in Latakia;
and Charles Dabbas and Emile Eddé in Lebanon.

Henri Ponsot, the new high commissioner, began by publishing
decrees abolishing the state of emergency and granting an amnesty to
some former rebels. The Bakri brothers, Fawzi and Nasib (maternal
uncles of Shukri al-Quwatli's future wife), were welcomed back to
Damascus and were carried shoulder-high by cheering crowds. Other
prominent nationalists, who had not actually taken up arms in the
Revolt, were also allowed to return. They included Faris al-Khoury,
Fawzi al-Ghazzi, Sa'dallah al-Jabiri and 'Arif al-Na'mani. These were
Riad el-Solh's closest friends. They were a small band of well-born and
highly educated prominent politicians, who shared the same patriotic
ideas and were on intimate terms with one another. There was much
movement at that time between Syria, Lebanon and Palestine by such
like-minded men. They also corresponded a good deal by courier,
although their letters were frequently intercepted by the French, with
unfortunate consequences for the bearers.

Riad had written a letter from Haifa in November 1926 to the
Tripoli notable, 'Abd al-Hamid Karami, to congratulate him on his
support for the nationalist cause, but also to request him to send some
money to the Delegation in Geneva. The bearer of the letter, Kamal Jabr –
member of a rich Beirut family of strong nationalist sympathies, who
had himself generously and valiantly sent Riad money many times when
he needed it – was searched at the Lebanese frontier and Riad's letter
was found on him. He and his brother Bashir were promptly arrested
and sent into exile to Qadmus in the Alawite statelet of north-west Syria.
Another letter from Riad, intercepted by the French at the same time,
was addressed to Shaykh Taj al-Din al-Hasani, who was of the same
family as Riad's maternal grandmother, and contained angry remonstra-
tions about Shaykh Taj's despicable collaboration with the French.[13]

---

[13] Consul General H. E. Satow to Secretary of State, Beirut, 6 December 1926 (FO
732/22/3).

Like most of his friends and colleagues in Damascus and Geneva, Riad had been deeply influenced by French culture and by the political and moral values of liberal Europe. He longed for these principles to be applied by the French in his own Levant as well. Instead, however, men like him were vilified, arrested, jailed and expelled from their countries. Steeped in the colonialist and racist mentality which prevailed in Europe between the wars, the British and French governments could only conceive of democracy for their own, supposedly superior, usage.[14]

On 27 October 1927, nationalists from different Syrian cities assembled in Beirut for what was to be the first Congress of the Syrian National Bloc (al-kutla al-wataniyya). The meeting had been made possible by a prior agreement between leaders from the rival cities of Aleppo and Damascus, which had each aspired to become the capital of Syria. The Aleppo strongman, Ibrahim Hananu, was an early driving force in the formation of the Bloc, his considerable organisation in the north giving it initial substance. To his great regret, Riad could not attend the Congress, as the French had not yet allowed him back to the Levant. Hashim al-Atasi from Homs was elected president of the Bloc. Other prominent members were Jamil Mardam from Damascus and Sa'dallah al-Jabiri from Aleppo. Faris al-Khoury, the Protestant lawyer from Damascus, was an influential voice. The Bloc was supported by the Istiqlal (Independence) group, led by Shukri al-Quwatli, and by many of the patriotic merchants (such as Tawfiq al-Qabbani, who was to be imprisoned several times by the French), who had called general strikes in the suq to support the nationalists. The Bloc's executive comprised seven members, including Riad's cousin, 'Afif el-Solh.

Although it was not a political party, but rather a loose alliance of prominent individuals, the Bloc managed, by 1928, to become the leading political formation in Syria. Many of its meetings were held in the leafy, jasmine-scented courtyard house, in the passionately anti-colonial Shaghur quarter, of the committed Damascene nationalist, Tawfiq al-Qabbani, father of the poet, Nizar Qabbani (who, in photographs of the period, can be seen sitting, as a sweet-faced toddler, among the crowd of eminent politicians, most often being addressed by the eloquent Fawzi al-Ghazzi).[15] The Bloc's main demand was the

---

[14] Fleury, 'Le Mouvement national arabe', p. 354.
[15] Photos in the possession of the author.

return to Syria of the coastal towns and the four *cazas* which had been annexed to Greater Lebanon. Branches were set up in these 'disputed territories'.

To underline its commitment to the cause of 'Syrian unity', the Bloc was eventually to add eight Lebanese Arab nationalists to its Council of thirty-eight members: Riad el-Solh and 'Abd al-Rahman Bayhum from Beirut; the Emir Amin Arslan and the Emir Shakib Arslan from Mount Lebanon; Sa'id Haidar from Baalbek; and 'Abd al-Rahman Karami, Muhammad 'Arif al-Hasan and 'Abd al-Latif al-Bissar from Tripoli.[16] At their first Congress in Beirut, members of the National Bloc agreed to talk to the French, in the hope 'of achieving their aspirations and the recognition of their national sovereignty'.[17] The French, in turn, watched these developments with keen interest, as they were well aware that they needed an elite group with whom they might be able to come to an accommodation.

Riad el-Solh was with the National Bloc, but perhaps not entirely of it. Being from Beirut gave him a certain distance from the rivalries of Damascene and Aleppan politics. He saw himself as the voice of Syria abroad, the champion of the cause of Arab independence. He famously articulated nationalist goals – the removal of French rule; the restoration of Syrian unity, and its membership of a wider Arab family. He had become a figure of some international renown. Great nationalist hopes were placed on the influence he could wield in Paris. In those days, when only elites enjoyed access to education and international travel, European capitals like Paris and London, then the centres of imperial power, seemed distantly out of reach. To be at ease in them, as Riad evidently was, could not but confer authority, and a certain glamour too.

In addition to the National Bloc, which dealt with Syrian affairs, Lebanese Arab nationalists created another forum in Beirut known as the Conference of the Coast, of which the main focus of interest was the 'disputed territories'. Convened by Salim 'Ali Salam, 'Abd al-Hamid Karami and Riad el-Solh, it met three times in 1928, and twice in 1933. Its main political grievance was the arbitrary enlargement by the French of the *Petit Liban*, and the dismemberment into mini-states of what had remained of Faysal's Arab kingdom. But

---

[16] Raghid el-Solh, *Lebanon and Arabism: National Identity and State Formation*, London 2004, p. 53, n. 51.
[17] Mahafzah, 'La France et le mouvement nationaliste arabe de 1914 à 1950', p. 301.

this initiative faced immense opposition from a dominant Maronite community which, until the mid-1930s, sought by all possible means to exclude Lebanese Arab nationalists from the politics of the country.[18]

Riad Bey's triumphant tour

Before setting out to meet those patriots eagerly awaiting him in Syria, Riad was fêted like a hero in Sidon. Celebrations in his honour were crowned by a tea given by his father in the last week of May 1928, to which were invited the newly elected nationalist members of Syria's parliament, representing Damascus, Aleppo, Homs and Hama, as well as many leading journalists. To placate his father, and in order not to arouse the hostility of the French High Commission, Riad had begun by being reasonably cautious. But, on this happy occasion, he let rip and delivered a bold rhetorical speech, which hailed the nationalists' victory at the April elections in Syria. 'We have finally won the contest', he cried, 'and must now consolidate our gains. We must secure the complete sovereignty and independence of Syria! I have not returned from exile to abandon my struggle for the total triumph of our plans . . . I share the hope that France and her representative in Syria will respond positively to our demands'. These words, the French noted, caused a great impression among the deputies present. An anxious High Commission reported to Paris that the nationalists' dream was to see

> all the mandated territories freed from the Mandates and joined together to form a large Eastern power . . . Riad el-Solh's activity in Lebanon is inspired by this principle alone . . . [The nationalists] hope that Lebanon will be the first state under the Mandate to detach itself from France and demand its annexation to Syria, while retaining a certain regional autonomy . . . It is difficult to calm the impatience of the Muslim regions of Tripoli, south Lebanon and the Biqa'. A meeting was held in Baalbek attended by Riad el-Solh, Fawzi al-Ghazzi and others on the invitation of the Haidar family. Demonstrators shouted

---

[18] Raghid el-Solh, *Lebanon and Arabism*, pp. 8–9.

their wish to be united with Syria before being dispersed by the police.[19]

Early in June, the High Commission reported to Paris that

the Lebanese government has become alarmed by the activities of Riad el-Solh since his return and by demonstrations in his favour in Sidon, Baalbek and Beirut. His encounters with Damascus nationalists and his inflammatory speeches have created a profound impression on those Muslim, and even Christian, elements who favour Syrian unity, but who had come to accept the current regime and who, at least for the moment, had rallied to the Lebanese Republic. The Muslims of Tripoli and Beirut have been astonished at the freedom with which the young Riad has expressed himself. The neutrality of the Mandate authorities towards him has encouraged them to express their desire for union with Syria.

The French High Commission also added that these nationalist moves had greatly disturbed many Lebanese ministers, who had held a secret meeting attended by the deputy Emile Eddé.

They discussed what measures should be taken to defend the integrity of Lebanon in the face of such subversive manoeuvres. It was decided to summon an extraordinary session of the Chamber and table an immediate bill, which would authorise legal proceedings against any person working to overthrow the existing regime and dismember Lebanese territory. The law would also forbid the holding of any meeting judged to be subversive. The coming debate is likely to be stormy, but the majority around Eddé will ensure the success of the government against such nationalists as 'Umar Bayhum and Ahmad Da'uq.
    Riad el-Solh's attitude has become provocative. Last night, a group at the Restaurant Français listened

---

[19] MAE, Nantes, Fonds Beyrouth (Amb.), série 199A4, carton 20, undated but probably end May 1928.

*to him avidly as he discussed the disarmament of France
and, as he said, the casual appearance of the French army
in contrast to the smart appearance of the Italian army,
which gave an impression of strength and superiority.
In all the public places where he appears, he affirms his
freedom to criticise, saying that no one would dare check
him because his powerful friends in Paris and at the
League of Nations would defend him.*[20]

But this was not quite so. Riad el-Solh was now seen as a major threat by the French government in Paris, as well as by the French-backed government in Beirut. He had aroused so much popular enthusiasm that he could no longer easily be reined in. Uncertain as to how much support Riad actually had in French political circles, the local French authorities decided to act prudently, with High Commissioner Henri Ponsot adopting a policy of non-interference, of nonchalance even. This aroused the fury of his French officers, who itched for a far more muscular response to Riad's 'provocations'. E. C. Hole, the British consul, reported to London that French officials interpreted Ponsot's aloofness as 'a complete incapacity to make up his mind'.[21] Evidently, no one knew quite what to do with Riad.

Cheered by a vast crowd, he made a triumphal entry into Damascus on 20 June 1928, in a convoy of several hundred cars. Several Syrian members of parliament had gone out to meet him on the Beirut road, together with delegations of students, notables and merchants. Not everyone, however, was overjoyed at the sight. The Bakri brothers, for example, resented Riad's popular acclaim. After all, *they* had fought in the Syrian revolt, risked their lives, seen their grand houses destroyed and their fertile lands confiscated, while he walked off with the prize!

More ominously, shortly before Riad was due to arrive at the Orient Palace Hotel – then the leading place to stay in the city – a young man, widely suspected to be in the employ of the French, accidentally dropped a small home-made bomb he was carrying. It exploded, tearing its bearer's clothes. He was at once arrested. Another bomb – made up

[20] MAE, Nantes, Fonds Beyrouth (Amb.), série 199A4, carton 20, renseignment d'une source sérieuse, 9 June 1928.
[21] Consul E. C. Hole to Sir Austen Chamberlain, Damascus, 2 June 1928 (FO 371/13076).

of a mixture of small stones and explosives, and wrapped in a piece of cloth – was thrown at the prominent nationalist, Fawzi al-Ghazzi, also on his way to greet Riad, but luckily failed to injure him.

The situation in Damascus was particularly tense, because the nationalists had decided to flex their muscles. A mere two months after the April elections, a Syrian parliamentary committee, chaired by Ibrahim Hananu, was charged with drafting a Constitution. Its author was Fawzi al-Ghazzi. His text pointedly made no mention whatsoever of the Mandate or of French interests. Article 2 defined Syria as an 'indivisible' entity, which included Palestine, Transjordan and Lebanon. It provided for a Muslim head of state, a Chamber elected for four years by universal suffrage, and empowered to sign treaties and name representatives abroad; a government responsible to parliament; religious freedoms and the equality before the law of all citizens, whatever their ethnicity. It gave Syrian women rights unequalled in any Arab constitution. It stipulated the creation of a national army. Everything about this Constitution was totally unacceptable to France, which angrily set out to sabotage it. Fawzi al-Ghazzi, the enlightened writer of this pioneering text, was much respected for standing up bravely to the French, who did everything they could to pressure him to make changes in their favour, but failed to sway him.

Such was the heated political atmosphere in Syria in the summer of 1928, when Riad was honoured by a number of grand receptions at which his efforts in Europe to challenge the Mandate were hailed, and to which he responded with rousing speeches – all carefully monitored by agents of the French *Sûreté Générale*. On 30 June, 'Abd al-Karim al-'A'idi gave a reception for him in Damascus attended by 700 people, including all the great names of the nationalist movement. On 3 July, he was the guest at a dinner given by Muhammad 'Ali al-'Abid. On 4 July, he called on the deputy Lutfi al-Haffar at his house in that same Shaghur quarter of Damascus, which so prided itself on its unyielding stand against the French. There, some thirty people had assembled to meet him. Lutfi al-Haffar then accompanied him to the neighbouring house of Shaykh Salim al-Tibi – another nationalist and a relative of Tawfiq al-Qabbani – where 400 notables and young people were waiting for him, and where he was greeted with long applause and cries of 'Long live Riad el-Solh!' In reply, he praised the courage and spirit of sacrifice of the Shaghur, and saluted the memory of Hassan Kharrat, leader of a resistance group during the Great Syrian Revolution. On

9 July, he attended a banquet at the Hotel Victoria, given by Mikhail Ilyan, a Christian nationalist from Aleppo.

On 10 July, Hashim al-Hakim gave a banquet in his honour at his house in the Midan quarter attended by 200 people. The inhabitants of Midan were particularly famous for their extraordinary hospitality, and the delicious, substantial and labour-intensive cooking of their womenfolk. The men were tough and used to having their way. Sarcastic Syrians quip that you should 'marry Midan girls, but keep your daughters from marrying Midan boys' (*Khod minhum wa la ta'tihum*). Be this as it may, the quarter had paid dearly in lost men and livelihoods during the Revolution.

Hashim Bey's son, Wahid, gave the address of welcome. 'We are celebrating tonight', he said, 'the arrival among us of the standard-bearer of nationalism, the flame of freedom and independence, Riad Bey el-Solh! A man who has chosen devotion as his principle and patriotism as his religion deserves to be welcomed by this honourable gathering.' In a touching flight of hyperbole, the young and excitable Wahid compared Riad to Bismarck, to the Egyptian nationalist Zaghlul Pasha and to Turkey's Mustafa Kemal, calling on him to rally the nationalists, too often divided by misunderstandings and personal conflicts. This way Syria's voice could be heard at the League of Nations, and her misfortunes become known to the world.[22]

Amid frenetic applause, Riad mounted the platform and began his speech with these words:

> *Throughout history, nations leap for joy when certain*
> *words are uttered. Italians, for example, cannot contain*
> *their enthusiasm when you speak to them of Rome, their*
> *Eternal City. For me, on the other hand, the simple word*
> *'Midan' arouses sentiments which I cannot begin to*
> *describe. Whatever I say about this quarter – or indeed*
> *about this city, which one cannot enter without feelings of*
> *immense veneration for the memories it evokes – whatever*
> *I say about Midan, can never do justice to its purity and*
> *nobility. Its reputation has spread far and wide, even*
> *to Palestine which, in spite of everything, has remained*

---

[22] MAE, Nantes, Fonds Beyrouth, série B, carton 20, Service des renseignements, Damas Ville, 18 July 1928.

Syrian. Our brothers there have been inspired by the deeds
of heroic Midan . . . Glory to you, dear sons of Midan!
We are at a critical stage in our struggle. I call
on you to rally as one man around our standard – the
standard of the National Bloc!

The Shaghur, home to so many National Bloc politicians and activists, and to their *Istiqlal* Party supporters, most notably Shukri al-Quwatli, had already done so unstintingly. With these flattering words, Riad was no doubt hoping that the still reluctant Midan would follow Shaghur's lead and do the same.

In speeches such as these, Riad declared time and again that the nationalists should all unite around the National Bloc. This was the way to triumph over the intrigues of their enemies. He often mentioned the French Radical Party – 'the strongest and richest party in the whole of France' – which had actually called for an agreement with the Syrian nationalists. Indeed, he said he was soon returning to Europe to carry on the fight there.

With these numerous social appearances and public speeches, Riad breathed fresh life into a resistance movement which – after the defeat of the Great Syrian Revolution – was still counting its losses and binding its wounds. At such meetings, proud and once well-to-do men were often painfully compelled to ask for aid to rebuild family homes vindictively burned down by the French. But there was also a new spirit of daring in the air. As guests filed out of the Hakim house to the applause of the inhabitants of the quarter, Fakhri al-Barudi cried: 'A little while ago we could not even have uttered the word "homeland" without some wretched spy denouncing us. Today, we have no fear of spies – or of lackeys of the French!'

Money and other problems

Three issues preoccupied Riad during his triumphal visit to Syria in the spring and summer of 1928. The first was the need to raise money to finance his continuing campaign in Europe. The records of the French police refer repeatedly to his request for donations to enable him to continue his work in Paris and Geneva. He was said to be seeking up to 3,000 Egyptian pounds. He had so far been largely self-financing and was now running out of all family and personal funds. His second preoccupation was his wish to explain to the Syrian public the nature of his work abroad, and the third was his contribution to the debate about how, and by whom, Syria was to be governed.

Before he returned to Europe that September, Ahmad Da'uq gave a farewell dinner for him at his house in Beirut. Riad chose the occasion to give a summary of the finances of the Syro-Palestinian Delegation in Geneva. 'Like my colleagues at the Delegation', he said, 'I am well aware of the importance of economic questions, but I must admit that economics is not my favourite subject'. In the eight years of its existence, he explained, the Delegation had spent some 15,000 Egyptian pounds, drawn largely from the private resources of the Emir Shakib Arslan, Ihsan al-Jabiri and himself. This did not include living or travel expenses. The Delegation, he said, had no regular income of its own. The total donations it had received amounted to 1,687 Egyptian pounds, of which the Lutfallahs had contributed 653 pounds. The association of Syrian merchants in Cairo had donated 100 pounds; the Syrian Independence Party of Argentina, 100 pounds; an anonymous Syrian patriot, 100 pounds; and the Arab Association of Australia and the Arab colony of New York had together raised 190 pounds. The clear implication of his remarks was that, if his work was to continue, fresh funds would need to be found as a matter of urgency.

As for the nature of his activities, Riad was anxious to make clear that he had no mandate to negotiate with the French government on Syria's behalf. That was the role of the National Bloc, 'whose patriotic stance was an honour to the country'. If the Bloc were to send a delegation to France, he would do everything in his power to help it. 'There have been many rumours about the nature of my mission in Europe', Riad declared. 'Some have said that I had gone to sound out the Quai d'Orsay about a visit to Paris by a delegation from Syria's Constituent Assembly'. But diplomacy was not his role, he stressed. His task was one of providing political information. It was to persuade French politicians and the French public that the Mandate was not in France's long-term interest, and that it should be given up as soon as possible.

His insistence on this point suggests that he may have been stung by the remarks of Sa'id Mahassen, who, in an article in the Syrian press, had accused Riad el-Solh of conducting negotiations over the future of a country 'of which he does not own a single piece of land'. This accusation was not only bizarre in its association of patriotic commitment with landownership, but inexact, as Riad was from a family that was part Syrian, and considered himself to be Syrian both politically and socially at this stage. 'I am going to continue the task which I have begun', Riad declared, 'which consists of working tirelessly to secure the realisation of our national aspirations'. French opinion did not yet know the true situation. There was still a great deal more to be done. He was going to ask the Socialist and Radical Parties of France to implement their promises regarding Syrian independence.[23] As it happened, on 30 November of that year, a Socialist member of the French Chamber of Deputies did propose the abandonment of the Syrian Mandate. He was promptly and firmly silenced by the prime minister.[24]

There was, nevertheless, some French uncertainty about the future of Syria. How was it to be governed? How could the Mandate win acceptance from a hostile population? What changes needed to be made for it to do so? High Commissioner Henri Ponsot may have had some reformist ideas, but he was held in check and undermined – as his predecessors had been before him – by the colonial and military party in Paris, which was still gloating over the crushing of the Great Syrian Revolution. Following heavy-handed instructions from Paris, Ponsot demanded the removal of the offending articles from the Constitution which Fawzi al-Ghazzi had written. But, when neither al-Ghazzi himself nor yet the Syrian parliament agreed to budge on this issue – which was vital to a sense of national dignity – Ponsot was swift to act. He adjourned Syria's parliament by decree for three months, and then dissolved it altogether.

In November, Consul E. C. Hole reported to London that the rejection of the Constitution had

> created an atmosphere of tension comparable only to the period of the rebellion. French troops are kept in readiness for immediate action . . . The population of certain villages are confined to their homes on pain of being shot, and irrigation is rendered impossible. Many villagers in panic have removed their belongings to Damascus . . . The Druze

---

[23] MAE, Nantes, Fonds Beyrouth (Amb.), série 199A4, carton 20, 12 September 1928.
[24] Sir W. Tyrrell to Sir Austen Chamberlain, Paris, 3 December 1928 (FO 371/13074).

of the Mountain are in a condition of extreme want . . .
Large numbers have come to the city to obtain work as
day-labourers.

Some months later, and to the great shock of opinion in the city, Fawzi al-Ghazzi died agonisingly of poisoning. His death was widely attributed in nationalist circles to French agents. Medicines which had been mixed for him by a cousin, who was his habitual pharmacist, were later found to have been tampered with en route to his house. What was almost certainly a political assassination of this unyielding man was dressed up to seem like a crime passionnel, and Ghazzi's highly strung and confused wife, Lutfiyya al-Yafi, was accused of the crime and imprisoned for years in the Damascus citadel, although she continued to swear her innocence, including in front of her entire family and with the Qur'an before her, as she lay on her deathbed many long years later.[25]

Coming as it did in the wake of brutal colonialist actions, Fawzi al-Ghazzi's untimely and mysterious death could not but be seen as highly suspicious, as it does to this day. His death deprived Syria of a potential leader, who had fought the French Mandate and conceived the blueprint of a constitutional democracy, which he had hoped would come into being immediately after Independence – a hope that still remains unrealised.

In this confused and miserable period, all sorts of ideas were being aired for Syria's future governance. Was it to be a republic or a monarchy? Most nationalists now favoured a republican regime. Riad was said to be campaigning for the election to the presidency of his colleague and friend, the Emir Shakib Arslan. Other reports, however, suggested that he might be supporting the candidacy to the Syrian throne of the Emir Zayd, younger brother of King Faysal of Iraq, and that he had received a deposit of 3,000 gold pounds to promote the Hashemite cause.[26] Yet another rumour had it that Riad actually favoured a Saudi prince – the Emir Faysal – one of the sons of 'Abd al-'Aziz al-Sa'ud. Other even more far-fetched candidates were said to include the son of the Bey of Tunis, or a member of the Husayni family of Morocco.

[25] Editorial pinning the blame for Fawzi al-Ghazzi's death on High Commissioner Henri Ponsot, in *al-Hadith*, Aleppo, 8 August 1929; interview with his grandson, Dr Hassan al-Ghazzi, 27 October 2007.
[26] MAE, Nantes Ambassade, série 199A4, carton 20, Sûreté Générale, Damascus, 4 July 1928.

Local British consular officials struggled to follow these Byzantine intrigues. On a visit to Damascus in January 1929, a Foreign Office inspector, the emphatically named Mr Hall-Hall, reported to London that E. C. Hole, the hard-pressed consul, was suffering greatly from over-strain:

> But . . . one sees French . . . officials at the Holes' house frequently. The men may be somewhat attracted by Mr Hole's French wife, who is lively and entertaining, though perhaps lacking in some of the dignity desirable in consular officers' wives . . . Mr Hole's languages (in order of proficiency) are French, Greek, Italian, German, Turkish, Arabic; also some knowledge of Spanish, Persian, Russian, Dutch, Portuguese and Romanian! Mr Parr, the vice-consul, has to be injected with strychnine every three days. Mr Pott, a probationer, seems an intelligent young man, although suffering from a kind of nervous illness. He is smitten with a most extreme form of shyness and therefore avoids company.[27]

Riad's triumphal visit to Aleppo

By this time, Riad was back in Paris, continuing his work of disseminating information and, as his letters imply, scoring considerable success with the French Radical and Socialist Parties. In April 1929, he hurried back to Lebanon, having received a wire from his father saying 'Ma santé est inquiétante' (my health is cause for concern). On his arrival in Beirut, a correspondent of al-Qabas wanted to know from him how the Syrian question was viewed in Paris. 'If the principle of independence is not conceded', Riad replied, 'there can be no satisfactory solution'.[28] But he was optimistic, convinced that the French public was on his side.

Riad then threw himself into his usual activities of speech-making and journalism, spending a great deal of time at the editorial

---

[27] Report by Mr Hall-Hall, a Foreign Office inspector, January 1928 (FO 369/2110, 2111).

[28] MAE, Nantes, Fonds Beyrouth (Amb.), série 199A4, carton 20, Service de presse du Haut-Commissariat, 11 April 1929.

offices of *al-'Ahd al-Jadid*, where he mounted a press campaign against Robert de Caix, the former secretary-general at the High Commission in Beirut, whose policy had led to the hateful fragmentation of Syria, and who had then been appointed French representative on the Permanent Mandates Commission. When violent clashes occurred between Arabs and European Jews in Palestine in 1929, Riad took the lead in organising demonstrations in Beirut in support of the Palestine Arabs. A French police report described him as *le turbulent agitateur nationaliste*. In a speech at the Hotel Gebeili in the Lebanese mountain village of Aley, Riad declared: 'The demonstrations have taken place in response to the persecutions suffered by the Arabs of Palestine. They have given us the chance to show the French and the world that the Lebanese and the Syrians are members of the same Arab family, and that they know how to stand together against their enemies'.[29] A correspondent of a nationalist newspaper, *al-Ahrar*, who interviewed Riad at his seafront home at 'Ayn al-Mrayseh in Beirut, described him as 'the soul of the nationalist movement'.[30]

In November, Riad set off on another triumphal visit to Syria, this time to Aleppo, where he was fêted by the leading nationalists – Sa'dallah al-Jabiri, Dr 'Abd al-Rahman al-Kayyali, Ibrahim Hananu, Dr Nazim al-Qudsi – as well as by the Christian notables, Mikhail Ilyan, Edmond Homsi, Na'im Antaki and Edmond Rabbath. French intelligence reported that the aim of his visit was to raise funds for the Syrian delegation in Europe and for his Beirut newspaper, *al-'Ahd al-Jadid*. He also hoped to heal rifts between nationalist leaders, who were not always at one with each other. Supporters of Sa'dallah al-Jabiri were at odds with those of Ibrahim Hananu and 'Abd al-Rahman al-Kayyali. Riad saw it as his task to make peace and bring them together.

A meeting held in Riad's honour at the Café Imperial on 26 November was characteristic of the many such gatherings he attended. It was opened by Dr 'Abd al-Rahman al-Kayyali, who hailed Riad's leading role in the cause of Syrian independence, and listed the sacrifices he had made to bring nationalist demands to the notice of ruling circles in the West. There followed a rousing poem by 'Umar Zayni; then a speech by Mikhail Ilyan; then another poem by Yusuf Hassir, mourning the martyrs who had been put to death by the Turks (which,

---

[29] MAE, Nantes, Fonds Beyrouth (Amb.), série 199A4, carton 20, note de l'Inspecteur-Général des Polices, Beirut, 31 August 1929.
[30] *Al-Ahrar*, Beirut, 22 October 1929.

French intelligence reported, 'moved the audience profoundly'). This was followed by a long speech by Dr Kayyali about the work of the Syrian delegation abroad and how it had suffered from lies put about by intriguers against its mission. 'Umar Zayni then declaimed another poem on the theme of freedom, which was received with great enthusiasm.

Riad rose to tell the meeting that he was carrying a letter from the French Socialist Party stating that it had decided that Syria was ready for independence and for membership of the League of Nations. Syria, Riad said, wanted Western-style independence, not 'Oriental' independence! He compared French policy in Syria unfavourably with British policy in Iraq, where the Mandate was being given up. He attacked Robert de Caix. He called for unity between Christians and Muslims, which, he said, was necessary to thwart Western attempts to divide them. His speech made a strong impression on the audience. The French *Sûreté Générale* had kept ten policemen in reserve at a nearby station, but, to its relief, they were not needed, as there was no disturbance to public order after the meeting.[31]

The next day, 27 November, the veteran nationalist leader Ibrahim Hananu gave a tea party at which Riad declared that 'The Syrian delegation has pledged never to cease to demand independence for Syria so long as any of its members are alive!' He returned to the theme of the need for Christian–Muslim entente. He observed that on the coast in Lebanon there was now complete understanding between Christians and Muslims. They were brothers bound together by their common link to their country. 'We must first give satisfaction to the Christians living among us', he declared. Unity demanded sacrifices and Muslims should be the first to assume them. This theme was to form the bedrock of his policy for Lebanon from then on.

In a vibrant tribute to Aleppo, he said that he could never forget those who had consoled him as he passed through the city on his way to exile in 1916. In the weeks he spent in Aleppo, Riad was a frequent visitor to the Jabiri household, where he virtually became one of the family. French intelligence reported that he had become engaged to Fayza, daughter of the late Ottoman parliamentarian Nafe' Pasha al-Jabiri, a leading Sunni Muslim notable. She was one of many heirs to

---

[31] MAE, Nantes, Fonds Beyrouth, série B, carton 20, Sûreté Générale, Aleppo, 28 November 1929.

his immense fortune, estimated at 200,000 gold pounds.[32] Indeed, Riad el-Solh was to marry Fayza al-Jabiri a few years later.

Dissensions in the Arab camp were numerous too. In Lebanon, pro-French Maronite politicians schemed to keep Arab nationalists out of politics altogether. In Syria, the nationalist movement was deeply divided: the Bakris sniped at the Solhs; Shahbandar intrigued against Shakib Arslan; Prince Michel Lutfallah had become bitter at the evaporation of his hopes for a Levant principality; republicans feared Hashemite royal ambitions; Aleppo sought to rival Damascus. The Great Syrian Revolution had left profound scars. Even the French themselves were uncertain as to how to proceed. They had brutally crushed the insurgency, but had failed to devise any sort of political settlement. Whenever one of their high commissioners attempted a creative political negotiation, he was soon brought down, either by the French military stationed in Beirut or by the colonial party in Paris.

And yet Riad el-Solh continued somehow to convey the fervour of nationalist commitment, as well as the hope that the longed-for goals of unity and independence could one day soon be realised. By 1928–29, he had become one of the most prominent Muslim political figures in Lebanon and Syria. His bold and tireless campaigning in Paris and Geneva had won him more attention than any other of his contemporaries. At a time of great confusion and despondency, when some began to feel that perhaps they had no option but to submit to French rule, he pledged to continue the fight.

[32] MAE Fonds Beyrouth, série B, carton 20, deuxième bureau, Beirut, 26 December 1929.

CONGRES SYRIO-PALESTINIEN
25 Août - 21 Septembre 1921
GENÈVE

26 – The Syro-Palestinian Congress in session at Geneva in 1921. It was the first organised Arab protest against the Mandates. At the centre of the top table is Prince Michel Lutfallah, president of the Congress; to his right is Shaykh Rashid Rida, vice-president. At the far end of the side-table to their right is the Emir Shakib Arslan, secretary-general. Riad el-Solh is at the table opposite, second from the right at the near end. At the small table in the middle of the room is Ali al-Ghaïaty, the only journalist allowed to follow the proceedings from inside the conference hall. (By kind permission of the Otrakji family collection at www.creativesyria.com.)

27 – The Druze Emir Shakib Arslan (1869–1946), a leading pan-Islamic political activist and man of letters. Exiled from Lebanon by the French, he spent most of the interwar years lobbying the League of Nations in Geneva on behalf of Islamic and Arab causes. His closest colleagues were Ihsan al-Jabiri, former chamberlain of the Emir Faysal in Damascus, and Riad el-Solh.

28 – General Maurice Sarrail (1856–1929), the French high commissioner who tried to introduce liberal reforms in Syria, but ended up ordering the bombardment of Damascus in 1925. (By kind permission of Sami Moubayed at www.syrianhistory.com.)

29 – The Druze leader Sultan Pasha al-Atrash (1891–1982), in bitter exile after the defeat by the French of the Great Syrian Revolution of 1925–27, which he had inspired and led. (By kind permission of the photography department of the American Colony in Jerusalem.)

30 – Dr 'Abd al-Rahman al-Shahbandar (1880–1940), a medical doctor and prominent Syrian nationalist of uncompromising views, who joined Sultan Pasha al-Atrash's Great Syrian Revolution in 1925, and helped spread it from the Jabal Druze to the rest of Syria. He was jailed on the island of Arwad, off the Syrian coast. In June 1940, he was assassinated in mysterious circumstances. (By kind permission of Sami Moubayed at www.syrianhistory. com.)

31 – Three rebels hanged by the French in al-Marja square in Damascus during the Great Syrian Revolution of 1925–27. Corpses were often left on view to intimidate the population. (By kind permission of Sami Moubayed at www.syrianhistory.com.)

32 – Fawzi al-Qawuqji (1890–1977), an ardent Arab nationalist and soldier-of-fortune, who fought the French in Syria in 1925–27, the British in Palestine in 1936–39, and the British again in Iraq during Rashid 'Ali al-Gaylani's coup of 1941. In the 1948 Arab-Israeli war, he commanded the volunteer Arab Liberation Army, and shared in the Arab defeat. (By kind permission of Sami Moubayed at www.syrianhistory.com.)

33 – Shaykh Taj al-Din al-Hasani (1885–1943), a pliant pro-French politician, who served the French repeatedly – as prime minister, as interim head of state in 1928–31, and as president of Syria in 1941–43. He was reviled by the nationalists, particularly by Riad el-Solh, who was distantly related to him. (By kind permission of Sami Moubayed at www.syrianhistory.com.)

34 – Fawzi al-Ghazzi (1891–1929), an outstanding anti-French lawyer and politician, who won fame in Syria by drafting a constitution, following the nationalists' victory at the April 1928 elections. Since his draft made no mention of the Mandate, it was angrily rejected by the French. Shortly afterwards, al-Ghazzi died of poisoning. His wife was accused of the murder and was sentenced to long years in jail, but the crime was widely attributed to French agents. (By kind permission of Dr Sabah Kabbani.)

9 MAN OF THE PEOPLE

The late 1920s and early 1930s were difficult times for Riad and for the Arab national movement to which he had dedicated his life. For one thing, there was a great deal of misery in Syria and Lebanon. The world recession had had a catastrophic impact on living standards there. Deflation in Lebanon in 1929–1930 had brought about a collapse of wages by 50 per cent. The average pay for an unskilled worker in 1932 was 11 francs for a ten-hour day (6 francs for women and 3 for children). Since 1914, the value of money in the Levant states had fallen by 500 per cent.[1] Quite apart from the hardships suffered by the working class, to which Riad was sensitive, the causes for which he had fought were languishing badly. There was a general sense of defeat and foreboding in the nationalist camp. In Syria and Lebanon, the French presence seemed immovable, while in Palestine, Britain was helping the Zionists establish their 'national home', to the great distress of the local Arab population. Riad watched anxiously as his friend, the Hajj Amin al-Husayni, Mufti of Jerusalem, struggled desperately to stem the relentlessly swelling tide of European Jewish immigration.

The one consolation Riad derived from these difficult times was a personal one. He was building a reputation as a prominent leader of his generation. In 1929, by the age of 35, he had gained an international reputation as a scourge of the French and British presence in the Levant, and an eloquent advocate of Arab liberation. Vigorous, charismatic, sharp-witted and at the height of his youthful powers, he was not only fêted in nationalist circles in Syria, Lebanon and Palestine, but was well known as a political activist in Paris and Geneva too. He

---

[1] Jacques Couland, *Le Mouvement syndical au Liban 1919–1946*, Paris 1970, p. 137.

was on easy terms with French journalists and parliamentarians, and was a thorn in the flesh of the Permanent Mandates Commission of the League of Nations, which had become more than familiar with the flood of impassioned letters and petitions addressed to it by Riad el-Solh and his two hardworking colleagues, Shakib Arslan and Ihsan al-Jabiri, of the Syro-Palestinian Delegation.

But behind the brave front he always liked to put on, all was not well with Riad. In his home base of Beirut, he was confined to the margins of political life by France and its local allies. As a Sunni leader with strong Arab nationalist views, he was deliberately excluded from mainstream politics, which remained the protected domain of politicians prepared to collaborate with the French. The all-powerful French High Commission, and the colonial secret services, considered him a dangerous agitator and kept him under very tight surveillance. Riad el-Solh's loyal following at this time was on the street, in the radical press and in the nascent labour unions. It was certainly not in parliament or in the other French-serving institutions of *Le Grand Liban*, still less in the *Sérail*, the compromised seat of government.

In Syria, although Riad was intimately connected with the leaders of the National Bloc, and was honoured and applauded by them, he remained, as a Lebanese, an associate member rather than a full member of their group. At its conference in Homs in 1932, the Bloc had indeed established a permanent secretariat (*al-maktab al-da'im*) composed of seven elected members: Hashim al-Atasi, president; Ibrahim Hananu, *za'im* (leader); Sa'dallah al-Jabiri, vice-president; Faris al-Khuri, *'amid* (doyen); Jamil Mardam, Shukri al-Quwatli and 'Abd al-Rahman Kayyali, members. Riad and two other Lebanese notables, 'Abd al-Rahman Bayhum and 'Abd al-Hamid Karami, had been named associates.

Goodbye to Geneva

By 1930, Riad had come to feel that his constant lobbying of the League of Nations at Geneva had been an exhausting and ultimately futile exercise, which had achieved little of political substance. Petitioning the League's Permanent Mandates Commission had turned out to be an expensive waste of time, since all appeals addressed to it had been callously brushed aside. In Europe between the wars, as rival imperial powers fought over their spheres of influence, there was little sympathy for the Arab struggle to throw off colonial rule in the Levant or in North Africa.

Riad had been profoundly influenced by his association with the Emir Shakib Arslan, a poet, man of letters and gentleman-revolutionary, some twenty-five years his senior, who treated him like a younger brother or son. The emir knew that Riad was always short of funds and that he was financing himself by selling off family land and assets. In one of his letters, he urged Riad not to dispose of everything he owned with no thought for the future.

> I don't want my paternal words to be a burden to you, but I would urge you not to sell your remaining property and deprive yourself of all your assets, even if the cause is our own.
>
> If one day, God forbid, you were to find yourself in need, no one would remember your services to the Arabs, or your expenditure. Try to hold on to what you still have, so as to live free and independent of others.[2]

Riad's temperament did not allow him to heed this concerned advice. He continued running up debts as quickly as ever. He would remain in loyal contact with Shakib Arslan and with Ihsan al-Jabiri for the rest of their lives, but 1930 was the last year in which he was to spend much time with either of them. In his last months in Geneva, he helped edit the French-language *La Nation arabe*, a 'monthly journal of political, literary, economic and social affairs', described as 'the organ of the Syro-Palestinian Delegation to the League of Nations serving the interests of the Arab countries and those of the East'. It contained numerous memoranda signed by Arslan, Jabiri and Solh, addressed to the League and to other bodies, about the colonial misdeeds of the British in Palestine and the French in Syria and Lebanon. The journal was edited from the Delegation's offices at 16 boulevard Helvétique, Geneva, and it was there, for weeks on end, that Riad went to work. In all, thirty-eight issues of *La Nation arabe* were published between 1930 and 1938.[3] In September 1931, there was a change of address and the

---

[2] Alia el-Solh, *Le Jour*, 7 December 1965.

[3] Fleury, 'Le Mouvement national arabe', pp. 329–54. All thirty-eight issues of *La Nation arabe* were published in 1988 in four facsimile volumes by Archives Editions, Farnham Common, Buckinghamshire, UK.

reference to the Delegation was dropped, but by that time events on the ground in both Lebanon and Syria had claimed Riad's attention.

Shakib Arslan and Ihsan al-Jabiri soldiered on alone. A Swiss intelligence report of 1 November 1933 remarked that 'thanks to the presence in Geneva of Emir Shakib Arslan and his close colleague Ihsan al-Jabiri, the threads of all the affairs of the Arab world pass through Geneva'.[4] The British Foreign Office took a less sanguine view, describing *La Nation arabe* as 'an incendiary and puerile journal'.[5] The very fact that a journal based in Geneva promoted the cause of Arab independence was evidently not welcome to an imperial power like Britain.

As the 1930s wore on, the journal and its editors were often accused of siding with the Fascists, even though their own struggle for Arab emancipation had long predated the rise of either Mussolini or Hitler. Obviously, some Arab nationalists did turn for help to either Italy or Germany, in the hope that these powers would put an end to the great oppression imposed on them by the British and the French. But these were in a minority. Arab patriots struggling for independence – whether they were Egyptian, Syrian, Tunisian, Algerian or Moroccan – found far more support on the Left than they did on the Right. Between the wars, Communist-front organisations, such as the League of Oppressed Peoples, became so identified with the cause of colonial liberation that, by extension, Arab nationalists came to be regularly denounced as 'Communist agitators'.

It was no small paradox (and one that was regularly seen among Italian Communists from aristocratic backgrounds) that militant Arab nationalists from patrician backgrounds – like Riad el-Solh, Shakib Arslan and Ihsan al-Jabiri – looked for support from revolutionary movements whose objectives were opposed to the actual interests of their own families. Arslan, for his part, had sought support for his cause where he could find it, on the Left as well as on the Right. He was a personal friend of the ex-German emperor, Wilhelm II. He had been the guest of the Soviet government in 1927, as well as of various American states. He had held meetings with Mussolini, but had also been invited to attend the Socialist Congress in Brussels in 1928, where, a year earlier, he had taken part in an anti-imperialist

[4] Ibid., p. 345.
[5] Foreign Office Records of Leading Personalities in Syria and Lebanon, 14 March 1938 (FO371/21914–115136).

congress. He knew the French Communist Senator Marcel Cachin and the editor of *L'Humanité*, Gabriel Péri. Many of these contacts he passed on to Riad, who greatly admired his political dedication and personal integrity.

Whenever he was accused of being an agent of Bolshevism or of Fascism, Arslan would reply: 'We hate all dictatorships without exception – whether Fascism, Kemalism, Bolshevism or French militarism in Syria and North Africa, or any other regime of this sort. We put them all in the same category and call on the conscience of the world to judge them as they deserve'.[6] This was very much Riad el-Solh's own position too.

A show of force in Riad's favour

A curious incident occurred at about this time which, although little more than a storm in a teacup, was to throw light on the tenor of Beirut public life and Riad's extraordinary popularity. It will be recalled that Sami el-Solh, by now a judge at the Appeal Court, was married to Riad's sister, Balqis. The son of 'Abd al-Rahim el-Solh, Ahmad Pasha's brother, he was Riad's cousin as well as his brother-in-law. Sami was known for his short temper, and had often been involved in disputes with French officials. On one occasion, he had had a violent quarrel with a French officer who had insulted him. Sami ended up slapping his face. Under French rule, this was a highly dangerous thing to do, which could easily have landed him in jail or worse. Hurrying home, he told his wife to pack their things immediately. 'We're leaving!' he cried. 'We have to get out.' But Balqis knew the wife of the French high commissioner, whom she had met socially in one of the city's salons. She decided to go at once to call on Madame Ponsot.

'What would you do', she asked her, 'if a man insulted you and your country?'

'Why, I would slap his face!' the spirited Frenchwoman replied.

The matter was settled there and then.

On another occasion, in December 1932, Sami el-Solh was incensed to learn that Mumtaz, his younger brother, had been harshly

---

[6] *La Nation arabe*, March–April 1932.

interrogated by Alfred Thabit, a pro-French judge at the Criminal Court. This was in connection with a real estate scandal in which, it was alleged, Mumtaz was involved. Sami went to confront Thabit at his office and, after a heated altercation between them, he rushed off to complain to President Charles Dabbas of what he considered a deliberate slight against the entire Solh family. Anxious to calm things down, Dabbas received Riad el-Solh at his house that afternoon to hear the family's side of the story, and then sent for Thabit for his version of the affair. Thabit was then persuaded to call on Riad and to tell him that he had never meant to insult Mumtaz at all. Riad took him at his word and, so far as he was concerned, the incident was closed.

But, for others, it was not. The following day, when Riad happened to be at the *Palais de Justice*, chatting with friends and lawyers as he waited for Sami to join them, a young man ran up to him and cried, 'Which one of you is Riad el-Solh? The Solhs seem to want a fight! We'll show them! We'll break the biggest head among them!' Smiling at this rude outburst, Riad asked the young man whether 'this head-breaking business was to take place at the *Palais de Justice*'. After some scuffles, the young man – who turned out to be Alfred Thabit's younger brother, George – was overpowered and thrown out of the law courts. Within hours, word of the incident had spread all over Beirut.

A crowd started to gather outside Riad's office in Allenby Street in downtown Beirut. Friends and acquaintances came to lend their support and reporters hurried to the scene. When Riad returned home that evening, he discovered that there had been a further unfortunate twist to the silly affair. Alfred Thabit had been beaten up in the street by two young members of the extended Solh family, Hasib and 'Imad el-Solh, who had even the cheek to go home to lunch before thinking of giving themselves up to the police.

Riad was called in to headquarters by the chief of police, 'Izz al-Din al-'Umari. When word got out that Riad was at the station on the Place des Martyres, large numbers of his supporters started to gather outside the building. From the pavement opposite, they could see Riad walking back and forth in the chief's office. From time to time, he would come to the window and wave, as if to reassure them that all was well.

But, by this time, news of the incident had spread beyond Beirut to other towns of Lebanon and Syria, where it was interpreted as a fight between the nationalists and the French. Delegations of Riad's supporters started pouring into Beirut from outlying parts of Lebanon and Syria, from as far away as Tripoli, Damascus and Hama. Shaykh Yusuf al-Khazen, head of an important Maronite family, led a large delegation from the Kisrawan region north of Beirut. The congestion was such that traffic was disrupted, while Riad's house overflowed with well-wishers. Full coverage of these events – inevitably with a slant in Riad's favour – was provided daily in *al-Nida' al-Qawmi*, a newspaper owned and edited by Kadhim el-Solh, another of Riad's cousins, where-upon the authorities closed it down.[7] Seizing on the chance to blast the repressive mandatory power, nationalist papers in Damascus took up the cudgels on Riad's behalf.[8] Najib al-Rayyes, editor of *al-Qabas*, accused the authorities of 'besieging' the nationalist hero. 'Those who wish to break the head of Riad el-Solh', he thundered, 'have not come into existence – either in Beirut or in Damascus.'[9]

The incident gave rise to no fewer than three court cases: Riad el-Solh versus Alfred and George Thabit; Alfred Thabit versus his young aggressors, 'Imad and Hasib el-Solh; and the mandate govern-ment versus *al-Nida' al-Qawmi* and its owner Kadhim el-Solh. Over one hundred lawyers from Lebanon and Syria volunteered to defend the Solhs. Twice that number attended the hearing to show their soli-darity with them on 27 January 1933. The court ruled in the Solhs' favour, although a disciplinary committee did blame Sami el-Solh for having created the disturbance in the first place. Publication of *al-Nida' al-Qawmi* was suspended until March. The young Solh stal-warts, 'Imad and Hassib, were released from jail on payment of a fine, which people pressed to pay in their stead. They were acclaimed at the prison gates by their supporters, who cheered their two cousins, Riad and Sami el-Solh, and sang the Syrian and Lebanese anthems before dispersing.

Riad opens a law office

It was in early 1933 that Riad decided it was time to earn a living. As usual, he was in financial trouble. Much of his property had been mortgaged or sold, with the money spent on journalistic and political

---

[7] *Al-Nida' al-Qawmi*, 27 December 1932.
[8] See *al-Qabas* and *al-Ayyam* from 25 December 1932 to the end of January 1933.
[9] *Al-Qabas*, 26 December 1932.

ventures. Petitioners were never sent away without a gift. For some years now, his reckless liberality had put Riad's relations with his father under strain, with the result that Rida and Riad never completely made it up. In his later years, Rida did take a house in Beirut but, more often than not, his wife Nazira would leave him in it and go to stay with her adored son.

Conscience-stricken at having dissipated the family wealth, Riad may have felt that it was time to shoulder some financial responsibility towards his parents and sisters. Very probably his legal wrangle with the Thabits had put him in mind finally to begin a career in law. Twenty years earlier, he had earned a prestigious law degree in Istanbul and, once settled in Beirut, he had registered at the Lawyers' Association (*L'Ordre des Avocats*) and been officially notified of his right to practise. He had so far chosen not to do so. But, influential and eloquent as he was, with a wide circle of friends and supporters, he felt that, even if his knowledge of the law was rusty, he could not fail to succeed. 'Do you like your new profession?' his father had asked him one day. 'I don't like it, but I make use of it! I have no legal ambitions. I've emigrated to the Bar just as one might emigrate to America – to make money.'

Opening a law office seemed the way to do it. His mother sold an emerald bracelet to provide the furnishings – rosewood panelling and green velvet furniture. Set on a plinth in a prominent place in the room was a marble copy of the *Lion de Belfort*, given him by Lebanese students in Paris as a tribute to his lion-like defence of the Arab homeland. (The original lion, a vast stone monument, had been erected at Belfort in eastern France to commemorate the city's heroic resistance during the Prussian siege in the 1870–71 war.) Riad was at first full of enthusiasm. He hired two young lawyers as assistants and set to work. But after a few months, the running of the office was left to them. The only evidence of him there was his polished brass nameplate on the door.

One incident, however, testified to his popular prestige, if not to his success as a lawyer. When the chief French prosecutor attempted to have Riad removed from the Bar, the Lawyers' Association immediately threatened to go on strike. Taken aback by this show of solidarity, the French sensibly decided to back down.[10]

---

[10] Alia el-Solh, *Le Jour*, 12 December 1965.

Champion of the workers

An important reason for Riad's immense popularity with the poor of Lebanon was his championship of the rights of the working class. He was perhaps the first nationalist politician of his generation to grasp that the struggle for workers' rights was a vital part of the struggle for independence. In this, he may have been influenced by what he had seen of trades unions in Europe. In any event, he was way ahead of most of his contemporaries on this issue, but, here too, he was up against great odds. The French High Commission identified any attempt by workers to organise in defence of their rights as 'nationalist agitation' or 'Communist subversion'. A decree of November 1930 made 'revolutionary propaganda' punishable by five years of hard labour; another decree in June 1931 prohibited all public meetings; and a third decree in September 1932 made it obligatory to bring before the courts any landlord who allowed 'unlawful meetings' to take place on his premises.[11]

Undeterred by these harsh measures, and no doubt influenced by the Syrian revolt across the border, 400 workers of a French concessionary company, the *Société des tramways et de l'éclairage de Beyrouth* (Beirut tram and lighting company) had, from 1 to 17 July 1926, struck for higher wages and better working conditions, calling on other workers to join them. Stoppages had taken place among printers, shoemakers, and wood and tobacco workers. The French reaction had been immediate and punitive. Twelve 'strike leaders' were arrested and three members of a new *Commission d'organisation syndicale*, a trades union committee, were deported to a fortress on the island of Arwad, where Riad el-Solh himself had once been held. They were to remain there for two long and terrible years, until amnestied in 1928 by High Commissioner Henri Ponsot.

Beirut's main utilities – water, electricity supply, public transport, posts and telegraphs, the management of the port – were run by French concessionary companies and were overseen by the French High Commission, which had appointed itself the legal heir to the Ottoman Empire. Even after the abolition of the Capitulations, the High Commission had remained responsible for foreign nationals and for the protection of their commercial and financial assets. A special

---

[11] I am indebted to Couland, *Le Mouvement syndical*, for the following account of the labour movement in Lebanon.

office known as the *Service de contrôle des sociétés concessionaires et des travaux publics* had been attached to the High Commission and would later be affiliated to what was to become known as the *Service des Intérêts Communs*, a body managing utilities and other facilities of joint interest to Syria and Lebanon.[12]

It was perhaps inevitable that French concessionary companies would become the main targets of the incipient trades union movement. Braving French repression, the trades union committee – the *Commission d'organisation syndicale* – was reconstituted underground with help and guidance from the Syrian Communist Party, whose central committee was composed of Fu'ad Shimali, Artin Medoyan, Hikazun Boyadjian and Farid Tu'meh. Shimali, who had represented the Syrian Communist Party at the VI Congress of the Communist International in Moscow in 1928, was undoubtedly its leading light. In 1929 he published a seminal work, *Niqabat al-'Ummal* (Workers' Trades Unions), and founded a newspaper, *Sawt al-'Ummal* (The Workers' Voice), of which four numbers appeared before the authorities closed it down.

By the late 1920s, the centre of gravity of the Arab workers' movement had moved from Haifa to Beirut, and had taken root in the tobacco industry, where the mechanisation of cigarette manufacture – cutting, rolling and packing – had deprived thousands of men and women of their livelihood, forcing them to move from their native mountain villages to the coastal towns in search of work. In May 1930, hundreds of tobacco workers had demonstrated in front of the seat of government in Beirut, prompting the authorities to respond with the usual harsh arrests and jail sentences.

In April 1931, a 'popular committee' launched another boycott of the *Société des tramways et de l'éclairage de Beyrouth*, which the Beirut Municipality said was making excessive profits. The city was in uproar. Several locally owned companies offered to supply electricity at much cheaper rates. The boycott of trams and electricity spread to Damascus, Aleppo, Homs and Hama, although it petered out before it managed to secure significant concessions from the company.

Such a boycott, however, did signal the rise of the urban proletariat as a new force in Arab politics. This was very different from the advocacy of traditional notables, who, in Ottoman times and after, had

---

[12] Carla Eddé, 'La Mobilisation "populaire" à Beyrouth à l'époque du Mandat: le cas des boycotts des trams et de l'électricité', in Méouchy, *France, Syrie et Liban*, p. 350.

been the main intermediaries between the population and the authorities.[13] Even though they came from families of notables in the old tradition, Riad and his two cousins, Kadhim and Taqi al-Din el-Solh, were accused by the French authorities of being the leading instigators of the boycott.

The movement had meanwhile spread to print workers who, in 1929, had started publishing a monthly journal called *al-Yaqadha* (The Awakening), with clear pan-Arab aspirations. It described itself as the 'organ of Arab workers everywhere' – and more particularly of printers in Syria, Egypt, Iraq and Palestine. In Lebanon, *al-Yaqadha* had campaigned against the High Commission's frequent suspensions of nationalist newspapers – a censorship which sometimes lasted for months, throwing printers arbitrarily out of work with no compensation. In the third issue of the printers' journal, Riad el-Solh had sprung to their defence, declaring that their union played an essential role in the struggle against French-owned concessionary companies – and against the French Mandate itself.

A taxi-drivers' union, which was formed in 1929, and became known as *jam'iyyat ta'adud al-sawwaqin* (Drivers' Solidarity Association), was another important centre of militant activity. It recruited hundreds, and eventually thousands, of members, including owner-drivers, hired drivers, car mechanics and even garage owners. Its members had gone on strike early in 1929, and then again in August 1930, seeking redress from heavy taxes, fines and discriminatory traffic regulations. On 28 January 1932, vast numbers of taxi-drivers travelled in convoy to Bkerké, seat of the Maronite patriarch, Antun 'Arida, hoping to secure his support – but failed to get it.

It was largely due to encouragement from Riad el-Solh that the Drivers' Solidarity Association had then grown from a purely professional body into an organisation seeking to achieve nationalist economic goals. A sign of this evolution was its protest against competition from the French-owned railway line, DHP (*Damas-Homs et Prolongements*) and from *L'Autoroutière*, a French-financed transport company. On 6 March 1933, the Drivers' Solidarity Association called a general strike, which was kept by 8,000 drivers in Lebanon and Syria. Shopkeepers in the coastal towns came out in support, bringing the country to a standstill.

---

[13] Ibid., p. 364.

On 19 March, Monsignor Ignatius Mubarak, the Maronite archbishop of Beirut, agreed to appear in public side by side with Riad el-Solh, in a gesture of solidarity with the strikers – earning sharp reproofs from Patriarch 'Arida and President Dabbas, both in league with the French. The defiance of the taxi-drivers inspired the printers to call a strike over their main grievance – the suspension of newspapers by administrative decree and the hardship this inflicted on print workers. On 22 March, 400 Beirut printers downed tools for twenty-four hours, forcing the government to pay compensation – in the event a paltry 100 lira – to printers who had lost their jobs. In August, the printers struck again, this time demanding, more ambitiously, a 50 per cent increase in wages, an eight-hour day, a government unemployment fund, indemnity for work accidents, hygienic working conditions and a ban on child labour.

Militancy had spread throughout the working classes. Cooks and waiters, silk weavers and woodworkers, fishermen and bank clerks, cement workers at the Chekka plant and men building the airport at Tripoli, even lawyers, doctors and pharmacists, had all started to organise themselves in the early 1930s, if still without adequate reference to each other.

Riad was one of the very few nationalist leaders to support this wide-ranging workers' movement. No doubt he had seen in the work stoppages – conducted sometimes in competition with the Communists, sometimes in collaboration with them – an opportunity to win a popular platform for his beliefs. It was natural for the strikers, in turn, to look for help from a prominent politician such as himself. He had, for instance, grasped the importance of trying to draw the highly influential Maronite patriarch, Antun 'Arida – a champion of the French presence in Lebanon, who had shown no sympathy for the workers' movement – into this struggle and onto the workers' side.

When a dispute broke out between High Commissioner Damien de Martel and the patriarch over the high commissioner's decision to award a tobacco monopoly in Mount Lebanon to a French company, the *Compagnie Libano-Syrienne des Tabacs*, Riad seized his chance. Racing to Damascus, he persuaded the principal leaders of the National Bloc to call on the patriarch. Accordingly, a highly eminent group of men, which included Shukri al-Quwatli, Jamil Mardam, Fakhri Barudi, Lutfi al-Haffar, Nasib al-Bakri and other prominent leaders, travelled to Lebanon, where, together with Riad, they set off for the patriarch's seat at Bkerké. The visit turned into a nationalist rally at which the flattered patriarch, amazingly enough, was moved to denounce the Mandate, even calling on the French to leave the country. The impact of this sea change on public opinion was electrifying.

With this significant coup, Riad managed to rally part of the upper and middle classes – including many Maronites, the traditional allies of France – to the side of the workers. He had turned the protest into a significant political revolt against the mandatory power. For he had understood how strikes and boycotts – which brought together members of Lebanon's different communities in common opposition to France's monopoly of public utilities – could be made into important landmarks on the road to independence.

The High Commission was outraged. On 15 April 1935, Damien de Martel ordered the closure of the drivers' union office and had Riad el-Solh deported to Qamishli, the remote town in the far north-east of Syria, where he was placed under house arrest. This provoked a storm of protest. The High Commission was deluged with telegrams from all over Syria and Lebanon, each bearing dozens of signatures. Several petitioners made the point that Riad's deportation was contrary to both law and human rights, and that such a violent act would only breed more violence. The Association of Arab Students in Toulouse, for example, sent an overheated message to say that, faced with France's illegal stance, Syrian youths there would be obliged to respond in kind with 'all legal and illegal measures'![14] Even the French Foreign Ministry in Paris and the League of Nations in Geneva were forced to take note of the affair.

Two months later, Damien de Martel relented and ordered Riad to be brought back to Beirut. As he reported to the foreign minister in Paris:

In my letter of 21 June, I judged that it was not timely to bring Riad el-Solh back from Qamishleh because of the danger his presence might cause at a moment when we were not sure that the boycott [of the Damascus tram and lighting company which lasted three months] might spread to Beirut.

[14] MAE, Nantes, Fonds Beyrouth (Amb.), série 199A4, carton 20, 17 May 1935.

> *As this peril has not occurred, at least for the time being, I have instructed that Riad el-Solh be brought back to Beirut. The secret was well kept and his return took place in the night of Sunday, 30 June, without professional agitators being able to arrange to give him a triumphal welcome.*
>
> *For several days running, ceremonies marking the mowled [or Mawlid al-Nabawi, the Prophet's birthday] were held in certain mosques of the Basta [a Muslim quarter of Beirut] to celebrate his return . . . The outpouring of joy was expressed by a display of fireworks and the explosion of crackers.*[15]

France's vain search for a treaty

Political debate in the decade that followed the Great Syrian Revolt was dominated by two apparently contradictory questions: what institutions would best prepare Syria and Lebanon for self-government; and, at the same time, how France was to secure its long-term interests in the region. Many French officials were convinced that the best way to perpetuate French control was by means of bilateral treaties with the two countries, binding them to France and reinforcing the terms and obligations of the Mandate. Nationalists like Riad el-Solh and his friends in the National Bloc, however, demanded independence for a 'Greater Syria', as a first step towards a wider Arab union. The gap between these two positions was unbridgeable.

High Commissioner Henry de Jouvenel had been more liberal, or simply more realistic, than his masters in Paris. He was certainly more open-minded than his military predecessors, Generals Gouraud and Sarrail, had been. He understood that, to have any chance of securing the acquiescence of the nationalists, a treaty would have to go well beyond Mandate terms – indeed, would have to replace them altogether. But he was unable to make headway against powerful officials such as Robert de Caix, who, as France's representative on the Permanent Mandates Commission, remained an influential voice on

---

[15] MAE, Nantes, Fonds Beyrouth (Amb.), série 199A4, carton 20, Damien de Martel au Ministre des Affaires Etrangères, 5 July 1935.

Levant affairs at the Quai d'Orsay. Having lost his argument in Paris, Henry de Jouvenel resigned in July 1926, after a mere eight months in office.

He was replaced by Henri Ponsot, who dissolved the Syrian parliament sine die in February 1929, after Paris rejected Fawzi al-Ghazzi's nationalist Constitution, which had categorically refused to accept the Allied carve-up of the region. Paris had rightly seen al-Ghazzi's Constitution, which pointedly omitted any mention of the Mandate, as a threat. It was a threat not only to its hegemony in Syria, but to the artificially constructed Greater Lebanon, as well as to the separation of Palestine from Syria, which the French had agreed with the British. In writing this brave – and to the French utterly outrageous – document, Fawzi al-Ghazzi may well have been signing his own death warrant.

Just over a year later, in May 1930, after al-Ghazzi's mysterious murder – which conveniently rid the French of a major challenger – Henri Ponsot unilaterally promulgated constitutional statutes for both Levant states. He modelled the statute for Syria loosely on the aborted Constitution of 1928, but removed Article 2, which had clearly referred to the unity of Greater Syria. Ponsot then went on to add Article 116, which insisted that nothing in the Constitution could be in opposition to the 'obligations' which France had contracted with the League of Nations regarding Syria. Such an extraordinary euphemism for occupation thereby guaranteed France's continuing position as a mandatory power. Mr Meade, Britain's acting consul in Aleppo, reported to London that local wits had derided Ponsot's Constitution as the 'Constipation'. Article 116, he added, was angrily seen as having completely negated the rest of the text.[16]

Ponsot also promulgated constitutional settlements for the sanjaq of Alexandretta, for the Alawite territory and the Jabal Druze. He vainly imagined that these measures would provide a basis for negotiating a treaty – if not with 'extreme' nationalists – then at least with the 'moderates' among them. Commenting from Paris on 23 May 1930, the British ambassador, Lord Tyrrell, expressed the belief that France was mainly concerned to pass the scrutiny of the League of Nations, rather than to make any real political progress.[17]

---

[16] Acting Consul Meade to Foreign Secretary, Aleppo, 6 June 1930 (FO 371/14554).
[17] FO 371/14553.

In 1931, Ponsot made yet another attempt to persuade the Syrians to accept a treaty institutionalising their subservience. The Anglo-Iraqi Treaty of June 1930 had made a huge impression on him. After all, it had managed to establish a 'close alliance' between Britain and Iraq, and it provided for 'full and frank consultations on all matters of foreign policy', as well as for 'mutual assistance' in case of war. Iraq had 'granted' the British the use of airbases near Basra and at Habbaniya, as well as the right to move troops freely about the country. It was agreed that the treaty, good for twenty-five years, would come into force when Iraq was admitted to the League of Nations – which occurred on 3 October 1932.

On a visit to Baghdad in late April 1931, Henri Ponsot confided to the British High Commissioner, Sir F. H. Humphrys, that he thought the treaty was 'a generous and statesmanlike endeavour to meet the legitimate aspirations of the Iraqis towards independence'. A flattered and no doubt surprised Humphrys was quick to report to London that Ponsot

> was convinced that British policy was right and should
> be generally followed in Syria . . . There was no doubt
> left in his mind that the policy of holding down a
> mandated territory by sheer force of arms was a negative
> policy, which held out no promise of a satisfactory
> dénouement. What was the alternative for Syria? To
> hold down with overwhelming force a sullen population
> that was ready to revolt and claim its rights whenever a
> favourable opportunity should present itself? He believed
> it was far preferable to grant these rights peaceably and
> ungrudgingly, as the British were doing, than to allow
> them to be eventually extracted by threats and disorders
> . . . The difficulty, however, was to bring the Quai d'Orsay
> to the same way of thinking.[18]

In spite of obstruction from Paris, Henri Ponsot decided to model his actions on Britain's policy in Iraq. On 19 November 1931, and without further ado, he dismissed the Prime Minister Shaykh Taj

---

[18] Sir F. H. Humphrys, High Commissioner in Iraq, to Foreign Secretary, Baghdad, 1 May 1931 (FO 369/2111, 371/15364).

al-Din al-Hasani, and announced that elections would be held in December–January 1931–32, with himself assuming, in the interim, the functions of head of state. Following the elections, a pro-French government was formed and the terms of a draft treaty 'agreed'. The draft was then presented to parliament for approval on 21 November 1933. It provided for a twenty-five-year alliance with France, to come into force once Syria became a member of the League; a French military presence in certain precise locations, just as in the case of the British in Iraq; and the transfer of power from the French to the Syrians after a four-year transitional period. Paris was adamant, however, in insisting on a separate existence for the Druze and Alawite states, where French governors continued busily to encourage separatist sentiment. But, since such dismemberment of Syria was not acceptable to the Damascus nationalists, the treaty remained nothing but ink on paper.

Ponsot did not fare much better in Lebanon. The statute he put in place was, in effect, a revised version of the 1926 Constitution, which had restricted Lebanese sovereignty in favour of the mandatory power. Lebanese Arab nationalists like Riad el-Solh were hostile to it because France retained control of foreign policy and of defence, while Article 95 enshrined the principle of sectarianism in Lebanon's political system. Many far-sighted Lebanese wished to end the confessional system there and then – Riad was first among them. He held several meetings with Henri Ponsot about this subject, and felt at times that he was making headway. But the meetings proved distressingly confusing: Ponsot would give the impression of being open-minded, but then clam up as strict guidelines from Paris gave him little room for manoeuvre.

Thereafter, French strategy was to use constitutional amendments to restrict the powers of both parliament and government – bodies where they had met opposition – and to enhance those of President Charles Dabbas, who was more easily controllable. Thus, in April 1929, Ponsot extended the president's term of office from three to six years and gave him the right to choose ministers free of parliament, and to dissolve the Chamber without seeking government approval. On 9 May 1932, the Constitution was suspended and all formal power was concentrated in the hands of the president (a state of affairs which would last until January 1934). However, all real power remained with Ponsot himself. He declared himself resolved to reform Lebanon's institutions, and to cut through client networks to end the corrupt division of spoils, which the confessional system had always encouraged. However, it was clear to many Lebanese that his real goal was to prevent any political advance towards autonomy, let alone independence.[19] Riad was intensely disappointed by the outcome of these talks. Ponsot's supposedly enlightened intentions had resulted in nothing but further political deadlock.

Ponsot did, however, put in hand a census which showed that Christians – *including* diaspora Lebanese and newly arrived Armenian refugees – had only a slender majority of 52.5 per cent out of a total population of 861,000. With a higher birth rate, Muslims, at 46.2 per cent, seemed certain to overtake Christians within a relatively short time. The census was the last of its kind ever attempted in Lebanon. Indeed, establishing exact numbers for the various communities became, thereafter, too explosive a political exercise ever to be contemplated again.

From Henri Ponsot to comte Damien de Martel

Unable to make political headway in either Syria or Lebanon, and trapped in an angry atmosphere punctuated by strikes and demonstrations, Henri Ponsot left his post in the late summer of 1933. The Levant had become a political graveyard for French high commissioners. Ponsot's bitter and foolhardy instructions to his successor, comte Damien de Martel, were to bypass the nationalists altogether. Upon his arrival in October 1933, de Martel set about liquidating his predecessor's policy – as advised by his predecessor Ponsot himself! He promulgated 'Constitutions' for both Syria and Lebanon. He attempted to force the Syrian parliament to ratify a treaty, which was nothing other than the 1930 statutes. But agitation in the street and opposition in parliament were so strong that he had to suspend the Syrian parliament altogether and withdrew the project in December 1933. On 2 January 1934, he decreed that executive powers in Syria would be placed in the hands of a personality appointed directly by the French high commissioner and responsible to him alone.

Elections were organised for a Chamber, now reduced to only twenty-five members, of whom seven were appointed. Those candi-

---

[19] Mizrahi, 'La France et sa politique de mandat', p. 52.

dates favoured by the High Commission proved successful. In March 1934, Damien de Martel called back the ever-amenable Shaykh Taj al-Din al-Hasani at the head of a caretaker ministry and, in November, suspended parliament indefinitely. In Lebanon, an elderly Maronite, Habib Pasha al-Sa'id, was appointed president in place of Charles Dabbas, who had retired after seven and a half years in office. As chief executive, the president was to be assisted by a Muslim secretary of state, in this case, 'Abdallah Bayhum. But, as British consular officials observed, the French tendency in both Syria and Lebanon was to bypass even puppet governments and exercise increasingly direct control. After ten years, no progress had been made either with institution-building or towards the conclusion of a treaty. The situation regressed to where it had been in 1926, but was made a great deal worse by a grave economic crisis and the events in Palestine.

Riad el-Solh takes a wife

Some months before being sent by the French to exile in Qamishli, Riad had married. It was a marriage that had been long in the making. Many years earlier, in 1912, when the Solhs were still living in Istanbul, Riad had gone out boating on the Bosphorus with his friends, Sa'dallah al-Jabiri and Raghid Kikhia. The wash from a passing steamer had suddenly capsized their boat. Sa'adallah could not swim. 'Save me!' he cried. When Riad and Raghid finally managed to haul him back on board, wet and flustered, he gratefully promised to marry each of them to one of his nieces, the two most beautiful girls in Aleppo.

In 1928, when Riad reached the age of 34, his parents decided that it was high time he was married. They chose a bride for him from the wealthy 'Azm family of Damascus, who were generally known to be personally haughty and lukewarm about the nationalist cause (with one or two glowing exceptions). Riad had reservations as to what such a union might entail. On 8 July 1928, he wrote anxiously though tactfully to his parents from Paris:

> I've already said that I won't disobey you about my
> marriage. In fact, I'm ready to give up political work
> for the duration of the engagement, and even for some
> time after the marriage itself. As to where I'm to live,

I would prefer Beirut, for reasons which I won't conceal.
I have simply come to believe that living in Beirut will
be an absolute necessity for me, and for my Lebanese
compatriots, for many years to come.

Nevertheless, if you really like the 'Azm girl, and
if you think it's worth the sacrifice, I would agree to live
in Damascus for a spell, leaving the future in the hands of
God.[20]

But this marriage never did take place. The girl and her family insisted that Riad el-Solh give up politics for an easy life in Damascus. He was, of course, far too committed to the Arab liberation struggle even to envisage such a fate, and Beirut was categorically his home base, whatever he might say in an obedient letter to his parents. After this failed first attempt to find him a bride, Riad thought it prudent to give his parents clearer guidelines for any further search. 'Whatever your choice,' he wrote,

you must explain to my future wife that life with me will
never be an agreeable boat trip, but rather a long and
arduous journey by road.

I can promise her neither jewels nor travels, but
only that one day she may be proud of me. She must be
intelligent enough to understand this, ambitious enough to
join in the struggle, funny enough to divert me. Above all,
she must be an orphan, because I don't want to have to
face eternal rivals. Fathers are my real worry.

Fayza al-Jabiri, Sa'dallah's niece, was just such an orphan, who had lost her father and her mother too. Daughter of the late Nafi' Pasha al-Jabiri, her mother had died giving birth to her, and her father a few years later. The absence of both parents may have accounted for her somewhat melancholy disposition. She was brought up by an older half-brother who had married her mother's sister. She was, in fact, one of seventeen girls and boys – brothers and half-brothers, sisters and half-sisters – from her father's three marriages. As a child, she had been sent to board with German nuns in Aleppo, where she learned German and was taught to play the piano. An accomplished girl, she also spoke French, Turkish and Arabic.

Fayza had seen Riad only twice before their marriage, once when she was a small child, and then again when she was a teenager. On this second occasion, her family had planned a party as a reward for her diligence in learning the first part of the Qur'an. She had been given a beautifully embroidered chiffon veil to wear for her big day. But her festivities were overtaken by Riad's triumphal visit to Aleppo in 1928. Arches had been erected for him in the street, a tribute to the huge reputation he had made as an advocate of the Arab cause in Europe. His friend Sa'dallah, the youngest of the Jabiri brothers and Fayza's uncle, gave a grand reception for him at the house of Fayza's late father, who had been the patriarch of the Jabiri family. This was attended by all the leading nationalists of the town. Riad's actual arrival at the house was greeted with applause and a great hubbub of animated conversation. As a result of all this excited commotion, Fayza's party was completely forgotten about. Upstairs in the women's quarters, she was so furious that, when she caught a glimpse of him in the courtyard below, she mischievously spat at him from one of the ornately carved balconies. She was just 17 when she married Riad el-Solh in 1930. By then, he was about twenty years her senior.

10 RIAD EL-SOLH, ZIONISM AND THE HAJJ AMIN AL-HUSAYNI

In Damascus in 1918, Riad el-Solh met and befriended Amin al-Husayni, a young Palestinian who, like himself, had rallied to Emir Faysal's banner and was soon to play a central role in Palestinian politics. No doubt they recognised in each other qualities of energy and leadership. Both were sons of prominent families, educated and highly politicised. Having made the transition from Ottomanism to Arab nationalism, they found themselves up against the harsh reality of British and French colonial power, and of Zionist ambition. Born around 1897, Amin had the conventional education of a Palestinian notable: Arabic and Islamic studies at a Muslim religious school; Turkish at a state school; French at a school run by Catholic missionaries; then a spell in Cairo studying with Shaykh Rashid Rida, the leading Islamic modernist of his day. This was followed by a pilgrimage to Mecca, which earned him the title of 'Hajj', which he chose to retain from then onwards.

As the half-brother of the Mufti of Jerusalem, the city's leading Muslim cleric, the Hajj Amin was steeped in Muslim learning and tradition. In 1914, he joined the Ottoman army as a junior officer and served the early years of the war in Anatolia, only to desert from the army in 1917 when on leave in Jerusalem. Inspired by the Arab Revolt, he raised some Palestinian volunteers for the Emir Faysal's forces and was in Damascus when the emir formed his government in 1918. He eventually made his way back to Jerusalem, where he founded the local branch of the Arab Club, the overt political manifestation of the secret society, *al-fatat*.[1]

---

[1] Laurens, *La Question de Palestine*, vol. I, pp. 425–6. For the Hajj Amin's career, see also Ibrahim Abu Shaqra, *al-Hajj Amin al-Husayni munthu wiladatihi hatta thawrat 1936*, Latakia, 1998; J. C. Hurewitz, *The Struggle for Palestine*, New York 1950;

In 1921, once Britain had established its rule over Palestine, High Commissioner Sir Herbert Samuel appointed the Hajj Amin to the office of Grand Mufti of Jerusalem at the remarkably young age of 24. A year later, he was appointed chairman of a newly formed Supreme Islamic Council in charge of *waqf* properties and Muslim religious courts. He thereby secured a commanding position at the centre of the spiritual, material and political life of the Palestinian Muslim community, and rose to the occasion. His particular concern – which was to prove a constant preoccupation throughout his life – was to safeguard the *Haram al-Sharif*, the Noble Sanctuary, from falling to the Zionists.

The enclosure of the *Haram* contains two great mosques – the al-Aqsa Mosque and the Dome of the Rock – as well as many smaller shrines and monuments, which together form a holy complex second only in importance for Muslims to the mosques at Mecca and Medina. Jewish zealots were suspected of plotting to destroy the mosques in order to build a temple on the *Haram*. To counter this threat, the Hajj Amin hired British and Turkish architects to restore the site and set about raising funds from Muslims around the world, thus promoting himself as the leading representative in Palestine of both pan-Arabism and pan-Islam.

At the heart of the *Haram* stands the Dome of the Rock, the first major example of Islamic architecture and one of the most revered of Muslim sanctuaries. It is an octagonal building of Byzantine design and Islamic decoration, built by Syrian craftsmen between 685 and 691, under the rule of the Caliph ʿAbd al-Malik. Its essential function was to protect the Holy Rock – an ancient oblong stony mass measuring 18 by 14 metres, to which the Prophet Muhammad, riding on the miraculous steed *al-Buraq*, travelled on his Night Journey from Mecca to Jerusalem, whence he made his Ascent to the Divine Presence in the upper heavens. In his time, the Caliph ʿAbd al-Malik was said to have employed fifty-two cleaners to wash the Holy Rock in rosewater, mixed with saffron, musk and ambergris. Five thousand lamps burning

Francis R. Nicosia, *The Third Reich and the Palestine Question*, Texas 1985; David Hirst, *The Gun and the Olive Branch: The Roots of Violence in the Middle East*, London 1977 (rev. expanded edn New York 2003); Maurice Pearlman, *Mufti of Jerusalem: The Story of Haj Amin al-Husseini*, London 1947; Joseph Schechtman, *The Mufti and the Führer: The Rise and Fall of Haj Amin al-Husseini*, New York 1965.

jasmine oil perfumed the shrine. The Dome of the Rock's octagonal structure became the model for domed sanctuaries and Saints' tombs from Morocco to China – as well as for traditional baptismal fonts.

By virtue of their common heritage of language, religion and way of life – and, not least, because of the dramatic political events they had witnessed and in which they had played a part – the Hajj Amin and Riad el-Solh shared from an early age a sense of being potential leaders of the emerging Arab nationalist movement, which was then struggling to formulate its aims. If there was a difference between them it was that the Hajj Amin was the more Islamic, whereas Riad, who had been brought up in Lebanon where Western influence was deep-rooted, was the more secular.

The acute grievance Riad shared with the Hajj Amin, and with other nationalists like themselves, was that the fate of their region was being decided by Britain and France in total disregard of the wishes of the local population. The former Arab provinces of the Ottoman Empire had been savagely dismembered. What had been a single physical, economic and cultural space, stretching from the Taurus mountains in the north to Sinai in the south, with Damascus at its centre, was now sliced up by the arbitrary and artificial frontiers of the Mandates. The Balfour Declaration had pledged British backing for the creation of a 'Jewish national home' in Palestine – that is to say, in southern Syria – while the creation of Greater Lebanon had stripped Syria of much of its Mediterranean coastline, including the important ports of Tripoli, Beirut and Sidon. What was left was then further subdivided into statelets, in which the French actively encouraged the separatist sentiments of minority communities like the Alawites and the Druze.

It was not surprising, therefore, that Riad and the Hajj Amin were united in opposition to the British and French Mandates, and to the menace inherent in the Balfour Declaration. For them, Palestine was an integral part of the Arab world, its independence as central to Arab prospects as that of Syria or Lebanon. If this crucial land bridge between Arab Asia and Arab Africa were to fall into foreign hands, irreparable damage would be done to the security of the entire Arab nation. No account of Riad el-Solh's life from the 1920s onwards would be complete without reference to his far-sighted anxiety concerning the Zionist project in Palestine.

Under British protection, the Zionists were steadily taking over Palestine, to the distress of its Arab inhabitants. Even as Riad challenged the French, he knew that their colonial hold over Syria and Lebanon was, by its very nature, temporary. There were no French settlers buying up land in Syria; no displaced and devastated Arab peasantry; no long-term colonisation project being planned and funded by France. Sooner or later, the French would have to depart – and he was determined to speed them on their way. But Palestine was a far more desperate case. Its ancient Arab character was being subverted in order artificially to accommodate an alien European population. No development anywhere in the region was more existentially disturbing to Arab nationalists than what was happening to Palestine, and none roused them to greater and more desperate measures.

Riad had grown up knowing Jews and learning something about Zionism. As a young boy early in the century, he had often been taken by his mother to winter on a farm in Jericho, which was owned by the Husaynis, who were close friends of hers. It was there that Riad met Musa Shertok – who, as Moshe Sharett, was later to serve as Israel's foreign minister from 1948 to 1956, and prime minister from 1954 to 1955. Shertok's parents had emigrated to Palestine from Russia in 1906. His father had found work as a smallholder on the Husayni family estate, where Musa Shertok spent his early years, mingling with Arab boys and learning to speak Arabic. Riad and Musa, both born in 1894, met each other at that time and, in the years before the First World War, attended the same faculty of law at Istanbul University.

Another young Jew whom Riad came across in Istanbul, who was also studying law, was David Ben-Gurion, later to become Israel's first prime minister. But no more than a casual acquaintance developed between them as Riad was only 17 at the time, while Ben-Gurion, already in his twenties, was deeply involved in Zionist politics. Born in Poland in 1886, Ben-Gurion arrived in Palestine in 1906, the same year as the Shertok family. He had been sent to study in Istanbul after the Young Turk revolution of 1908. Politically ambitious, he hoped to become a member of the Ottoman parliament – even a minister in the Turkish government – with the far-reaching aim of becoming an advocate of Zionism among the new-guard Turks, who were generally sympathetic to Jews.

In his book, *My Talks with Arab Leaders*, Ben-Gurion mentions his contacts with Turkish and Arab students during his Istanbul years. In the summer of 1914, he and another law student, Itshak Ben-Zvi, made their way back to Palestine for the summer holidays. But they were unable to stay there for long because, once war broke out that August, their names were discovered on a list of delegates to a Zionist Congress. They were interrogated by the Turkish authorities and banished from the Ottoman Empire on orders from Jamal Pasha, the newly arrived commander-in-chief and ferocious governor of the Damascus vilayet, who was determined to quash any manifestation of local nationalism, whether Jewish, Arab or – most awfully – Armenian.[2]

Riad became aware of the Zionist threat to Palestine in his teenage years. His own father, Rida el-Solh, had in the Ottoman parliament aired the danger posed by well-funded, organised and ever-accelerating Jewish settlement. From the moment, therefore, that the new system of post-war Mandates was announced, Riad was concerned to learn what the Zionists wanted in Palestine, and how far their British backers intended to go in support of them. It was with these questions in mind that, aged 28, he set off for London in November 1921, to offer his services, and his knowledge of international affairs, to Musa Kadhim al-Husayni, a former Palestinian mayor of Jerusalem, who was engaged in talks under British auspices with the Zionist leader, Dr Chaim Weizmann. The talks were being held against a background of extreme tension, with repeated clashes between Arabs and Jews in Jerusalem in the run-up to the anniversary that November of the Balfour Declaration. As the son of Faysal's former minister of interior, and as a rising politician in his own right, Riad attracted Weizmann's attention. He clearly thought him of sufficient interest to hold private talks with him.[3]

A meeting was arranged on 7 November, attended on the Zionist side, in addition to Weizmann, by James de Rothschild and Itamar Ben-Avi, editor of the paper *Doar ha-Yom* and an activist of the *yishuv*, the Jewish community in Palestine. As a basis for their discussions, Ben-Avi had drafted a document entitled 'Proposed Arab-Jewish Entente', of which the main thrust was a suggested trade-off: the Zionists would give the Arabs 'moral and material support' in realising their 'legitimate national aspirations', while the Arabs, in exchange, would support the Jews in establishing a 'national home' in Palestine.

In agreeing to meet Weizmann, Riad was mainly concerned to see whether the political influence of the Zionists could be mobilised to

---

[2] David Ben-Gurion, *My Talks with Arab Leaders*, Jerusalem 1972, p. 4.
[3] Neil Caplan, *Futile Diplomacy*, 2 vols, London 1983–86, vol. I, pp. 54 ff.

prevent the ratification of the League of Nations Mandates over Syria and Lebanon. Like other Arab nationalists at that time, he wanted the Mandates cancelled and replaced by a federal Arab state. If the Zionists were to help the Arabs secure this vital objective, he was prepared to agree to limited Jewish immigration into Palestine. But the talks got absolutely nowhere. Riad insisted that Ben-Avi's draft include a clause ruling out the creation of a Jewish state in the future. It was no surprise that Weizmann, whose entire political energies were devoted to this very end, insisted that, on this particular issue, it was best to 'let sleeping dogs lie'. He could not, he said disingenuously, make a commitment on behalf of future generations of Jewish immigrants. Riad retorted that he believed that Weizmann's ultimate objective was a Jewish state.[4]

Riad was not overawed by the Zionist leader, who, somewhat uncharacteristically, gave him what appears to have been a respectful hearing. In his dealings with Arabs, Weizmann was inclined to be arrogant, even imperious, as if addressing an already defeated enemy. Apart from his personal achievements, both scientific and social – of which he was very proud – his sense of superiority sprang from his remarkable success in having won crucial support for Zionist ambitions from the greatest imperial power of the day. He fully expected Britain to force the Arabs to accept the Zionist programme, whether they liked it or not. Nevertheless, always careful not to arouse unwelcome Arab hostility, he rarely revealed the full extent of his ambition, which, in his own phrase, was to make Palestine as Jewish as England was English or America American. Riad's discussions with Weizmann in 1921 gave him an early suspicion that the Zionists were actually seeking a state of their own.

His contacts with the Zionists were resumed in Cairo in March 1922, and then again a month later, when he joined Shaykh Rashid Rida, Kamil al-Qassab and Emile Khouri – who described themselves as the Executive Committee of the Syrian Union Party – in a further round of talks.[5] But by June, these, too, had reached an impasse, largely because the Zionists were afraid of alienating their British patrons, having worked so hard to cultivate the relationship. They had no intention of cancelling the League of Nations Mandates, as

[4] Laurens, *La Question de Palestine*, vol. I, p. 592.
[5] Caplan, *Futile Diplomacy*, p. 55.

the Arabs demanded, since they needed the protection of the Palestine Mandate for their own Zionist project. Nor could they, in the circumstances, afford to offend the French by challenging their Mandates over Syria or Lebanon. In fact, they decided that mere contact with Arab nationalists such as Riad el-Solh threatened to put them in the anti-French camp, and they backed off.

In the confused situation of the time, when the new map of the Middle East was still being drawn, a subject of heated debate among nationalists like Riad el-Solh and the Hajj Amin was whether to adopt a position of total opposition to the mandatory authorities in Damascus, Beirut and Jerusalem, or whether to try to cooperate with them in the Arab interest. Throughout the interwar years, Riad never deigned to play France's political game in Syria and Lebanon. He was, however, always ready to engage in discussion with French officials and politicians, and was keen to seek to sway French public opinion by every possible means. The Hajj Amin's position was somewhat different. The British had appointed him Grand Mufti on the explicit condition that he would use his influence to preserve public order in Jerusalem. Although he defined himself as an Arab nationalist and a Palestinian patriot, he had agreed nevertheless to engage in a certain cooperation with the mandatory power. He kept his side of the bargain – until, that is, massive Jewish immigration and land purchase made his position intolerable, and he rebelled.

The attempt to contain the Zionists

In the early 1920s, the Emir 'Abdallah, third son of King Husayn of the Hijaz, seemed to offer the Palestinians a crutch on which to lean. 'Abdallah had appeared in Transjordan via the Hijaz railway and had set up a modest administration in Amman. From there, he threatened to march on Damascus to reclaim from the French the lost throne of his brother, Faysal. To persuade him to stay put, the British gave him a small subsidy, but not enough to keep him out of the hands of the Zionists. Eager to match Faysal's achievement – the British had placed him upon the throne of Iraq after he had been toppled by the French in Syria – 'Abdallah's ambition was to be named king not just of Transjordan but of Syria and Palestine as well. In return, he was ready to fall in with the project of a 'Jewish national home' in Palestine – or at any rate not to oppose it. He was widely suspected of having accepted funding from the Zionists, after he had held several secret meetings with Weizmann in London in October 1922.

If they recognised his authority and granted him subsidies, 'Abdallah was ready to grant the Zionists extensive rights, even to the extent of allowing them to buy land in Transjordan. The British eventually vetoed such transactions.[6] His father, King Husayn of the Hijaz, may have shared his views, because, when he visited Amman on 18 January 1924 and was asked by Sir Herbert Samuel to receive a Zionist delegation, he decided to decorate the Chief Rabbi accompanying the delegation with the grand cordon of the Order of Arab independence![7]

Aware of these contacts, Riad el-Solh needed to explore whether an accord between the Hashemites and the Zionists would protect core Arab interests, or whether it would sabotage them. He travelled to Amman a number of times in the early 1920s to try to probe what such a deal would involve. He was inclined to think that if the Zionists were to lend their support to the creation of an Arab union, to include Syria, Palestine and Transjordan, room might perhaps be found in such a structure for an autonomous Jewish enclave. With this in mind, he even agreed to act on occasion as an intermediary between 'Abdallah and the Zionists.[8] It may have been at this time that he was approached by A. N. Kalvarisky, head of the Arab Department of the Jewish Executive, to whom the Zionist leadership had given the task of finding Arab interlocutors prepared to engage in discussions with them. Riad and Kalvarisky became acquainted, and were to hold a number of meetings over the years, none of which yielded anything apart from talk, as their political positions were simply too far apart.

Chaim Weizmann was attracted by the idea of a deal with the Hashemites, but he naturally put his own far more ambitious slant on it. He made it clear that he was ready to offer economic and political assistance to a potential Arab federation, if the Arabs, in turn, were to

[6] See Mandel, *The Arabs and Zionism*; N. Weinstock, *Le Sionisme contre Israël*, Paris 1969; Avi Shlaim, *Collusion Across the Jordan: King Abdallah, the Zionist Movement, and the Partition of Palestine*, Oxford 1988; Henry Laurens, *La Question de Palestine*, vol. II, 1922–1947: *Une Mission sacrée de civilisation*, Paris 2002, pp. 289–90.

[7] Laurens, *La Question de Palestine*, vol. II, p. 52.

[8] MAE, Nantes, Jerusalem, 101, Bulletin de Renseignements, no. 54, 17 September 1923. Quoted in Laurens, *La Question de Palestine*, vol. II, pp. 51–2.

grant generous space for a 'Jewish national home'. But his proposed trade-off was basically flawed. The Arabs were being asked to make major territorial concessions to the Zionists in exchange for airy, insubstantial promises of help for a putative Arab federation.

In any event, the Hashemite cause was to suffer a devastating setback a few months later, with the humiliating defeat of King Husayn of the Hijaz. When Mustafa Kemal, leader of the new Turkish Republic, abolished the Ottoman Caliphate on 3 March 1924, Husayn saw his chance to proclaim himself Caliph instead, asking the Muslim world to say prayers in *his* name. But such pretension aroused the hostility of India's Muslims, as well as of Egypt's King Fu'ad (who may have had ambitions of his own in this direction), and especially of Ibn Sa'ud, the rising leader of the Arabian Peninsula. Ibn Sa'ud urged Husayn to renounce the Caliphate, as well as any attempt to impose his hegemony over Arabs and Muslims. When his appeal went unheeded, Ibn Sa'ud sent his Beduin fighting force, the *Ikhwan*, to attack the Hijaz. By the end of 1925, the Hashemites had been driven out of Mecca, Medina and Jiddah. The Hijaz as a whole was swiftly brought under Ibn Sa'ud's rule.

In spite of this massive blow to his family fortunes, the Emir 'Abdallah – now based in Amman – continued for many years to entertain the hope of uniting the Levant under his throne, but the hostility of Ibn Sa'ud, the Egyptians, France and the Syrian nationalists; the coolness of the British; as well as the formidable advance of the Zionists, were to rob his ambition of any real credibility. Many Arab nationalists, the Hajj Amin among them, distanced themselves at this time from the Hashemites and instead pinned their hopes on Ibn Sa'ud. King Faysal of Iraq continued to be held in some esteem, but the same could no longer be said of his brother 'Abdallah, or of their father Husayn, perhaps because of their unbecoming readiness to get into bed with the Zionists. Riad el-Solh was reluctant to commit himself to either the Hashemite or the Saudi camp, but he was acutely aware that their bitter quarrel gravely weakened the Arab position and could only help the Zionist cause.

In early 1924, as he awaited a French amnesty to allow him back into Syria and Lebanon, Riad rented a room in a family pension on Mount Carmel in Haifa. Learning from the Husayni family that he was there, Musa Shertok called on him, and persuaded him to accompany him to Jerusalem for another interview with Dr Weizmann. On the road, Shertok pointed out to Riad the burgeoning Jewish settlements, or *kibbutzim*, being built on the plains by active teams of men, women and children. The journey to and from Jerusalem – and the meeting with Weizmann – brought home to Riad the unstoppable determination of European Jews to establish their hold over Arab Palestine, and the tragic incapacity of the Arabs to face up to the threat.[9] He now grasped that Zionist ambitions were far greater than *he* had imagined: they wanted the *whole* of Palestine, on *both* banks of the Jordan – or at least as much of it as they could seize. It was not until 28 February 1928 that Britain separated Transjordan from Palestine by treaty, recognising the former as an independent state within the framework of the Mandate.

The years 1924–27 were, in fact, the period of the fourth *aliya*, which saw thousands of Jewish immigrants from Europe and Russia flowing into Palestine, together with substantial funds to subsidise their settlement. By this time, the divide between the Arab and Jewish communities could no longer easily be bridged. Herbert Samuel left Palestine on 1 July 1925, only a few weeks before the outbreak of the Syrian revolt, which was to destroy his French counterpart in Damascus, General Sarrail. Throughout these years, Riad had to wrestle with the difficult dilemma of whether to declare his total opposition to the very notion of a 'Jewish national home', as his instinct dictated, or to adopt a more cautious, and politically more level-headed, recognition of the realities of power. He was enough of a pragmatist to realise that, by the mid-1920s, the British-backed Zionist project was already so well entrenched that it would be difficult, if not impossible, for the Arabs – in their divided state – to uproot it altogether. From the end of the First World War to 1925, the number of Jews in Palestine had trebled from 55,000 to over 150,000. They already accounted for 16 per cent of the population. As it was no longer possible to defeat the Zionists, Riad judged that the urgent task was to try to contain them. This became depressingly clear when, with the ratification of the charter of the Palestine Mandate on 22 July 1922, Britain reaffirmed its commitment to the Balfour Declaration.

Riad's strategy, then, became to try to protect essential Arab interests by restricting Zionist ambitions within an Arab framework. The struggle against the growing Zionist presence, together with

---

[9] Alia el-Solh, *Le Jour*, 14 November 1965.

stirring events such as the Syrian revolt and Abd el-Krim's rebellion in Morocco against France and Spain, roused him and the Hajj Amin to demonstrate against Britain and France, to call for resistance, to organise movements of international solidarity and generally to earn themselves a reputation as flag-bearing champions of the Arab cause. Their dream was of a united Arab nation strong enough to stand up to the Western Powers *and* to the Zionists at once. It was a vision that reached out beyond the artificial frontiers of the Mandates to the whole Arab world. Riad greatly admired the Emir Shakib Arslan, head of the Syro-Palestinian Congress, and worked at his side for several years, not only because of Arslan's unfailing patriotism and personal commitment, but also because he, too, saw the Arab countries, indeed the Islamic world, as a single body facing the same threat.

Over the following decade, Riad argued that, if the Zionists could be persuaded to throw their political and financial weight behind the cause of an independent Arab grouping of Syria, Lebanon, Palestine and Transjordan, he would produce an 'Arab Balfour Declaration', which would grant the Jews a 'home' within such a large and confident Arab entity. He made this offer to David Ben-Gurion and Musa Shertok in 1934, and to Chaim Weizmann himself in 1936, believing that he could convince the Palestine Arabs to accept it. But the Zionists had far wider aims in mind. They wanted the *whole* of Palestine, not a small enclave within an Arab federation, and certainly not one that would be dependent for its survival on Arab goodwill.[10]

Throughout the 1920s and well into the 1930s, Riad remained persuaded that dialogue was the best means to arrive at a formula for Arab-Zionist coexistence. But it was soon to become blindingly clear to him that the Zionists, in spite of their willing rhetoric, had no interest whatsoever in compromise with the Arabs. By the time of the outbreak of the Palestine Arab revolt of 1936 – crushed by the British with great brutality – the situation had deteriorated beyond all hope of repair. The full scale of Zionist ambitions was no longer in doubt to anyone, least of all Riad. By way of these abortive contacts, however, Riad el-Solh came ruefully to understand the extent to which the Zionists had managed to rally European and American opinion in their favour, and how feeble the Arabs had been in putting their case to the

[10] Laura Zitrain Eisenberg, *My Enemy's Enemy: Lebanon in the Early Zionist Imagination, 1900–1948*, Detroit 1994, p. 66; Beydoun, 'Riad el-Solh et les élections législatives de 1943', p. 405, n. 10.

world. It was an imbalance that he still hoped to rectify. He learned a great deal about political lobbying from what he observed of Zionist methods. In winning British support, culminating in the crucial Balfour Declaration of 1917, Chaim Weizmann had made his pitch, not in Palestine but in London – and at the very highest level. This lesson was certainly not lost on Riad.

Weizmann's 'Greater Palestine'

An issue of particular concern to Riad el-Solh was the Zionist ambition to establish Jewish colonies beyond Palestine's borders in Syria and in South Lebanon. Weizman had long been thrilled by the idea of a 'Greater Palestine', and had repeatedly attempted to persuade the French to allow Jewish settlement on the Golan and the Hawran, as well as in Lebanon up to the Litani river. Some wealthy Syrian Jews, who were affiliated to the Zionists, had sought to buy land in these regions. The Zionist press clamoured for their annexation.

In Paris, Weizmann put his case to Henry de Jouvenel, the French high commissioner in Syria and Lebanon, whom he met in November 1925 at the house of the French socialist leader, Léon Blum, who was himself a Jew of Zionist sympathies. In April 1926, Weizmann had another meeting with Jouvenel, this time in Beirut, following an official visit which the French high commissioner had paid to Palestine a month earlier. Once again, Weizmann tried to persuade Jouvenel to agree to Jewish settlement in the French Mandated territories. But, as the French were already struggling to put down the Syrian revolt, they were reluctant to make concessions to the Zionists that would further infuriate the Arabs. Jouvenel left his post in October 1926, and the idea was dropped by his successor. Weizmann, however, was not ready to give it up.

The notion of extending Jewish settlement across the border into Syria and Lebanon flowed naturally from the large land purchases which Zionist bodies, such as the Jewish National Fund and the Palestine Land Development Corporation, had been making in northern Palestine. They had found sellers because they were prepared to pay higher than market prices, but even more crucially because the artificial frontiers of the British and French Mandates had cut off Syrian and Lebanese landowners from their estates in Palestine. In the key years

1920–27, the great majority of land sales to the Jews were made by absentee non-Palestinian landowners. One very big transaction was the Zionist purchase of some 240,000 dunums (about 32,000 square kilometres) in the region between Haifa and the Jordan valley.[11] Later on, in the 1930s, the sellers tended to be peasant smallholders crippled by debt and forced to sell. Purchases accelerated as Jewish capital fled from Germany to Palestine, greatly facilitated by the *Haavara* transfer agreement that was struck between the Nazis and the Zionists.[12] Jewish philanthropists like the Rothschilds and the Montefiores provided a great deal of the funds, while Britain provided physical security and political cover. The idea of a 'Jewish national home' was quickly being turned into a reality.

The surge in Jewish immigration in the 1930s encouraged Weizmann to revive his idea of a 'Greater Palestine', to include parts of Syria. He came to Paris in June 1933 to persuade the French government that it could ease the suffering of European Jewry by allowing Jewish refugees to settle on the Syrian side of the Tiberias and Huleh lakes. Alternatively, he 'helpfully' suggested, France could 'transfer' Palestine Arabs to these Syrian regions, in order to make more room for European Jews in Palestine! A short while later, he was back in Paris to seek Léon Blum's support for the idea. Blum advised him privately to buy as much land as possible in Syria and Lebanon so as to create facts on the ground.[13] But the French Foreign Ministry remained unconvinced. When Damien de Martel, the high commissioner in Beirut, paid a visit to Palestine in January 1934, he told his British counterpart that it was out of the question for the French to allow European Jews to settle in Syria, as the local population would never accept it. As for transferring dispossessed Palestinian farmers to Syria and Lebanon, this would only cause Arab outrage, and justifiably so. Indeed, responding to his own worries about such designs, as well as to the fears of the local population, Damien de Martel passed a long-sighted decree on 18 January 1934, establishing administrative control over all land sales on the Syrian and Lebanese borders with Palestine.

---

[11] Laurens, *La Question de Palestine*, vol. II, pp. 145–7.
[12] Edwin Black, *The Transfer Agreement: The Dramatic Story of the Pact between the Third Reich and Jewish Palestine*, Washington 1984 (new edn 1999); Nicosia, *The Third Reich*; N. Weinstock, *Le Sionisme contre Israël*.
[13] Laurens, *La Question de Palestine*, vol. II, p. 268.

Weizmann, however, was not about to be so easily defeated. Early in 1934, he busied himself raising funds for the purchase of a large Syrian estate close to the Palestine border, declaring that the French authorities had already agreed to the transaction. When challenged by the French high commissioner in Beirut in March 1934, he pretended instead that no such purchase was being considered. That same month, however, he told the French consul in Jerusalem that strong Jewish colonies in Syria could provide security for Jewish immigration to Transjordan, where Jews could be settled in groups of 10,000 at a time! Weizmann's persistence in promoting his plans aroused a good deal of irritation at both the Quai d'Orsay in Paris and the French High Commission in Beirut, where he came to be considered an undesirable pest.

While steadily expanding their holdings in Palestine, the Zionists tried to sell Arab leaders the idea that the Jewish Agency would finance the resettlement outside Palestine of Arab farmers and their families who had lost their land. It was thus that the concept of 'transfer' was raised for the first time, with the Zionists arguing that Transjordan and even Iraq constituted a reserve that could be used to house dispossessed Palestinian peasantry. A. N. Kalvarisky, whose task it was to sound out Arab opinion on such issues, contacted Riad el-Solh to persuade him of the 'benefits' of such Arab-Jewish cooperation. Needless to say, Riad was intensely hostile to this argument.

Aware that he was fighting a losing battle in Palestine, the Hajj Amin wrote to Riad in Beirut, urging him to intervene to prevent Zionist expansion into Syria and Lebanon. One of his letters reads as follows:

> His Excellency, the great and respected patriot, Riad Bey el-Solh,
>
> We have learned that certain faithless people are proposing to sell a large tract of land at Manara and Hunayn in the region of the Huleh, transferring property rights from Arab into Jewish hands.
>
> If this transaction were to go through, God forbid, it would be a grave, a very grave, danger for the region, as it would modify its Arab character and give it a Jewish complexion, while provoking the exodus of hundreds of Arab families who live there and cultivate the land.

That is why we beg you to deploy the maximum
of efforts to block this attempt by the Jews and their
supporters, and to maintain these lands in Arab hands. We
are firmly of the hope that your efforts will be fruitful and
will result in the preservation of this land.
The President of the Supreme Islamic Council
Muhammad Amin al-Husayni.

The crisis over the Wailing Wall

An even more inflammatory issue which was to bring the Hajj Amin and Riad el-Solh together was the dispute over the status of the western wall of the *Haram al-Sharif* – or the 'Wailing Wall' – a last vestige of the Second Temple, where Jews had come to pray since the late Middle Ages. For Muslims, this was an integral part of the al-Aqsa mosque complex, since it had been established in the reign of Saladin as a Muslim endowment, or *waqf*, for the benefit of Moroccan pilgrims. The violence which was to erupt in 1929 at this spot was fuelled by Arab anger and frustration at large-scale Jewish immigration and land purchase, which were dispossessing Palestinians.

The crisis may be said to have started the previous August, when the Hajj Amin staged a grand celebration to mark the completion of the first phase of the restoration of the *Haram's* two mosques, attended by prominent Muslims from many parts of the world. The Zionists found the celebration offensive and chose that very moment to press their claim to the Wall. The Muslim *waqf* authorities had allowed Jews to pray at the Wall for centuries, but not to bring in screens, seats or other objects that might be seen as creating a synagogue, and thereby establishing a permanent Jewish right to the site.

On 23 September 1928, during Yom Kippur, and in a deliberate challenge to this ancient arrangement, European Jews set up a screen at the Wall to separate men from women. Local Arab inhabitants immediately alerted the Muslim religious authorities, whereupon the British governor ordered the police forcibly to remove the screen. The Zionists then demanded that the mandatory authorities expropriate the entire Maghrebi quarter flanking the Wall (which Edmond de Rothschild had tried to acquire in 1918), claiming that the removal of the screen threatened the whole project of a 'Jewish national home'.

The Hajj Amin's response was to summon an Islamic Congress in Jerusalem in November, which passed a resolution affirming that the Palestinians were the guardians of Jerusalem's Holy Places on behalf of the worldwide Muslim community. Many Syrian nationalists attended the Congress, while, from their headquarters in Geneva, Riad el-Solh, and his two colleagues in the Syro-Palestinian Delegation, the Emir Shakib Arslan and Ihsan al-Jabiri, lent their strong support. In a letter on 7 November, they drew the attention of the League of Nations to the great anxiety that the Islamic Congress had expressed over a law, passed by the Palestine government in 1924, which authorised the expropriation of property in the general interest. Would this law now allow the Jews to take possession of Muslim holy sites? Muslims wanted the law amended, together with the appointment of 'a totally impartial attorney general determined to uphold the principle of absolute religious neutrality'.[14]

When the new British High Commissioner Sir John Chancellor arrived in Jerusalem in December, he was besieged by Zionist petitions demanding the expropriation of the entire *waqf*. British legal experts ruled that, since Jews had the right to pray there, the Wall could not be considered a 'purely Moslem sacred shrine', whereupon the Hajj Amin produced an Ottoman ruling of 1912, which barred Jews from bringing any objects to the Wall. From the start, Muslims saw the Jews' attempts to expand their rights at the Wall as an opening move to seize the *Haram*, destroy the mosques and build a Jewish temple on the site. Arab passions were further aroused by the announcement of the creation of the Jewish Agency in June 1929, as a quasi-governmental organisation to promote the cause of the 'Jewish national home' during the British Mandate – a decision formally ratified a month later at the sixteenth Zionist Congress in Zurich, which marked a summit of Chaim Weizmann's political career. In fact, the Jewish Agency seems to have been in existence since 1923, if not earlier, when it took over from the Zionist Commission the task of representing and administering the growing Jewish community.

In any event, the Zionists' steady political and territorial gains, and the corresponding alarm and dispossession of the Arabs, had largely destroyed any hope of peaceful coexistence between them. The stage was set for a conflagration. In mid-August, a Zionist demonstration at

---

[14] Ibid., pp. 153–4.

the Wall by young Jews of the strident Betar movement was followed the next day by a counter-demonstration of some two thousand Muslims at the Dome of the Rock on the *Haram*. Almost at once, pernicious rumours were spread of an imminent massacre of Jews by Muslims, and of an assault by Jews on the *Haram*. After prayers on Friday, 23 August, an angry mob attacked the Jewish quarter, killing passers-by and destroying property. At the same moment, some Arabs were murdered by Jewish youths. The police were soon overwhelmed as the violence spread to Hebron, where sixty-seven Jews were killed; then to Safed, where another twenty Jews were killed; and then on to Haifa. Muslims claimed that the Zionists had deliberately provoked the troubles in order to have an excuse to seize the *Haram*. The whole week of 23–30 August was marked by terrible scenes of carnage. In all, 135 Jews and 136 Arabs were killed – the latter mainly by British police – while another 340 Jews and 240 Arabs were wounded.[15]

Emotions ran high across the Arab world. A demonstration in Damascus on 26 August in solidarity with the Palestinians, in which cries of 'Down with the Balfour Declaration' were heard, ended in clashes with the French police and some loss of life. In Jerusalem, High Commissioner Sir John Chancellor came to the conclusion that the main source of tension was land sales to the Jews. He wanted to pass restrictive legislation, but faced stiff opposition from Norman Bentwich, his attorney general, himself a Jew of strong Zionist sympathies. Arab peasants, driven off their land, found refuge in the slums and shantytowns of Haifa, from where the more militant among them launched sporadic attacks against the new Jewish settlements.

The mutual killings of 1929 dissipated any illusion that European Jews and Arabs could cohabit peacefully in Palestine. Inevitably, Oriental Jews in Arab countries now began encountering suspicion and outright hostility. An appeal to world Jewry to stand by the *Yishuv* was matched by an affirmation of Muslim solidarity and pan-Arab identity. Thus began the confrontation between the world of Jewry and the world of Islam, which continues with ever greater virulence to this day.

Weizmann, who had far greater access to Western statesmen than all Arab leaders put together, told the British that the answer

---

[15] For a contemporary report of the 1929 violence by the remarkable American foreign correspondent, James Vincent Sheean, see his *Personal History*, New York 1935.

to the crisis lay in transferring the Palestine Arabs to Transjordan. At a meeting in London with the British Prime Minister Ramsay MacDonald, he demanded an independent commission of enquiry to establish responsibility for the troubles and punish the culprits. He brazenly asked for more immigration visas, a bigger role for Jews in the Palestine administration and a purge of all officials hostile to Zionism. The British kowtowed to his demands. On 17 June 1930, three Arabs were executed for crimes committed in August 1929, while the only Jew sentenced to death was soon amnestied. Inevitably, there were angry demonstrations in honour of the 'martyrs of Islam'.

In constant touch with Riad el-Solh and other pan-Arab nationalists, the Hajj Amin used the crisis to strengthen his own position on the Palestinian and Arab political scene. Adopting an anti-British tone, he now declared that Palestine would achieve independence only through the union of Arab countries which, he predicted airily, was soon to come about. Independence could be won only by force. In much the same way as Riad had acquired a considerable reputation for his struggle against the French Mandate, so the Hajj Amin's defence of the *Haram al-Sharif* in Jerusalem earned him a reputation well beyond Palestine. To counter what he saw as a Zionist threat, he decided to turn the site into a Muslim necropolis where important personalities could be buried. Their funerals would, he believed, provide occasions for Muslim leaders to come to Jerusalem, to meet and exchange views. In 1931, twenty thousand people attended the funeral of a prominent Indian Muslim, Muhammad Ali, and in the same year, the Sharif Husayn, the former king of the Hijaz, was also buried on the *Haram*.

The General Islamic Conference and its abortive sequel

In that year also, the Hajj Amin and Riad el-Solh conceived the idea of convening a major pan-Islamic conference to focus Muslim attention on Palestine, where continued Jewish immigration was creating an explosive situation. To avoid arousing the hostility of Indian Muslims, General Sir Arthur Wauchope, the new British high commissioner, who had taken up his post in November 1931, gave his assent. Riad went to Cairo to discuss the project with members of the executive committee of the Syro-Palestinian Congress and other leading figures, and to establish the conference agenda.

The General Islamic Conference opened in Jerusalem on 7 December 1931 – the anniversary of the Prophet's Night Journey – and remained in session for ten days. It was attended by some 130 delegates from twenty-two countries, united in a great élan of Muslim solidarity. Many came from Palestine and Syria; others from Iraq, Iran and India. The French historian of Palestine, Henry Laurens, described the Congress as 'a crucial moment in the history of twentieth-century Islam'.[16] Arab delegates saw it also as an occasion to celebrate pan-Arab achievements – in great part the fruit of the tireless campaigning by the three stalwarts of the Geneva-based Syro-Palestinian Delegation. To their great regret, Riad's two colleagues, Shakib Arslan and Ihsan al-Jabiri, were unable to travel to Jerusalem, but – as they wrote in a note appended to the list of delegates – Riad was there to represent them.[17]

The declared goals of the Congress were the defence of the Western Wall and Jerusalem's other Muslim Holy Places; the founding of a company to safeguard Palestinian land; the creation of a Muslim university of al-Aqsa (as an answer to the newly opened Hebrew University on Mount Scopus); the restoration of the Hijaz railway; the rejection of Britain's pro-Zionist policy; and the continued struggle against Jewish immigration and settlement. Riad played a prominent part in the proceedings. He was in fact entrusted with 'external propaganda', that is to say, the task of making known the dangers facing Palestine and its Arab inhabitants.[18] The Hajj Amin, Grand Mufti of Jerusalem, won personal acclaim, acquiring a pan-Islamic aura well beyond Palestine's borders.

Among the resolutions passed was one calling for the convening of an Arab conference, with the aim of holding in check the Zionist

---

[16] Laurens, *La Question de Palestine*, vol. II, p. 227.

[17] At the end of a long list of delegates is the following note in French:

> Nous [Shakib Arslan and Ihsan al-Jabiri] avons été invités, nous deux, membres de la Délégation syro-palestinienne, à prendre part à ce Congrès, mais pour certaines raisons et à notre grand regret, nous n'avons pas pu nous y rendre; et avons prié notre collègue Riad Bey Solh de représenter la Délégation, ce qu'il a fait avec toute la dignité et la capacité qui ne lui ont jamais fait défaut.

(We [Shakib Arslan and Ihsan al-Jabiri], members of the Syro-Palestinian Delegation, were both invited to take part in this Congress, but for certain reasons and to our great regret, we were not able to attend. We asked our colleague, Riad Bey Solh, to represent the Delegation, which he did with the dignity and ability which have never failed him.)

[18] Alia el-Solh, *Le Jour*, 14 November 1965.

seizure of Palestine. But where was this second conference to take place? Britain and France would not allow it to be held in countries under their control – such as Palestine itself, or Syria and Lebanon. Egypt was ruled out because of its still hesitant awakening to Arabism, and also because its leadership was paralysed by a struggle between the palace and the nationalist *Wafd* Party. Iraq was seen as a more promising venue, especially as it was about to become independent from Britain. Many of the men around King Faysal were militant pan-Arabs. In fact, a leading Iraqi politician, Yasin al-Hashimi, travelled to Jerusalem in mid-1932, with the welcome news that Iraq had agreed to host the conference.

When King Faysal visited his brother 'Abdallah that year, Riad el-Solh raced to Amman to seek an audience and receive the king's personal assent. Preparations for the conference proceeded over the next eighteen months. Emissaries were sent to reassure the Saudis that their Hashemite enemies would derive no political benefit from the conference, and, in the early winter of 1932–33, Ibn Sa'ud gave his agreement. The date of the conference was fixed for the spring of 1933. It was then learned, however, that Faysal was planning to travel abroad for urgent medical treatment. The conference was postponed, only to be abandoned altogether when Faysal died in Switzerland in September 1933. In any event, the British had by then made it clear that they would not allow such a conference to be held in Baghdad.

For Arab nationalists such as Riad el-Solh, Faysal's death, followed by the cancellation of the conference, was one more in a long list of bitter defeats and disappointments suffered since the First World War. When Faysal's body arrived at Haifa by ship for its over-land journey to Baghdad, vast crowds came out to pay homage to his memory and to his contribution to the nationalist cause.

Arab hopes pinned on Germany

Many Arabs welcomed Hitler's rise in January 1933, as it seemed to promise a change in the international balance of power.[19] It was thought that Nazi Germany could provide a counterweight to Britain and France. Some even hoped that a new war in Europe would

---

[19] Nicosia, *The Third Reich*, pp. 85 ff.

weaken the imperialist powers, and allow the Arabs to accede to real independence, strip the Zionists of British protection, and thus put an end to the very notion of a 'Jewish national home'. At several meetings with Heinrich Wolff, the German consul general in Jerusalem, the Hajj Amin expressed his support for certain Nazi policies and, in particular, the anti-Jewish boycott.

Riad el-Solh's colleague, the Emir Shakib Arslan, went to Berlin in November 1934 in an attempt to win over Germany to the Arab cause.[20] Fawzi al-Qawuqji, the Arab guerrilla leader who was later to command Arab volunteers in Palestine, pleaded with Fritz Grobba, the German ambassador in Baghdad, for German weapons.[21] Riad himself travelled to Ankara in the mid-1930s for a meeting with the German ambassador, no doubt to explore what support the Arabs could expect in their struggle for independence.[22]

In requesting German aid, the invariable Arab argument was that an independent Arab state in Palestine would be Germany's ally, whereas an independent Jewish state would be Germany's enemy. But, to their surprise and disappointment, the Arabs made little or no headway with the Germans. They were slow to grasp that the Nazis were exceedingly careful not to do anything that might antagonise the British or undermine the security of the British Empire. An accommodation with Great Britain had been a cornerstone of Hitler's strategic and ideological calculations since the early years of the Nazi movement, and would remain so until the outbreak of the Second World War. One of Hitler's supreme priorities was to make Germany *judenrein* (free of Jews), not to challenge British or French control over Arab territories. Jewish emigration from Germany (*restlose Auswanderung*), mainly to Palestine, was to be actually encouraged, rather than stopped.[23]

Zionist leaders did not challenge this aspect of Nazi policy, since it helped them strengthen the Jewish presence in Palestine. Indeed, the *Haavara* agreement, reached between the Nazi government and the Zionists, led to the transfer of over 100 million Reich marks of blocked Jewish assets to Palestine in the form of German exports

[20] Ibid., p. 88.
[21] Ibid., pp. 101–2; see also Khayriyya Qasimiyya (ed.), *Filastin fi mudhakkarat al-Qawuqji*, Beirut 1975.
[22] Interview with Alia el-Solh, Monte Carlo, 5–6 October 2004.
[23] Nicosia, *The Third Reich*, p. 122; Laurens, *La Question de Palestine*, vol. II, pp. 259–60.

sold locally, and the corresponding emigration of about 8,000 Jews a year between 1933 and 1939 (although this number was halved in the two years 1937 and 1938).[24] For Jews throughout Eastern Europe, and especially in Poland, the rise of Nazi terror made Palestine seem more than ever the haven they longed to reach. Whether legally or clandestinely, some 30,000 Jews managed to enter Palestine in the year 1933 alone.

In despair at this rising tide of Jewish immigration from Europe, the Arab Executive staged demonstrations and, on 13 October 1933, called a general strike which resulted in clashes with the police. Palestinian anger was directed at the British, the great imperial power which they felt had so utterly betrayed them. No Jews were molested. A further demonstration on 27 October led to more serious clashes, and the liberal use of gunfire against unarmed Arab demonstrators. By the time the strike was lifted on 3 November, nearly thirty Palestinians had been killed and hundreds wounded. The agitation spread to Transjordan and led to angry protests in Syria and other Arab countries.

The Hajj Amin was absent from Palestine during these events, but when he was received by Sir Arthur Wauchope on 3 December, he urged him to order a halt to Jewish immigration and land acquisition. Firing on demonstrators was a grave political mistake as well as a crime, and the families of the victims should be compensated at once, he advised. The Supreme Islamic Council should be given means to resettle peasants stripped of their land. Sooner or later, he told the British high commissioner, the Zionist project would have to be considered accomplished. Wauchope was given similar advice by Musa al-'Alami, another prominent Palestinian from a well-known Jerusalem family.[25] Of the same generation as the Hajj Amin, he had served in the Ottoman army in the First World War and then studied at Cambridge University before returning to Palestine in 1924, where he was employed in the legal department of the Palestine government. In 1933, the British high commissioner appointed him one of his private secretaries, with responsibility for Arab affairs. Musa al-'Alami was soon to become related to Riad by marriage, as they both found brides from the same affluent Aleppo family, the Jabiris. Musa married the

---

[24] Nicosia, *The Third Reich*, app. 7 and 8.
[25] Geoffrey Furlonge, *Palestine Is My Country: The Story of Musa Alami*, London 1969; Laurens, *La Question de Palestine*, vol. II, pp. 266–7.

daughter of Ihsan al-Jabiri, Riad el-Solh's friend and colleague in the Syro-Palestinian Delegation.

There was much talk at the time of dividing Palestine into Arab and Jewish cantons. Musa al-'Alami's pragmatic advice to Wauchope was that part of the Palestine coast – where Jews had already settled in large numbers – should become an autonomous Jewish canton, into which immigration would be free. The rest of Palestine should be put in the hands of an Arab government, with Jewish representation only on a proportional basis. Needless to say, the Zionists strenuously opposed any proposal that might limit their expansion. The true scandal of the period was British complicity with Zionist designs. Those British offi-cials who wished to strike a more neutral stance were shunted aside or 'purged' – to use Weizmann's sinister term – leaving the field to those of Zionist persuasion. Even a man like T. E. Lawrence, long romanticised as being on the 'Arab side', has recently been depicted as having tilted towards the Zionists.[26] He had been instrumental in persuading the Sharif Husayn to agree to the principle of a 'Jewish national home' in Palestine, in return for British political favours (most of which failed to materialise).

Palestinian factional politics

Riad el-Solh was much involved in the early 1930s in patching up quarrels between squabbling Palestinian leaders. Then, as now, the Palestinian national movement was gravely weakened by the plague of factional in-fighting. In particular, two leading Palestinian clans, the Husaynis and the Nashashibis, had for years been locked in political rivalry. The Nashashibis had done everything they could to prevent the convening of the 1931 Islamic Conference, well aware that it would give their rival, the Hajj Amin al-Husayni, a considerable boost. Indeed, the Mufti's soaring prestige was achieved largely at their expense. In Palestinian society, the Husayni clan's prestige rested largely on its claim of descent from the Prophet, whereas the Nashashibis, of more recent origin, had become rich from tax farming in the late Ottoman period. Politically more moderate than the Husaynis, they collaborated with

---

[26] Interview with Martin Gilbert about his book, *Churchill and the Jews*, New York 2007; *Jerusalem Post*, 23 February 2007.

the British authorities and favoured the creation of a British-backed Hashemite monarchy to rule over Palestine and Transjordan. This was the programme of their political party, the Party of National Defence (*hizb al-difaʿ al-watani*), which was violently opposed to the Mufti.

Another intra-Palestinian conflict was that between the Hajj Amin and a group of Palestinian activists led by ʿAwni ʿAbd al-Hadi, who had been one of the Emir Faysal's private secretaries in Damascus, where Riad had first met him. Exasperated by the paralysing rivalry between the Husaynis and the Nashashibis, ʿAbd al-Hadi had formed a political party, the *Istiqlal* (Independence), which launched an active campaign against Jewish immigration and settlement and called for peaceful civil disobedience on the Gandhian model. Palestine, it declared, was a pivotal Arab country and an inalienable part of Syria. The always paranoid French saw the *Istiqlal* as the creation of British intelligence. To oust the party from the Palestinian political scene, the Husayni clan eventually launched its own 'Arab Party of Palestine' at a congress in Jerusalem on 26–27 March 1935, with anti-Zionism as the main plank of its platform. These were some of the factions which Riad, with no little exasperation, tried to bring together. He paid several visits to Palestine in the early 1930s in an attempt to reconcile them, but with no lasting success.

At much the same time, he was busy mediating between squabbling Syrian nationalist leaders too. Shortly after returning to Beirut in 1935 from his spell of house arrest in Qamishli, he was called upon to sort out a quarrel in Tripoli between the supporters of ʿAbd al-Hamid Karami and those of Dr ʿAbd al-Latif al-Bissar. Clashes had taken place between the two groups. ʿAbd al-Hamid Karami had been set upon and beaten up by four of al-Bissar's men, when he was returning home from a call on Fakhri Barudi, who was then visiting Tripoli. Riad headed a delegation to mediate between the two clans. As he wrote to his friends Nabih and ʿAdil al-ʿAzma on 27 July 1935, 'I have just returned from Tripoli where I spent two sleepless nights in an attempt to resolve the great difficulties of the task. Now that I have returned [to Beirut], I believe that I can arrive at a negotiated solution within a week'.[27] These persistent squabbles in Palestine and Syria brought no profit, to say the least, to the Arab cause.

---

[27] Khayriyya Qasimiyya (ed.), *al-Raʾil al-ʿarabi al-awwal. Hayat wa awraq Nabih wa ʿAdil al-ʿAzma*, London 1991, p. 268.

11 BEN-GURION AND THE ARABS

In the mid-1930s, Riad el-Solh and a number of leading Palestinian and Arab personalities were drawn into discussions with David Ben-Gurion, who had recently been elected to the Zionist Executive, the movement's governing body. With his colleague, Moshe Shertok – Riad's boyhood acquaintance – Ben-Gurion was responsible for political affairs. By 1934, when the Jewish community in Palestine had grown to some four hundred thousand, Ben-Gurion decided that the time was ripe to explore the possibility of an agreement with the Arabs, seeing that he could now confront them with a fait accompli. Moreover, the British High Commissioner General Arthur Wauchop had resolved, on the advice of his hardline and pro-Zionist advisers, to crack down hard on the Arab opposition, much as the French had done in Syria. In such circumstances, Ben-Gurion thought that the Arabs might be ready to do a deal.

But with whom was he to talk? There was no single, all-powerful leader able to speak for all Arabs. Among Palestinians, the Hajj Amin was the most influential figure, but in view of the ever-widening chasm between the Arab and Jewish communities in Palestine, Ben-Gurion thought it best not to approach him. He decided instead to make contact with half a dozen distinguished and influential Arabs, representative of well-born and educated nationalist opinion, whom he imagined he could win over to his way of thinking. They were Musa al-'Alami, Riad el-Solh, 'Awni 'Abd al-Hadi, the Emir Shakib Arslan, Ihsan al-Jabiri and George Antonius. It was striking that only two of the group – Musa al-'Alami and 'Awni 'Abd al-Hadi – were native-born Palestinians. In those days, particularist sentiment had not yet set in, and it was natural that prominent pan-Arabs like Riad el-Solh, Shakib Arslan and Ihsan al-Jabiri should feel themselves authorised to discuss the future of Palestine, and equally natural for Ben-Gurion to sound them out.

To each of them, although in a somewhat different form, he put a two-stage plan, which he hoped would win their acceptance, even their support. The first stage of his plan was the creation of a Jewish state once the Jews had become a majority in Palestine and Transjordan. In a second stage, he anticipated that a link could be forged between this Jewish state and a federation of Syria and Iraq, so as to reassure the Palestine Arabs, who would by then be a minority in the Jewish state, that they would still be part of an Arab majority in the wider region.

On 20 March 1934, Ben-Gurion met Musa al-'Alami at Moshe Shertok's house in Jerusalem. 'I put to him the crucial question', Ben-Gurion wrote later.[1]

> 'Is there any possibility at all of reaching an understanding with regard to the establishment of a Jewish State in Palestine, including Transjordan?' He replied with a question. Why should the Arabs agree? Perhaps the Jews would manage to achieve this even without Arab consent, but why should they give their consent to this? I answered that in return we would agree to support the establishment of an Arab Federation in the neighbouring countries and an alliance of the Jewish State with the federation, so that the Arabs in Palestine, even if they constituted a minority in the country, would not hold a minority position, since they would be linked with millions of Arabs in the neighbouring countries.

Would the Arabs, Ben-Gurion then asked, accept parity in the Palestine Legislative Council, which the British were thinking of setting up? Musa al-'Alami rejected the very idea. 'Why should they, he asked? Did the Arabs not constitute four-fifths of the country's population? Were they not the indigenous population? Why should they make such a concession?'

On 26 March, less than a week after this deadlocked exchange, Musa Kadhim al-Husayni, the head of the Arab Executive – whom

---

[1] Ben-Gurion, *My Talks with Arab Leaders*, pp. 16–21.

Riad had attempted to assist in his negotiations with Weizmann in London in 1921 – died at the age of 83. His funeral on the *Haram al-Sharif*, which the Hajj Amin had succeeded in turning into a necropolis for Muslim personalities, was the occasion of a huge popular demonstration. But, because of the Husayni–Nashashibi quarrel, and the *Istiqlal*'s nationalist overbidding, no one was able to take his place at the head of the Arab Executive. The truth was that, gravely weakened by internal squabbles and confronted by the rising power of the highly organised Zionists, the Arabs were already losing the struggle for Palestine.

Such was the background to Ben-Gurion's meeting with Riad el-Solh on 15 June, for which Moshe Shertok had prepared the ground by visiting Riad in Lebanon. Although by this time deeply suspicious about Zionist intentions, Riad was nevertheless prepared to explore whether any essential Arab interests could still be protected by an eleventh-hour understanding with the Jews. He wanted to know in detail just what sort of an agreement Ben-Gurion had in mind. The Zionist leader put to him a somewhat more elaborate plan than the one he had proposed to Musa al-'Alami, summed up this time in five consecutive stages:

- Unlimited freedom for Jewish immigration into Palestine and Transjordan.
- The Palestine Arabs to remain in the country and be given help to improve their economic and cultural situation.
- Jews and Arabs to participate in government on a basis of parity for the duration of the Mandate.
- The creation of an independent Jewish state in Palestine.
- A link between this Jewish state and an independent Arab union of the neighbouring countries.

Ben-Gurion's five points confirmed Riad el-Solh's worst fears: the Zionists intended to turn the whole of Palestine and Transjordan into their independent Jewish state! But how was this project, so destructive of Arab national interests, to be thwarted, or at least held in check? He asked for Ben-Gurion's proposals in writing, and undertook to discuss them with other Arab leaders. He told the Zionist leader that France, jealous of its hold on Syria, would oppose the entry of that mandated country into any Arab union or federation – particularly one dominated by Britain. It would require a world war, he remarked, with no little prescience, to transform the situation and bring the Mandates to an end.[2]

Ben-Gurion's next Arab interlocutor was the *Istiqlal* leader, 'Awni 'Abd al-Hadi, whom he met on 18 July, and to whom he once again outlined his vision of a large Jewish state on both banks of the Jordan, linked to an Arab federation. 'Abd al-Hadi was unimpressed. 'The Jews were buying up the best lands and dispossessing the Arabs', he told Ben-Gurion. 'Weizmann and others were always proclaiming goodwill toward the Arabs – but where was this goodwill . . .? Do you think you can fool us with sweet-sounding proclamations . . .? The settlement of the Jews undermines the existence of the Arabs. It is of no benefit to us'. 'Abd al-Hadi asked Ben-Gurion whether the Zionists would help the Arabs rid themselves of the imperialist powers. Ben-Gurion was frank enough to admit that the political liberation of the Arabs would have to wait until later. The Zionists certainly would not fight the highly accommodating British on their behalf![3]

At another meeting with Musa al-'Alami on 14 August, Ben-Gurion again outlined his plan of a Jewish state linked to an eventual Arab federation. 'Alami replied that without a firm guarantee regarding the federation, the Arabs could not accept unlimited Jewish immigration, or the creation of a Jewish state. He suggested, however, that Ben-Gurion's proposals could best be put to the Hajj Amin, the Grand Mufti. At a further meeting on 27 August, and having consulted the Mufti in the meantime, 'Alami posed a number of questions. If European Jews became the majority and Palestine was declared a Jewish state, who would guarantee the security of the Dome of the Rock on the *Haram al-Sharif*, the holiest Muslim shrine outside the Hijaz? This, he explained, was the Mufti's main concern. Ben-Gurion sought to be reassuring. Only Orthodox Jews believed that the Temple should be rebuilt, he told 'Alami, and then only after the coming of the Messiah. A guarantee of the security of the site could be given, if the Arabs required one.

'Alami then enquired whether Ben-Gurion would agree to Palestine, Iraq and Transjordan forming a single state. Ben-Gurion's reply was firmly in the negative. The independence of the Jewish people was inconceivable, he insisted, without an independent political

---

[2] Ibid., pp. 17–18.
[3] Ibid., pp. 18–21.

state of their own. Palestine and Transjordan had to be part of the Jewish state, with Iraq as the other partner in the federation. Would Ben-Gurion restrict Jewish immigration for a decade, so as to limit the Jewish population to no more than one million by the end of that period? Once again, Ben-Gurion refused, as unlimited immigration was the central pillar of his policy.[4]

Ben-Gurion next arranged to interview the Emir Shakib Arslan and Ihsan al-Jabiri, Riad's colleagues in the Syro-Palestinian Delegation, whom he met in Geneva on 23 September. To them, too, in discussions which lasted until dawn, he repeated his belief in the absolute necessity, indeed the inevitability, of creating a Jewish state in Palestine and Transjordan. The Jews would soon be a majority in Palestine, he claimed. That could no longer be prevented. But it was necessary to reach an agreement with the Arabs. If a Jewish state were part of a wider Arab federation, the Palestine Arabs would not feel in a minority. Arslan was taken aback by such naked ambition. In his mind, there was no question of either a Jewish majority or a Jewish state. He was not prepared even to consider entering into serious discussions with the Zionists, unless they assured him that the Arabs in Palestine would be allowed to remain a majority. The Arabs, he said, would never tolerate a Jewish Palestine; nor had the Jews any right to settle in Transjordan, over which they had absolutely no possible claim. Ihsan al-Jabiri attempted to be somewhat less abrasive than Arslan – but even he could not hold out for long in the face of Ben-Gurion's unabashed triumphalism.[5]

A couple of days after the meeting, the indefatigable Ben-Gurion was in Warsaw, where, in a crowing speech, he announced that an agreement was about to be reached with the Arabs on the basis of his plan. Arslan and Jabiri were outraged by this leaked disinformation. To safeguard their reputations, they immediately published in *La Nation arabe* their version of the 'exchange of views' with the Zionist leader.[6] They had asked Ben-Gurion how many immigrants the Zionists planned to bring into Palestine, and what was his estimate of the country's maximum capacity of absorption. Ben-Gurion had replied that Palestine and Transjordan could absorb six to eight million Jews. He had come to ask what compensation the Arabs would require to give

[4] Ibid., pp. 24–33.
[5] Ibid., pp. 35–7.
[6] *La Nation arabe*, no. 2 (December 1934), pp. 145–6.

their consent to the creation of a Jewish state in these territories. Those Arabs who did not wish to emigrate could remain there, and their land would not be taken from them, he had said.

> We could hardly refrain from smiling at such enormities . . .
> nevertheless we asked Mr Ben-Gurion what compensation
> the Jews would offer the Arabs in exchange for such
> sacrifices. He answered: 'We will give the Arabs political
> and economic aid. Political aid will consist of mobilising
> Jewish power in favour of the Arabs of Syria; as for
> economic aid, it would consist of investing capital in
> Mesopotamia, the Saudi region and Yemen in order to
> contribute to their economic development.'
>   'In sum,' we replied, 'you are asking for the
> evacuation of a country . . . in exchange for an offer of
> uncertain political aid and for a financial contribution for
> which none of the Arab countries has a pressing need.'

Arslan and Jabiri reminded Ben-Gurion that France was beginning to recognise Syria's ability to govern itself; that Iraq had recovered its independence and was in full economic expansion as a result of its oil resources; and that the Hijaz and the Yemen had no intention of accepting foreign capital, least of all Jewish capital. His offer, they told Ben-Gurion, was totally inadequate to persuade

> one and a half million Arabs to resign themselves to giving
> up their homeland, the sacred land of their fathers, and to
> emigrate into the desert; and for the Arab nation of some
> twenty million people to accept the shame of counter-
> signing the evacuation of this most sacred territory,
> each clod of which was steeped in the blood of their
> ancestors . . . With ideas as excessive and insolent as these,
> Ben-Gurion should not think of seeking the consent of his
> adversaries. It was better for the Zionists to rely on British
> bayonets to create their Jewish kingdom rather than seek
> an agreement with the Arabs.

In their account of the interview, they rightly concluded that it was active British encouragement combined with Arab lethargy that had given Ben-Gurion the temerity to make such 'puerile and insubstantial' proposals. His approach had revealed the Zionists' true aim, which was to create a Jewish majority in Palestine. Arslan accurately foretold what would then happen: 'Once they have a majority, *c'est fini pour les Arabes*.'[7]

In April 1936, buoyed up by a record influx of 65,000 Jews the previous year, Ben-Gurion had three long discussions with yet another prominent Arab. This time his interlocutor was George Antonius, a Cambridge-educated, Greek Orthodox intellectual of Lebanese-Egyptian parentage, who had acquired Palestinian citizenship in 1925. He had worked for the British Mandate government, but had resigned in disgust in 1930, in protest at Britain's glaring bias in favour of the Zionists. In 1938, as Palestine was slipping out of Arab hands, he published a seminal book, *The Arab Awakening*. It was immediately recognised as a classic of Arab nationalism.

With Antonius, Ben-Gurion's central argument was that there was no essential contradiction between the national aspirations of the Arabs and those of the Jews. The Jews were interested only in 'Eretz Israel', which he defined as 'the land between the Mediterranean to the West and the desert to the East, and between Sinai to the South and the source of the Jordan to the North' – an area which included Transjordan and parts of Syria and Lebanon. Even if the Arabs found themselves a minority in this area, they would still be members of the greater Arab nation. He would accept no limitation on Jewish immigration, but argued instead for an 'active agreement' between Arabs and Jews. 'We would help the Arab people to attain its maximum productivity', he declared patronisingly. 'We would aid it morally, politically, financially and organizationally. And the Arabs would help us in developing Eretz Israel to the utmost, so that they would have a good life in this country and so that we might bring in the maximum number of Jews'.[8]

In that same year, 1936, Riad el-Solh had a meeting with another leading Zionist representative. This time, his interlocutor was not the pugnacious David Ben-Gurion, but the more moderate Nahum Goldman, a lifelong Zionist who had just helped set up the World Jewish Congress, over which he was to preside for many years.

---

[7] Cleveland, *Islam Against the West*, p. 78.
[8] Ben-Gurion, *My Talks with Arab Leaders*, pp. 42–4.

Their meeting took place in Paris, where Riad was advising the Syrian delegation on its treaty negotiations with Léon Blum's Popular Front government. Riad was in an angry mood. He had devoted his whole life to the cause of Arab independence, only to learn that Chaim Weizmann had, in secret, urged Blum *not* to grant independence to Syria. If the Jews wanted an understanding with the Arabs, he told Goldman, they had better first publicly declare their support for the Arab liberation movement. Only then would it be possible to discuss anything at all.[9]

In Paris, Riad was unaware that Weizmann had also pressed Léon Blum to resist any attempt by the Syrians to challenge the expanded frontiers of Greater Lebanon, as drawn by the French in 1920. Weizmann hoped that Zionists and Maronites would be able to cooperate to confront 'the fanatical Muslim masses' of the interior.[10] He wanted Blum to authorise the settlement of thousands of Jews between the Palestine frontier and Beirut. At his request, a French lawyer, Cadmi-Cohen, went to Beirut to propose that the Jews and the Lebanese conclude a 'gentleman's agreement' based on Jewish settlement in South Lebanon. The Jews would recognise the expanded international frontiers of Lebanon, while Lebanon would recognise the Zionists' right to Transjordan and the Sinai peninsula. No agreement was reached, although a small Maronite fringe – worked upon by the idea of creating a 'Christian national home' in Lebanon – viewed the idea with sympathy.

By this time, Riad had given up all hope of reaching any acceptable accommodation with the Zionists, as their demands were simply too outrageous. Moreover, they seemed to enjoy steely British backing. The Arabs, on the other hand, were squabbling and faction-ridden, as concerned to put each other down as they were to fight the Zionists. What advice was he to give his Palestinian friends? He was all too aware that events were pushing the Hajj Amin towards greater and greater radicalism. There were forces in the Palestinian camp, and indeed in the Arab world at large, that favoured a recourse to arms against both the British and the Zionists. The scholarly Antonius himself had told Ben-Gurion that, with European Jews flooding unchecked into the country, the Arabs had no option left but to fight. If the Zionists wanted 'a one

[9] Ibid., p. 70.
[10] Laurens, *La Question de Palestine*, vol. II, p. 326.

hundred per cent Jewish State', there was absolutely no possibility of reaching any understanding with them.[11]

Riad was full of foreboding. He had seen the ruthless way in which the French had routed the Syrians at Maysalun in 1920, and had then crushed their Revolution in 1925–26. A brutal imperial power like Britain would have no qualms whatsoever about using great force against rebellious natives. Its response to any Arab unrest in Palestine was unlikely to be different from that of the French in Syria. Rather than risk another armed clash with the French, Riad had argued in favour of a campaign of propaganda and persuasion, of reaching out to French opinion through his contacts with politicians and the press in Paris. His efforts were beginning to bear fruit. The French had agreed to treaty negotiations with the Levant states which, it was hoped, would bring the Mandates to an end and lead to independence. But Palestine was different. While the Arabs quarrelled among themselves, the Zionists were driven by a single-minded determination to take over the whole country. They were already a community of close to half a million Jews, largely of European origin, educationally and economically superior to the Arabs, and greatly increasing in numbers, as well as in possession of land and wealth, literally by the day. What was to be done?

Ben-Gurion's offer to his various Arab interlocutors had been basically the same: give us Palestine and Transjordan as a Jewish state, and we will help you set other Arab countries on the path to development and some sort of federation. But Riad fully understood that, in view of the Zionists' dependence on Britain and their fear of offending the French, the political offer they were making to the Arabs was nothing but a hollow one. It was mere dust in their eyes. For his part, Ben-Gurion had also known that the Arabs would never agree to 'sell' Palestine to the Jews. A Jewish state, he now concluded, could be had only by a decisive show of military strength.

The Palestine Arab rebellions of 1936–39

In the early 1930s, a group of young Arabs decided to form a secret organisation, *al-jihad al-muqaddas* (the sacred struggle), to prepare

---

[11] Ben-Gurion, *My Talks with Arab Leaders*, p. 49.

for armed revolt. Under the impulse of their leader, 'Abd al-Qadir al-Husayni, son of Musa Kadhim al-Husayni, the former head of the Arab Executive, cells were created and funds collected. The Mufti was informed and cautiously urged them not to act until they were ready.

At about the same time, a similar organisation was being created in northern Palestine by 'Izz al-Din al-Qassam, a devout Syrian from the Latakia region, who had studied at the Azhar in Cairo, taught at a religious college, fought the French and been condemned to death by them in absentia. He had fled to Haifa, where he had set up a night school for the illiterate and begun to preach, thus gaining a following among uprooted peasants.[12] Organising them in a network of secret armed cells, he prepared to wage jihad against the Zionists, the British and their Arab collaborators.

Men like Qassam were driven by a fierce spirit of patriotism and self-sacrifice. They were responding to persistent rumours that the Zionists were now forming and arming their own underground forces. In October 1935, the British police had uncovered large-scale trafficking of German weapons through the port of Haifa, which had been sold to the Zionists with the approval of the Nazis. Arabs like 'Izz al-Din al-Qassam became resolved to acquire weapons themselves – and to use them. With eleven of his followers, he decided to go underground and launch military operations. They were soon located and surrounded. Qassam was killed in a gun battle with the police on 21 November 1935. As befitted a national hero, his funeral in Haifa was the occasion for a huge political demonstration. More than seventy years later, his name was given to the primitive, home-made rockets which the desperate Palestinians – under siege in Gaza – were to lob defiantly, if ineffectually, at Israel.

Qassam's movement was to survive his death. On 15 April 1936, a band of Palestinian rebels held up a bus on the road from Nablus to Jaffa and killed two Jewish passengers. Jewish reprisals quickly followed. Two Arabs were assassinated in a banana plantation, and thirty thousand Jews from Tel Aviv clashed with the police. To coordinate local Palestinian resistance, activists in Nablus formed a national committee, a move followed by other Arab towns and villages. To take command of the whole burgeoning movement, the Hajj Amin set up a Higher Arab Committee on which the five main Palestinian

---

[12] Hirst, *The Gun and the Olive Branch*, p. 199.

political parties were represented under his chairmanship, and which the *Istiqlal* leaders joined a little while later. The Committee called a general strike which, it declared, would not end until Jewish immigration and land purchase were halted and the Mandate replaced by a national government. Ironically enough, the strike ended up benefiting the Jewish economy, by enabling it to become more self-sufficient. Jewish workers replaced Arabs on Jewish-owned citrus plantations, while port facilities at the Jewish city of Tel Aviv were created and expanded, to reduce dependence on the old Arab port of Jaffa.

When the British High Commission refused to yield to the strikers, sporadic acts of violence occurred, soon escalating into open rebellion. Armed men attacked Jewish colonies and ambushed British forces. Roads were mined, trains derailed, telephone wires cut and traffic between cities disrupted by sniper fire. To raise funds and weapons for the insurgents, 'Committees for the Defence of Palestine' sprang up all over the Arab world – in Syria, Iraq, Egypt, Transjordan, Kuwait and Lebanon, where Riad el-Solh was very active. Arab volunteers began to infiltrate into Palestine, where they were organised into paramilitary units by Fawzi al-Qawuqji, now a generalissimo of the Palestine revolution, whose varied career had included fighting the French in Syria, advising Ibn Sa'ud on military matters, and teaching at the military academy in Baghdad. Swept along by the current, the Hajj Amin's own role quickly evolved from that of a traditional notable, usually called upon to calm tempers and act as an intermediary with the authorities, to that of the outright leader of an armed uprising.[13]

On 2 September, the British cabinet took the decision to crush the rebels by force. A division of British troops was sent out to Palestine. Urged on by the Zionists and by his own pro-Zionist advisers, Sir Arthur Wauchope authorised the arrest without warrant of suspected rebels, the internment and deportation of strike leaders, the seizure of buildings and vehicles, and the collective punishment of hostile villages. Arming Jewish settlers was legalised, while nearly three thousand supernumerary Jewish police were recruited and trained. To protect scattered Jewish colonies, the British began cooperating with the *Haganah*, the Jewish underground army, which, by the summer

---

[13] Hurewitz, *Diplomacy*, vol. II, p. 69; Laurens, *La Question de Palestine*, vol. II, p. 319.

of 1936, had grown into a sizeable military force. Alarmed at this dangerous turn of events, government ministers in neighbouring Arab states and other leading figures tried to persuade the Higher Arab Committee to end the strike, but the Hajj Amin and the fighters insisted that Jewish immigration had to be suspended first. This, however, was totally rejected by the Zionists. Moshe Shertok even told Musa al-'Alami that Jewish immigration was as sacred to the Zionists as the Dome of the Rock was to the Muslims.

How was the situation to be brought under control? Was there a role for an external mediator? In regular contact with the Hajj Amin, yet increasingly preoccupied by his espousal of what he feared would prove to be self-defeating violence, Riad el-Solh thought to intervene with the British High Commission. He feared that the Palestinian rebellion against the British would merely drive them further into the arms of the Zionists – which is indeed what happened – and lead to an even harsher repression of the Arabs. He wished that the Palestinians could have adopted the tactics of persuasion and dialogue which he had sought to use with the French. He advised them to appeal more forcefully to British public opinion, rather than to allow the Zionists to monopolise the field completely. But, at this critical juncture, Riad was called to Paris to advise the Syrian delegation on its treaty negotiations with the French. A Franco-Syrian draft agreement was signed on 9 September 1936. It was seen at the time as a great triumph for the Syrian National Bloc – and for Riad el-Solh himself.

Riad was one of the few Arabs at that time who understood that great efforts had to be made to influence and win over international opinion, if the Arab case was to be heard. His colleague, the Emir Shakib Arslan, was another such rare exception. By personal advocacy and in the columns of his journal, *La Nation arabe*, Arslan tirelessly defended Arab and Muslim interests throughout the 1930s. But it was all uphill work. The cause of Arab liberation was unpopular in Europe. The Palestine Arabs had made no attempt to influence opinion in any non-Arab country. No Arab state was represented on the Permanent Mandates Commission. In spite of some modest progress towards political independence, most Arab countries were still under the jackboot of the Western Powers.

The Jewish Agency, on the other hand, had had permanent offices in London and Geneva for a long time, and had successfully cultivated a host of influential people. Zionist leaders had regular access to European statesmen. Zionist branches in many countries had mobilised opinion in favour of the 'Jewish National Home'. Indeed, very large sums had been collected for precisely that purpose. It was not until 1936 that a small Palestine Information Centre was opened in London, but its impact was extremely limited. Politically and financially, the Zionists were already far more influential than the Arabs could ever hope to be.[14]

Egypt's political leaders could have served as potential mediators, but, much like the Syrian delegation in Paris, the Wafdist government had little time for Palestine, as it was absorbed in the final stage of negotiating the Anglo-Egyptian treaty of 26 August 1936. It was then that Iraq's Foreign Minister General Nuri al-Sa'id, a pillar of British policy since the time of the Arab Revolt, entered the scene. No doubt he thought he could put his credit with Britain to work in the service of the Palestinians in their hour of need. Proposing himself as a mediator, he came to Jerusalem that August to see if a settlement could be reached. Before setting out for Palestine, he consulted Riad el-Solh – they had been friends since their youth in Istanbul – because the solution he wanted to propose was modelled on the same one that Riad had been urging for a decade, namely the creation of a large Arab federation, in which room could be found for a 'Jewish national home' in the form of a canton in the coastal areas of Palestine, where most of the Jews had settled. Nuri went to Cairo to reassure the Egyptians that the creation of such a large Arab state would not challenge Cairo's predominance in the eastern Mediterranean.

In Jerusalem, Nuri had meetings with Sir Arthur Wauchope, who appears to have encouraged his efforts, and also with Moshe Shertok of the Zionist Executive. The strike would be called off, he told the latter, if Jewish immigration were suspended so as to allow talks to take place on all contentious issues. But Shertok would have none of it. Immigration, he contended irritably, was an absolute Jewish right.[15] When the British allowed Nuri to meet the *Istiqlal* leaders in their internment camp, he was rash enough to suggest to them that Britain would be ready to suspend Jewish immigration and grant a general amnesty to the rebels, if they were prepared to end their violent rebellion.

---

[14] Hurewitz, *Diplomacy*, vol. II, pp. 85 ff.
[15] Ibid., p. 70.

Word of these exchanges so alarmed the Zionists that they acted quickly to nullify Nuri's efforts. In London, Weizmann persuaded William Ormsby-Gore, the British colonial secretary, to issue a communiqué saying that neither the high commissioner in Palestine nor the British government had agreed to the suspension of Jewish immigration, or to a permanent Iraqi mediation in Palestinian affairs – a declaration which left the unfortunate Nuri out on a limb. The Arabs saw it as yet another example of British perfidy and of the manipulative power of the Zionists. In any event, a military coup in Iraq on 29 October 1936 by Bakr Sidqi, the acting chief of the general staff, overthrew Yasin al-Hashimi's nationalist government. Nuri al-Sa'id went prudently into exile, and that was to prove the end of his hapless mediation.

By this time, British troops in Palestine, numbering about twenty thousand, had managed to break all organised Arab resistance. At the insistent urging of Arab leaders, the Mufti's Higher Arab Committee finally agreed to call off the strike. It had lasted 176 days and claimed the lives of up to 1,000 Arabs, 37 Britons and 69 Jews.[16] Fawzi al-Qawuqji's Arab volunteers were made to leave the country. They were allowed to cross into Transjordan and then go on to disperse in Iraq. The Jews, on the other hand, refused to relinquish their weapons.

The Peel Commission and the rebellion's second phase

Though Riad el-Solh was not a leading actor in the Palestine drama, he remained throughout in close touch with its protagonists. The fate of the Palestinian Arabs, dispossessed by the Zionists and violently repressed by the British, was not something that he could for a moment ignore. The brutal creation of a 'Jewish national home', in a hostile Arab environment against the will of the indigenous population, ignited a raging fire of irreconcilable nationalisms. It was to cast a dark cloud over his entire career, as it did over that of every Arab leader from that day onwards.

The British government then decided to appoint a Royal Commission to 'investigate causes of unrest' in Palestine. Composed

---

[16] Hirst, *The Gun and the Olive Branch*, p. 209.

of six eminent persons, it was led by Lord Peel, a former secretary of state at the India Office. He was the grandson of Sir Robert Peel, the great British statesman of the first half of the nineteenth century and the founder of the Conservative Party. The Commission arrived in Palestine on 11 November 1936. Outraged that, despite its arrival, Britain had not stopped the issuing of entry permits to European Jews, the Hajj Amin's Higher Committee foolishly decided to boycott it – much to the Palestinians' disadvantage. On the urging of Arab leaders, the boycott was eventually lifted in January 1937, but only after the Commission had already held fifty-five sessions. In contrast to Arab silence, Weizmann gave a masterly three-hour performance, in which he 'portrayed the Jewish tragedy in the light of history with the zeal and assurance of a great artist'.[17] He had been scathing and dismissive of the Arabs: their nationalism was a crude borrowing from Europe, an expression of force with no spiritual or cultural content, whereas Zionist interests were identical to those of the British Empire.

While the Commission was still considering its report, the Hajj Amin went to Saudi Arabia in February 1937 to meet Ibn Sa'ud and perform the pilgrimage. He was accompanied by 'Izzat Darwaza, a Palestinian activist from Nablus, who had been prominent in the Arab nationalist movement since the First World War.[18] They flew to Cairo and, before taking ship from Suez for the Hijaz, they had pro-longed discussions with Riad el-Solh and Nuri al-Sa'id (who was still in exile), both of whom had come there to meet them. The four men had been friends since the heady days, almost twenty years earlier, of Faysal's rule in Damascus. Riad's advice to the Mufti was to resort to diplomacy rather than to war. But the Hajj Amin was by this time persuaded that there was no justice to be had from the British and that the Palestinians had no alternative but to take to arms.[19] In Mecca, he asked Ibn Sa'ud for guns and money, which the king agreed to provide if fighting resumed, but on condition of absolute secrecy. In fact, violence erupted that February, with bomb-throwing and a spate of mutual killings.

Published on 7 July 1937, the Peel Commission's report reached the grim but realistic conclusion that the Palestine Mandate was unworkable. The conflict between Arabs and Jews had become

---

[17] Christopher Sykes, *Crossroads to Israel*, London 1965, p. 197.
[18] Muhammad Izzat Darwaza, *Mudhakkarat*, 2 vols, Beirut 1993.
[19] Laurens, *La Question de Palestine*, vol. II, pp. 338–9.

irreconcilable and was only likely to get worse. Neither side would ever agree to be the minority. The Palestine Arabs wanted independence. They hated and feared the fact of a 'Jewish national home'. They were all the more frustrated by the progress towards independence of neighbouring Arab states. As for the Jews, their worsening situation in Europe would inevitably lead to further pressure on Palestine. The only hope for a peaceful solution lay in partition.

Accordingly, the Commission recommended that Palestine be divided into three parts: a sovereign Jewish state of about 5,000 square kilometres, comprising Galilee, the Jezreel valley and much of the coastal plain – but not including the Jewish quarters of Jerusalem, where some 70,000 Jews lived, out of a total then approaching half a million; a sovereign Arab state of about 12,500 square kilometres, including 6,000 in the Negev desert, which would be united with Transjordan; and lastly, a British mandatory zone – in effect, a pear-shaped corridor stretching from Jerusalem and Bethlehem to a point on the Mediterranean coast just south of Jaffa. Britain would also retain control of strategic airfields and of the ports of Haifa and 'Aqaba, to which both Arabs and Jews would have access.

Neither the Arabs nor the Jews were at all happy with these proposals. The Arabs' worst fears were confirmed by them. The coastal region, which had been the focus of Arab development for a century, and was the spectacularly beautiful part of Palestine, was to be given to the Jews, with only Jaffa and Gaza remaining in Arab hands. Jerusalem was to be placed in a corridor outside the future Arab state. The Palestinian political class was to be dispersed, with leadership passing to the Emir 'Abdallah, and his far more backward Transjordan. 'Abdallah was indeed the main beneficiary of the Peel plan.

The Hajj Amin's Higher Arab Committee rejected the partition plan and called on Arab heads of state to do the likewise. Instead, it demanded total independence for Palestine, the abolition of the Mandate and the end of the experiment of a 'Jewish national home'. However, the Palestinians were divided among themselves. The Hajj Amin's Nashashibi rivals were inclined to accept partition, provided that Palestine was merged with Transjordan under 'Abdallah. It was their foolish way of defeating the Mufti.

In the Jewish camp, Vladimir Jabotinsky's Revisionists insisted on the Jews' 'inalienable right' to the whole of Palestine, and to Transjordan as well. Weizmann and Ben-Gurion were more pragmatic.

Choosing to see the plan as yet another opportunity proffered them by the British, they gave grudging acceptance to the principle of partition, but only on condition that the proposed Jewish state was greatly expanded. They demanded the whole of the Palestine coast, from Gaza to the Lebanese frontier; Galilee and the whole of the north; as well as part of the southern desert – in all, about 10,500 square kilometres. This was a considerable retreat from the claim the Zionists had made at the 1919 Peace Conference, which was for a Palestine stretching north to the Litani river in Lebanon, and including the Golan and the Hawran in Syria, the most fertile part of Transjordan and a part of Sinai – in all about 50,000 square kilometres! The Zionists had persistently sought a foothold in Syria and Lebanon, and were only held in check by the vigilance of the French mandatory authorities, who saw them as an extension of British machinations.

In the early summer of 1937, the Hajj Amin went to Syria for further meetings with Riad el-Solh and with the National Bloc, which was now in power in Damascus. In his absence, Moshe Shertok and the Emir 'Abdallah both denounced him separately to the British as a dangerous troublemaker. Weizmann even warned Léon Blum by telegram that the Mufti was planning a revolt in Palestine with Syrian help.[20] Shertok urged the British to deport him. The Zionists believed that if the Hajj Amin were removed from the scene, 'Abdallah and the backstabbing Nashashibis would consent to partition and would agree to the redrawing of the map of Palestine to the Zionists' advantage. The British Colonial Office, in turn, became convinced – under relentless Zionist pressure – that the Hajj Amin was the real obstacle to the implementation of the Peel plan.

The Hajj Amin escapes to Lebanon

Learning that the British were about to arrest and deport him, the Mufti moved himself and his family into the *Haram al-Sharif*, where British troops could not enter. From this sanctuary, he continued to orchestrate the campaign against partition. Violence erupted again that August, with persistent reports of arms trafficking and the formation of armed bands in the countryside, especially in the north of Palestine,

[20] Ibid., p. 346.

where al-Qassam guerrillas were still active. In the first phase of the rebellion, Palestine Defence Committees in Iraq, Syria, Lebanon and Egypt had managed to send funds and volunteers to Palestine, but once the British army had broken Arab resistance, these had lain dormant. Now, in the summer of 1937, they sprang to life again around a project to organise a pan-Arab conference, which, it was hoped, would rally Arab governments and public opinion to the Palestine cause. The plan was to hold the conference in Palestine itself, but the British authorities refused to allow it. The Damascus Committee then approached the French, who agreed to the meeting being held in Syria, but under stringent conditions. There was to be no participation of the Syrian government, and no questions raised concerning the French Mandate, the status of Alexandretta, or the expanded frontiers of Greater Lebanon.

Despite these limiting conditions, this proved a high point of pan-Arab concern for Palestine. It was a genuine revolt against the hated imperial power that had occupied Egypt, betrayed the Sharif Husayn and opened the way for Zionist immigration. It captured the Arabs' imagination. Under tight French surveillance, nearly four hundred delegates gathered for the opening ceremony on 8 September 1937, at the mountain resort of Bludan, an hour's drive from Damascus. 'Izzat Darwaza, the prominent Nablus activist, headed the Palestinian delegation. Riad el-Solh led a large group of Sunni Lebanese politicians. Iraq, where Nuri al-Sa'id and the Arab nationalists were back in power, was strongly represented. Indeed, a former Iraqi prime minister, Tawfiq al-Suwaidi, was elected conference president. His vice-president was Alluba Pasha, a former Egyptian minister. The Egyptians were, in fact, far more in evidence in Bludan than they had been at the General Islamic Conference in Jerusalem of 1931. The Emir Shakib Arslan also attended the Bludan conference. In his committed vision, Palestine was the crucible in which Arab-Islamic determination would be tested; it was the measure of whether the Arab nation was willing to transform itself through sacrifice – to become in the future what it had been in the past.[21]

On 10 September, resolutions were passed unanimously declaring Palestine an integral part of the Arab homeland; no part of it could be alienated or detached. Partition was rejected, as was the creation of a Jewish state. Immigration and the sale of land had to stop. The

[21] Cleveland, *Islam Against the West*, p. 81.

Balfour Declaration had to be annulled. The Mandate had to be abrogated and replaced by an Anglo-Palestinian treaty guaranteeing the independence and sovereignty of Arab Palestine. The Jewish minority, however, would have the same rights as the Arab majority. Britain was told that it had to choose between the Arabs and the Jews. If it did not change its policy in Palestine, the Arabs would be free to turn for help to powers hostile to it. Nazi Germany and Fascist Italy were, in fact, already actively seeking to undermine British (and French) influence in the Mediterranean region.

Although he was known as an outstanding figure of militant pan-Arabism, Riad el-Solh at Bludan sought to preach the virtues of persuasion and diplomacy; but he was going against the grain and could no longer stem the tide of violence. A mere two weeks after the delegates dispersed, Lewis Andrews, the British acting district commissioner of Galilee, was assassinated on 26 September by four members of an al-Qassam band. He had been closely associated with Lord Peel's partition plan. Britain's reaction was immediate. The Hajj Amin's Higher Arab Committee was outlawed, and several of its members arrested and deported in chains to the Seychelles. The Zionists were exultant. Hiding in the *Haram*, the Mufti himself managed to escape arrest, but he was stripped of all his functions. On the night of 13–14 October, disguised as a Beduin, he managed to slip through the cordon around the *Haram* and escape by fishing boat up the coast to Lebanon.[22] It was the exact reverse of the sea journey which Riad, then under sentence of death by the French, had made from Lebanon to Palestine in 1920.

From Lebanon, the Hajj Amin attempted to cross over the mountains to Syria, but he was intercepted by the French police and interrogated by Monsieur Colombani, the powerful head of the *Sûreté Générale*, who placed him under house arrest in the coastal village of al-Zuq, a Christian area north of Beirut.[23]

There, to Britain's extreme annoyance, the French allowed him to continue to direct the Palestine resistance movement. No doubt they were happy to pay the British back for *their* attitude during the Syrian revolt of 1925–26, when Syrian rebels had mounted raids against French positions from the safety of British-occupied Transjordan. In

---

[22] Amin al-Husayni, *Mudhakkarat al-hajj Amin al-Husayni*, Damascus 1999, p. 32.
[23] Laurens, *La Question de Palestine*, vol. II, p. 374; Hurewitz, *Diplomacy*, vol. II, p. 82.

any event, Paris had already dismissed the Peel Commission's partition plan as a British manoeuvre. By raising the prospect of an Arab union, they said, the British sought to distract the Arabs from the huge loss of Palestine. In any event, the idea of such an Arab union was certain to raise French hackles, as it was considered a British plot to oust them from Syria, which in certain ways it was. There was another French consideration. The Mufti had become a Muslim hero, widely seen as a victim of Zionist intrigue and British duplicity. He enjoyed the support of Muslim leaders like Riad el-Solh in Beirut and the National Bloc in Damascus, whom the French were, by this time, anxious to try to conciliate. It was not, therefore, in France's interest to seek to restrain him. In the months of crisis which led to the outbreak of war in September 1939, the Mufti's stay in Lebanon was to become an increasing source of friction in Franco-British relations.

The second phase of the revolt

In Palestine, violence erupted more fiercely than ever in October 1937, with armed bands launching attacks on British troops and Jewish settlements, as well as on those Arabs who were inclined to collaborate with the British. Among these were the Nashashibis and other Arab opponents of the Hajj Amin. The rebellion was thus in part, and shockingly so, an Arab civil war. It grew over the next couple of years into a murderous inter-Palestinian blood feud, similar to that which was to convulse the Palestinians in 2007–9. About a quarter of those Palestinians who lost their lives in the late 1930s were killed by their own people.[24] This time, the Husaynis declined to call on the services of the veteran guerrilla leader Fawzi al-Qawuqji, who was now considered too close to the Emir 'Abdallah and their Nashashibi foes. Operating mainly in the Jerusalem area, the Hajj Amin's followers joined forces with the al-Qassam guerrillas. 'Izzat Darwaza – appointed by the Hajj Amin to take charge of military operations – divided Palestine into distinct operational zones and tried to set up a central leadership.

The British army found itself dealing with almost continuous guerrilla warfare, waged by some three thousand rebels in the countryside and about a thousand in the cities. A further six thousand peasant

---

[24] Sykes, *Crossroads to Israel*, p. 218.

fighters were able and ready to join in if required.[25] Palestine support committees in Damascus, Cairo, Baghdad and elsewhere redoubled their efforts to raise funds and smuggle weapons into the country. By the summer of 1938, the rebels had more or less taken control of the central mountain area of Galilee, and also, if only intermittently, of main cities such as Hebron, Nablus, Beersheba, Jaffa, Tiberias and old Jerusalem.

Britain responded with a ferocious campaign of counter-terror: mass arrests without trial, destruction of suspects' houses, beatings, humiliations and collective punishments. Military courts were set up and innocent civilians herded into concentration camps. Carrying bombs or firing guns was decreed punishable by death. To the shock of the Arab population, one of the leaders of the al-Qassam group, the old and greatly admired Shaykh Farhan al-Sa'di, was put on trial, sentenced and hanged – one of the 112 Arabs to be hanged by the British before the revolt was finally crushed.[26] Showing which side they were on in this gruesome gallows game, the British hanged only one Jew for 'terrorism'. As the violence escalated, so did the British repression of it. Torture became systematic. The horrifying practice was adopted of tying bewildered peasants to the front of vehicles as 'human shields' against mines and ambushes. What was, in effect, a spontaneous peasant revolt was cruelly put down in great blood by a reigning imperial power. The Palestinians had been driven to desperation by unchecked Jewish immigration and land purchase, as well as by Britain's untempered bias in favour of the Zionists. But challenging British military power proved to be a strategic mistake – as grave a one as the Syrian armed revolt against the French army more than a decade earlier. Riad el-Solh's foreboding was to prove justified. The Palestinian uprising was, in the sad words of John Marlowe, yet another 'of the blind alleys of Arab nationalism doomed . . . to failure'.[27]

While the Arabs were ruthlessly put down, Jewish rural police grew from 3,500 in 1936 to 5,000 by 1938. A further 1,000 Jewish volunteer guards were enlisted in Jerusalem. British cooperation intensified with the *Haganah*, which by now was a substantial underground

---

[25] Laurens, *La Question de Palestine*, vol. II, p. 388; Hirst, *The Gun and the Olive Branch*, p. 212, puts the rebel figure at 'up to 15,000 men'.

[26] Hirst, *The Gun and the Olive Branch*, p. 216.

[27] John Marlowe, *The Seat of Pilate: An Account of the Palestine Mandate*, London 1959, pp. 137–8.

army of 15,000 men and women. The British came to rely on armed Jewish settlers, and turned a blind eye to *Haganah* operations of 'aggressive defence', which consisted of pre-emptively taking the war to the Arabs rather than merely defending Jewish colonies – a policy that Israel has continued to adopt ever since. This 'forward strategy' was further elaborated and given a cruel edge by Captain Orde Wingate, a young British intelligence officer with a passion for Zionism, who trained and led 'special night squads' of *Haganah* and British troops. Their speciality was to ambush and kill Arab fighters and their leaders. Moshe Dayan was one of several future Israeli officers who, under Wingate's command, learned the lessons of derring do, quick mobility and deep penetration, which were to shape Israel's future military strategy.[28]

Surprise attacks by mobile Jewish commando groups, the assassination of Arab leaders and the brutal treatment of Arab civilians were to become hallmarks of Israeli practice from that moment onwards.[29] The violence escalated further in midsummer 1938, when a terrorist Jewish organisation, the Irgun, started launching retaliatory raids against Arab civilians, such as the repeated explosions in the fruit market at Haifa, which killed and maimed hundreds of people. The uprising itself and its vicious repression destroyed the Palestinian economy. More than 5,000 Arabs were killed and another 14,000 wounded.[30] Several hundred more fled the country, especially those financially able to do so. The British lost 101 men and the Jews 463. In such conditions of chaos and death, Lord Peel's partition plan became yet another of Palestine's miserable casualties.

Britain changes course

Throughout the Arab world, a chorus of protest arose at the brutal repression in Palestine. Opinion in important countries like Egypt and Iraq ran strongly against Britain. The High Commission in Jerusalem reported that the trial of strength was turning into the greatest anti-colonial revolt Britain had faced since the First World War. In London, the Foreign Office grew alarmed at the impact on Britain's position in

[28] Hirst, *The Gun and the Olive Branch*, p. 228.
[29] Laurens, *La Question de Palestine*, vol. II, p. 392.
[30] Walid Khalidi, *From Haven to Conquest*, Beirut 1971, pp. 846–9.

the region. Finally, anxious to preserve some friendship of Arabs and Muslims, Foreign Secretary Anthony Eden grew increasingly critical of the pro-Zionist bias of William Ormsby-Gore at the Colonial Office. Far from protecting Egypt – the main reason it had been conquered in the first place in the First World War – Palestine had become a zone of extreme vulnerability for the British. It was threatened internally by the Arab uprising, and externally by Italian naval and air power. Indeed, Fascist Italy had begun to pose a disturbing challenge to Anglo-French hegemony in the Mediterranean. In an attempt to woo Muslim opinion to the side of Mussolini, Radio Bari had started broadcasting propaganda in Arabic as early as March 1934.[31] Riad's friend, the Emir Shakib Arslan, was received by the Duce in 1934. He was one of many Arabs who considered that Fascist Italy posed far less of a danger to Arab vital interests than did either imperial Britain or France.

In London, geopolitical considerations were now uppermost in official minds, and in particular the need to secure Middle East oil resources, military bases and lines of communication to India and beyond. The Iraq Petroleum Company's pipeline carried indispensable oil to Haifa on the Mediterranean. If Palestine were to fall, it was feared that British power in the whole Middle East would collapse. An immediate worry was that the overstretched British army was finding it difficult to reinforce its troops in Palestine. Indeed, following Germany's annexation of Austria in March 1938, the threat of a European war was such that Britain was forced to start bringing troops home from Palestine.

These were some of the factors which robbed the Palestine partition plan of its relevance. Eden was opposed to partition, but even when he resigned in February 1938, in protest at Neville Chamberlain's expedient political tolerance of Fascist Italy, opposition to the Peel plan continued to gain ground and was further accelerated by a reshuffle of senior officials. On 1 March, Sir Arthur Wauchope was replaced in Jerusalem by Sir Harold MacMichael, a former governor of Tanganyika; while in London, Ormsby-Gore – the main champion of partition – resigned in May and was replaced at the Colonial Office by Malcolm MacDonald, son of the former prime minister. A British commission, sent to Palestine to examine how partition could

---

[31] Callum A. MacDonald, 'Radio Bari, Italian Wireless Propaganda in the Middle East and British Countermeasures, 1934–38', in *Middle Eastern Studies*, 17 (1977).

be implemented, reported back that the scheme should simply be scrapped. The British government, therefore, decided promptly to jettison it, and, by the summer of 1938, the partition plan was stone-dead. Britain now had other pressing priorities.

To find a way out of the impasse – but with the undeclared aim of strengthening imperial defences in the Middle East – the British government called a round-table conference in London, which was opened by Prime Minister Neville Chamberlain on 7 February 1939. It was attended by Palestine Arabs and by the Jewish Agency, as well as by representatives of Egypt, Iraq, Syria, Transjordan and Yemen. The Mufti was short-sightedly barred from attending. Relations between the Arabs and the Jews had, by this time, become so bad that they refused to sit together in the same room. The British declared that a total of only 75,000 Jews would be allowed into Palestine over the five years beginning on 1 April 1939. Measures would be taken to prevent further immigration, now to be considered illegal, while Jewish land purchase would be regulated, even prohibited altogether in certain regions. None of these proposals had any chance of being implemented by the Zionists. Indeed, all of them were spectacularly breached. The conference ended with no agreement on 17 March.

Two months later, on 17 May, the British government published a White Paper which, although calling for safeguards for the 'Jewish national home', nevertheless dealt a severe blow to Zionist ambitions by declaring that it was 'not part of [British] policy that Palestine should become a Jewish state'. This categorical statement was breathtaking in its dishonesty, because, by brutally crushing the Arab revolt, killing its fighters and driving its most effective leaders into exile, and by encouraging dissension in Palestinian ranks, Britain had indeed done everything possible to lay the groundwork for the swift post-war emergence of a Jewish state.

The 1939 White Paper's proposals bore little connection to the facts on the ground. It proposed the gradual establishment, over a decade, of a Palestinian state that was to be governed jointly by Arabs and Jews. Full independence, it asserted, would be conditional on good relations between the two communities. The Jewish Agency denounced the White Paper as treachery, and vowed to oppose it implacably. Indignant at this reversal of British policy in 'favour' of the Arabs, the Zionists now accelerated the process of Jewish militarisation, which was eventually to be used as much against the British – who had created and strengthened it in the first place – as against the Arabs. In 1939, Britain had suddenly understood that it would soon be preoccupied in fighting for its own survival as a nation and an empire. In the all-important Middle East, its primary goal was therefore to check and reverse pro-Axis feeling, while seeking to mobilise the Arabs for its war effort. Winning the war overrode all other considerations.

The Hajj Amin's Higher Committee repudiated the White Paper for not going far enough in meeting Arab demands. He himself moved in October 1939 from Lebanon to Baghdad, where he acquired considerable influence, taking the lead in pro-Axis activities and attempting to incite further rebellion against the British in Palestine. He hoped a German victory would provide great gains for the Palestinians, and perhaps even put him at the head of a large Arab state. However, when Rashid 'Ali's revolt in Iraq was put down in 1941, the Mufti had to flee, first to Iran and then to Italy. In November, he met Hitler in Berlin and joined the Axis propaganda effort as a director of a special Arab Office, broadcasting programmes to the Arab world.[32]

In their very different ways, the Hajj Amin al-Husayni and Riad el-Solh remained pan-Arab champions, but they were eventually compelled by the pressure of events to focus their struggle on a much narrower compass – the Hajj Amin on Palestine and Riad on Syria-Lebanon. They continued to live and dream the cause of Arab independence and unity, but they parted political company when the Hajj Amin put his faith so utterly in Nazi Germany, hoping thus to stem the Zionist tide in Palestine. Riad chose to look to Britain instead, to help break France's grip on the Levant. For all his courage and patriotism, the first ended his life in exile, reviled for his alliance with Hitler. The second, on the other hand, came to be hailed as the principal architect of Lebanon's independence.

---

[32] Hurewitz, *Diplomacy*, vol. II, pp. 147 ff.

12 THE MAKING OF A LEBANESE PATRIOT

By the mid-1930s, Riad el-Solh had emerged as the virtually undisputed leader of the Sunni community of Lebanon. It was by no means an easy position to occupy. To be an Arab nationalist in *Le Grand Liban* between the two world wars was to be an alien in a country whose frontiers one had great difficulty recognising, whose state ideology one could not but find repellent, and from whose politics one was deliberately excluded. It was a state which threatened every aspect of one's identity. The Sunnis of Lebanon did not like to think of themselves as being merely 'Lebanese', since their real *patrie* was the far wider Arab world. They were hardly reconciled to finding themselves citizens – and second-class citizens at that – of a French-protected Christian state, which had been carved out of the heart of 'geographical' Syria by General Gouraud on 31 August 1920, and proclaimed to the world as a fait accompli on the following day.

Riad's family had been landed notables, high-profile members for many generations of the Ottoman ruling classes. Even though their roots were in Sidon, they felt as much at home in the Syrian interior as they did on the coast. Indeed, the Sunnis of Sidon, like those of Beirut and Tripoli, considered themselves to be an integral part of Syria's majority Sunni community, with which they had intimate family, commercial and political ties. Riad's grandfather, Ahmad Pasha, had married a daughter of the Mufti of Damascus; his father had served the Empire as a district governor, as a member of the Ottoman parliament and then, when the Empire collapsed, as the Emir Faysal's minister of interior in Damascus. Riad himself had married into the prominent Aleppo family of the Jabiris. In sentiment, outlook and national feeling, he was as much – and perhaps far more so – Arab as he was 'Lebanese'.

However, literally by the stroke of a pen – that is, upon signing decree no. 318 creating Greater Lebanon – General Gouraud reduced Riad el-Solh from being a member of the Arab world's dominant Sunni majority to a member of a Sunni minority in a new Maronite-dominated state. Overnight, the rulers had become the ruled. Members of the old urban Sunni elite – who had been the traditional intermediaries between state and society – now found themselves a subservient minority. They now had to learn to live under Christian rule, just as the Christians had learned to live under Muslim rule until France's colonial intervention made it otherwise.[1] The Sunnis, to say the least, found this sudden change of their status profoundly uncomfortable and unwelcome.

The issue of the 'disputed territories'

The decision to create a Greater Lebanon within enlarged frontiers had been the direct outcome of General Gouraud's victory over the Emir Faysal. It had also been highly influenced by Robert de Caix, secretary-general at the High Commission in Beirut and champion of France's colonial mission. He favoured a policy of divide and rule, based on playing on ethnic and religious minorities. In first place came France's faithful Maronite clients of Mount Lebanon; but almost as important to their strategy were the heterodox Alawites of north-west Syria; the Druze of southern Syria; and the Kurds of the Jazira. Sunnis in both Syria and Lebanon detested the way the French dealt separately with these various minorities. More particularly, they regarded the Maronite claim to an enlarged independent Christian state under French protection, not as a legitimate aspiration, but as a French plot to deny the Arabs their national independence.[2] The rift thus created between Arab nationalists and Lebanese nationalists was to overshadow Riad's life for much of the interwar period. Seeking to bridge this divide was to be one of his main contributions to modern Lebanon's political life.

It will be recalled that, when he came to draw the expanded boundaries of Greater Lebanon, Gouraud saw fit to attach great swathes of Syrian territory – including much of the Mediterranean

[1] Hanna Ziadeh, *Sectarianism and Intercommunal Nation-Building in Lebanon*, London 2006, p. 108.
[2] Meir Zamir, *The Formation of Modern Lebanon*, New York 1988, p. 59.

coastline – to the core of Mount Lebanon. This unilateral act radically transformed the nineteenth-century Ottoman *mutasarrifiyya* of Mount Lebanon into *Le Grand Liban*. In July 1920, the size of Mount Lebanon had been no more than 4,500 square kilometres; a month later, at 10,452 square kilometres, Greater Lebanon was made twice as big. The annexed territories included the sanjaq of Beirut in the centre; that of Sidon in the south (amputated of its southern region, which was attached to Palestine); and that of Tripoli and its hinterland in the north. In addition, the four *cazas* of Biqa', Baalbek, Hasbaya and Rashaya to the east and south-east of Mount Lebanon were detached from the vilayet of Damascus and attached to the new state.

Before the First World War, Mount Lebanon's Maronites were a clear majority, comprising 58 per cent of the population; compared to the Greek Orthodox, 12 per cent; the Druze, 11 per cent; and the Sunnis and Shi'is together a mere 8 per cent. By 1921, the confessional composition had changed dramatically. With the addition of the new territories, the Maronites, numbering 176,000, now accounted for only 31.3 per cent of the total population. At 300,000, all the Christian sects together totalled 53.4 per cent, only slightly more numerous than the 262,000 Muslims (Sunnis, Shi'is and Druze), who totalled 46.6 per cent.[3]

Most of the Sunni and Shi'i Muslims who lived in the coastal towns and in the four inland *cazas* rejected the French Mandate and rebelled against their forced integration into Greater Lebanon. They wanted to be reunited with the Syrian homeland. As a sign of their hostility, they largely boycotted the consultations which led to the drafting of the Lebanese Constitution of 1926, which they saw as legalising their separation from Syria. On 9 January 1926, the Sunni Mufti of Beirut, Shaykh Mustafa Naja, sent a letter to Musa Nammur, chairman of the constitutional commission, informing him officially that Muslims wanted nothing to do with the new institutional arrangements.[4]

The issue of the 'disputed territories' which had been annexed to Mount Lebanon dominated the political debate in the Levant for many years. Were they to be returned to Syria, as the nationalists demanded; or had they become an inalienable part of the new state, as the Maronites insisted, and Article 2 of the 1926 Constitution

---

[3] Jacques Séguin, *Le Liban Sud: Espace périphérique, espace convoité*, Paris 1989, pp. 42–4.

[4] Nadine Méouchy, 'Le Pacte national 1943–1946: Les ambiguïtés d'un temps politique d'exception', in Khoury (ed.), *Sélim Takla*, p. 467.

affirmed, when it declared that 'No part of the Lebanese territory may be alienated or ceded'?

As a leader of Lebanon's Sunni community in the 1930s, Riad el-Solh's dilemma was how to reconcile Arab nationalism – the very bedrock of his being from his early years – with the new sentiment of Lebanese patriotism, which had inevitably grown up and taken root within the new frontiers. His efforts over the next decade were directed at winning support for the proposition that Lebanese patriotism and Arab nationalism were neither incompatible nor irreconcilable; that loyalty to the new state of Greater Lebanon could be squared with a belief in Arab independence and unity; indeed, that Lebanese independence was a necessary step towards the greater Arab goal. This new-fangled notion was, to say the least, not readily acceptable to diehards on either side.

At the time, Lebanon's actual separation from Syria was largely a fiction. The politics of the two countries remained intertwined. Their economies were linked by a customs union and by innumerable ties of trade, and of financial and family relations. Both were ruled by the same French High Commission in Beirut. The same French concessionary companies supplied electricity to both, ran the tramways and managed the railways. A single French bank, the Banque de Syrie et du Liban, issued the volatile paper currency. Visits were frequently exchanged between Lebanese and Syrian Arab nationalists. Riad was as much at home in Damascus and Aleppo as he was in Beirut. The two countries were like connecting vessels: whatever happened in one had an immediate impact on the other.

Hananu's death and the forty-day strike

This connection was soon to be demonstrated by an event in Syria of capital importance: the death on 21 November 1935 of Ibrahim Hananu, the uncontested leader of the National Bloc, with whom Riad had been closely associated for many years. From his home base in Aleppo, Hananu had been an active leader of the Great Syrian Revolution of 1925–26, but, following the ferocious crushing of that revolt, he had more recently – like Riad himself – tempered his position by insisting on the need for dialogue with the mandatory power in pursuit of the goal of independence.

This attitude set the tone for the speeches at his funeral, which was attended by delegations from all over Syria. Riad led a large group from Beirut. A notable feature of the funeral was the public association of Christian and Muslim clergy and the fact that Christian as well as Muslim symbols were used in the design of the floral tributes carried in the vast procession of thirty thousand mourners, which spread over some 2 kilometres.[5]

Unfortunately, the imperious High Commissioner comte Damien de Martel was too obtuse to seize the occasion of Hananu's death to reach out to the nationalists. Instead, he opted for stern measures to quell the ferment then much in evidence throughout the country. Arming himself with a host of statutory powers, he threatened to send into exile anyone who might dare to challenge him in word or deed. His stern authority, however, was somewhat upstaged by his lax and colourful private life. He was often to be seen in Beirut's bars and cabarets, and was known to be having a torrid liaison with the Russian wife of a foreign consular official. His own wife, la comtesse de Martel, who arrived in Beirut that winter, seemed far more interested in horses than in her husband's dalliances, and indulged her passion at Beirut's febrile weekly races.

On 10 January 1936, forty days after Hananu's death, massive street demonstrations took place in Damascus and soon spread to all Syrian cities. They were immediately followed by a general strike. The agitation was intended to press for a unitary Syrian state, to be ruled from Damascus, and to include the minorities which the French had schemed to deal with separately – Druze, Alawites, Turks (of the sanjaq of Alexandretta) and Kurds (of the Jazira). The high commissioner responded by sending police to raid the nationalists' headquarters and deport Fakhri Barudi, the 'theoretician' of the National Bloc and a leading nationalist intellectual, to Qamishli in Syria's far north-east. Barudi, who had narrowly escaped execution during the Great Syrian Revolt, had a notable rhetorical talent for inflaming the crowd, which the French high commissioner found particularly enraging.

The comte de Martel came himself to Damascus to deal with the situation. But a meeting with moderate nationalists ended in an angry altercation. He arrogantly warned Fayez al-Khoury, leader of the

---

[5] Robert Parr, British consul in Aleppo, to Sir Samuel Hoare, 29 November 1935 (FO 371/19022).

Damascus Bar – and brother of Faris al-Khoury, the prominent National Bloc politician – that he had only to give word to the Senegalese sentry at the door for Khoury to be sent off to join Barudi in the far north![6] All attempts at conciliation failed. The patriotic shopkeepers, setting aside all notion of profit, declared their determination to carry on the strike to the bitter end. Craftsmen and factories followed suit. Prices began to rise, adding to the suffering of the poor. Soon the demonstrations turned violent. Several rioters were killed in Damascus in clashes with the police and soldiery. In Hama, a crowd attacked a troop of French cavalry, which, firing back with live ammunition, killed seven of the assailants and wounded scores of others.

The task of restoring order was, on 10 February, given to General Charles Huntziger, commander of the French Army of the Levant, who established his headquarters at the Orient Palace Hotel near the Hijaz railway station, then the best hotel in Damascus. Senegalese sentries, armed with long curved knives known as *coupe-coupes*, kept pedestrians off the pavement in front of the building, to the outrage of the proud Damascenes. Huntziger imposed martial law on the city and warned the population that his soldiers were on the alert to return blow for blow. Newspapers were shut down, as were schools and Damascus University itself. Prominent nationalists, including Jamil Mardam and Nasib al-Bakri, were arrested and sent into exile.

But, to the consternation of the French, the demonstrations then spread to Beirut, Sidon and Tripoli, where shops closed down and students went on strike in solidarity with their Syrian brothers. Money and food were gathered and sent from Lebanon to Syria. This development could no longer be ignored, as it was the first time opponents of the French-imposed status quo in Lebanon had taken to the streets to demonstrate against the French Mandate.[7]

On 19 February, the French high commissioner invited the president of the Damascus Chamber of Commerce, 'Arif al-Halbuni, to meet him, along with a delegation of merchants, expecting that they would ask for French help to crush the nationalists. Instead, as a condition for their return to work, the angry merchants repeated the nationalists' demands in toto: the immediate release of all prisoners arrested during the riots; the prompt removal of Shaykh Taj al-Din

---

[6] Consul Gilbert Mackereth to Anthony Eden, 21 January 1936 (FO 371/20065).
[7] Raghid el-Solh, *Lebanon and Arabism*, pp. 21–2.

al-Hasani, the collaborating and despised French-appointed prime minister (who, on being dismissed four days later, quickly fled to Paris); the restoration of Fawzi al-Ghazzi's Constitution; the reopening of the Syrian parliament; and the negotiation of a treaty along the lines of the Anglo-Iraqi Treaty of 1931. As a result of his admirable – and, to the French, surprising show of strength – the affluent Halbuni has gone down in Syrian history as a nationalist hero.

On 28 February, the fortieth day of the general strike, the highly committed nationalists organised a colossal demonstration, which once again led to violent clashes with the police. Many rioters were killed by French live fire. The British consul reported to London that the poor were on the verge of starvation, but had developed what he described bizarrely as 'a dangerous degree of fanatical asceticism'. It was to prove to be the tipping point.

The French decide at last to negotiate

In Paris, the French government was pressured on one side by colonial officials and military officers, who continued to dream of empire and feared the loss of lucrative posts, and, on the other, by left-wing pressure groups, anxious to relieve French taxpayers of the unprofitable burden of ruling an increasingly unruly Syria. It therefore decided to talk its way out of the escalating crisis. Instructions in this sense were sent to the high commissioner. On 1 March 1936, de Martel was forced to issue an undertaking to restore constitutional life. He also authorised a delegation to travel to Paris in order to negotiate a treaty.

The French were no doubt galvanised into changing course in Syria by mounting dangers in Europe, by Italy's imperialist expansion and by the signing of an Anglo-Egyptian Treaty in July 1936. At a meeting with a group of nationalists comprising Hashim al-Atasi (who had replaced Ibrahim Hananu as leader of the National Bloc in January 1936), Dr 'Abd al-Rahman al-Kayyali, Fayez al-Khoury and Riad's cousin, 'Afif el-Solh, the high commissioner agreed to declare an amnesty for all persons arrested or exiled in connection with the disturbances, and the nationalists agreed to call off the strike.

The next day, 2 March, marked the beginning of the 'Id al-Adha – the Feast of Sacrifice which brings to a close the annual Pilgrimage to Mecca. It was the occasion in Damascus for four days of incessant parades, by processions representing every guild and quarter of the city. The British consul reported scenes of the greatest jubilation. The nationalist leaders, 'who had led the nation to victory', were, of course, accorded special ovations. The consul noted, not without admiration, their remarkable powers of organisation and command in controlling the crowds, both in its anger and in its joy.

It was agreed that a treaty, which would be no less favourable to Syria than the Anglo-Iraqi Treaty had been to Iraq, would be negotiated forthwith in Paris. The nationalists chose Hashim al-Atasi, Faris al-Khoury, Jamil Mardam and Sa'dallah al-Jabiri as their representatives. These were Riad's closest friends, his comrades in the struggle for independence. To temper their nationalist ardour, the French High Commission insisted on adding two 'moderate' government ministers to the delegation: Edmond Homsi, an Oxford-educated Christian banker from Aleppo, and the Emir Mustafa al-Shihabi, a French-trained agronomist. Also attached to the delegation were two secretaries, the European-educated lawyers Edmond Rabbath and Na'im Antaki, both from elite Christian families in Aleppo.[8]

Born about 1865 into the landed aristocracy of Homs in central Syria, Hashim al-Atasi was a brave and gentlemanly nationalist. He had served as prime minister and president of the Constituent Assembly under the Emir Faysal, and had been one of the three mediators in the conflict between the Imam Yahya of Yemen and Ibn Sa'ud. His patrician and moderating influence was to be of considerable assistance to the Syrian delegation in Paris.

Riad el-Solh was asked by his friends to go ahead to France before the Syrian delegation, in order to gauge the political climate there and prepare the ground for the delegation's arrival. He was to be the nationalists' principal adviser in their negotiations with the French. But, in his usual, highly energetic manner, he did not set sail for France directly, but first went down the coast to Palestine, in one of his endless attempts to mediate between warring Palestinian factions. The situation was particularly explosive there, as the 1936 rebellion against Britain was on the verge of breaking out. Far from healing the differences between Palestinian factions, the rebellion was to sharpen the feud between the militant Husayni faction and the collaborating Nashashibi one.

---

[8] Khoury, *Syria and the French Mandate*, p. 464; Consul Gilbert Mackereth to Foreign Office, Damascus, 17 March 1936 (FO 371/20065).

From Palestine, Riad then travelled to Istanbul in order to enquire into Turkish designs on Alexandretta, Syria's north-western region, which – because it was partly inhabited by Turks – the Ankara government was scheming to annex. Riad gloomily suspected that the French might be prepared to let it go, without even consulting the Syrians. In Istanbul, he called at the literary club *al-muntada al-adabi*, one of his old haunts, which, in the years before the First World War, had contributed to the nationalist awakening of the Arab provinces and the revival of the Arabic language. He was mortified to discover that the increasingly anti-Arab Turks had turned it into an institute for the study of Urdu.

En route at last for Paris, his train stopped briefly at Lausanne, where he was able to spend a few minutes with his former colleagues of the Syro-Palestinian Delegation, the Emir Shakib Arslan and Ihsan al-Jabiri. Riad gave them news of what was happening in Palestine and Syria. After these diversions, he travelled on to the French capital, arriving there on 12 March 1936, some ten days ahead of the Syrian delegation, which set out from Beirut on 21 March, amid scenes of great public enthusiasm.

Emile Eddé versus Bishara al-Khoury

On setting out on his travels, Riad had left behind a Lebanese political scene that was wholly dominated by the Maronites. On 20 January 1936, at the height of the nationalist disturbances in Syria, a prominent Maronite lawyer, Emile Eddé, was elected president of Lebanon, defeating his Maronite rival, Bishara al-Khoury.

Eddé was on friendly terms with Riad and with other prominent figures in the Muslim and Arab nationalist camp, but, politically, he represented everything that they detested. He was a staunch champion of Lebanon as a Christian state under French protection; he was viscerally opposed to Syrian and Arab unity; and he even aspired to make French the official language of the state, so anxious was he to sever Lebanon from Arab culture and political connection. From the creation of the state in 1920, right up to the end of 1935, Eddé and men like him, strongly backed by the French authorities, had managed to exclude Arab nationalists from any role in Lebanon's political life. This exclusion applied not only to Riad, but also to other prominent

Sunni notables of Arab nationalist conviction, such as the Salams of Beirut and the Karamis of Tripoli.

By 1936, however, the spill-over into Lebanon of the anti-French riots in Syria, as well as the increasingly vital social contacts and commercial ties between notables of all confessions, made such discrimination more or less untenable. In a mood of overdue self-assertion against the long-dominant Maronites, Muslims, both Sunni and Shi'i, began to demand a voice and a space of their own in the Lebanese political arena.

To a manner still true today, Lebanese society in the 1930s revolved around a score of families, whose prestige depended on their prominence in their respective communities; on their wealth or owner-ship of land; on their inherited religious functions; or, in the case of the bourgeois elites of the Lebanese coast, on their business activities as commercial agents, bankers and intermediaries between Western suppliers and Arab markets. Then, as now, their names were familiar to everyone.

Members of the Beirut elite, both Christian and Muslim, who owed their distinction to wealth, real estate holdings and business activities, included the Sursock, Pharaon, Bayhum, Da'uq, Hoss, Salam, Na'mani and Ghandur families. Some Sunni Muslim families, whose social prominence was derived from their traditional religious duties, included the Tabbara, Fakhuri, Naja and Yafi families in Beirut; and in Tripoli, the Karami, Jisr and Ahdab families. To cite a single example, 'Abd al-Hamid Karami was the Mufti of Tripoli, a post which had been held by his father and grandfather before him. In the Shi'i community, prominent notables included the As'ad family of Jabal 'Amil in South Lebanon, the Sharaf al-Din family in Tyre, and the Hamadeh family of the northern Biqa'.[9] The Druze community was led by the rival clans of the Jumblatts and the princely Arslans.

The confessional system lent importance to the heads of the most prominent families, who were the acknowledged leaders of their communities. These were the outstanding figures of Lebanese society with whom the Solhs – a landed family from South Lebanon, who moved to Beirut in the late nineteenth century and won respect in the service of the Ottoman Empire – had to relate and compete. Riad el-Solh himself had captured the limelight by the international reputation he

---

[9] Qasimiyya (ed.), *al-Ra'il al-'arabi al-awwal*, p. 272.

had acquired lobbying for the Arab cause in Geneva and Paris; by his championship of the working class and of the nascent trades union movement in Lebanon; and by his pan-Arab nationalist activities in Syria, Palestine and, further afield still, in North Africa. When General Franco tried to mobilise Moroccans in his bid to overthrow the republican Spanish government, Riad issued an impassioned appeal in which he denounced Fascism and defended the cause of the Spanish Republic. 'The Arabs', he declared, 'have never been mercenaries. They cannot participate in the massacre of a people struggling to defend its freedom and independence. They cannot defend the fascist Franco who has betrayed his homeland and is plotting with Hitler and Mussolini'.

But even Riad's considerable international achievements were not enough to breach the fortress of Maronite supremacy in his own country! In Lebanon, the institutional framework of political life had been laid down by the French-inspired 1926 Constitution, which placed the president of the Republic, invested with full executive powers, at the heart of the system. He was invariably a Maronite, except for the very first incumbent, Charles Dabbas (1926–32), who was a member of the Greek Orthodox community. The president could name and dismiss ministers, dissolve parliament and, if he so wished, even rule by decree. On paper, he was all-powerful; in practice, his powers were subservient to the will of the French high commissioner.

Modelled on the 1875 Constitution of France's Third Republic, the 1926 Constitution declared *Grand Liban* to be an independent republic, with Beirut as its capital. In recognition of the country's mosaic of sects and communities, Article 95 conceded that 'As a transitional measure . . . the communities shall be equally represented in public posts and in the composition of ministries'. This Article perpetuated the confessional system inherited from the Ottoman *mutasarrifiyya*, but did little to dent Maronite hegemony, which was backed by the French. It was only with the appointment of a Sunni prime minister in 1937 that the Muslims began to wrest a measure of executive power from the Maronites, although, like all other cabinet members, the prime minister was always in danger of summary dismissal by the president.[10]

As a result of these givens, Lebanese politics consisted of mere jousting between rival Maronite leaders and their respective camps – a contest which largely excluded all other communities. Of these jousts,

[10] Méouchy, 'Le Pacte national', p. 464, n. 8.

none was fiercer than that between Emile Eddé and Bishara al-Khoury, since these two presidential contenders were so similar and had been so intimately connected. Eddé was born in Damascus in 1883, where his father had been a dragoman at the French consulate. Khoury was born in the Lebanese village of Rishmayya in 1880. His father, Shaykh Khalil, had been head of the Arab Secretariat under the Ottoman *mutasarrif.*

Both Eddé and Khoury were schooled by the Jesuit Fathers in Beirut and then studied law in France, where Eddé gained a doctorate from Aix-en-Provence and Khoury a degree from the University of Paris. On returning to Lebanon, Khoury joined Eddé's law practice as a trainee, where he stayed until the outbreak of the First World War in 1914. When Turkey entered the war on Germany's side, Eddé and Khoury fled to Egypt to escape Turkish repression. They practised law in Cairo and Alexandria, before returning to Lebanon in 1919, when Eddé took Khoury back as head of his law firm, the most prominent in Beirut at the time.

Both men entered politics and both married into leading Lebanese Christian families, whose members, whether brothers, brothers-in-law, cousins or associates, mobilised support for them and helped finance their political careers. Eddé married Lodi Sursock in 1912, while Khoury married Laure Chiha in 1922. Laure was the sister of Michel Chiha, who was a writer, poet and ideologue of Lebanese nationalism, as well as a newspaper proprietor and partner in the Banque Pharaon et Chiha, a leading Lebanese bank during the Mandate and the early years of independence. Chiha had been secretary of the commission which drafted the 1926 Constitution, and was considered its most active member.[11]

While Eddé practised at the Lebanese Bar in the 1920s, 'where he became identified with the French omnipresence in the area',[12] Bishara al-Khoury entered the judiciary, rising to become president of the Court of Appeal and then director of justice. In 1926, when the Constitution of the Lebanese Republic was adopted, he was appointed

---

[11] For a detailed analysis of the 1926 Constitution, see Edmond Rabbath, *La Formation historique du Liban politique et constitutionnel*, new edn Beirut 1986, pp. 379–400; Ziadeh, *Sectarianism and Intercommunal Nation-Building*, pp. 86–101.

[12] Raghid el-Solh, *Lebanon and Arabism*, pp. 14 ff.; Michael Johnson, *Class and Client in Beirut: The Sunni Muslim Community and the Lebanese State, 1840–1985*, London 1986, p. 119.

minister of interior in the first cabinet of Auguste Pasha Adib. In due course, he engineered the overthrow of Adib Pasha's ministry and was then called upon by President Dabbas to form the second government of the Republic. One of his first acts as premier was to appoint his brother, Sami al-Khoury, as director of justice. In that post from 1926 to 1939, Sami was well placed to help Bishara in his various commercial enterprises, which included the award to the Chiha-Pharaon group of a fifty-year concession in the area of the Place des Canons, Beirut's main square, which had belonged to the former Compagnie française de la route de Damas, and on which lucrative real estate was soon to be erected.[13]

If there was a difference between Eddé and Khoury, it was that the first was totally committed to Lebanon's French connection and to French culture more generally, while the second was far less attached to a perpetual alliance with France. Having chosen to master the Arabic language, Bishara al-Khoury had an affinity with Arab culture and with Islam. He also understood the need to reach out to those Lebanese citizens beyond his own, narrow Maronite community. As president of the Republic in 1943, Khoury was to become Riad's partner in the struggle for independence.

On the morning of 20 January 1936, at an extraordinary session of the Lebanese parliament, Emile Eddé defeated Bishara al-Khoury for the presidency of the Republic, in spite of the latter's intense election campaign, which had been largely financed by his wife's cousin, Henri Pharaon. The first ballot gave Eddé fourteen votes and Khoury eleven, but, since Eddé had failed to obtain the necessary two-thirds majority, a second ballot was then held. It gave Eddé the absolute majority of fifteen votes to ten for Khoury.[14] In these contests, each leader could count on a loose group of parliamentary supporters. Eddé's friends were known as the Unionist or Eddéist Bloc, while Khoury's friends had formed a group known as the Constitutional Bloc. These two, largely Maronite, groupings were both in the *kiyanist* tradition – from the Arabic *kiyan*, or 'entity' – meaning that they were committed to the geographic and political entity of Greater Lebanon.

Curiously enough, Eddé won the presidency thanks largely to the efforts of a Muslim. This was Khayr al-Din Ahdab, who, having

---

[13] MAE, Nantes, Fonds Beyrouth (Amb.), série 199A4, carton 20, Note de Beyrouth, 25 August 1941.

[14] Consul General Havard to Mr Eden, Beirut, 23 January 1936 (FO 371/20065).

been elected to parliament in 1934, managed to rally several unde-cided deputies to Eddé's camp. Once he assumed the presidency, Eddé, in turn, began paving the way for Khayr al-Din to become prime minister – which he did in January 1937, the first Muslim to hold such a post. Khayr al-Din Ahdab had been Riad el-Solh's partner in a jour-nalistic venture – the launching and editing of their newspaper, *al-'Ahd al-Jadid*, in the 1920s. At that time, Khayr al-Din had been a staunch Arab nationalist. But once he had his sights on the prime minister's office, he drifted away from Riad and renounced his earlier commit-ment to Arabism and Arab unity. The powers and the privileges of the premiership, and the close collaboration with the French that it then entailed, may simply have proved too great a seduction to Ahdab. Not surprisingly, Riad took this as a personal and political betrayal.

The Conference of the Coast

On 10 March 1936, leading Muslims from Lebanon's coastal cities held a conference in Beirut – the 'Conference of the Coast' (*mu'tamar al-sahil*) – to demand the return to Syria of Beirut, Tripoli and Sidon, as well as the four *cazas* which had been attached to Lebanon in 1920 – the so-called 'disputed territories'. In a word, the Conference called for the dismantling of the French-created Greater Lebanon. This was a repeat of two earlier conferences that coastal leaders had held, in 1928 and again in 1933, with much the same unionist aims.[15] Riad el-Solh did not attend the 1936 meeting. He had already set out on his circuitous journey to France, his mind preoccupied with the treaty negotiations which the Syrian nationalists were about to conduct with the French.

But there was another even more important reason why he chose not to be there. He was gradually coming to the conclusion that Greater Lebanon – fifteen years after its creation – was already something of a fait accompli. Its frontiers could no longer realistically be challenged. Riad was a political pragmatist, with an acute sense of what was achievable and what was not. When Greater Lebanon was first created in 1920, he had, like other Muslims, totally opposed it. But, several years later, his views had begun to alter. In 1928, he was

---

[15] Raghid el-Solh, *Lebanon and Arabism*, pp. 22 ff.; Hilal el-Solh, *Tarikh rajul wa qadiyya*, p. 274; Johnson, *Class and Client*, p. 25.

quoted as saying that he much preferred 'to live in a hut inside an independent Lebanese homeland, than to live in an Arab empire under colonial rule'.[16] Such a remark suggested that his priorities were changing. He had by no means given up his lifelong goal of Arab independence and unity, but Lebanese independence had become the immediate priority of his political life.

A long observer of his career reported that, on his return from Qamishli, where the French had deported him in 1935 for supporting the militant trades union movement, he seemed less of a firebrand and more of a statesman.[17] By the mid-1930s, he had come to realise that Lebanese patriotism – however much it was despised by Arab nationalists who derided it as a French creation – was a powerful force which needed to be conciliated rather than confronted. This led him to seek to consolidate his relations with leaders of other communities, notably with Patriarch Antoine 'Arida, a central political and spiritual figure in the Maronite camp. In this, as in so much else, Riad was well ahead of Muslim opinion in Lebanon, and of that of his peers in his own Sunni community. He was therefore forced to tread carefully.

Salim 'Ali Salam, in whose house and under whose chairmanship the Conference of the Coast took place, was a Sunni notable and traditional Arab nationalist with a long and commendable political record. He had attended the first Arab Congress in Paris in 1913 as a delegate of the Beirut Reform Committee. He had represented the Beirut vilayet in the Ottoman parliament in 1914. On the collapse of the Empire, he had been a member of the General Syrian Conference of 1919, held in Damascus during Faysal's brief rule. (This had also been attended by Riad, his father, Rida, and his cousin, 'Afif.) Other notables who were now present at the Conference of the Coast, and who shared Salam's unionist passions, included 'Abd al-Hamid Karami from Tripoli, 'Adil 'Usayran from South Lebanon, Naji al-Fakhuri and three members of the Bayhum family from Beirut.

Salam and his fellow Arab nationalists had called the Conference because of their anxiety concerning the negotiations that Syria and Lebanon were about to conduct with France. They feared that any treaty, once it was signed and ratified, would from then on cement the existing frontiers – thereby destroying any hope of securing the return

---

[16] Basim al-Jisr, *Mithaq 1943, limadha kana wa limadha saqat?*, 2nd edn Beirut 1997, p. 81.

[17] Hilal el-Solh, *Tarikh rajul wa qadiyya*, p. 274.

of the disputed territories to Syria. To the alarm of these notables and traditionalists, therefore, one member of the Conference, Kadhim el-Solh, struck a discordant – even dissident – note.

Kadhim el-Solh's rebellion

Kadhim was Riad el-Solh's young cousin. He was a lawyer, an intellectual and the proprietor of the daily newspaper, *al-Nida'*, which he had launched in 1931 with three of his brothers, 'Adil, Taqi al-Din and 'Imad. As the son of Monah el-Solh and the grandson of Ahmad Pasha, he was attending the Conference as a Sunni representative of South Lebanon. Together with other young radicals, such as Farid Zayn al-Din and Shawqi al-Dandashi, Kadhim el-Solh and his brother Taqi al-Din had, the year before, in 1935, formed an Arab Nationalist Party (*al-hizb al-qawmi al-'arabi*).

On Riad's prompting, as well as out of personal conviction, at the Conference Kadhim voiced the heretical view that calling for the dismantling of Greater Lebanon might actually be doing a disservice to the Arab nationalist cause. The more the Arab nationalists pressed their demand for the return to Syria of the disputed territories, the more the Christians would run for shelter into the arms of the French, thereby fatally damaging the prospect for any future unification of Lebanon with the rest of the Arab world. A wiser policy would be to seek to persuade the Maronites and the other Christians to join their Muslim brethren in the struggle for Lebanese independence – as a necessary first stage towards the unity and independence of the wider Arab homeland.

In other words, Kadhim argued, a compromise needed to be struck between coastal Muslims from Sidon and Tripoli such as themselves, who wanted unity with Syria, and Lebanese Christians, who sought French protection for *their* Christian-dominated state. Such a policy, he warned, would not be cost-free. It would undoubtedly require Muslims to make substantial concessions. Indeed, he proclaimed controversially, the only way to win over the Christians to the Arab cause was to drop altogether the demand for the return of the disputed territories to the Syrian motherland.

Kadhim's views ran totally counter to majority Muslim opinion. The task of the Conference, he pleaded, should be to accelerate the process of Lebanon's cooperation with the Arab world, rather than risk hardening positions on either side of the Lebanese divide by demanding the dismantling of *Le Grand Liban*.[18] Such was the startling premise which became the basis of Kadhim's celebrated text, *Bayna al-ittisal wal-infisal fi Lubnan* (The choice between connection and cleavage in Lebanon), first published in the Beirut daily *al-Nahar* in March 1936, and then as a pamphlet in April 1937.[19]

True to his beliefs, Kadhim refused to sign the Conference's final declaration, which predictably called for the return of the disputed territories to Syria. Needless to say, he did not make any converts to his views, which were angrily dismissed in Muslim circles in Beirut. But he did start a trend that was slowly to gain momentum, at least among the educated elite, if not yet among the Muslim masses.

From a distance, Riad el-Solh was quietly applauding. His brave cousin Kadhim had been his advance guard, his stalking-horse even. With Syrian Treaty negotiations about to take place in Paris, Riad knew that this was no time to ruffle French feathers by adopting a hardline Arab position. He thought it politic to dissociate himself – and dissociate the Syrian delegation too – from the dogmatic position adopted by the Conference of the Coast.

Riad had spent a great deal of time and effort courting French politicians of the Socialist and Radical parties. He did not want to dissipate all the French goodwill he had earned by voicing maximalist demands at this critical moment. It was noteworthy that some prominent members of Syria's National Bloc had come to share his more pragmatic analysis. On their way to Paris for the long-sought negotiations, they understood that this was no time to provoke the French, or indeed the Lebanese Patriarch, who himself had considerable influence in Paris.[20]

In Lebanon, changes were taking place which were eventually to make the Solh formula more acceptable. Younger members of both the Sunni and the Christian bourgeoisie were beginning to discover that they had much more in common than they had been led to believe. Socially, they belonged to the same world; so much so that some intermarriages – totally unheard of before – began to take place

---

[18] Raghid el-Solh, *Lebanon and Arabism*, p. 33.
[19] Ziadeh, *Sectarianism and Intercommunal Nation-Building*, pp. 104, 199, n. 65. See also Kadhim el-Solh's article in a special issue of *al-Nahar*, Beirut, January 1975, pp. 67 ff., 'La Constitution, le pacte national, la formule libanaise'.
[20] Raghid el-Solh, *Lebanon and Arabism*, p. 36.

between them. Christian businessmen began to recognise the folly of seeking to separate Lebanon from the Arab hinterland, where they had such important trading and financial interests. They no longer accepted as a matter of course the dependent relationship with France, which their fathers had so agitated for, as they now considered that it restricted their business with other Western nations. In fact, they were beginning to resent French mandatory practices altogether, especially the naked greed of French concessionary companies. These wanted exclusive control of Syrian and Lebanese markets. In their turn, Muslim businessmen came to see that the well-established links that the Christian Lebanese had with Europe could be turned to their advantage too. They began to consider cooperation with the Christians in a *Lebanese*, rather than a Syrian, context. In both camps, there developed an inclination to build bridges across the confessional divide.

In July 1936, for example, just four months after acting as secretary of the Conference of the Coast, a young Sunni leader, Salah Bayhum, wrote a letter to the French-language Beirut newspaper, *L'Orient*, calling for 'an effective union of all communities, necessary for the security of our national existence'.[21] This was still a daring idea for most coastal Muslims to embrace, especially in places such as Sidon or Tripoli, where Syria rather than Lebanon was still considered the motherland.

In Paris, with the Syrian delegation

Franco-Syrian talks were formally opened in Paris on 2 April 1936, but were almost immediately adjourned in stalemate. The imminent prospect of French general elections, which were to be conducted in two stages on 26 April and 3 May, absorbed the full attention of Prime Minister Albert Sarraut, and indeed of the whole French political class. As a result, Foreign Minister Pierre-Etienne Flandin, who headed the French team to the talks, could do nothing more than mouth a hardline, uncompromising position. With the outcome of the elections highly uncertain, no French government could afford to envisage a radical change of policy in the Levant.

The Syrians soon learned that the negotiations were going to be far more difficult than they had anticipated. This early setback took

[21] Johnson, *Class and Client*, p. 25.

much of the wind out of their sails. Having few influential friends in Paris, the Syrian delegation relied on Riad el-Solh's extensive network of contacts, especially on the Left. Knowing that he could hope for nothing from the colonialist, military and Catholic right wing, he had long cultivated the Socialists and the Communists. So he now set to work again, mobilising the press and arranging meetings with prominent left-wing French politicians. He managed to secure a desk at the offices of the Communist daily, *L'Humanité*, where he took to supplying its editorial writers with a steady stream of advice and information about the Syrian cause.

It was at this time, on 7 April, that Riad sent a letter from Paris to Nabih and 'Adil al-'Azma, two of his Syrian friends then in Palestine, outlining the complicated situation as he saw it.

> *I arrived in Paris on a Monday morning, twenty-six days ago, and since my arrival, I have been studying and searching and following the exchanges between the Syrians and the French.*
>
> *I have noticed that, in spite of the preoccupation of the people here with great political issues on the eve of the parliamentary elections, the Syrian question has not been put aside. Some attention is being given to it, although I have also noticed intrigues in the ministry of foreign affairs, in the ministry of war, and in the hidden depths of clerical and financial opinion. What is strange is not that these intrigues occur but that they are out of sight . . . Such machinations work opaquely and in secret. It is proof of their weakness – but also proof that most, if not all, of those on the French side dealing with this matter [the talks with the Syrians] seem to want to arrive at a solution.*
>
> *This is the visible face of the Syrian question. From this visible face, other matters may be deduced, formal in nature perhaps, but important nevertheless. The real solution may lie, more than one might think, in matters of detail – in the <u>form</u> of the negotiations. Who will negotiate for the French? Should the talks be suspended [in Paris] and continued back home? Should one await the results of the parliamentary elections?*

Before the delegation arrived, I had come to the conclusion that the Ministry of Foreign Affairs, which remains a prisoner of old ideas and habits, was rather inclined to keep the negotiations within a bureaucratic framework, restricting the small number of people involved – essentially the High Commissioner in Syria and a few of his colleagues. It also wanted a speedy conclusion.

Parliamentary deputies [on the other hand] – and primarily the chairman of the foreign affairs committee – took the view that [High Commissioner] de Martel should not participate in the talks and that these should, in any event, be postponed until after the elections.

These were the two views I found on my arrival.

My own feeling was that, if the Ministry were to accept our demands, the best solution would be to conclude the talks speedily and return [home] at once. In that case, the presence of de Martel in the negotiations would be acceptable.

But, if neither the Ministry nor de Martel were ready to accept our demands, then we should wait for the right moment, find out how best to work, probe [the other party] but without breaking contact, impose ourselves but without undue speed. I began to lean towards this latter solution and I imagined that events would decide the matter. That, in effect, is what has happened.

De Martel and the Ministry have been in a state of paralysis as they wait for the upheaval of the elections, which could well result in a change of personnel and of method. They might themselves be the victims of change. The discussions [I have had] seemed to point in that direction . . .

Thank God, our brothers [in the Syrian delegation] are united, attentive and prudent. We meet regularly and everyone expresses his opinion. While I work to collect information, they follow the right course. I really believe I will soon have less work to do. I have great hopes in the outcome of the elections – even though the essential point for us, as you know, is the statement I made twenty years ago which is now on the lips of all our brothers:

'It is easier for France to leave the country [Syria] than to deprive it of its freedom and independence – a course which would dishonour its representatives on the ground.'
The matter of these representatives is, in a word, THE question at issue: they exert pressure here in this country, they send lying reports, and they deceive people. I do not believe that negotiations based on their reports can possibly yield us any results. The left-wing parties say they will change this way of behaving, but the truth is that France is still stuck in its old and outdated ways.
Please show this letter to His Excellency the Hajj Amin, but do not give it to the press.[22]

Léon Blum and the Popular Front

Riad el-Solh's evaluation of the situation in France was both accurate and shrewd, as events were to prove. The general elections brought the Popular Front to power, a left-wing coalition of Radical Socialists, Socialists and Communists, headed by the Socialist Party leader, Léon Blum, then aged 64. For constitutional reasons, the new government could not assume office until the Sarraut government had resigned on 1 June. From the Syrian point of view, this new government was a good deal better than its predecessor. Riad, however, was not reassured. He did not believe that any mainstream French politician could easily abandon French interests in the Levant. Blum's mind was focused on the social and economic transformation he hoped to bring about in France, by means of a raft of radical reforms. He was hardly preoccupied by colonial questions.[23]

Born in Alsace to a family of Jewish shopkeepers, Blum was under constant pressure from his co-religionist, the Zionist leader Chaim Weizmann, not to grant independence to the anti-Zionist Damascus nationalists, but to concentrate instead on allowing the settlement of Jews on Syrian and Lebanese territory bordering Palestine.[24]

---

[22] Qasimiyya (ed.), *al-Ra'il al-'arabi al-awwal*, p. 272.
[23] W. B. Cohen, 'The Colonial Policy of the Popular Front', in *French Historical Studies*, 7 (spring 1972), pp. 369, 388, quoted in Khoury, *Syria and the French Mandate*, p. 485, n. 2.
[24] Laurens, *La Question de Palestine*, vol. II, pp. 326, 341.

Similarly, Lebanese nationalists in Beirut feared that Blum might make concessions to Syria at Lebanon's expense. The Maronite archbishop of Beirut, Musa Mubarak, hurried to Paris, and at a meeting with Blum on 27 May, asked for guarantees of Lebanon's expanded frontiers. Although he did not quite get the firm pledge he was seeking, Blum did assure him that he would make no commitment to the Syrians, without giving the Lebanese question careful study first. Negotiations with the Syrians were then suspended for the entire month of May, pending the assumption of office by the new government.

Accompanied by Riad, the Syrian delegates seized the opportunity to head for Geneva to discuss the situation with the two nationalist sages, the Emir Shakib Arslan and Ihsan al-Jabiri. They returned to Paris in good time to resume the talks, once Blum had formed his government on 4 June, and had won a vote of confidence in the National Assembly the following day. Riad's assiduous courting of the Left was rewarded with an invitation to address the Socialist Party Conference in Paris on 30 May to 1 June, which had been convened to salute the victory of the Popular Front. Eloquently, Riad el-Solh pleaded the cause of Syrian independence and unity, winning an ovation and a promise of support, even though France's attention was decidedly elsewhere.

Blum's left-wing coalition had triumphed on the crest of a wave of French working-class hopes, and in an international context of extreme tension. Hitler and his Nazi Party had come to power on 30 January 1933, imposing Fascist rule throughout Germany. A year later, on 6 February 1934, French Fascists, hoping to replicate the German experience, had marched on the National Assembly, creating a riot and forcing the resignation of Prime Minister Edouard Daladier. The Left replied with a general strike – which closed down 12,000 factories, of which 9,000 were occupied by the strikers. Massive demonstrations followed, which brought tens of thousands out on the streets, representing all left-wing parties and factions. This formidable show of force marked the true birth of the Popular Front, at least at mass level, if not yet among politicians.

On 27 June 1935, Socialists and Communists concluded an anti-Fascist pact, followed on 14 July by a large grouping – a *rassemblement populaire* – of Socialists, Communists, Radicals and the two major trades union movements, the CGT and the CGTU. On 13 February 1936, Léon Blum – already the target of a carefully orchestrated and vicious anti-Semitic hate campaign in the right-wing press – was physically assaulted and only narrowly escaped lynching. His car was stopped and wrecked on the Boulevard Saint-Germain by a crowd of *Action française* thugs, who had been waiting for the funeral cortège of the royalist historian Jacques Bainville to pass. Dragged from his car, beaten and abused, a bloodied Blum managed to take shelter in a nearby building. The awful assault was to put him in hospital for several weeks.[25]

But on 7–8 June, within days of forming his government, Blum reached a historic agreement with employers and unions on a series of revolutionary measures – the so-called Matignon Accords. These were passed into law by the National Assembly, and by huge majorities. They were radically to change the life of the French working classes: a forty-hour working week; holidays with pay; collective bargaining; the nationalisation of the arms industries; the extension of compulsory schooling; a statute for the Bank of France; and, on 19 June, the dissolution of the right-wing Leagues, whose marches had brought such ugly mayhem to the streets and had threatened the very life of the Republic.

A month later, on 17–18 July, General Franco's seizure of power unleashed the Spanish Civil War, plunging the French Left into an agonising debate about whether or not to rush to the help of the Spanish Republicans. But, when Britain decided to stand aloof – as did Radical Socialist ministers in his own government – Blum found himself, to his great regret, having to agree a policy of 'non-intervention'.

Such was the overheated atmosphere in which members of the Syrian delegation attempted to negotiate their country's independence from France. They derived some cheer from the appointment of Yvon Delbos as French foreign minister, and Pierre Viénot as under-secretary of state for foreign affairs, both of whom were somewhat more open to Syrian aspirations than their predecessors had been. Viénot was to conduct the talks. But, once again, these appointments aroused the fears of Lebanese nationalists, who suspected that the Blum government might come to be persuaded to return the 'disputed territories' to Syria. As it so happened, having been cast down by the first round of negotiations, the Syrians chose not to raise the matter of the territories when talks resumed in June. Nevertheless, the fact that the talks were taking place at all in an atmosphere of mutual confidence, as well as

[25] See Serge Bernstein, *Léon Blum*, Paris 2006, pp. 426 ff.

the widely publicised reports of Riad's speech at the Socialist Party Conference, incited President Emile Eddé to send a telegram of protest to the French government. The Blum government found it necessary to placate him.

Accordingly, Viénot sent Eddé a telegram in which he recalled that the Mandate charter had given both Syria and Lebanon a 'parallel vocation for independence', underpinned by international guarantees. Among these guarantees figured 'the territorial statute . . . which, in the case of Lebanon, was defined on 31 August 1920'. Viénot further proposed to negotiate a treaty with Lebanon which would provide for its accession to the 'international status of an independent state'.[26] It was only then that Hashim al-Atasi, leader of the Syrian delegation, addressed two letters to the comte de Martel, in which he reserved the right to raise the issue of the disputed territories at a later date. He was careful, however, to avoid making any specific claims.[27] Much as they wanted to recover the territories, the Syrian nationalists did not wish to risk the total collapse of their talks with France at this point. Nor did they want to be seen to be making claims over Lebanon, at a time when they were still having great difficulty persuading the French to agree to the extension of Syrian authority over the French-run Alawite territory and the Jabal Druze.

If Lebanese nationalists were reassured by Viénot's telegram to Eddé, the same could not be said of Arab nationalists. They were further incensed by reports that a Lebanese delegation – then being formed to negotiate a treaty with France – appeared to exclude the Syrian 'unionists' of Lebanon. As an indication of Sunni anger, a violent demonstration took place in Sidon on 12 July. It was only dispersed with live fire. A general strike was then called, which quickly spread to other Lebanese cities. In Beirut, a delegation went to protest the brutality of the gendarmerie to the French High Commission.

The signing of the Franco-Syrian Treaty

Finally, after weeks of talks and the drafting of numerous letters which were attached to the final document, a twenty-five-year Franco-Syrian

---

[26] Mizrahi, 'La France et sa politique de mandat', p. 61.
[27] Raghid el-Solh, *Lebanon and Arabism*, p. 43.

Treaty of 'friendship and alliance' was initialled on 9 September 1936 in the Salon de l'Horloge at the Quai d'Orsay in Paris.[28] Its declared aim was to 'define, on the basis of complete freedom, sovereignty and independence, the relations which would subsist between the two states after the end of the Mandate'. The two countries were to consult on all matters of foreign policy that might affect their common interests. They pledged to come to each other's aid in the event of a conflict with a third country. If war were ever imminent, Syria would supply France with all possible facilities on its territory, including the use of railways, rivers, ports, aerodromes and other means of communication.

Ratification of the treaty by the Syrian and French parliaments was to be followed by a three-year probationary period, during which powers would gradually be transferred. At the end of this period, the treaty would come into force on the day that Syria was admitted to membership of the League of Nations. Attached to the treaty was a Military Convention, under which France would provide a military mission to train Syria's army, gendarmerie, navy and air force – but at Syria's own expense. Local troops were to pass under the control of the Syrian defence ministry, but instructors and equipment would be exclusively French. France would be allowed to maintain two airbases in Syria at agreed locations, and not less than 40 kilometres distant from Syria's four main cities.

The attachment of the Alawite territory and the Jabal Druze to Syria was recognised only in principle. They were to continue to enjoy a degree of autonomy on the model of the sanjaq of Alexandretta, the extent of which was to be determined by decree of the French High Commission. In the meantime, and for the duration of the three-year probation period, administration of the two territories was to be shared between the Delegate of the French High Commission and a *mutasarrif* appointed by Damascus. France was to maintain troops in the Alawite territory and the Jabal Druze for a period of five years, starting from the entry into force of the treaty.

In a dispatch from Damascus to the Foreign Office on 27 October, Consul Mackereth reported that 'The Moslems remain suspicious about the military convention in which the Christians see their only ray of hope'. Far from loosening Syria's ties with France, the treaty seemed to bind them ever closer. Before there could be any semblance

---

[28] For the text of the Treaty, see Hourani, *Syria and Lebanon*, pp. 313–33.

of real independence, the hurdle of ratification had to be cleared and the three-year probationary period successfully navigated.

Nevertheless, the Syrian delegation returned to a tumultuous welcome in Damascus on 29 September. Triumphal arches were erected on the route from the railway station to the *Sérail*, where the comte de Martel was waiting for them. But when the train arrived, members of the delegation and those that were meeting them were swept along the platform and out of the station by an unruly if highly enthusiastic crowd. The procession to the *Sérail* developed into a surging mob.[29]

Yet, as the treaty was open to widely divergent interpretations, it did little to appease intercommunal tensions. Neither Arab nationalists nor Lebanese nationalists had in the end got what they wanted. The former had failed to secure the return to Syria of the disputed territories – there was, in fact, no mention of them at all in the treaty – while the latter feared that France's concessions to Syria had endangered its long-term connection with Lebanon. Sadly, and only a few days after the delegation's return, rioting broke out between Muslims and Christians in Aleppo, leaving eight dead and some one hundred and fifty wounded.[30]

Riad, who did not like flying, returned by sea to Beirut, where he, too, was rapturously received. He was showered with flowers as he drove up from the port. The text of the treaty was published in the Lebanese press. It was rumoured that Muhi al-Din Nusuli, owner of the newspaper *Bayrut*, had purloined the document from Riad el-Solh's briefcase during the voyage. But, despite appearances to the contrary, Riad was rather pleased with the leak. He certainly wanted the terms of the treaty to become known as widely and as soon as possible.

Most Syrians welcomed the treaty as a great achievement of the National Bloc, which won an overwhelming majority at elections in November. Jamil Mardam became prime minister and formed a government composed of Sa'dallah al-Jabiri (minister of internal and external affairs), Shukri al-Quwatli (minister of finance and defence) and 'Abd al-Rahman al-Kayyali (minister of justice and education). Faris al-Khoury became speaker of the National Assembly. All these men, by then in their mid-forties, had been at the forefront of the Syrian national movement for years. Like Riad el-Solh, their close

---

[29] Acting Consul J. C. Ogden to Foreign Office, 3 October 1936 (FO 371/20066).
[30] Consul Robert Parr to Mr Eden, Aleppo, 13 October 1936 (FO 371/20066).

associate in Lebanon, they had been persistent enemies of the Mandate and had done their utmost to bring it to an end. A month later, on 21 December 1936, the National Bloc leader Hashim al-Atasi was elected president of the Republic. On 27 December, the treaty was approved by the new government, and the following day, it was ratified unanimously by the Syrian parliament – which was at long last meeting, after a French-imposed suspension of twenty-five months.

For this historic sitting in the Chamber, a prominent place was reserved for members of the diplomatic corps. However, the place of the French delegate was removed from a seat on the government bench to a railed-off loge at the side.[31] The nationalists' victory may have been partial and uncertain, but they were nevertheless determined to celebrate it for all it was worth. The formation of the Popular Front government in France, and the conclusion of the Anglo-Egyptian and the Anglo-Iraqi treaties, led many Syrian nationalists to believe that their own independence would no longer be delayed.

Riad el-Solh knew, however, that the battle was far from over. Syrian unionists in Lebanon were deeply disillusioned by the treaty, while radical Arab nationalists in Syria – especially supporters of the exiled Dr 'Abd al-Rahman Shahbandar – denounced the National Bloc members as traitors for what they deemed amounted to no better than collaboration with France. Always looking for a workable compromise, Riad preached that Lebanon's relations with both Syria and France should be decided by dialogue rather than coercion. Searching for a formula that the Maronites might agree, he came up with the idea that Syria and Lebanon should join together in a confederation. His hope was that this would be more acceptable to the Maronites and the French than outright unity with Syria. But some Lebanese nationalists viewed even this modest idea with suspicion, while Arab nationalists were split between the hardline 'unionists' of Tripoli (Karami, 'Abd al-Latif al-Bissar and their friends) and the more moderate 'confederalists' of Beirut (the Solhs, the Salams and the Bayhums).

To promote the idea of a confederation, this latter group organised a week-long Muslim national conference (*al-mu'tamar al-qawmi al-islami*), held from 23 to 28 October at the house of 'Umar Bayhum, and under the chairmanship of Salim 'Ali Salam. A final memorandum affirmed the participants' wish to see Syria and Lebanon join in as wide

---

[31] Damascus Consulate to Foreign Office (FO 371/20848).

a confederation as possible (*ittihad bi-awsa' ma yumkin min ashka-lihi*), provided that the Franco-Lebanese Treaty guaranteed administrative decentralisation of the two regions and equality between the two communities.[32] In a speech at the conference, Riad el-Solh addressed his remarks to Lebanese nationalists: 'We are not forcing you to enter into a union', he declared, 'but on what basis do you insist that unionists must accept a separate Lebanon, since they are no less numerous than you are?'[33] Riad led a delegation to the French high commissioner, to promote the confederal idea and to ask for the participation of Arab nationalists in the Franco-Lebanese negotiations. But his requests fell on deaf ears.

The Franco-Lebanese Treaty and its opponents

In the event, concluding a Franco-Lebanese Treaty proved a simple affair. Comte de Martel and a Lebanese delegation headed by President Emile Eddé began talks in Beirut on 20 October 1936 – without the participation of any Arab nationalists. A treaty was initialled on 13 November and was ratified by the Lebanese parliament on the 17th. Unlike the treaty with Syria, the Lebanese treaty was renewable for a second twenty-five-year term, while French bases were to remain in Lebanon with no time limit. The speed with which matters were settled reflected the harmony of views between Lebanese nationalists and majority opinion in France, which held that Lebanon should remain a centre of French influence and a base for France's Mediterranean forces for the foreseeable future. The Popular Front government was as deeply convinced of this as were its right-wing opponents.

On a visit to Paris some months later as the guest of the French government, Eddé made his profession of faith: 'The Lebanese knew', he declared, 'that their national independence was only possible within the framework and under the guarantee of the alliance with France'. Lebanon was France's main *foyer de rayonnement* in the Near East and Central Asia. To the *Echo de Paris*, Eddé said that 'the Lebanese consider their agreement as a new historic bond with France. They have concluded a treaty which will be in force for twenty-five years,

---

[32] Méouchy, 'Le Pacte national', p. 468.
[33] Raghid el-Solh, *Lebanon and Arabism*, p. 46.

but what they really desire is one in perpetuity'. Asked whether he saw any objection to a French naval base in the Levant, he replied that the whole of the Lebanese coast might be considered a French maritime base.[34]

The Christians of Lebanon were thus delighted with the treaty, but the Muslims gave it a stormy reception. Tripoli closed down for a whole month in protest against the city's retention inside Lebanon. Syrian flags were hoisted on its mosques. At least six rioters were killed and many others gravely injured. The three principal Muslim leaders, including Karami himself, were arrested and taken to jail in Beirut. But there, too, Muslim malcontents clashed repeatedly with Christians. Coming out of the Basta mosque, Muslim worshippers took up arms and marched to the centre of Beirut. They were there dispersed by French troops, but not before they had smashed up the city square, torn up the Lebanese flag and attacked several Christian passers-by. Running battles between demonstrators and police left four people dead and hundreds more wounded.

In retaliation against the Muslims, Armenian Christians then attacked the quarters around the Basta area, which were vigorously defended by their inhabitants. Outside Beirut, there were several instances of attacks on Christian property.[35] Alarmed at this outbreak of communal violence, notables of all confessions attempted to cool the hotheads and mediate between them. In this, Riad el-Solh played a prominent role, as did his fellow Sunnis, Salim 'Ali Salam, 'Umar Bayhum and 'Umar al-Da'uq. They were joined by Bishara al-Khoury (Maronite), Henri Pharaon (Greek Catholic), Habib Trad, Jean Tueni and Habib Abu Shahla (Greek Orthodox).[36]

The conclusion of the treaties, the intercommunal distur- bances that followed, and the proposal for a confederation which Riad was advocating, combined to bring about some evolution in Muslim opinion in Lebanon. Up to the end of 1936, Arab nationalists had focused on the issue of the disputed territories, but following the conclusion of the treaties with Syria and Lebanon, Lebanese Muslims

---

[34] Eric Phipps, British Ambassador in Paris, to Foreign Office, 5 July 1937 (FO 371/20848).

[35] Acting Consul General G. W. Furlong to Mr Eden, Beirut, 17 November 1936 (FO 371/20067); Consul General G. T. Havard to Mr Eden, Beirut, 24 November 1936 (FO 371/20066); Pierre Rondot, *Les Institutions politiques du Liban*, Paris 1947, p. 15.

[36] Johnson, *Class and Client*, pp. 19, 22, fn.

became aware that this issue was no longer of pressing importance in either Paris or Damascus. Indeed, Lebanese Sunnis had to acknowledge to their chagrin that, on this issue at least, they could no longer count on their Syrian 'brothers'. In fact, wanting to protect their own treaty with France, the National Bloc sent a delegation to Tripoli, made up of Jamil Mardam, Sa'dallah al-Jabiri and 'Afif el-Solh, to seek to calm things down and end the strike. The upshot was that Lebanese Muslims came gradually to accept the existence of Lebanon as an Arab state among others, while continuing to entertain the hope that, once its full independence was achieved, it would join its neighbours in some form of entente based on Arab nationalist and non-sectarian principles.[37]

The destruction of the Syrian Treaty

The three-year probation period that had been agreed by French and Syrian negotiators gave the colonial party time to mobilise against the treaty. A press campaign was launched, backed by some sixty French trading and industrial companies operating in Syria and Lebanon, among them the Banque de Syrie et du Liban and the concessionary companies running the railways and the trams, and providing electricity to Damascus, Beirut and Aleppo. All the old arguments – depressingly familiar since the First World War – were now rehashed and revived. France had to stay in Syria to maintain its regional influence; to remain a great power in the Muslim world; to prevent the spread of pan-Arabism to North Africa; to protect Lebanon from Syria, and the religious minorities from the 'tyranny' of the Muslim majority; to safeguard French interests against the perfidious British.[38]

To make things worse, the Blum government soon found itself in trouble. Blum was regularly pilloried as a traitor, a homosexual and a Jew. Another target was his minister of interior, Roger Salengro, the Socialist mayor of Lille, whom the far right had never forgiven for dissolving the Leagues. A vicious campaign, falsely accusing him of desertion during the Great War, so unhinged this susceptible man, that he ended up gassing himself in his apartment.

---

[37] Raghid el-Solh, *Lebanon and Arabism*, p. 50.
[38] Khoury, *Syria and the French Mandate*, p. 486.

A flight of capital, a fall in industrial output and a renewed outbreak of strikes forced Blum on 13 February to announce a 'pause' in his reforms. A prey to internal feuds, his left-wing coalition was in real danger of falling apart altogether. Struggling in April to cope with a flood of bad news, he asked parliament to grant him full economic powers, but the Senate – where he had lost his majority – refused his request. Blum resigned on 21 June 1937. He returned to power some eight months later on 13 March 1938, only to leave office for good within less than a month, on 8 April. His policies were gradually abandoned by Edouard Daladier and his Radical Party, which rose to power on the ruins of the Popular Front.

The collapse of the Popular Front doomed the Syrian Treaty and gave heart to all those who wished to perpetuate the Mandate – the colonial party, colonial administrators, concessionary companies, clerics – that motley crew who claimed to be concerned for the safety of Levantine minorities. They were joined, most crucially at this strategic juncture, by military officers, who were then increasingly worried by confronting an expansionist Italy, as well as by the looming threat of an all-out European war. The Levant, after all, was a key French military asset, which could not, in such dangerous circumstances, be expected to be given up.

Jamil Mardam went twice to Paris, in a desperate attempt to save the treaty – first in November 1937, and again in August 1938, when he stayed for three months. On each occasion, he was forced to make more concessions and give further pledges: to protect minority rights, and in particular those of the Christians; to renew the privileged status of the Banque de Syrie et du Liban; to guarantee the teaching of French in Syrian schools; to grant a permit to France for oil exploration; and a great many things besides.[39] On 1 September 1938, General Huntziger, the former commander-in-chief of the French Army of the Levant and a member of the Higher War Council, categorically informed Mardam – in the presence of Foreign Minister Georges Bonnet – that new clauses had now to be added to the already agreed military convention. French forces were to stay in Syria for the full duration of the treaty; the budget and the administration of local troops were to remain in French hands; French agents were to be stationed in the Jazira and the Syrian interior. Bonnet insisted that

---

[39] Ibid., pp. 489 ff.

without these military upgrades, there was no chance at all of the treaty being ratified.

What is more, on 14 December, under insistent pressure from the military and right-wing groups, Bonnet told the Foreign Affairs Commission of the National Assembly that the French government no longer intended to ask parliament to ratify the treaties. This was a lethal blow to the nationalist government in Damascus, whose whole programme was based on reaching such an agreement, which they had hoped would finally set Syria on the path to independence. The truth was, however, that the new military clauses had already robbed the treaty of all political significance. This was immediately clear to the nationalist politician Shukri al-Quwatli, who now saw the need to attack the very principle of the treaty, rightly arguing that it could no longer credibly be seen as a step towards ending the Mandate.

The struggle to tame the separatists

Quite apart from its devastating failure to get France to ratify the treaty, Jamil Mardam's government was beset with grave internal problems. Of these, the most pressing was the need to bring the Druze, the Alawites and the other religious and ethnic minorities of the Jazira under the rule of Damascus. The separatist sentiment in these regions, long encouraged by the French, had been gravely underestimated. In 1937, the Kurdish townspeople and Turkoman tribes in the Jazira rebelled, demanding separation from Syria and autonomy under the French Mandate. Because of its chronic insecurity, this region had been sparsely populated until the French arrived to 'pacify' it. France had then encouraged the emergence of a Kurdish-Christian alliance, welcoming in for the purpose thousands of Kurdish refugees from Anatolia, as well as Chaldean Assyrian Christians, who had fled repression in Iraq in 1933, with the result that by the mid-1930s, some 150,000 people had moved into the Jazira region – these being Kurds, Circassians, Armenians, Jacobite and Assyrian Christians, Yezidis and Turkomans. All these disparate groups were united in their vociferous detestation of the government in Damascus. They even petitioned the League of Nations to demand local autonomy.

After two years of anti-government agitation, the Jabal Druze expelled the Syrian officials sent to govern it. In 1939, it even proclaimed its independence. In the Alawite region – where Syria's governors had never managed to extend their authority beyond the coastal towns – a separatist revolt broke out in early 1939. In May, the new French High Commissioner Gabriel Puaux – who had replaced Damien de Martel in January 1939 – officially restored the system of regional autonomy for the Alawites and the Druze, and was preparing to extend it to the Jazira, which he placed under French military government.

As if all this were not enough, the nationalist government had then to wrestle with the question of the sanjaq of Alexandretta in north-west Syria. Because this territory contained a large Turkish minority, it had been granted a special status – determined by international agreement – to which Turkey was a party. A census in 1933 established that, out of a total population of 186,800, there were 89,500 Arabs, 70,800 Turks and 25,000 Armenians, Kurds and Circassians. But, after the conclusion of the Franco-Syrian Treaty, Turkey began claiming that Turks were now in the majority there, and it demanded special treatment for the sanjaq. As France was anxious to reach a political and military agreement with Ankara, it gave weight to Turkey's politically motivated and unfounded claims. In agreement with the League of Nations, a statute for the sanjaq was proposed in May 1937, under which it would remain linked to Syria while enjoying wide autonomy. But the Syrian parliament, sensing danger, refused to recognise the new proposed statute.

As preparations to hold elections were made in the sanjaq, the local Turks began to agitate, and Turkey carried out threatening troop movements in their support. Despite such clumsy, heavy-handed Turkish pressure – which France and its local representatives appeared happy to tolerate – the electoral rolls failed to indicate any Turkish majority. The registration of voters was therefore deliberately suspended so that Turkish troops could enter the sanjaq on 5 July 1938, with the blessing of France. That way, the electoral rolls were suddenly made to show that Turks accounted for 63 per cent of the population!

Having illegally ceded it the territory, France quickly proceeded to sign a Treaty of Friendship with Turkey on 4 July 1938, which it had long sought to do. The sanjaq was gradually integrated into Turkey, and in June 1939 was renamed the Turkish province of Hatay. Some 20,000 terrified refugees – Arabs, Armenians and Greeks – fled to Syria and Lebanon, leaving all their possessions behind. In an account of these events, the French historian André Raymond commented that giving the sanjaq to Turkey was 'a flagrant act of political immorality' on the part of France. It 'was in contradiction with the wishes of the majority of the population and with the obligations France had assumed towards Syria as the mandatory power'.[40]

These events had a profound impact on Syria, where both the political debacle and the human catastrophe were naturally blamed on the government. It was accused, no doubt somewhat unfairly, of having failed to defend Syrian rights.[41] Dr Shahbandar – one of the shrillest critics of the nationalist government – accused Jamil Mardam of having surrendered Alexandretta to the Turks, and of having made too many concessions to the French. Jamil Mardam was defeated – by both an enraged opinion at home and a perfidious French government in Paris. He resigned on 18 February 1939. President Hashim al-Atasi, in turn, withdrew from public life on 7 July, in protest against this unwarranted return of the French mandatory regime.

Using the excuse of the absence of a Syrian interlocutor, High Commissioner Puaux high-handedly dissolved parliament, suspended the Constitution and appointed a council of directors-general to rule by decree.[42] He claimed there was now an 'imperial duty' to maintain public order and the French presence. Most of the nationalist leaders suddenly found themselves in prison or in exile once again. They had to face the grim fact that Alexandretta was lost; that Syria was once again dismembered; and that the treaty they had worked so hard to negotiate had been tossed into the dustbin of history. The clock had been turned back to 1920.

One way or another, all the great efforts of Riad el-Solh and his nationalist colleagues had proved to be in vain. Their resulting sense of failure was extreme. In the 1930s, Riad had spared no effort to prepare the ground for a negotiated settlement with France, which would lead to Syrian independence. He had argued that dialogue rather than armed conflict was the only policy that could yield results. By direct contacts with French politicians and the press, he had sought to persuade French opinion that the Mandate – and the very crude way that it was being applied – had *damaged* rather than enhanced French

[40] Raymond, 'La Syrie, du Royaume arabe à l'indépendance', p. 75.
[41] Mizrahi, 'La France et sa politique de mandat', pp. 64 ff.
[42] Méouchy, 'Le Pacte national', p. 469.

interests in the region. His repeated visits to Paris had given him some insight into the turbulent world of French politics, where left and right, freethinkers and clericals, liberals and imperialists, debated and fought in ways reminiscent of the old Ottoman parliament that his father had known in his youth.

At the same time, in Lebanon, in order to mobilise the Christians to the cause of independence, Riad el-Solh had pioneered the notion of a Muslim-Christian entente. As a child, he had been taught to take pride in the efforts of his grandfather, Ahmad Pasha, then *mutasarrif* of Acre, to rescue and give succour to the desperate Christian refugees of the 1860 massacres. Those actions had come to constitute an essential part of Solh family lore. Also, as a result of his early schooling by Jesuits, and of a young manhood spent in the cosmopolitan environment of Istanbul, Riad el-Solh had acquired knowledge of Western ways and of Christian beliefs, as well as an understanding of the not too far-fetched fears of the Christian minority in the Arab East. Riad's own cast of mind was resoundingly secular. There was no hint of Muslim fanaticism in his personal make-up, nor was there any, he added confidently, in the Arab nationalism to which he now invited his Christian compatriots to adhere.

What Riad el-Solh achieved at this early stage was a measure of Muslim–Christian cooperation within a Lebanese framework. It was driven essentially by an understanding between notables of different confessions, and was financially underpinned by cooperation in Beirut's business community, between those Muslims and Christians who had increasingly important commercial interests in common. Among intellectuals, on the other hand, there was a bond of a different nature forming, regardless of their confessional background – a common appreciation of the revival of the Arabic language in journalism, higher education, literature and publishing. This was to make of Beirut the most exciting of cities and the unrivalled intellectual capital of the Arab world for a long time to come.

Because of such evolving attitudes – to which Riad made a significant contribution – Muslims, with himself foremost among them, no longer took to presenting themselves as inhabitants of a coastal region, who demanded to be reunited with Syria; but, rather, as members of the Muslim community of Lebanon – a community which now began demanding the same rights as its Maronite fellow citizens, and an equal voice in public affairs. As a leading Sunni politician, as an Arab nationalist of international renown, and as a Muslim who understood the mental make-up of both the local Christians and the Western world, Riad el-Solh was well placed to champion a vital coexistence between the two all-powerful currents in Lebanon's political life – Arab nationalism and Lebanese patriotism.

13 COMPETING IDENTITIES: THE BATTLE FOR MEN'S MINDS

As Riad el-Solh climbed to a commanding position on the Lebanese and Arab scene in the 1930s, an important source of his power and prestige was undoubtedly his impeccable pan-Arab pedigree, acquired in his struggle against the Turks and then against the French and British Mandates. His anti-imperialist stance in the 1920s and 1930s, and his participation in the pan-Islamic and pan-Arab conferences – convened by the Hajj Amin al-Husayni in Jerusalem in 1931 – had brought him into contact with the leading activists and anti-imperialist thinkers of both the Mashrik and the Maghrib, in addition to those of India, Transcaucasia and the Indonesian archipelago.

In the eastern Arab world, he was a member of a network of political leaders who already were – or were soon to become in the immediate post-Second World War years – at the centre of power in Beirut, Damascus, Riyadh, Amman, Baghdad and Cairo. He knew them all personally and had had constant political dealings with most of them since before the First World War. Members of this network, by and large, spoke the same political language, seeing the regional and international scenes through remarkably similar lenses. In addition, Riad had married a member of the Jabiri family of Aleppo, which had brought him into the fold of the extended contacts of this distinguished Syrian clan. No other Lebanese leader enjoyed his particular combination of assets.

Another source of Riad's power was his solidarity with the deprived, with those at the bottom of Lebanon's social pyramid. Whereas he was certainly in his element when talking to kings, presidents and pashas, he was – and to his credit – even more at ease and content when he was meeting with labourers, shopkeepers and peasants. This was in striking contrast to many of the haughty notables of the period. Riad liked to call on his working-class constituents at their dwellings, attend their weddings and their funerals, receive them graciously in his home; find their children jobs, and help them iron out the endless problems they encountered in a deeply hierarchical country, with everything from the courts to the schools, to hospitals and the police, as well as the Byzantine government bureaucracy.[1]

This brought him into close contact with the nascent trades union movement and with the Communist Party of Syria and Lebanon, which began to gain considerable momentum from 1935 onwards. The party had been founded in Beirut in 1930 and had had some success in organising industrial strikes and supporting political demonstrations. Whereas its early founding members had been mostly Armenians, they were supplanted, after some tension and acrimony, by Khalid Bakdash, a (somewhat vainglorious) Soviet-educated Kurd, and by a number of Arabs, notably Farajallah al-Hilu, Mustafa al-'Aris, Fu'ad Qazan, Nicola Shawi and Antun Thabit. This group of dedicated men inspired the Anti-Fascist League in Beirut in 1936, and published a newspaper, the *Voice of the People*, from 1937 until the outbreak of war, together with a stream of leaflets and manifestos and translations of Marxist texts. Party branches were opened in all the main cities. Although opinion in the party was at first divided on whether to collaborate with nationalists like Riad el-Solh, a clear political decision was taken by the party in 1936 to support him.[2]

Riad el-Solh was unique among the notables in Lebanon at the time in grasping that the assertion of working-class rights – and especially the strikes mounted against French concessionary companies – was an integral part of the anti-colonial struggle. No doubt, his close links with the Popular Front in France, and his observation of Léon Blum's reforms in favour of the working class, had helped frame his political understanding of social problems and his natural sympathy for the underprivileged.

The years in Lebanon immediately before the Second World War were racked by great social unrest, sparked by the spiralling cost of living and an economy in free fall. Strikes often paralysed the country. Riad's support for these strikes caused him to be banished by

---

[1] Letter from Professor Walid Khalidi, 3 February 2007, to whom I am greatly indebted for the first three paragraphs of this chapter.
[2] Stephen Hemsley Longrigg, *Syria and Lebanon under French Mandate*, Oxford 1958, p. 227.

the French to the town of Qamishli in Syria's far north-east for some months in 1935. Ironically enough, Qamishli was a town that was itself very sympathetic to Communism, being home to a reasonably organised peasantry, and to several ethnic and religious minorities who were all highly politicised. Not being Arab, they were not attracted to that ferment of Arab nationalism which had drawn to it so many other Syrians of the period.

Riad's failed bid for parliament

When Riad stood for parliament at the October 1937 elections, he did so with the support of the Communists, and also of Salim 'Ali Salam and the Islamic Council. He stood in Beirut on a list with another Sunni notable, 'Umar Bayhum. Opposite them was an Eddéist coalition, led by the Muslim but pro-French 'Abdallah al-Yafi. These rival lists demonstrated the division of the Sunnis of Lebanon's coastal regions. On the one hand, there were diehard opponents of the Mandate, such as the Solhs and the Salams in Beirut, and the Karamis in Tripoli. On the other hand, a number of Sunni figures had thrown in their lot with President Eddé, such as 'Abdallah al-Yafi himself. Then there was Muhi al-Din Nusuli, member of a well-known Sunni family of Beirut who, early in 1935, had started publishing a mildly nationalist newspaper, *Bayrut*;[3] or Prime Minister Khayr al-Din Ahdab, Riad's former friend and journalistic colleague, with whom he was now at political loggerheads.

The French – and the Lebanese authorities acting hand in glove with them – were determined to undermine the Solh–Bayhum list. As the gap between the Eddéists and the nationalists widened, Bishara al-Khoury's Constitutionalists tried to explore the possibility of an electoral cooperation with the nationalists. But, on instructions from Paris, the French High Commissioner de Martel warned Bishara al-Khoury not to cooperate with such men under any circumstance. The nationalists were to be kept out of parliament altogether. Rather, he urged the Eddéists and the Constitutionalists to enter into an electoral alliance *against* Riad el-Solh. To achieve this aim, de Martel issued a decree on 6 October 1937, extending Eddé's presidential term to six

[3] Raghid el-Solh, *Lebanon and Arabism*, p. 76.

years and increasing the number of deputies to 63 – 42 to be elected
by direct vote, and 21 to be appointed by the president, but actually by
the French themselves. The authorities' campaign against Arab nationalists culminated in the insidious offer of cooperation, which Eddé and
Ahdab made to the Salams and the Bayhums, on condition that they
drop Riad el-Solh from their list and replace him with a more amenable
candidate. Needless to say, this shameless and French-inspired proposal
was contemptuously turned down by the two proud patriots.

To be entirely certain that Riad would not stand a chance
of winning, the French went so far as to rig the elections. Prominent
journalists were promised parliamentary seats and high administrative posts, if they consented to attack the nationalists in their writings.
A mind-boggling 270 of the nationalists' electoral agents were jailed
on the eve of the poll. Others were harassed by the police – even man-
handled – at the doors of the actual polling stations. Ballot papers were
duplicated. As a result of these French shenanigans, Riad's bid was
clearly going to be unsuccessful – as was that of the Communists. He
thus found himself forced to withdraw.

The pro-French list in Beirut won 22,671 votes and the
Arab nationalists a mere 1,608. The outcome was hailed by narrow
Lebanese nationalists and the pro-French press as a decimating
defeat for pan-Arabism itself and a victory for the Lebanese cause.
L'Orient, the French-language daily of Georges Naccache and Gabriel
Khabbaz, crowed that Riad el-Solh had been beaten even on his
own terrain of Beirut! In contrast, al-Nahar, the leading Arabic-
language newspaper – founded by the Greek Orthodox and far more
open-minded and inclusive Ghassan Tuéni – attacked President Eddé
and Prime Minister Ahdab for their 'Phoenicianism'. This was a deri-
sive shorthand term for all those who sought to turn their back on
the Arab world, in order to pursue instead a narrow sectarian agenda,
anchored in murky mythologising about Phoenicia and Phoenicians.

The first sitting of the new parliament took place on 29
October 1937, when Pierre Trad was elected president of the Chamber.
The next day, Prime Minister Khayr al-Din Ahdab tendered his resignation to the president of the Republic. Eddé refused to accept it, and
asked him to form another cabinet, which he did, ensuring for himself
a large parliamentary majority.[4]

---

[4] Ibid., p. 79.

Faced with implacable French hostility, and with the French-backed Eddé–Ahdab edifice of power, Riad was up against overwhelming political odds. In the few years before the Second World War, French policy was in the grip of a rigidly conservative coalition of military officers, colonial administrators and clerics, all of whom favoured a perpetuation of the French presence in the Levant. They continued to see Greater Lebanon as a loyalist Christian island in a sea of hostile Muslims, and as a base from which to project French power in the Eastern Mediterranean against ambitious rivals such as Italy.

The French authorities in Beirut failed to understand that part of the Sunni establishment in Lebanon was now ready to be reconciled to Lebanon's 1920 frontiers. Or indeed, that men like Riad el-Solh had, by the 1930s, moved away from their utter rejection of Lebanon's expanded borders, to something like resigned acceptance of them, and even integration into the new Lebanese state. It was, after all, on the basis of such an evolved political sentiment that the Syrian nationalists had in 1936 embarked on treaty negotiations in Paris, in the expectation of achieving independence. They very much hoped to be able to achieve an acceptable compromise with the French.[5]

The French, however, remained sceptical of any national-ist change of heart. High Commissioner comte Damien de Martel suspected that Riad's acceptance of Greater Lebanon's borders was opportunistic and insincere, as he suggested in a triumphant comment after the elections: 'The most notable result', he declared, 'is the defeat of all Muslim and unitary irredentism, even though Riad el-Solh tried to rally votes . . . by proclaiming himself a partisan of the Lebanese state infused by an Arab spirit'.[6] For the French, Arab nationalism remained the enemy to be kept at bay, a view very much encouraged by their local Maronite clients. Such intransigence led to a hardening of battle lines between Arab nationalists and Lebanese nationalists – and, more ominously, between Muslims and Christians.

This was a time of near political anarchy in Lebanese affairs. Although the Maronite Lebanese nationalist Emile Eddé had been elected president in January 1936, his contest with his Maronite rival, Bishara al-Khoury – who was more tolerant of Arab nationalism – continued unabated. It split the political class from top to bottom.

---

[5] Méouchy, 'Le Pacte national', p. 465.
[6] Raghid el-Solh, *Lebanon and Arabism*, p. 80; Consul General Havard to Foreign Office, Beirut, 2 November 1937 (FO 371/20849).

The treaty negotiations which Syria and Lebanon had conducted with France had become a source of bitter discord. Lebanese Muslims – particularly in cities like Tripoli, where Sunni Muslim religious sentiment was strong – feared that their hopes of being reunited with Syria would now be dashed forever. This brought them out onto the street in violent demonstrations.

Meanwhile, in Syria, as France dragged its heels in ratifying the 1936 treaty, the independence for which the National Bloc had fought so hard, and suffered so much, was fast turning into a shivering mirage. To the profound frustration and outrage of Arab nationalists, French colonialism was being boldly reasserted, as if nothing had happened to concentrate French minds in the seventeen years since the start of the Mandate.

At the same time, opinion in Lebanon and across the whole of the Arab world was inflamed by the Palestinians' unequal struggle against the British and the Zionists. Support for the Palestinian rebellion, which broke out in 1936 and continued in spasms until 1939 – and which British troops put down with such heavy-handed cruelty and brutality – became one of the great hallmarks of Arabism. In this angry atmosphere, Prime Minister Ahdab fell foul of nationalist opinion by failing to denounce the Peel Commission's partition plan, and by giving his consent to Lebanon's participation in the 1936 Tel Aviv Zionist Fair, which all other Arab states had decided to boycott. He was accused of having financial interests in certain Zionist companies, an accusation that he sought somewhat awkwardly to refute, by reminding critics that he had once given refuge in Lebanon to the former Mufti of Jerusalem, the Hajj Amin al-Husayni.[7]

These local conflicts and frustrations had an unsettling impact on Levant society. But perhaps the greatest disturbing influence on local opinion as the 1930s drew to a close was the rise of Fascism in Europe. With little to show for their long battle against the Mandates, and feeling utterly betrayed by the perfidy of both Britain and France, Arab nationalists began desperately to hope that the rising power of Germany and Italy might finally manage to break the British and French hold on the Levant.

Soon noisy youth movements, paramilitary organisations and ideological parties sprang up in imitation of their Fascist European

---

[7] Raghid el-Solh, *Lebanon and Arabism*, p. 82.

counterparts, venting their frustration at the political impotence of their elders. Politics in Lebanon in the late 1930s was no longer the exclusive preserve of older notables, as it had indeed been for so long. New actors emerged on the scene, sharpening the divide between rival national identities, and carrying what was an increasingly bitter competition into the street.

The debate about Lebanon's identity

The 1937 elections were not primarily about economic or social issues. Rather, the main underlying theme was a debate about Lebanon's national identity. Was Lebanon an Arab country, an integral part of the wider Arab world; or did it have a separate, non-Arab identity, shaped by its Christian and Western connections, by its long-standing opening to the rest of the Mediterranean world, by its political history of occasional autonomy within the Ottoman Empire, and even by its more ancient historical origins? The battle was waged between opposing camps in the press, on the street and even in the salons of the elite. This was no polite affair of little consequence. Rather, for many, it was a life-and-death issue, affecting the very core of their being, and setting the stage for the civil war that would rage so bitterly forty years later.

Indeed, the question of national identity, which has plagued Lebanon since its creation as a modern state in 1920, remains largely unresolved to this very day. If anything, it seems at times to become more acute and divisive than ever, as a result of the political and military intervention of rival external powers, each tempted to enlist local proxy forces. The ensuing clashes often play on historical divisions and serve to entrench a culture of violence.

'All states are artificial in the literal sense', Albert Hourani once remarked in one of his essays.[8] 'That is to say, they have been formed by specific historical processes, by human acts within a given physical environment over a period of time.' There is, indeed, nothing cast in stone about national identities. Rather, nations are complex evolutionary creations, made of internal turbulences and external interventions;

---

[8] Albert Hourani, *Political Society in Lebanon: A Historical Introduction*, Oxford 1986, p. 2.

of the often arbitrary drawing of frontiers; of historical or geographical accident; of myth; of the way people think and feel about themselves and their history; and of many other factors – of which by no means the least important are the abstract formulations of intellectuals. In Lebanon, as elsewhere, the sinister ideologues of 'national identity' have much to answer for.

Riad el-Solh's Arab nationalism had been given a bitter edge by several decades of painful defeats. Although Sunni Muslims, such as himself, were heirs of the Ayyubid and Mamluk dynasties, of 400 years of Ottoman rule from 1516 onwards, and of the Arab Revolt of 1916, they had been kept out of Lebanese politics by the French-backed Maronites for virtually the whole of the interwar period. From being the majority community of the Arab world, they had found themselves reduced to a minority within a Greater Lebanon created by the French. Yet, in spite of this adversity, Arab nationalism remained the only ideology Riad el-Solh ever truly believed in. It was his spiritual and intellectual inheritance. His ambition was to alter the course of his country – to win over Lebanon to a non-confessional Arab national-ism, in which both Christians and Muslims would find their home. His lifelong conviction was that the goal of the emancipation of the Arab world should be shared by every single Arab, including the Lebanese of all confessions. Whatever their backgrounds, they were all comrades-in-arms. Each individual had to be committed and concerned. After all, he had seen with his own eyes exactly what such commitment and hard work had earned for the Zionists.

In view of the dispiriting events he had lived through, it took considerable self-confidence and grit to continue to hold unswerv-ingly to this position. Both he and his father had been incarcerated in a grim Turkish military prison at Aley, and had only narrowly escaped death by hanging. Several of the early nationalists they had known and loved had died appalling deaths on the gallows in public squares in Damascus and Beirut in 1915 and 1916. Riad had had to witness his father, and so many other loyal, lifelong imperial offi-cials, struggle in vulnerable middle age with the countless dilemmas posed by the traumatic transition from Ottomanism to Arabism; watched as their fortunes and privileges collapsed beneath them with the defeat of the Empire in the First World War. Then, just as the dream of Arab independence and unity seemed within reach, came the carving up of the Arab provinces by Britain and France to suit their mutual imperial interests, followed by the forced imposition of colonial Mandates on the area. Other disasters followed thick and fast: the crushing of the Great Syrian Revolt of 1925–26; the inexorable, British-backed tide of Jewish settlement and the murderous defeat by Britain of the Palestinian rebellion of 1936–39; France's refusal to ratify the 1936 treaties, and its full restoration of the hated Mandate.

This grim catalogue of events only confirmed the ever-optimistic Riad el-Solh in his belief that independence was the ultimate destiny of the Arab people – and that he himself had a significant role to play in bringing it about.

The South Lebanon connection

There was a further dimension to Riad's nationalism. Although he was a Sunni Muslim, his roots were in South Lebanon, which was and remains a predominantly Shi'i Muslim area. It was no accident that Ahmad Pasha, his landowning grandfather, had insisted, in a gesture to his Shi'i friends and retainers, that Riad be given the name of 'Ali – after 'Ali ibn Abi Talib (598–661), cousin and son-in-law of the Prophet Muhammad, and Islam's fourth Caliph. In Shi'i doctrine, 'Ali is believed to be the first Imam – in the special sense in which the Shi'is understand this term – that is, the unique intermediary between man and God. According to the Shi'i heterodox interpretation of Islamic doctrine, the Imam is necessary for salvation. In his youth, Riad often signed himself as Riad 'Ali, although once he became a public figure he decided to drop this second name.

South Lebanon is a region of steep hills separated from each other by valleys and deep gorges, a fractured landscape which, over the centuries, provided protection for minority communities such as the Shi'a. Having challenged the basic tenets of Sunni Muslim faith, they were seen by majority Sunni Islam as a dangerous and unwelcome threat to the established religious and political order in Damascus and Baghdad. As a result, the Shi'i community could not but face oppression and persecution.

With rare exceptions, the Shi'is of Lebanon have been on the defensive throughout their history, retreating into their mountain refuge of Jabal 'Amil in the far south, named after the Bani 'Amila, an Arab tribe of Yemeni origin.[9] Their oppressors were not only the Mamluks – those former military slaves who seized power in both Egypt and Syria in the fourteenth century – or the Ottoman Pashas from the sixteenth century onwards, but also local opponents, such as the Maronites and the Druze. These latter two minorities, after establishing themselves in the central region of Mount Lebanon, made repeated forays outside it. The Maronites were members of a schismatic Christian movement, which, from the sixth century onwards, made its way into Lebanon from Antioch. They were to benefit, some centuries later, from waves of European occupation in the bloody form of the Crusades. The Druze, another heterodox sect, founded in Cairo by a disciple of the sixth Fatimid Caliph, al-Hakim, appeared on the Lebanese scene in the ninth century. During the four centuries of Ottoman rule, these two rival communities, the Maronites and the Druze, achieved a dominant position over Mount Lebanon, even at times a form of quasi-autonomy, relegating the Shi'is in the south to insecure and impoverished marginality. The Shi'is thus became 'Lebanon's forgotten citizens'.[10]

They were not, however, entirely deprived of external support. When Shah Isma'il made Shi'ism the official religion of Persia in the early sixteenth century, he imported Shi'i scholars and religious functionaries from Iraq, Bahrain and South Lebanon. Ties were thus forged which were to grow closer over the years, and have been vigorously reactivated in our own day. The great mosque and *madrassa* of Shaykh Lutfallah in Isfahan, for example, are named after an immigrant from a southern Lebanese village. In the words of Albert Hourani, 'The link between Shi'is and Iran, like the link between the Maronites and the papacy, helped to define the space within which Lebanon was to live and move'.[11]

Changes in the geopolitics of South Lebanon were greatly to affect the fortunes of the Solh family. Before the building of the Damascus–Beirut road in the 1860s, the Lebanon and anti-Lebanon mountain ranges were a formidable barrier between inland Syria and

---

[9] Séguin, *Le Liban Sud*, Paris 1989, pp. 29–46; see also M. Jaber, *Pouvoir et société au Jabal Amel de 1749 à 1920 dans la conscience des chroniques chiites et dans un essai d'interprétation*, Paris 1978; Chibli Mallat, *Shi'i Thought from the South of Lebanon*, Oxford 1988.

[10] Chalabi, *The Shi'is of Jabal 'Amil*, p. 2.

[11] Hourani, *Political Society in Lebanon*, p. 6; see also Albert Hourani, 'From Jabal 'Amil to Persia', in *Bulletin of the School of Oriental and African Studies*, 49 (1986).

the Mediterranean. It was no easy journey to scale the peaks or cross the mountain passes. Trade from Damascus and the Syrian interior to the coast had to skirt the mountain ranges from the south to reach Sidon via Jezzin or Nabatiyya. As the terminal of the only 'easy' route from Damascus to the Mediterranean, Sidon was to grow into a flourishing trading centre, becoming Syria's principal Mediterranean port. It reached the peak of its fortunes in the first decades of the seventeenth century, during the reign of the Druze Emir Fakhr al-Din. He made Sidon his political and commercial capital, thus opening Mount Lebanon to the world of the western Mediterranean. For a while, therefore, Sidon's commercial importance shifted the region's geopolitical centre of gravity towards the south.

From his fief in the Shuf region of Mount Lebanon, Fakhr al-Din extended his domain eastwards towards Damascus and south-wards as far as Safad in Palestine. To secure the Damascus–Sidon road, he settled minorities along its route – both Shi'i peasant families and Maronite families from the southern reaches of Mount Lebanon. Many Christian villages in the region today still bear witness to that ancient resettlement. So flourishing did Sidon become under his rule, that a Florentine consulate was opened there in 1630.

But the extent of his glittering conquests started to alarm the Sublime Porte. Indeed, Fakhr al-Din found it prudent to seek shelter for a while with his friends the Medici in Florence. (Wonderfully, he was so impressed by the buildings and gardens that he saw there that he sought to reproduce something of their splendour in his own country upon his return.) The Ottoman Sultan, however, would not leave him alone. Angered by the revival of the emir's fortunes, he had him arrested in 1635 and brought to Istanbul, where, after a long impris-onment, he was hanged. Some years after his death, the Sublime Porte created a new Ottoman vilayet, with Sidon as its capital. It included central Lebanon and northern Palestine, and was ruled by Syrian governors who were appointed directly from Istanbul. In this manner, South Lebanon gradually reverted to being a peripheral region halfway between Egypt and Turkey, forever torn between submission to Mount Lebanon to the north or to the Ottoman pashas of Syria-Palestine to the south.

Sidon's fortunes were finally dashed for good by the building of the Beirut–Damascus road, which robbed the town of most of the traffic between inland Syria and the coast. This shift in the pattern of trade became even more pronounced when the railway was built in 1895, moving Lebanon's centre of gravity decisively towards the north. Economic activity was henceforth centred on Beirut, as well as on Mount Lebanon and its Christian community. Beirut replaced Sidon as the trading capital of Syria – a commercial supremacy it has largely managed to retain in the face of astounding odds. Sidon was reduced to the status of 'small town', losing the important political and economic role it had once played, when it was still the terminal of the natural route from the interior to the Mediterranean.[12]

It was undoubtedly these developments that caused Riad's grandfather, Ahmad Pasha, and his great-uncle, 'Abd al-Rahim, to move from Sidon to Beirut in the mid-nineteenth century. They did not, however, sever their ties to the south, which continued to play a large part in their lives. After all, home for them was still there, as were their estates, friends and the members of their extended family.

On the Solh family's return to Lebanon from Istanbul in 1913, Rida and Riad el-Solh spent a good deal of time in South Lebanon in discussions with 'Abd al-Karim al-Khalil and other local notables. Khalil was a young nationalist, who seems to have been the main inspiration behind a shadowy 'Arab Revolutionary Movement' based in Sidon. They were all rounded up by the Turkish authorities, and taken to be jailed at Aley. Rida and Riad el-Solh managed to escape the gallows, but Khalil was hanged. Once the Turks were defeated and the Emir Faysal established his rule in Damascus, Rida el-Solh became his minister of interior, and Riad, aged just 24, was sent to run Sidon on the emir's behalf.

France disapproved of ties between the population of South Lebanon and the government in Damascus, and did its best to sever them. This angered the Shi'is, who reacted violently. Armed bands attacked Christian villages and harassed French troops. The French then supplied the Christians with weapons, which led to clashes between Shi'i and Christian villages in May 1920. The French eventually separated the combatants, and sent troops to occupy and 'pacify' the villages of South Lebanon.

Much like the Sunni population of Tripoli and other coastal towns, the Shi'i population of the south was bitterly opposed to incorporation into France's 'Greater Lebanon'. Having suffered from the control of Sunni Ottoman governors and having been excluded from

---

[12] Séguin, *Le Liban Sud*, pp. 29–46.

the economic prosperity of Beirut, the Shi'is opposed their annexation to Mount Lebanon. They feared that this would lead to their domination by the Maronites and the Druze. Some took up arms, but were soon subdued by the French. Many hoped that a large Arab state of nationalist temper would allow their community to retain its confessional identity, while escaping from the political inferiority and economic neglect of the past. But it was not to be. Nevertheless, it was from South Lebanon that Riad was finally elected to parliament in 1943, his stepping-stone both to the premiership and to the fight for the independence of Lebanon.

The rise of Lebanese nationalism

The Lebanese nationalism with which Riad had to contend was the very opposite of everything he himself stood for. It was totally opposed both to Syrian unity and to pan-Arab nationalism; it was fearful of being swamped by Islam; it was obsessively attached to France and to the French language, and it looked to Paris for protection against its Arab hinterland. Its war cry was the defence of the Lebanese *kiyan*, or entity – that is to say, the Greater Lebanon within its French-expanded borders – that very same entity that Arab nationalists still hoped to dismantle. Above all, it was essentially Christian, viewing Lebanon as the 'national home' – very much under Maronite leadership – of Lebanese Christians of all denominations.

The Maronite Church had indeed played a decisive role in shaping Lebanon's identity over many centuries. Links with Christian Europe were forged at the time of the Crusades, when a minority among the Christians of Syria found kindred spirits in a number of Crusader enclaves established at the end of the eleventh century, foremost among them the Kingdom of Jerusalem and the County of Tripoli. Early in the twelfth century, the Maronite Church made contact with the papacy and accepted Catholic doctrine. As for the link with France, it was forged as early as 1553, when Paris secured from the Ottomans the right to extend French protection to Latin Christians and Catholic establishments within the Empire, an arrangement that was then extended informally to native Christians as well. From the time of Louis XIV onwards, French policy in the Levant was always concerned with the protection of the Maronite Church.

It was not, however, until the early twentieth century that the notion of a Greater Lebanon emerged and took root. In 1908, a certain M. Jouplain published a large tome in Paris under the title of *La Question du Liban: Étude d'histoire diplomatique et de droit international*, in which he called for the creation of '*le Liban de la grande époque*', which he named specifically as '*Le Grand Liban*', within what he termed its natural and historic frontiers. Eleven years later, in August 1919, a Beirut journal, *La Revue phénicienne*, published an article entitled 'La Question du Liban', in which the author, Bulus Nujaym, confessed that it was he who had written the earlier volume. But what exactly were those 'natural and historic frontiers' to which Nujaym had referred, and how had they come about?

The reference is thought to be to the borders of the domains which had first been carved out by Fakhr al-Din, and then by Bashir II, and which were later incorporated in the staff maps of the French Expeditionary Force, which was sent to Syria after the 1860 massacres. As we have seen, the Emir Fakhr al-Din of the Ma'nid dynasty was the Druze ruler of the Shuf, who had managed to extend his rule in the first half of the seventeenth century over much of what was later to become Lebanon and Syria. Bashir II (1788–1840) was the great prince of the Shihab dynasty who, in turn, extended his rule over the whole of Mount Lebanon from north to south in the early nineteenth century.

Lebanese nationalists consider these two rulers the founding fathers of the Lebanese nation. Nujaym was particularly enamoured with Fakhr al-Din, who, he wrote, 'fashioned a powerful and well-organised state with Lebanon as its centre . . . It was no longer a Turkish province but a state with a life of its own, resembling more the civilised countries of Western Europe than a vilayet of the Sublime Porte. Led by an Enlightened Despot, it experienced the splendour of an Italian Renaissance.'

There was much wishful thinking in such an account. Although Fakhr al-Din certainly won a measure of independence from Istanbul for a limited period of time, his power was exaggerated by those who later used him to forge their founding myth. Albert Hourani wrote of him that 'The state he created was a personal one. It did not express itself in institutions and it did not last long'.[13] On his defeat and death, Istanbul reasserted its central control, but in even stronger form than

---

[13] Hourani, *Political Society in Lebanon*, p. 7.

before. The role claimed for the princes of the Shihab family has also been much inflated. While they succeeded in bringing Maronites and Druze together under one government, it is questionable whether they managed to shape a Lebanese entity separate and distinct from the rest of Syria in the eighteenth century.

As the century wore on, part of the Shihab family gradually converted from Sunni Islam to Maronite Christianity, and, partly as a result, a transfer of hegemony took place from the Druze to the Maronites. At the same time, the Maronite Church strengthened its position with a formal agreement with the papacy in 1736. These developments reached their nineteenth-century flowering in the long reign of Bashir II, who strengthened his army, extended his power and built the palace of Beiteddine. But, like Fakhr al-Din before him, Bashir II's achievement did not outlast him, and he, too, came to grief.

In 1830, Ibrahim Pasha, son of the master of Egypt, Muhammad Ali, invaded Syria and occupied the Lebanese mountains. Bashir II made the strategic blunder of siding with him against the Ottomans. For a while, they triumphed. But the Egyptian invaders underestimated the cohesion of the local communities. When they attempted to impose conscription, a revolt broke out. And when the Ottoman Sultan made war on Muhammad Ali, the European Powers – with the exception of France – sided with the Sultan. In 1840, Ibrahim Pasha was forced to withdraw from Syria, and his ally, Bashir II, was defeated by the Ottomans the following year. His Lebanese emirate collapsed and he died in exile.

Ottoman rule was restored. The Porte replaced what it saw as a disloyal Shihab regime with a system of two cantons, one Druze, the other Maronite. This was the so-called double *qa'im maqamiyya* of 1842. But disturbances and violent clashes between the two communities over power-sharing soon broke out, reaching a savage climax in the intercommunal wars of 1860, when Christians were massacred by Druze in the Lebanese mountains, the killing spreading to Damascus, causing France to send an expeditionary force to the Levant under General Beaufort d'Hautpoul.

Ottoman officials and European representatives held a conference in Beirut and another in Istanbul at which, under a series of organic statutes in 1861 and 1864, it was agreed that Mount Lebanon would have a special status as an autonomous province, or *mutasarrifiyya*, within the Empire. It would be ruled by a non-Lebanese Christian governor, appointed by the Ottoman government with the consent of the European Powers. The governor was assisted by an administrative council of twelve members, representing the six principal communities of the Mountain. With its own police force and system of justice, autonomous Mount Lebanon was to enjoy fifty years of peace and prosperity until the First World War. The cultivation of silk there for the Lyon market, for example, reached its height in the 1860s.

But the new autonomous province was not as large as the old domains of the Ma'nid and Shihab emirates had been. The Biqa' valley and Wadi al-Taym were amputated, as well as the district of Sidon and the city of Beirut, all of which were incorporated into the neighbouring Ottoman provinces. Advocates of Greater Lebanon would later campaign for the recovery of these important territories.

Nevertheless, in the view of the Lebanese historian Kamal Salibi, Lebanon's identity was, for the first time, given legal definition by the establishment of the *mutasarrifiyya*. To be 'Lebanese' was to enjoy citizenship in the autonomous province, and the various privileges that went with it.[14] A sense of Lebanese identity developed most strongly among Maronites, who, in the decade 1850–60, managed to establish their hegemony over the Mountain, thus sending the Druze into irreversible decline. The Shi'is of South Lebanon had sided with the Druze, and now shared in their defeat and decline. Christian power took hold, together with a sentiment of Lebanese national separateness, inspired at least in part by the rise of Serbian and other Christian and anti-Ottoman nationalisms in the Balkans.

Nadine Picaudou, a French historian of Lebanon, takes a somewhat different view from that of Kamal Salibi. Rather than seeing the *mutasarrifiyya* as a founding moment in the forging of Lebanon's distinct identity, she sees it instead as an institutional device by the Ottoman Empire to restore its control after the 1860 massacres.[15] No notion of Lebanese citizenship transcending the sectarian communities was promoted during the period of the *mutasarrifiyya*. On the contrary, the old legacy of confessionalism – now under Christian leadership – became further entrenched.

---

[14] Kamal S. Salibi, 'The Lebanese Identity', in *Journal of Contemporary History*, 6(1), p. 78.
[15] Nadine Picaudou, 'La Question libanaise ou les ambiguïtés fondamentales', in Khoury (ed.), *Sélim Takla*, p. 44.

The lure of Phoenicianism

Curiously, this legacy of Christian fanaticism and domination has, in modern times, coexisted alongside a strong dose of paganism in the form of a claim, first advanced in 1919, that Lebanon was no less than a reincarnation of ancient Phoenicia – a polity which had existed some five thousand years earlier on a coastal strip of the east Mediterranean, very much where the Lebanese coast lies today. For some Lebanese Christians, this claim of descent from the Phoenicians represented an opening to the sea and to the commercial world beyond. But, more significantly, in their view, it was a link to something non-Arab – to the Christian victors of the Great War, to 'modernity', even to Western civilisation itself.[16]

The Phoenicians are thought to have arrived in the eastern Mediterranean around 3000 BC. No one is quite sure where they hailed from, though some scholars think they may have come from the Persian Gulf. In subsequent centuries, they extended their influence from Biblos and Beirut southwards to Jaffa and Acre – and across the Mediterranean to Carthage (founded about 814 BC), to Cyprus, even to Andalusia. They were clearly a remarkable people. They developed an alphabet; they were gifted seafarers, navigating by the stars; they taught the West accounting and book-keeping, which they learned from the Babylonians; they were traders and colonisers, famous for their gold- and metalworking, their glass-blowing, their ivory- and woodcarving and their brilliant dyes and covetable dyed cloth. One way or another, they played an important role in the ancient history of the world. For four and a half centuries, they held complete mastery over the Mediterranean. They were the unrivalled and undisputed trading nation between East and West. In due course, however, they were subdued by the Assyrians in the ninth century BC, by the Persians in the sixth century BC, and by Alexander the Great, before finally being incorporated into the Roman province of Syria in 64 BC.[17]

'Phoenicianism' was adopted by many Christians as a Lebanese identity myth, largely as a result of the advocacy of Charles Corm, a Lebanese intellectual who passionately promoted the idea in four issues of a journal, *La Revue phénicienne*, which he published in Beirut

---

[16] Asher Kaufman, *Reviving Phoenicia: The Search for Identity in Lebanon*, London 2004, pp. 87, 141–2.
[17] See Dimitri Baramki, *Phoenicia and the Phoenicians*, Beirut 1961.

in 1919. He was to remain a tireless champion of Phoenicianism until his death in 1963. Riad el-Solh and Charles Corm got to know each other at school, having sat next to each other on the same bench at the Lazarist college of 'Aintura in the Lebanese mountains.

Born in Beirut in 1894 – the same year as Riad – Charles Corm was the son of a well-known Lebanese artist. He had gone on to make a fortune as the agent of the Ford Motor Company in Syria and Lebanon, before retiring from business to become a poet, *homme de lettres* and thinker. In February 1934, he launched his Editions de la Revue Phénicienne, a publishing house that became the major outlet for 'Phoenician' works in the 1930s and 1940s. Corm was also a firm supporter of President Emile Eddé, whose anti-Arab cultural and political orientation he shared. Like Eddé, he refused to use anything but French as his means of written communication. (It is no small irony that one of his sons, David, went on to marry the Palestinian Arab Muslim granddaughter of the Hajj Amin al-Husayni.)

Phoenicianism was given a further lease of life with the publication in Beirut between January 1938 and July–August 1939 of thirteen numbers of the magazine *Phénicia*, of which a leading contributor was Michel Chiha, brother-in-law of Bishara al-Khoury, President Eddé's Maronite rival. Chiha and Khoury had spent three years of the First World War in Alexandria, where they became firm friends. Chiha was later to become a champion of the idea that Lebanon was in essence a Mediterranean country, linked (in his words) by an 'identity of soul and thought' to the Latin West, and to France in particular. As a Christian Lebanese – and as the secretary of the committee which drafted the 1926 Constitution – he was largely responsible (and disastrously as it turned out) for the character of Lebanon's constitutional arrangements. Through the editorials of *Le Jour*, the French-language newspaper he founded in August 1934, Chiha built a reputation as one of the country's foremost political ideologues. In developing the ideology of an independent Lebanon, he was joined by the banker Henri Pharaon, who shared both his philosophy and his financial acumen. Together they founded the powerful Chiha–Pharaon banking partnership.[18]

After the Second World War, the Phoenician idea as a basis for Lebanon's national identity continued to win devotees, as may be seen from a series of occasional lectures given in Beirut from 1946

---

[18] Johnson, *Class and Client*, p. 120.

until the mid-1970s, later published as *Les Conférences du Cénacle*. The underlying theme of several of these lectures was that multi-lingual, entrepreneurial, market-oriented Lebanon, situated on the Mediterranean seaboard like Phoenicia before it, should be considered the obvious and privileged partner of the West.

But, by claiming Lebanon as a creation of the Mediterranean world, the Phoenicianist formula ignored another major strand of Lebanon's identity – that of Mount Lebanon as a fortress closed in on itself, a refuge for minorities, where Maronites and Druze survived over the centuries, if not always in harmony, at least in irritable coexistence.

Most people, and Muslims especially, dismissed Phoenicianism as laughable nonsense. As the historian Kamal Salibi has remarked, Sunnis had early on denounced Phoenicianism as a French imperialist conspiracy against Arab nationalism. The notion was, in any event, intellectually questionable, as it ignored the country's important Arab heritage. 'No theory of Lebanese nationality', the (Christian) Salibi writes, 'could be valid if it did not take into consideration the fundamental historical and cultural connection between Lebanon and Arabism'.[19]

The point was also made by the Lebanese sociologist Ahmad Beydoun, in an essay published in Paris in 2000, in which he analysed the fascination that the notion of Phoenicianism exercised on Lebanese Christian minds from 1919 up to the 1970s.[20] Corm's immediate priority in 1919, Beydoun explained, was to remove Syria from the orbit of the Emir Faysal's Hijaz, which he saw as a mortal threat to the Westernised, French-speaking Levantine society he so cherished. 'What do we have in common with the Beduin?' Corm exclaimed in one of his articles. 'The Lebanese and the Syrians are not Arabs!'[21] At a later stage, he went further still, seeking even to tear Lebanon away from its Syrian hinterland.

But, as Beydoun pointed out, the Phoenician model had two major flaws: the Mountain and Islam. The Mountain refused to

---

[19] Salibi, 'The Lebanese Identity', p. 84.

[20] Ahmad Beydoun, 'Extrême méditerranée: Le libanisme contemporain à l'épreuve de la mer', in Elias Khoury and Ahmad Beydoun, *La Méditerranée libanaise*, Paris 2000.

[21] Charles Corm, 'Méditations nationalistes', in *La Revue phénicienne*, no. 3 (September 1919), pp. 174, 175, 178, quoted in Beydoun 'Extrême méditerranée', p. 34.

recognise the coast as the centre of Lebanon's identity, while thirteen centuries of Islam in the country could hardly be dismissed as a mere parenthesis. Those who thought of themselves as 'Mediterranean' had to come to terms with strong pan-Arab and pan-Syrian influences, which were plainly incompatible with 'Phoenicianism'. The Lebanese search for Phoenician ancestors had, indeed, no basis in historical or regional facts on the ground. In other words, Phoenicianism was a myth, alluring to some, but an outright myth nevertheless.

Like their alleged Phoenician forefathers, some modern Lebanese continue to feel that they, too, have been called upon to play a role as cultural intermediaries between East and West. That is probably as far as this historical comparison can be stretched.

Riad el-Solh was well aware that he could not confront head-on the powerful current of Lebanese nationalism, with its multiple strands – Maronite, French, *kyanist*, Mediterranean, Phoenician – as well as its veneration for Fakhr al-Din and Bashir II, supposedly the princely founding fathers of the Lebanese nation. As Lebanese nationalism could not be defeated, it would have to be conciliated and co-opted instead. The independent Lebanon Riad envisaged – and which he eventually managed, against immense odds, to bring into being – had therefore to be a Christian–Muslim partnership in the fullest sense of the word.

14 THE POLITICS OF THE STREET

Pan-Arab nationalism and 'Greater Lebanon' patriotism, the two main political ideologies of the time, found themselves challenged on the Syro-Lebanese scene by another political movement, which was viscerally opposed to both of them.[1] This was Antun Sa'ada's Syrian National Party (*al-hizb al-qawmi al-suri*), known more widely by its French name of *Parti populaire syrien*, or PPS. Sa'ada recognised neither the existence of a Greater Lebanon separate from Syria, nor the Arab character of Syria as an integral part of the wider Arab world. His central tenet was that the 'Syrian nation' was not Arab at all, but constituted a distinct entity of its own, shaped over the millennia by its unique geographical environment. There was an 'organic correlation', he argued, between the Syrian nation and its physical homeland. Such radical views ruled out compromise or cooperation with other movements and ideologies.

The challenge from Antun Sa'ada's Pan-Syrianism

The 'organic unity' of Syrian society, Sa'ada wrote, was not based on race or blood, but was the result of the 'long history of all the people who have settled in this land, inhabited it, interacted and finally become fused into one people. This process started with the peoples of the Neolithic age . . . and continued with the Akkadians, Canaanites,

---

[1] *Qawm* means 'people', but the French mistranslated *qawmi* as 'populaire', so the party came to be known as the *Parti populaire syrien*. The word 'Social' was later added to the party's name so that its official designation in English became the Syrian Social Nationalist Party, or SSNP.

Assyrians, Aramaeans, Ammorites and Hittites'.[2] He defined the 'natural boundaries' of the homeland as extending

> from the Taurus range in the north-west and the Zagros mountains in the north-east to the Suez Canal and the Red Sea in the south and includes the Sinai Peninsula and the Gulf of Aqaba, and from the Syrian sea [the Mediterranean] in the west, including the island of Cyprus, to the Arch of the Arabian Desert and the Persian Gulf in the east. This region is also called the Syrian Fertile Crescent, the Island of Cyprus being its star.[3]

Antun Sa'ada was a geographical determinist of a mystical (and, some would say, confused) sort. In an interview with the author in the early 1960s, Michel 'Aflaq, the founder of the Ba'th Party – a bitter ideological opponent of the PPS, and which was later to become no less strident in its repressive organisation – summed up Sa'ada's party in the following terms:

> The whole movement was an odd mixture of modernism, of scientism, with something extremely old, even archaeological; a resurrection of the local past and grudges a thousand years old. Among the many movements of Arab rebirth, this was one which aborted and lost itself in unhealthy romanticism, due perhaps to the fact that Sa'ada's mind was directed mainly towards the past.[4]

Sa'ada was no mere armchair theorist, however. He built a secret, authoritarian, rigidly hierarchical movement, united around a strong cult of the leader, and equipped with a paramilitary arm, which was to have a disturbing effect on Lebanese and Syrian politics both before

---

2 Antun Sa'ada, The Principles of the Syrian Social Nationalist Party by The Leader (n.d.), p. 14. See Patrick Seale, The Struggle for Syria: A Study of Post-War Arab Politics, Oxford 1965 (new edn London and New Haven 1986), pp. 64–72.
3 Sa'ada, The Principles, p. 22. The 'geographical homeland', as defined by the party in the 1930s, made no mention of Cyprus and listed the Tigris as the eastern boundary. It was expanded in 1947 to include Cyprus and the whole of Iraq. See Antun Sa'ada, al-Ta'alim al-suriyya al-qawmiyya al-ijtima'iyya, 4th edn Beirut 1947, p. 18. See also Antun Sa'ada, Nushu' al-umam, vol. I, a book he started in prison and published in Beirut in 1938.
4 Seale, The Struggle for Syria, p. 68.

and after the Second World War. Born on 1 March 1904 into a Greek Orthodox family at Dhur al-Shwayr in Mount Lebanon, Antun Sa'ada was the son of Dr Khalil Sa'ada, a medical doctor and graduate of the American University of Beirut, who, early in the century, had emigrated first to Egypt, where he is best remembered as the author of a two-volume English–Arabic dictionary. He then went to Brazil, leaving his family behind in Lebanon. He took with him to Latin America a strong belief in Syrian nationalism, which was current in the Near East in the previous half-century, ever since the vilayet of Damascus was renamed the vilayet of Syria in 1864.

Like others at the time, Khalil Sa'ada was influenced by the work of a French geographer, Elisée Reclus, who, in his *Nouvelle Géographie Universelle*, published in Paris in 1884, had written of the existence of a Syrian race, circumscribed within the limits of geographical Syria, and utterly distinct from the Arab race.[5] In Brazil, Dr Sa'ada started a magazine in which ideas of this nature were expounded.

The young Antun joined Dr Sa'ada in São Paulo in the early 1920s and worked for a while on his magazine. Without any means of support in Lebanon, he had been unable to continue in full-time education. He must have fallen out with his father, however, because after a few years spent in Brazil, he headed to Europe towards the end of the decade, spending a year or more in Germany. He returned to the Near East in July 1930. He was 26, and his financial situation was still precarious. In Syria, he found employment for a short spell on a Damascus newspaper, *al-Ayyam*. But Syria under French rule was intellectually suffocating as well as poverty-stricken, so he moved to the more congenial atmosphere of Beirut. He had no money or profession, and supported himself by giving private lessons in Arabic and German, usually conducted in a tree house – just a few planks, a camp-bed and a folding table – which he erected on a piece of land owned by the family in the village of al-Arzal close to Dhur al-Shwayr.

The American University of Beirut was an intellectual centre of Beirut, and Sa'ada, although never formally attached to the college, often found his way to the staff common room, where tea was served at 4 p.m. He wore a full beard like a priest, attracting some ridicule on account of the obstinate insistence with which he defended his views. It was then, in about 1931–32, that the idea of creating a secret political organisation

---

[5] Kaufman, *Reviving Phoenicia*, p. 8.

appears to have taken root in his mind. He talked for hours in the common room, went swimming with the students, and gathered his first disciples. He may well have been inspired by the ideas of a Jesuit priest, Henri Lammens, a professor of oriental studies at Beirut's University of Saint Joseph, who, in 1921, published a two-volume work, *La Syrie: Précis historique*, in which he argued that the Syrians had been historically in existence as a people long before the coming of the Arabs, and that they had all the potential to develop into a nation of their own.[6]

According to internal party documents, Antun Sa'ada's party was officially constituted on 21 November 1934, but it only came to the attention of the French authorities a year later, in November 1935. It was then that the French *Sûreté Générale* discovered that a seemingly innocuous trading company, the Société Syrienne de Commerce, with offices in one of Beirut's main streets, was in fact the headquarters of a revolutionary political movement, which seemed to be preparing to overthrow the government. The discovery of the party by the government led to an attempt to suppress it. On 5 November 1935, Sa'ada was arrested with ten of his colleagues and sentenced early in January 1936 to six months in jail and a fine of 25 Lebanese pounds. A brief sentence was also passed on his principal lieutenant, Ni'mat Thabit, for violations of public order.

The trial attracted considerable publicity for the party. In court, Sa'ada was far from penitent: when his name was called out as Antoine Sa'ada he would give no reply until the Syriac 'Antun' had been substituted for the Gallic 'Antoine'. When charged with conspiracy against the state, he threw back at the prosecutor that it was the French who were the real conspirators, since they had signed the Sykes–Picot Agreement with Britain. Searches in the homes of party members uncovered what were said to be incriminating documents, including sketches and maps of the military aerodrome at Rayak and the sites of barracks and ammunition dumps in various parts of the country. The documents revealed that Antun Sa'ada was the supreme leader – or *Raïs* – of a semi-clandestine party of some five or six thousand members in Lebanon and Syria, divided into a great many sections and subsections. Only the chief of each subsection knew the identity of the members in the section immediately above him.

<hr />

6 Kamal Salibi, *A House of Many Mansions: The History of Lebanon Reconsidered*, London 1988, p. 132.

Sa'ada was assisted by a central committee of twelve 'counsellors', with titles such as counsellor of the interior, of finance, of war, and so forth. Under interrogation, the counsellor of war confessed that the party's programme foresaw the need to create a militia able to maintain order in the country once the Mandate had come to an end.[7] Party members were to be found in the big cities of the Levant – in Beirut, Tripoli, Damascus and Aleppo. But they were also to be found mainly among minorities in more remote regions – in Marj 'Ayun and the Matn, home to large Greek Orthodox populations; among the Druze in the Shuf; among the Alawites on the Syrian coast at Tartus and Safita; and in the region of Kura, south-east of Tripoli.

While its strict discipline, modelled on Fascism – with its brown shirts, rigid principles and leader worship – enabled the PPS to organise impressive parades, and to have a say on most occasions, it was nevertheless weakened by government repression, by the secession in 1937–38 of some of its prominent members, and by the frequent imprisonment of its leader. The mass of the population seemed indifferent to Sa'ada's esoteric doctrines, but may have been impressed by the party's organisation, which, at a time of acute economic crisis, was able to replace public services and provide a wide range of jobs (much as Hizballah was to do some decades later). From the very start, Sa'ada gave priority to the creation of a paramilitary organisation. Seized during searches were several documents, written in his own hand and dating back to 1935, which contained details about 'military affairs'.

Shortly after his release in 1936, Sa'ada was arrested a second time, when members of his party beat up two Lebanese journalists who had written critical articles about the movement. Nevertheless, a party decree dated 30 January 1936 named the *Raïs* as commander-in-chief of the party's troops, assisted by a war council. About a year later, on 21 February 1937, some four hundred party members paraded in a demonstration of strength at Bikfaya in Lebanon, only to be dispersed by gendarmes after a brief scuffle. In November of that year, Sa'ada set out on a propaganda tour of Syria and Lebanon to the rapturous applause of his followers. At Tartus on the Syrian coast, the road he took was lined by units of his militia, some on foot, others on horseback.

[7] Consul General G. T. Havard to Foreign Office, Beirut, 2 December 1935 (FO 371/19022).

Government pressure on the party increased when, in March 1936, Sa'ada petitioned the French high commissioner for a Syro-Lebanese union. He and some of his lieutenants were imprisoned for a few weeks, and an official investigation into the party's activities led to renewed persecution. This met with violent opposition by a membership which was growing rapidly, and which was by no means confined to Lebanese. Sa'ada was arrested a third time on 7 March 1937, but freed two months later – when the government of Khayr al-Din Ahdab sought, and apparently obtained, the support of his party for the government list in the elections of that year.

However, in June 1938, threatened again with arrest, Sa'ada thought it best to leave the country in something of a hurry, obtaining a visa for Cyprus, via Palestine, from the British consulate. The party issued a grandiloquent statement on 15 August 1938, explaining away their leader's hasty exit as being designed to bring the Syrian cause to the attention of the world community, and to organise overseas members into a body able to contribute to the party's work. The statement ended thus: 'Let us be ready for the day when our Leader will call us to the field of freedom and honour. Let our hearts accompany the national hero on his travels and uphold him at every moment with our thoughts and feelings.' After Sa'ada's departure, however, the party became dormant. In the autumn of 1939, its premises were occupied and its leaders arrested for being pro-German.

From Cyprus, Sa'ada went to Berlin, where he conferred with the PPS group in that city and where the Nazi authorities are believed to have given him a warm welcome. He then passed through Budapest and Berne, made radio broadcasts from both cities, before going on to Rome. From Italy, he took ship for Latin America towards the end of 1938. In Brazil in 1939, he issued a proclamation which was nothing less than a call to insurrection – and was recognised as such by the French authorities, as well as by the party faithful in Syria and Lebanon. In his proclamation, Sa'ada addressed himself to the 'men in brown uniform', a reference to his militia, and to the men of the 'red storm', his elite storm troops. 'The French government', he wrote, 'is at present studying a project for a new dismemberment of Syria, dividing the State of Syria into four regions to be governed by French advisers with the help of certain Syrians who are always ready to sell out the interests of the Syrian people'.

He insisted on the need

to oblige the nations and the powers to recognise our
nation and our state, our right to live among the nations
and the powerful . . . The world is moving rapidly towards
a final decision . . . Everyone must be ready when the signal
is given, and you will know what I mean by that . . . The
present circumstances of our nation will decide the outcome
of a struggle between life and death . . .

    Comrades, from this hour our great work begins.
The policy of patience and tolerance is at an end. Stand
ready at your posts![8]

The publication of this proclamation in the form of a tract was one of the charges brought on 3 October 1939 against forty-two persons (thirty-one Lebanese and eleven Syrians) by a French military tribunal, which, the following August, passed sentences on the accused varying from one year in prison to twenty years of hard labour and prohibition of residence in countries under the French Mandate. Antun Sa'ada was sentenced in absentia. His closest associate, Ni'mat Thabit, was given ten years. The PPS was now considered a serious threat to the Lebanese state. But the sentences did not cause the party to interrupt its activities altogether. A defiant tract was published on 28 August 1940: 'The authorities had thought that by arresting some leaders they would paralyse the action of the party and terrorise its members. But the party is alive in the heart of the Nation . . . The newly appointed Higher Executive Committee will . . . continue the struggle until the final victory.'

    After the outbreak of war, Sa'ada wrote an ardently pro-Nazi article on 11 November 1939, in the *Diario Syrio* of São Paulo, while a few days later, on 16 November, the whole paper was devoted to the party, with Sa'ada's picture appearing on the front page under a picture of an eagle. Sa'ada was to return to the Near East after the Second World War, when his movement was to have a baleful, and ultimately devastating, impact on Riad el-Solh's political career and life.

---

[8] MAE Fonds Beyrouth, série B, carton 5, dossier 61, 13 September 1940.

Sa'da's challengers: the *Phalanges* and the *Najjada*

In 1936–37, Sa'ada's movement was challenged in Lebanon by a number of rival youth movements, of which the most important were the *Phalanges libanaises* (the *Kata'ib* in Arabic), militant champions of Lebanese nationalism, and their Muslim counterparts, the *Najjada*. Led by Pierre Gemayel, a physically robust young Maronite, the *Phalanges* were adamantly opposed both to the Arab nationalism of Sunni leaders like Riad el-Solh, and to Sa'ada's pan-Syrianism – indeed, to anything that might threaten the entity of the Greater Lebanon that was forged by the French in 1920. The conservative Phalangist slogan was 'God, Family and Homeland', and its vigorous paramilitary organisation indicated that it was a good deal more than the athletics club it pretended to be.[9]

The *Najjada* (the Rescuers), originally a Muslim Boy Scout movement founded by Muhyi al-Din al-Nusuli, was far less effective or long-lived. Its headquarters were in the heart of Muslim Beirut, in the *Basta*, and its Arab nationalist colouring led to frequent clashes with the *Phalanges*. Pierre Gemayel, founder and leader of the *Phalanges*, and Husayn Saj'an, who was to head the *Najjada* in 1939, had both attended the Berlin Olympics of 1936. They were greatly taken with the order, discipline and manic nationalism of the Nazis.[10]

These movements were essentially youth protests against their elders. But they were also mutually competitive, and, with their uniforms, parades, salutes and cult of the leader, they were modelled on the youth movements of the Fascist and Nazi regimes of Italy and Germany.[11] Their appearance in Syria and Lebanon in 1934–37 suggests that they satisfied a certain psychological need of many young men at the time. Like their PPS opponents, the *Phalanges* and the *Najjada* recruited among the same pool of lower middle- and working-class youths, who, often unemployed and frustrated, were anxious for status and for any sort of work. It was they who were attracted by the squads of these paramilitary movements.

Some members, however, were drawn not so much to the parades and the uniforms, but to the ideas and political programmes of these movements, no doubt as a result of the spread of mass education

---

[9] Longrigg, *Syria and Lebanon*, p. 226.
[10] John P. Entelis, *Pluralism and Party Transformation in Lebanon: al-Kata'ib 1936–1970*, Leiden 1974, p. 46.
[11] Longrigg, *Syria and Lebanon*, p. 225.

between the world wars, and of an active, boisterous and often vociferous press. Recruits of this sort reflected the new political modernity of the 1930s, with its acute anxieties about how the Arab region might fare in a world threatened by war.[12] At any rate, they signified the entry into political life of a new generation, ready to break deliberately with the client networks which older notables had nourished to secure their political base. Indeed, these notables soon found that the younger movements had taken control of the street. There was, of course, no clear-cut transition from one form of political organisation to another. Much like the parliamentary blocs of Emile Eddé and Bishara al-Khoury, the new movements also benefited, among other things, from primary solidarities and client networks in specific quarters of the city.

Much the same political phenomenon could be observed in other Arab countries. This was the era of the multicoloured marchers: of the blue and green shirts in Egypt (the Blue Shirts, for example, were a nationalist youth brigade, particularly active in Cairo); of the grey and white shirts in Syria; the khaki shirts in Iraq; and Sa'ada's brown shirts in Lebanon. The Communist Party was at loggerheads with all these proto-Fascists, as it was also with all Catholic institutions and organisations.

Alarmed at the threat posed by these mushrooming movements to public order and the state's authority, President Eddé issued a decree on 18 November 1937 dissolving the 'coloured shirt' organisations and declaring illegal all the military-like formations that had sprung up over the previous two years. Only sporting clubs were allowed to continue in existence. Pierre Gemayel at once published a violent protest in the Beirut press, vehemently denying that the *Phalanges* intended to play any military role whatsoever. His movement's aim, he declared, was to root out 'anarchy' from the country. Its members were the 'elite' of Lebanese youth, inspired by patriotism of the most sincere kind. If the government wished to destroy this ideal, it would have to suppress 8,000 young men. His statement ended with the words, '*Comarades, à demain!*'

Indeed, the next day, as the British consul general reported to London, hundreds of *Phalanges* members suddenly appeared in Beirut's main square, resisting attempts to disperse them by the few policemen on duty at the time. In due course, reinforcements of police and gendarmerie arrived, as well as detachments of other 'coloured shirt' groups, some of them armed. A considerable amount of stone throwing and

[12] Méouchy, 'Le Pacte national', pp. 470, 473.

some firing ensued, and a riot developed which was not quelled until French military detachments arrived on the scene with machine guns.

By midday the square had been cleared and several arrests made. There were many wounded on both sides. One hapless Senegalese soldier under French command was killed by a ricochet. On government orders, no account of the riot was allowed to appear in the morning press the next day. Needless to say, the Phalangists continued to meet in secret and, like other movements, remained underground until Lebanon's independence in 1943.[13]

Syria's 'Iron Shirts'

In Syria, too, leaders of the National Bloc watched with interest the emergence of youth movements in Germany and Italy – both enemies of France that was colonising them – and attempted to transplant this model of discipline and esprit de corps to their own country. The 'Iron Shirts' (al-qumsan al-hadidiyya), the Bloc's paramilitary youth group, first appeared in Damascus on 8 March 1936, when the nationalists, once they had called off their successful General Strike, prepared to conduct treaty negotiations with France. In no time, branches sprang up all over Syria. By April, the Iron Shirts' programme had been formulated, with an emphasis on the struggle for independence, guided by 'sacrifice, discipline and devotion to the nation'. These Iron Shirts – trained in part by ex-Turkish officers – proved as attractive to young Syrians as the *Phalanges* were to Christian youth in Lebanon. Every Syrian city had its drilled and uniformed squads, who were in evidence, parading and saluting, on every public occasion. They were frequently in trouble with the local French-controlled police and with the French themselves. Their uniforms were iron-grey shirts and trousers, a belt, a black tie and the *sidora* cap that had been popularised by the Iraqi army. Their insignia was a torch-bearing hand and their salute the Fascists' raised arm. The threefold '*Heil*' of the Nazis was converted into a threefold '*Jihad*'. The Iron Shirts' objective was to act as the Bloc's instrument among the young, to attract support away from rival formations, and to mobilise a pool of recruits for a potential national army.

---

[13] Consul General Havard to Foreign Office, Beirut, 22 November 1937 (FO 371/20849).

On 29 September 1936, the Iron Shirts staged a 'victory' parade with which they greeted the Syrian delegation on its return to Damascus from the negotiations in Paris. They failed, however, to control the unruly crowd which accompanied the delegation to the *Sérail*. Present at the scene, a strait-laced British consul was scandalised to note that some of the Iron Shirts on parade were actually smoking cigarettes![14] By the end of 1936, the Executive Committee of the Iron Shirts claimed to have 15,000 recruits, including some 4,000 in Damascus alone. The patron of the Damascus branch was Fakhri al-Barudi, whose influence among the educated youth of Damascus was unrivalled and who dreamed of creating a national army, while effective leadership was in the hands of the Secretary-General Munir al-'Ajlani, a supporter and son-in-law (at that time) of the radical nationalist, Dr 'Abd al-Rahman al-Shahbandar. As in Lebanon, it was the thirst for employment which drew so many jobless youth into the Iron Shirts, no doubt in the hope that, if and when the cause triumphed, they would be given employment as gendarmes, policemen or government clerks of one sort or another.[15]

Writing about something else altogether, the historian Sir Lewis Namier nevertheless captured the conditions which are apt to produce authoritarian movements. He wrote that they arise 'amid the ruins of an inherited social and political structure, in the desolation of shattered loyalties – it is the desperate shift of communities broken from their moorings'. The members of such movements are 'disappointed, disillusioned men, uprooted and unbalanced, driven by half-conscious fears and gusts of passions, frantically seeking a new rallying point and new attachments. Their dreams and cravings projected into the void gather round some figure . . . it is the frenzy of the worshippers which imparts to him meaning and power'.[16]

Riad el-Solh's position on the scene

These, then, were some of the various parties, movements and paramilitary forces in Lebanon and Syria, with which a leading politician

[14] Acting Consul J. C. Ogden to Foreign Office, Damascus, 3 October 1936 (FO 371/20066).

[15] Khoury, *Syria and the French Mandate*, pp. 472 ff.; Longrigg, *Syria and Lebanon*, pp. 226–30.

[16] Sir Lewis Namier, in an essay on Napoleon III, 'The First Mountebank Dictator', in his *Vanished Supremacies*, London 1962, p. 73.

like Riad el-Solh would have to deal as he made his way to the front of the stage. In the ebb and flow of politics over the coming years, Riad was to make use of most of them at one time or another, although he was perhaps closest to the *Najjada*. He himself never formed a party or militia of his own. His political history, which stretched back to Ottoman times, his lifelong commitment to the Arab nationalist cause, and his belonging to an Arab generation for whom political parties in the modern sense were still largely unknown, or suspect, may have been the reason for this. The Syrian National Bloc, with which he was intimately associated, was not really a party, but more a collection of individualistic notables. Often at odds with each other, they frequently required Riad's patient mediation. In Lebanon, Bishara al-Khoury's Constitutional group and Emile Eddé's Unionist Bloc were also not parties in the modern sense, but merely gatherings of ambitious men around a leader who, they hoped, might eventually be able to put some political or commercial advantage their way.

Nevertheless, and no doubt influenced by his dealings with Léon Blum's Popular Front in Paris, and by his relations in Lebanon with the trades unions and the Communist Party, Riad considered forming a left-wing political grouping under his leadership, but he never did so. He was fortunate in having what was, in effect, his own private 'party' or think tank, staffed mainly by younger members of his family, many of whom were clever, dynamic, politically astute and organisationally gifted. Among these were his cousins, Taqi al-Din el-Solh – a future prime minister – and Kadhim el-Solh, later ambassador to Iraq, as well as these men's younger brothers. Together, they formed a closely knit, unconditionally loyal group. They brought Riad intelligence and gossip, and helped him draft his formal speeches. They spread his thought, offered advice, sang his praises or maligned his opponents in the press and in their own extensive circles of contacts.[17]

Kadhim el-Solh edited a newspaper, *al-Nidal al-Qawmi*, and ran an embryonic party of the same name. He, Taqi al-Din and other activists and intellectuals, such as Farid Zayn al-Din and Shawqi al-Dandashi, had, in 1935, formed an Arab Nationalist Party (*al-hizb al-qawmi al-'arabi*), which was little more than a discussion group. It was not unlike another nationalist gathering of the time, the League of National Action (*'usbat al-'amal al-qawmi*), formed in 1933 by

---

[17] Letter to the author from Professor Walid Khalidi, February 2007.

students and teachers at the American University of Beirut, such as Constantine Zurayq and Fu'ad Mufarrij. All these men and groups provided Riad el-Solh with an invaluable support network.

Although Riad had no militia or political party of his own, he did have a source of muscular power provided him by the *qabadayat*, the salty, neighbourhood strongmen. Riad knew who they were in every lane of Beirut, as he did in his home town of Sidon. He took great care to cultivate their friendship, massage their prickly egos and nurture their fierce loyalty through all manner of reciprocal services, both symbolic and material. At parliamentary elections – and especially at the crucial elections of 1943 – he was to use these *qabadayat* as his 'electoral keys' to muster votes. They not only served as important allies, but also, when necessary, as enforcers of his political authority. They were his buddies, who, if need be, could be counted on to serve as his bullies.[18] A study in 1943 by the Lebanese police identified eighty-one *qabadayat* in the city of Beirut: fifty-one were for Riad el-Solh; nine were for 'Abdallah al-Yafi; and seven were for Ayyub Thabit.[19] Such was Riad el-Solh's political environment on the eve of a world war, which was to throw the Middle East into the most bitter turmoil. But it was also to open the way for the independence, which had been so long struggled for and desired.

[18] Ibid.
[19] CADN, Inventaire 2, *Sûreté Générale*, carton 47, Information Beyrouth, 22 February 1943, quoted in Méouchy, 'Le Pacte national', p. 470, n. 23.

15 THE CHANGING FORTUNES OF WAR

Riad el-Solh's political career was to be profoundly influenced by the titanic struggle of the Western allies against Hitler. He was able to make a bid for power only after Britain had expelled the Germans and the Italians from the Middle East and defeated Vichy France in the Levant. When the Axis Powers were sweeping all before them, many Arabs jumped on the German bandwagon – like the Hajj Amin al-Husayni, who, embittered by Britain's unwavering support for the Zionists, had staked all on a German victory. Riad had the political sense not to follow suit. He believed in an Allied victory. But he must at times have wondered whether there was anything to be gained from the adamantly colonial Western Powers, who were evidently more concerned to protect their own Middle East interests than to satisfy the Arab wishes for national independence.

Despite his banking on the Allies, Riad's impatience with the French knew no bounds. Consistently refusing to accept the reality of Arab nationalism, they had deliberately, and over several decades, frustrated the legitimate political ambitions of the majority Sunni Muslim elite – of which Riad was a prominent member. They divided the Levant into mini-states and autonomous regions, carving out a Greater Lebanon for the benefit of their Maronite clients. This was France's major error. By giving the Maronites a dominant position in a strategically vital area, capable of serving as a base from which to control inner Syria, France incurred the implacable enmity of Sunni Muslims, while greatly setting back the chance of any meaningful Muslim–Maronite entente.

French schools and colleges had, since the nineteenth century, sought to play a leading role in the educational revival of both Syria and Egypt. But a movement to reclaim and revive the

Arabic language and Arab culture soon gathered pace, especially in Syria, and made France's pretension to cultural dominance an irksome imposition. The sophisticated and much-travelled Muslim families of Beirut and Damascus, who had been used to high office in the former Ottoman administration, were affronted at having to deal – on a daily basis – with mediocre, vulgar and often venal French officials, who had the arrogance to treat *them* with disdain. Riad el-Solh himself was a Francophile, very much at home in Paris; yet his personal and political relations with the overbearing bureaucracy of the French High Commission in Beirut became execrable nevertheless.

When the French crushed the Great Syrian Revolution of 1925–26, Riad had been one of the first nationalists to argue that the time had come for a change of strategy. Instead of resorting to arms – a futile and suicidal enterprise against the overwhelming military might of the French Empire – he argued that it was wiser to seek to persuade the French public that its government's colonial policies were profoundly mistaken. In a campaign of information and propaganda, he had expended great efforts in putting the Arab case to French parliamentarians and journalists. His efforts had seemed to bear fruit in 1936, when Léon Blum's Popular Front government agreed to negotiate treaties with Syria and Lebanon, which promised to set them on the road to independence. Riad had put his considerable knowledge of French affairs at the service of the Syrian delegation, and had joined in the popular euphoria once an agreement had been reached.

But when France refused to ratify these 1936 treaties, hope gave way to a bitter and turbulent mood. Riad and his friends in Syria's National Bloc (*al- kutla al-wataniyya*) were suddenly discredited. They were exposed to violent criticism from more extreme nationalists, in particular from Dr 'Abd al-Rahman al-Shahbandar, who had played a leading role in the 1925 revolt. The sense of failure was further sharpened when, in an act of political cynicism, France ceded Syria's north-western province of Alexandretta to the Turks in 1939, thereby amputating an important part of Syrian territory, without even bothering to consult the Syrians! Many nationalists, Riad among them, came to the hard conclusion that a war between European Powers might well be their only chance to throw off France's hated rule.

British and French Imperial Policy

Riad el-Solh was well aware that Britain and France were uneasy neighbours in the Middle East. The French made no secret of their conviction that the British were conspiring to evict them from Syria and build an Arab empire under British control, while the British were convinced that France delighted in stirring up anti-British trouble. Anglo-French rivalry was a fact of life, as every Arab politician knew. The question was how to put this rivalry to Arab advantage.

One of the reasons for the mutual suspicion of Britain and France lay in their different conceptions of imperial policy, as illustrated by their differing responses to nationalist pressure. Britain's overall strategy was to pretend to yield to nationalist demands, hoping that this would allow it to maintain order with a minimum of force in the territories under its control. It liked to show that it wished to reconcile Arab aspirations with its own strategic needs, although of course this could never be done smoothly. In Palestine, certainly, Britain's biased and catastrophic imperial policy set the stage for the terrible bloodletting that continues to our own day.

The French, in contrast, persisted in seeing Arab nationalism as an enemy to strike down – and as brutally as possible. They kept a large garrison in Syria in the fear that any concession there might encourage agitation in their North African territories, where they were intent on repressing the great nationalist movements, as they had done so savagely in Algeria. In the words of a self-satisfied (and disingenuous) British report, 'The British tried to transform mandates into alliances; the French seemed, at least, to be trying to transform them into colonies'.[1]

Britain's seemingly more flexible approach could claim some successes, at least for its own empire. The most notable of these were the treaties with Iraq of 30 June 1930 and with Egypt of 26 August 1936. The Iraq treaty provided for a twenty-five-year alliance, assigning two airbases to the RAF – one on the middle Euphrates, the other at Basra. It guaranteed Britain's military and transport facilities in times of war. It affirmed 'the permanent maintenance and protection

---

[1] Report by FRPS, 4 November 1940 (FO 371/27308). See also A. B. Gaunson, *The Anglo-French Clash in Lebanon and Syria, 1940–45*, New York 1987; and Aviel Roshwald, *Estranged Bedfellows: Britain and France in the Middle East during the Second World War*, Oxford 1990.

in all circumstances of the essential communication of His Britannic Majesty'. In return, Iraq was granted, not full sovereignty, but some considerable freedom of political and diplomatic action, both internal and external. Similarly, the Egyptian treaty established a perpetual alliance with Great Britain and made temporary provision for the stationing of British naval, military and air forces in Egypt for the defence of the Suez Canal.

In French eyes, Britain's policy of fostering 'independence' in Iraq and Egypt set a destabilising precedent for France's own presence in Syria. The French resented Britain's close and harmonious relations with the Emir 'Abdallah of Transjordan, a country which they saw as providing a base for subversive operations against their own rule in Syria.

Riad el-Solh was well aware of Britain's greater political, military and commercial power in the area – its control of Egypt, Palestine, Transjordan, Iraq and the Arabian Gulf – but it was France with which he had to deal in Lebanon and Syria. To his alarm, therefore, when war seemed imminent in 1939, France started to strengthen, rather than relax, its hold over the Levant, thus dealing a further blow to Syria's hopes for independence.

Weygand and the Army of the Levant

On 25 August 1939, General Maxime Weygand, who had been French high commissioner in Beirut in 1924, was brought urgently out of retirement in Brittany, in order to assume command of French forces in the eastern Mediterranean. He was given authority over the incumbent French High Commissioner Gabriel Puaux (who had been French ambassador in Vienna at the time of the *Anschluss*).[2]

Weygand was a small, spry, sharp-eyed man of 71, who, in spite of his advanced age, remained highly energetic. Reaching Beirut on 30 August via Marseilles, Tunis, Malta and Alexandria, he flew off to Cairo the very next day for a meeting with General Sir Archibald Wavell, commander-in-chief of British forces in the Middle East. Only a day later, on 1 September 1939, the Germans attacked Poland and war was declared.

---

[2] See Maxime Weygand, *Mémoires*, vol. III, *Rappelé au service*, Paris 1950; Henri de Wailly, *Syrie 1941: La guerre occultée, Vichystes contre Gaullistes*, Paris 2006, pp. 19 ff.

In this fevered atmosphere, Weygand's urgent task was to rebuild the Army of the Levant, which, ill-equipped and flabby from long years of routine existence, was in no fit state to fight. Most of its officers and NCOs – veterans of the First World War – were now too old for strenuous physical activity. Some had become so corpulent that they were unable even to buckle their service belts. They had come to the Levant to avoid barrack life in France, and had seen no military action since the crushing of the Great Syrian Revolution of 1925. Many of the French troops had been turned into cooks, grooms, drivers, secretaries and doormen, who were mainly good at adopting an insolent and racist manner in their dealings with the Syrians. Their wives, too, were particularly offensive. On paper, however, their numbers looked impressive: 1,686 officers and 40,000 men. A further 300 officers, only 50 of whom were French, commanded locally raised units of 15,000 men.[3]

This army was, by any reckoning, an eccentric multi-ethnic and multi-religious patchwork of colonial North African units, colonial Senegalese battalions and local Arab levies, the so-called *Troupes spéciales du Levant*. These consisted of Lebanese and Syrian recruits, mainly from minority peasant backgrounds. They included Alawites from the mountains above Latakia, as well as Christians of Assyro-Chaldean origin from the Euphrates region. The French had also formed a dozen cavalry squadrons of Circassians, Druze and Kurds, who, when in the field, were given a daily wage and food allowance, but who were expected to scrounge around for forage for their mounts.[4]

Made slothful by the clement weather and the easy living, the Frenchmen in command of this motley force took their duties lightly. They spent much of their time in cafés, playing cards, playing tennis or betting on horse races on Sundays. Their worn and antiquated military equipment contributed to the general air of debility. The French officers, sergeants and corporals were mostly volunteers who had sometimes had to wait two or three years for these soft and highly prized Levant postings. With tax-free pay, subsidised meals, free housing and health care, as well as numerous perks and allowances, a Frenchman could be at least twice as well-off living in Beirut, Aleppo or Deir ez-Zor as

---

[3] Maurice Albord, *L'Armée française et les états du Levant, 1936–1946*, Paris 2000, pp. 26–35.
[4] De Wailly, *Syrie 1941*, p. 25.

he would be in a garrison town in France. Such were the attractions of the Levant postings that the inclination was to stay on as long as possible, for a third, fourth or even a fifth tour of duty. Some men spent their entire military career in Syria and Lebanon, and were therefore inevitably wedded to the notion of 'direct rule' over the natives, since it served their own pockets before anything else. It was rare, however, for such men to bother to get to know an Arab family, let alone to consider learning any Arabic while en poste.

The widely held view in the French Army of the Levant at the time was that Syria and Lebanon were an integral part of the French Empire, to be defended against all-comers and at all costs. The underlying principle of the Mandate, with its declared mission of 'preparing' the locals for independence, struck many of them as a betrayal of their private interests, dolled up as France's 'civilising mission'. It was a period of profound stagnation, due to the lack of will or political imagination in Paris and the debased French representatives on the spot.[5] The French had, in fact, comfortably settled down between the wars to running a colonial-style regime in Syria and Lebanon, backed by military force.

Weygand's task was to turn these disparate and hopeless units of the Army of the Levant into an effective fighting force. Given the obstacles facing him, he managed to work wonders. Within six months, and with reinforcements and equipment summoned from France, he put together a force of 50,000 men, well structured, well equipped and reasonably well led, which he named the GFML – *Groupe des forces mobiles du Levant.*

All this was terrible news for Riad el-Solh and his nationalist colleagues. They were now compelled to lie low. Once France was at war with Germany, the French suspended the Levant constitutions indefinitely, and cracked down on all hint of political agitation. The police were placed under French military command, the press was heavily censored and limited to a single sheet a day. Listening to German and Italian radio broadcasts, to which many locals were addicted in defiance of their French oppressors, was banned on penalty of three months' to three years' imprisonment, and fines ranging from 20 to 200 Syrian pounds. Street lighting was almost entirely suppressed

---

[5] Raymond, 'La Syrie du Royaume Arabe à l'indépendance', p. 71.

and vehicles were permitted to use only subdued headlamps.[6] A military tribunal was set up to try opponents of French rule – of whom Riad was a prime suspect.

On 10 May 1940, Hitler launched his *Blitzkrieg* against Belgium and France, and, within days, the war was lost. On 17 May, Paul Reynaud, who had replaced Edouard Daladier as French prime minister in March, summoned General Weygand urgently back to Paris where, two days later, this hard-pressed man was given the impossible task of taking charge of an already collapsed situation. Dunkirk fell on 4 June and the Somme front a week later. On 14 June, Paris – which had been saved from wanton destruction by being declared an open city – was handed over to the Germans at a sombre ceremony at the Hôtel de Crillon on the Place de la Concorde. In less than a month, 70,000 French soldiers had been slaughtered in a vain attempt to check the German onslaught. On 22 June, France signed an armistice with Germany.

In 1939, Britain and France were still ruling over the two greatest empires of the world. Only a few months later, one of them was roundly defeated while the other seemed destined to suffer the same fate. These fast-moving and dramatic events strained the already doubtful loyalty of the Arabs towards their cruel French colonial masters. It was said at the time that when Syrians wished to speak favourably of Hitler, and bypass the French censor, they would refer to him as Abu Rashid. In Lebanon, he was known as Abu Sa'id.

The impact of the French defeat

The defeat of the French army – followed closely by Marshal Philippe Pétain's armistice – caused incredulity, consternation and grief in the French community of the Levant. Pétain, an aged First World War hero, had replaced Paul Reynaud as prime minister on 16 June. The armistice terms he managed to secure were not quite as humiliating as might have been expected. Even though France had surrendered to Germany, it could still retain its fleet and its empire. And although half of it was occupied, it could keep its flag, its administration, its political autonomy, its diplomatic representatives and its merchant shipping. No doubt, the relatively lenient armistice terms were a pointer that, in Hitler's mind

---

[6] Political report: Syria, Damascus, 28 May 1940 (FO 371/24591).

at least, this was a mere interim measure. He expected Britain to fall within weeks, when he would put his new European order in place.

In Lebanon, distraught Maronites prayed for the salvation of France in an atmosphere of deep mourning. Women even put away their jewellery. Some 14,000 summer visitors from Egypt and neighbouring countries scrambled to get home from the resorts of the Lebanese mountains. As sea communications were briefly interrupted, many had to go through Palestine by land. The child king of Iraq, disappointed at having to cut short his holidays, left for Baghdad on 8 September.[7] Attitudes towards France began to change, even among its former clients and most fervent supporters. Looking for a new protector to guarantee Lebanon's safety and independence, some Maronites turned to the Italians, others to the Germans. A handful even travelled to Ankara to confer with Franz von Papen, the influential German ambassador there.

Encouraged by this change in public attitudes, Arab nationalists began to renew their activities in the hope that liberation was at hand. Riad el-Solh organised political meetings to mobilise opposition to the French, whose presence in the Levant, after the German occupation of their home territory, seemed increasingly untenable. The local Muslim population was now inclined to pin its hopes on Germany, and even Riad must have been tempted to look in that direction.[8] Those Arab regimes that were under Britain's control were encouraged to perceive France's collapse as a golden opportunity to destroy the French Mandates once and for all. Prime Minister Nuri al-Sa'id of Iraq urged Britain to force France to grant Syria and Lebanon immediate independence, no doubt in the hope of bringing Syria into a Baghdad-led pan-Arab confederation. The Saudis expressed their fear of an Italo-Turkish partition of Syria, while their rival, the Emir 'Abdallah of Transjordan, fretted that the Saudis might exploit a power vacuum in Syria to enthrone a Saudi prince there.[9]

---

[7] Consul General Havard to Foreign Office, Beirut, 13 September 1939 (FO 371/23277).

[8] Raghid el-Solh, *Lebanon and Arabism*, pp. 113 ff., 116; Raymond, 'La Syrie du Royaume Arabe à l'indépendance', p. 77.

[9] Roshwald, *Estranged Bedfellows*, p. 16. Supporters of Ibn Sa'ud working for this cause were said to include Shaykh Yusuf Yasin in the Hijaz; Dr Midhat Shaykh al-Ard (Jamil Mardam's brother-in-law), who became Ibn Sa'ud's influential physician in the Hijaz; Khalid al-Hakim and Hussein al-'Uwayni, of the Beirut firm of Bahsali & 'Uwayni.

In France, the new Pétainist government, first at Bordeaux, then at Vichy, struggled to consolidate its authority over an empire decapitated by the collapse of the French homeland. In far-flung places like Indochina, Morocco and West Africa, French proconsuls wrestled with the painful dilemma of having to choose between Marshal Pétain's legitimacy, and the daring call of General Charles de Gaulle – broadcast over the BBC from London on 18 June 1940 – to repudiate the Franco-German armistice and continue the fight against Nazi Germany under his leadership. Most governors and senior officers chose to side with Pétain. General Georges Catroux was one of only three French generals who rallied to de Gaulle. Catroux had been governor-general of Indochina at the time of the fall of France. He had already served twice in the Middle East, as head of the French military mission to the Hijaz in 1919–20, and then as chief of intelligence in Syria and Lebanon in 1926–28. He was soon to reappear in the Levant.[10]

In Beirut, there was a moment of utter confusion in the French ranks. General de Gaulle was an unknown quantity. Few of the French in the Levant had actually heard his broadcast. To rally to him was to risk putting one's entire career at stake. The commander-in-chief of French forces, General Eugène-Désiré Mittelhauser, a large, choleric Alsatian, hesitated, as did the more timid High Commissioner Gabriel Puaux. In both, an instinct to fight on clashed with a deeply ingrained sense of obedience to political masters. Deeply shocked by the armistice, their first thought was to reject it, a rebellious attitude encouraged by younger officers, including the Chief of Staff Colonel Edgard de Larminat, who plotted to take the whole Army of the Levant over to the British in Palestine.

Then came orders from Bordeaux to stand firm. Mittelhauser clicked his heels and obeyed. He had Larminat arrested and sentenced to thirty days' detention in the Damascus citadel. But freed by junior officers, the colonel managed to flee to Palestine, along with many Spanish Republicans, Central European Jews, Hungarians, Portuguese, Czechs and others in France's Foreign Legion. A Polish brigade under the command of General Kopanski, haunted by the fear of being handed over to the Germans, was clemently allowed to cross the border with its vehicles and weapons intact.[11] In all, about 900 men,

---

[10] Vichy condemned him to death in absentia on 10 April 1941. Gaunson, *The Anglo-French Clash*, p. 14; de Wailly, *Syrie 1941*, pp. 469, n. 16, 470, n. 24.
[11] De Wailly, *Syrie 1941*, pp. 33 ff., 47.

including some officers, out of the 50,000 stationed in French Syria and Lebanon, managed to slip away to British Palestine. The rest remained loyal to Vichy. In any case, the Royal Navy's pre-emptive attack on the French fleet at Mers-el-Kebir (Oran) on 3 July 1940, little more than a week after the signing of the armistice – which killed 1,500 sailors and sank or damaged several French ships – prompted Vichy France to break off relations with Britain. This put an abrupt end to French forces trying to escape to Palestine. Many who had thought to join de Gaulle in England now had second thoughts.

Once Puaux and Mittelhauser bowed to Pétain's orders, they found themselves under enormous economic pressure, since Britain began to blockade French-held territories by land and by sea, causing considerable hardship in Syria and Lebanon. The price of medicines, coal and wood soared dramatically, while staple items such as sugar, rice, petrol and fuel oil became largely unobtainable. Syrian producers started to hoard flour, forcing many Beirut bakeries to close. The French made a point of openly blaming the British for these supply problems.[12] The nationalists, however, saw these same problems as a source of encouragement and defiance. Many felt that the moment had come to exploit the confusion in the ranks of the Army of the Levant, divided as it was between Pétainists and Gaullists, and to look to Britain for deliverance. But they were to be disappointed.

What Riad el-Solh and his friends failed to grasp was that Britain was not willing to intervene in the Levant – at least not yet. London was being ultra-cautious: it needed a stable Levant while it concentrated its forces elsewhere for the life-and-death struggle against Germany. While supporting de Gaulle's Free French movement, it wished to avoid a direct military clash with Vichy, as it simply did not have enough troops available for one. Britain's overriding concern was to ensure that the French in Beirut would not give the Axis a foothold in their territory. Indeed, seeking to placate Vichy so as to keep it neutral, the British gave assurances that 'We covet no inch of French territory for ourselves'. They went so far as to pledge that the French Empire would be restored once victory was achieved. In return, Vichy was asked to keep the Germans out of French overseas bases, especially in the Levant.[13]

---

[12] Raghid el-Solh, *Lebanon and Arabism*, p. 114.
[13] Roshwald, *Estranged Bedfellows*, p. 19.

Seen from London, the Levant States assumed an increasingly dangerous significance after June 1940, when Mussolini belatedly backed Hitler, thereby threatening the whole British position in the Mediterranean, the Middle East and East Africa. Archibald Wavell, the British commander-in-chief in the Middle East, had a mere 50,000 troops stationed locally, while Italian forces in Libya, Eritrea and Ethiopia, backed by a strong navy and air force, numbered nearly half a million. The Italian presence in Eritrea especially threatened Britain's vital Red Sea communications with India, Singapore and Australia.[14] Italy had seized Libya from the Ottoman Empire in 1911 and then had vigorously colonised it. By 1938, some 90,000 Italians had settled in Libya, concentrated in Tripoli, Benghazi and in the Gefara plain of Tripolitania. In 1935–36, Mussolini had also invaded Ethiopia, with the vainglorious aim of uniting it with Eritrea and Italian Somaliland to establish a 'neo-Roman' East African empire.[15]

The British Foreign Office warned the War Cabinet that if enemy forces secured facilities in the Levant, the British would be outflanked and the whole British position in the Middle East, including in Egypt and Arabia, would be at risk.[16] The chiefs of staff agreed with this assessment. 'We cannot tolerate the replacement of French authority [in Syria and Lebanon] by either German or Italian administration or influence', they wrote in a memorandum.

> *On military grounds it is of the utmost importance that Syria and Lebanon remain properly administered by an administration favourably disposed towards ourselves. Our policy must therefore be directed*
>
> - *towards bolstering up the French to keep their administration going;*
> - *to giving active assistance to the French should their administration degenerate;*
> - *to the supersession by British administration should that of the French collapse.*

[14] Gaunson, *The Anglo-French Clash*, pp. 4, 11.

[15] Wm. Roger Lewis, 'The Colonial Empires of the Late Nineteenth and Early Twentieth Centuries', in Lewis, *Ends of British Imperialism: The Scramble for Empire, Suez and Decolonization. Collected Essays*, London 2006, pp. 39–40.

[16] Foreign Office to War Cabinet, 9 May 1940 (FO 371/24591); Foreign Office to War Cabinet, 1 July 1940 (FO 371/24592).

The memorandum added that as the French had no lines of communication for the replenishment of warlike stores and supplies, and had no means of leaving Syria, they were dependent on the British – 'we should encourage this dependence'.[17]

Italy's entry into the war shocked the Syrians and Lebanese, who, almost without exception, resented the Italians for their brutal conquest and colonisation of Libya. The war was now on their doorstep. The need for stricter air-raid precautions became obvious. Lighting restrictions were tightened and trenches appeared in public gardens and on any spare ground. A British consular official in Damascus noted with wry amusement that 'the French Delegate and his staff descended to the trench which had been dug for them on an adjoining piece of ground and spent an unpleasant half-hour in the blazing sun to the accompaniment of odours which left no doubt as to the use to which the trench had been put during the previous night'.[18]

Since British policy was to prop up the local Vichy regime, relations between the British and their French counterparts in the Levant remained reasonably good. Consul General Godfrey Havard reported to London on 14 July 1940 that 'my relations with the authorities are still friendly and, whilst sometimes obstructive and always suspicious of British intrigue in Syria, the French will probably continue to do what they can to maintain an atmosphere of cooperation so as long as they have hope of economic assistance from His Majesty's Government'. Two weeks later, he described a 'frank and cordial' discussion with High Commissioner Puaux.

> *Whilst he left me in no doubt as to his personal sentiments which he expressed frankly in words – 'Every true Frenchman can but hope for a British victory' – he was equally frank in stating that he would submit to all orders from Vichy. At the same time he gave me to understand that he would seek from Vichy as few instructions as possible in the hope that he would be left alone to carry on administration of these territories as unobtrusively as possible.*[19]

---

[17] Chiefs of Staff Committee to War Cabinet, 22 July 1940 (FO 371/24592).
[18] 21 June 1940 (FO 371/24591).
[19] Consul General Godfrey Havard to Foreign Office and War Cabinet (FO 371/24593).

Apart from the blockade – which the British eased from time to time – the war brought few immediate changes. Trains from Palestine to Iraq crossed the French-mandated territories, and British consulates in Damascus and Beirut remained open, as did the French consulate in Jerusalem. This British policy aroused the furious impatience of General de Gaulle, who was itching to expel Vichy and establish his Free French movement in the Levant.

It was also incomprehensible and profoundly disappointing to Riad el-Solh and the nationalists. As they saw it, Vichy was collaborating with Germany – a power with which Britain was at war. Yet in Beirut and Damascus, British and Vichy officials were, inexplicably, on amicable terms! Nationalists who had hoped for liberation were confused and frustrated by the continued solidarity of these two imperial powers.

The Axis propaganda war

Although Riad el-Solh met several prominent German visitors to the Levant in the late 1930s and in the early years of war, he was careful never to commit himself to the Axis cause. As his formative years had been spent in Istanbul and Geneva, his instincts were democratic and his political education both Ottoman and French. He found most aspects of Hitler's regime utterly repellent: the cult of the leader, the 'Aryan' racism, the aggressive militarism, the brutal crushing of all dissent. He knew, however, that if Germany were to win the war, he would have to be prepared to deal with it. But it was not a prospect that he relished. In any event, Germany's interest in the Arab world seemed to him at best half-hearted. Indeed, Hitler's attention was focused primarily on Central and Eastern Europe. He did not wish either to challenge Britain's imperial interests in the Arab world, or to antagonise Mussolini and disturb his grandiose regional ambitions. The British, however, always anxious to protect their vital Middle East assets – oil, the Suez Canal and imperial communications to India and the Far East – kept a sharp eye on German activities in the area.

In December 1937, a visit to Syria by Baron Baldur von Schirach, a Nazi Youth leader, had been followed by that of other German propaganda agents. In June 1938, Herr Walter Beck, a senior German official, had selected some seventy Syrians for education in Germany, with the German government paying the full cost of their board, lodging and fares. In December 1938, Consul Gilbert Mackereth reported that the German Legation in Baghdad had become the directing centre for German political activity in Syria, Lebanon, Palestine, Transjordan and Iraq.[20] In Damascus, a centre of German propaganda was the *Nadi al-'arabi*, or the Arab Club, whose president, Dr Muhammad Sa'id Fattah al-Imam, was known as a Germanophile, in constant touch with the German consul general in Beirut. The British continued to puzzle over the origin of his ample funds. When Baron von Flugel, a German resident in Beirut, arrived in Damascus with Princess Hohenlohe on 19 January 1939, Dr Fattah al-Imam acted as their guide.

Such German manoeuvres had begun to alarm the French, who feared that Hitler might be planning to foment trouble in Syria and Lebanon. On the outbreak of war, the Arab Club was closed down and, on 3 September 1939, members of the local German community – businessmen, archaeologists, as well as outright spies – were interned. A number of Germans were also expelled and the residence permits of others were not renewed.[21] But following Marshal Pétain's armistice of June 1940, the Germans were let out and immediately resumed their activities. An Italian Disarmament Commission under General Giorgis arrived in Lebanon on 28 August to monitor the demobilisation of French forces, account for their equipment and weapons and de-sequester Italian and German properties. A gossip related that when the Italian general arrived at Rayak aerodrome, he offered his hand to the French receiving officer – who refused it. 'You are ungracious to your conqueror,' the Italian insisted, whereupon the Frenchman retorted, 'I'm sorry, I didn't realise you were German.'[22] Faced with hostility and contempt from the French as well as from the local population, the Italians soon gave up their heel clicking, Fascist salutes and elaborate uniforms, choosing instead to appear more anonymously in civilian clothes.

In February 1941, the Italian army was broken and driven out of Cyrenaica (Libya) by Wavell. But the Germans soon lent a hand to the Italians, sending Rommel's mechanised contingent to Libya. When

[20] Consul Gilbert Mackereth to Foreign Office, Damascus, 1 December 1938 (FO 371/21914).
[21] Political Report: Syria, Damascus, 28 January 1939 (FO 371/23276).
[22] Beirut Weekly Appreciation, 10 September 1940 (FO 371/24595).

London ordered Wavell to stop the British offensive, and send an expeditionary force to Greece instead, Rommel seized his opportunity. Turning an armoured reconnaissance into an audacious assault, he managed to drive the British out of Libya. By mid-April, only Tobruk still held.[23]

Once a German liaison mission was attached to the Italian Commission in Beirut, German influence quickly outstripped that of the Italians. Its first organiser was Roland Eilander, a well-known Beirut-born German, who had links with a number of prominent Lebanese families. Then Rudolf Roser, a German intelligence officer, arrived in September 1940. The French alleged, somewhat improbably, that he controlled a network of 1,500 agents from his room at the Hôtel Metropole. A little while later, Major Van Prat and three German officers travelled to Abu Kamal, a small town in Syria opposite Iraq on the Euphrates, to study the situation on the Iraqi border. The British and French started to suspect that the Axis Powers were preparing to open a new front against the Allies.

This suspicion was confirmed by a month-long visit to the Levant by Herr Werner Otto von Hentig, head of Section VII of the German Foreign Ministry, which was responsible for a vast area extending from Turkey to India.[24] He was considered the best oriental expert in the German service, having served in Peking, Tehran and Istanbul. In the First World War, he had been sent by the German Foreign Ministry to stir up Central Asian tribes against the British.

Von Hentig arrived in Beirut from Turkey on 15 January 1941, armed with a visa given him by Vichy for a 'political and cultural' mission. The British were persuaded that his real aims were to make contact with the nationalists; spy out the general political situation, including the state of local Anglo-French relations; and start an anti-British propaganda campaign. It was, no doubt, with this in mind that von Hentig approached Riad el-Solh, with whom he had several long conversations. He also saw 'Umar Bayhum, 'Umar Da'uq and 'Adil Arslan. To all of them he preached the advent of a German era. If Germany won the war, he promised, it would grant independence to all the Arab countries. But if Britain won the war, she would give southern Syria to the Zionists and northern Syria to the Turks. With

23 Gaunson, *The Anglo-French Clash*, p. 12.
24 Werner Otto von Hentig, *Mein Leben. Ein Dienstreise*, Göttingen, 1962; de Wailly, *Syrie 1941*, p. 469, n. 9.

such a message, he set about rallying opinion against Britain. At the Hôtel Metropole on 25 January 1941, he organised a showing of *Sieg im Westen* (Victory in the West), a film which graphically portrayed France's defeat, to rally opinion against the French.

His visit aroused considerable excitement and undoubtedly increased sympathy for Germany. This was probably the high point of German influence on the nationalists. Just as the Normandy Hotel was considered the headquarters of the Italian Commission, so the Hôtel Metropole now became, in the alarmist words of the British consul, 'a notorious German centre'. The British suddenly found themselves marginalised. Vichy ordered the British consulate to leave Beirut for the outlying village of Aley, where it was kept under close surveillance and denied diplomatic bag facilities.[25]

Von Hentig spent 26–30 January in Damascus, where he met Shukri al-Quwatli, Nabih al-'Azma, Adib Khayr and other nationalists. He also met a number of Syrian Germanophiles. Prominent among them was Sa'di Kailani, a nobleman of Afghan origin, who was married to a German woman and who, like von Hentig himself, had been sent between the wars to foment trouble among the tribes of Waziristan in north-western India, until the British paid him off to leave the area.[26]

Accompanied by Rudolf Roser, von Hentig then set out on a number of journeys through Syria, where he made a point of meeting tribal leaders, religious dignitaries and other notables. In discussing the country's future, he regularly expressed the view that after the war, Germany would unite the various Arab states (excepting Saudi Arabia) into a confederation under German influence. Alexandretta was to be returned to Syria and the Zionists expelled from Palestine. In a hotel register in Palmyra he described himself as the *Gauleiter* of the Near East (*Gauleiter* bring a Nazi Party title for the political boss of a region). A Syrian tailor was even commissioned to make large numbers of Nazi flags, apparently for imminent use.[27]

Despite the 'rosy' future which von Hentig painted for the Arabs, there is no evidence that Riad el-Solh or Shukri al-Quwatli ever strayed beyond careful neutrality in their discussions with him. Quwatli was deeply disturbed by the fact that the German was always

[25] Consulate General (Aley), Beirut Appreciation, 1–12 January 1941 (FO 371/27327).

[26] Roshwald, *Estranged Bedfellows*, p. 51.

[27] Consulate General (Aley), Beirut Appreciation, 1–14 March 1941 (FO 371/27327).

accompanied by the conspiratorial figure of Sa'di Kailani, who always did his best to discredit the National Bloc. Under Kailani's influence, von Hentig was quoted as saying that the only Arab leader in whom the Germans had any faith was the Hajj Amin al-Husayni. Riad el-Solh was courted by von Hentig but did not succumb. Indeed, at the time of von Hentig's visit, he thought it best to make overtures to the British, who were feeling the German pressure.

That February, the British consulate general in Lebanon reported to London that

> *some prominent Lebanese Arab Nationalists like Riad el-Solh and 'Adil Arslan think that His Majesty's Government should make some declaration touching the independence of certain Arab states like Syria and the Lebanon after the war. The silence observed by HMG in this connection leads them to believe that HMG are indifferent to Arab aspirations. Riad el-Solh . . . deplores any such indifference on the part of HMG towards the future of the Arabs, as it will only tend to make German blandishments to the Arabs more acceptable.*[28]

Von Hentig left for Ankara on 13 February, doubtless to report to Ambassador von Papen on the results of his visit.[29]

Beirut intrigues

While the Germans were making the running in the Levant, General Charles de Gaulle was pondering how to seize the initiative in the mandated territories, which he wanted at all costs to retain for France. Always suspicious of British intentions, he decided to send General Georges Catroux, his representative in the Middle East, to defend French interests on the spot. Anxious to evade the attention of the Vichy representative accredited to Egypt, Catroux landed in Cairo on 27 September 1940, in the guise of a Monsieur Chartier, a French-speaking Canadian businessman. His ambitious plan was to

---

[28] Consulate General (Aley), 14 February 1941 (FO 371/27327).
[29] Beirut Appreciation, 28 January – 3 February 1941 (FO 371/27327).

rally the Army of the Levant, topple the Vichy administration in Syria and Lebanon, and bring the mandated territories over to de Gaulle by means of an armed coup. He believed the Arab inhabitants could be won over by a promise of independence. All he needed was a little British support.

British policy, however, remained ambivalent. London would have welcomed a Free French coup which restored French forces to the Allies, but it nevertheless feared that if Vichy was weakened in the Levant, internal security would collapse. British forces were simply not available to deal with such an outcome. Britain was also aware that Arab aspirations for independence would have to be met, however nominally, if they were to be weaned away from the Germans. These contradictory British objectives pleased no one. The Gaullists cried perfidy while Vichy was darkly suspicious, seeing Britain's patronage of Arab aspirations as a plot to manoeuvre France out of the Levant. In turn, Riad el-Solh and the nationalists were dismayed by Britain's reluctance to challenge the status quo.

However, the changing fortunes of war brought about a vast swing in public opinion. The success of the Royal Air Force in the Battle of Britain, the postponement of Operation Sealion (the planned German sea and airborne invasion of the British Isles), the revolt against Vichy in some French Central African colonies, as well as innumerable letters from France describing the deplorable state of affairs under German occupation, all contributed to a striking change of sentiment towards Britain among French officers and officials. Britain's will and ability to resist aroused admiration and excitement, and led to a surge of support for de Gaulle. Among Lebanese and Syrians, opinion also moved in favour of the British – with the exception of some Maronites who had made advances to the Italians, and some Muslims who had pinned their hopes on Germany, largely because they were outraged by Britain's support for the Zionists in Palestine.

Beirut started to buzz with rumours of an imminent coup. To improve its prospects, the British hastened the repatriation to France of as many French reservists as possible.[30] Alarmed at the spreading dissidence, Vichy sent Colonel Bourget to the Levant with full powers to rid the country of Gaullist influences. Shortly after his arrival,

---

[30] Beirut Weekly Appreciation, Aley, 10 September 1940 (FO 371/24595); and Beirut Weekly Appreciation, Aley, 17 September 1940 (FO 371/24595).

Bourget – who had been General Weygand's chief of staff – spread instant panic in the French community by decreeing that all French officers who were known to have mistresses would be tried by a disciplinary court, whether they were married or unmarried. Among the victims of his more political interrogations was Madame Cointet, wife of the assistant French director of education, who was thrown into prison with prostitutes and common criminals, because he suspected her of helping a demobilised French aviator, Captain Bonafé, to escape over the border to Palestine. She was believed to have taken the captain to the frontier in her own car, on the pretence of a fictitious shooting expedition. One way or another, Colonel Bourget's Gestapo methods drove the Free French movement underground. In an attempt to protect Gaullist sympathisers, the British warned the French High Commission that safe-conducts would not be given to French ships if any persons were sent to France, other than soldiers for demobilisation.[31]

But the changing fortunes of war intervened again. The progress of the Italians in the Western Desert disconcerted the local French community and led to a loss of confidence in Britain, as well as a surge of sympathy for Vichy. In Beirut and Damascus, Marshal Pétain's portrait began to reappear in offices and shop windows. Throughout these uncertain times, Riad el-Solh held anxious meetings with his supporters and with neighbourhood strongmen, to brief them on political developments and instruct them on what line to adopt.

Gaullists rejoiced when Vichy axed Monsieur Colombani, the head of the *Sûreté Générale* in Beirut, a brutal and treacherous French Corsican official. Riad el-Solh and the nationalists rejoiced as well, as he had been particularly assiduous in harassing them. Colombani had been offered a bribe of a million francs by an over-zealous emissary from the Gaullist Committee in Cairo to turn a blind eye to General Catroux's preparations for a coup. But, true to his character, Colombani had betrayed the movement in the hope of even greater reward.

Colombani's background was unsavoury. He had been involved in the Stavisky scandal of 1934 – the sordid case of a notorious embezzler, Alexandre Stavisky who, after peddling millions of francs' worth of dud bonds, was found dead. Jean Chiappe, the fanatically right-wing police prefect of Paris at the time, was suspected of having ordered his killing to protect influential people. The scandal brought down the

---

[31] Beirut Weekly Appreciation, Aley, 1 October 1940 (FO 371/24595).

government. One of the first acts of the new Prime Minister Edouard Daladier was to sack Chiappe. But Chiappe's career was revived when Vichy sent him as high commissioner to Beirut to replace the vacillating Gabriel Puaux. Colombani, however, was not at all anxious to be reunited with Chiappe,[32] and was spared that ordeal when, on its way to the Middle East, the latter's aircraft was shot down by a British fighter.[33]

Colombani ran amok after his dismissal and, in the course of three days, managed to get himself beaten up by French officials whom he had sought to try for treachery. His wife – colourfully described in a British consular report as 'a massive product of the Istanbul underworld' – was assaulted by one of the High Commission typists. The family was due to leave for France by ship, but Colombani refused to embark unless given written assurance from the British that he would not be captured en route. London agreed on the grounds that Colombani in France would be less of a nuisance than on the loose in Syria. The British had come to the conclusion that he was an accredited Italian agent. Riad el-Solh was hugely relieved by Colombani's departure, as word had reached him that the Corsican had been planning to arrest him.[34]

The British watched the evolving situation with considerable nervousness. Sir John Shuckburgh chaired a committee which, on 18 October 1940, outlined a number of options for the War Cabinet:

(a) *If General Catroux achieves a successful coup d'état, the question of policy will be greatly simplified, and we need probably only concern ourselves with the attitude of the new French Administration to Arab aspirations in Syria. On this point, General de Gaulle's attention has already been drawn to the importance of adopting a conciliatory attitude towards Arab nationalist aspirations . . .*

(b) *If, however, General Catroux advises that any attempt at a coup d'état should be abandoned or indefinitely postponed, or if a coup d'état is attempted and fails, it will be necessary to reconsider our whole attitude towards the*

---

[32] Beirut Weekly Appreciation, Aley, 28 November 1940 (FO 371/27327).
[33] Beirut Appreciation for period 28 November – 10 December 1940, Aley, 11 December 1940 (FO 371/27327).
[34] Interview with Alia el-Solh, Monte Carlo, 4 October 2004.

> *French Administration in Syria. It will be for consideration whether we should adopt an aggressive policy perhaps even involving the occupation of Syria, with or without Turkish cooperation, or whether we should maintain the present policy either intensifying or relaxing economic pressure. The problem clearly involves military considerations of the first importance.*[35]

The Committee decided that it would be unwise to stir up Arab disaffection against the French, unless it was possible to support such action by military force. For the time being, economic pressure on Syria would continue, but care would be taken not to force the French authorities into active hostility. Trade across the Palestine frontier would be restricted, but not prevented altogether.

In December 1940, General Henri-Fernand Dentz, the commander-in-chief of French forces in the Levant, was appointed high commissioner as well. He had been head of intelligence (the *Service des renseignements*) in Syria and Lebanon in 1924, when his misreading of Druze sentiment and his poor advice to General Sarrail had helped trigger the Great Syrian Revolution of 1925–26. In 1940, it was Dentz who had been chosen to hand Paris over to the Germans at the Hôtel de Crillon. Catroux had tried to win him over to the Allied cause, but Dentz was a confirmed Pétainist and would not budge. The British considered him an honest, if blinkered, soldier, who blindly obeyed Vichy's orders. On his arrival in Beirut, Dentz told his officers: 'Put it into your heads that what you are defending here is not Syria, but North Africa'. He was convinced that if Vichy failed to defend the Levant against the British, the Germans would invade French North Africa and the 'free zone' in France itself.[36]

Then came yet another swing in the rollercoaster of public opinion, as a result of British military successes in Egypt. All classes of the population in Syria and Lebanon now rallied to the Allies once more. Some amusement was caused in Beirut by young newspaper sellers who trumpeted the taking of 20,000 Italian prisoners with the cry of *Inkasar Macaroni!* (Macaroni is defeated!).[37]

---

[35] Official Committee on Questions Concerning the Middle East, 18 October 1940 (FO 371/24594).
[36] De Wailly, *Syrie 1941*, p. 73.
[37] Beirut Appreciation, 11 December – 20 December 1940 (FO 371/27327).

The killing of Dr Shahbandar

Riad el-Solh and his nationalist friends in Syria were then thrown into violent disarray by a political murder in Damascus which was to reshuffle the cards in the nationalist camp. Dr ‘Abd al-Rahman al-Shahbandar was assassinated on 6 July 1940 in murky circumstances. He had been a key figure in the Great Syrian Revolution of 1925–26, when his newly formed People's Party had linked up with Druze chieftains in their violent revolt against the French – who had never forgiven him.

He had also incurred the anger of Jamil Mardam, Sa‘dallah al-Jabiri and the *kutla al-wataniyya* as a whole, by his relentless campaign of sabotage against the 1936 treaty, which the Bloc had negotiated with France. He had continued acidly to denounce it as inadequate, even treacherous. When, having been amnestied by the French, the doctor returned briefly to Syria in May–June 1937, the nationalists tried to placate him by offering him the presidency of the Chamber, and conferring on him the title of 'Sole Leader' at a ceremony at the Damascus Municipality. But Shahbandar had far wider ambitions. He believed he could rally the whole of Syria around his person. Back in Cairo, he resumed his sniping at the nationalists, and they responded in kind, accusing him of trying to rob them of the fruits of their long struggle for independence from the French.

As an atheist, a self-regarding and Western-educated physician and outspoken political personality, Shahbandar was admired by his many devoted followers. Born in Damascus in 1879, he had graduated as a doctor of medicine from the American University of Beirut and had spent the First World War in Egypt. As a fervent enemy of the French Mandate, he was repeatedly sentenced by French military courts, first to death, then to hard labour, and was held for a while in a fortress on the island of Arwad off the Syrian coast, only to be pardoned afterwards. This allowed him to resume his political activities. Condemned to death once again, he fled to Cairo, where he became a member of Prince Michel Lutfallah's Syro-Palestinian Committee, and where, between 1926 and 1937, he ran a successful medical clinic, which earned him a considerable fortune.

In July 1938, Dr Shahbandar wound up his affairs in Cairo and returned permanently to Syria. But the nationalist leaders blocked him in the mountain village of Bludan. Apparently, some of them spent large sums to persuade the inhabitants of the feisty Midan from welcoming him in their quarter. Some of his followers were arrested and newspapers favourable to him were closed down. He responded from Bludan with a violent diatribe against Jamil Mardam personally, who was his main political rival.[38] It was not until October that Shahbandar managed to overcome the *kutla*'s obstacles and finally enter Damascus.

Quite apart from the onslaught it faced from Shahbandar, the *kutla* had become fractured by internal disagreements. Jamil Mardam faced a challenge from Shukri al-Quwatli, whose *Istiqlal* Party was attempting to reform the *kutla* from the inside. There was tension between the members from Damascus and those from Aleppo. Two prominent *kutla* members from Aleppo, Dr 'Abd al-Rahman al-Kayyali and Sa'dallah al-Jabiri – the latter, Riad's old friend and the uncle of his wife – had lost general esteem for having failed to prevent France from ceding the sanjak of Alexandretta to Turkey. The public feared that, in the event of further pressure from Turkey and its pro-German officer corps, France might cede still more Syrian territory, which their ineffective leaders might once again be unable to prevent.

The *kutla* government fell from office in March 1939, sealing the fate of the treaties. High Commissioner Puaux then dissolved parliament, clamped down on the nationalists, and installed a Council of Directors headed by Bahij al-Khatib, a Syrian official of Lebanese origin who was opposed to the *kutla*. The French suspected Shahbandar of having had close ties with the British, to the point that they considered him to be Britain's man in Syria. He was also a friend of the Hashemites and had gone to great lengths to secure British support for a confederation of Syria, Lebanon, Transjordan and Palestine under the rule of the Emir 'Abdallah. In June 1939, he had led a large delegation to Amman and, in a toast to the emir, had declared unilaterally that 'Syrians extend to the Emir the allegiance which in the past they extended to King Husayn and then to King Faysal',[39] thus crossing a red line as far as the French were concerned.

By the time France capitulated to Germany in June 1940, Dr Shahbandar had outstripped his nationalist rivals because of such manoeuvring and was considered by the British to be the leading political figure in Syria. His murder, therefore, provoked intense

---

[38] MAE, Fonds Mandat Liban/Syrie, Série Beyrouth, 3e version, no. 23/271, Service des renseignements, Damascus Bureau, 24 November 1938.

[39] MAE, Fonds Mandat Liban/Syrie, Série Beyrouth, 3e version, no. 23/271.

emotion and feverish speculation about who might lie behind it. Pro-Shahbandar opinion in Damascus sought to pin the blame on Jamil Mardam himself. Others believed that certain Iraqi personalities, or even the Hajj Amin al-Husayni, may have been implicated in the murder. The British resident in Amman reported to the Foreign Office that the money for the assassination may have been provided by the Iraq government and forwarded to Damascus through 'Adil al-'Azma, the head of the Palestine Defence Committee in Syria.[40] By the end of July, the Syrian police had charged five persons, one of whom, 'Asim al-Na'ili, had been Mardam's secretary. Shahbandar's family in Cairo offered a reward for any information. The old Druze warrior, Sultan Pasha al-Atrash, led a delegation to Damascus to pay homage to Shahbandar, in loyal memory of the ties they had forged during the 1925 revolt.

Dr Shahbandar's widow arrived in Damascus from Egypt to attend memorial celebrations on 17 August. For his part, Khaled al-'Azm, a wealthy Syrian politician with ambitions to rule, who was utterly opposed to the *kutla*, took to spreading the rumour that the nationalists had killed Shahbandar.[41] But 'Izzat Qabalan, Shahbandar's cousin and former aide, told the British consul in Damascus on 17 October that the plot to murder Dr Shahbandar had been hatched in the Iraqi consulate in Damascus at the time of a visit by the Iraqi premier, Nuri al-Sa'id.[42]

Who was responsible for Shahbandar's murder? Philip S. Khoury, the leading historian of the French Mandate, has speculated that the killers might well have been French intelligence agents sympathetic to Vichy, who wanted to eliminate a man who was both an extreme nationalist and a suspected British agent; Italian agents for much the same reasons; the Mufti, who wanted to block the Emir 'Abdallah's bid for a Syrian throne; Iraqi agents who also wanted to

---

[40] British Resident in Amman to Foreign Office, 17 August 1940 (FO 371/24594).

[41] Khaled al-'Azm, *Mudhakkarat*, 3 vols, Beirut 1973, vol. I, p. 158; British Consul Gardner to Foreign Office, Damascus, 14 August 1940 (FO 371/24593).

[42] Members of the Shahbandarist party were as follows: the acting president was Nasuh Babil, editor of *al-Ayyam*, while leading members were Darwish al-Ajlani (a wealthy Damascene), Fawzi and Nasib al-Bakri (who resigned from the *kutla* after Shahbandar's murder), Munir al-Mahayri (Shahbandar's nephew), 'Izzat Qabalan (his cousin and former aide), Dr 'Abd al-Qadir Zahra (a well-known doctor in Damascus) Rashid Baqdunis, Shafiq Diab, and various members of the Atrash family, including Sultan, Zayd and 'Abd al-Ghaffar. Political Report: Syria, Damascus, 21 October 1940 (FO 371/24591).

thwart 'Abdallah; or, lastly, the leaders of the *kutla* who were engaged in a power struggle with Shahbandar.[43]

The Damascus newspapers of 17 October 1940 published a list of the suspected murderers and their accomplices. The list included Ahmad 'Assassa, who was charged with premeditated murder, as well as Shaykh Saleh Ma'tuq, Ahmad Tarabishi, 'Izzat Shamma, 'Asim al-Na'ili, Fawzi Qabbani – and even the three *kutla* leaders, Jamil Mardam, Lutfi al-Haffar and Sa'dallah al-Jabiri! These three eminent gentlemen were forced to flee to Iraq on 18 October as a result of this damaging smear, apparently tipped off that charges were about to be brought against them in the French-controlled courts.

Baghdad was a centre of Arab nationalist agitation, but it was also a haven for men who, by 1939–40, no longer felt safe in French-occupied Syria or Lebanon. The Mufti of Jerusalem had made a dramatic escape from Lebanon to Iraq in October 1939, once he became aware that the British were pressing the French to have him arrested. The veteran freedom fighter Fawzi al-Qawuqji was also in Baghdad, together with other Palestinians close to the Mufti. Riad's cousin, Kadhim el-Solh, had fled to Baghdad from Lebanon, as had Farid Zayn al-Din from Syria. They were joined there by the three *kutla* leaders.[44] Shahbandar's supporters were certain that French officials had been involved in the murder plot. They also chose to believe that the French had allowed Mardam and the others to escape, as it suited them to be rid of these three important nationalist leaders.

Although Shahbandar had been assassinated in June 1940, the trial of the suspected murderers did not begin until 9 December. It ended on 7 January 1941 after several adjournments (for the purpose of consulting the French mandatory power). Presided over by a Frenchman, the court conducted its proceedings in an atmosphere of great tension. No appeal was allowed against its judgements. To general surprise, the public prosecutor displayed a pronounced bias in favour of 'Asim al-Na'ili, Jamil Mardam's secretary, although rumours had spread that he was the intermediary between the nationalist leaders and the actual killers. Indeed, at the last moment, charges against 'Asim al-Na'ili

---

[43] Khoury, *Syria and the French Mandate*, pp. 588 ff. See also Beirut Weekly Appreciation, Aley, 22 October 1940 (FO 371/24595); Beirut Weekly Appreciation for the period 28 November – 10 December 1940, Aley, 11 December 1940 (FO 371/27327).

[44] Raghid el-Solh, *Lebanon and Arabism*, p. 111.

and the three nationalist leaders were dropped altogether. A British consular official reported that the Prosecutor's indictment, in which he withdrew charges against the nationalists, had been prepared even before the charges had been fully heard.

The court refused to allow questions to be raised on the political aspects of the case – in particular the allegation that Dr Shahbandar had been a British spy – or indeed on its religious aspects. When the defence attempted to prove that Shahbandar had been murdered because he was an 'enemy of Islam', the Shahbandarists put forth a statement by the leading 'ulema of Damascus, strongly refuting the accusation. Having thus disposed of both the political and religious aspects, the court concluded bizarrely that there remained only one possible motive for the crime, which was *'mistaken* religious zeal'.[45] The death sentence was passed on Ahmad 'Assassa and three others – and they were duly executed on 4 February. Colonel A. J. Gardiner, the British consul general, commented: 'I am inclined to agree with the view held by Nazih Bey al-Mu'ayyad, the victim's brother-in-law, who considers that the crime was probably hatched in Baghdad by the Hajj Amin al-Husayni and his following, possibly with the approval of Italy. The latter country has certainly shown great interest in the case'.[46] Italy was widely thought to have provided the cash to pay the defence lawyers' fees.

The crime was never fully elucidated. At any rate, the Shahbandarists – both the family and the party – were deeply dissatisfied with the outcome of the trial. When, in a gesture of condolence and reconciliation, Shukri al-Quwatli placed a wreath on Shahbandar's grave, Shahbandar's son brusquely ordered it to be removed. The trial, he declared, had failed to identify his father's real murderers.

What was the local upshot of Dr Shahbandar's murder? Jamil Mardam and his colleagues ended up in Baghdad, far away from the Syrian political scene. In Damascus, Shukri al-Quwatli was thus able to make his bid for the leadership of the national independence movement.[47] In a manifesto in March 1941, he called for the formation of a national government. Much like Shukri al-Quwatli in Damascus,

---

[45] Note by Vice-Consul R. A. Beaumont, Damascus, 11 January 1941 (FO 371/27330).

[46] Consulate General (Aley), Beirut Weekly Appreciation, 1–12 January 1941 (FO 371/27327).

[47] Khoury, *Syria and the French Mandate*, p. 590.

Riad el-Solh in Beirut was now the major nationalist leader whom the Germans sought to court and with whom the French and the British eventually had to deal.

The nationalists make their bid

Like most of his colleagues in the nationalist movement, Riad el-Solh considered that the French were finished. He planned to force concessions from them by inciting a popular revolt, which he reckoned the weakened French forces would not be able to put down. The conditions seemed propitious. In both Syria and Lebanon, the population was restive because of the grim social and economic conditions. The cost of living had soared, with the price of bread increasing fourfold. Sugar, rice and paraffin were virtually unobtainable, and petrol extremely scarce. Every night saw power cuts. Trade had ground to a halt because of the British blockade, and many workers were no longer able to feed their families. The number of unemployed in Damascus alone was said to have reached 50,000. Syrian labourers could no longer reach Palestine for temporary work, as they had been used to doing when times were hard. On 10 January 1941, Dentz reported to Paris: 'I must absolutely win the battle for wheat, but I've got everyone against me . . . the population . . . the merchants . . . the British . . . and, of course, the Germans'.[48]

Dentz's real attention, however, was elsewhere. He had a visceral suspicion of the British and was convinced that they planned to squeeze the French out of Syria in order to seize it for themselves. He had harboured these suspicions since being en poste in Damascus during the 1925–26 revolt. He now feared that a British invasion was imminent. Instead of setting up some sort of nationalist government – as some of his advisers urged – he tightened the screw, giving wider powers to the *Deuxième Bureau*, the hated military intelligence service. A Gestapo atmosphere came to reign.[49]

It was then that Riad in Beirut and his nationalist associates in Damascus decided to call a general strike in the two countries. Political agitation had been fuelled by the deplorable economic

---

[48] De Wailly, *Syrie 1941*, p. 94.
[49] Beirut Appreciation for the period 28 November – 10 December 1940, Aley, 11 December 1940 (FO 371/27327).

situation. Demonstrations against the food crisis began in Damascus, and quickly reached Homs and Aleppo. A general strike in Syria was proclaimed at the end of February and spread to Beirut, Tripoli and Sidon by early March. Dentz called out the armoured cars. Several demonstrators were killed in Damascus and in other Syrian cities. In Beirut, on 1 April, a demonstration of hungry Muslim women and children soon turned into angry riots. The French police opened fire, killing two people and wounding half a dozen. The French-appointed Lebanese Council of Directors resigned in protest. There were fears of a new Revolt on the model of 1925. When the dreaded Senegalese colonial troops were deployed in the streets, the Imam of the great mosque at Aleppo made a violent denunciation of France's colonial oppression. More clashes followed, leading to several more deaths in Aleppo and Damascus.

While Riad directed the disturbances in Beirut, Shukri al-Quwatli emerged as the leader of the uprising in Damascus. The Mandate, he declared, was no longer legitimate and the 1936 treaty should be reinstated.[50] He told the US consul general that the nationalists intended to press for immediate and complete independence, since they could no longer trust the French to grant it to them after the war.

In London, the troubles prompted a re-examination of the economic blockade of the Levant states. General Archibald Wavell and Sir Miles Lampson, the British Ambassador in Cairo, recommended that it be lifted and replaced by clearing agreements with Palestine and Egypt. The consulate general in Beirut agreed, fearing that a continued boycott would drive the French into the arms of the Germans, thus turning Syria into a military base for the Axis Powers.[51]

On 25 March, General Delhomme, the French military commander, proclaimed a 'state of siege': public meetings were banned and private meetings subjected to military approval; gatherings in the street of more than five people were forbidden; cafés had to close by 8 p.m.; telegrams and trunk calls between Syrian towns were discontinued, and all exit from, or entrance to, Damascus was controlled by the police. No one was allowed to travel by car without a permit. On the night of 25–26 March, some eighty nationalist agitators, mostly headmen of districts, were arrested and threatened with deportation without trial.

---

[50] Raghid el-Solh, *Lebanon and Arabism*, pp. 117 ff.
[51] Beirut Appreciation, 15–21 March 1941 (FO 371/27327).

Sa'dallah al-Jabiri, who had fled to Iraq during the French-controlled Shahbandar trial, tried to return to Syria on 28 March, but the French authorities turned him back at the frontier.[52]

A rattled Dentz tried to come to terms with the strikers, but found no one ready to collaborate with him. He issued a declaration in which he said that France sympathised with Syrian aspirations, and would grant independence 'once the international situation stabilised'. He was prepared, as a gesture, to replace the Council of Directors by a ministry led by a head of government. This would be assisted by a Consultative Assembly 'composed of the principal representatives of the country's political, economic and cultural life as well as of the younger generations', which would be given legislative powers as well as control over *ravitaillement*, the provision of supplies. He announced an immediate economic and social programme to relieve unemployment. The following day, 2 April, he appointed Khalid al-'Azm, president of the Damascus Chamber of Commerce and Industry – a politician who was opposed to the National Bloc and sympathetic to the French – as head of government and minister of interior.

This move calmed passions in Damascus somewhat, but riots broke out elsewhere. In Hama, three demonstrators were killed and eighty-five wounded on 18 April, while in Aleppo on 22 April, crowds, angered by the continued shortage of bread, resorted to widespread looting. Two rioters were killed and many were injured in what were considered the worst riots in living memory. The whole city was shut down.

At the same time in Lebanon, Emile Eddé, president of the Council of Directors, resigned and was replaced as head of state by Alfred Naccache, a Maronite magistrate, with Ahmad Da'uq as his deputy.[53] On 18 April – in a move which seemed to rob its presence in the Levant of any legal basis – France withdrew from the League of Nations, the body which in 1919 had entrusted it with the Mandate.

Both Riad el-Solh and Shukri al-Quwatli denounced these changes as mere window-dressing and refused to participate in either government. They sent the French high commissioner a note demanding an immediate return to constitutional life. But they also decided to lift the strike. They may have been prompted to do so by the return to Syria from Vichy France of Shaykh Taj al-Din al-Hasani, the former

[52] Beirut Appreciation, 22–31 March 1941 (FO 371/27327).
[53] Beirut Appreciation, 1–12 April 1941; Raghid el-Solh, *Lebanon and Arabism*, p. 119; Raymond, 'La Syrie du Royaume Arabe à l'indépendance', p. 77.

collaborationist prime minister, who, at a meeting attended by two thousand people in the Midan quarter, immediately attacked the nationalists, no doubt at French instigation. Fearing that the French were about to set up a government under their dependable man, Shaykh Taj – or govern directly through Bahij al-Khatib, another compliant official – the nationalists preferred to make a show of support for al-'Azm, even though they had no political liking for him, losing no opportunity to demonstrate that it was they who held the reins.[54]

Such was the turbulent state of the Levant in early April 1941. Disgusted with the French and disappointed with the British, Riad el-Solh and the other nationalists were immensely heartened by the news from Iraq that an anti-British coup had at long last challenged the Anglo-French grip on the Arab world.

[54] Consulate General (Aley), Beirut Appreciation, 13–24 April 1941 (FO 371/27327).

16 RASHID 'ALI AND 'OPERATION EXPORTER'

By the spring of 1941, Riad el-Solh had come to believe that France would not relinquish control of the Levant without a fight, and that Britain was determined to prop up the Vichy regime of General Henri-Fernand Dentz. Turning their backs on the nationalists, the imperial powers now thought of nothing but military bases, access to oil and safe communications. In their eyes, the aspirations of the local inhabitants to independence were insignificant at best, and a spanner in the works in what were difficult times. Britain and France might normally be colonial rivals, but in an emergency they closed ranks. Oliver Harvey, a senior British Foreign Office official, wrote pragmatically in his diary that 'Our long term interests and those of the French are identical', and, a little while later, 'If we weaken the French in Syria, we weaken our own position'.[1]

In such frustrating circumstances, it was hardly surprising that many Arabs began to look to Germany for deliverance from Anglo-French machinations. As Field Marshal Rommel took Benghazi in early April, driving Wavell's forces back into Egypt, and as German armies advanced into Greece and Yugoslavia, never had a German victory seemed more likely. It was at this very moment that a *coup d'état* took place in Baghdad, which seemed to break Britain's hold over Iraq. This, after all, was a major Arab country and a major player in the field of Arab nationalist activity. Nationalists in Syria and Lebanon read the Iraqi coup as a prelude to their own liberation from France. It raised the heady possibility that an Iraqi-Syrian federation might soon be

---

[1] *Oliver Harvey Diaries*, 4 December 1943, British Library Add. MSS 56400; *Oliver Harvey Diaries*, 29 October 1944, British Library Add. MSS 56400, quoted by Wm. Roger Lewis, 'The British and the French Colonial Empire: Trusteeship and Self-Interest', in Lewis, *Ends of British Imperialism*, pp. 279 ff.

proclaimed. Nationalist hearts – and Riad's first among them – thrilled at the prospect.

Rashid 'Ali al-Gaylani, author of the Baghdad coup, was a veteran nationalist, then almost 50 years old. He had never accepted the Anglo-Iraqi Treaty of 1930, which Nuri al-Said's government had signed. In Gaylani's view, this subjected Iraq to Britain's direct imperial control, under the guise of an 'alliance' between the two countries. The accommodating Nuri believed in Iraqi self-government under a British protective umbrella, but Rashid 'Ali wanted full independence, free from the humiliating presence of foreign troops. Born into a prominent Baghdad family in 1892, he was two years older than Riad, and had, like him, studied law. His family was descended from the prominent Sufi order of the Gaylaniyya, which administered a large *waqf* (or religious endowment) in Baghdad. In the nineteenth century, his grandfather had been the *naqib al-ashraf*, or representative of the leading religious families in their dealings with the Ottomans – an official position similar to that held by the Hasani family of Damascus, into which Ahmad Pasha, Riad's grandfather, had married.

Rashid 'Ali had graduated from the Baghdad Law School in 1914, and joined the Ottoman bureaucracy at Mosul. After the collapse of the Ottoman order, Gaylani returned to Baghdad where he practised and taught law, until he was appointed judge in the Court of Appeal at the remarkably young age of 27. He began his career in politics in 1924 as minister of justice in the first government of Yasin al-Hashimi, an ardent nationalist like himself. Together, they formed the Party of National Brotherhood (*al-ikha' al-watani*), to promote nationalist aims and challenge Britain's imperial interference in Iraq's internal politics.

Rashid 'Ali served as prime minister for the first time in 1933, when, on the sudden death of King Faysal, he had the delicate task of overseeing the transition of the Crown to King Ghazi. Unlike the sage and prudent Faysal, Ghazi was rash and impetuous, with an unseemly passion for fast cars. His reign was to prove turbulent and brief. On 29 October 1936, Iraq's constitutional life was shattered by a military *coup d'état* led by General Bakr Sidqi. This was the first of a series of military interventions in politics in the modern Arab world which have proved so catastrophic to the region ever since. Yasin al-Hashimi's government was overthrown and his Minister of Defence Ja'far al-Askari was killed. King Ghazi had rashly sanctioned the coup, but Bakr Sidqi's excesses soon alienated even his military supporters, and he was murdered by a group of officers in August 1937.

The following year, King Ghazi decided to try to realise his ambition of annexing Kuwait to Iraq (an ambition that Saddam Hussein would later share), before merging them together into a Fertile Crescent federation with Syria and Palestine. But, just as Iraqi troops massed on Kuwait's border in an intimidating show of force, Ghazi died suddenly, apparently when he drove his car into a lamppost on 3 April 1939. His infant son, Faisal II, aged only 4, succeeded him, under the regency of his uncle, the Emir 'Abd al-Ilah, who became de facto ruler of Iraq.

'Abd al-Ilah shared Nuri al-Sa'id's belief in the need for British imperial protection. As a result, they both found themselves increasingly at odds with the profoundly anti-British sentiment of the younger officers in the armed forces, and, indeed, of Iraqi opinion at large, which was inflamed by Britain's brutal repression of the Palestinians. The militant mood in Baghdad had much to do with the presence of a vocal group of Arab exiles, led by the former Mufti of Jerusalem, the Hajj Amin al-Husayni. As a result, a powerful wave of nationalist protest soon swept Nuri al-Sa'id from power and carried Rashid 'Ali to the premiership in 1940.

Hoping to free Iraq from British control, Rashid 'Ali called for a revision of the Anglo-Iraqi treaty, imposed restrictions on British troop movements, refused to break off relations with Italy and, in a bid to win German support, sent his Minister of Justice Naji Shawkat to meet the German ambassador Franz von Papen in Ankara. These policies so alarmed both the Regent and Nuri that, with British backing, they forced Rashid 'Ali to resign on 31 January 1941. He was replaced by General Taha al-Hashimi, whose Foreign Minister Tawfiq al-Suwaydi was summoned to Cairo in March 1941, to be sternly told by Britain's Foreign Secretary Anthony Eden, that Britain required a more cooperative attitude as well as the breaking off of relations with Italy. The shaken Suwaydi went home and persuaded Taha al-Hashimi that it would be best to suppress the rebellious officers. But the move was to backfire spectacularly.

On 1 April 1941, the army surrounded the royal palace in Baghdad. Hours earlier, the Regent had managed to escape to the British base of Habbaniya, and from there to Basra and thence to Amman. Backed by four generals known as the 'Golden Square',

Rashid 'Ali seized power again on 3 April – and deposed the absent Regent. One of his first acts – designed to be highly provocative to the British – was to send an Iraqi artillery unit to face the RAF base at Habbaniya. In the following days, substantial Iraqi ground forces were moved to the plateau overlooking the base, where Britain kept 2,200 troops, 12 armoured cars and 96 mostly obsolete aircraft, used primarily for training purposes. Rashid 'Ali demanded that British aircraft be grounded and all troop movements halted.

The impact of Rashid 'Ali's coup

These dramatic events in Iraq were followed with passionate interest in Syria and Lebanon, where Riad el-Solh presided over excited meetings held to pledge solidarity with Rashid 'Ali. In Damascus, students demonstrated outside the British consulate, even breaking its windows. To the great irritation of the British, the French authorities allowed the Syrian and Lebanese press to carry Rashid 'Ali's exultant statements, while in Baghdad itself the Mufti's Arab Guard, a radical youth movement, published a pamphlet proclaiming that all Arabs were now engaged in a jihad against the British.[2] Local British officials in Beirut and Damascus were well aware that the Iraqi situation provided a great opening for Axis propaganda, and decried the lack of a British counter-effort. They believed that it was time for London to make a public pronouncement in favour of Syrian independence. But Britain was too inhibited by the ambivalent policies it had seen fit to pursue. It was reluctant to arouse all-too-ready French suspicions of British political intrigue. It therefore supported de Gaulle, while continuing to support Dentz. In addition, General Wavell was determined to safeguard his available military resources for the defence of Egypt, rather than disperse them in any other intervention further east in the Arab world.

Meanwhile, German armies were advancing on all fronts. Believing in an imminent German victory, King Farouk refused to declare war on the Axis. Britain's vital lines of communications – to Egypt, the Persian Gulf, India, Malaysia and Australia – seemed in deadly danger. Italy was in control of both shores of the central Mediterranean, threatening the Royal Navy's historic domination of the

[2] Consulate General (Damascus), April 1941 (FO 371/27327).

area. In the Nile valley, Britain had only 55,000 men and 200 ancient planes to counter the better-armed and far more numerous Germans in Libya and Italians in Ethiopia and Eritrea. With the looming threat of a potential Axis pincer movement, the British brooded that Rashid 'Ali's coup might be no accident, but rather proof of a concerted plan to trigger an Arab insurrection in the whole region. Then, as now, Iraq was possessed of vital resources which the West coveted. It was a major supplier of oil to British forces, as well as a key land-bridge between Britain's stronghold in Egypt and its indispensable imperial reservoir of fighting men in India. Britain fretted that, thanks to the insurrection in Iraq, its whole strategic perimeter was shrinking before its very eyes.[3]

In the highly charged years of 1940–41, Rashid 'Ali's coup was a small event compared to the many larger ones that came to shape our world. For example, Mussolini's decision to enter the war on Hitler's side changed the course of the conflict. Hitler's half-baked decision to invade the Soviet Union, without having first defeated Britain, no doubt lost him the war. And Churchill's bulldog determination to keep on fighting, even when Hitler had subdued half of continental Europe, saved the world from Nazi domination – and had a strong bearing on the muscular response he adopted in Iraq.[4]

Rashid 'Ali had actually taken both the Germans and the British by surprise. Neither had been given advance warning of his coup and both now scrambled to react – the Germans to give him military support and the British to bring him down. By arming Rashid 'Ali, the Axis Powers had placed themselves in the immediate proximity of the Levant. Believing he could not afford to delay in responding to this threat, Churchill decided on immediate action.

The British ambassador to Iraq, Sir Kinahan Cornwallis (who had arrived in Baghdad on the very day of the coup), informed Rashid 'Ali that Britain needed to land Indian troops in Basra in order to reinforce Wavell's position in Palestine. If he respected British treaty rights, Britain would recognise his government. But if he refused, this would be considered a violation of the treaty and would trigger a severe military response. Under this pressure, the Iraqi cabinet agreed to cooperate with the British request, and the Indian 20th Infantry Brigade

[3] Gaunson, The Anglo-French Clash, p. 12.
[4] See Peter Calvocoressi's review in the Financial Times, 4–5 August 2007, of Ian Kershaw, Fateful Choices: Ten Decisions that Changed the World, 1940–41, London 2007.

disembarked at Basra on 19 April. But when Rashid 'Ali demanded the rapid movement of these troops out of Iraq, the British brushed him aside. He retaliated by refusing permission for a second troop convoy to land at Basra. As far as he was concerned, the treaty was now null and void.

On instructions from London, the British consul general in Beirut warned the French high commissioner on 29 April that the Germans might be planning to occupy Syrian airbases with airborne troops. British intelligence had reported that 500 troop-carrying machines, capable of bringing in 5,000 men and their equipment, might already be concentrated in the Dodecanese. General Dentz replied that his orders were to defend the mandated territories against external aggression, whatever its source.

The British worried that the Reich might persuade Marshal Pétain not to resist a German occupation of Syria.[5] They had learned that the Germans, who were evidently anxious to come to Rashid 'Ali's aid, were negotiating with Vichy for the use of Levant airfields. They had asked that their aircraft be allowed to land in Syria, refuel and take off for Iraq. In return, Vichy wanted Germany to release French prisoners of war. This negotiation was seen by Britain as a development of the utmost gravity. If the Luftwaffe were to obtain free use of Syrian and Lebanese airfields, the whole British position in Egypt might become militarily untenable, and the Suez Canal and the whole of the Mediterranean could be lost. The mood in London was grim because, by 30 April, the Germans had overrun Greece, where they had subjected British forces to a Balkan Dunkirk.

So, on urgent instructions from Churchill, the British gave Rashid 'Ali an ultimatum. The Iraqis were to withdraw from the proximity of the Habbaniya base by the early hours of 2 May or face attack. Once the ultimatum expired, British aircraft began to bomb and strafe Iraqi troops. On the second day of the fighting, Blenheim fighter bombers arrived on the scene to destroy the Iraqi air force and decimate Iraqi airbases. This was followed by a ground attack, which forced the Iraqis back to Falluja. The siege of Habbaniya was lifted.

It was not until 9 May that a solitary German aircraft landed at Mezze airport in Damascus with Major Axel von Blomberg on board, together with half a dozen other German officers. After

---

[5] Beirut Appreciation, 25 April – 8 May 1941 (FO 371/2732).

spending the night at the Orient Palace Hotel, they flew on to Iraq the next day. On 10 May, three further German aircraft landed at Aleppo, one of them crudely painted in French colours. It carried F. Grobba, the German ambassador in Baghdad, who was returning to his post; Rudolf Rahn, a German diplomat who had served with Ambassador Abetz in Paris; and a number of Vichy emissaries.[6] At a meeting in Beirut with the French commander, General Henri-Fernand Dentz, the Germans demanded that the military stocks of the Army of the Levant be delivered forthwith to the railhead on the Turkish border for immediate transfer to Iraq. Within days, some 20,000 rifles, 200 machine guns, 5 million rounds of ammunition, and 56 truck-loads of aviation fuel were loaded onto trains for Iraq. In exchange, Iraq sent Syria train-loads of wheat, oil, butter, dates, fruit and vegetables, which had an instant salutary effect on prohibitive local prices. At his trial in France after the war, Dentz claimed, in his own defence, that most of the materiel dispatched to Iraq was either obsolete or defective.

In the following weeks, more German aircraft transited through the airfields of Damascus, Aleppo, Rayak and Palmyra on their way to the battlefield in Iraq. From 14 May onwards, these airfields came under frequent RAF attack, but no French targets were hit. Wavell and Dentz evidently sought to avoid an Anglo-French clash. Yet, behind the scenes, there was a furious debate. De Gaulle wanted the British to help the Free French evict Vichy from the Levant. He argued that Dentz could not be relied on to oppose either Vichy or the Germans – as indeed proved to be the case. Only Free French control of the Levant could do that. But Wavell, desperate to halt the German advance on Egypt, was not yet ready to spare the men and materiel to take Syria. His instinct was to continue to strengthen Dentz against the Germans. He therefore told an impatient de Gaulle that no operation against Vichy in Syria could be envisaged for the time being.[7]

In all, about one hundred German – and a smaller number of Italian – aircraft passed through Syria in May and June, serviced by some two hundred German mechanics on the ground, although the heat and the long flight to Iraq took their toll in numerous break-downs and losses. The Axis managed to mount half a dozen raids on Habbaniya and on British reinforcements racing across the desert to

[6] See Rudolf Rahn's memoirs, *Rubeloses Leben*, Düsseldorf 1949, pp. 149 ff., quoted by de Wailly, *Syrie 1941*, p. 474, n. 2.
[7] Gaunson, *The Anglo-French Clash*, p. 30.

Iraq, but these were not militarily significant. Dentz reported to Vichy that the German effort seemed largely improvised and had no real impact on the situation in Iraq.[8]

Meanwhile, a hastily assembled Anglo-Arab column, jauntily named Habforce ('Hab' for Habbaniya), crossed 500 miles of desert from Palestine and reached Habbaniya on 18 May. Another column, KingCol, travelled from Transjordan. Additional Indian forces arrived in Basra. Driven out of the town of Falluja, Rashid 'Ali's troops were pursued along the river valley to Baghdad, which fell on 30 May. This cleared the way for the restoration of the Regent, the Emir 'Abd al-Ilah, who returned to Iraq on 1 June and formed a pro-British government under Nuri al-Sa'id. A British military presence remained in place to uphold them.

Swift and ferocious British action had broken Rashid 'Ali. Preoccupied with the situation in Greece, Crete and Libya, the Axis had been unable to give him more than limited help. He was forced to flee to Iran on his way to Germany, where he spent the remaining years of the war broadcasting to the Arab world. He then escaped to Saudi Arabia, where he was granted political asylum. When the Iraqi monarchy was overthrown in 1958, Rashid 'Ali returned to Baghdad and once again attempted to seize power. But he failed and was sentenced to death. He was later pardoned, and returned to live in exile in Saudi Arabia, where he died in 1965.

For Riad el-Solh, and for other Arab nationalists in the Levant, Rashid 'Ali's downfall was a shattering blow. Having themselves failed to loosen France's grip on Syria, they had hoped that a nationalist triumph in Iraq would open the way for their own independence. A few enthusiastic souls even travelled to Iraq to fight with Rashid 'Ali. Meetings of solidarity with him were held at Riad's house, including a very large one on 4 May 1941. Subscription lists were opened in favour of 'the Arab victims of British imperialism', and collections were made in Lebanon's main towns. But the disappointment at his fall was intense, reopening wounds the nationalists had suffered from the failure of their own interwar struggle. They compared the dashing of their aspirations in Iraq to the debacle of an earlier generation, when King Faysal's government in Damascus was destroyed by the French in 1920.[9]

---

[8] De Wailly, *Syrie 1941*, pp. 148, 158. See Air Vice-Marshal A. G. Dudgeon, *Hidden Victory: The Battle of Habbaniya*, London 1941.

[9] Raghid el-Solh, *Lebanon and Arabism*, p. 132.

The sight of German aircraft operating from Syrian bases had given the British a real scare, as it looked as if the Germans had come close to establishing their influence in Iraq, Syria and Lebanon. Had they succeeded, they could from there have launched attacks against Egypt and against Britain's other positions in the Middle East and beyond. This grim prospect convinced the British that, while they fought the Germans in the Western Desert, they could no longer tolerate the existence of a Vichy regime in the Levant. The two situations had become utterly incompatible. On orders from Vichy, Dentz had allowed German and Italian planes to refuel in Syria. He had allowed the Germans to use Syrian railways to send fuel and armaments to Iraq.[10] Vichy's alleged neutrality in the mandated territories had proved to be a sham. Wavell's policy of propping up Dentz was now discredited and had to be swiftly abandoned. In a sharp reversal of policy, London ordered Wavell to respond forcefully to the threat posed by Vichy's collaboration with the Axis. Indeed, Vichy had to be expelled from the Levant.[11]

Britain drew another lesson from the Iraqi emergency, which was that the political aspirations of the Arabs could no longer be so callously ignored. Arab opinion had to be conciliated and won over, even if this meant inevitable tensions with the French. The mobilising power of Arab nationalism had to be taken into account, as local popular Arab sentiment suddenly became a key to British security.

Defeating Vichy in the Levant

Even before the fighting in Iraq was over, Churchill ordered Wavell to prepare to move into Syria and Lebanon at the earliest possible opportunity, and with the largest possible force – without prejudicing the security of the Western Desert.[12] By 27 May, Wavell presented London with an outline of 'Operation Exporter'. On the same day, Anthony Eden explained to the War Cabinet the urgent need to seek to win over Arab nationalist opinion to the Allied side. He launched the effort in a speech at the Mansion House in London – the official residence of the Lord Mayor of the City of London – on 29 May. 'Many Arab thinkers',

---

[10] See Compton Mackenzie, *Eastern Epic*, London 1951, p. 107.
[11] Raghid el-Solh, *Lebanon and Arabism*, pp. 139 ff.
[12] Gaunson, *The Anglo-French Clash*, pp. 31 ff.

he declared, 'desire for the Arab peoples a greater degree of unity than they now enjoy . . . His Majesty's Government for their part will give full support to any scheme that commands general approval.' No doubt he hoped that these cautious words would conciliate the Arabs without unduly alarming the French.

In a four-pronged attack at dawn on 8 June 1941, Allied troops crossed the border into Syria and Lebanon and were immediately to encounter stiff resistance. On the first day of the war, General Georges Catroux issued a proclamation which he hoped would ensure the neutrality of the local population. 'I have come', he declared, 'to terminate the mandatory regime and proclaim you free and independent. You are henceforth sovereign and independent peoples . . . Your independent and sovereign status will be guaranteed by a treaty which will define our respective relations'.[13] Churchill welcomed Catroux's statement, which de Gaulle communicated to the National Bloc in Syria via Jamil Mardam: 'The proclamation whose spirit and terms I have approved will be made in my name and the name of Free France, that is to say of France.'

Britain proposed to issue a guarantee of Catroux's declaration. But de Gaulle flatly rejected the idea of a joint proclamation, viewing the British proposal as a presumptuous intrusion into France's sphere of influence. His view was that 'the word of France had no need of a foreign guarantee'. This veto of de Gaulle forced the British to issue a separate statement endorsing Catroux's proclamation, while denying that they themselves had any further ambitions in the Levant.[14] Indeed, on the eve of the attack, Churchill sent de Gaulle a conciliatory message in which he declared:

> *You know that we have sought no special advantage over the French Empire and have no intention of exploiting the tragic position of France for our own gain. I welcome therefore your decision to promise independence to Syria and Lebanon, and as you know I think it essential that we should lend to this promise the full weight of our guarantee.*

---

[13] FO 371/27214/E2915; General Georges Catroux, *Dans la bataille de la Méditerranée*, Paris 1949, pp. 137 f.

[14] Gaunson, *The Anglo-French Clash*, pp. 41–2.

But Churchill's real intentions can far better be judged from a message he sent to Oliver Lyttelton, Britain's minister of state, who arrived in Cairo on 5 July to represent the War Cabinet and handle the relationship with the Free French. Churchill insisted to him that 'the main point' was

> to gain the Arab world by establishment and proclamation at earliest of Syrian independence in whatever form is most acceptable . . . Our policy is to give the Syrian Arabs independence . . . the Arabs bulk far more largely in our minds than the Free French, and there can be no question of any lengthy delay in negotiating treaties which satisfy them and convince them that they have not merely exchanged one set of Frenchmen for another.[15]

The Syrian campaign

The battle plan for the Allied invasion of Syria and Lebanon was drawn up by General Henry 'Jumbo' Wilson, commander of Operation Exporter. It unfolded as follows:

- Crossing the Syrian border from Palestine, the 5th Indian Brigade Group headed for Quneitra and Dar'a, opening the way for elements of the 1st Free French Division to advance on Damascus.
- The Australian 7th Division headed for Beirut along the coastal road from Haifa, opening the way for the Australian 21st Brigade to take the city. These Allied ground forces were supported by shelling from Royal Navy and Royal Australian Navy ships. At the same time, the Australian 25th Brigade attacked the Vichy airbase at Rayak.
- The 10th Indian Infantry Division advanced up the Euphrates from Iraq towards Deir ez-Zor, Raqqa and Aleppo, with the aim of cutting Vichy communication and supply lines.[16]

Having crushed the Iraqi revolt, a Habforce brigade gathered near the Transjordan border in western Iraq and advanced north-west into

---

[15] Ibid., pp. 53–4.
[16] Andrew Mollo, *The Armed Forces of World War II*, London 1981; de Wailly, *Syrie 1941*, p. 68.

Syria to take Palmyra and secure the Haditha-to-Tripoli oil pipeline. Meanwhile, Vichy strong points and communication links were raided by British paratroopers from No. 11 Commando and by members of *Palmach*, a unit recruited from the Zionists in Palestine. *Palmach* also provided some of the interpreters and guides used by the Allied units. This was how Moshe Dayan, later to become a famous Israeli general, lost an eye to a Vichy sharpshooter.

The Army of the Levant under Vichy command numbered some 35,000 regular troops. It consisted of four battalions of the Foreign Legion – the best troops available; three battalions of the 24th Colonial Infantry Regiment, which were brought up to strength by being amalgamated with two garrison battalions of colonial Senegalese troops; and contingents of mounted North African cavalry – the so-called *spahis* – of some 7,000 men. In mountainous country, the horse was still a useful instrument of war. In addition, there were several locally recruited infantry battalions, the so-called *Troupes Spéciales*, composed mainly of 'Alawis, with a sprinkling of Turkomans, Druze and Kurds, of indifferent fighting ability. Dentz's army had 14 artillery batteries, 90 tanks, 70 armoured cars and more than 250 aircraft, although many would soon be destroyed on the ground. It had enough petrol and munitions for six weeks of combat.

The five-week campaign turned out to be harder and longer than the Allies had expected, with particularly bitter fighting between Gaullists and Pétainists. General Dentz's troops fought hard. Among numerous lesser engagements, the highlights were the battle for the Litani River (9 June); the battle of Jezzine (13 June); the battle of Kisweh (15 June); and the battle of Damascus (18 June). The fall of the city was marked by the ceremonial entry of the two French commanders, General Catroux and Major-General Paul Louis Legentilhomme, escorted by Circassian cavalry (*Gardes Tcherkess*).

The British commander-in-chief reported to the War Office that the Free French Division had fought well, but that 'the fratricidal aspect on tired troops has made them unreliable and unfit for further heavy fighting'. Politically and psychologically, he continued, the Free French were almost universally unpopular with the French community in Syria. The officers of the Vichy Army were implacably hostile to the Free French, whom they considered to be traitors. As for the Syrian population, it had welcomed the British as liberators, but this attitude was 'undergoing considerable modification as a result of what they regard as the replacement, with British connivance, of one set of French by another'. The Syrians, he added, were 'gravely disappointed at the absence of any sign of implementation by French of the guarantee of independence'.[17]

Following the capture of Damascus, the key engagements were the battle of Merj 'Ayun (19 June); the battle of Palmyra (1 July); the battle of Deir ez-Zor (3 July); the battle of Damour (5 July); and, finally, the battle of Beirut (12 July). By the time Beirut fell, Dentz had lost 6,000 men, of whom roughly 1,000 had been killed. The vast majority of Dentz's troops were taken prisoner. On 12 July, his envoys approached the British for an armistice. It was signed at Acre on 14 July, bringing the war to an end.

The terms of the armistice suggested that General 'Jumbo' Wilson disliked having to side with Gaullist military upstarts against the professionals of the Vichy army. As a soldier of conventional upbringing, he treated Dentz's defeated army with deliberately exaggerated chivalry. Indeed, the armistice document he drafted made no reference at all to the Free French. The French Mandate was not mentioned in the document, but nor, for that matter, was the independence of Syria. Not only would he not allow Catroux to sign the armistice document, but, in a secret protocol, Wavell also denied him the means to recruit Vichy troops into Gaullist ranks. Instead, he insisted on their repatriation to France. All personal contacts between Gaullists and Pétainists were banned. In their attempt to win troops over to the Gaullist side, Free French representatives were restricted to the use of pamphlets, loudspeakers and wireless – a farcical arrangement which ruled out genuine individual choices. It thus put an end to Free French recruitment in the region. The armistice amounted to a transfer of Syria and Lebanon from France to Britain. Catroux had evidently been the wrong man to represent de Gaulle at Acre.

The Lyttelton–de Gaulle agreement

De Gaulle saw it as a conspiracy. Arriving in Cairo from Brazzaville on 20 July in a towering rage, he immediately set about amending the

---

[17] Most secret cipher telegram from C. in C., Middle East, to the War Office, 27638, 16 July 1941, St Antony's College, Middle East Library, Private Papers.

Acre agreement. He brushed aside the inconvenient fact that his own plenipotentiary had accepted it. This high-handed behaviour so irritated the British that, at one point, they seriously considered keeping him out of Syria altogether. It was suggested that he be denied the use of wireless and telegraph, and would, if necessary, be deposed in favour of Catroux – in which case de Gaulle would have been locked up in a British prison! These drastic measures were not needed after all, because de Gaulle soon proved himself to be somewhat more amenable.

After three days of intense haggling, an agreement was thrashed out on 25 July between de Gaulle and Oliver Lyttelton, the British minister of state, consisting of an 'interpretation' of the Acre armistice, as well as two enclosures on the subject of 'Collaboration between British and Free French Authorities in the Middle East'. These provided for a somewhat muddled division of authority, whereby political and administrative control of the Levant territories would be the concern of the French, while effective power lay with the British, since they controlled all aspects of the military situation. The 'condominium' was never satisfactory and led to violent disputes. De Gaulle interpreted the agreement to mean British recognition of France's entire sovereignty over the Levant states.[18] A major point of contention was the extent of independence that each side believed should be granted to these states. Should the Iraqi model be followed, as advocated by the British, or should 'independence' be no more than an even more restricted version of the 1936 treaties, as the French demanded? In the ensuing uproar, Churchill and de Gaulle embarked on a long and famous feud.

Operation Exporter inevitably diminished France's position in the Levant. De Gaulle started to regret the promise of independence he had made. He was tormented by having to fight his old comrades and so incur the charge of betraying French interests. He hated the idea that Vichy troops would be sent back to France. 'This should not be accepted at any price', he wrote to Churchill. But, at Wavell's headquarters, there was a firm conviction that the Army of the Levant had to be repatriated as soon as possible. There was the need to stabilise the Levant and reduce the demands on Wavell's resources. Some Allied forces in Syria were badly needed in the Western Desert, where Wavell's latest offensive (Operation Battleaxe, 15–17 June) was ending

---

[18] Gaunson, *The Anglo-French Clash*, pp. 60 ff.

in a precipitate retreat from the Halfaya Pass.[19] Alone in its struggle against the Axis, Britain did not think this was any time to drive Vichy further into the arms of Hitler. A generous treatment of captured Vichy troops was therefore decided. In the event, only 5,500 men out of a total of 35,000 chose to join the Free French.

De Gaulle had wanted to appoint Catroux high commissioner in the Levant, but Churchill persuaded him not to. Instead, in a letter to Catroux, de Gaulle named him delegate general, and instructed him to negotiate 'treaties instituting the independence and sovereignty of the Levant states, together with the alliance of these states with France, and safeguarding the rights and interests of France'. The starting point of the negotiations was to be the 1936 treaty. In spite of his title, Catroux was to assume 'all the powers' of a high commissioner of France. 'The Mandate entrusted to France by the League of Nations . . . has to run its full term', de Gaulle wrote.

De Gaulle now sought to set limits to the unconditional independence which Catroux had pledged. He had to take into account the impact on French opinion of a hasty withdrawal. *La France Libre* could not make reckless concessions or renounce the Mandate until the League of Nations, or some successor organisation, decided it must.[20] De Gaulle longed to reach Beirut and Damascus, patch up the French image and reassert France's 'historic mission' in the Levant – a mission that he dreamed would be controlled by France alone, with no interference from Britain, the United States or any international body. For de Gaulle, the union of the Empire and of metropolitan France was one of the keys to the restoration of French grandeur. It was, in his view, tangible evidence of France's rank as a world power, and he was not about to give it up.[21] Indeed, he would remain a colonialist for many years to come, until rivers of Algerian blood finally stained his conscience.

Riad el-Solh and the nationalists had been passive spectators of the war, but they derived no comfort from its outcome. De Gaulle's posturing filled them with foreboding. They soon saw that no trust whatsoever could be put in Catroux's declaration of 'independence', which was being contravened every day by French officials. The very same ones who had served Vichy were now back at their posts, serving

---

[19] Ibid., pp. 47 ff.
[20] Raymond, 'La Syrie, du Royaume arabe à l'indépendance', pp. 77 ff.
[21] Gaunson, *The Anglo-French Clash*, p. 29; Lewis, 'The British and the French Colonial Empire', p. 285.

the Free French. Evidently, for the nationalists, the battle was far from over. Luckily for them, France was no longer the preponderant power in the Levant that it had been before the war. For Riad, there was a glimmer of hope in the person of General Edward Louis Spears, Churchill's special envoy to the Free French.

17 RIAD BEY AND GENERAL SPEARS

Major-General Edward Spears knew next to nothing about the Middle East when he landed in Cairo with General de Gaulle on 1 April 1941, just two days before Rashid 'Ali's coup in Baghdad. But he had other compensating qualities. He was strong-willed and fearless; he was a skilled politician, used to dealing with important people; he loved France, spoke beautiful French and was devoted to Anglo-French solidarity (as Conservative Member of Parliament for Carlisle, he was jokingly referred to at Westminster as 'the Member for Paris'). He was also a close personal friend of Winston Churchill, Britain's wartime leader. It was said that in 1922, Spears had offered to step down from his newly won parliamentary seat, so as to give Churchill the chance to win an easy by-election. Although Churchill declined Spears's offer, he was never to forget this generous personal and political gesture.

During the First World War, Spears had served as liaison officer between British and French military intelligence and, later, between the two military commands. He was, therefore, in May 1940, Churchill's natural choice as his personal envoy to France's embattled Prime Minister Paul Reynaud. When France collapsed before the German onslaught in June, Spears took charge of General de Gaulle and flew him to England from Bordeaux under the nose of Marshal Pétain's new government. Churchill made Spears head of the British Mission to the Free French.[1] Later, and throughout his spell in the Middle East, from 1941 to 1944, Spears enjoyed the inestimable advantage of being able to report directly to Churchill, over the head of the Foreign Office and of all other departments of state. In any event, he had nothing but scorn for the Foreign Office, which he considered invariably

---

[1] Roshwald, *Estranged Bedfellows*, p. 86.

wrong-headed and chicken-hearted. This unusual soldier-diplomat provides a striking example of how the bold intervention of a single individual can alter the course of events. He was to play a decisive role in bringing both Syria and Lebanon to independence – in close collaboration with Riad el-Solh.

General Spears's American wife, the daughter of William Borden of Chicago, was equally enterprising. She had directed a mobile hospital in the First World War, a feat she even managed to repeat in the Second World War, though all her equipment was lost during the French retreat. With help from the Americans, she then had a new medical unit equipped, which she gave to General de Gaulle, and which accompanied the Free French to Africa and took part in the Syrian campaign.

Spears arrived in Cairo a fervent Gaullist, deeply impressed by the Frenchman's defiance, and determined to do his utmost to help him launch the Free French on their way to national revival. He had a good grasp of geopolitics, and was one of the first to warn of the danger to the vital Suez Canal artery, to the British fleet at Alexandria, to Cyprus, to the oil pipeline from Iraq – indeed, to the whole British position in the eastern Mediterranean – if German planes were allowed to operate from Syrian and Lebanese airfields, no more than an hour's flying time away. Spears joined his voice to de Gaulle's to urge General Archibald Wavell, the British commander-in-chief, to expel the Vichy regime from Syria at the earliest possible opportunity.

But Spears soon began to notice that de Gaulle's priorities were markedly different from his own. De Gaulle's chief concern, it emerged, was to restore French control over the Levant states. It was to be the first hint of disagreement between them.

In Cairo, Spears and de Gaulle discovered that Britain had set up what amounted to a regional government, of which the pivot was Oliver Lyttelton, who, from his previous job as president of the Board of Trade, had been appointed British minister of state for the Middle East in June 1941. Around Lyttelton, three important bodies had been formed with the aim of uniting the scattered British military and civilian forces in the Middle East. There was a Middle East War Council, which was the highest political authority; a Middle East Defence Council, which was a subcommittee of the War Council; and a Middle East Supply Centre, which developed into a vital regional hub. Spears got on well with Lyttelton. The 'Spears Mission' was, in fact, designed to serve as liaison between these three departments and de

Gaulle, with its main task being to aid the Free French in securing their military needs. It established branches in the various areas where Free France was operating.[2] At full strength, it numbered 131 members; 25 of these were officers, the rest other ranks, and 37 civilians. After the occupation of Syria and Lebanon, the Spears Mission moved its regional headquarters from Egypt to Lebanon. Although its seat was in Beirut, it had representatives in Tripoli, Zahleh and Sidon, as well as in Damascus, Aleppo, Hama, Latakia, Suwayda, Deir ez-Zor and Hasaka.[3]

Three days after General Dentz surrendered at Acre, Spears outlined, in his usual robust style, how he saw his task in Syria and Lebanon: 'I am in complete and absolute agreement with the Minister of State [Lyttelton] on all subjects. All agree that the Syrian Mission presents the greatest difficulties imaginable. Success difficult to achieve. Disaster possible. If my relationship with the Minister of State were interfered with, would feel unable to undertake this difficult task.' This was an early indication of Spears pre-empting any attempt at interference by officials from London.

Spears continued:

The problem is

To prevent the country going up in smoke.
To help to make out of Syria a solid bloc which will provide a safe basis for our armed forces to operate from whatever the circumstances may be.

This object is to be achieved in a country where

(a) *Native interests often are in conflict with each other.*
(b) *Population is now to a great extent armed.*
(c) *French of all categories intensely disliked.*
(d) *Free French very jealous of the British.*
(e) *Free French authorities are often in conflict with each other.*
(f) *Complete dearth of administration officials.*
(g) *A great many British unconnected elements intensely distrusted by the French upon whom the natives will endeavour to play.*

[2] Raghid el-Solh, *Lebanon and Arabism*, pp. 143 ff.
[3] Eyal Zisser, *Lebanon: The Challenge of Independence*, London 2000, p. 251, n. 13.

*Out of this some sort of order is to be created keeping
the country as French as possible while safeguarding vital
British interests.*

*Above all it is necessary to avoid civil disturbances
which would in all likelihood spread beyond Syria and
which would involve us in using force against those very
Arabs whose goodwill we are so anxious to cultivate.*

*A further elementary difficulty is de Gaulle himself.
He returns here on Friday intending to go to Syria and . . .
may attempt to repudiate the Armistice if he is not satisfied
over the terms for winning over French troops.*

*De Gaulle will require most careful handling . . .
if he were given a free hand in Syria in the mood in which
he now is, the country would be out of hand within a
fortnight.*[4]

On arrival in the Levant, Spears was predisposed to be suspicious of those Arab nationalists who, as had been reported to him, were friends of the Hajj Amin al-Husayni and had backed Rashid 'Ali in his challenge to Britain in Iraq. They were said to have flirted with both Germany and Italy. Since the British security services considered Riad el-Solh and his friends to be dangerous men, Spears decided to keep them at arm's length. His Mission also boycotted Syria's Arab nationalists for about a year. When Sa'dallah al-Jabiri attempted to return to Syria from Iraq, he was turned back at the border. Riad, in turn, kept a low profile, fearing arrest.

Spears took quickly to Levantine politics. To initiate him into its complexities, he relied on Furlonge and Gardiner, British consuls in Beirut and Damascus, both well versed in local affairs and familiar with the local personalities. In the meantime, he needed to get the measure of Catroux and see whether de Gaulle could be tamed.

The leader in waiting

By 1941, Riad Bey – as he was universally known – was widely recognised as the main Lebanese Muslim leader of his generation, and a

[4] General Spears to Foreign Office (via Cairo, 2252), 17 July 1941, St Antony's College, Middle East Library, Private Papers, Spears Box 1, GB 165-0269.

pan-Arab figure of the first importance. The French – whether Gaullist or Vichy – identified him as their principal opponent, while privately recognising his merit, as may be seen from a report sent to Paris in September 1941 by the French authorities in Beirut:

> *Riad el-Solh is a politician who enjoys great influence*
> *in Arab circles. He has worked for union for the past*
> *twenty years. Originally very rich, he has spent his fortune*
> *on his political activities. He has never been willing to*
> *collaborate with the mandatory authorities . . . He is a*
> *skilful* manoeuvrier *and his duplicity is baffling. It has*
> *not been possible to determine whether he is xenophobic,*
> *pro-British or pro-German. He has managed to seem all*
> *three at once. He is closely linked to the Syrian, Iraqi and*
> *Palestinian nationalists . . . [He] works for Syrian unity, as*
> *a first step towards a greater Arab union.*[5]

Riad, his wife Fayza and their five daughters were then living in a rambling apartment above a row of shops in the Ras al-Nab'a quarter of Beirut, which they had rented from Milhem Bey Hamadeh (grandfather of the present-day Druze politician, Marwan Hamadeh). There, on 'Umar ibn al-Khattab Street, Riad was at home. The *qabadayat*, or local street heads, protected him, and he used them in his battles with the French.

When he first married Fayza al-Jabiri in 1930, Riad and his wife had moved in with his parents, into the house on the Beirut seafront at Minat al-Husn, which his mother had inherited and where he had spent so much of his childhood. Built like an Italian palazzo, it had spacious rooms and a wonderful view of the sea, ebbing and flowing on the rocks below. Riad particularly loved this view. But when the French took action against him in 1935, deporting him to Qamishli for his role in the taxi-drivers' strike, they sequestered those of his properties which had not already been sold – the land in South Lebanon and the house at Minat al-Husn – and put them up for forced sale. The Beirut house was sold to an Italian-Jewish family, the Giustinis, who promptly

---

[5] MAE, Nantes, Fonds Beyrouth (Amb.), série 199A4, carton 20, note sur Riad el-Solh, de la Délégation Générale de la France Combattante au Levant, 23 September 1941. Translation from the French by the author.

pulled it down and built an apartment block on its plot. A nightclub called the Domino opened on the ground floor.

As Riad rose in the Arab political firmament, his wife Fayza was no doubt proud of him. He had the charm, the wit and the political power to be irresistible. But she was perhaps not as fulfilled as she might have liked to be. Riad was often away or in exile. Throughout the Mandate, the French, who considered him their enemy, gave his family a hard time. For long periods, no one would dare call on them. And when he was home, he was usually busy downstairs with his supporters and with the street heads of Beirut's Muslim quarters. Loud, rough men came and went, while Fayza played her Chopin upstairs. She brought up her daughters more or less by herself, and, as money was short, she knitted or sewed clothes for them. She was a brave but reserved woman, even with her own family.[6]

Zuhayr 'Usayran, a friend and neighbour, remembered Riad el-Solh at that time.

> He was always well dressed, sported a small moustache and wore a tarbush (always at a rakish angle). Our house was close by. The demonstrations would begin and end at his place. He was the leader who had fought the Mandate. I noticed that he liked to ride horses and read Arab history. He loved poetry, especially al-Mutanabbi and Imru' al-Qays, and he had a great appreciation of classical music.[7]

The Spears Mission could not afford to ignore Riad and the nationalists forever. A first attempt to mediate on their behalf with the Allies was made by two Iraqi politicians who had come to power under British auspices following the overthrow of Rashid 'Ali – namely Prime Minister Jamil al-Madfa'i and Foreign Minister 'Ali Jawdat al-Ayyubi.[8] These men had been members of Arab nationalist organisations before the First World War and had served as officers in the Sharifian forces. They had then joined Faysal's administration in Damascus. As a result,

[6] Interview with Alia el-Solh, 4–5 October 2004, Monte Carlo.
[7] Article about Riad el-Solh by Huda al-Husseini, based on the reminiscences of Zuhayr 'Usayran, an older journalist, in the Lebanese magazine al-Shira', no. 848 (7 September 1997).
[8] See Raghid el-Solh, Lebanon and Arabism, pp. 147–51 for the following passage.

they had a strong natural interest in Arab politics and a regional network of contacts and friends. In Lebanon, their link was with Riad el-Solh, the representative of the Arab nationalist mainstream, rather than with the rival faction of Karami and his Beirut allies, the Salams and the Bayhums.

Riad el-Solh in Beirut and Shukri al-Quwatli in Damascus welcomed this offer to plead their case with the Spears Mission. Their contact with Jamil al-Madfa'i and 'Ali Jawdat al-Ayyubi in Baghdad was made through the Iraqi consulates in Beirut and Damascus, as well as through Riad's cousin, Kadhim el-Solh, who was then living in Baghdad. On 14 July 1941, Kadhim submitted a memorandum to Madfa'i, for him to pass on to the British, in which the demands of the nationalists were spelled out. These were independence and free elections for Syria and Lebanon; France to refrain from encouraging separatist and confessional movements; and Britain and France to accept the entry of Syria and Lebanon into an Arab alliance or federation.

Riad then wrote Kadhim a letter in which he reiterated the nationalists' goals of independence and unity. He expressed his appreciation for Anthony Eden's Mansion House speech and General Catroux's 8 June 1941 proclamation of the independence of the Levant states, as well as the statement the same day by Britain in which it associated itself with the French pledge. Riad proposed holding a plebiscite in Lebanon on the issue of Arab unity, under the auspices of an international body, to include Iraq and Saudi Arabia.

The Iraq government adopted Kadhim el-Solh's memorandum and communicated it, with some amendments, to Sir Kinahan Cornwallis, the British ambassador in Baghdad. Similar memoranda were submitted to representatives of President Roosevelt and to General Catroux. Ibn Sa'ud himself offered to mediate with the British on behalf of Riad el-Solh and Shukri al-Quwatli, but the British declined his offer. Nevertheless, because of all this activity, the Spears Mission was by this time fully acquainted with Riad's views.

An intermediary who helped ease Riad el-Solh's entry into the confidence of the Spears Mission was Captain Marun 'Arab, a member of the Greek Orthodox community and an astute observer of the Lebanese political scene. He and Riad were friends and would speak Turkish together. Marun had served at the British embassy before the war as an adviser on local affairs, joining the Spears Mission as Furlonge's assistant after the Allied occupation. As Riad el-Solh's daughter, Alia, was later to joke to the author: 'Il se dit capitaine, militaire il n'est pas; Maroun il se dit, Maronite il n'est pas; Arab est son nom, mais arabe il n'est pas'.[9]

Direct contact was eventually made through another of Furlonge's associates, Yusuf Salem, who was also a friend of Riad. When Furlonge informed Salem that Riad would shortly be sent to jail because of his cooperation with the Germans in Iraq, Salem hurried to warn Riad of what was in store for him. He then arranged for Riad to meet Furlonge. The consul repeated the charge that Riad and his National Bloc friends in Syria had cooperated with the Germans, but a three-hour discussion ensued, during which Riad was able to convince Furlonge that any contacts that had been made had not been intended to harm British interests, but were solely with the aim of liberating Syria from the French.

Riad then made the consul an offer. 'Let us agree to put the past behind us and talk only of the future. If you help us end the French Mandate, we will be on your side.' The very next day, Riad asked his journalist friend, Hanna Ghusn of *al-Diyar*, to write an editorial under the heading, 'Why we stand with Britain'. It spelled out the nationalists' new relationship with the British.[10]

Like most Arab nationalists, Riad could not help feeling a deepseated mistrust of Britain for having given Palestine to the Zionists and Syria to the French, thus betraying its wartime pledges to the Arabs. His hostility to Britain had been reinforced by the crushing of Rashid 'Ali's uprising in Iraq and the humiliation of Farouk of Egypt, when British tanks had surrounded the king's palace, and forced him to appoint the Wafdist leader Nahhas Pasha as prime minister. Moreover, Britain's continued political and military control of Iraq, Transjordan, Palestine and Egypt thwarted the Arabs' aspirations for independence and unity.

Nevertheless, Riad was a pragmatic politician. He recognised that Britain's 'Arab policy' remained somewhat more liberal than that of France. Moreover, his close personal ties with Ibn Sa'ud in Arabia, Nahhas Pasha in Egypt, the Hashemite camp of the Emir 'Abdallah in Transjordan and the Iraqi Regent 'Abd al-Ilah – all of whom had

[9] Interview with Alia el-Solh, 4–5 October 2004, Monte Carlo.
[10] Hilal el-Solh, *Tarikh rajul wa qadiya*, p. 80; Yusuf Salem, *Khamsun sana ma' al-nas*, Beirut 1975, pp. 111–15 (2nd edn 1998).

collaborated closely with Britain during the war – may well have mitigated his own anti-British stand.[11]

Spears's conversion from Gaullism to Arabism

General Spears was a man of strong emotions, as passionate in his attachments as he was in his hates. Having been a devoted Gaullist, he was transformed within weeks of his arrival in the Levant into one of de Gaulle's most ferocious opponents, even hinting to London that it would be best if the French leader were excluded from the area altogether. The reasons for such a sudden and radical change of heart were numerous and deeply felt. Spears was outraged by de Gaulle's feud with his own hero, Winston Churchill. He also had a profound distaste for de Gaulle's notorious rudeness – indeed he was to write of 'the insane assaults of de Gaulle's ugly temper'.[12] He was affronted by the brutal way in which the Frenchman had savaged the July 1941 Armistice. Spears also had a general contempt for French colonial methods, which to him seemed to represent the blinkered nationalism of a bygone era, a view which earned him a rare admonishment from none other than Churchill himself, who warned him that 'We should discourage the throwing of stones since we have greenhouses of our own – acres and acres of them.'[13] Perhaps what was truly intolerable to a staunch patriot like Spears was that de Gaulle seemed more concerned with retaining France's hold over the Levant than with winning the war. Spears was candid enough to describe this metamorphosis in himself: 'A lifetime steeped in French feeling, sentiment and affection was falling from me. England alone counted now.'[14]

By the autumn of 1941, Spears had become thoroughly disillusioned with the Free French leader. As General 'Jumbo' Wilson, commander of Operation Exporter, commented wryly: 'Within a few weeks of the signing of the Armistice at Acre [Spears] suddenly turned bitterly

---

[11] Meir Zamir, 'An Intimate Alliance: The Joint Struggle of General Edward Spears and Riad al-Sulh to Oust France from Lebanon, 1942–1944', in *Middle Eastern Studies*, 41(6) (November 2005), pp. 811–32, at p. 816.

[12] Major-General Sir Edward Spears, *Fulfilment of a Mission: Syria and Lebanon 1941–1944*, London 1977, p. 142.

[13] Quoted by Zamir, 'An Intimate Alliance', p. 812.

[14] Major-General Sir Edward Spears, *Assignment to Catastrophe: The Fall of France, June 1940*, Melbourne 1954, p. 48.

anti-French. Up to that time, nothing could be too good for them.'[15] And by the end of that year, a new General Spears had emerged. He was now very much inclined to tilt towards the nationalists, since he judged that, at this stage of the war, it was more important for Britain to secure Arab goodwill than to improve relations with Free France. Spears was convinced that British interests required him to extract independence for the Levant states from the reluctant Free French, who continued to insist that the Mandate was still valid.

Spears was incensed by the way the Free French set about running things. They installed paper republics in Beirut and Damascus, and, lacking administrative manpower, they left most Vichy officials in place, merely removing a handful of the more vocal Axis sympathisers. In fact, Spears could hardly spot the difference between the Free French in the Levant and Vichy. For their part, the French saw Spears's encouragement of local nationalism as a perfidious British attempt to bring Syria and Lebanon into Britain's sphere of influence. Instead of being an instrument of Anglo-French cooperation, the Spears Mission turned into a source of some considerable friction.[16]

It was left to Churchill to calm French fears. On 9 September 1941, the prime minister rose in the House of Commons to define Britain's position on the Levant question. 'We have no ambitions in Syria', he declared.

> We do not seek to replace or supplant France, or substitute British for French interests in any part of Syria. We are only in Syria in order to win the war. However, I must make it quite clear that our policy, to which our Free French allies have subscribed, is that Syria shall be handed back to the Syrians, who will assume at the earliest possible moment their independent sovereign rights. We do not propose that this process of creating an independent Syrian Government – or Governments – because it may be that there will not be one Government – shall wait till the end of the war. We contemplate constantly increasing the Syrian share in the administration. There is no question of France maintaining the same position which she exercised

---

[15] Quoted by Gaunson, *The Anglo-French Clash*, p. 66.
[16] Raghid el-Solh, *Lebanon and Arabism*, p. 143.

*in Syria before the war, but which the French government
had realized must come to an end. On the other hand, we
recognize that among all the nations of Europe the position
of France in Syria is one of special privilege, and that in so
far as any European countries have influence in Syria, that
of France will be preeminent.*

    [Hon Members: 'Why?']

    *Because that is the policy which we have decided
to adopt. We did not go there in order to deprive France
of her historic position in Syria, except in so far as it is
necessary to fulfill our obligations and pledges to the
Syrian population. There must be no question, even in
war-time, of a mere substitution of Free French interests
for Vichy French interests. The Syrian peoples are to
come back into their own. This is fully recognized in the
documents that have been exchanged between the Minister
of State [Lyttelton] and the Free French.*

    *I was asked a question about our relations with
Iraq. They are special; our relations with Egypt are special,
and, in the same way, I conceive that France will have
special arrangements with Syria. The independence of Syria
is a prime feature of our policy.*[17]

This ambiguous statement was puzzled over by the French and the
nationalists alike, satisfying neither party. The Arabs thought it brazenly double-tongued. Churchill was, after all, an unrepentant imperialist, whose notion of Arab 'independence' was based on the shackling
treaties that Britain had concocted with both Iraq and Egypt in the
1930s. These gave Britain sovereign influence in both countries, as
well as a clear right to military bases. By the 1940s, Arab nationalists
in Syria and Lebanon were not at all prepared to accept the sort of
nominal independence which had been granted to Iraq and Egypt.

    Churchill's statement was in fact deeply contradictory. Syria
was to be independent, but the French were to retain their special
position in it. To support the aspirations of the Syrians *and* uphold the
privileged position of France was well-nigh impossible, because the
essential Syrian aspiration was to be rid of the French entirely. Britain

[17] Hansard, 9 September 1941, Prime Minister's Statement on British Policy in Syria.

claimed to have no imperial ambitions, but, in reality, its whole Levant policy was crafted in such a way as to create compliant Arab 'leaders' in its own British-controlled 'Muslim' empire.[18]

In order to encourage the French to give some ground to the nationalists in the Levant – as Britain believed it had itself done in Iraq and Egypt – the Foreign Office then went back on its word to the Syrians and Lebanese. It informed General de Gaulle privately that it recognised his right to exercise the powers granted to France under the Mandate, and it agreed that the Mandate would be terminated only when it was replaced after the war by treaties binding Syria and Lebanon to the French Republic! Obviously enough, this position was in flagrant contradiction with the declarations made by the Free French and the British on 8 June 1941.[19]

Churchill's bizarre statement to the House of Commons, and the Foreign Office's edifying 'clarifications', encouraged General Catroux to issue a manifesto of Syrian independence on 27 September 1941, in which – exploiting the conciliatory contradictions in the British position – he coolly sidestepped the whole question of independence. There was to be no restoration of constitutional processes and no meaningful shift of power to the Syrians. Catroux was to remain high commissioner in all but name: he would continue to govern by decree; he retained control of the *Troupes Spéciales*, of the *Sûreté Générale*, of the *Intérêts Communs*; and, with the aid of 'advisers' to the ministries, he would exercise powers which made a sham of all promise of independence. The new regime he set up was nothing but an elaborate and manipulative puppet show.[20]

In Syria, Catroux nominated Shaykh Taj al-Din al-Hasani as president – a man notorious for his servility to France – and Hasan al-Hakim as prime minister. In Lebanon, Alfred Naccache was given the title of president, and a new cabinet was formed on 1 December 1941 under Ahmad al-Da'uq. Spears's reaction was scathing. On Naccache's appointment he wrote graphically to Lyttelton: 'One feels as if we were holding down the Lebanon to be raped by Free France'. He found it 'singularly unpleasant' to be 'the embodiment of such a policy'.[21] Although the British considered that they had not been adequately

---

[18] Gaunson, *The Anglo-French Clash*, p. 78.
[19] Raghid el-Solh, *Lebanon and Arabism*, p. 154.
[20] Gaunson, *The Anglo-French Clash*, p. 80.
[21] Ibid., p. 82.

consulted in these arrangements, they duly recognised the two governments, formalised in a letter of congratulations which King George VI was asked to send to the president of the Syrian Republic on 29 October, which went as follows:

> *It is with great pleasure, Mr. President, that I have learned of the proclamation of the 27th September, 1941, declaring the independence of Syria and also of your assumption of the distinguished office of President of the Syrian Republic, and I send you my warmest congratulations on this auspicious occasion, with my best wishes for your health and happiness and for the welfare and prosperity of Syria and its citizens.*
>
> *It is my earnest wish that the friendly relations between our respective peoples may become increasingly close and cordial to the benefit of their mutual interests and for the development of the high principles which they hold in common. George R. I.*[22]

A similar message was sent to the president of Lebanon.

The French did not appreciate such courtly diplomatic gestures, which they read as further proof that Britain was muscling in on their turf. For their part, the nationalists found Catroux's statement and his subsequent actions wholly unacceptable. They wanted France to honour at once the promise it had made, rather than to defer major issues to a negotiation of uncertain outcome at the end of an unpredictable war.

Riad's memorandum of December 1941

Early in December, the French had word that Riad was planning to respond to Catroux's declaration. As their Beirut representatives reported to de Gaulle:

> *The extremist Muslim leader Riad el-Solh is preparing an appeal to the Allies. In his appeal, he is believed*

---

[22] Annex to an aide-mémoire handed to General de Gaulle on 28 October 1941, by the Secretary of State for Foreign Affairs. Spears Papers, St Antony's College, Middle East Library, Spears Box 1, file 4, GB16S-0269.

to criticize the new regime of Lebanese independence which, he claims, is not in conformity with the statements and promises made by Great Britain to the Lebanese and Syrians. He says it is a lame independence because the government has been chosen by General Catroux rather than elected by the people and, moreover, that the government is in possession of no official document, apart from General Catroux's statement, to consecrate the principle of independence. M. Riad el-Solh is also demanding the achievement of Syrian union.[23]

While Riad was still working on his memorandum, however, General Spears left Beirut for London on 11 December to put his views to British officials in his usual forthright manner. In his absence, Riad completed his memorandum and copies were sent to the legations and diplomatic missions of Britain, the United States, Turkey, Iraq, Saudi Arabia and Egypt. The Spears Mission took particular note of it, since Catroux's declaration of Lebanon's independence had already been the subject of a bitter dispute between Spears and de Gaulle.[24] It fell to one of Spears's assistants, John Hamilton, to receive Riad's memorandum and forward it to the minister of state in Cairo. Hamilton commented: 'It is a well-reasoned petition and it is worthy of being placed on record against the time when further decisions regarding the future of this country will be taken.'[25]

Dated 20 December 1941, Riad's memorandum was a thoroughgoing critique of General Catroux's policies and a clear statement of the Arab nationalist position. Catroux's proclamation, he declared, contradicted the promise of independence made by Catroux himself, and later reiterated by de Gaulle, Churchill and Eden, as well as the declarations made by the French and the British on 8 June 1941. He disputed Catroux's assertion of France's *droits historiques* in Lebanon, and rejected his proposal that the Mandate be replaced after the war by a treaty based on the 1936 Franco-Lebanese treaty. Any such treaty, he argued, would rob Lebanon of its sovereignty and prevent it from taking

---

[23] MAE, Nantes, Fonds Beyrouth (Amb.), série 199A4, carton 20, Délégation Générale de la France Combattante au Levant, 5 December 1941.

[24] Zamir, 'An Intimate Alliance', p. 816.

[25] Letter from Hamilton to Minister of State with Solh's petition attached (FO 371/31469/592), quoted by Zamir, 'An Intimate Alliance', p. 817. See also Alia el-Solh, '*Indama dakhalu al-tarikh*, Beirut 1959; Hilal el-Solh, *Tarikh rajul wa qadiyya*, pp. 82–7.

part in the realisation of Arab unity – as encouraged by the British government itself. Far from abolishing sectarianism and helping Lebanon to emerge as a unified Arab country, the regime proposed by the French would entrench confessional and regional divisions. Casting scorn on the 'consultations' that had preceded Catroux's declaration, he regretted that the French authorities had not allowed free elections to be held. Addressing Catroux himself, Riad declared: 'You refused to listen to those who sought to draw your attention to the real wishes of the country.'

In his memorandum, Riad deliberately avoided any reference to the controversial issue of Syrian unity, to the problem of the 'disputed territories' or to any demands of an 'Islamic' nature. Rather, he sought to express the spirit of compromise and reconciliation, which had begun to take hold among Arab nationalists in the mid-1930s, and was continuing to gain ground in the changing circumstances of the war.[26]

From an early age, Riad had been concerned to soothe Christian Lebanese fears of being swamped in a wider Muslim world. With their anxieties very much in mind, he began to recommend a gradualist and democratic approach to Arab unity, rather than anything more coercive. The result of such a delicate approach was promising. Some Maronites began to reconsider their hostile attitude towards Arab nationalism, and felt less apprehension about forging closer relations with neighbouring Arab states. Free French attempts to rekindle Maronite fears and to exclude Arab nationalists from the political process were far less effective than they had been in the past. Indeed, at a public meeting at Bkerké, the Maronite Patriarch himself denounced Catroux's plans and called for real independence for Lebanon. Far from finding themselves isolated, as the French had hoped, Arab nationalists were now at the very centre of political activity.[27]

Riad's memorandum was much debated, but it was not published in the Beirut press. Wartime censorship, as well as a shortage of newsprint, had reduced Beirut newspapers to a mere page or two, which were largely devoted to the war, to reports of rationing and other similar items of popular interest.[28] Fear of French reprisal also inhibited local

---

[26] Raghid el-Solh, *Lebanon and Arabism*, pp. 157–8; Cairo to London, 13 January 1942 (FO 371/31469); Zamir, 'An Intimate Alliance', p. 816.

[27] Raghid el-Solh, *Lebanon and Arabism*, p. 159.

[28] There was no mention of Riad's memorandum in *Beirut*, the newspaper owned by his close friend, Muhyi al-Din Nsouli, nor in *al-Nahar*, *L'Orient*, *Le Jour*, *al-Nida'* (which was closed down between 1937 and 1949) or *Lisan al-Hal* (closed down between 1932 and 1960).

editors from publishing Riad's views. He had to resort to other methods to reach a wider audience. In an article in *al-Shira'* on 7 September 1996, the Lebanese reporter, Huda al-Husayni quoted the veteran journalist Zuhayr 'Usayran as saying: 'The first political event which consolidated [my relations with Riad Bey] took place in 1941, when General Catroux published his proclamation of Lebanon's independence. Riad el-Solh refused to recognise this proclamation. He drafted a hostile response to it, but the Lebanese press refused to publish it. He asked whether I could go to Palestine and give it to the correspondent there of [the Egyptian newspaper] *al-Ahram*, which I did.'

A knighted Edward Spears returns to the Levant

Spears returned to Beirut in March 1942 with a new title and wider powers, his prestige further enhanced by Churchill's continued personal backing. In London, he was knighted – and was now known as General Sir Edward Spears. Moreover, as well as retaining his old position as Britain's chief representative to the Free French in the Levant, he was also appointed British minister to the Syrian and Lebanese republics. Within days of his return, he presented himself formally to their two presidents, but pointedly neglected to pay Catroux the official visit which the latter, as representative of the French Mandate, might well have expected. The message was clear – Spears no longer recognised the Mandate. His strategy was now to take 'independence' literally. He even demanded that Catroux refrain from invoking the Mandate at all, since it was a 'legal fiction'. He thus determined to harry the French, encourage the Syrians and the Lebanese in their quest for independence, and make the Levant an asset for the wartime Allies. De Gaulle and Catroux inevitably drew dark conclusions from these developments. Catroux complained to Lyttelton that 'Spears had acted . . . in a discourteous and threatening manner'.[29]

Riad el-Solh's relations with the Spears Mission started to blossom in the early summer of 1942. After he had held further meetings with Geoffrey Furlonge, a new tone emerged in British dispatches about him. In a memo to Spears about the situation in the Muslim community, Furlonge wrote: 'Riad Bey . . . is their only

---

[29] Gaunson, *The Anglo-French Clash*, pp. 81 ff.

notable of any calibre'.[30] A few weeks later, another dispatch reported that Riad was now convinced that the Allies would win the war and was prepared to cooperate.[31] The British began to dismiss French accusations that Riad had cooperated with the Germans and gave greater weight to Riad's own argument that the Muslims had been unfairly smeared as being pro-Axis and that they had only tilted towards the Germans in the hope of ending French control. Riad pleaded for British support for Lebanon's Muslims – of far greater strategic importance to Britain, he argued, than a small number of Lebanese Christian separatists.[32]

Spears now came to share the nationalists' view that the Mandate had had no legal foundation since April 1941, and that it had been terminated de facto by the defeat of Vichy France, if not by the Free French proclamation of independence for Syria and Lebanon. All that remained to do was the transfer of powers. But this could not be linked – still less subjected – to the conclusion of a treaty. After so many bitter experiences, the Syrians were in no mood to conclude any more treaties with France. They wanted to free themselves completely from whatever post-war pressure would be brought to bear upon them. These ideas formed the basis of Riad's entente with Spears. So began a close relationship which was to last for the next two and a half years.

By this time, Oliver Lyttelton had left Cairo to become minister of production in the UK. He was replaced briefly as minister of state by Sir Walter Monckton, and then by R. G. Casey, formerly Australia's minister in Washington. This was the new man whom Spears had now to convert to his views.

Sami el-Solh's premiership

When the Lebanese Prime Minister Ahmad Da'uq resigned in July 1942, Spears wanted Riad el-Solh to succeed him. But the French were determined to prevent it. Catroux preferred 'Abdallah al-Yafi, who was known to be pro-French and had married into the wealthy Syrian 'Azm

---

[30] Furlonge to Spears, Beirut, 8 June 1942 (FO 226/233); Zamir, 'An Intimate Alliance', p. 817.
[31] Beirut Political Officer, 23 July 1942 (FO 226/306).
[32] Zamir, 'An Intimate Alliance', p. 817.

family. Yafi had already served as a compliant prime minister before the war. Furlonge sent Spears another memo:

> *There is only one Sunni Moslem who has the necessary*
> *ability and force of character to lead the Ministry and to*
> *prevent the President from encroaching on its preserves.*
> *This is Riad el-Solh, who is disliked by the French and*
> *was at one time considered suspect by some of our*
> *security organizations. All recent reports indicate that he*
> *is nowadays convinced of an ultimate Allied victory and is*
> *prepared to cooperate loyally with us; he took the trouble*
> *to visit me and express these sentiments on the day when*
> *the recent news from Egypt was at its worst. [By early July*
> *1942, Rommel was only 60 miles from Alexandria.]*
>
> *He has the great advantage, at the present time, of*
> *having close connections with, and considerable influence*
> *on, Syria. I consider that we might be well advised to make*
> *the attempt to induce the French to accept him on these*
> *grounds. If, however, they refuse point blank, his cousin*
> *Sami el-Solh would not be wholly objectionable.*[33]

In the event, Sami el-Solh was chosen. He gave up the presidency of the Criminal Court for the prime minister's office.[34] Spears was harshly criticised by de Gaulle, and even frowned upon by his own British Foreign Office, for his intervention on behalf of Riad, and of Sami el-Solh. Riad did not mind his cousin's appointment. Quite to the contrary: he told President Naccache that he and his cousin were one, and it was enough to have one of them in power.[35] To Catroux, he remarked sarcastically that he was delighted that, after twenty years, the French had finally decided to end their boycott of the Solh family!

In any event, Riad remained highly influential behind the scenes. Under his influence, Sami pressed ahead with some Arab nationalist demands, such as the use of Arabic to replace French in official documents; the appointment of nationalists to judicial and

---

[33] Furlonge to Spears, Note for His Majesty's Minister, Beirut, 23 July 1942 (FO 226/233).

[34] Sami el-Solh, *Ahtakimu ila al-tarikh*, Beirut 1970, p. 48.

[35] Hilal el-Solh, *Tarikh rajul wa qadiyya*, p. 82; *al-Hawadith* (Beirut), no. 1087 (9 September 1977).

municipal posts; and the need for some government institutions to pass into Lebanese control. Beirut witnessed a surge of Arab nationalist sympathy. In Sidon, the Solhs and their allies the 'Usayrans celebrated Lebanon's Arabism, while in the Biqa', the Haydars rekindled unionist ideas among the inhabitants of the *caza* of Baalbek.[36] Indeed, Sami el-Solh's eight-month premiership in 1942 paved the way for Riad's own nomination to the post in the following year.[37]

The crisis over wheat

As politicians and foreign powers squabbled over ministerial appointments, the people went hungry. Lebanon was afflicted by a prolonged wheat crisis: grain was scarce because the 1941–42 winter crop had been poor and because ruthless merchants hoarded stocks in the expectation that prices would soar. But food shortages were dangerous, as they risked sparking disorder at a time when the British faced an imminent threat in Egypt from Rommel. Spears's successful resolution of the crisis was to enhance his reputation and strengthen his hand in his duel with both de Gaulle and his petulant critics in London. It was also to provide a favourable context for his emerging alliance with Riad el-Solh.

Spears's solution was to collect wheat directly from growers in exchange for cash. The total tonnage to be collected from each region was estimated and an official price fixed. The scheme was administered by the Wheat Office, or *Office des céréales panifiables* (OCP), established in May 1942 with representatives from Britain, Free France, Syria and Lebanon on its board. Spears and Catroux, however, had the final word. The key difficulty was ensuring that grain targets were met, since black market sales and smuggling across the Turkish border could not be stopped entirely, nor could the bribing of local officials. Spears's tactic was ingenious. He decreed that, from then on, offenders would be exiled to the inhospitable Red Sea island of Kamaran.

Calling on the Syrian Prime Minister Husni al-Barazi – himself a rich and powerful landowner – he gleefully told him that he would be the first to be sent to Kamaran if the quotas for his region were not

---

[36] Raghid el-Solh, *Lebanon and Arabism*, p. 166.
[37] Zamir, 'An Intimate Alliance', p. 818.

met! He added that he and Catroux would be accompanying him the following day on a visit to a grain-growing area, to see for themselves if the wheat was coming in. The results were simply miraculous. Grain poured in at a faster rate than the amazed OCP could bag it.[38] But the problem of adequate wheat supplies continued to preoccupy the British, the French and the local authorities until the very end of the war.[39]

De Gaulle's controversial visit

On 11 August 1942, General de Gaulle came to Lebanon, as he declared, 'to take men and affairs in hand . . . and demonstrate the predominance of France'.[40] In a series of grandiloquent speeches, he repeated his intention of maintaining French control over the Levant, and, in stark contrast with the prevailing mood, he sought to lessen the independence of Syria and Lebanon, strengthen the Mandate and postpone general elections indefinitely.[41] His pronouncements naturally alienated nationalist opinion and offended the general public. His arrogant assertion that France would regain its all-powerful position in the Levant, and his insistence on a treaty, persuaded some Christian politicians, including Shaykh Bishara al-Khuri, quickly to reconsider their support for Britain. In contrast, Prime Minister Sami el-Solh chose to coordinate his policies closely with the Spears Mission throughout de Gaulle's month-long visit.[42]

On 12 August 1942, the Free French leader set off on a regal progress through the Levant states, in which he treated local notables with great pomp and ceremony, while studiously ignoring some British personnel and openly insulting others. His imperial pitch was that 'the time had not yet come' for independence in Syria and Lebanon, 'and might not come for many years'. On 14 August, he sent Churchill a formal protest about the state of affairs in the Levant, alleging that the British government was breaking its agreements by constantly interfering in the internal affairs of the region. Churchill replied on 22 August that Britain had committed itself before the whole Arab

---

[38] Gaunson, *The Anglo-French Clash*, pp. 89–90.
[39] Raghid el-Solh, *Lebanon and Arabism*, pp. 164 ff.
[40] Catroux, *Dans la bataille de la Méditerranée*, p. 272.
[41] Raghid el-Solh, *Lebanon and Arabism*, p. 167.
[42] Zamir, 'An Intimate Alliance', p. 818.

world to ensuring that the French proclamation of independence was carried out.

By September, de Gaulle's volatile presence in the Levant had become an issue in itself, threatening the Allies' relations with the Arabs and straining Churchill's patience to breaking point.[43] The British prime minister therefore resorted to financial sanctions. Britain had agreed to give the Free French £300,000 on the 9th of each month and another £200,000–300,000 later in the month, specifically for their Levant expenses. As instructed by Churchill, Eden commanded the Treasury not to pay the Free French their monthly subsidy until de Gaulle agreed to return to London.[44] Under such pressure, de Gaulle finally consented to return to Britain at the end of September 1942, only to engage with Churchill in a bitter exchange over Spears's allegedly anti-French policies. Churchill's mood was not improved by a personal confrontation with de Gaulle on 30 September, when both leaders lost their temper and harsh words were exchanged.

De Gaulle wanted Spears, his bête noire, removed from the Levant – and believed himself to be on the point of securing his dismissal. He considered Spears's activities a flagrant violation of French sovereignty and a concerted effort to undermine France's position. Catroux, in turn, complained to Richard Casey, the new minister of state, that Spears 'is now the man who has assigned himself the task of destroying French influence in Syria and Lebanon'. As a result, Casey began to think that Spears may have gone too far. As for the timorous officials at the Foreign Office, they would have been most happy to be rid of Spears, whom they considered a dangerous maverick.

Beyond irritation at Spears's determined independence, there was an important disagreement of substance. Several senior Foreign Office officials did not consider themselves to be at war with French colonialism. Rather, they shared de Gaulle's conventional belief in a European colonial mission. Men like Oliver Harvey did not want the French to be kicked out of the Levant, because they thought that the British might soon require bases in Syria, which would be in the gift of the French.[45] The Foreign Office, therefore, backed de Gaulle in stressing the continued validity of the Mandate. Some officials even argued abstrusely that Catroux's declaration of June 1941 meant 'to start on

---

[43] Gaunson, *The Anglo-French Clash*, pp. 95, 96, 97, 98, 100.
[44] Ibid., p. 207, n. 48.
[45] Lewis, 'The British and the French Colonial Empire', pp. 284, 287.

a course which would bring the Mandate to an end, *not* to end the Mandate there and then'. De Gaulle therefore had support in Whitehall for his view that the legality of the Mandate had been unaffected by Catroux's dramatic declaration of June 1941.

But, as Casey cautioned the Foreign Office:

> *It is essential to preserve confidence that we shall not again abandon Syria to the French at the end of this war. If that confidence is seriously shaken, the last reason for Syrian attachment to the Allied cause will have vanished. We cannot then blame them if they put their money on Germany. Moreover . . . the fulfillment of war promise in Syria materially affects the attitude of Iraq and other Arab countries.*

In other words, Casey was arguing that Catroux's proclamation of independence and the British guarantee could not be dismissed except by a naked betrayal of 1919 dimensions.[46] Spears was then saved from dismissal when Churchill minuted that 'Spears has certainly defended, with great energy and ability, British rights in Syria'. This ended this particular 1942 campaign to dislodge him.

It had been a close run, but in the end it backfired. Wounded by de Gaulle's efforts to have him dismissed, and even more so by the arch criticisms of Anthony Eden and other Foreign Office officials, Spears became more determined than ever to work closely with Riad el-Solh and force the French out of Syria and Lebanon for good.[47]

[46] Gaunson, *The Anglo-French Clash*, p. 104.
[47] Zamir, 'An Intimate Alliance', p. 818.

35 – Riad el-Solh in Damascus *c.*1932, with his closest political allies, the
leading members of Syria's National Bloc. Front row from left: Sa'adallah
al-Jabiri, Faris al-Khouri, Ibrahim Hanano, Hashim al-Atasi, Riad el-Solh,
two unidentified persons, Jamil Mardam Bey. Second row from left: Sa'id
al-Ghazzi, 'Abd al-Rahman Kayali, unidentified person. Third row from left:
unidentified person, Najib al-Rayyes, Fayez al-Khouri, unidentified person,
Zaki al-Khatib, Tawfiq Shishakli, Nasouh Babil, Mazhar Raslan, Na'im
Antaki, Ihsan al-Sharif, Shukri al-Quwatli. (By kind permission of Dr Sabah
Kabbani.)

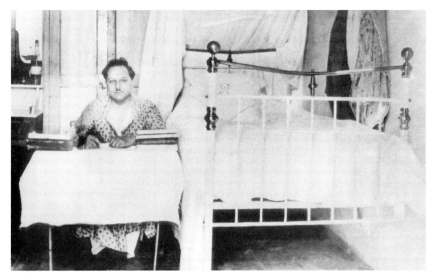

36 – Riad el-Solh under house arrest in 1935 at Qamishli, a town in the Syrian north-east, to which he was banished by the French High Commissioner comte Damien de Martel, for his support of Lebanon's nascent trades unions. (By kind permission of Ghassan Tuéni and *al-Nahar*.)

37 – Riad el-Solh (in a hat, on the far left), with the Syrian delegation, which had come to Paris in 1936 to negotiate a treaty with France. (From the Otrakji family collection at www.creativesyria.com.)

38 – The signature on 9 September 1936 of the ill-fated Franco-Syrian Treaty, in the Salon de l'Horloge of the Quai d'Orsay in Paris. The Syrian delegation comprised, from left to right, Edmond Homsi and Mustapha al-Qusari, as well as four leading nationalists, Sa'dallah al-Jabiri, Jamil Mardam Bey, Faris al-Khouri and Hashim al-Atasi (signing the document). Next to him is Pierre Viénot, secretary of state at the French Foreign Ministry, who conducted the negotiations with the Syrians. To Viénot's left is Prime Minister Léon Blum, head of France's Popular Front government. (By kind permission of the Archives of the French Ministry of Foreign Affairs, Fonds Wormser.)

39 – As Grand Mufti of Jerusalem from 1921 to 1948, Hajj Muhammad
Amin al-Husayni (1895–1974) played a leading role in opposition to
Zionism. He sided with Germany in the Second World War in the belief that
a German victory would stem the flood of Jewish immigration into Palestine.
(Reproduced from www.passia.org, by kind permission of Muhammad Abu
Rumieleh, webmaster.)

40 – Emile Eddé (1884–1949), a fervently pro-French Maronite lawyer and politician, who served as president of Lebanon from 1936 to 1941. His bitter rival, Bishara al-Khoury, was elected president in 1943, and named Riad el-Solh as his prime minister. (Photograph by John Phillips for *Life* magazine, Beirut, November 1943, copyright Time Inc.)

41 – General Henri-Fernand Dentz, Vichy's high commissioner for Syria, commanded the troops that fought the British and the Free French in the bitter war of 1941. (By kind permission of Sami Moubayed at www.syrianhistory.com.)

42 – General de Gaulle inspecting tribal forces during his regal visit to Syria in 1942. (By kind permission of the Bibliothèque de Documentation Internationale Contemporaine, Paris.)

43 – President Bishara al-Khoury of Lebanon with members of Riad el-Solh's first cabinet in 1943. From right to left, 'Adil Usayran, Camille Chamoun, Habib Abi Chahla, President Bishara al-Khouri, Riad el-Solh, Salim Takla, the Emir Majid Arslan. (By kind permission of Ghassan Tuéni and the publisher of *Le Livre de l'indépendance*, Dar al-Nahar.)

44 – Riad el-Solh addressing a cheering crowd from a balcony, on his return to Beirut in 1943, after his incarceration by the French in the fort at Rashaya. (By kind permission of Madame Leila Hamadi el-Solh.)

45 – General Sir Edward Spears and General Charles Catroux in Beirut in 1943. Having been a passionate Gaullist, Spears then became an equally passionate convert to the cause of Arab nationalism, providing Riad el-Solh with invaluable support in the struggle for Lebanese independence. (By kind permission of Sami Moubayed at www.syrianhistory.com.)

46 – Dr Chaim Weizmann (1874–1952), the long-serving Zionist leader and first president of the State of Israel. (Photograph by Bernard Hoffman, 1943, for *Life* magazine, copyright Time Inc.)

47 – David Ben-Gurion (1886–1973), under a portrait of Theodor Herzl (founder of political Zionism), reading Israel's declaration of independence on 14 May 1948, at a museum in Tel Aviv. Ben-Gurion led Israel to victory in the 1948 war, and served as prime minister from 1948 to 1963, except for a period of nearly two years in 1954–55. (Photographer, Zoltan Kluger/GPO.)

48 – Shukri al-Quwatli and Bishara al-Khouri, the presidents of Syria and Lebanon, flanked by their two prime ministers, Jamil Mardam and Riad el-Solh, at a meeting on 1 January 1947 to celebrate the departure of French troops from the Levant. They chose a historic spot on the banks of *nahr al-kalb* (the Dog river), where other conquerors had left their mark. (By kind permission of Ghassan Tuéni and the publisher of *Le Livre de l'indépendance*, Beirut 2002).

49 – Riad el-Solh with Lebanese officers in the 1940s. (By kind permission of Madame Leila Hamadi el-Solh.)

50 – Riad el-Solh with Sa'dallah al-Jabiri (1891–1948), his lifelong friend and uncle of his wife. Sa'dallah al-Jabiri was prime minister of Syria from August 1943 to October 1944, and again from October 1945 to December 1946. His early death at the age of 57 opened the way for Shukri al-Quwatli to assume the leadership of the nationalists. (By kind permission of Madame Leila Hamadi el-Solh.)

51 – Shukri al-Quwatli (1891–1967) was elected president of Syria in 1943, and then again in 1948. He was overthrown by Colonel Husni-al-Za'im in a military coup in March 1949. Voting next to Quwatli is Tawfiq al-Qabbani, the nationalist merchant from Shaqhur, and father of the poet Nizar Kabbani. (By kind permission of Dr Sabah Kabbani.)

52 – President Bishara al-Khouri and Riad el-Solh with Colonel Husni al-Za'im, author of Syria's first military putsch in 1949, for whom they had the greatest distaste. Za'im was himself overthrown and murdered by another colonel four months later. (By kind permission of Madame Leila Hamadi el-Solh.)

53 – Antun Sa'ada (1904–49), founder and leader of the *Parti populaire syrien* (later the Syrian Social Nationalist Party), in a Beirut courtroom, about to be sentenced to death for sedition in 1949. He was executed by firing squad a few hours later. (By kind permission of Ghassan Tuéni and *al-Nahar*.)

54 – President Bishara al-Khouri and Prime Minister Riad el-Solh in Beirut in the late 1940s. (By kind permission of Madame Leila Hamadi el-Solh.)

55 – King 'Abd al-'Aziz al-Sa'ud and Riad el-Solh, during one of the latter's visits to the Saudi Kingdom in the 1940s. (By kind permission of their grandson, HRH Prince Alwaleed bin Talal.)

18 THE ELECTORAL CHALLENGE

In the spring of 1943, Riad el-Solh had a sense that years of effort were about to bear fruit. The time had come, he believed, to make a bid for power through the Lebanese electoral process. He was a few months short of his fiftieth birthday. It was a moment of enormous exhilaration for him, although he could not entirely dispel a certain anxiety that French obstruction could yet shatter his ambition. He retained the memory of his first attempt to stand for parliament in 1937, when he had been forced to make a humiliating withdrawal on the very same morning of the poll, once it became clear that the French would rig the vote in order to keep him out.

This time, however, there were a number of factors distinctly in his favour. For one thing, Britain had become all-powerful in the Middle East. Its military predominance was such that it was recognised as the supreme arbiter of the situation, even by the reluctant French themselves. The British minister of state in Cairo was the ultimate regional authority. By contributing to regional integration through its Cairo-based Middle East Supply Centre, Britain had encouraged many Arab nationalists, including Riad el-Solh, to believe that an Arab union or a federation was a serious possibility.

Britain's Foreign Secretary Anthony Eden appeared to favour some form of Arab unity. His statement on the subject in the House of Commons on 24 February 1943 was deciphered optimistically, triggering a great surge of Arab diplomatic activity – although it was even more cautiously phrased than his Mansion House speech of 29 May 1941 had been. Eden declared that the initiative for Arab unity should 'come from the Arabs themselves', adding, however, that 'no such scheme which could command general approval has yet been worked out'. Nevertheless, the Arabs took these non-committal remarks to mean that Britain welcomed closer ties between Arab countries, and sought to endorse the aspirations of Syria and Lebanon for independence. They failed to grasp that Eden, an old-fashioned imperialist, did not wish to offend France – the other great European imperial power – nor endanger British cooperation with the Free French in the French-occupied Levant.

Spears and Arab nationalism

The nationalists had a precious asset close to home in the person of General Sir Edward Spears, now British minister to the Levant states. With all the fervour of a new convert, Spears had become a zealous Arabophile and a champion of Arab independence. Arab nationalism seemed to have filled the vacuum left by his previously passionate pro-French ideals. The aspirations of the Syrians and Lebanese – whom he now saw as victims of French oppression – were irresistible to him, and in this his conviction was genuine.[1] His motives, however, were complex ones. They seemed to include contempt for France's moral turpitude in the struggle against the Axis; disgust at its brutal colonial policies (conveniently forgetting Britain's own equally abhorrent colonial record); and rage at General de Gaulle's presumptuous arrogance in his dealings with Britain, a power on which the Free French movement was utterly dependent.

Spears seemed to relish every aspect of the Levantine environment in which he found himself, and in which he was treated like a prince. He shot quail on the estates of Arab notables; he was fêted in drawing rooms where society hostesses hung on his every word, delivered in his faultless French; and he engrossed himself in the Byzantine intrigues of local politics, enjoying the considerable powers that were at his disposal. What Spears seemed to delight in most was outwitting the French Delegate General Georges Catroux, while also keeping at bay his political masters at the Foreign Office in London, whose pussyfooting and cowardice he so disdained.

In dealing with the Foreign Office, Spears's temperamental inclination was to act first and justify later. But this frequent departure from normal diplomatic practice caused exasperation in Whitehall.

[1] Gaunson, *The Anglo-French Clash*, p. 70.

Some officials even thought that he was conducting a personal vendetta against de Gaulle. Internal Foreign Office memos called for him to be reined in:

> *If we are to go on with General Spears as our representative in Beirut, it seems very necessary that a firm effort should be made to rid him of his obsession over the Free French. A member of his staff . . . said that he had never known what was meant by animals eating their young until he had seen Sir E Spears devouring the Free French movement.*[2]

Another memorandum complained:

> *I know of no instance in which he may be said to have helped [the Free French] except when his assistance could be used to boost his own position, his solicitude for which is based either on personal egotism or on Empire-building proclivities, which are some two hundred years out of date. Or both . . . We have had the interesting comment from an American source that Sir E. Spears' real objective is, through the instrumentality of his over-elaborate Mission, to duplicate the French administrative system and to squeeze them out much as Clive squeezed the French out of India'.*[3]

In contrast to such pompous phraseology, Spears's own language was blunt and colourful. For example, in one of his dispatches he described Lebanon's President Alfred Naccache as 'showing something of the dangerous courage of a demented sheep'. Spears certainly was no diplomat, but a bold and skilful politician. He was able to survive in his vulnerable post because of the strong Allied interest in both Syria and Lebanon as a war base. Or because, as he never tired of reminding London, he was fulfilling the mission Britain had undertaken on 8 June 1941, when it gave the Levant states guarantees of independence. Above all, he survived because he enjoyed Churchill's personal

---

[2] Internal Foreign Office document, 28 June 1942 (FO 371/31473).
[3] Internal Foreign Office memorandum, 12 August 1942 (FO 371/31474).

support. Spears's view was that Britain's promises had to be honoured, if local opinion was to remain on the side of the Allies. Accordingly, and to the great satisfaction of Riad el-Solh and the nationalists, he maintained firm pressure on France and its local representatives to hold free and fair elections in Syria and Lebanon as soon as possible. Indeed, Spears's commitment to the Arab cause provided Riad and his associates with an opportunity which they exploited for all it was worth. Haunted by the memory of the First World War, when Britain had abandoned the Levant to the tender mercies of the French, they feared that, this time too, British interest would simply fade away after the war. Indeed, they would have liked Britain to take an even more active part in their affairs than Spears himself was ready to contemplate.

The French fight back

Although the British were militarily dominant, the French were still very present in the Levant and fought tooth and nail to protect what they saw as their vital interests. The Lyttelton–de Gaulle agreement of 25 July 1941 created a division of authority, which had given them the lead role in the civil administration of Syria and Lebanon. Determined to maintain France's hold over these states, de Gaulle sought to bind them to France by treaty, as he had made clear during his regal progress in August 1942. He had dismissed all notion of elections as premature, no doubt suspecting that a free vote would bring to power an anti-Mandate government.

In the same arrogant vein, General Catroux told Spears that the Levantines 'were not really interested in freedom'. He belittled the Syrian nationalist hero Shukri al-Quwatli as 'a plausible orator and a demagogue'.[4] By the spring of 1943, Catroux was still extremely reluctant to restore constitutional life to the Levant. To fix a date for elections, he argued, would lead to agitation. Such elections, he informed Spears, were not really necessary from an internal point of view. The pressure for them was due to the external influence of Iraq and Egypt, both of which could be safely ignored.

---

[4] Record of 7 March 1942 meeting with General Catroux about Shukri al-Quwatli (FO 371/31481).

Catroux's inclination was to recall the submissive 1937 Chamber, which he thought would head off British intervention. He also hoped it would check what the French considered an unfortunate trend among some Christians, to reach an entente with the Muslims, on the basis of a Muslim acceptance of Greater Lebanon.[5] Parroting Catroux's ignoble position, Syria's French-appointed President Shaykh Taj al-Din al-Hasani, and Lebanon's pro-French President Alfred Naccache, both strongly objected to the holding of elections. The latter even had the gall to tell Spears that elections would merely inflame local passions and would serve no useful purpose whatsoever.[6]

Yet, in spite of Spears's support, the nationalists still faced an uphill struggle. For, by 1943, when the German threat to the Middle East had been largely dispelled, Eden was no longer as anxious to conciliate Arab opinion as he had been in 1941. As the fighting shifted from the Middle East to Europe, London began to review its priorities, and the Arab world suddenly seemed far less important. Britain had now to focus on its post-war relations with the French. Eden and the Foreign Office were coming round to the view that it might be better to keep the Mandate system in place, and not disturb the French position in the Levant. France should be allowed to retain its local privileges, London started to argue – and certainly in Lebanon. This cynical sentiment ran contrary to Spears's passionate belief in Arab independence, and was inevitably to lead to a clash.

Riad el-Solh, in the meantime, knew that the French were still powerful enough to make his life very difficult. Only by winning an election could he manage to come to power, but this was where France's control of the bureaucracy, and indeed of the whole electoral process, might thwart him. He could not afford to confront the French head-on. He certainly wished to take full advantage of Spears's political sympathy for the nationalist cause, but not in such a way as to offend the French, who would then move heaven and earth to keep him from office. It was now time to dissemble. Riad would have to manoeuvre skilfully between Spears and Catroux. But even before that, he would have to get himself onto an electoral list.

[5] Beydoun, 'Riad el-Solh et les élections législatives de 1943', p. 409.
[6] Spears to Foreign Office, 21 February 1942 (FO 371/31471).

The local political scene

Several mutual antagonisms complicated the Lebanese political scene. President Naccache was hostile to Patriarch Antoine 'Arida, the powerful Maronite prelate, as well as to Shaykh Bishara al-Khoury and his Constitutional Bloc. Patriarch 'Arida, in turn, was hostile to General Catroux, to the point that, in April 1942, he cancelled the traditional Easter Monday Mass, rather than suffer the presence at it of the French delegate general.[7] Relations between the Patriarch and the French had been strained ever since the tobacco crisis of the mid-1930s, when France had sought to impose a *Régie* monopoly.

The crisis had worsened over the following years, reaching a peak with the spectacular rapprochement – engineered by Riad el-Solh – between the Patriarch and the Muslim leaders of both Lebanon and Syria. At a meeting at the Patriarch's seat at Bkerké on Christmas Day 1941, 'Arida had joined the nationalists in calling for a restoration of the Constitution and for 'true independence' for Lebanon.

But by 1943, this rapprochement had worn thin, and confessional polarisation had once again reasserted itself. The upshot was that Riad could no longer count on the support of the Christian clergy.[8] Indeed, the Patriarch was now solidly opposed to the allegedly 'pro-Muslim' policies of Prime Minister Sami el-Solh, who was, ironically enough, also under pressure from members of his own Muslim camp, who felt that he had failed to protect *their* interests. And some Muslim leaders, who had become jealous of his tenure of office, were plotting to replace him. In short, Sami's political power had seriously deteriorated. This was not good news for the Solh family in general – nor for Riad in particular.[9]

The overall situation was also plagued by unresolved problems of a more fundamental nature. Did the Mandate still have any legal or de facto relevance? Should the nationalists commit themselves to negotiating a new treaty with France, as the French were now demanding as a precondition for holding elections? Lebanese and Syrian nationalists were unanimous in rejecting this demand, as Lieutenant-Colonel Geoffrey Furlonge, Britain's political officer in Beirut, reported to the Foreign Office on 28 February 1943.

---

[7] Spears Mission weekly summary, Syria and Lebanon, 9 April 1942 (FO 371/3471).
[8] Beydoun, 'Riad el-Solh et les élections législatives de 1943', p. 409.
[9] Spears Mission weekly political summary, 3 February 1943 (FO 371/35174).

Riad Bey Solh visited me yesterday on his return from Damascus . . . He had enquired among the [Syrian] Nationalists their present views on the conclusion of a treaty with the French and had found them all of the opinion that there could be no question of discussing that now . . . The first thing, in their opinion, was to get constitutional government re-established in Syria.[10]

Spears concurred with this position. He reported to London that 'the great bulk of the native populations in both states would be strongly opposed to the conclusion of treaties of any sort with the Fighting French chiefly because . . . they hope that the end of the war will somehow bring them complete emancipation'.[11]

There were other contentious questions. Should the old Chamber of Deputies be recalled and a Senate nominated, or should a fresh start be made with new elections? Spears pressed for new elections, but Catroux dragged his feet. Should a third of the deputies be nominated, or should all the deputies be elected? The Lebanese electoral law had always made provision for a certain number of nominated deputies. The principle of having one-third of the Chamber nominated was introduced in 1927, but the overall number of deputies had varied: forty-six in 1927, forty-five in 1929 and twenty-five in 1934. In 1937 the number was raised to sixty-three, of which one-third was, as usual, nominated. The nomination of deputies had been a device by the party in power to consolidate its position. If, for example, it found itself in a minority in parliament, it would dissolve the Chamber and arbitrarily increase the number of deputies, of which it would then nominate one-third to suit its purpose. What was to be done about this stain on the parliamentary record? Anxious to strengthen his own position, President Naccache was naturally in favour of the practice continuing. But the nationalists, and indeed most progressive elements in the body politic, felt that there was no place for such a risible system of nominated deputies.

Riad el-Solh wondered, in turn, if truly free elections could indeed be held, or if the old French habits of bribery, intimidation and vote-rigging were by now so deeply entrenched as to make real

[10] G. W. Furlonge to Foreign Office, 28 February 1943 (FO 226/240).
[11] Spears to Foreign Office, 10 March 1943 (FO 371/35175).

change unlikely. In the run-up to previous Lebanese 'elections', the usual practice had been for the entire Civil Service to be subjected to a veritable reign of terror. All officials suspected of sympathy for the opposition – or of simply holding lukewarm sentiments towards the government – were brutally dismissed and replaced by electoral agents of the governing party. These then set about distributing sinecures on a lavishly corrupt and highly corrupting scale. Ministers standing for re-election stopped at nothing to frustrate their opponents. When, and in spite of such blatant measures, the government's majority was still looking fragile, it breezily eliminated the danger by duplicating the ballot papers![12]

Although the Fighting French – *La France combattante*, as de Gaulle had dubbed his movement – had now replaced Vichy, the local administration was still riddled with all manner of abuse. French corruption, as the holier-than-thou Geoffrey Furlonge now reported, was rife in the fields of justice, supply services, concessionary companies, funds of Common Interest and domestic morals. 'The moral corruption of the French authorities has always been a by-word and the Fighting French are not a whit better than their predecessors', he wrote primly.

Petticoat influence on promotions, appointments and concessions is too obvious and too widespread to be in doubt. In the past, the most notorious case was probably the liaison between the comte de Martel, the French high commissioner, and the wife of the then Belgian consul general, who secured the appointment of a Lebanese prime minister and the issue of a large wheat contract to two of her friends in return for large payments. Amongst the Fighting French, domestic fidelity seems to be the exception rather than the rule and in certain branches, particularly of the Fighting French military forces, officers' promotion appears largely to depend on the willingness of their wives to oblige their chiefs.[13]

An example was set at the top of the local French administration in 1943, when Jean Helleu, who replaced Catroux as delegate general,

---

[12] G. W. Furlonge to Foreign Office, February 1943 (FO 226/240).
[13] G. W. Furlonge to Foreign Office, 4 October 1942 (FO 371/31479).

installed his mistress in an office of the *Sérail* within a few weeks of the arrival of his wife.[14]

The general tension and uncertainty in Lebanon in 1942–43 were compounded by the grim economic situation, which Spears blamed squarely on 'the shockingly incompetent administration of Catroux's own puppets'. The cost of living had soared. Merchants hoarded key supplies such as wheat in order to manipulate prices. In the summer of 1942, the price of wheat on the black market had risen to four times the controlled price, causing Spears to take draconian measures.[15] In January 1943, he deported a number of prominent hoarders, including Shaykh Muhammad al-Faraj, head of the Wulda tribe in the Jazira, for failing to deliver the wheat quota imposed on his villages. 'Similar action', Spears told London, 'will be taken against other notables, unless they comply with the demands of the *Office de céréales panifiables* within a specified time-limit'.[16]

These problems and tensions led to disputes within the French camp itself, suffering as it was from the continued feud between Gaullists and Pétainists. Monsieur Lépissier, secretary-general at the *Délégation Générale*, warned Spears that Vichy elements continued to be active in the Levant states, posing a danger to the Allied cause. He pointed an accusing finger at Blanchet, head of the *Cabinet Militaire*, Boegner, head of the *Cabinet Politique*, Gautier, head of the *Sûreté Générale*, and Buis, the *Sûreté* chief in Damascus, claiming he was certain that these men continued to be in touch with Vichy. Catroux, he explained,

had given his full support to these individuals firstly, because they flattered him and he was a very vain man, and secondly, because, largely thanks to Madame Catroux [who was certainly no Gaullist] he had always wished to maintain the door ajar to Vichy . . . Madame Catroux kept on making the most violent attacks on General de Gaulle to M. Helleu, who was naturally much embarrassed.[17]

Anthony Eden had grown weary of Spears's repeated complaints of French misbehaviour. He reprimanded him for allegedly suggesting to

---

[14] HM Chargé d'affaires, Beirut, to Foreign Office, 17 July 1943 (FO 226/240).
[15] Spears to Foreign Office, 16 July 1942 (FO 371/31474).
[16] Spears to Foreign Office, 9 January 1943 (FO 371/35174).
[17] Spears to Foreign Office, 9 January 1943 (FO 371/325174).

a French representative that the Lyttelton–de Gaulle agreement was no longer valid. Spears heatedly rebutted the charge, maintaining that 'the mistaken and malicious interpretation [of his remarks] had emanated from a "Mafia" within the *Délégation*'. The problem, he added, was that 'the principal French representative [Helleu] is powerless in the hands of ill-intentioned subordinates'.[18] But this did not satisfy his critics in London.

Riad el-Solh and General Catroux

As the situation developed, a great deal came to depend on the evolution of Catroux's own thinking, as well as on the instructions he received from the French National Committee in Algiers – and indeed, from de Gaulle himself. In December 1942, Catroux seemed inclined to make concessions to the nationalists. Spears reported, for example, that in a brief meeting with Riad el-Solh and Bishara al-Khoury, Catroux had been anxious to seem friendly. '"What do you want?" he had asked. "Everything!" Riad had replied with a grin. Catroux grinned back and indicated, with a wave of his hand, that there should be no difficulty about it. He did not mention the question of a treaty'.[19] Things seemed to be moving in the right direction. Indeed, by February 1943, Spears reported that Catroux had

> *largely lost interest in the affairs of these countries and is thinking in the main of North Africa and of his schemes there. For instance, talking of the elections, he told me that he was fed up with the whole question and wanted it out of the way. This should greatly facilitate matters and I only hope that the Mafia will not manage to work up his old suspicions and inhibitions.*[20]

But, when Riad had a long interview with Catroux in early March 1943 – only the second time he had had a real discussion with him – he came away disappointed. As he told Furlonge, he had put his views to

---

[18] Spears to Anthony Eden, 8 February 1943 (FO 371/35175).
[19] Spears to Foreign Office, reporting what Furlonge had told him, 17 December 1942 (FO 226/242).
[20] Spears to Foreign Office, 21 February 1943 (FO 371/35175).

Catroux clearly and forcefully, and had explained to him that he and his associates were opposed to the recall of the 1937 Chamber. They wished to be assured instead that any government formed to conduct elections would be chosen from all important elements of the country – including the Muslim opposition. The latter had a right to be represented in any future Chamber, and insisted on being given the chance to voice its views, like any other group.

Riad had then gone on the offensive, telling Catroux that he had proof that Monsieur Pruneaud, the French *Conseiller* at Sidon, had publicly stated that Riad's candidature had to be opposed by all possible means, and that he (Pruneaud) had prepared a list of candidates, whom the French would support. Catroux was embarrassed and promised to investigate. Riad had gone on to tell Catroux that, while he and his associates were in favour of Lebanese independence, they opposed any 'dismemberment' of the country.

This was a clear shift in the nationalists' position. Previously, they had wanted the 'disputed territories' returned to Syria. But now that they had entered the Lebanese political arena, they were anxious to protect the integrity of Greater Lebanon. This was because they knew that the only regions that were liable to secede were the predominantly Muslim ones. Any secession on their part would leave the remaining Lebanese Muslims in a position of hopeless political inferiority to the Christians.

Riad el-Solh now joked to Catroux that he had no doubt heard him described as a dangerous enemy of France. It was true that he had much with which to reproach the French. Nevertheless, he recognised that the Lyttelton–de Gaulle agreement had accorded France a privileged position in the country. He, for one, was prepared to concede it a cultural, and even an economic, pre-eminence, provided that Lebanon's sovereign independence was not compromised.

But Riad had been dismayed by Catroux's reaction to his remarks. He had felt that 'the General was preparing to act on lines far removed from any that a Nationalist could approve, for he had given not one indication of any genuine sympathy for Lebanese aspirations towards independence'.[21] Despite Riad's pessimism, however, Catroux was soon to give the nationalists an agreeable surprise.

---

[21] G. W. Furlonge to Foreign Office, 4 March 1943 (FO 226/240).

The launch of the election campaign

On 24 January 1943, the French National Committee in Algiers – no doubt under British pressure – gave Catroux the green light to restore constitutional life in the Levant states.[22] Accordingly, in a broadcast from Beirut on 18 March 1943, Catroux announced that he had issued three decrees: the first restored the Lebanese Constitution, and was to come into effect on the day the president of the Republic was elected by the Chamber of Deputies. The Chamber itself was to emerge from general elections to be held within three months. This was later amended on 25 March to specify that the three-month limit was not for the election of a parliament but for the convocation of electoral colleges. No date was fixed for the elections themselves, quickly raising fears that the French might once again seek to delay them.

Catroux's second decree established a non-political provisional authority to conduct the general elections, 'immune from extraneous influences and conducted in a spirit of freedom, good order and respect for the opinions of others'. His third decree named Dr Ayyub Thabit as head of this provisional authority, with the twin titles of head of state and head of government. He was to be assisted by two ministers, Jawad Bulos and Khalid Chehab.[23]

Spears immediately claimed credit for this French volte-face. 'Catroux's proclamation', he crowed to London,

not only contains every one of the points I have contended were essential or important if Lebanese independence was to be real, but both in his appeal to the people and in his reference to the freedom they will achieve he expresses views which we can wholeheartedly support. He has in fact been extremely responsive to my suggestions. The result justifies the very hard and prolonged struggle I have had in the past.[24]

The expectation of an early return to constitutional life aroused intense excitement throughout Lebanon, as well as a surge of political activity.

---

[22] See Rabbath, *La Formation historique du Liban*, p. 474, for the statement by the National Committee. Rabbath's monumental work is an indispensable source for the history of Lebanon from the earliest times to independence.

[23] Summary of declaration by General Catroux, 18 March 1943 (FO 371/35176).

[24] Spears to Foreign Office, 19 March 1943 (FO 371/35178).

Political parties started marshalling their forces for the coming struggle and intriguing for French and British support. Electioneering was soon in full swing in all five *muhafazats* (administrative districts), where candidates now jockeyed for position.

Meanwhile, Jean Helleu – who had served in Beirut in the 1930s under High Commissioner Ponsot – was appointed to succeed Catroux as delegate general and plenipotentiary for the Fighting French in the Levant. Catroux was transferred to Algiers as commissioner for Muslim affairs.

Helleu was deeply suspicious of the British, and his appointment was therefore a setback for the nationalists. He was no doubt influenced by a report he had received of the proceedings of Britain's Middle East War Council, which, at its meeting in Cairo on 10–13 May, had resolved that

The continued presence of France in the Levant is incompatible with our political and military interest in the Middle East, as well as with the peaceful development and well-being of the Arab countries . . . Any form of closer political association between the Arab states, or even between the states of Greater Syria, a development to which HMG has declared themselves sympathetic, is hardly possible as long as the French maintain any direct influence, political or military, in Syria and Lebanon.[25]

This uncompromising statement did not actually reflect the views of the conciliatory Foreign Office. It was the views of Spears and of Britain's new minister of state in the Middle East, Richard Casey. Helleu, however, could not have known that. It was hardly surprising, therefore, that he encouraged his newly appointed head of state, Dr Ayyub Thabit, to take an even harder pro-French line.

At 73, Thabit was already well advanced in age. Born in Beirut in 1870, he had graduated from the Syrian Protestant College (later the American University of Beirut), and studied medicine in the United States before returning to Beirut just before the First World War. There, he had become secretary of the Reform Committee (*al-jam'iyya al-islahiyya*), had attended the Arab conference in Paris of 1913, and

[25] Raghid el-Solh, *Lebanon and Arabism*, p. 174.

had held various ministerial posts between the wars.[26] Spears reported to the Foreign Office that Thabit was a Protestant of considerable integrity and independent mind, but added shrewdly that he was short-tempered and had proved difficult to work with in the past.[27] Indeed, the view soon took hold in Lebanese political circles that Dr Thabit was dictatorial by nature, and was so avid for power that he would make every effort to postpone the elections so as to remain in office as long as possible. He outraged the nationalists by denouncing Riad el-Solh and 'Abd al-Hamid Karami as 'anti-Lebanese'. This easy insult caught the ear of Patriarch 'Arida, who was by now so suspicious of Muslim politicians that he wanted all candidates in the forthcoming elections to swear an oath of loyalty to the *kiyan* – that is to say, to the 'entity' of Greater Lebanon.[28]

Worse was to follow. On 17 June, Thabit issued two decrees, numbers 29 and 50. The first ordained that those overseas Lebanese, who had kept their Lebanese nationality (and were mostly Christian), would be included in any count of Lebanon's population, thus increasing the Christian element in the electorate. The second changed the confessional distribution in the five *muhafazats* in favour of the Christians. The total number of deputies was increased from forty-two to fifty-four (thirty-two Christians and twenty-two Muslims). Of the twelve new deputies, ten were Christian and only two Muslim (with one a Sunni and one a Shi'i).

It was obvious that the French mandatory power and its hardline Christian clients were determined to ensure a parliamentary majority, which would uphold the French presence and perpetuate French protection for a Christian-dominated Lebanon.[29] Thabit then announced that he was delaying the elections until September, arguing unconvincingly that the summer was the busiest time of the year, with the tourist season in full swing and the harvesting of wheat and silkworm growing at their peak. Spears and Furlonge accurately considered Thabit's moves to be grave errors of political judgement.

His arbitrary decrees plunged the country into a bitter confessional crisis. Riad and other Muslim leaders met at the Lebanese Mufti's house on 19 June, and demanded that the French cancel Thabit's

---

[26] Ibid., pp. 169 ff.
[27] Spears to Foreign Office, 10 March 1943 (FO 371/35175).
[28] Raghid el-Solh, *Lebanon and Arabism*, p. 173.
[29] Beydoun, 'Riad el-Solh et les élections législatives de 1943', p. 410.

decrees. Failing that, they would insist on a new census. Otherwise they would boycott the elections altogether. They set up a committee which sent a formal protest to the French, British, American, Egyptian and Iraqi representatives in Beirut. Furlonge reported to London that

> *in conversation on June 20, Riad el-Solh, who is the strongest personality on the committee, stated that, in view of the barefaced manner in which the Christians had manoeuvred in the matter of these decrees, he felt that the Muslims could no longer usefully participate in the elections and should return to their previous attitude of aloofness and non-cooperation with the Lebanon, and should maintain their demands for the return to Syria of the four cazas attached to Lebanon after the last war.*[30]

Angry and gloomy, Riad el-Solh, 'Abd al-Hamid Karami and Sa'ib Salam visited Furlonge on 29 June, in order to inform him that they had come to the conclusion that Muslims could not hope for a fair deal in Lebanon, since the French were adamant in upholding Christian domination. Invoking the ideals of the Atlantic Charter, they called for British intervention. Furlonge felt obliged to point out that the Atlantic Charter 'was hardly applicable to a state in which the two main halves of the population wanted totally different ways of life'.[31]

The Lebanese crisis gave Egypt's *Wafd* Party, and its leader Mustafa al-Nahhas, an opening in which to emphasise Egypt's central role in Arab affairs. When the Germans were threatening to invade Egypt, the British had forced King Farouk to call on Nahhas Pasha to form a government, and he had won an overwhelming majority at elections in March 1942. Nahhas Pasha now wished to enhance his party's image and his own prestige as the defender of the Arab nationalist cause. He was, therefore, happy to respond to a call for help from Riad el-Solh and to offer his services as a mediator in the Lebanese crisis. Spears, too, hurried to intervene. He put maximum pressure on Helleu to abrogate Thabit's decrees, warning that the crisis posed a threat to the country's security – and therefore to the British war effort.

---

[30] G. W. Furlonge to Foreign Office, 21 June 1943 (FO 226/240).
[31] G. W. Furlonge to Foreign Office, 29 June 1943 (FO 226/240).

Alarmed at this turn of events, Catroux also entered the fray. To calm inflamed Muslim passions, he suggested that the formula proposed by Nahhas Pasha be accepted, namely that of a 5:4 ratio in the Chamber between Christians and Muslims, which would result in twenty-nine Christian seats and twenty-four Muslim seats. He also promised to conduct a general census after the elections. But when this proposal failed to win general approval, Spears stepped in to arbitrate. His formula of a 6:5 ratio between Christians and Muslims proved to be the winning one, and was to result in thirty seats for the Christians and twenty-five seats for the Muslims (Sunni, Shi'i and Druze). It fact it was to remain in force until the Lebanese Constitution was amended following the Ta'if accord of 1989. Spears also managed to persuade Helleu to abolish the principle of nominated deputies, which had given supporters of the French Mandate a built-in majority. The door was thus opened wide for an electoral contest in which Britain – posing as the champion of free and fair elections in Lebanon (despite its tarnished record elsewhere in the world) – now had the star role.

Riad el-Solh and his associates were given further encouragement by the victory of the National Bloc at Syrian elections in July. His friends had triumphed. The nationalist hero Shukri al-Quwatli was elected president, and promptly named Sa'dallah al-Jabiri as Prime Minister. Jamil Mardam became foreign minister; Lutfi al-Haffar, minister of interior; Khaled al-'Azm, finance minister; and Dr 'Abd al-Rahman Kayyali, minister of justice. Spears assured Anthony Eden that the elections were the fairest that had ever been held in Syria, and that the overwhelming majority of the Syrian electorate was in favour of the National Bloc. The Syrian results seemed to foreshadow Riad el-Solh's own bid for power. It seemed as if liberation was at hand for the long-suffering Levant!

The turning point in Riad's relations with the French came on 14 July 1943, when Catroux – then on a brief visit to Beirut from Algiers – asked Riad to call on him. They had a long and unusually friendly discussion. According to Riad's account to Furlonge the next day, Catroux had not spared his criticism of Dr Ayyub Thabit for promulgating his controversial decrees and postponing the elections. Riad raised with Catroux the question of his own candidature and that of 'Abd al-Hamid Karami, the nationalist leader from Tripoli. They represented, he argued, an important section of Lebanese opinion and could not, for any valid reason, be excluded. Catroux had given Riad the impression that he agreed with him, even hinting that France might perhaps have followed a mistaken policy in Lebanon – a reference to its exclusive support for the Maronites. As Furlonge commented wryly: 'All this came well from the Co-ordinator of Muslim Affairs, and certainly pleased Riad'.[32] Even more encouraging was Catroux's frank criticism of Helleu, for mismanaging the situation and posing such an unwarranted challenge to Muslim opinion.

On 21 July, Jean Helleu promulgated a decree replacing the now thoroughly unpopular Dr Thabit by Butros ('Petro') Trad as head of state, with 'Abdallah Bayhum as secretary of state. Trad was a Paris-educated lawyer from a prominent Greek Orthodox Beirut family, who had been a member of parliament since 1922. His low-key approach was very different from that of Thabit, and helped at once to reduce confessional tensions.[33] It was then announced that elections would be held on 29 August and 5 September, followed by presidential elections on 19 September.

Politicians turned their attention to the composition of electoral lists. For Riad el-Solh, it was still not plain sailing. As the Spears Mission reported to London, 'We still have very good reason for entertaining fears about [French] interference in the forthcoming elections. In particular, the French *Conseillers* in North Lebanon (Dementsys) and South Lebanon (Pruneaud) have beyond the slightest doubt been intriguing, threatening and bribing most actively; and Helleu's repeated promises to call them to order have so far had no effect'.[34] Riad was encouraged by Spears's sustained efforts to loosen France's grip on Lebanon's political life. But with the elections now fast approaching, he had some important decisions to make.

The choice of South Lebanon

Riad was determined to enter parliament, but where was he to stand? Should he attempt to get elected in Beirut, or might his chances be better in South Lebanon? In Beirut, his prospects did not seem particularly good. The Christians of the city – half the electorate – were

---

[32] G. W. Furlonge to Foreign Office, 16 July 1943 (FO 226/240).
[33] Raghid el-Solh, *Lebanon and Arabism*, p. 178.
[34] D. W. Lascelles of the Spears Mission to the Foreign Office, 9 August 1943 (FO 226/240).

largely hostile to him. His entente with the Patriarch, which had lasted eighteen happy months, had ended. 'Arida had even given fervent support to Thabit's decrees.[35] Nor could Riad count on solid backing from his own Sunni community, since men like 'Abdallah al-Yafi and Sa'ib Salam, and even his own cousin, Sami el-Solh, aspired to gain the premiership for themselves and could not be expected to make way for him.[36] They knew, as did everyone else, that if Riad el-Solh were to win an election in Beirut, he would at once become the uncontested leader in the capital, because of his greatly superior Arab and international renown. All others would be left with no choice but to defer to him.

Riad had also to consider that his image had been somewhat tarnished by wounding accusations – put about by his enemies – that he had profited from Sami el-Solh's premiership. The French *Sûreté Générale*, which loathed him, bruited it about that his house was always besieged by jobseekers, or by plaintiffs before the courts, who had come to solicit his intervention with the authorities – for which they were prepared to pay.[37] For all these reasons, Riad decided to leave to Sami the task of representing the Solhs in Beirut. In the event, two lists were formed in the capital: one led by Sami el-Solh, with Naccache as its nominal Christian leader; the other led by 'Abdallah al-Yafi, with George Thabit as its nominal leader.

In early August 1943, Riad made a firm decision to stand in South Lebanon. He had for several weeks been keeping a close eye on the unfolding campaign there and had noted that no other Sunni figure of national stature had decided to stand. This was plainly to his advantage. In the South, the Shi'is had six seats, reflecting their demographic weight, while the Greek Orthodox, Greek Catholics, Maronites and Sunnis had one seat each. The Sunni seat was the one Riad had to win. The incumbent after the 1937 elections had been the Emir Khalid Chehab of Hasbaya, who had been France's closest Muslim supporter in the creation of Greater Lebanon.[38]

Riad had been utterly engrossed in Arab affairs for all of his political life. He had not immersed himself enough in the detail of life

[35] Beydoun, 'Riad el-Solh et les élections législatives de 1943', p. 417.
[36] Ibid., p. 419.
[37] CADN, Fonds Beyrouth, carton 21, Information, *Sûreté Générale*, Beirut, 17 September 1942.
[38] Beydoun, 'Riad el-Solh et les élections législatives de 1943', pp. 443–4.

in South Lebanon, and had failed to cultivate close ties with the local notables and families – an essential prerequisite for victory. He could not be certain of winning. But his family rallied round to help. His cousin, Kadhim el-Solh, started paying weekly visits to Sidon to mobilise support for him, while Mamduh el-Solh, Sami el-Solh's brother, also stopped at the town for discussions with local people on his way to his property at 'Arnun, near Nabatieh. Riad himself concentrated his efforts on Sidon, where he was able to win support from his wealthy, landowning Jawahiri cousins – Yusuf Jawahiri had represented Sidon on the Administrative Council of Greater Lebanon in 1920 – and from two other leading families of the town, the Zayns and the Mahjubs.[39] He still had to contend with the French, however, whose local officials were determined by threats and bribes to keep the nationalists out of parliament and the Mandate in place. Some officials even talked openly of a 'French list of candidates', which a committee composed of Messrs Baelen, Boegner and Rozek (key figures in the *Délégation Générale*) was drawing up, and which the *Délégation* would support.

G. W. Furlonge feared that the local population would form the impression that nothing had changed, and that Lebanese 'independence' was just a cloak for continued French domination. He reported to London that

> *In South Lebanon, the activities of M. Pruneaud, the French* Conseiller, *have passed all permissible limits. He has already formed his list (composed for the most part of sycophantic nonentities), is engaging in constant consultation with notables, and is using every means in his power to impress upon the public that his candidates must be elected, and that anyone standing against them will be opposed by the* Délégation Générale, *which he openly states 'will run the elections.' The powers which he can exercise through the* Gardes Mobiles, *the* Sûreté, *etc, and in such matters as car-restrictions and supplies, are sufficiently great to enable him to intimidate most electors.*

Furlonge noted that Pruneaud's influence was particularly directed against Riad el-Solh, a nationalist leader whom he considered dangerous,

---

[39] Ibid., p. 441.

and against 'Adil 'Usayran, whom he believed to be pro-British. Pruneaud was chiefly concerned to ensure that Ahmad al-As'ad, the only powerful South Lebanon candidate amenable to his influence, would not join either Riad el-Solh or 'Adil 'Usayran on a common list.[40] 'Adil 'Usayran and Ahmad al-As'ad were indeed to be the two poles around which Riad el-Solh was to conduct his campaign, and which were ultimately to determine its outcome.

The emergence of a 'unified list'

'Adil 'Usayran – nephew of Najib 'Usayran, a notable who had been a member of previous Lebanese parliaments under the French Mandate – had emerged on the South Lebanon scene during the tobacco crisis of the 1930s. He had backed the proposal for a *Régie* monopoly, which the French had sought to impose, and was at the time on close and friendly terms with Zinovi Pechkhoff, the French *conseiller* who ruled the South like a personal fief. The adopted son of the Russian writer Maxime Gorki, Pechkhoff was later to have a remarkable career as a Gaullist general and as French ambassador to Japan, immediately after the Second World War.

But when the tobacco crisis degenerated in 1936 into armed clashes at Bint Jbeil, resulting in casualties and arrests, 'Adil 'Usayran changed camps. Turning against the French, he became a fervent advocate of Syrian unity and allied himself with Kadhim el-Solh in the National Call Party (*hizb al-nida' al-qawmi*). He was married to Nadia, a refined and beautiful daughter of the Khalil family of Tyre, Riad el-Solh's powerful allies in that coastal town.

When 'Adil made a violent speech against the *Régie* and in support of the tobacco growers, the French had him arrested and sent for trial. They were convinced that the entire tobacco protest movement had been incited by Riad el-Solh and the Syrian delegation, which was then negotiating their ill-fated treaty in Paris.[41] In 1943, eight years later, the French still considered 'Adil 'Usayran an enemy.

The case of Ahmad al-As'ad was altogether different. He was an establishment figure, heir to one of the most powerful families of

---

[40] G. W. Furlonge to Foreign Office, 10 February 1943 (FO 226/240).
[41] Beydoun, 'Riad el-Solh et les élections législatives de 1943', pp. 420–1; Chalabi, *The Shi'is of Jabal 'Amil*, pp. 137–8.

the Jabal 'Amil, who had cooperated with the Turks and then with the French. Ahmad al-As'ad's father, 'Abd al-Latif, had represented the family in the parliaments of the French Mandate. On his death in 1935, Ahmad had taken over the leadership of the family, entering parliament in 1937 and serving briefly as a minister in Ahmad Da'uq's government in 1941–42.

Ahmad al-As'ad was the nephew of Kamil al-As'ad, Rida el-Solh's rival in South Lebanon in the early years of the First World War. It will be recalled that Kamil had denounced Rida to the Turks for nationalist activities, which had resulted in Rida and his son Riad being sent for trial to Aley.

Against this background, it might have been supposed that Riad el-Solh would keep well away from Ahmad al-As'ad, his family's traditional opponent, and line up with 'Adil 'Usayran, now his comrade in resistance to the Mandate. But it did not happen that way. With characteristic political shrewdness, Riad decided that it would not be in his interest to join 'Usayran on an overtly anti-French list. Seeking to reassure the French, he preferred to ally himself with this more powerful Shi'i notable, Ahmad al-As'ad, whom the French considered reliable. But how was such an alliance – which seemed almost against nature – to be realised?

The key intermediary between them was Yusuf Salem, an old parliamentarian who had first been elected in 1925 and was considered something of an expert at putting electoral alliances together. He was the man who had persuaded the British in 1941 that Riad el-Solh and the National Bloc in Syria were not implacably hostile to British interests. He had urged Furlonge to meet Riad rather than arrest him, and bring him over to the Allied side (as he was later to recount in his book, *Khamsun sana ma' al-nas* – Fifty Years with the People). It was Yusuf Salem, too, who had organised meetings at his home between Furlonge and the Syrian nationalist leaders, Shukri al-Quwatli and Sa'dallah al-Jabiri. Furlonge's entente with Riad el-Solh had been somewhat easier to arrange because, unlike the other two, he had not gone to Baghdad at the time of the Rashid 'Ali uprising, although he had certainly organised meetings in support of the brave Iraqi nationalist.

Yusuf Salem now moved to bring Riad el-Solh and Ahmad al-As'ad together.[42] He proposed that they engage in a preliminary

---

[42] Beydoun, 'Riad el-Solh et les élections législatives de 1943', pp. 425, 430.

dialogue with a view to concluding an electoral pact. A dialogue accordingly took place. No doubt the declining influence of the French *Délégation Générale* and the growing influence of the Spears Mission persuaded Ahmad al-As'ad that a list with Riad had a much better chance of victory than a totally pro-French one. There was, however, some resistance to the idea of a pact with Riad from members of the Shi'i electorate, who feared it would lead to Sunni domination. They had not welcomed Riad's earlier suggestion of a merger of Sunni and Shi'i community institutions, so as to form a Muslim bloc able to challenge the Maronites. In fact, they reacted by reinforcing their own community institutions and creating a Shi'i Supreme Council, chaired by Ahmad al-As'ad himself.

Nevertheless, in the first week of August 1943, and after much preliminary discussion, Riad el-Solh's place on Ahmad al-As'ad's list was announced. To general surprise, 'Adil 'Usayran himself then rallied to this same list – together with three of his supporters, Kadhim al-Khalil, Rashid Baydun and 'Ali 'Abdallah – in the apparent conviction that it was futile to fight the strong combination of Ahmad al-As'ad and Riad el-Solh. Ahmad al-As'ad, in turn, preferred this combination to an alliance with Najib 'Usayran and Yusuf al-Zayn.

Alarmed at this unexpected line-up, Pruneaud, the French *conseiller*, desperately tried to form an opposing list around Zayn, but it lacked substance or credibility. The result of Riad el-Solh's political activities was the creation of a 'unified list', which was formally announced on 17 August at a mass meeting at Taybeh, ancestral home of the As'ad family. Ahmad al-As'ad's decision to throw his weight behind this list was to have a determining impact on Riad el-Solh's future political career.

An angry Pruneaud rightly read the creation of the 'unified list' as a serious setback for France in South Lebanon.[43] Riad el-Solh was well aware that he could still be dangerous, and had to be conciliated. He turned for help to Emile Eddé, one of France's most loyal supporters, who now set about persuading Pruneaud and the *Délégation Général* that it was best for them to remain neutral in the upcoming elections. Eddé's intervention was not entirely selfless. He had long dreamed of being elected president of the Republic once more, and he needed a prominent Sunni, like Riad, at his side in his contest with his main rival, Shaykh Bishara al-Khoury. Riad thus incurred a political debt towards Eddé, which he was to repay some months later.

[43] Ibid., pp. 433–5.

With the approach of the poll, all parties jockeyed furiously for position. The French did not dare oppose Riad el-Solh too openly, for fear of pushing him into the arms of the British. To disarm the French, the canny Spears pretended he did not want Riad to win, and, for his part, Riad pretended to vouch publicly that he would be guided by French interests. A week before the election was due to take place, members of the 'unified list' held a meeting at the house of Kadhim al-Khalil. There, they made to discuss who, in the event of victory, they would back for the post of president of the Republic. Riad el-Solh loudly declared, with a mischievous grin, that they should vote for the candidate of the representative of France! No sooner had he uttered these words, than they were transmitted to Jean Helleu, the *délégué général* – which, of course, was Riad's intention.[44]

The decisive vote

The elections were preceded by a period of intense campaigning, during which the 'unified list' held large meetings at Sidon, Khiam, Taybeh and Jezzine. At Taybeh – where there were no French flags in evidence – Ahmad al-As'ad declared that Lebanon was an 'Arab country', a declaration which the French authorities found highly annoying. Riad el-Solh's campaign culminated with a speech he delivered in the Maronite village of Jezzine, which was in some way an answer to Patriarch 'Arida and his bishops. These had been angered by the *Délégation Générale*'s tolerance of the unified list. In his speech, Riad recalled that he had in the past been an enemy of the French Mandate. He was now, he said, a champion of Lebanon's independence and a friend of the democratic nations of the world. He expressed the fervent hope for an Allied victory in the war, and for a union of all Lebanese in attachment to their country. He repeated a sentiment that he had voiced before, namely that he preferred to live in a village that was independent rather than in an empire under foreign control. This remark was widely taken to mean that he now preferred Lebanese independence to Arab unity. He intended that his Christian critics would hear his words as a gesture of reassurance and conciliation.

---

[44] Ibid., p. 429.

For the purpose of the elections, the same division of the country was adopted as in 1937, with Lebanon's five *muhafazats* – Beirut, North Lebanon, South Lebanon, the Biqa' and Mount Lebanon – counting as separate constituencies. A simple majority was necessary to be elected at the first round, while the second round allowed for abstentions and last-minute electoral pacts. It is perhaps worth recalling that Lebanon's total population at that time was a mere 1,150,000 (and that of Syria 2,700,000).[45]

On the morning of 29 August – the day of the first round of the elections – Riad published a statement in *al-Diyar*, a newspaper owned and edited by his friend Hanna Ghusn, which read like a programme of government. Riad's tone indicated clearly that he was aiming for the premiership. 'We are entering a new world,' he wrote,

> *in which the great and the small, the strong and the weak, will enjoy the benefits of freedom . . . Our national sovereignty is based on solid guarantees . . . on the Atlantic Charter, that landmark in the history of civilisation, and also on the many further guarantees specifically given to us by General de Gaulle, the leader of the Fighting French, as well as by the Prime Minister of Britain and the President of the United States . . . My programme is that of a loyal and devoted person who loves his country. This is not the place to go into details. I will merely say that my programme will serve to consolidate our independence and national sovereignty. As for our external policy, it will aim to bring Lebanon into the circle of countries that work to build this new world of freedom, justice, law and prosperity, a world of the four freedoms proclaimed by President Roosevelt.*[46]

The 'united list' won more than three-quarters of the votes cast. Out of a registered electorate of 37,661 in South Lebanon, 24,393 went to the polls, a major turnout of 66 per cent. The well-liked 'Adil 'Usayran came first on the list, with 20,011 votes, followed by Rashid Baydun

---

[45] Gabriel Menassa, Memorandum dealing with the Lebanese electoral problems and the introduction of necessary reforms, Beirut, 16 January 1943 (FO 226/240).

[46] MAE, Nantes, Fonds Beyrouth (Amb.), série 199A4, carton 20, Statement by Riad el-Solh in *al-Diyar*, 29 August 1943.

with 19,483 and Ahmad al-As'ad with 19,424 – who was livid at having come third on a list he had been instrumental in having drawn up! Riad el-Solh secured the Sunni seat with 19,406 votes. The French failed miserably to ensure the victory of their man, the Emir Khalid Chehab.

Elsewhere in the country, Muslim leaders did very well. Sami el-Solh, 'Abdullah al-Yafi and Sa'ib Salam were elected in Beirut, and 'Abd al-Hamid Karami in North Lebanon. The Shi'i notable Sabri Hamadi was elected in the Biqa', and the Druze notable Kamal Jumblatt in Mount Lebanon. They were joined, among the total of fifty-five deputies, by leading figures from other communities, such as the Greek Catholic Salim Takla, and the three leading Maronites, Bishara al-Khoury, Emile Eddé and Camille Chamoun, in Mount Lebanon; the Greek Catholic banker Henri Pharaon in the Biqa'; the Greek Orthodox notable Habib Abi Chahla, the Maronite Alfred Naccache and the Protestant Ayyub Thabit in Beirut.

But it was the triumphant entry of Riad el-Solh and of other leading Muslims into parliament for the first time that was to change the political and sectarian balance of power in Lebanese politics for good.

19 THE COMPROMISE OF THE NATIONAL PACT

Riad el-Solh's election to the Lebanese parliament in August 1943 carried him a significant step closer to the premiership. But the prize was still tantalisingly out of reach. Under the Lebanese system, the president of the Republic appoints the prime minister – but a president had yet to be chosen by the Chamber. That choice was not due to take place until 21 September. From Riad's standpoint, everything depended on the outcome of that contest. But which of the two well-connected Maronites vying for the top job would best serve his purpose?

Emile Eddé and Shaykh Bishara al-Khoury had spent much of the 1930s in fierce competition. With French support, Eddé had defeated Khoury for the presidency in 1936 – a presidency interrupted by the war – and he now hoped to do so again. The two men seemed evenly matched. Each had a large network of backers, friends and relations, and both had married into rich and powerful Beirut families. Each was the leader of a parliamentary grouping: Emile Eddé was master of his National Bloc, and Bishara al-Khoury of his Destour (Constitutional) Bloc.

Although both were committed to Greater Lebanon within its expanded 1920 borders, they differed significantly over what they thought the role of France should be in Lebanese affairs, as well as over Lebanon's relations with its Arab neighbours. Eddé wanted France to remain engaged in Lebanon – politically, militarily and culturally so – in order to protect it from its Arab neighbours, and especially from Syria, which he tended to perceive as menacing. Khoury wanted freedom from French control, so as to allow Lebanon to take what he believed was its natural place in its larger Arab and Muslim environment. As a passionate Francophile, Eddé preferred to write and speak in French,

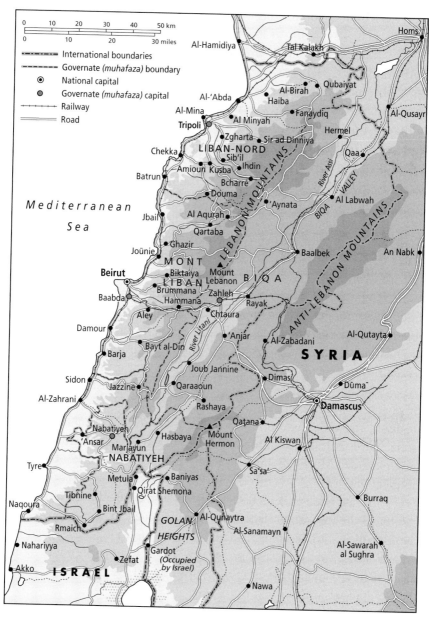

3 – The Republic of Lebanon

whereas Khoury, who had been educated in the Arabic language as well as in French, was totally at home in Arab culture.

Riad el-Solh had to wrestle with the question of which of these two Maronite leaders was more likely to appoint him prime minister, and, more importantly, to be a committed partner in the struggle for independence, which would certainly involve a bruising confrontation with the French. Bishara al-Khoury's pro-Arab sentiments marked him out to be Riad's obvious choice. The paradox, however, was that Riad was personally closer to Eddé. Whereas his relations with Khoury were cordial enough, he found Eddé the more congenial of the two. After all, Eddé was highly entertaining company: he was intelligent and sophisticated, and with a pronounced sense of humour much like Riad himself. Eddé was also refreshingly direct: he did not attempt to fudge or conceal his attachment to France. One knew exactly where one stood with him.

In any event, the issue was by no means black and white, since Eddé had chosen to make conciliatory gestures to the Muslim community. As president of the Republic in 1936, he had appointed Khayr al-Din Ahdab, Riad's former partner in their joint journalistic venture, to the post of prime minister – the first time that a Muslim had risen to such heights under the French Mandate. But, to Riad's great surprise and disappointment, Ahdab made no political capital out of his position, choosing instead to water down his Arab nationalist convictions. Nevertheless, his appointment did mark the formal entry of the long-excluded Muslim community into the upper echelons of Lebanese political life.

Emile Eddé also rendered Riad el-Solh a valuable service in the run-up to the legislative elections of August 1943, when he persuaded the French not to campaign openly against him. He had assured the French – no doubt on Riad's prompting – that Riad el-Solh was by no means Britain's man. This certainly helped dispel the grave reservations they had about him.

Meanwhile, the French – who demanded blind loyalty from all Maronite politicians – had turned resolutely against Bishara al-Khoury. They considered him an opportunist for selling out, in their estimation, to the British. A jaundiced French official wrote that Bishara al-Khoury 'was French when he believed in the predominant position of France in the Levant; Arab as soon as he sensed that France's Popular Front governments favoured nationalism; Anglophile when British troops entered Lebanon'.[1] By 1943, the French had become decidedly peeved with him. 'Since the arrival of Allied troops', another disgruntled French official reported to Paris,

> *Bishara al-Khoury has judged the time ripe to make a bid for power. With his Pharaon relatives – who have secured large British contracts for the building of roads and air strips – he has thrown open his house to British officers, giving them lavish receptions, and making himself agreeable to the Spears Mission and to the staff of General Wilson [commander of Britain's Ninth Army]. He sings the praises of everything British and denigrates the 'degenerates' of the twenty-year French Mandate. However, when General Catroux toured the country to sound out the wishes of the population regarding the choice of President, Bishara al-Khoury always arranged to have someone there to whisper to the General that Bishara was the most popular and the best-qualified person for the job.[2]*

As well as deploring Khoury's contacts with the British, the French were unhappy at the close relations he had forged with Nahhas Pasha in Egypt and with members of the National Bloc in Syria. These, after all, were the leaders of the two Arab states most able to exert influence on Lebanese affairs. It was not surprising, therefore, that the French threw their weight resolutely behind Emile Eddé for the presidency.

Riad el-Solh's dilemma was acute. On personal grounds, he preferred Eddé, but on political grounds, he had serious doubts about him. He judged that Eddé might accept a certain distance from France, but how far would he actually go? Would he be prepared to press for a total withdrawal of French troops from Lebanon, a necessary condition, in Riad's view, for real independence? Would he accept the notion of Lebanon's 'Arab identity', which Riad el-Solh was determined to affirm?[3]

Riad thought it over and consulted his friend, the Iraqi Consul General Tahsin Qadri, whom he had known as a young man in Istanbul,

---

[1] MAE, Nantes, Fonds Beyrouth (Amb.), série 199A4, carton 20, 25 August 1941.
[2] MAE, Nantes, Fonds Beyrouth (Amb.), série 199A4, carton 20, 20 February 1943.
[3] Interview with Alia el-Solh, Monte Carlo, 4–5 October 2004.

and who was now the doyen of the diplomatic corps in Beirut. Because of his acquaintance with all the leading politicians – and indeed because of Iraq's prestige – Qadri was able to play a considerable role in Lebanese affairs. Riad's daughter Alia, then a child of about 10, recalled that he called at their house one day with a message for her father. Taking an empty cigarette packet out of his pocket, he flattened it, and then scribbled: *Tea at Qadri's at 5 tomorrow*, entrusting it to her to give to Riad. When Riad el-Solh went to the consul's house the next day, he found Bishara al-Khoury already there – in a meeting designed to bring them together. 'It was the first time in Lebanese history that a would-be prime minister chose a would-be president, rather than the other way round,' Alia el-Solh commented with a chuckle.

The 19 September 1943 meeting

Tahsin Qadri was not the sole go-between. In an interview before his death, Nasri Maalouf, a lawyer and former deputy who had been one of Riad's close friends, made a record of how the alliance between Riad el-Solh and Bishara al-Khoury actually came about.[4] Maalouf had first met Riad in Damascus in the early 1930s, on one of the latter's visits to his nationalist friends there. Having just graduated from Damascus University, Maalouf was introduced to Riad by his law professor, the eminent politician Faris al-Khoury, who persuaded Riad to employ the young Maalouf in his law office in Beirut. In this way, Maalouf came to know Riad's cousins, Kadhim and Taqi al-Din el-Solh too, eventually joining them as a trusted member of Riad's inner circle of speechwriters, cheerleaders and advisers.

In the days of feverish activity between the second round of legislative elections on 5 September and the presidential elections on 21 September, the key question these men found themselves asking was this: how could Riad even consider joining forces with Emile Eddé – a man who wanted only limited independence from the French – while Bishara al-Khoury had no Muslim partner of weight, although he stood for total independence? Indeed, the only significant Muslim in Bishara al-Khoury's Destour camp was the Emir Khalid Chehab

---

4 Nasri Maalouf, 'Riad el-Solh doit être avec Béchara el-Khoury', in Khoury (ed.), *Sélim Takla*, pp. 510–16. Farès Sassine conducted the interview with Maalouf on 12 July 2002; Gérard D. Khoury translated the Arabic text into French.

of South Lebanon. He was an honest enough man, but had become politically tainted by his collaboration with France.

At a meeting in Kadhim's office, Maalouf pleaded with the others: 'Just give me twenty-four hours to confer with the friends of Bishara al-Khoury – but without for the moment alerting Riad or asking anything of him'. Once the others had agreed to this *démarche*, Maalouf called on Salim Takla, one of Bishara al-Khoury's closest friends and most respected advisers, who was known as the 'brain of the Destour bloc'.

Maalouf said to him: 'The British and the Lebanese are agreed in wanting Lebanese independence. In fact, we entirely support Bishara al-Khoury in his demand for total independence. Riad, however, prefers Emile Eddé. The only Muslim in the Destour Bloc is the Emir Khaled Chehab, a man with no popular following in Beirut.'

'What are you trying to say?' Salim Takla asked.

'I'm saying', Nasri Maalouf replied, 'that Riad el-Solh should link up with Bishara al-Khoury.'

'What a dream that would be!' Salim Takla responded enthusiastically. 'I would certainly be for it.'

'I've come to say to you that we should work together to bring it about,' Nasri Maalouf continued.

'But what are *they* asking for?' Salim Takla asked. [By this he meant Riad el-Solh and his camp.]

'Riad doesn't yet know of this proposal. However, if your side were to open the door to him, I believe you could draw him in towards you. We would then set to work on our side,' Nasri Maalouf replied confidently.

Salim Takla thought this was a great idea. But how to carry the project forwards? Believing that Bishara al-Khoury would welcome the prospect of an alliance with Riad, Maalouf and Takla agreed that Salim Takla was the person to put the suggestion to him. Takla, however, was reluctant to undertake the mission by himself. He felt he needed the support of another prominent Maronite close to Bishara, such as Camille Chamoun. So Takla arranged for Maalouf to sound out Chamoun. The latter's response was immediate and enthusiastic. 'Go and speak to Riad,' he urged.

Maalouf was a careful lawyer. The main obstacle to an alliance between Riad el-Solh and Bishara al-Khoury was Riad's friendship with Emile Eddé, and his loyalty to him. Maalouf felt he could not approach

Riad el-Solh until Bishara al-Khoury's camp had formally endorsed the idea of an alliance with him. Chamoun then gave his personal backing to the initiative and urged Maalouf to waste no time in putting it into effect, since the presidential election was fast approaching.

So, as a first step, Maalouf arranged for Riad to meet Salim Takla, and, once that meeting had gone well, Takla and Chamoun proceeded to cement ties between the two political camps. 'When we told Riad how we had gone ahead without his knowledge', Maalouf said later, 'he listened in silence, but made no comment'.[5]

These Byzantine preliminaries set the stage for a historic tête-à-tête between Riad el-Solh and Shaykh Bishara al-Khoury, which took place on 19 September at the house of a mutual friend in the cool mountain town of Aley (where the Solhs, *père et fils,* had once awaited trial for their anti-Turkish activity). There is no record of what took place. Riad wrote down nothing about it, and the meeting gets only a brief mention in Bishara al-Khoury's own memoirs. It later emerged that they reached an unwritten gentleman's agreement to the effect that, if Bishara al-Khoury were elected president, he would appoint Riad el-Solh as his prime minister. They agreed to share power, with the aim of creating a solid political platform from which to make a bid for independence from France.

'I decided', Bishara al-Khoury wrote, 'to entrust the post [of prime minister] to Riad el-Solh, a man of great intelligence and rare courage, who was well-regarded in Lebanon and in the Arab countries. We met two days before the [presidential] elections and we agreed on this point'. Khoury added that 'the [19 September] meeting remained secret and I did not reveal my intentions, even to the persons closest to me'.

Thus was established the broad principle of Lebanese independence on the basis of Christian–Muslim coexistence. The understanding between the two men was fleshed out a few days later in Riad el-Solh's first statement to parliament as prime minister – a programme of government which came to be known as the National Pact, *al-mithaq al-watani.* How exactly they struck their deal, however, and what they said to each other at that historically crucial meeting, remains shrouded in mystery.

---

5 Bishara al-Khoury, *Haqa'iq Lubnaniyya,* 3 vols, Beirut 1960, vol. II, p. 17.

Background and significance of the Pact

The political compromise between Maronites and Sunni Muslims, embodied in the National Pact, was evidently the work of these two principal actors. Together, president and prime minister were able to achieve independence for Lebanon, putting an end once and for all – after a bitter struggle with France – to the oppression and stagnation of an entrenched colonial regime. Their partnership was made possible because of their exceptional givens. Riad had from an early age developed an understanding of Christian anxieties, and a personal sympathy for them, while Bishara al-Khoury had the independence of mind to understand that he needed to look for support outside his narrow Maronite community. This allowed him to see the usefulness of an alliance with Riad el-Solh, a Sunni leader who had acquired great influence with the Muslim population of Lebanon and other Arab countries. The Pact established a new pattern of communal coexistence in which, for the first time, the urban Sunni Muslim leadership rose to a position of full power-sharing with the Maronites, who had previously dominated the political scene. It thereby radically transformed the power structure which the French had put into place.

Riad's alliance was not only with Bishara al-Khoury himself. It was also with his Destour Party and its powerful backers, such as Henri Pharaon and Michel Chiha, pillars of Lebanon's financial and cultural life. These affluent men must have grasped – however reluctantly – that, since the French could no longer guarantee them Christian pre-eminence, the time had come for some sort of compromise with their country's Muslims. They were ready to put some distance between themselves and the French, and to draw closer to the Arab world. In any event, concentrating the minds of Bishara al-Khoury and his commercially canny friends was the fear that, if the French ever regained the upper hand in Lebanon, Emile Eddé, their political rival, would come to power, and *his* entourage alone would enjoy the spoils.

The alliance between Riad el-Solh and Bishara al-Khoury might never have taken place, and would certainly not have yielded the results that it did, had it not been underpinned by General Spears. This powerful British minister to the Levant states was determined that France should be made to honour the pledge it had given to grant independence to both Syria and Lebanon – a pledge which Britain itself had guaranteed. Riad el-Solh and General Spears had achieved, over the previous year, a political understanding and a degree of strategic complicity which neither felt it wise fully to avow.

Riad's skill was to have seized the right moment for his bid for power and his challenge to the French. His many years of exile in Switzerland and France had given him a more sophisticated understanding of European politics than many of his Lebanese and Syrian contemporaries. It helped him grasp how the international balance of power might be put to the service of Lebanon. Above all, it helped him understand how to handle General Spears, as well as his key adviser, Geoffrey Furlonge, whom Riad was now seeing almost daily. Riad was well aware that Spears's unusually robust championship of the cause of Lebanese and Syrian independence – and his stubborn readiness to confront both General de Gaulle and his own British Foreign Office – were precious assets which needed to be exploited to the full, and quickly.

There were, of course, other elements in the equation. Riad was encouraged and emboldened by the electoral victory of his nationalist friends in Syria. They, in turn, helped to bring about his rapprochement with Bishara al-Khoury. A Syrian delegation led by Lutfi al-Haffar came to Beirut to persuade Sunni notables to support Khoury's candidacy, and put an end to Eddé's ambitions. Egypt's Prime Minister Nahhas Pasha was also committed to Khoury's election, and instructed the Egyptian consul in Beirut, Ahmad Ramzi, to influence Muslim opinion in Khoury's favour. And there was Riad's determination to throw into battle all the prestige, popularity and pan-Arab credentials he had painstakingly amassed over the years.

The political question that faced both Riad el-Solh and Bishara al-Khoury was the extent to which each could compromise in sharing state power.[6] The key to their entente was the acceptance by Muslims of Greater Lebanon within its expanded 1920 frontiers, and the parallel acceptance by Christians of Lebanon's place within the Arab family. Thereafter, Lebanese Muslims no longer presented themselves as the inhabitants of regions demanding to be reunited with Syria, but rather as members of Lebanon's Muslim community, a community which now demanded equal – or almost equal – rights with the Maronites.[7] This, then, was the central theme of the National Pact. It expressed Riad el-Solh's acceptance that the independence of Greater Lebanon

[6] Zisser, *Lebanon*, p. 56.
[7] Méouchy, 'Le Pacte national', p. 468.

was the immediate goal, displacing any notion of union with Syria. Bishara al-Khoury accepted in turn that, since independence from France was the goal, he and his fellow Christians had henceforth to dispense with the protection and privilege which French patronage had so long accorded them.

Both sides made major concessions. The Sunnis gave up all idea of dismantling the French-created and anti-Arab entity of Greater Lebanon, and the Christians acknowledged that, whatever their cultural, political and trading ties with the West, Lebanon was essentially an Arab country. This was where their future lay. An answer was thus provided to the existential question which had plagued Greater Lebanon from its very beginnings: whether the enlarged state was a purely temporary phenomenon, or whether it would endure for the foreseeable future within its expanded borders. The voluntary commitment by both Muslims and Christians to Greater Lebanon, as embodied in the National Pact, was to guarantee its metamorphosis into a durable modern state.[8]

Riad el-Solh's endorsement of this 'Lebanese solution' lent political gravitas to the growing collaboration between Christian and Muslim merchants, financiers and political brokers. The National Pact had not, after all, emerged fully formed from a vacuum, nor was it merely a convenient arrangement concocted between two ambitious men. It represented the gradual convergence over several years of a number of social, economic and political trends, both local and international, of which the most important was the growing realisation by Lebanon's Muslim and Christian elites that they had much more in common than they had long wished to suppose. Socially, at the very least, they belonged to exactly the same world.

Indeed, they had begun to move closer together since the 1930s, as they gradually came to realise that there was no real contradiction between the Sunnis' commercial ties with the Arab world, and the Christians' ties with their Western trading partners. Both sets of relations could be put to work for the greater benefit of a common middle class. Its future prosperity would depend on the successful development of Beirut as a trading and banking centre, strategically poised between the markets of the Arab world and the West. The National Pact was, to a great extent, an expression of these tempting joint financial interests.[9]

[8] Ibid., p. 463.
[9] Johnson, *Class and Client*, pp. 26, 117–18.

In the words of Ghassan Tuéni, the veteran editor of *al-Nahar* and a prominent political figure on the Lebanese scene for more than half a century, the participation of the Sunni elites in Lebanon's leadership transformed the economic interests of the new governing alliance, its objectives, its social outlook, and even its internal and external economic policies.

> *Tremendous, though at times slow, change occurred, moving the Lebanon of 1943 away from an economy based exclusively on tourism, services, trade, craftsmanship and agriculture that had shaped its modest image under the French Mandate. A new middle class was born which, along with the growing professional and intellectual classes, was soon to become the real social foundation of the new democracy.*[10]

Both sides were to derive substantial reassurance from the new arrangement. The Christians no longer required French guarantees for the existence of their state. They dared emerge at last from their closed confessional shell, and – moderating, nevertheless, their sense of difference from the Muslims – they reached out avidly to the wider Arab world. Lebanon's Muslims, in turn, felt that they were no longer an alien and despised minority in a foreign-created and Christian-dominated state, but had at last achieved the status of full citizens.

This accord between the elites was underwritten by new forces and pressure groups at the popular level, and in particular by the paramilitary movements which had emerged in the Levant in the late 1930s. These expressed the needs and frustrations of an emerging younger generation. Once the battle with France became a joint one, these youth movements brought their members out in bold demonstrations against the mandatory power. They even wrested control of the street from the authorities themselves. From 1943 onwards, for example, Pierre Gemayel's *Phalanges libanaises* and the Sunni *al-Najjada* were to serve as intermediaries between the *petit peuple* and the older notables, both Christian and Muslim, who had traditionally dominated the political scene through *their* respective networks of patronage.

[10] Ghassan Tuéni, in *Beirut Review*, no. 6.

Amazingly enough, these rival youth movements began to cooperate in 1941 in delivering supplies to the hard-pressed population. They then started sending delegations to each other's demonstrations, and, in 1943, they went further still by embarking on joint political action. The *Najjada*'s Jamil Makkawi proposed to Pierre Gemayel that they join forces in backing certain candidates at the August parliamentary elections, an alliance which yielded very positive results. Without the streetwise muscle of these youth movements in favour of the National Pact, the coming trial of strength with the French might not have been successful.[11] The National Pact provided the essential bedrock for Bishara el-Khoury's candidature as president. Intense bargaining between deputies, religious leaders and political notables produced an outcome which finally outwitted the French. They were made to think that the British wanted Camille Chamoun, known for his strong pro-British sentiments, to be elected president. Although this was an unfounded rumour, it caused the French to switch their support from their own man, Emile Eddé, to Bishara al-Khoury, who they were led to believe was a 'compromise candidate', who alone was capable of keeping Chamoun from office. Emile Eddé thus found himself defeated even before any election had taken place – and defeated by the very mandatory power in which he had so totally put his trust!

On 21 September, the Lebanese parliament elected Shaykh Bishara al-Khoury president of the Republic. On taking the oath of office, he gave a clear indication of the policies he planned to pursue. While paying tribute to the principle of Arab solidarity, he declared that he intended to inaugurate a new era of freedom and national sovereignty. The next day, he appointed Riad el-Solh as prime minister.

[11] Méouchy, 'Le Pacte national', pp. 471–2, 480.

20 THE DECISIVE BATTLE

On the afternoon of 21 September 1943 – on the very day Bishara al-Khoury was elected president of the Lebanese Republic – Riad el-Solh went to see Geoffrey Furlonge, Spears's political adviser. He already knew that he would be appointed prime minister the next day, and he wanted to brief Furlonge on how he saw the situation, as well as giving him a preview of the policies he intended to pursue. Nothing could better illustrate the working relations Riad had established with the Spears Mission. He had been in the habit of seeing Furlonge, or his assistant Captain Marun 'Arab, almost every day, as well as holding regular meetings with General Spears himself. In preparing for the decisive battle to break the French grip on the Levant, Riad el-Solh and General Spears were allies. They pooled their information and coordinated their strategy.

Riad told Furlonge that he planned to move fast. His aim was to extract as many concessions as he could from the French in the shortest possible time. The French were weaker than they had ever been, but the fighting mood of the Lebanese parliament could not be expected to last for more than a few months. He would not accept French dictation in his choice of ministers, but intended to adopt a firm policy from the very start and form as independent-minded a government as possible.[1] Spears was delighted when Riad's appointment was confirmed. 'He is undoubtedly the best man among a very limited number of Sunni Muslims available', he wrote to Harold Macmillan, the British representative to General de Gaulle's Committee of National Liberation in Algiers. Spears knew that Riad el-Solh was de Gaulle's bête noire – an enemy who dared challenge the French presence in the Levant. Spears,

[1] G. W. Furlonge to Spears, 21 September 1943 (FO 226/241).

4 – The contemporary Middle East

therefore, wanted to provide Macmillan with adequate ammunition with which to counter French objections to Riad's appointment.[2]

On 25 September, Riad formed his government, with himself as prime minister and finance minister, and Habib Abi Chahla (Greek Orthodox) as deputy prime minister, as well as minister of justice and education. Abi Chahla was a member of Emile Eddé's National Bloc – the only one in the cabinet – but he was known to hold much more progressive views than Eddé did on the important and controversial subject of Arab unity. The four other ministers were Salim Takla (Greek Catholic), foreign affairs and public works; Camille Chamoun (Maronite), interior and posts and telegraphs; the Emir Majid Arslan (Druze), defence, agriculture, health and social services; and 'Adil 'Usayran (Shi'i), supply, economy, trade and industry. All the principal religious confessions were thus represented. Spears reported to the Foreign Office that the new government was 'strong and homogeneous'.

'The appointment of Chamoun to Interior', he added, 'is an excellent step, well calculated, in view of his outstanding honesty, to break the system of administrative favouritism which has led to so much inefficiency in the past'. Among Lebanese politicians, Chamoun was one of Spears's favourites. For one thing, he and his wife *looked* so very British, Spears liked to tease. More seriously, he counted on Chamoun to 'break the underground web with which the French have entangled this country'.[3]

Indeed, Spears could barely contain his satisfaction – nor his sense of personal achievement – at the formation of Riad el-Solh's government. He congratulated himself that it was largely the result of his own work. To Richard Casey, the British minister of state in Cairo (with whom he had formed an alliance against those he considered to be the weak-kneed Francophiles in the Foreign Office), he wrote happily on 28 September:

> *The appointment of the Riad el-Solh ministry means that*
> *everything has ended infinitely more satisfactorily than*
> *I ever dared hope for. I have felt all along as if I were*
> *building a house of cards and that an additional card was*

[2] Spears to Resident Minister, Algiers, 24 September 1943 (FO 660/36).
[3] Spears to Foreign Office, 27 September 1943 (FO 226/241).

likely to bring down the whole structure. Yet until the last tier was in position nothing had been achieved . . .

It was very curious to observe how complete the French discomfiture in the Lebanon has been. The money they have spent, the pressure they have brought to bear, the open cheating in the elections, helped them little . . . I have the impression that the French are feeling very piano indeed and are accusing each other of false manoeuvres. Meanwhile we sit very pretty.[4]

Riad's landmark speech

Riad's ministerial speech on 7 October won him vast applause in parliament and across the country, consecrating his reputation as the prime architect of Lebanese independence. It was a long and carefully phrased address, to which he gave a note of great solemnity by declaring at the very start that Lebanon was entering a 'critical and dangerous period, such as it had never known before'. This was his warning that the battle with France was about to begin. For the first time in twenty-five years, he said, the elections had made the Lebanese people the real source of power – thus opening the way for true independence.

'We want true independence', he cried, 'we want total national sovereignty. We want to dispose of our resources as we see fit, and as our national interest alone dictates. This is the political watchword of this government, which I have had the honour to form and to lead'. The gauntlet was thus thrown down to the French.

Riad el-Solh then proceeded to outline the principal changes he was intending to make. The Constitution would be amended to remove those articles which were not compatible with true independence, since they gave others – and by others, he meant, of course, the French – authority over Lebanese affairs. The Constitution had to be freed from all such constraints. The Arabic language was to be the only official language, rather than Arabic *and* French. In agreement with Syria, his government proposed to take over the management of the so-called *Intérêts Communs*, that wide range of revenue-producing activities of

---

[4] Spears to R. G. Casey, Minister of State, Cairo, 28 September 1943 (FO 226/241).

vital interest to both Syria and Lebanon – the customs administration, the railways, the tobacco monopoly, the ports, the telephone network, the antiquities service – which France had striven to keep so firmly in its own hands.

Riad declaimed the word 'independence' in his maiden address nearly thirty times. He did not simply ask for independence, or wait for France to concede it, or for the Great Powers to bestow it: he outlined concrete steps to secure it. That was the true novelty of this stirring speech.[5]

The Chamber was, of course, eager to hear what Riad had to say about Lebanon's relationship with the Arab world, since it had always been a principal source of discord between Christians and Muslims. It was not disappointed. 'Lebanon's geographical situation', Riad declared, 'the language of its people, its culture, history and economic situation, all demand that it place its relations with its sister Arab countries at the very top of its major preoccupations'. But he then added, 'The government will establish Lebanon's relations with the Arab states on a solid foundation, which will guarantee their respect for Lebanon's independence, full sovereignty and territorial integrity, because Lebanon is a country with an Arab face, which draws from Western civilisation what is good and useful'.

This last key phrase – greeted with loud cheers in the Chamber and subsequently much quoted – sweetly summed up the groundbreaking compromise between Muslims and Christians, which lay at the very heart of the National Pact.

'Our brothers in the Arab countries', Riad continued,

> *only want from Lebanon what its own proud and patriotic sons want for themselves. We do not want a Lebanon which is a fiefdom of the colonialists, and they do not want a Lebanon which might serve as a conduit for colonialism to their countries. Both of us – we and they – want Lebanon to be proud, independent, sovereign and free.*

It was a skilful message of reassurance, addressed both to Lebanon's mosaic of religious communities and to its vigilant Arab neighbours.

---

[5] Ghassan Tuéni, *Le Livre de l'indépendance*, Beirut 2002, p. 30.

Riad had a good deal more to say on many other topics. He promised to reform the electoral law and to carry out a population census (always an explosive subject in Lebanon, where the Christians were fiercely attached to preserving their increasingly fragile majority). He called for the early suppression of the confessional system, which, he warned, was an obstacle to national progress. It damaged Lebanon's reputation, poisoning relations between its various religious communities. He intended to reform the civil service and make sure that the judiciary became fully independent. He would seek to guarantee an adequate supply of wheat; tackle the cost of living; improve roads and support agriculture. He also hoped to ensure social justice; see to the advancement of women; improve the press and the educational system; make contact with overseas Lebanese and free all political prisoners. 'Who better than I, who have spent part of my life in detention and another part in exile, can understand the sufferings and miseries of prisoners? I will not sleep until the last prisoner has rejoined his family'.

Riad was happy to announce that Egypt had recognised Lebanon as an independent state – a decision of immense benefit for Lebanon. He expressed his thanks to 'sister Egypt', to its government and its people. As for France – 'a country to which Lebanon is bound by ties of friendship' – and Allied states such as Great Britain and the United States, his government would seek to forge the best possible relations with them, relations that were founded on friendly respect.

The Chamber gave Riad el-Solh an overwhelming vote of confidence. It was a tremendous personal triumph for him. Only one deputy, Alfred Naccache, abstained, and one other, Dr Ayyub Thabit, recorded a vote against the government, leaving before the motion was put to the house. No doubt in a bid to 'manage' the French, Riad made no mention in his speech of the *Sûreté Générale*; of the hated officers of the *Services Spéciaux*, of the Mixed Courts or concessionary companies – subjects which his more excitable supporters wanted him to attack.

In the prolonged debate that followed Riad's speech, the opposition tried to postpone the vote of confidence, but its motion was defeated and the vote was taken. Belgrave, the acting British political officer, commented that the historic session 'showed that the young parliament can talk; it remains to be seen how far it will walk'.[6] Spears

---

[6] Squadron Leader R. Belgrave, Acting Political Officer, to Foreign Office, 8 October 1943 (FO 226/241).

hastened to congratulate Riad on his maiden speech – he had earlier been briefed on its main themes – and immediately received a note back from Riad which expressed great appreciation for Spears's invaluable help, and counted on him for future support. 'In carrying out the task I have undertaken, I am counting on the support of all the friends of Lebanon, of whom you are the very first'.

The first round

Evidently, the French were utterly enraged by the speech. Five days after it was delivered, Jean Helleu, the *délégué général*, and his principal advisers, Chataigneau and Boegner, forced themselves to dine with Bishara al-Khoury and Riad el-Solh. French tempers had not cooled by then, and it was not an amicable supper. When Bishara raised the question of the concessions, which he was expecting the French to make towards Lebanese independence, Helleu – evidently acting on instructions from de Gaulle, transmitted through Chataigneau, who was just recently back from Algiers – retorted that *nothing whatsoever* would be conceded until the Mandate had been terminated by the conclusion of a treaty.

Riad immediately protested that the French themselves had proclaimed Lebanon's independence in 1941, long before there was any talk of a treaty to terminate the Mandate. Although Helleu was unable to deny this, he continued to insist that there would be no transfer of powers, at any rate during the course of the war. What had the war to do with it? Riad asked. After all, the conclusion of a treaty would in no way affect the position of Lebanon in relation to the actual war. By this time, Helleu was beginning to show signs of discomfort and embarrassment. The French were prepared, he repeated, to sign a treaty at once, but Riad countered that the French Committee in Algiers was in no position to conclude treaties in the name of the whole of France. Helleu protested that he and General de Gaulle would give their word of honour that any instrument signed now would later be ratified by France. Riad was quick to remind him that the French parliament had failed to ratify the 1936 treaty, even though a French government of the time had signed it. How, then, could the French Committee give any such guarantee? To this lucid question, Helleu had no reply.

Both Bishara al-Khoury and Riad el-Solh stressed to Helleu that they were nationalists, committed before their public opinion to carrying out their nationalist programme. Parliament would insist that they keep their promises or resign, and so French concessions were essential. All that Helleu could find to say was that they should 'govern with wisdom' (*sagesse*). Angered by his inflexible pomposity, Bishara and Riad declared that they would rather cut off their right hands than sign a treaty with the French! On this defiant note, the difficult dinner ended.

'In a state of mind verging on despondency', Riad gave Spears a full account of the impasse with the French. The French had even accused Britain of being the real obstacle to Lebanon's independence, he told him. Indeed, while Riad and Bishara were arguing with Helleu, Boegner, further down the dinner table, was busy telling a Lebanese minister that Britain was pressing for Lebanese independence, in order to take over the Levant for itself. Lebanon's independence, he predicted sourly, would certainly then be cancelled.[7]

Spears was now beginning to fear that Riad el-Solh might not survive a head-on clash with the French. Some British officials were already worried that Riad was moving a bit too fast. Belgrave, the cautious acting political officer, feared that Riad's excessive speed 'might put the new Lebanese motorcar in the ditch'.[8] But Riad remained adamant about amending the Constitution quickly. With considerable foresight, Spears warned London that if the French persisted with their 'completely intransigent and unjustified attitude', they would run into very stiff opposition from both the Lebanese and Syrian governments. Neither government had any intention of allowing itself to be fobbed off with offers of a treaty; Lebanese public opinion was fully aroused. He urged London to make every attempt to convince René Massigli, de Gaulle's Commissioner for Foreign Affairs, that the French were heading for 'total disaster' in the Levant, if they continued to maintain their present line.

D. W. Lascelles, a member of the Spears Mission, reported from Damascus that a Franco-Syrian dinner had gone off no better than the one held in Beirut. With the Syrians, as with the Lebanese, Helleu again insisted that there would be no French concessions without the signing of a treaty.[9]

---

[7] Spears to Foreign Office, 16 October 1943 (FO 226/241).
[8] British Consulate General, Beirut, to Foreign Office, 1 October 1943 (FO 226/241).
[9] D. W. Lascelles to Spears, 21 October 1943 (FO 226/241).

The second round

Relations grew even frostier when, on 22 October, Helleu wrote Bishara al-Khoury a letter, stating bluntly that France would not accept Riad el-Solh's constitutional amendments, as an 'international undertaking' could not be revoked by a unilateral act! The Mandate, Helleu asserted, continued to exist in law since France had not been relieved of it by the League of Nations. 'Grave consequences' would follow, he threatened, if the proposed changes were implemented. To this undignified threat, Riad's robust reaction was to ask Yves Chataigneau, Helleu's deputy, to seek authority from his superiors to withdraw Helleu's letter. At the same time, he handed Chataigneau an official note, which made three specific demands:

(1) The transformation of the *Délégation Générale* into a diplomatic mission, 'compatible with the independence of Lebanon'.
(2) All attributes of sovereignty on Lebanese territory to be exercised exclusively by Lebanon's constitutional authorities.
(3) The Lebanese government to take over all interests and services at present administered on Lebanon's behalf by the *Délégation Générale*. Syria and Lebanon had agreed that they would jointly administer the revenues deriving from the *Intérêts Communs*.

Although the note was firm, it was couched in polite language. In step with the Lebanese, the Syrian government sent Helleu a similar letter. Chataigneau professed himself to be unaware of the existence of Helleu's threatening letter. He undertook to raise the matter with him before Helleu's departure for Algiers on the morning of 28 October. On the evening of the 27th, he informed Riad that the letter would not be withdrawn. Riad replied that, in that case, he would have to give full publicity to it, as well as to his government's reply.

Riad was convinced that the French were playing for time in the hope that some as yet unforeseen event, or even the end of the war, might somehow strengthen their hand. He was well aware that the *Délégation* was doing its best to undermine his authority by playing on traditional Christian fears. Yet in spite of these French intrigues, he was determined to move ahead, he told Spears. He set Thursday, 28 October as the date when parliament would debate Helleu's letter, as well as his government's reply to it. In what seemed to be something of a panic, Chataigneau then sent Riad an urgent message, requesting him *not* to read the exchange of letters in parliament before Helleu's return from Algiers.[10]

When Chataigneau's request was conveyed to him, Riad replied with a display of nationalist fireworks:

> *I am determined to execute my programme to the very last, no matter what happens and even if I remain alone in the field. I said yesterday that I had devoted my blood to independence when under age, and that my blood was nearly shed when I was a young man [a reference to his trial by the Turks]. I am not going to spare my blood now that I am an adult . . .*
>
> *I am not simply a politician. I am a fighter! I am going to execute my programme. I will read all the correspondence [in the Chamber] and disclose everything, if and when I find it necessary to do so . . .*
>
> *I am proud to say that I have kindled in Lebanese hearts the fire of independence, which will never be extinguished. I am proud of having gathered Christians and Muslims together under the banner of independence.*[11]

The third round

At noon on Friday, 5 November, members of the Beirut press corps were summoned to the French embassy, where Monsieur Goulmier, the head of the *Délégation*'s press department, handed them a toughly worded communiqué from the French Committee in Algiers. So long as the Mandate was in force, it stated, no amendments to the Constitution could be made without the explicit consent of the French authorities. Monsieur David, the *délégué* for Lebanon, handed the government a copy of the same communiqué.

---

[10] Spears to Foreign Office, 28 October 1943 (FO 371/35183); Belgrave to Spears, 29 October 1943 (FO 226/241).
[11] R. Belgrave to Spears, 30 October 1943 (FO 226/241).

Riad immediately called his ministers together. Changes to the Constitution, they decided, were fully within the government's competence under Article 76 of the Constitution itself. The proposed amendments were then circulated to the deputies at noon on Saturday, 6 November, and a parliamentary session set for the afternoon of Monday the 8th. That morning, however, Monsieur David conveyed to President Bishara al-Khoury a verbal message from Helleu in Algiers, earnestly requesting him to postpone consideration of the amendments until Helleu's return to Beirut.

On receipt of this message, Bishara summoned Riad and the ministers to his office. They unanimously resolved that there was no ground for Helleu's request, and asked Monsieur David to come to the presidency at 3 p.m. to receive their reply. When he read their statement, he expressed a mixture of pain and indignation. He had failed in his mission, he cried, and would have to resign the next day. (In the event, he did not.) No parliamentary vote could be free, he exclaimed heatedly, when deputies were under pressure from the mob! Riad coolly suggested that Monsieur David take a walk around the parliament building, so that he might observe for himself the complete calm in the city. He might even like to attend the debate, to judge the atmosphere in which it was conducted.

The Lebanese parliament met at 3.30 p.m. and passed the constitutional amendments by an almost unanimous vote of forty-eight (two members abstained, and two others withdrew before the vote was taken). Riad el-Solh received a rousing ovation. The session was entirely orderly. Crowds outside the Chamber were kept strictly controlled by the Lebanese police.

The French immediately imposed a ban on any mention of the debate or the vote in the local press, and put a complete stop on all outgoing press telegrams on the subject.[12] Feeling the need for external support at this critical moment, Riad turned at once to Spears. Could not a question be asked in the House of Commons, he enquired, to solicit a statement from the British government in support of his constitutional amendments? The French were forever telling the Lebanese that they would shortly be dropped by the British, he said, so any evidence to the contrary would be extremely welcome.[13]

[12] Spears to Foreign Office, 9 November 1943 (FO 371/35183).
[13] R. Belgrave, Consulate General, Beirut, to D. W. Lascelles, British Legation, Beirut, 9 November 1943 (FO 226/241).

The fourth round

General de Gaulle's intransigence had put Jean Helleu in an impossible position. He was a weak character, given to strong drink. At moments of tension, he was known to slip away *pour un petit whisky*. But on Tuesday, 9 November, his courage pumped up by de Gaulle, he arrived back in Beirut in combative mood. His first move – which was petty in itself – was to cancel invitations which the *Délégation* had sent out to Lebanese ministers and deputies to attend the Armistice Day parade on 11 November – commemorating the Allied victory in the First World War – as well as the ball at the French Club the same evening. When Bishara al-Khoury heard of this undiplomatic cancellation, he informed the *Délégation* that he would not attend either.

Acting on a suggestion from George Wadsworth, the American minister in Beirut, Spears called a meeting of the Diplomatic Corps at the British Legation, where it was decided that foreign diplomats would not attend either. Only their military attachés would go to the parade, since it was a commemoration of an Allied victory. Rumours began circulating in Beirut that Helleu was planning a *coup de force*.[14]

On the morning of 10 November, Spears happened to find himself with Helleu as they waited together at Beirut airport to greet the king of Yugoslavia, who was paying a brief visit to Lebanon at the invitation of the French. They exchanged a few words. Helleu was amiable and made no reference to the crisis. They were due to meet again later that night at a dinner party Spears was giving in honour of the king, to which Salim Takla, the Lebanese foreign minister, had also been invited. Spears sat the king on his right and Helleu on his left. The Lebanese question was discussed. In view of the alarming rumours circulating in Beirut, Spears seized the opportunity to sound out Helleu on his intentions. He was reassured to hear Helleu give him his word of honour that no violent measures would be taken which might disturb public order. Helleu repeated the pledge several times.

Once the main guests had departed, Spears told Takla what Helleu had said, and Takla conveyed the message late that night to Bishara al-Khoury. Khoury, in turn, informed Riad el-Solh. Thus reassured, they all went to bed.[15] The opposition leader, Emile Eddé, spent

---

[14] Spears to Foreign Office, 10 November 1943 (FO 371/35183).
[15] Spears to Foreign Office, 11 November 1943 (FO 226/241).

the evening attending a French play at the West Hall of the American University of Beirut. He did not seem to be enjoying himself. One observer noted that he looked pale and distraught, as if seriously unwell.[16]

The fifth round

Before dawn on Thursday, 11 November, the President of the Lebanese Republic Bishara al-Khoury, his Prime Minister Riad el-Solh, and two members of the cabinet – Minister of Interior Camille Chamoun and Minister of Foreign Affairs Salim Takla – were arrested at their homes by a combined force of French marines, Senegalese colonial troops and agents of the *Sûreté Générale*. A third minister, 'Adil 'Usayran, was arrested later in the day at Aley.

The arrest of President Bishara al-Khoury was carried out with great brutality. Troops overpowered the guard, broke into the presidential residence and started searching the rooms. Hearing the sound of kicks and rifle-butts on their bedroom door, Bishara and his wife attempted to barricade themselves in by pushing their iron bedstead against the door. But when they heard shouts coming from the room of their 12-year-old daughter, Bishara's wife ran through the adjoining bathroom and saw two French marines, one holding a pistol and the other a rifle with a fixed bayonet, demanding that the child tell them where her father was to be found. Huguette Khoury (later to become a famous artist) said that her father was sleeping in his room. 'That's not true', the soldier shouted roughly. 'He's upstairs.' The girl replied that the floor above was not his.

Meanwhile, the president's bedroom door had been forced open and the room filled with soldiers. In a rage, Madame Khoury called them cowards, brutes, savages. Even the Gestapo would not have been so brutal! The officer in charge produced a signed order from Jean Helleu to arrest the president. As Bishara al-Khoury did not have his glasses, his wife read the arrest warrant aloud, whereupon the soldiers gave the president five minutes to get ready, during which, humiliatingly, he was made to dress under threat of their weapons. They then took him by force to a car outside and drove him away into the night.

---

[16] Tuéni, *Le Livre de l'indépendance*, p. 36.

The soldiers demanded that Madame Khoury open the safe in their room, or they would force it open. They seized some papers from it. They then rampaged through the house, breaking valuable objects, forcing open the doors, and overturning the armchairs. Once they had gone, the houseboy came in tears to Madame Khoury, to say that the soldiers had stolen his savings of 1,695 lira.

The president's son, Khalil, was forced down into a dark cellar with blows of rifle-butts, and cries of 'Son of a dog!' He was kept there under guard until a little before five o'clock in the morning. When he was released, he ran off to rouse General Spears from his bed.

Much the same drama was enacted at Riad el-Solh's house, which was broken into by some thirty soldiers, many of them Senegalese colonial troops. Surprised in bed together, Riad and his wife thought they were about to be killed. A devout Muslim woman, who never showed herself in public without a veil, Fayza el-Solh was deliberately humiliated and forced to walk barefoot in her nightdress. Riad was dragged from bed and bundled into a car.[17]

A day later, French and Senegalese troops once again broke into the Solhs' house and, training their weapons on Madame Solh and her five daughters, gave the place a havoc-causing search. It was not made clear whether they were looking for something in particular, or whether it was simply further harassment of Riad's family. After this experience, Madame el-Solh and her children took refuge in the residence of their friend, the Iraqi Consul General Tahsin Qadri.[18]

Also before dawn on 11 November, 'Abd al-Hamid Karami's house in Tripoli, where he lived together with his brother and their respective families, was invaded by Senegalese troops under the command of French officers. The troops forced their way into the bedrooms, terrorising the women and children by training their guns on them. Other soldiers wandered through the house, pillaging, helping themselves to forks and spoons, beating up servants – one suffered a broken rib – and stealing their savings. They seized 'Umar, 'Abd al-Hamid's 7-year-old son, pressed their pistols to his head, and threatened to kill him if he did not tell them where his father was.

As it happened, 'Abd al-Hamid Karami had gone the previous day to visit one of his estates in the mountains. Having finally elicited

---

[17] Spears to Foreign Office, 14 November 1943 (FO 226/241).
[18] Spears to Foreign Office, 15 November 1943 (FO 226/241).

where he was, the troops made for the village. They broke open the door of the house where he was sleeping and woke him up at the point of their bayonets. On hearing that he was about to be arrested, he leaned forwards to reach for his dentures but collided violently with the gun barrel of a Senegalese soldier, suffering a head wound. The soldiers ransacked the house, breaking into cupboards and stealing everything of value, including Karami's spectacles and whatever cash they could find. One of his servants was relieved of 28 pounds sterling, a small fortune in his eyes. Karami, a prominent nationalist leader and deputy, was led away in his night clothes, bare-headed without his turban – a humiliating predicament for this former Mufti. He was kept in handcuffs for the drive over the mountains to the fort at Rashaya, more than a hundred kilometres south-east of Beirut.[19]

When, shortly after 5 a.m., General Spears was woken by Khalil, the president's son, he attempted to telephone George Wadsworth, but found that his line had been cut. Hurrying to his office, he managed to reach Richard Casey, the minister of state in Cairo, on his secure phone at about seven o'clock, and gave him a report of what he had managed to piece together of the night's events. Outraged by Helleu's violence, Spears asked Casey to give him authority to have martial law proclaimed. Britain, he suggested, should take over the government. But the more cautious Casey felt that this risked bringing British troops into conflict with the French. He instructed Spears to warn Helleu instead of the possibility of martial law, and to stress that the arrest of the president and his ministers posed a threat to Britain's strategic interests.[20]

At 8 a.m., Radio Beirut broadcast a speech by Helleu. The time had come, he declared, to put an end to Riad el-Solh's 'dictatorial regime'. Solh was a friend of the Germans, as could be seen from their broadcasts, hailing him as a great leader and applauding his actions against France. He had been a Lebanese patriot for only six weeks, having spent the previous twenty years conspiring against Lebanon! With Solh out of the way, talks would start that very day 'in a friendly and co-operative atmosphere', to implement France's promise to grant independence to Lebanon.

The *Marseillaise* was then played and two *Arrêtés* were read out over the radio. The first stated that the constitutional amendments

[19] Spears to Foreign Office, 29 November 43 (FO 226/242).
[20] Minister of State, Cairo, to Foreign Office, 11 November 1943 (FO 226/241).

of 8 November were a violation of the Constitution and of international agreements and would not be recognised. They were from that moment annulled. The Chamber of Deputies was suspended and fresh elections promised. Executive power was placed in the hands of a head of state and head of government, who would rule by decree. A second *Arrêté* named the pro-French Emile Eddé to the dual post.

It soon became apparent that these measures had been decided upon as early as 9 November, since the *Arrêtés,* broadcast on the 11th, were dated the 10th. Emile Eddé, France's man in Lebanon, had been seen on the 9th going to the Résidence des Pins (which to this day remains the splendid official residence of the French ambassador) and had not returned home until after midnight.

Spears poured out his contempt, telling the Foreign Office that Emile Eddé was regarded by the whole population as a traitor. He had always been a complete French stooge, and when he last held presidential office was 'exceptionally corrupt and under strong suspicion of trafficking in narcotics, though this was never definitely proved. There can, of course, be no question whatsoever of recognizing him'.[21]

The sixth round

Early on the morning of 11 November, shortly before Helleu's 8 a.m. broadcast, a small group of men gathered at Spears's house for a council of war. Wadsworth was there, as was Habib Abi Shahla, the deputy premier; the Emir Majid Arslan, the defence minister; Tahsin Qadri, the Iraqi consul general; and British service chiefs. Abi Shahla, who had escaped arrest during the night, announced his determination to fight on, a sentiment echoed by the Emir Majid – whose upward-curling waxed moustaches, something of a personal trademark, contributed to the martial appearance of this Druze chieftain. His men in the mountains, he said, were ready to fight.

The next day, Abi Shahla and Arslan left Beirut for the neighbouring mountain village of Bshamoun, which had been chosen for its strategic location – close to the capital, yet astride the roads which led to the south, to the north and to the Biqa' valley. Nestling in the mountains close to Aley, it was well placed to resist attack. There

---

[21] Spears to Foreign Office, 11 November 1943 (FO 226/241).

they formed a 'provisional government', setting up their headquarters in a house, situated high in the village, belonging to a local notable, Hussein al-Halabi. A small room in one wing of the house was named the *Sérail*, the new seat of government, and was guarded by two young men. No one was allowed to enter without a permit. The other wing served as reception room, where a steady stream of well-wishers was received. At night, it was turned into a dormitory. The ministers bedded down on mattresses on the floor. A 'national guard' was formed, under the command of former journalist Na'im Mughabghab. Armed men flocked to join them from all over Mount Lebanon.

Meanwhile, back in Beirut, the speaker, Sabri Hamadi, attempted to hold an emergency session with a few deputies who had managed to force their way into parliament through a cordon of French troops. One deputy, Sa'di al-Munla, climbed over the outside wall and crawled into the building through a back window.[22] A Memorandum of Protest was sent to the Allied Powers by the speaker and six deputies – Sa'di Munla (North Lebanon); Henri Pharaon (Biqa'); Sa'ib Salam (Beirut); Marun Kan'an, Muhammad Fadl and Rashid Baydun (South Lebanon). It expressed 'horror and loathing' at the 'disgraceful deed' of the French, in preventing lawful deputies from entering the Chamber.

The deputies then turned their attention to devising a new flag. The old Lebanese flag had been the French tricolor, with a green cedar tree on the central white band. They decided to keep the cedar on the white band, but flank it by two red bands instead. (When Spears heard about this later, he was quick to note the importance of the flag as a symbol of the new Lebanon, now symbolically freed from centuries of French tutelage.)

A French officer then stormed in and ordered them all out, whereupon the deputies decided to resume their session elsewhere. Their first thought was to go to the residence of the president at Qantari, but when they discovered that it, too, was under siege, they went to the house of Sa'ib Salam, a large white edifice at Mussaitbeh (the same house where Salim 'Ali Salam, Sa'ib Salam's father, had once chaired the 1936 Conference of the Coast). The following day, 12 November, no fewer than thirty-three deputies managed to make their way there and gave a vote of confidence to the provisional government at Bshamoun.

---

[22] Tuéni, *Le Livre de l'indépendance*, p. 16. See also the Lebanese newspaper, *al-Diyar*, of 25 November 1943.

They also ordained: that no money be paid by the Treasury to the Eddé government; that the Banque de Syrie et du Liban refuse to honour any drafts signed by Eddé; and that all civil servants be ordered not to cooperate with him. Crippled by these measures, Eddé was unable to form an administration. He did not even dare go to his office without an escort of armoured cars.

Some four hundred prominent Beirut citizens then formed a 'National Congress' under the leadership of Michel Pharaon and the former prime minister, Ahmad Da'uq, in order to organise passive resistance. Subcommittees were set up to raise funds for tradesmen crippled by the strike; to provide first aid to those wounded in confrontation with the French; to collect political intelligence; and to keep in touch with foreign diplomats, as well as with the provisional government at Bshamoun.

Meanwhile, the whole town was in uproar. Tramcars were overturned and set on fire. French vehicles were vandalised. A large picture of General de Gaulle, on top of a building at the corner of rue Allenby, was torn down, disconnecting some wires as it fell, and putting Radio Beirut temporarily off the air. Stones were thrown at French military personnel, who opened fire, wounding a number of demonstrators and killing two of them. Diplomats and religious leaders crowded into the houses of the arrested president and ministers in order to express their support.

Calling on the president's wife that afternoon, Lady Spears found to her horror that the flight of steps outside the residence was running with fresh blood. Senegalese colonial troops on housetops had been firing through its windows, and several people had been gunned down. Madame Khoury was invited to move with her family into the Spears household, but courageously decided to stick it out in her own home instead.[23]

The seventh round

A significant aspect of the crisis was the sudden alliance that was forged between the Christian *Phalanges* and the Muslim *al-Najjada*, which together brought their troops onto the streets in violent defiance of

---

[23] Spears to Foreign Office, 11 November 1943 (FO 226/241).

the French. Declaring a general strike, they closed down the town and mounted joint demonstrations in front of parliament. The *Phalanges* leader, Pierre Gemayel, and the *Najjada* leaders, Jamil Makkawi, Anis al-Saghir and 'Adnan al-Hakim, formed a high command, with Gemayel at its head. Three hundred young Muslims even enrolled under the *Phalanges* banner![24]

These youth movements had tremendous latent power. The *Phalanges* were said to have 35,000 members, mainly in Beirut and the Biqa', and the *Najjada* another 10,000.[25] Their alliance mirrored the pact between Christian president and Muslim prime minister. French intelligence reported that Riad el-Solh had given Gemayel 50,000 Lebanese lira to meet his new commitments, with a promise of a further million lira once his government took control of the *Intérêts Communs*.[26] However, on the afternoon of 13 November, Pierre Gemayel was arrested when he went out to observe French tanks and machine guns on the Place des Canons – and to photograph the dead and wounded. The athletic and tough Gemayel – in the manner of Hollywood films – had to be assaulted by a dozen French soldiers before he could finally be handcuffed and taken away. Elias Rababi, editor of the Phalangist organ, *L'Action*, was also detained.

The eighth round

When Yusr el-Solh heard that her cousin Riad had been arrested early that morning, she ran with the news to Najla Sa'ab, head of the Women's Union (*al-ittihad al-nisa'i*). Although seven months pregnant at the time, Najla immediately started rallying other prominent women from all communities and confessions. By the next morning, two hundred of Beirut's leading women, escorted by three hundred youths, as well as numerous political and business leaders, made their way to the British Legation. A chosen delegation of Lebanese ladies then called on General Spears.[27] For well-born Arab women at that time, such a bold venture

---

[24] Méouchy, 'Le Pacte national, p. 480.
[25] Ibid., p. 481.
[26] M 484, CADN, Inventaire 2, *Sûreté Générale*, Beirut, carton 81, Information, 14 November 1943.
[27] It included Mme Evelyn Bustros, Mme Linda Sursock, Mme Shafiqa Diab, Mme Anna Thabit, Mlle Jacqueline Thabit, Mme Rose Zakkour, Mme Alice 'Achou (Salim Takla's mother-in-law), Mme Renée Takla (Salim Takla's wife), Mme Camille

into the public domain was a considerable break with tradition. On the way to the Legation, they were grossly insulted by Senegalese colonial troops, who were under French orders to call them the foulest of names. They looked to the British, they told Spears, to stop the massacre of their children. A country that produced such splendid women, Spears replied with characteristic gallantry, deserved to be free.[28]

The crowd of women with their entourage – some five hundred people – then headed for the American Legation, where the same smaller delegation now called on George Wadsworth. Others overflowed down the front steps into the garden and onto the street, where they were addressed, from time to time, by one of their leaders from the wall of the Legation garden. Suddenly, Wadsworth later reported to Washington,

> *two French Army troop-carrying lorries drove up, each*
> *containing 16–20 black troops and 2 or 3 French noncoms.*
> *All were fully armed with machine guns, bayoneted rifles*
> *or drawn revolvers. The women had gathered behind the*
> *garden wall, insulting and spitting (even the best of them)*
> *at the troops and screaming that the Senegalese would*
> *shoot. The street was eventually cleared.*

More violent incidents followed. On 13 November, a detachment of French marines (*fusiliers marins*) opened fire at point-blank range on a group of students, mainly from the American University of Beirut, who had assembled outside the British Legation. 'Part of the crowd took to their heels while others threw themselves on the ground', Spears reported to London. 'Not less than 40 rounds of ball ammunition were fired and one marine with a Hotchkiss gun emptied it into the crowd. The casualties were taken to the American Hospital. One was very seriously wounded'.[29]

In Sidon, French troops opened fire on a crowd of demonstrators, composed largely of schoolchildren, wounding about sixty. Spears reported that 'the crowd besieged the gates of the British hospital to

---

Chamoun, Mme Wadi' Na'im (wife of a deputy), Mlle Ibtihaj Qaddura, Mlle Clodagh Thabit, Mme Emile Lahhoud (wife of a deputy) and Mme George Kfuri (wife of a former minister under Sami el-Solh).

[28] Interview with Yusr el-Solh, London, January 2004.

[29] Spears to Foreign Office, 13 November 1943 (FO 371/35185).

take refuge. When it was decided that only the wounded could be admitted, many people smeared themselves with blood to order to enter. There were four deaths, with the youngest a girl of seven. British troops of the Northumberland Fusiliers volunteered to give blood transfusions. Nineteen pints of blood were obtained, which the medical officer believed to have saved the lives of at least seven of the wounded children'. Spears was certain that Pruneaud, 'the notorious *Conseiller* in South Lebanon', was responsible for ordering the crowd to be dispersed by such ugly force. In Tripoli, French Bren-gun carriages fired at close range on a crowd, wounding eleven, of whom seven were young children. Three died on their way to hospital.[30]

The ninth round

In the early hours of 11 November, President Bishara al-Khoury's car was the first to reach the Rashaya citadel. He was confined to the room of the military commander of the fort, who had loyally given it up. It was not a very large room, but it had a mat on the floor, a sofa and armchair facing the bed and was reasonably well heated. Riad el-Solh was less fortunate. Although his room was large, it was also bare and dirty, with no furniture of any sort. The three ministers – Chamoun, Takla and 'Usayran – were all crowded into one small cell, in which four beds had been jammed together, with no space between them. Who, they wondered, would be the fourth occupant? They did not have to wait long to find out. From the window of their cell, they saw a half-naked, barefooted figure, smeared in blood, staggering towards them, being pushed and shoved by Senegalese troops with fixed bayonets. It was only when he entered their cell that they were able to recognise the Tripoli strongman, 'Abd al-Hamid Karami.

As it happened, a sergeant in the guardroom had caught a glimpse of the president and the ministers on their arrival, and, thinking that it was an official visit, hurried to ring up the commander of the gendarmerie at Rashaya, who in turn rang up the *qai'm maqam*. Both hurried to the citadel to welcome the honoured guests. They were soon to learn their mistake. The sergeant was placed under arrest for his pains, and transferred to Beirut.

---

30 Ibid.; Spears to Foreign Office, 3 December 1943 (FO 226/242).

The president and prime minister were not allowed to communicate with each other, but within a few days, Riad el-Solh had
managed to form a network of informers, no doubt recruited from
among the prison guards. From them, he learned of the strikes, of
the provisional government at Bshamoun, of the National Council
and of international reactions to the crisis. The four ministers spent
their time playing tric-trac, drinking coffee and smoking. At their own
expense, they arranged for a cook to be brought in from the village
to prepare meals, under the refined supervision of Camille Chamoun,
who designated himself 'chief cook'. His culinary services were much
appreciated, except by the hapless Karami, who was unable to chew on
anything substantial. Deprived of his false teeth, which had been stolen
by the soldiers who had come to arrest him, he had to subsist on a little
soup and juice during his whole time in detention.

They were not the only inmates at Rashaya. Thirty-five other
prisoners were overjoyed to see the new arrivals, as it broke the
monotony of their own detention. Most of them were there for 'stirring up trouble' against the French. One of the political prisoners was
none other than the Syrian journalist, Najib al-Rayyes, owner of the
Damascus newspaper, *al-Qabas*, who had had a long career fighting
both the French and British Mandates. Others were members of Antun
Sa'ada's *Parti populaire syrien*, including Ni'mat Thabit, Zakariya
Lababidi and Anis al-Fakhury.[31]

The tenth round

On the day following the arrests, Spears sent an official letter of
protest to Jean Helleu. He did not conceal his outrage at the *délégué*'s
actions.

> M Jean Helleu, Ambassador of France and Delegate
> General, 12 November 1943.
> Your Excellency,
> The Minister of State in Cairo, with whom I have
> been in telephonic communication, instructs me to inform
> you that he has learned with the utmost concern and

---

[31] Tuéni, *Le Livre de l'indépendance*, p. 80.

indeed indignation of the measures taken by the French authorities in the small hours of this morning, consisting inter alia of the arrest of the lawfully elected President of the Republic and the majority of the members of the Lebanese Government and the forcible closing of the Chamber of Deputies by French black troops. Some of these arrests – notably that of the President himself – were effected in a manner which cannot fail to revolt public opinion not only in these States but throughout the civilized world.

I would remind Your Excellency that no later than at midnight last night I was insisting with you on the vital importance of avoiding anything liable to disturb the peace. You gave me your word of honour, repeated several times, that no measures were in contemplation which were liable to disturb public order or in any way interfere with the war effort.

Others must be left to judge of the interpretation to be placed on your action in giving this undertaking a few hours before it was broken. It is difficult to imagine steps more likely to break the peace and interfere with and impede the war effort in these countries than those which you have taken. Already, according to reliable information which has reached me, at least three persons have been killed including one child in demonstrations which have taken place outside the Parliament building. Not only have these actions of your subordinates created the very greatest indignation amongst the population of these States; but they will also inevitably arouse the consternation and wrath of the entire Arab world. The indignation of the religious leaders, both Christian and Moslem, has already been expressed to me and to my diplomatic colleagues in the strongest possible terms.

I leave it to you to imagine the effect which these inadmissibly dictatorial measures, taken against a small and defenceless people, will inevitably have upon enlightened public opinion in the great Democracies which have publicly declared it to be their aim to combat precisely such measures.

To this, Helleu replied defensively and in uncertain English.

> *Your letter today being couched in discourteous terms, I*
> *have the honour to inform you that I consider it as not*
> *received.*
> > *I have no need of lessons concerning my honours.*
> > *The version you have given me of language I*
> *drafted and of facts which you mention is inexact.*[32]

In Algiers, Roger Makins, a member of the British liaison office with the French, called on General de Gaulle and René Massigli, at their request, on the evening of 12 November. He found them subdued, though still not ready to give way an inch. Makins gathered that Helleu had acted on instructions from de Gaulle himself.

De Gaulle said that he knew the French position was weak: they could not move a ship or a man without the approval of the Allies. But, he added petulantly, if Britain forced the issue in Lebanon, he would give orders to withdraw all French officials and troops from the Levant and wait upon events, publishing the French case to the world. De Gaulle reserved his sharpest criticism for his former friend, General Sir Edward Spears, who was now his most bitter enemy. He would not even admit that Spears had a right to be considered on a par with Jean Helleu, France's plenipotentiary and delegate general in the Levant, let alone to interfere in Lebanese affairs.

The French position, de Gaulle insisted with stubborn persistence, was based on the Mandate, which could not be legally terminated during the war. Syria and Lebanon had been promised independence. In Syria, the undertaking had been honoured; in Lebanon, elections had been held. But the government which emerged from the elections had proceeded to provoke the French at the very moment when they had decided to negotiate on the basis of the 1936 treaty. In the face of this provocation, the French had no choice but to exercise the rights to which they were entitled under the Mandate. He was sending General Catroux back to the Levant with the appropriate instructions – but what these were, he did not care to say.[33]

---

[32] Spears to Foreign Office, 12 November 1943 (FO 371/35184).
[33] R. Makins, Algiers to Foreign Office, 12 November 1943 (FO 226/241).

When Catroux reached Beirut on 16 November, it became apparent that his instructions were to reinforce Emile Eddé and face down Riad el-Solh, and, if possible, evict him from office altogether.

The eleventh round

Sabri Hamadi, the parliamentary speaker, had by now managed to slip out of Beirut and join the provisional government in Bshamoun, where the Emir Majid Arslan had assembled some two hundred Druze fighters, armed with rifles and hand grenades. More armed men, Christian as well as Druze, had poured into the neighbouring villages of Shwaifat and 'Ain 'Anub, as well as the surrounding hills.

A French force attacked the village in mid-November, but was forced to fall back under a hail of bullets. When the French attacked again a few days later, a member of the local guard, Sa'id Fakhr al-Din, was killed as he tried to throw a bomb at a French tank. He was a member of Antun Sa'ada's *Parti populaire syrien*. His family was awarded 5,000 Lebanese lira. When she came to visit the government at Bshamoun, Laure al-Khoury, the president's wife, herself contributed 500 Lebanese lira. Madame Riad el-Solh, accompanied by Lady Spears, also visited the village in order to congratulate the fighters.[34]

Catroux sent Monsieur Bart, the new French *délégué* for Lebanon, to Bshamoun to parley with the members of the provisional government. He attempted to make light of the crisis and asked why they did not come down to Beirut, since nobody wanted to arrest them. They replied that they took with the utmost seriousness this culminating episode of twenty-five years of French rule. When asked what their terms were, they said no negotiation was possible until all the ministers were released. Those French officials who had shed Lebanese blood would all have to be dismissed. Bart invited the provisional government to visit Catroux in Beirut, but the invitation was rejected on the grounds that they could place no trust in a French safe-conduct. When Bart suggested a meeting with Catroux at Aley, they replied that if Catroux had anything to say to them he should come himself to Bshamoun.[35]

---

[34] Tuéni, *Le Livre de l'indépendance*, p. 50.
[35] Spears to Foreign Office, 17 November 1943 (FO 371/35187).

Spears then had a long conversation with Catroux, reminding him that the British government had expected the release of the imprisoned ministers at least twenty-four hours earlier. Catroux said he was unaware of any time limit, and would not have come had he known there was an ultimatum. Spears told him that if he were to order the immediate release of the government, and a return to pre-11 November conditions, there was still a possible chance for the French to retrieve their position. Otherwise, in his view at least, the French position was lost.[36] The British government, he insisted, would not give way on the question of the immediate release of the imprisoned ministers and the re-establishment of a constitutional regime: the longer the delay, the greater the blow to French prestige. The one way left to maintain Catroux's own personal position, as well as that of France, was to lay the blame for the tragedy on Helleu, and order an immediate return to the pre-11 November position.

Spears's blunt remarks aroused consternation in some parts of the Foreign Office. The head of the Eastern Department was particularly scathing:

> *It will be seen how this remarkable representative of ours has exceeded his instructions at every turn in what ought to have been an important conversation.*
>
> *Catroux has been given the impression that we started him off under a time limit ultimatum. The only time limit ultimatum we set at the beginning of this affair was when we said that we expected Catroux to be in Beirut not later than Monday. He eventually reached there on Tuesday.*
>
> *Spears urges a return to 'pre-November 11th conditions.' He has had no possible sanction for such a demand. 'Pre-November 11th conditions' would imply (a) the immediate restoration of the Chamber which we have specifically said we are not asking for, and (b) the re-establishment of the Government in their functions, which we have also said is another matter that must wait a little.*

[36] Ibid.

> *Spears tells Catroux that His Majesty's*
> *Government will not give way 'on the question of the*
> *immediate release of the imprisoned Ministers and the*
> *re-establishment of the constitutional regime.' This is*
> *another way of saying the same thing and of making*
> *absolutely certain that Catroux makes his decision under a*
> *complete misapprehension of what he is being asked to do.*
> *The point, of course, is that it is not practicable*
> *to restore, or to expect the French to restore, the*
> *constitutional regime until we have established the basis of*
> *a* modus vivendi *between that regime and the French.*[37]

Such views demonstrated the pro-French bias of some Foreign Office officials, and their racist contempt for Lebanese aspirations. They seemed unwilling to grasp that a trial of strength was already under way in Lebanon, and that the French were losing it. They also seemed unable to comprehend that Spears was not about to allow his enormous and persistent efforts over the preceding two years to be undone by some lily-livered officials in London.

Following his interview with Spears, General Catroux attempted to negotiate his way out of the impasse by holding separate meetings, in the greatest secrecy, with both Bishara al-Khoury and Riad el-Solh. The president was taken to Beirut at night to meet Catroux on Thursday, 18 November, followed by the prime minister on the 19th. Neither knew of the other's journey. Catroux clearly hoped to open a breach between them, in accordance with the formula de Gaulle had come up with. This was to return Bishara al-Khoury to the presidential palace – he was, after all, a man with whom the French had done business in the past – but to keep Riad out of government altogether. De Gaulle was counting on the Francophiles in the Foreign Office to prevail over the more radical Spears, Casey and other British officials and service chiefs in the field in the Middle East. But the scheme fell apart when Bishara al-Khoury nobly refused to be separated from Riad el-Solh.

After his interviews with them, Catroux himself became persuaded that there would be no solution to the crisis without the return to power of the Bishara–Riad duo.[38] Hoping to soften their boiling

---

[37] Maurice Peterson, Memorandum, 8 November 1943 (FO 371/35187).
[38] Tuéni, *Le Livre de l'indépendance*, p. 118.

resentment against France, he gave orders to 'relax' their prison regime at Rashaya. The prisoners were allowed to talk to each other, and were let out of their cells for an hour in the morning and another in the afternoon.

The twelfth round

Catroux, however, was soon faced with an altogether more threatening situation. Word had reached London that there was a plan afoot to transfer the prisoners from Rashaya to Algiers. Even the pro-French party in the Foreign Office realised that this could ignite an explosion of mob violence across the Middle East, forcing Britain's hard-pressed troops to intervene to restore order. London asked Richard Casey to put British forces in Egypt on the alert. The decision was then taken to bring matters to a head by means of an ultimatum to Catroux.

On the afternoon of 19 November, Catroux was invited to Spears's home, where Casey handed him a stern aide-mémoire: if at 10 a.m. on 22 November the British government had not received a favourable reply to its demand to replace Helleu and release the president and the Lebanese ministers, Britain would declare martial law for reasons of strict military necessity. British troops would then release the prisoners themselves and the Commander of the Ninth Army would take control of the country.[39]

Catroux found himself caught in a vice between Britain's ultimatum and de Gaulle's continued intransigence. This bred in him a feeling of humiliation and powerlessness. He was later to say that the word that sprang to his mind, when Casey gave him the aide-mémoire, was 'Fashoda'. (This was the name of a fort on the Upper Nile where, in 1898, British and French forces, in their imperial 'scramble for Africa', engaged in a battle of wills. To the fury of the French, Britain got the upper hand.) Hoping to have it out with Casey, Catroux went to see Spears again on 20 November, but Casey had already left for Cairo. A by-now weary Catroux confessed to Spears that the ultimatum should have more properly been addressed to de Gaulle, rather than to himself. He did not have the authority to receive it, nor the power to take decisions concerning it. The crisis had by now moved well beyond him.

[39] Ibid., p. 116.

The French made one last attempt to tough it out. On 21 November – one day before the British ultimatum expired – Massigli sent Macmillan a communiqué for transmission to Casey. The substance of it was that the French National Committee did not think it would be right for Riad el-Solh and members of his government to be brought back to power *at present*. If a conference were necessary to regulate relations between France and Lebanon, such a conference should be purely Franco-Lebanese – that is to say, without British participation. The 1941 Lyttelton–de Gaulle agreements did not give the British Command the right to proclaim martial law. If the British government put its threat into effect, it would have to bear the entire responsibility for what might follow, and for the impact on the future of Franco-British relations.[40]

Learning of the French communiqué, Spears feared that the London Francophiles might now take fright. For a moment, he felt in danger of being outmanoeuvred, and having all his efforts turned to dust. Outraged by the French move, he gave the Foreign Office a lecture: 'I leave you to imagine', he wrote, 'what the rest of the world would think of our connivance at such a grim farce in which the Lamb would sit down alone with the Wolf at the conference table'. Piling on the pressure, he told London that the Lebanese, in their thousands, were now defying the French curfew. There were sounds in Beirut of very large crowds gathering and the roar of shouting could be heard all over the town. The French had to give way or the situation might become uncontrollable.

Catroux came to see Spears that night. He was in an agony of indecision. He had had no reply from Algiers to his urgent messages. Could he take matters into his own hands? Unless he received an absolute veto from the French National Committee, he was inclined to reinstate the Lebanese government. Spears had to remind him that, according to the letter of the law, it was not up to him to *reinstate* the Lebanese government, since it had been illegally suspended. Unless Helleu's decrees of 11 November were abrogated, Britain would be obliged to declare martial law the next day. He urged Catroux to release the prisoners, to ask Emile Eddé to withdraw from the scene, and to send Helleu out of the Levant altogether. A defeated and exhausted Catroux gave in. In view of the deafening silence from

---

[40] British Legation, Beirut, to Foreign Office, 22 November 1943 (FO 226/242).

Algiers and the unrelenting pressure from Spears, he had simply run out of options.[41]

Meanwhile, with a manic persistence, Spears piled the pressure on London to ensure that there would be no softening of the British line. He reported that a large delegation of deputies had come to the Legation to say that, if the French insisted on Catroux negotiating a return to constitutional life with Bishara al-Khoury alone – in other words, excluding Riad el-Solh – there would be 'no possibility of holding the mob tomorrow'. Leaders of the northern Biqa', he warned, were prepared to 'die fighting'. One family alone had already mobilised 400 armed men. In the southern Biqa', the Druze were organised under their family chiefs and were in touch with the minister of defence, the Emir Majid. They had at least 500 rifles in their possession and would rise to a man when the signal was given. In Sidon, notables were planning to blow up the French Marine barracks and the French *conseiller*'s house. Coordinated uprisings were being planned all over Lebanon, with, as their primary objectives, French arms and ammunition dumps. Leaders of rural communities were proceeding with the organisation of their forces in order to take early action should the French refuse to restore the situation. The purpose in all this, he cunningly added, was to create a state of affairs which would force the British to take over armed control. Spears knew very well that this last argument would sound alarm bells in London.[42] Indeed, that very night, numerous explosions were heard in Beirut, with Emile Eddé's house among the targets. In the early hours of 22 November, Eddé escaped to an unknown destination in a French van.

The thirteenth round

On Sunday night, 21 November, the BBC broadcast news of the imminent release of the arrested ministers, sparking an explosion of joy throughout Lebanon. Immense crowds, tens of thousands strong, started moving about the town. They were largely armed. There was continuous and very heavy shooting in the air. The vast demonstrations continued over the next day. Carrying deputies shoulder-high,

---

[41] Spears to Foreign Office, 21 November 1943 (FO 226/242).
[42] Spears to Foreign Office, 22 November 1943 (FO 226/242).

the crowds converged on the parliament buildings, tore down the old Lebanese flag and hoisted the new flag. Similar scenes were enacted at the *Sérail* and the Beirut Municipality. As French and colonial Senegalese troops were confined to their barracks, there were no violent incidents. The only acts of defiance were the tearing down and trampling of French flags.

On Monday morning, 22 November, people flocked to the houses of the president, the prime minister and the other arrested ministers, to await their arrival from Rashaya. The prisoners were released at around 11 a.m. and headed for Beirut, accompanied by the French *délégué*, Monsieur David, and the head of the Lebanese gendarmerie, Colonel Nawfal. At about 2 p.m., Bishara al-Khoury and Riad el-Solh, the two heroes of the hour, rode side by side into Beirut, to scenes of popular elation. Monsieur David had wanted to sit next to the president on the journey from Rashaya – no doubt in the hope of restoring some shred of French prestige – but the president, keen to put him off acting so distastefully, told him that if they were seen entering Beirut together, David would certainly be lynched by the mob.

A vast cheering crowd carried the president up the steps of his residence at Qantari. The same car then took Riad el-Solh to his home at Ras al-Naba', where, after an emotional welcome from his wife and daughters, he addressed the cheering crowd from the balcony of his house. He then made his way back through the throng to the president's residence.

General Catroux arrived there a few minutes later. But the house was so teeming with well-wishers that there was no room to receive him. He was taken into Bishara al-Khoury's bedroom, where he was received *très froidement*. The interview lasted about an hour. Hoping to rescue something from the wreckage of French policy, Catroux began by insisting that the president arrange for the Solh government to resign. It was absolutely essential that Bishara al-Khoury make a gesture of reconciliation and show consideration for French feelings (*des égards pour la France*). Bishara's refusal was cutting and categorical: public opinion would never tolerate it, he said, even if he were prepared to make such a gesture, which he was not. In any case, no conciliatory move was due to the French at a moment such as this.

Seemingly worried and depressed, Catroux then asked that Riad el-Solh be brought into the conversation. To them both he said: 'As you refuse to dissolve the Government, at least give me time to telegraph to Algiers for fresh instructions. I will strongly recommend that you, Riad el-Solh, should be permitted to remain in office. I hope to receive an answer tomorrow.'

Catroux requested that, in the meantime, the president go down to the *Sérail* alone on the morrow, keeping the government in the background 'for the next few days'. Bishara al-Khoury replied that this was quite impossible. He had indeed intended to go to the *Sérail* with *all* the ministers, but they were too exhausted, not by the ill treatment that they had suffered at Rashaya, he said triumphantly, but rather from the sleepless excitement of the reception they had received in their homes upon their return. He had decided, nevertheless, that two ministers – most probably Camille Chamoun and Selim Takla – would go to the *Sérail* the next day, and that he would go down there officially with all his ministers on Wednesday morning, and hold a review of troops. This was his firm intention, whatever the reply from Algiers. Catroux's eleventh-hour effort had failed.

Meanwhile, the released ministers were so harried by their admirers that they had to seek refuge in Henri Pharaon's house for some much-needed food and rest.[43] 'Abd al-Hamid Karami returned to Tripoli, where he was greeted by enormous crowds. Habib Abi Chahla returned to Beirut from Bshamoun, but the Emir Majid Arslan decided to remain there for a day longer, as a precaution, until he was sure that everything was satisfactorily cleared up. Abi Chahla, Salim Takla and 'Adil 'Usayran then went up to Bshamoun to escort him back to Beirut. Accompanied by a great number of armed supporters and still wearing his traditional Druze battlefield outfit – flowing headdress, white breeches, high boots, a pistol in his belt and an ammunition belt slung across his chest – he made his ceremonial way to the *Sérail*.[44]

On 24 November, Catroux paid an official visit to the *Sérail*, and handed the president a letter confirming that the National Committee in Algiers had annulled Helleu's *Arrêtés*. De Gaulle had at last climbed down. The situation thus reverted to what it had been on 10 November.

There was, however, a further murky subplot. Riad el-Solh learned that, the night before they were to be released, a French hit team, led by Colonel Boisseau, had arrived at Rashaya with the

[43] Ibid.
[44] Spears Mission to HM Minister, 23 November 1943 (FO 226/242).

intention of kidnapping and killing them, rather than allowing them to be set free. He was persuaded to leave the fort for Beirut only after a senior French officer conveyed orders to him from General de Gaulle himself. Bishara, on the other hand, had heard of a plot by French extremists to kidnap Catroux in his residence in East Beirut, in order to prevent him from freeing the prisoners.

Yves Chataigneau was appointed *délégué général* in place of Helleu. However, the French-controlled press in Algiers pointedly published a telegram from de Gaulle to Helleu, in which he said: 'General Catroux will transmit to you the Committee's decision inviting you to return to Algiers for consultation. I shall myself be most interested to hear your report and meanwhile address to you an expression of my friendship.'

For his part, Spears – the hidden hand behind the momentous drama – was glad to learn that those he considered to be his particular enemies in the *Délégation*, Messrs Baelen and Boegner, were also headed for Algiers. 'I am now safe!' he happily joked to London.

The last round

Exhausted though he was, Riad el-Solh came to see his ally, General Spears, on the night of 22 November, and stayed with him for about an hour. How they must have savoured their triumph, although Spears refrained from recounting to London the glee with which they toasted their remarkable victory. He only reported that Riad was calm but very determined. Spears described the abominable way Riad had been treated at Rashaya. His room was damp, his bed filthy and the 'sanitary' arrangements beyond description. He was guarded by the roughest troops available. But despite all French precautions, he had managed to keep fully informed of what was going on outside. He was completely at one with the president, whose firmness and loyalty he could not praise highly enough. It had become abundantly clear, Spears commented, that the Lebanese government would not accept any French interference whatsoever with their complete independence.[45]

On 23 November, Spears called on President Bishara al-Khoury. The house was packed with deputations, from learned bodies

---

[45] Spears to Foreign Office, 23 November 1943 (FO 226/242).

to representatives of small shopkeepers. Women's delegations were also numerous. Spears listened to some of their speeches. He noted that all demanded complete and absolute independence. There was a great deal of cheering for Great Britain. He felt personally vindicated, and his patriotic satisfaction was complete.

With daring, determination and skill, Riad el-Solh and General Spears had forced the French to concede Lebanon's independence. For Riad, this was sweet compensation for the many blows, setbacks and disappointments he and his generation of nationalists had suffered: Jamal Pasha's hanging of their early martyrs; the slaughter of Syria's fledgling army by the French at Maysaloun; the dismemberment of Greater Syria; the savage crushing of the Great Syrian Revolution; the shipwreck of Arab hopes when Britain smashed the Palestinian uprisings of 1936–39; France's criminal cession of Syria's Alexandretta province to the Turks; the long and bitter ordeal of the Mandate, and many, many more. Now, he hoped, the tide was turning. He had seen how skilful the Zionists had been at harnessing Britain to their cause. He, Riad el-Solh, had also managed to harness a remarkable British proconsul to *his* national cause.

The dramatic events of November 1943 were hugely important for the future of Lebanon. They set it on the path to genuine independence – or at least an independence as genuine as a small and weak country could expect to enjoy, in view of its strategic position and its many internal weaknesses, which together made its neighbours and the great powers consider it a battleground on which to fight out their quarrels. In the words of the historian Albert Hourani, the events of November 1943 'left behind them a fragile sense of unity and triumph, from which the independent Lebanon and its government could derive something of the revolutionary legitimacy which is the basis of modern nation-states'.[46]

In a note to the Foreign Office on 25 November, Spears felt the need to explain at some length – even to justify – the reasons for his actions. The French contribution to the 1941 campaign had been minimal, he wrote. It was Britain that had wrested the Levant from Vichy. The Free French claim to have inherited France's former mandatory position was more than legally doubtful. In any event, they had

---

[46] Albert Hourani, 'Lebanon: Development of a Political Society', in Hourani, *The Emergence of the Modern Middle East*, p. 138.

pledged publicly to terminate the mandatory regime, and Britain had underwritten that pledge. But the Free French had obstinately refused to honour their promise.

Here, Spears could not resist putting in a word of congratulation for himself. 'It was only with the greatest difficulty', he wrote,

> *and as a result of nearly two years of diplomatic pressure, that we finally induced them to make a first step in that direction by permitting a return to constitutional and parliamentary life. The result was the emergence, despite every form of interference and pressure by the French, of a strongly nationalist Lebanese government and parliament, which proceeded to assert their undoubted right to revise their country's constitution. It was this action that precipitated the crisis of the 11th November.*

The measures taken by the French, he concluded, were 'unjustified on any conceivable legal basis and quite incompatible with the spirit of the Atlantic Charter . . . These measures definitely endangered the Allied war effort in the Levant'. Had the British not forced the French to revoke them, the result would have been a popular revolution, serious interference with Allied lines of communication, and a large-scale massacre of Frenchmen.[47]

It was a powerful political apologia for what had been a personal policy, fuelled by Spears's sudden and implacable hostility to the French, and fervent conversion to Arab nationalism.

Spears was unable, however, to escape scot-free. Anthony Eden had not wanted to make the French eat humble pie. To review the situation, he called a meeting at the British Embassy in Cairo on 7 December, attended by Richard Casey, the British minister of state in the Middle East; General Sir Edward Spears, Britain's minister to the two Levant states; Lord Killearn (formerly Sir Miles Lampson), the British ambassador in Cairo; Harold Macmillan, Britain's representative to General de Gaulle's Committee of National Liberation; and other British bigwigs, both civilian and military. Eden chaired the meeting. He was plainly unhappy at the outcome of the Lebanese

---

[47] A Note of the Reasons for British Action in the Lebanese Crisis, British Legation, Beirut, 25 November 1943 (FO 226/242).

crisis. It was not desirable, he said, with no small dose of imperial arrogance, that peoples under mandate should be permitted to terminate the mandatory arrangements without appropriate agreement with the mandatory power. It would set a dangerous precedent which might be followed elsewhere in the Middle East.

But terminate the French Mandate was what Spears had done. He knew that he had got his way, but now he was careful not to crow about it. Eden insisted that the Lebanese should not be given the impression that anything they did would enjoy British support – but that was precisely the impression that Spears had chosen to give them all along. Unable to contain himself any longer, Spears blurted out that he was certain that the Lebanese would insist on the French clearing out of the Levant after the war. But Eden would have none of this. His instructions were rather that Britain should use its authority with the Lebanese, to help in their relations with France and save French face as far as possible. An inflexible Eden was unable to grasp that such policy and such way of thinking had long since been overtaken by events.[48] Indeed, this mental limitation would prove to be his undoing in the Suez crisis of 1956.

It was by no means a satisfactory meeting. Spears had managed to anger a great many powerful people in London, including Anthony Eden himself. He was to be made to pay a price for his transgressions. Even his old friend, Winston Churchill, could not save him now. Nevertheless, it had been a fabulous adventure!

---

[48] Memorandum of Meeting held at British Embassy, Cairo, at 4.30 p.m. on 7 December 1943 to discuss the question of Syria and Lebanon (FO 226/242).

21 | PAINFUL AWAKENING

Hardly had Bishara al-Khoury and Riad el-Solh returned in triumph to Beirut from their incarceration at Rashaya than things started to go wrong. It soon became clear that the French were determined to fight back, and that British support for the nationalists could no longer be counted on. Moreover, sectarian fires in Lebanon were by no means extinct, and Arab unity, or even solidarity – which Riad had always believed to be an article of faith – was evidently little more than a mirage. The grandiose speechmaking of Arab leaders simply threw a veil over their deep-seated rivalries and mutual hatreds. Riad el-Solh and his cabinet were to have a painful awakening.

In Algiers, General de Gaulle was seething with anger that Riad el-Solh's 'provocation' had gone unpunished. How dare this defiant Muslim nationalist remove all mention of the Mandate from Lebanon's Constitution, putting an end to France's centuries-long privileges in the Levant? De Gaulle's mood was to blame the British, and especially that false friend, Sir Edward Spears, for whom he now felt nothing but implacable hostility. His instructions to General Catroux were to compel the Lebanese and the Syrians to sign a treaty with the Free French, which would restore France's pre-eminent position in the two countries – a pre-eminence which, he never failed to repeat, the British themselves had recognised in the Littleton–de Gaulle letters of 1941.

Catroux returned to Beirut on 16 December 1943 and, assisted by the *Délégué Général* Yves Chataigneau, and the new *délégué* for Lebanon, Count Stanislas Ostrorog – a recent defector from Vichy – immediately entered into negotiations with the Lebanese and Syrian governments. Catroux's tactic was to give some ground – he could not do otherwise in view of the nationalist fervour in Beirut and Damascus – while seeking to retain control of the real levers of power. Thus, on

22 December, an agreement was reached in Damascus for the transfer – in principle – of the *Intérêts Communs* to the two local governments, but each item had to be separately negotiated and separately agreed upon. This was followed on 3 January by the successful transfer of the customs administration and the tobacco monopoly, achievements that were greeted locally with great rejoicing. Riad el-Solh was rewarded by a motion of thanks in parliament. But, in fact, the transfer was largely a fiction, since the agreement was not to be fully implemented for another two years, and the numerous French officials employed in the various administrations were to remain very much in place.

Moreover, no progress whatsoever was made on the transfer to the Lebanese and Syrians of the *Sûreté Générale*, the *Gardes Mobiles* and the *Troupes Spéciales* – the French-officered local levies which were the real sinews of French power. It soon became evident that the *Troupes Spéciales*, in particular, were the instrument with which the French intended to pressure the local governments into concluding the treaties they demanded. The French had several cards up their sleeve. They knew that many Syrians and Lebanese in the *Troupes Spéciales* – many of them from minority backgrounds – were happy to remain under French command. They feared that if the levies were transferred to the local governments, their pay and conditions might deteriorate. Indeed, the Lebanese and Syrian governments would have been hard-pressed to find any money for the *Troupes Spéciales*, even had the French consented to hand them over. While the populations clamoured for the creation of 'national armies', the governments themselves knew that such demands could not yet be met. When Riad el-Solh's government presented its first budget to the Chamber in March 1944, national defence received a mere 22,000 Syrian pounds (about £2,000 sterling) out of a total of 34 million, suggesting that no financial provision could be made for a national army, beyond providing a salary for the minister of defence, and a small budget for his office.

On 10 March, General Paul Beynet arrived to take over from Chataigneau, whose term of office was coming to an end. The French wanted Beynet to have the twin titles of *délégué général* and commander-in-chief of French forces in the Levant. The Lebanese government immediately objected: these titles were no longer compatible with Lebanon's independent status. The French, they argued, should have appointed an ambassador, by agreement, in accordance with diplomatic norms. Beynet had to content himself with the sole title of *délégué général*. He tried to make himself agreeable, but only because there were sinister French plots being hatched behind the scenes.

Spears, for one, was convinced that France was planning a military coup. This seemed to be confirmed by the arrival of numerous French military officers – whom he described as 'of extreme right-wing tendencies' – and by reports that large numbers of colonial Senegalese troops were being moved from North Africa to the Levant.[1] It appeared that the plan was to create internal disorders 'necessitating French intervention'.[2] Spears reported that, according to a secret source in the *Délégation*, the organiser of the disorders would be Colonel Jouteau, head of a newly formed French battle school; General Montclar, 'a notorious fire-eater'; Colonel Vermeulen, commander of the *Troupes Spéciales*; and Colonel Angen, who 'had taken a particularly embittered line after the November crisis'.

Chataigneau, with whom Spears dined on 9 March, was 'fully aware that there was a French plot on foot'. He told Spears that 'a group of 147 French officers with leftist tendencies had been formed in opposition to the hitherto all-powerful Fascist military clique'. Chataigneau seemed certain that de Gaulle himself knew of the activities of the extremists. But in London, Spears's Foreign Office critics – led by R. M. A. Hankey, head of the Eastern Department – mocked 'the fearful fuss' Spears was making about French troop movements, and pooh-poohed his fears. 'It just shows again that where Frenchmen are concerned, we really cannot trust Sir E. Spears' judgment', Hankey minuted contemptuously in March.[3]

A serious incident on 27 April, however, gave substance to Spears's foreboding. Joseph Karam, the newly elected deputy for North Lebanon, came that day to Beirut to take his seat in the Chamber. He had been known as a French protégé, but, bowing to the prevailing climate, had renounced French support on the eve of the poll. Nevertheless, as his convoy approached Beirut, it was joined by large numbers of pro-French opposition elements, many carrying firearms and flying French flags on their cars. When Karam entered the parliament building, part of this crowd tried to force its way in with him. A corporal in French uniform then climbed up the ironwork over the main door and fixed a French flag over it. He was at

---

[1] Spears to Foreign Office, 9 March 1944 (FO 371/40311).
[2] Commander-in-Chief Middle East to War Office, 14 March 1944 (FO 371/40311).
[3] Minute by R. M. A. Hankey, March 1944 (FO 371/40300).

once shot at and wounded by someone in the crowd. The French later issued a warrant for the arrest of Na'im Mughabghab, on a trumped-up charge of attempted murder. He had been head of the small force which had protected the 'provisional government' in Bshamoun during the November crisis, and had earned French loathing. A general mêlée followed in front of parliament. A grenade was thrown, wounding the second-in-command of the Lebanese police and twenty other people, and killing four civilians and a gendarme. Spears reported that 'there seems to be enough evidence to show that the *Sûreté* had a hand in the affair'. But it was not clear whether this had been a clumsy attempt to overthrow the government or merely a *ballon d'essai* – a trial run.

Thoroughly alarmed, Riad el-Solh pledged that force would be used to suppress the troublemakers. He publicly deplored the fact that 'a group of traitors' was prepared to violate parliament and all it stood for. But privately, he and his colleagues were now understandably nervous regarding French intentions. Fearing arrest – and a possible replay of the events of the previous November – cabinet members spent the night of 4–5 May away from their homes. Commenting on these events, Spears reported to London that

> *since last November, the French have been pursuing two policies. The high authorities, Catroux, Chataigneau and Beynet, have been carrying out a policy of genuine transfer of powers. But, behind the scenes, a horde of French officials, officers and agents of the* Sûreté *have been working in exactly the contrary sense, and have been spending very large sums of money for this purpose. They have concentrated on arousing the fears of the Christians.*

The Syrian authorities were having much the same problems as the Lebanese. When they requested a thousand rifles for their grossly under-equipped gendarmerie, the French offered to sell them 400 used rifles, model 1904, at a cost of 400 Syrian pounds each, which, it was calculated, was the equivalent of five and a half times the cost of a new Lee Enfield. The ammunition the French offered was of 1884 manufacture, priced exorbitantly at 147 piastres (3 shillings and 4 pence) a round. Spears thundered that 'It is clear that the French have no desire whatsoever to see the local governments discharge efficiently their responsibility for maintaining internal security. Indeed, it would seem that the policy of Algiers is to make this impossible'.[4]

The liberation of Paris from the Germans, first announced on the BBC on Wednesday, 23 August 1944, was the occasion for great celebrations by the French in the Levant – and for anxiety on the part of the local governments. In Beirut, the French community attended a solemn mass of thanksgiving in the Church of St Antoine, while French flags hung from parachutes were dropped by French planes. Other French flags were pressed into the hands of civilians during the celebrations. In Damascus, a boisterous reception was held at the French Officers' Club, while an illuminated Croix de Lorraine, within a V-sign formed from burning mazout, shone out rather provocatively on Mount Qassiun, the hill that overlooks the largely Muslim city. Needless to say, the Syrian government had not been informed of this French initiative; nor had its agreement been sought. The attitude of the local French officers was: We are the masters now! Your independence is non-existent, and the British are merely trying to replace us.

On 24 August, a day after the liberation of Paris, René Massigli, de Gaulle's commissioner for foreign affairs, addressed a stiff note to Anthony Eden, complaining of British encroachments (empiètements) on France's 'pre-eminent position' in the Levant.[5] He demanded that instructions be given to British representatives not to interfere in the internal affairs of Syria and Lebanon. Some British authorities, he said – and he meant, of course, Sir Edward Spears – considered that these states were now fully independent, and that there was no further reason to end the Mandate by means of a treaty. Displaying the usual French paranoia regarding British intentions, he alleged that this situation would allow Britain to take advantage of France's 'momentary inferiority'. Massigli's most insistent demand was that Eden declare publicly that Britain supported the conclusion of a treaty between France and the Levant states.

Eden rejected the charge of British encroachments. It was normal, and indeed inevitable, he wrote in reply, that British representatives should be in close relations with the local governments. He firmly rejected the 'unwarranted suggestion' that Britain was seeking to

---

[4] Spears to Foreign Office, 24 June 1944 (FO 371/40312).
[5] René Massigli's note of 24 August 1944 and Anthony Eden's reply (FO 371/40302).

supplant France's influence in the Levant. But he then committed what was a major error of judgement. In a total disavowal of Spears's policies and recommendations – which had annoyed him almost as much as they had the French – Eden told Massigli that the British government 'would welcome an agreement between France and the Levant States freely to conclude the treaties foreseen in the Declarations of Independence, as a convenient method of determining their future relations'.

Eden was now saying that Britain supported France in wanting a treaty, whereas Spears had reported to London, time and again, that the Lebanese and Syrian governments had no intention whatsoever of concluding any sort of treaty with France, or of giving it any special privileges in their countries. This deviously contradictory policy from London – of backing France while pretending to recognise the independence of the Levant States – was greatly to weaken the position of both Riad el-Solh and of General Spears. It would also be the cause of much future trouble.

On firm instructions from Eden, Spears (trying hard to conceal his huge personal embarrassment and fury) had to travel to Damascus to inform Syria's President Shukri al-Quwatli that it was time for the Syrian government to consider the conclusion of an agreement with the French. Syria would need some economic and financial support, he said, and it was not British policy to take the place of France in any sphere. This line of argument – the opposite of all that Spears had advocated in the recent past – caused a furore. The Syrians, naturally, condemned it as a 'complete betrayal'. They understood that their independence depended on a balance between the British and the French: if the British withdrew their support, the Syrians would be lost. An angered Quwatli was driven to write letters to Churchill, Roosevelt and Stalin, denouncing the Eden–Massigli exchange, which he compared to the secret agreements of the First World War, which had led to the hated Mandate being imposed on Syria in the first place. Any negotiations with the French would be profitless, he wrote, because Syria 'does not want to grant France any advantage, whether cultural, material, political or military'. It wished to treat all nations, and especially the Great Powers, on a footing of complete equality.[6]

---

[6] Spears to Foreign Office, 23 September 1944 (FO 371/40203).

No illusions on the Arab front

While these confrontations with the French were taking place, Syria and Lebanon were also much preoccupied with inter-Arab relations. As a pan-Arab figure, Riad had for decades been on familiar terms with all the principal Arab rulers. Now, as prime minister of Lebanon, he was one of them, and, as the victor of the November contest with the French, he shone with particular brilliance. Congratulations and invitations poured in from across the region.

For months, ever since the elections of August 1943, Lebanon had been in the limelight, and throughout the November crisis had found itself on the front page of the world's newspapers. Although it was a very small country, it had become a test case for a whole series of stirring ideas. These included the right of small states to independence and democracy; the sincerity of Allied war aims and the Atlantic Charter – that ringing declaration made by Roosevelt and Churchill in August 1944, in which they affirmed 'the right of all peoples to choose the form of government under which they will live'. Riad el-Solh repeatedly invoked the Charter in his speeches, to justify Lebanon's demand for full independence from France.

On coming to office, Riad undertook a number of journeys to neighbouring countries, which were meant to symbolise Arab resurgence. He began with Cairo in January 1944, where he was a guest of King Farouk, and held talks with Prime Minister Mustafa Nahhas Pasha. Visits to Haifa and Damascus followed and, in April–May, to Baghdad and Riyadh as well. In each case, he and his delegation – which included Lebanon's Foreign Minister Salim Takla, and Musa Mubarak, President Bishara al-Khoury's *chef de cabinet* – were fêted and lavishly entertained.

On these voyages, the main subject of discussion was always the prospect for Arab unity. With the imminent end of the war, the subject had come very much to the fore. In theory, every Arab leader swore by Arab unity. In practice, it was a different story. Every single leader feared a union which might restrict his freedom of action, or even deliver him up to his enemies. Being an old hand at Arab politics, Riad el-Solh knew the secrets, rivalries and geopolitical concerns of the various Arab heads of state.

He knew, for example, as did every other politicised Arab, that the Saudi monarch, 'Abd al-'Aziz al-Sa'ud, was engaged in a bitter vendetta with the Hashemites. Their quarrel dated back to 1926, when Ibn Sa'ud's forces had occupied Mecca, and driven the Sharif Husayn out of his ancestral Hijaz and into exile in Cyprus. Ibn Sa'ud had then taken the Sharif's own title, king of the Hijaz, and added it to his own of Emir of Najd. He had then obtained official recognition from Britain, France and the Soviet Union, as well as Muslim acknowledgement of his new role as protector of Islam's holy cities and guardian of the hajj.

In spite of these successes, however, Ibn Sa'ud continued to entertain the greatest suspicion of the Hashemites, especially when one of the Sharif's sons, 'Abdallah, became emir (and later king) of Transjordan, and another son, Faysal, became king of Iraq. As a result of this great personal dislike of both father and sons, Ibn Sa'ud chose to keep aloof from schemes for Arab unity, seeing them as nothing more than Hashemite expansion on the approaches to his kingdom.

It was common knowledge that the Emir 'Abdallah's obsessive ambition was to occupy the throne of Syria, and then to merge that country with Transjordan, Palestine and Lebanon into a Greater Syrian union. 'Abdallah had nursed this ambition ever since his younger brother, Faysal, secured the throne of Iraq, a country which the General Syrian Congress in Damascus of March 1920 had originally earmarked for himself. For decades, 'Abdallah schemed persistently to draw Syria into his orbit, without, however, much success. His hopes revived when Faysal died in 1933, making him the leader of the Hashemite family, a position which he hoped would enhance his prospects for the Syrian throne. In July 1938, he suggested to Harold MacMichael, British high commissioner for Palestine and Transjordan, that the increasing difficulties of the Palestine question could be solved by the creation of an Arab kingdom comprising Transjordan and Palestine. In the summer of 1939, he launched a similar scheme, with an eye to including Syria and Lebanon as well in his proposed kingdom.[7]

But 'Abdallah's financial dependence on Britain and his suspected collusion with the Zionists gravely weakened his case. He was seen to be pursuing selfish, even mercenary, dynastic ambitions, rather than larger nationalist goals. He was opposed by the French, by Ibn Sa'ud, by the Syrian nationalists, while even Britain – his patron and backer – was not all that keen on his ambitions. It urged him to be

[7] Raghid el-Solh, *Lebanon and Arabism*, pp. 103 ff.

content with his desert fiefdom, which happened to serve Britain's interests as a base for the British-officered Arab Legion.

'Abdallah also faced fierce competition from Baghdad. There, the Hashemite Regent 'Abd al-Illah, his nephew, and Nuri al-Sa'id, Iraq's leading statesman, both saw Iraq as far more suited than backward Transjordan to take the lead of any proposed Arab union. Iraq had rising oil revenues, an expanded army, membership of the League of Nations, and a nationalist ideology of wide appeal outside its borders. However, both these rival Hashemite schemes faced great opposition, not only from Riyadh, Paris and London, but from Cairo as well.

In the 1920s and 1930s, Egypt had not been very interested in the affairs of other Arab countries. The sole exception was Sudan, which it had always considered its natural extension, since the security of the Nile was an intense and abiding Egyptian concern. But when Nahhas Pasha, the leader of the *Wafd*, came to power in 1942, he sought to enhance Egypt's regional position – as well as his own prestige – by taking the lead in the burgeoning debate over Arab unity. He had invited delegations from Arab countries to come to Cairo for discussions, in preparation for a conference which, he hoped, would produce a consensus on the form Arab unity should take.

Both Nahhas Pasha and King Farouk knew very well that Hashemite ambitions – whether pursued by the Emir 'Abdallah or by 'Abd al-Illah and Nuri al-Sa'id for Greater Syrian or Fertile Crescent unity – were contrary to Egypt's interests in its new ambitious role as the leading Arab power. Indeed, the emergence of a large bloc in Arab Asia would challenge Egypt's dominance in the eastern Mediterranean. It thus became an enduring principle of Egyptian foreign policy to prevent any such development taking place.

Egypt's policy thereafter was to oppose any form of union between two or more Arab states. It proposed instead something more modest: an extended family of individual Arab states, grouped loosely around the Egyptian 'elder sister'. This could then be mobilised at appropriate times in support of Egyptian national aims. This policy was to reach its peak when Gamal 'Abd al-Nasser was engaged in a struggle against Western Powers in the 1950s and 1960s. Nasser's own union with Syria (1958–61) was a brief departure from this policy, an aberration which even he came to regret. It was forced upon him by the Syrian military junta of the time, which felt the need for the popular Nasser's protection, as well as by the ideologues of the Ba'th Party.

In addition to such broad strategic differences between the principal Arab states, their relations were further bedevilled by a host of personal antipathies, which Riad had to take into account in his Arab contacts. King Farouk detested Nahhas Pasha, who had been foisted on him by the British when Rommel was at Egypt's door. When Riad and the Lebanese delegation were in Egypt, one of Farouk's courtiers described Nahhas to them as 'the Egyptian Emile Eddé', since he had taken office 'under the guns of British tanks'.

For Riad, one of the rare pleasures of his 1944 visit to Cairo was seeing his friend Makram 'Ebeid again. Ebeid was a brilliant, Oxford-educated lawyer and a luminary of Egypt's Coptic community. As secretary-general of the *Wafd*, he had negotiated the 1936 Anglo-Egyptian Treaty. But, after differences with some of Nahhas's associates, he had broken with the *Wafd* a year before Riad's visit and had founded his own splinter group, the *kutla wafdiste*. All the while, however, he had adhered fervently to the credo which had so attracted Riad el-Solh, namely that the Egyptians were Arabs, and that Arab unity and Arab solidarity were the essential prerequisites for an Arab renaissance in modern times.[8]

In Iraq, there were similar antagonisms. 'Abd al-Ilah and Nuri al-Sa'id hated each other. Yet they also needed each other as they strove to regain control of Iraq following Britain's crushing of Rashid 'Ali in 1941. Moreover, there was no love lost between the Iraqi Nuri and the Egyptian Nahhas. They were rivals, in that they were both aspiring to impose on the Arab world their own vision of the form unity should take.

Ibn Sa'ud – the dominant force in the Arabian peninsula – continued to view all these unity schemes with the greatest suspicion. In addition to his hostility towards the Hashemites, he had no time for the pan-Arab conference which Nahhas wished to convene. Ibn Sa'ud did have his favourites on the Arab scene. He liked and respected both Riad el-Solh and the Syrian President Shukri al-Quwatli, whose courage and patriotism he admired. But he was suspicious of Syria's Foreign Minister Jamil Mardam, whom he thought unduly influenced by Nuri al-Sa'id.

As if these inter-Arab squabbles were not enough, Riad's home scene in the Levant gave little ground for satisfaction. He was

[8] Ahmad Qassem Goudah (ed.), *al-Makramiyyat*, Cairo n.d., pp. 147–50, quoted in Anouar Abd el-Malek, *Anthologie de la littérature arabe contemporaine*, 2 vols, Paris 1965, vol. II, pp. 126–7.

discouraged to see his Syrian friends – the leaders of the National Bloc with whom he had worked so closely for decades – split down the middle by personal conflicts, and by the rival interests of the cities of Damascus and Aleppo. He sought repeatedly to mediate between them. His conciliation was also needed in Palestine, where the Husayni and the Nashashibi factions, among many others, continued to fight and often kill each other. This disastrous fragmentation was to make the Palestinians even easier prey for the Zionists.

Riad el-Solh's Arab journeys in 1944 provided him with a refresher course in these many antagonisms and rivalries. In Egypt, although both King Farouk and Nahhas Pasha went out of their way to welcome him, he was reminded of the grave tensions between them. Moreover, he noted that the Egyptians were then not particularly concerned with the Palestine question. At the formal meetings with Nahhas, Riad defended the Palestine cause, arguing that the Arab states should make contact with Palestinian leaders, adopt the solutions they recommended, try to prevent any further Jewish immigration and land purchases, and help form a Palestinian national government. He told the British Ambassador Lord Killearn, that 'discussions about Arab unity were useless if Palestinian representatives could not join in'.[9] The Egyptians' main priority, Riad noted, was not Palestine, but the frustration of any pan-Arab consortium in Asia, which Cairo feared would fall under Iraqi leadership.

On their return journey from Egypt, the Lebanese delegation of Riad el-Solh, Salim Takla and Musa Mubarak paused in Haifa to meet Palestinian leaders. To their surprise, they found Iraq's Nuri al-Sa'id convalescing in hospital there. He took the opportunity to expound to them his scheme for Fertile Crescent unity. This would extend, without the impediment of frontiers, from Iraq to Syria, and from Lebanon to Palestine. It would be a union in which Baghdad intended to play the central role. Anxious to preserve their own hard-won and still fragile independence, his Lebanese audience hardly warmed to his ideas.

Sadly, there were no tangible results from Riad's visits to Cairo, Haifa, Baghdad or Riyadh. On a visit to Damascus, he made a pledge to his nationalist friends that Lebanon would never sign a treaty with France, or accept a French military base in Lebanon, which might constitute a threat to Syria. This was what he had meant when he said in his first

---

[9] Killearn to High Commissioner, Palestine, 16 January 1944 (FO 371/39987).

ministerial statement – in a phrase he was often to repeat – that Lebanon would never serve as a 'conduit for colonialism' to its Arab neighbours.

In all these Arab capitals, Riad was once again reminded of the strict limits beyond which Arab leaders were not prepared to go where Arab unity was concerned. As a lifelong Arab nationalist, he was obviously disappointed by this, but as prime minister of Lebanon, this may have suited his country's interests well enough. Knowing the fear that Lebanon's Christians had of being swamped by Muslims, he noted wryly that Egypt's overly modest plan for a loose association of Arab states was just about what the Christians of his own country might be persuaded to accept.

Riad's own position had evolved considerably since the 1930s. In his youth, he had dreamed of Syrian unity as a first step towards a wider Arab union. But, once he entered the Lebanese political arena and set his sights on power in Beirut, he was forced to adjust his views to take local opinion into consideration, which included, to a great extent, Christian opinion. He was now called upon to champion Lebanese objectives rather than Arab nationalist ones. What he had thought a mere halt on the road was beginning to look like a final destination. It was therefore as a Lebanese patriot that he now championed Lebanon's independence within its expanded 1920 borders. His challenge was to draw the Muslim population of Lebanon behind him in support of the new Lebanese state.

Riad came to see, early on, that the quest for Lebanon's independence had to be grounded in Muslim–Christian power-sharing.[10] The National Pact, which he had forged with Bishara al-Khoury, was the expression of this entente, on which his whole political programme was founded. To keep the Christians on board, he found that he had no option but to oppose schemes for region-wide Arab union. He had to champion instead the sovereignty, independence and territorial integrity of Greater Lebanon. Within these strict limits, Lebanon was free to cooperate as much as possible with other Arab states. This cautious formula was the only way to keep his internal coalition in place. It was a politically difficult and often personally distressing tightrope act.

Some Christians remained convinced that Riad el-Solh's defence of Lebanon was not genuine. Some Lebanese Muslims, and many of his friends in Syria's National Bloc, were unhappy with his new position.

[10] See Nasri Maalouf's testimony, in Khoury (ed.), *Sélim Takla*, pp. 510 ff.

They accused him of having sold out his nationalist ideals for the sake of power. And yet, *no* Arab state was prepared to relinquish its *own* sovereign powers to a wider Arab union or federation. Lebanon was by no means an exception in wanting to safeguard its independence in much the same way. The endemic suspicions which Arab leaders harboured about each other ruled out the possibility of Arab union.

The Alexandria protocol

In August 1944, Riad delivered a speech at an Arab Lawyers' Congress in Damascus, in which he gave powerful expression to his views.

> *Lebanon is indeed an Arab country, as its Government declared in its ministerial statement, a statement which was approved in full by the* whole *of Lebanon and which has become its National Charter.*
>
> *Lebanon will never serve either as a fiefdom for colonialism, or as a conduit for colonialism to other Arab countries – that is to say to you!*
>
> *Independent Lebanon, whose independence you and other peoples have recognized, will go with you as far as you yourselves will go . . .*
>
> *I say this so that Lebanon should hear what I say, and that all Arab governments, Arabs and other peoples, should also hear . . . In my view, Arab unity is the guarantee of the independence of each country that embraces it, within the limits it sets for itself. Some people indulge in intrigues and concoct plots. They say that Syria and Iraq have reached an agreement to swallow Lebanon. That is a lie. It is a calumny. Nothing of the sort is happening, or will happen . . .*
>
> *In conducting my electoral campaign, I said to my brothers, who share my ideals: 'Lebanon is not on the road we would want. The Muslims follow one road and the Christians another. It is our duty to bring them together under the flag of independence.'*
>
> *It was on this basis that I conducted my campaign, that I accepted the premiership, and that I worked with*

*my brothers so that Lebanon would become independent.
We have reached our goal, and have hoisted aloft a
national flag, noble and glorious. We have given the first
place to the Arabic language, which has become the sole
official language of the country, and we have freed the
Constitution from all blemishes . . .*

*Let me sum up so that I may be heard in Lebanon.
My brothers in the Arab countries have recognized your
independence, on condition that Lebanon collaborates
with the Arab countries – within the limits of its
independence, its frontiers, and its integrity.*

*No doubt I will find myself in difficulty with
my companions in the struggle, who believe that I have
become a 'regionalist'. But I must tell the truth today.*
The truth is that all Arab countries understand unity in
the same way that Lebanon understands it. *That is the
truth!*[11]

At Egypt's invitation, Arab delegates met in Alexandria from
25 September to 7 October 1944, in what became known as the preparatory committee for the founding congress of the League of Arab
States.[12] Riad el-Solh led the Lebanese delegation to the Alexandria
Conference, and Salim Takla gave the opening speech for Lebanon.

The delegates debated three different models of association: a
centralised union, a federal union and a confederal one. Riad el-Solh
rejected any form of federalism. It would split Lebanon, he argued, at
a time when France was pressing it to conclude a treaty which would
guarantee the French the special privileges they had long enjoyed.
Lebanon had been able to resist these French pressures, thanks mainly
to the alliance between his own Arab nationalists and Bishara al-
Khoury's Destour Party. But if Arab nationalists were to press Lebanon
to accept a federal solution, the Destour Party would quit the alliance
at once. This would open the way for a treaty with Paris, which would
only consolidate French influence in the Levant – and pose a grave
threat to Syria.

[11] *Al-Bashir* (Damascus), 17 August 1944, report of Riad el-Solh's speech at the Arab Lawyers' Congress.
[12] Raghid el-Solh, 'Sélim Takla et la création de la Ligue arabe', in Khoury (ed.), *Sélim Takla*, pp. 341–3.

It soon became apparent that the Alexandria Conference would achieve only limited objectives. In so far as a consensus emerged, it was for an association of states even looser in form than a confederation. This was the real sense of the Alexandria Protocol, which was signed at the close of the meeting. After some further amendments later – and yet more dilution of unionist objectives – it served as the basis for the creation in Cairo in March 1945 of the League of Arab States.

The French fight back

Even though the results of the Alexandria Conference were extremely modest, the French – and their diehard Christian supporters in Lebanon – reacted violently to them. Emboldened by Eden's reply to Massigli – in which Britain supported France's demand for a treaty – General Beynet, the French *délégué général*, precipitated a crisis with the Lebanese government, by sending a rash and peremptory note to President Bishara al-Khoury. He claimed that the Alexandria Protocol had tied Lebanon's hands, ruling out the possibility of it ever concluding a treaty with France. As a result, the French now considered invalid General Catroux's declaration of Lebanese and Syrian independence of 1941.

This was too much even for the imperial-minded British. The Foreign Office hurried to instruct its Paris embassy to take the matter up with the new French Foreign Minister Georges Bidault.[13] 'In the view of His Majesty's Government', A. Holman, the British chargé d'affaires in Paris, wrote to Bidault, 'there is nothing in the resolutions of the Alexandria Conference which can be regarded as impairing the independence of the States concerned. HMG would not in any case accept the suggestion, implied by the language held by General Beynet to the Lebanese President, that the independence of the Levant States was subject to reconsideration'.[14]

The Lebanese promptly asked for Beynet's note to be withdrawn and Riad el-Solh made an impassioned statement in the Chamber:

We have become independent because we wanted to be independent, and because the Arab States and the great

---

[13] Foreign Office to Paris, 20 October 1944 (FO 371/40112).
[14] A. Holman, British Chargé d'Affaires to M. Georges Bidault, Minister of Foreign Affairs, 24 October 1944 (FO 371/401123).

Allied Powers have recognized our independence. This is a fact that cannot be challenged . . .

We shall hold on to our independence and defend it whatever the cost. November is, for us, an eventful month. We came out of last November safe and victorious, and we shall come out of this November, safe and victorious.

As for a treaty [with France], I have said – and the government has said – that Lebanon does not intend to conclude a treaty with any Power or State. We are determined to go to the Peace Conference free of all promises or treaties . . . There are no grounds for fear.

This declaration was received by the Chamber with prolonged applause.

To any observer witnessing the nationalist fervour in the Levant States – and the impatience of the great majority of the population to be rid of the French – it was clear that the blinkered Anthony Eden had made a grave mistake in encouraging the French to press the Levant states for a treaty. It would, of course, have been far wiser had he paid more attention to what Spears was reporting, and less to the armchair views of his prejudiced officials in London, and to his own racialist and anti-Arab instincts. Spears had quoted Riad el-Solh as saying that the Lebanese government had not recognised the Mandate and would never recognise it. He had quoted the Syrian Prime Minister Sa'dallah al-Jabiri, as telling the Syrian parliament, 'No treaty! No Mandate!'

But Spears's enemies were now gathering in London. His policies were being undermined by senior officials in the Foreign Office's Eastern Department, notably R. M. A. Hankey, who, as early as December 1943, had minuted:

The whole trouble is that Sir E. Spears is determined to get the French completely out of the Levant States, regardless of our conception in London of British interests, or the Secretary of State's or the Prime Minister's instructions. It is becoming futile to send Sir E. Spears instructions and he will certainly wreck the modus vivendi *negotiations [this was a euphemism for the preparation for the Treaty*

*negotiations that the French wanted] unless we recall him.
This is my considered advice.*[15]

And, most unfortunately for the Levant, Anthony Eden decided to heed it.

Riad's headaches as prime minister

Riad el-Solh did not have an easy time as prime minister. Quite apart from his prolonged struggle with the French, he was attempting to run a small country with few resources, little civic spirit, a quarrelsome political class, a great deal of corruption, and profound suspicions between Muslims and Christians. Within a few months of taking office, his government faced almost universal complaints of maladministration. The budget was slow in passing; there was a failure to impose new taxation; the cost of living was soaring, as was government expenditure; ministries became swollen with political appointees – often non-entities, with little knowledge or experience; ministers and department heads, altogether too accessible to the public, were plagued by constant demands for favours. Petty notables felt that they had right of entry into any government office at any hour. There was a general sense that the government was getting little done.

Some of these problems were endemic to the system. Jobs were given on the basis of religion rather than competence. This was because confessionalism – the tradition that every community had to be represented in proportion to its numbers in every type of public function – was engrained throughout the country. Inter-sectarian quarrels were still of too recent memory to allow the average Lebanese to sink his confessional rights in favour of rights as a Lebanese citizen.

Riad, too, had to bear his share of blame. He was the eloquent voice of liberation, the supreme political strategist – but he had no taste for administration. He diverted all economic and financial complaints onto the unfortunate 'Adil 'Usayran, head of *ravitaillement* – the supply chief – who became the butt of public criticism. Riad would say airily that he could not 'fight on two fronts' – against the French and against internal problems.

[15] Minute by R. M. A. Hankey, 3 December 1943 (FO 371/35194).

To ease the pressure from the public, the government resigned on 1 July 1944 and, as expected, President Bishara al-Khoury immediately asked Riad el-Solh to form a new government. Riad took for himself the portfolios of interior and supply, and gave assurances that he intended to overhaul the administration and direct internal affairs with a firmer hand. Hamid Frangieh (Franjiyyeh), a prominent Maronite landowning *za'im* from Zgharta, was brought in as minister of finance; Camille Chamoun left the government to take up his appointment as Lebanese minister in London; 'Adil 'Usayran was replaced by a young and unknown Shi'i from South Lebanon, Muhammad al-Fadl.

Riad may have been able to retain the premiership at this time of crisis largely because of the difficulty of finding a suitable Sunni to replace him. His main rival, the Tripoli leader 'Abd al-Hamid Karami, was considered too inexperienced, too uneducated and too suspect to the Christians; the unpopular 'Abdallah al-Yafi did not particularly want the office; Sami el-Solh knew to his cost by now that he would always be overshadowed by his cousin Riad; and Sa'ib Salam, though an excellent candidate for a junior portfolio, was thought to be as yet too young to be ready for the premiership.

But all was not going smoothly. Riad faced opposition inside and outside the Chamber from three distinct directions: from a group of pro-Eddé deputies led by Dr Ayyub Thabit and Alfred Naccache; from a number of South Lebanon deputies, led by Ahmad al-As'ad, who now revived the old rivalry between the Solhs and the As'ads; and by a raucous opposition faction led by Tawfiq 'Awad, who was believed to have received a large sum from French secret funds in order to create disorder.

Emile Eddé himself was believed to have had a series of meetings with unnamed 'French agents'.[16] Indeed, what to do about Eddé had become a real headache for Riad el-Solh. Some deputies wanted him put on trial for high treason, on a charge of conspiring with the French during the November crisis. Others wanted the government to pass a law expelling him from the Chamber. But Riad was anxious to placate Eddé's supporters, rather than inflame them. He also owed Eddé a favour for having persuaded the French not to oppose him too openly in the August 1943 elections. He repaid this debt by arguing

---

[16] G. W. Furlonge, British Consulate General, to British Legation, Beirut, 10 August 1944 (FO 226/252).

that Eddé's case was covered by a clause in the 1934 Electoral Law, which provided for the unseating of a deputy if he had accepted 'remunerative office' in either Church or State. Eddé, accordingly, lost his seat for having taken office from the French on 11 November 1943. This protected him from the far more serious charge of treason.

At the same time, desperate to reassert their cultural supremacy, the French were putting intense pressure on the Lebanese government to sign a *convention universitaire*, laying down the curriculum in Lebanese schools. France was attempting to impose the *baccalauréat* to the exclusion of all other school diplomas, and to persuade the government not to recognise the certificates of either the American or British schools. This would, in effect, have excluded from public employment all those who had not obtained a French educational qualification. They included the tens of thousands of Muslim Lebanese, who had had an education in Arabic or in English. Excluding them was no doubt the real reason for this French move.

The situation became so tense that Riad el-Solh even began to be concerned about his own personal safety. The four gendarmes guarding his residence were increased to twelve, and four additional bodyguards, armed with rifles and a machine gun, were put up in an adjacent building, with orders to come to the aid of the gendarmes in an emergency. Towards the end of the year, a French naval officer, Rear Admiral Auboyneau, called on Riad el-Solh at his office in the *Sérail* and invited him to attend a party on his cruiser, the *Emile Bertin*. 'I accept on condition that you remain on land,' Riad joked. 'Last time I was deported to Rashaya. This time it might be further away still!'

The fall of Edward Spears

Such personal alarms apart, Riad's greatest political problem was that the British – who had so far been his greatest support – were now cool and distant. Whereas the French were making obvious attempts to incite the Christians against the Muslims, spreading the word that the Christians were in danger of absorption into a British-inspired Muslim bloc from which only the French could save them, the British remained eerily silent. Spears had gone to London for difficult talks at the Foreign Office. In his absence, Gilbert Mackereth, the chargé d'affaires at the British Legation, was plainly hostile to Spears's policy.

When Riad el-Solh complained to Furlonge that the French were encouraging his opponents with money, arms and verbal propaganda, Mackereth chose to report to Hankey that 'We are constantly hearing this sort of thing – a string of unrealistic and unsubstantiated tales of French activities'.[17]

On Spears's return to Beirut at the end of August 1944, Anthony Eden decided to put an end, once and for all, to his career in the Levant. For Eden and for some of his senior Foreign Office officials, Spears was not only an incorrigible Arab-lover, but also a maddeningly independent envoy. He pursued his own political goals and refused to toe the official line, which he despised as being cowardly and wrong-headed. On 1 September, Eden wrote Spears a cold and unpleasant letter, which could only be taken as a dismissal.

With the end of the war in view, it is most important that our efforts should be used to the fullest possible extent to pave the way for an eventual agreement between the Levant States and the French, which will permit the conduct of their future relations on an ordinary diplomatic basis. I have not been able to convince myself that any less formal agreement than a treaty is likely to attain this object.

You will therefore neglect no opportunity of impressing on the local Governments that the conclusion of an agreement with the French is, in our view, not only the best, but perhaps the sole method, of securing full and unchallenged independence. You should also do everything possible to promote the establishment of a practical modus vivendi *between the States and the French, which will pave the way for such treaties . . .*

I shall shortly enter into communication both with the Minister Resident Cairo, and with yourself, in order to ensure that the Spears Mission shall be greatly reduced, whether by absorption into the Legation or as regards certain of its officers into the military command, or by simple suppression, so that the end of the war will find us in a position to conduct our relations with the Levant

<hr>

[17] G. Mackereth to R. M. A. Hankey, 5 September 1944 (FO 3761/40112).

States on a basis which is scarcely, if at all, different from
that of ordinary diplomacy.[18]

Spears waited a few weeks before replying to this outrageous repudiation of everything he had worked and pleaded for consistently over the
years. He felt obliged to reassure friends like Riad el-Solh that things
were not as bad as they actually seemed; say his many farewells; and
settle his affairs after four eventful years in Beirut. On 4 December,
the Foreign Office announced that Sir Edward Spears was anxious to
resume his duties as a Member of Parliament and had therefore asked
that his resignation as His Majesty's minister to the Levant states be
accepted, with effect from 15 December.

On 8 December, Spears sent a last, long dispatch to Anthony
Eden (of which the following are extracts). He robustly restated
his views and defended his actions. 'One sentiment is prevalent,' he
wrote,

> *throughout all classes in both countries; namely dislike*
> *of the French, individually and collectively. It is not*
> *universal, for certain sections of the Christians, particularly*
> *the Maronite clergy of Mount Lebanon and their closer*
> *adherents, and the minorities of North and East Syria,*
> *are imbued with French culture and have an atavistic but*
> *uncontrollable fear of Muslim domination, which leads*
> *them to imagine that a continuance of French control is*
> *preferable to independence . . . But the Muslims, who form*
> *some 75 per cent of the whole, and a large proportion of*
> *the Lebanese Christians, are possessed by a determination*
> *sooner or later, somehow or other, to be rid of the*
> *French. It is necessary to insist on this point, since it is*
> *fundamental. No freely-elected Government in either State*
> *can do otherwise, in the present state of feeling, than base*
> *its policy on this consideration.*
> *. . . All the indications are that the French are*
> *determined not only to exploit to the full the powers*
> *they still retain, but to force on the States, by any means*
> *open to them, treaties giving France a* de facto *control*

---

[18] Eden to Spears, 1 September 1944 (FO 371/40347).

far greater than that accorded to us in Iraq twelve years ago . . . it would be hard to point to one French official or resident in either country who has evinced the slightest sympathy for the evolution of Syria and the Lebanon.[19]

Spears then summarised the grievances of the local Arab population against the British: their resentment at having been abandoned to the French in 1920; their anger at Britain's pro-Zionist policy in Palestine; their shock in 1941 at having the Free French imposed on them – indistinguishable, in their eyes, from the detested Vichy regime; their disappointment at Britain's failure to force the French to implement the promise of independence they had made, and which Britain had under-written. In addition to all this, he said, there was a disastrous shortage of wheat and a rise in commodity prices.

'It required every effort on the part of myself and my staff', Spears wrote, 'to improve this unfavourable situation. Bound as we were by the Lyttelton–de Gaulle agreements, we were unable at first to control the errors and incompetence of the makeshift Free French organization'. He then described how he had been able to organise the supply of wheat and avert a possible famine. As for the political situation, it was only the 'unremitting pressure of His Majesty's Government on the Free French which finally induced the latter to consent to the restoration of the constitutions and the holding of elections'. When a clash with the French came, as the result of the new Lebanese government's determination to pursue its independence, it was only British action, he claimed, which had saved Lebanon from losing all it had gained.

Spears then reviewed the considerable problems facing both Syria and Lebanon, before coming to his conclusion.

The attitude of the French is the crux. The time when the French could have obtained preferential treaties went by in 1937, when they first declined to ratify the 1936 treaties they had signed in 1936 and then, by allowing the annexation of the Hatay [former Alexandretta] by Turkey, showed themselves incapable of assuring the protection of the States . . . The whole trend of French policy . . . leads to only one possible conclusion. The

---

[19] Spears to Eden, 8 December 1944 (FO 371/40307).

Délégation Général, *amplifying through their propaganda loudspeakers the clamant voice of the Christian minority under their influence, will sooner or later raise the cry of 'Protection for the Christians of the Levant' as a pretext for demanding the strengthening of their military forces, and will thereafter demand treaties on terms which will run wholly counter to legitimate Syrian aspirations.*

If France acted in this way and if Britain stood aside, Syria would call for help from the Arab states, the United Sates and the Soviet Union, and British influence 'would have irretrievably vanished'.

Spears concluded by declaring:

If, on the other hand, we are prepared to stand firm now and hereafter in support of the States until their aspirations are satisfied, I am convinced that we shall be able to build, on the base of the goodwill already achieved, a solid position for ourselves which will buttress the whole structure of our influence in the Middle East.

Throughout my term of office, I have been guided by two main objectives, which must, I submit, be ever present in the mind of His Majesty's Representatives in the Middle East: the successful prosecution of the war, and the preservation of our strategic position. How far I have been successful, and how far I have failed, I leave to others to judge. But the objectives are, I think, unimpeachable; and the policy which I have outlined in the preceding paragraphs is, I submit, the one best calculated to achieve them.

Eden totally ignored Spears's prescient words. He had already made up his mind that Spears was a troublemaker. He therefore instructed Terence Shone, Spears's replacement in the Levant, to facilitate the conclusion of 'a formal agreement between the Levant States and France . . . I can see no other satisfactory issue to the present position'. Eden revealed his innermost motives by adding, 'French and British interests in the Levant are not fundamentally opposed . . . There is, however, a long heritage of bad relations between France and Great Britain in the Levant. I am anxious to bring this state of affairs to an end'.[20]

[20] Eden to Shone, 20 December 1944 (FO 371/40347).

A short while later, Eden had to endure a blast from Lord Killearn, British ambassador in Cairo, even more toughly worded than Spears's own, carefully considered dispatch. By warning of the dangers of the policies Eden was pursuing, Killearn was in effect supporting Spears. 'We seem to have been pursuing two diametrically opposing policies at the same time,' he wrote.

> *On the one hand we have been encouraging the Arab Union and on the other we have been promoting Zionism in Palestine and French predominance in Syria. It seems a safe bet that our Syrian, Palestinian and our Arab Union policies will come into conflict before too long.*
>
> *As regards Syria and the Lebanon, I understand that our policy is to press these States to conclude treaties with France, which would give the latter a preferential position and presumably military bases. This policy will not be accepted except under duress by Syria or even by the Lebanon, however much internal division the French may be able to create.*
>
> *The Lebanese have signed a protocol which precludes them from signing any treaty with France which would make Lebanon a French military bridgehead against Syria, and they would hardly dare incur the open hostility of the surrounding Muslim world by breaking this agreement and siding with France . . .*
>
> *If we support France in the matter of the treaty, the French are bound to go ahead energetically with the business and, if opposition is encountered, the chances are that General de Gaulle, with his well-known inclination towards drastic measures, will use force at least against the Lebanon to impose a treaty, unless we stop him from doing so. Very little force would be necessary in the Lebanon. A naval demonstration with landing parties would be sufficient . . .*
>
> *We would become involved in a conflict with ninety per cent of the Arab world and sooner or later we shall end up losing the Middle East . . .*
>
> *All sorts of nationalist problems are boiling up in the Middle East and, even without the millstones of France*

and Zionism around our neck, we shall have quite enough to handle in straightforward clashes between ourselves and nationalist elements . . .

I have thought it permissible to sound this warning note in view of ominous signs of French truculence . . .
The visit of a French cruiser to Beirut may well be the first step in a French campaign of menace which may end in violence.[21]

Eden ignored this sound advice too, as he had ignored Spears's own warnings. In his reply to Killearn, he could only repeat his stubborn, threadbare formula: 'I cannot at present see any satisfactory alternative to our policy of facilitating an agreed settlement between the French and the Levant States, though this will clearly not be easy to arrange and will take time'.[22]

How was Eden's attitude to be explained? As the Suez crisis was clearly to demonstrate a decade later, it was compounded by a pronounced distaste for Arabs, as well as an imperialist fellow-feeling for France, a power similar to Britain itself, which was temporarily down on its luck. Eden's instinctive regard for France by far outweighed any concern for the distant, troublesome and relatively unimportant Syrians and Lebanese. Paris had just been liberated and the focus in London had shifted to post-war Europe. The Arab world had been reduced to an insignificant sideshow.

The Syrian and Lebanese governments could not conceal their dejection at Spears's departure. They gave him honours never before conferred on any foreigner. He was made an honorary citizen of both Syria and Lebanon. Syria's President Shukri al-Quwatli decorated him with the Order of the Umayyads, and Lebanon's President Bishara al-Khoury with the Order of the Cedar. At a farewell dinner (one of several) Riad el-Solh gave for him at the Normandy Hotel, Spears declared that he was almost certainly unique in the world in being a citizen of both Levant states! The fact that such an honour had been given to a single man was profound evidence, he said, of the fraternal feeling Syria and Lebanon felt for each other. This, he continued, was what actually pleased him most.

---

[21] Cairo to Foreign Office, 25 December 1944 (FO 371/114174).
[22] Foreign Office to Cairo, 5 January 1945 (FO 371/40307).

Once back in England, Spears continued in the House of Commons – and with much publicity – to defend Syria and Lebanon against the French. In an interview with the *Sunday Express* on 24 January 1945, he declared that the twenty years' experience of the Mandate had made Syria and Lebanon resolved 'never to place their heads in the noose again'. They were determined never to concede a predominant position to any one power. And, in a last dig at his former friend, General de Gaulle, he added: 'In the name of what principle for which we are fighting can a treaty be imposed on them?'

Spears's departure from the Levant marked the end of an era. Riad el-Solh himself resigned on 9 January 1945, brought down by widespread complaints over the soaring cost of living and government inefficiency, and by Christian fears that the Alexandria Protocol – signed by seven Arab states on 7 October 1944 – would put the Christians under Muslim domination. President Bishara al-Khoury then called on 'Abd al-Hamid Karami, Riad's main Sunni rival, to form a government, the first of three political leaders to occupy the prime minister's office before Riad's return to power on 14 December 1946.

The French rejoiced at the departure of Sir Edward Spears and Riad el-Solh. An exultant General Beynet reported to Georges Bidault that 'Riad el-Solh's open hostility to France was the real reason for his fall and disgrace . . . General Spears had given this Muslim national-ist full powers to direct a fifth column with the aim of bringing about the disappearance of the only remaining Christian homeland in the Levant'.[23]

The bombardment of Damascus

Beynet's analysis was to prove no more reliable than Eden's. Indeed, de Gaulle was shortly to behave in as brutal a manner as Spears and Killearn had predicted he would. In early January 1945, French tanks were moved to Damascus, while the French *Délégué* Colonel Oliva-Roget, sent a threatening note to the Syrian government, breaking off negotiations over the transfer of the *Troupes Spéciales*. The govern-ment replied expressing astonishment at the tone of the French note,

---

[23] MAE, Nantes, Fonds Beyrouth (Amb.), série 199A4, carton 20, Général P. Beynet à M. Georges Bidault, 12 January 1945.

and listing the many anti-Syrian actions the French had perpetrated in the previous months.

In late February, the British learned that the French planned to move three battalions of colonial troops to the Levant in two cruisers, to 'relieve and reinforce' French forces. One of the French cruisers, with 800 colonial Senegalese troops on board, was due in Beirut on 5 May. Alarmed at this development, the commander-in-chief of British forces in the Middle East informed the French commander, General Humblot, that he was not prepared to authorise these reinforcements of French forces 'unless the proposals and reasons for them were placed before him'.[24] In Paris, on 30 April, British Ambassador Duff Cooper warned General de Gaulle of the danger to public security if French reinforcements arrived in Beirut at a moment when Franco-Syrian discussions were about to be resumed. De Gaulle peevishly rejoined by complaining that since there were British troops in the Levant states, he was not prepared to reduce the number of French troops. He repeated his mantra that British policy was to seek to weaken the position of France in Syria, in order to replace her there.

On 8 May, General Beynet revealed French terms for the proposed treaty: the *Troupes Spéciales* were to remain under French command for an indefinite period, and would only be transferred, and French troops evacuated, after the Syrians concluded cultural, military, economic and diplomatic conventions with France. The Syrian and Lebanese governments naturally refused to negotiate on this basis. On 14 May 1945, the Lebanese government learned that French troops had sailed from Tunis to Beirut, where they landed a few days later.

Shortly afterwards, Lebanese and Syrian representatives met French delegates in Damascus, amidst strikes and disturbances in the city. The French repeated their hard, unreasonable demands. Lebanon and Syria refused to enter into negotiations, and instead condemned the troop landings. Violent demonstrations broke out, with bloody clashes between demonstrators and French troops in both Damascus and Beirut. Disorder spread all over the mandated territories. Within ten days, law and order had completely broken down.

On 27 May, the Syrian government told the British political officer in Damascus, Trevor Evans, that the situation was slipping

[24] Beirut to Foreign Office, Weekly Political Summary, 28 February 1945 (FO 371/45553).

out of control and that the formation of a revolutionary government, that would declare war on France, had become a real possibility. The only way out was for the *Troupes Spéciales* to be handed over and for French troops to be removed from the towns. Meanwhile, dozens of Syrian men were deserting every day from the *Troupes Spéciales* to the government side.

The French military command in Damascus was by this time in a state of high excitement. On orders from General de Gaulle to General Beynet, the French rashly decided to resort to force. On 29 May, a French artillery battery at Mezzé opened fire on the ancient Citadel, which was the headquarters of the gendarmerie – the only force at the disposal of the Syrian government. Several of the 150 gendarmes stationed there were killed or wounded, and the rest took flight. Their Armenian commander, Lieutenant Colonel Hrant, was wounded by shrapnel. This effectively put the gendarmerie out of action. A solitary French aircraft then bombed the same target, scoring a direct hit on the civil prison situated in the Citadel, and killing thirty-two prisoners. The doors of the prison were thrown open and the remaining prisoners allowed to escape. The French are believed to have whisked away some of the prisoners held there for the killing of Fawzi al-Ghazzi, perhaps better to camouflage their own possible involvement in his murder, several years earlier. With Lieutenant Colonel Hrant out of action, the only senior gendarmerie officer left in Damascus was Colonel 'Abd al-Ghani al-Qudmani, who headed a force of sixty gendarmes at the *Sérail*, the seat of government. They soon came under attack.

The French did not arrest President Shukri al-Quwatli or members of his government, having perhaps learned the lessons of the November 1943 crisis in Lebanon. Their main intention seems to have been to terrorise the city and force the government either to resign or flee. They would then have installed a puppet government. They warned that any quarter of the city that attempted to rise in rebellion against them would at once be obliterated.

Heavy firing recommenced around midnight. An hour later, at about 1 a.m. on 30 May, the French shelled the Syrian parliament building at point-blank range and, after heavy mortar fire, seized control of it. Its garrison of sixty-five gendarmes were either killed or captured, their blood spattering the walls inside and out. The elegant building was then ransacked by French troops. There was further artillery fire that morning and, in late afternoon, the Damascus Citadel was bombed once again.

During the night of 30–31 May, the Citadel was bombed for a third time, while artillery shells whistled over the town every three or four minutes, causing fires to break out. A British Red Cross ambulance train at the Hijaz railway station was destroyed by a shell, and a Syrian physician, Dr Muslim al-Barudi, was killed when the French fired on his ambulance, which was ferrying wounded civilians to the Victoria Hospital, run by British medical missionaries in Qassaʿ. Some of the more seriously wounded were sent to the British army hospital outside the city.

On the morning of 31 May, shelling and mortar fire continued, while French armoured cars roamed the streets, firing indiscriminately. The French then captured the Damascus police headquarters. During two brief negotiated truces on 30 May, and again the next day, British and Allied civilians were evacuated from the city, but both truces were broken by the French. There was also large-scale looting by French troops, often in the presence of their officers.

On 31 May, Anthony Eden announced in the House of Commons that Prime Minister Winston Churchill had that evening sent General de Gaulle the following message:

> *In view of the grave situation which has arisen between your troops and the Levant States, and the severe fighting which has broken out, I have with profound regret ordered the Commander-in-Chief, Middle East, to intervene to prevent further effusion of blood in the interests of the security of the whole Middle East, which involves communications for war against Japan. In order to avoid collision between British and French forces, we request you immediately to order French troops to cease fire and withdraw to their barracks. Once firing has ceased and order is restored, we shall be prepared to begin tripartite talks in London.*

At about 5 p.m. on 1 June, a British armoured column entered Damascus to the cheers of the much-tried population. While French troops were cleared from the streets, Britain briefly assumed military control until the Syrian government could resume its normal functions.

Always ready to spring to the defence of the Levant states – and no doubt to embarrass Anthony Eden – General Sir Edward Spears asked in the House of Commons whether the government could provide a figure for Arab casualties. The answer, conveyed by the prime minister on 5 June, was (in round numbers) 80 gendarmes killed, 400 civilians killed, 500 seriously maimed or wounded and another 1,000 injured. The *Mohafez* of Damascus estimated damage to property at 25 million Syrian pounds. Among the buildings seriously damaged were the parliament, the Citadel, the *Sérail*, the Orient Palace Hotel, the Jenkiz mosque, and hundreds of small factories, commercial shops and trading establishments. There was a small number of British casualties, including Major Scott-Nicholson, killed by a rifle shot outside the Orient Palace Hotel, and Mrs Grey, wife of the church army warden, who, having bravely declined to be evacuated, was killed by shrapnel on the roof of her house.

At a press conference in Paris on 2 June, General de Gaulle was unrepentant. French military and civilian establishments had been attacked, he claimed, and French troops had had to react to restore order. He blamed the crisis on 'the attitude taken either at the highest level by the British Government or at a low level by a mass of British agents'. France wished to safeguard her cultural, economic and military interests. But, he said bitterly, 'There are interests that are opposed to ours in a way which we cannot accept'. As for Churchill's message – to which he had thought it best not to reply – it 'had changed nothing and would change nothing' in the orders he would give to French troops.

General Beynet in Beirut was equally unashamed about the murderous bombardment of civilian Damascus. It was perfectly normal, he told a British envoy, to subdue the natives with a little shooting, if they caused trouble! It was ridiculous to talk about 'Syrian public opinion', since it did not exist. The affair was now over. The French were out and the British were in, as they had always planned to be.[25]

The bombing by the French of an open and defenceless city caused extreme bitterness throughout the Levant. Hatred for France reached the highest level ever known. President Shukri al-Quwatli, who had a long and prestigious history of fighting France and being

---

[25] Report by Mr Donald Mallett, Regional Press Officer at His Majesty's Embassy in Paris, on his visit to Syria and the Lebanon, 7 July 1945 (FO 371/45576); General de Gaulle's account of the Syrian crisis in his *Mémoires de guerre: Le salut, 1944–1946*, Paris 1959, pp. 186–96.

imprisoned by the French, now told the British Minister Terence Shone of his 'implacable determination' to rid his country of French influence, once and for all.

The outcome would have been different had Britain's Foreign Secretary Anthony Eden followed General Spears's advice and given firm support to the Levant states in their new-found independence, rather than encouraging the French to attempt to safeguard their 'pre-eminent position' by imposing a treaty that no self-respecting Syrian was willing to accept.

22 GOODBYE TO THE FRENCH

The British and French Mandates, which were imposed on the Arab provinces of the Ottoman Empire when it was dismembered after the First World War, were an unrelieved catastrophe. In Palestine, if seen through Arab eyes, the British Mandate was to result in the violent emergence of the State of Israel at the heart of the region, and its ruthless expulsion of much of the native Palestinian Arab population – with dire and enduring consequences for regional stability and international peace. In the Levant, the French Mandate was seen as a political and moral disaster of great magnitude. The local populations were made to suffer more than twenty years of ferocious repression, culminating in the wanton bombardment of the ancient city of Damascus in 1945, that final demonstration of the bankruptcy of French colonial policy.

The bombardment of Damascus was a crime, a racist spasm of a defeated imperial power. It ended, once and for all, France's ambition to remain the 'pre-eminent power' in the Levant, to retain cultural, political, economic and military privileges by means of treaties. Nor did the French go gracefully after the last fires had been put out, which left so many families, including old and important ones, homeless and destitute. It took nearly two more years of bitter negotiations before the last French soldier was to fly out of Beirut, on 31 December 1946.

The Lebanese and the Syrians were finally on their own. But they were as yet not quite able to govern themselves, and totally unable to defend themselves. Despite the stirring speeches of leaders like Riad el-Solh and Shukri al-Quwatli, the actual situation of their two countries was pitiable. As the French had insisted on running almost every aspect of the show themselves, few locals had been allowed to acquire any meaningful administrative experience. There was a grave shortage of trained men, and virtually no trained women available to slot into key jobs. On the eve of the Second World War, there were only 356 students in higher education in Syria.[1]

In a word, the French legacy to the Levant states had very little to commend it. The road network may have been extended somewhat; tracts of land in the Jazira may have been opened up to cultivation, and there was some little progress in health services and primary education. One bright spot, however, was the founding of Damascus University in the 1920s, the country's first institution of higher education, largely on the initiative of Dr Rida Sa'id and a group of like-minded medical doctors and academics. Dr Said became its first president.

On the whole, however, the legacy of the Mandate was calamitous. It was one of French-rigged elections, corruption and bribery, constitutional confusion and constantly changing administrative boundaries; of a parliamentary system flawed by nominated deputies, and by frequent dismissals of the entire Chamber, whenever the French failed to get their way. Force was used to hold down the territories, most strikingly in Syria in 1925–26, when the great uprising was put down in blood. In Lebanon in November 1943, the newly elected president and many members of his government were dragged from their beds in the middle of the night and thrown into jail, for daring to purge the Constitution of references to the hated Mandate (as Fawzi al-Ghazzi had done in Syria and had almost certainly paid for with his life).

Apart from these particular outrages, the constant intimidation of the population by the use of Senegalese colonial troops – who had orders to be as brutal as possible and to break all social taboos by entering the harem quarters of homes, to frighten and humiliate women and children – was much resented. It was an ugly indication of the depravity of the methods of empire – using one colonised people (in this case, African Muslims) to terrify and subjugate another. The Syrian and Lebanese elites, many of them refined and educated, found the daily denigration of being ruled by crass French *petits fonctionnaires* hard to bear.

Militarily, Syria and Lebanon were left with no armed services to speak of. Without French officers and French equipment, their national armies were paltry forces, scarcely able to keep order at home, let alone put up much of a fight a year or two later against

---

[1] Raymond, *La Syrie d'aujourd'hui*, pp. 82 ff.

the well-trained and armed Jewish state. Lebanon had scarcely 2,000 men under arms in 1945–46. Far from being reinforced, equipped and prepared for the looming emergency in Palestine, the Syrian army was *reduced* between 1946 and 1948, from 7,000 to 2,500 men, for a desperate lack of funds.[2] An added reason for this disastrous emasculation was that the Syrian politicians who came to power at independence – all drawn from elite families in Damascus, Aleppo, Homs and Hama – were rightly suspicious of the political and class loyalties of men who had served under the French flag, and who were mostly rural youths from minority backgrounds. The French had packed their *Troupes Spéciales* with such soldiery, and had done their best to wean them away from Arab nationalism and towards separatist allegiance, so that they had little in common with the dominant ideology of the urban notables.

Where the French went wrong

A great many mistakes lay at the root of the French failure. For one thing, Paris never took to its 'mandatory' obligations. Born after the First World War, of Wilsonian principles, the Mandates were supposed to be based on the notion that aid and advice from more advanced countries would guide the former Ottoman provinces to eventual independence. But the French substituted domination for tutelage, putting in place colonial regimes, similar to the ones they had imposed so harshly on North Africa. Indeed, throughout the years of the Mandate, the French were reluctant to soften their direct rule in the Levant, for fear that it might undermine their iron hold over their North African possessions.

In Beirut, the French high commissioner, assisted by a secretary-general, ran what was, in effect, a fully-fledged administration. High Commission *délégués* controlled the local governments; French 'advisers' were present in ministerial offices, while political officers for 'native affairs' ruled in outlying districts. The French army was in full control, assisted by the locally recruited but thoroughly colonial *Troupes Spéciales*. As for those economic services shared by both states – the so-called *Intérêts Communs*, primarily the customs

[2] Khoury, *Syria and the French Mandate*, p. 629.

administration – these remained throughout under firm French control, despite the fact that the officials running them were often incompetent or corrupt, and sometimes both.

From the moment Greater Lebanon was created, French policy was to back minorities against the majority, on the presumption that minorities would prove more loyal to France, providing the local underpinning for French rule. In Syria – under the influence of men like Robert de Caix, secretary-general at the high commission in the early years of the Mandate – the Druze in the south, the Alawites in the north-west, and a host of other minorities in the Jazira province of the far north, were given special preference over the Sunni Muslim majority. They were encouraged further to develop their existing separatist sentiments, and were groomed to view the nationalists of Damascus and other big cities as their enemy.

In Lebanon, the French favoured the Maronites, fanning the flames of Christian–Muslim antagonism so as to create a raison d'être for their own presence. Of course, the French did not invent the ancient ethnic and religious diversity and divergences of these countries, but they certainly aggravated and exploited them for their own ends. Forever harping on the fears of Lebanese Christians of being swamped by 'Muslim hordes' from the Syrian interior – a fate, they implied, from which French protection alone could save them – they fed Christian paranoia and greatly complicated the outlook for Muslim–Christian cooperation. Sectarianism, very much the product of French policy, became a feature of Lebanon's political system, and, to a lesser extent, Syria's too.

A regrettable result of these policies was that neither Lebanon, nor its inland sister Syria, was able to develop a coherent national identity that all its citizens could willingly espouse. Indeed, the Lebanese state which Bishara al-Khoury and Riad el-Solh inherited was far from being a united political society. Their main challenge was how to integrate the various communities into a nation, how to devise a regime that would enable the main sections of the population to live together, not merely in passive but in active amity, and in loyalty to that idea. When he first became prime minister in 1943, Riad el-Solh vowed to phase out the confessional system, which he described as a poison. But he found himself unable to do so, perhaps because it was already too deeply engrained. The unresolved contradiction between a society built on ancient confessional solidarities (*'asabiyyat*) and a nation state built on a shared national identity, continues to plague Lebanon to this very day.

The problem was not confined to Christian–Muslim relations in Lebanon, but involved Syria too. This was because, from the very start, the French saw Lebanon as a military bridgehead from which to control the Syrian interior. But this posed a tricky dilemma: for Syria to feel independent and secure, it was necessary that no foreign power be dominant in Lebanon. But if there were no foreign power in Lebanon – or at least none in a position to intervene if necessary – then Christians, or other anti-Syrian groups, felt under threat. This conundrum, in one form or another, continues to plague leaders of both countries today.

The French approach was flawed between the world wars because they refused to recognise – or perhaps failed to understand – that Arab nationalism was not merely the creation of Western-educated urban intellectuals, but had grown into the most widespread and deep-rooted ideology of the period. It had great mobilising power – especially, but by no means exclusively, among Muslims. More than 75 per cent of the Levant population considered the Mandate illegitimate. They did not want a Mandate, and they did not want a French one in particular. The result was a total breach between France and the nationalists.

The persistent Anglophobia of many French officials was a contributing factor too, because they were inclined to blame the nationalist ferment on British intrigues. Right up to the dying days of the Mandate, the French suspected the British of seeking to take advantage of their wartime weakness in order to supplant them, and bring the whole Middle East under British influence. This was General de Gaulle's persistent refrain. The ineradicable French conviction that Arab nationalism was being manipulated by the British led the French to miss important developments, which might have proved to their advantage. One was the evolution in the thinking of prominent Muslim Arab nationalists – Riad el-Solh first among them – who moved from a total rejection of Greater Lebanon's French-expanded frontiers, to their own integration into the new Lebanese state.[3]

The problem lay in Paris as much as it did in the French-administered Levant, and was largely the fault of French colonial, military and clerical lobbies. These were able to exert such great influence

[3] Méouchy, 'Le Pacte national', p. 465.

because the governments of the French Third Republic lacked a clear colonial policy. They had little understanding of which French interests had to be preserved and which could safely be discarded. By seeking to hold the Levant by such brutal force, they ended up losing it altogether.

The most glaring examples of policy blunders were the failure to ratify the 1936 treaty – the last time France might have secured privileges freely consented to by nationalist governments – as well as the illegal handing over of Syrian Alexandretta to the Turks in 1939, in contravention of France's mandatory obligation to protect the integrity of the territory entrusted to it. Another blunder was the attempt to 'safeguard the rights and interests of France' by forcing Syria and Lebanon to sign treaties in violation of the unconditional promise of independence given them in 1941. No doubt the French defeat of 1940, and the subsequent feuding between Gaullists and Pétainists, complicated the relationship between France and the Levant States. Anxious to win popular French opinion to his side, de Gaulle could not afford to be accused of seeming to liquidate the French Empire.

At the root of many of these problems lay the early dismemberment by Britain and France after the First World War of what had been considered natural or geographic Syria. Although administered as separate imperial provinces, Syria under the Ottomans was a single social, economic and political space, in which people and goods were able to move freely. In the late Ottoman period, and under great Western pressure, these Syrian provinces suffered their first dismemberment when Mount Lebanon was given an autonomous statute in 1861, and when Jerusalem first and later Beirut became centres of separate provinces in subsequent decades. But this was nothing compared to the amputation which, after the First World War, caused Syria to lose Mosul to Iraq and Cilicia to Turkey. What was left was then chopped up into disparate political units, which were to become, in due course, the Republics of Syria and Lebanon, the Kingdom of Jordan, the State of Israel – and the Palestinian Territories, still bleeding and occupied at the time of writing.

These four sovereign states – and a fifth still in the making – were carved out of the same flesh. They were all part of a region which, to an earlier generation, had been known simply as 'Syria' or 'bilad al-Sham'. They still have a unique relationship with one another, even though they have gone on to develop distinct ideologies and national identities. There is a sense that none of them can escape their common history and environment, however much one or the other might wish to do so.

Syrians especially have continued to suffer from a feeling that their country was made smaller than it was ever meant to be. The repeated amputations of the previous century created a yearning to be part of a larger unity. In the first half of the twentieth century, the urge to break out of Syria's artificially cramped space produced two rival doctrines: the pan-Syrianism of Antun Sa'ada, which was soon to have such a devastating impact on Riad el-Solh's life and career; and the pan-Arabism of the Ba'th Party, which was to have a profound, and not always benign, influence on the politics of Syria and Iraq.

But of all the complex Levantine relationships, none has remained more intimate, more incestuous, than that between Syria and Lebanon. The two countries are indissolubly linked by history, by dense family ties, by trade and by a shared geopolitical environment. Yet under the Mandate, they were made to develop separate identities and interests, in a deliberate, trouble-sowing French policy. A major headache which Riad el-Solh inherited from the French was Lebanon's vexed relationship with Syria – which remains to this day a central problem of Lebanese politics.

The beginnings of the quarrel with Syria

All his life, Riad el-Solh had campaigned for Syrian unity, as a first step towards Arab unity. Greater Syria was his homeland. Both he – and his grandfather, Ahmad Pasha – had married into prominent Syrian families. His closest political friends were the leaders of Syria's National Bloc. He was as much at home in Damascus and Aleppo as he was in Beirut and Sidon. It was, therefore, the bitterest irony that he should eventually find himself having to defend narrow Lebanese interests against those of his Syrian neighbour. This certainly had never been his intention when he set out in politics.

Indeed, within twenty-four hours of forming his first cabinet in September 1943, he had raced to Damascus and forged a common front against the French with both his old friend and comrade-in-arms, Syria's President Shukri al-Quwatli, and with Prime Minister Sa'dallah al-Jabiri, his wife's uncle. In October, he had made further frequent visits to Syria to coordinate their joint strategy. On 4 January 1944, he signed an agreement with the French, together with Syria's Finance Minister Khaled al-'Azm, which transferred control of some of the *Intérêts Communs* to their two respective governments – notably the directorate of customs and the tobacco monopoly. That same month, a Higher Council of Common Interests, which had earlier been set up, was due to start work.[4]

But almost immediately, Riad el-Solh ran into ferocious opposition from diehard Christian Lebanese nationalists – notably from the Maronite Patriarch Antoine 'Arida, and also from Alfred Naccache and others – who attacked the Higher Council as 'a government within a government', claiming that it paved the way for a union with Syria – a fate that Christian Lebanese nationalists dreaded above all things.

Riad el-Solh had to pay a long visit to the Patriarch in order to reassure him that there was nothing 'supra-national' about the Higher Council; that legislative authority over economic matters would remain firmly in the hands of the Lebanese parliament; and that no joint Syro-Lebanese institution would have independent executive powers. Fundamental problems remained, however, due to the different nature of the two states, as they sought to develop within the artificial boundaries imposed on them by the French.

The first problem Syria and Lebanon had to wrestle with was the division of customs revenues. A temporary agreement was reached whereby each state received 40 per cent, while the remaining 20 per cent was to be divided up on the basis of each state's actual consumption of imports. But this led to abuses and complications. As Syrian customs services and storage facilities were poorly developed, much of the trade for the two states was diverted to Beirut, where port facilities were better organised and equipped. Upon exhausting their own import licences, Lebanese merchants would often seek to purchase the licences of their Syrian counterparts. When the goods came through Beirut customs, they would be taxed in favour of the Syrian account – only to be diverted to Beirut and consumed there. Lebanese officials began fearing that this abuse of import licences would result in Syria getting the lion's share of the 20 per cent of revenues, which was due to be shared out. Accordingly, in December 1945, the revenue split was

---

[4] See Youssef Chaitani, *Post-Colonial Syria and Lebanon*, London 2007, for a detailed study of Syrian-Lebanese relations in the immediate post-Second World War period.

amended to give Lebanon 44 per cent and Syria 56 per cent. But this hardly resolved the growing problems between the two countries.

The heart of their disputes lay in the profound difference of their economies. Syria was essentially a food-producing country and also, in a small way, an incipient industrial country. It felt the need for import taxes and quotas with which to protect its agricultural and industrial production, especially such goods as grain, flour, dried and canned fruits, vegetable oil, ghee, nuts, as well as cotton, yarn and textiles. Lebanon, on the other hand, produced little of anything, and it therefore favoured a laissez-faire policy of unrestricted imports, so as to be able to provide cheap goods for its hard-pressed population. A clash of interests was inevitable, primarily because excessive Syrian protectionism caused prices to soar in Lebanon – and for so vital an item as grain.

The disparity in price was flagrant. In 1945–46, a kilo of bread cost 125 piastres in Beirut against only 80 in Damascus and 50 in Palestine. Many a Lebanese working-class family was forced to spend its entire daily wage on one meal's worth of bread. Lebanon clamoured for the freedom to import grain on the international market, whereas Damascus insisted that Lebanon honour its agreement to be supplied only by Syria – even at prices well above the international level!

There was a host of other disputes, as much political as economic. Lebanon held that Beirut was the natural port for both countries, and Lebanese merchants the natural importers. But in Syria, pressure was mounting to develop the port of Latakia, so as to free Syrian merchants from both physical and economic dependence on Beirut's port facilities. In the resentful words of 'Arif al-Lahham of the Syrian Chamber of Commerce, 'Syria is living in a house with only one door, of which the key is in Lebanon.' Underlying these disputes was the usual political tension between Christian Lebanese, distrustful of Syria, and Syrians vexed by the hostility of Lebanese Christians to Arab nationalism. The quarrel was sadly to rumble on for the next several years, damaging Riad el-Solh's relations with his historic political partners in Damascus and Aleppo.

Bishara al-Khoury and Riad el-Solh

The French-devised Lebanese political system granted the president far greater powers than the prime minister – indeed powers which resembled those of the French high commissioners under the Mandate. Whereas the president was elected for a fixed term of six years – which gave his position great stability – the prime minister served at the president's pleasure and could be dismissed at any moment. Weaker prime ministers had to live in constant fear of being sent home.

The president could adjourn or dissolve parliament, appoint top officials in the bureaucracy, veto legislation or rule by decree. He had ultimate control over the distribution of state patronage, a vital prerogative in a country where the wheels of the political system were lubricated by the giving and receiving of favours.[5] But whether the president was always able to exercise these wide powers depended on his strength of character, and on his relationship with his prime minister. It was no secret that Riad el-Solh was a stronger personality than Bishara al-Khoury. His long political innings had given him great political weight. Indeed, Riad was only able to serve under Bishara al-Khoury because the latter was not a dominant president.

After two years of close partnership with Khoury, Riad left office on 9 January 1945, no doubt feeling in need of a rest after the long tussle with the French. Over the next two years, the prime ministerial chair was occupied in succession by 'Abd al-Hamid Karami, Sami el-Solh and Sa'di Munla – all of whom had to put up with constant sniping from Riad, who greatly enjoyed the freedom of being in opposition. 'Our friend Riad el-Solh will not leave me in peace for a single day,' Karami would often complain.

Even though he was out of power for most of 1945 and 1946 – only resuming the premiership on 14 December 1946 – Riad el-Solh remained at Bishara al-Khoury's side throughout, helping him with his choice of ministers, with the distribution of portfolios, and with more general political advice. Whereas Riad el-Solh had emerged invigorated from the crisis with the French, Bishara al-Khoury, who was of less vigorous health, was tired and shaken. In mid-December 1944, he fell in the street and broke an arm. While suffering insomnia brought about by pain, he had to undergo the further strain of a change of government – of Riad el-Solh's resignation and his replacement by 'Abd al-Hamid Karami. Confined to his room by doctor's orders, he was unable to attend to government business or receive his ministers. He then suffered a serious psychological blow with the sudden death on

11 January of his lifelong friend and closest collaborator, Salim Takla. It began to be rumoured in Beirut that the president was suffering from a form of melancholia so acute that it was beginning to prey on his reason.[6]

Bishara al-Khoury was in fact having a nervous breakdown. Quite apart from the political stress he was under, he had been deeply disturbed by the suicide of his wife's niece, Magda, a young woman who had been like a daughter to them. She was the child of Marie Chiha Haddad, sister of Laure Chiha, Bishara's wife, and of Michel Chiha, Bishara's loyal friend and supporter. Michel Chiha was a prominent banker and intellectual and the publisher of the Francophone daily *Le Jour*. The paper had supported Bishara al-Khoury in his climb to power, in opposition to George Naccache's *L'Orient*, which had backed Emile Eddé and his policy of close ties with France.

Although no one was allowed to see the ailing Bishara al-Khoury, for fear of disturbing him further, Riad insisted on paying him a visit. He gave a short account afterwards of what had transpired: 'I greeted him. He did not answer. His doctor (Dr Ba'qlini) said to him: "Do you recognize him?" He moved his head and said, "Yes, it is Riad el-Solh." But he had hardly uttered these words than he began to sob. Dr Ba'qlini then signalled to me to withdraw.'

It was decided that Bishara al-Khoury should leave Beirut for Tiberias, in Palestine, where it was hoped that the thermal waters would do him good. In Haifa, he was treated by Dr Hermann Zondek, a German Jewish psychiatrist.[7] The Prime Minister 'Abd al-Hamid Karami visited him in February and reported that he was making a good recovery. Some weeks later, in March 1945, Bishara al-Khoury was well enough to return to Lebanon and resume his duties. Riad was once more at his side in a supporting role. On 11 November, the two men paid an emotional visit to the fortress at Rashaya, where they had been incarcerated together only two years earlier.

Quite apart from his own increasingly fragile health, Bishara al-Khoury was plagued by the misdeeds of members of his family. His son, Khalil al-Khoury, offended local conservative opinion by often sharing the back seat of the president's official car – a Lincoln convertible – with a notorious cabaret dancer. One of the president's

---

[6] Syria and Lebanon Weekly Political Summary, 31 January 1945 (FO 371/45553).
[7] MAE, Nantes, Fonds Beyrouth (Amb.), série 199A4, carton 20, Sûreté aux Armées, Beirut, 30 January 1945.

brothers, Salim al-Khoury, was even more of a problem. He nakedly exploited his brother's position as head of state for his own political and financial gain. Known as 'the Sultan', he was the disreputable éminence grise of the regime. Another of Bishara al-Khoury's brothers, Sami, was also no great asset to the family. On 5 October 1945, a presidential decree appointed him as Lebanon's minister to the Egyptian Court. He had been director of justice from 1926 to 1939, then president of the Council of State and then director at the Foreign Ministry – owing his career, in every case, to his brother's influence rather than to any of his own talents. A French report described Sami al-Khoury as being 'slow of thought and withdrawn, lacking initiative and general culture. At the Foreign Ministry, he displayed no excessive fondness for work, preferring to sit at a gaming table until dawn. His ponderous appearance, clumsy manners and lack of conversation are unlikely to make him shine in diplomatic circles or among the Lebanese community in Egypt'.[8] Yet, in spite of these grating burdens and liabilities, Riad el-Solh continued to defer to Bishara al-Khoury. He sought to build him up in his own speeches, always referring to him as the 'national leader' who had brought the country to independence.[9]

Getting the French out

After the bombardment of Damascus in May 1945, the Syrian and Lebanese governments decided that, whether Paris liked it or not, they could wait no longer to take control of the problematic *Troupes Spéciales*. Faced with this decision on the part of these governments, and under considerable international pressure in the wake of their criminal folly, the French finally agreed to proceed with the transfer, which was effected over the following months. Funding for the force, however, was a problem for the Syrians and Lebanese. Vindictively, France even attempted to get them to repay 50 million Syrian pounds, allegedly what had been spent on the *Troupes Spéciales* over the years, in order to repress the local population.

[8] MAE, Nantes, Fonds Beyrouth (Amb.), série 199A4, carton 20, Sous-Délégation du Liban Sud, Saida, 13 June 1946.
[9] MAE, Nantes, Fonds Beyrouth (Amb.), série 199A4, carton 20, note on Bishara al-Khoury's family.

There were difficulties over the transfer of other French-controlled items too, such as the telephone service and the local radio station, Radio Levant, for which the French were asking the Lebanese to cough up ridiculous sums. Further irritation was caused by French delays in transferring major public buildings, such as the *Grand Sérail* itself, which the Lebanese government desperately needed to house its scattered departments.

These disputes were overshadowed by the much bigger problem of the evacuation of French troops from the Levant, which the Lebanese and Syrians considered the essential prerequisite of real independence. But France was evidently in no hurry to pull out, and seemed intent on reinforcing its forces instead. The Lebanese government – and the British military authorities for that matter – suspected the French of wishing to consolidate their hold over the two main Levant airfields, Rayak in Lebanon and Mezzé in Syria, by flying in additional air force personnel.

Meanwhile, French ships continued to bring in more colonial troops. The French claimed that this was a routine rotation of existing forces, but it struck the Lebanese as odd that the French were busily renting new houses for the families of their officers. It seemed as though they had no intention of leaving at all. 'They love us too much,' President Bishara al-Khoury joked to Terence Shone, the British minister in Beirut.[10]

Such was the background to the decision of the Lebanese and Syrian governments to seek the help of the newly created United Nations Organisation to bring about the withdrawal of foreign troops from their countries. As it happened, London was the venue in January 1946 for the first meeting of the UN General Assembly and Security Council. To house this international gathering, the Methodist Church granted the British government use of its vast meeting place, Central Hall, Westminster. The Lebanese delegation sent to London consisted of Foreign Minister Hamid Frangieh, assisted by Riad el-Solh and Yusuf Salem (the Greek Catholic politician from Tyre, of strong Arab nationalist sympathies, who had played an important role in forging the alliance between Riad el-Solh and Bishara al-Khoury at the time of the 1943 elections). In attendance on the delegation was Lebanon's Minister in London Camille Chamoun. They were put up at the

---

[10] Beirut to Foreign Office, 13 February 1946 (FO 371/52479).

Mayfair Hotel, which was comparatively warm, despite severe fuel rationing.

Riad el-Solh was not in the habit of keeping a regular diary, but on this occasion – perhaps because of its importance – he did make some notes, beginning with his flight from Beirut to Cairo, and then from Cairo to London.

> *3 January 1946*
> *We arrived in Cairo. Our aircraft carried the name of Beit ed-Din [Lebanon's famous early nineteenth-century palace built by the Emir Bashir II, who ruled for more than half a century]. I have a feeling that this journey will bring to an end the struggle I have waged for political independence, which will be completed only with the evacuation [of French troops]. But are we truly at the end of our struggle?*
>
> *5 January 1946*
> *Today, I took a plane from Cairo to London. It was my first long journey by air. When the plane took off, I thought my heart would stop beating. But when the aircraft gained height, I felt more confident than some of the others. That is what we are like: we fear something before it happens. Does man fear death because he has not experienced it? If we were to undergo death, would it no longer frighten us?*
>
> *9 January 1946*
> *We, the delegates of 51 nations, met at 4 p.m. in the vast chamber of Central Hall, Westminster, to inaugurate the session of the UN General Assembly.*
> *I felt that Lebanon was for the first time entering an international conference by the main door. At previous conferences [of the League of Nations] Lebanon had to stay outside. We used to beg foreign delegates to stop so that we could put our case to them. Most of them rejected us, and turned away. Some politely bid us leave. Only a very few stopped to hear what we had to say.*
> *This time, I was myself stopped by the representative of an oppressed people. I took the time to hear him out, because I had the feeling that I was hearing*

myself when, just the other day, we were in the same unfortunate position.[11]

King George VI welcomed the delegates with an uplifting speech. 'The greatest and most dangerous conflict of all ages has been triumphantly surmounted,' he declared. 'Our enemies lie prostrate. But it is on the conquerors – the United Nations – that the responsibility for reconstruction now falls. It is for us to lay the foundations of a new world where such a conflict will be impossible'. That night the king gave a state banquet for the delegates at St James's Palace. *The Times* described the scene:

> *The King, in the service uniform of an Admiral of the Fleet, sat in the centre of a long table, with four other tables leading from it at right angles. On each, tall candles burning in candelabra of solid gold shed a mellow light on the white damask cloth and shone on massive gold vases filled with pink chrysanthemums and pink and white orchids.*[12]

Although the invitation was in principle reserved for heads of delegations, Riad el-Solh was nonetheless included. As Lebanon's most prominent statesman, he was given special attention. He soon found that many people wished to meet him. For example, with his active input, the Arab and South American delegations established close contact and arranged to give each other mutual support. General Sir Edward Spears was on hand to look after Riad and initiate him in the complexities of British politics. Riad had previously been used to the French-speaking world of Paris, Geneva and Beirut. In London, he marvelled at the stoicism of the British people who accepted cuts to their already meagre wartime rations. He admired their political sense, in July 1945, at voting out Winston Churchill, the larger-than-life victor of the war against Hitler, to replace him as prime minister by the Labour leader, Clement Attlee. Attlee was clearly more suited, the electorate understood, to the task of post-war reconstruction and to the alleviation of working-class poverty, so candidly described in *Freedom from Want*, the celebrated Beveridge Report of 1942.

---

[11] Extracts from Riad el-Solh's notes, published in the Egyptian newspaper, *Akhbar al-Yom*, 30 March 1946.
[12] *The Times*, 10 January 1946.

A first taste of the cold war

Riad's interest in Britain, which Spears had carefully fostered in Beirut, was now consolidated.[13] Not only did he and his colleagues get a proper feel for a Britain that was struggling to rise from the ruins of war, but they also gained an insight into the tense post-war mood of international relations. The Levant was to provide one of the very first diplomatic battlefields for the contest between former allies, which was soon to become known as the cold war. Riad had a ringside view of the jousts between such international figures as the Soviet delegate, Andrei Vyshinsky, and the British Foreign Secretary Ernest Bevin.

The Foreign Office went to some pains to help the Lebanese and Syrian delegations draft the letter which they sent to the UN secretary-general on 4 February, in which they complained that the presence of French *and* British troops on their territory was an infringement of their national sovereignty. They requested the Security Council, under Article 34 of the UN Charter, to demand the complete and simultaneous withdrawal of these foreign forces. The French were upset – with Foreign Minister Georges Bidault pretending to 'sorrow and surprise' that Lebanon should have chosen to associate itself with the Syrian complaint.

Count Stanislas Ostrorog, the new French secretary-general at the *Délégation Générale* in Beirut, arrived in London on 1 February, hoping to engage the Lebanese in negotiations before their application could be heard by the Council. But Hamid Frangieh – as he told Sir Alexander Cadogan, the head of the UK delegation – refused to enter into negotiations with Ostrorog, or indeed with Georges Bidault himself, unless the French, at the outset, would give him assurances of the early withdrawal of their troops, together with a tangible date of completion.[14]

On 14 February, the Council examined the Syrian and Lebanese complaint; on the 15th, the heads of the two delegations put their case to the Council, and discussions then continued on the 16th. An American senator, Arthur Vandenberg (R. Michigan), who witnessed these events in London, gave this report to the US Senate:

Two of 'the newest, smallest and humblest of countries,'
he said, 'petitioned for relief against two Great Powers.'

[13] Report by G. W. Furlonge, Beirut, 4 April 1946, on his conversations with Riad el-Solh and Yusuf Salem (FO 371/52480).
[14] Memorandum by Sir Alexander Cadogan, 1 February 1946 (FO 371/52479).

Ernest Bevin announced that that he was willing to withdraw British troops at once, so that Georges Bidault of France had to follow suit. Edward Stettinius, the U.S. delegate, then proposed a resolution which took note of these British and French assurances, expressing confidence that foreign troops would be withdrawn from Syria and Lebanon 'as soon as practicable.' The parties were to start negotiations without delay.[15]

The matter seemed to have been promptly and happily resolved. 'The dove of peace flew in at the window', Senator Vandenberg declared, 'but it then quickly flew out again', since the Soviet Commissar, Mr Vyshinsky, was evidently in no mood for such easy peace. He insisted on amending the American resolution – which most members of the Council considered unwarranted – resulting in two more days of 'intense and futile debate' before a vote could be taken. Vyshinsky demanded that France and Britain should abstain from voting since they were parties to the dispute. The two nations agreed to abstain, and the Soviet amendment was voted down, with only its author supporting it. The American resolution was given the seven affirmative votes required by the Charter. But Vyshinsky still refused to yield! He used his one vote to veto the entire proposal. He was evidently far less interested in helping Syria and Lebanon than he was in baiting Britain and France.

'That left little Lebanon and little Syria just where they started. But then came a thrilling climax. Bevin, for Britain, and Bidault, for France, magnificently asserted that they would *voluntarily* accept the terms of the Resolution. I was proud of Western democracy that night!' Senator Vandenberg declared. But, he then asked with some plaintiveness, 'What is Russia up to?' It was an American question that was to be posed again and again, angrily and insistently, over the five decades to come.

The French proposed that the negotiations between the parties should take place in Paris. This came as a bit of a shock to the Syrian and Lebanese delegations. The Syrians, in particular, were hesitant to go to the capital of a country which had so recently bombed their own. Ernest Bevin strongly advised them to go, but Spears – very anti-French

---

[15] Report of Senator Vandenberg's speech in *The Daily Telegraph*, 28 February 1946.

and no doubt still smarting at his treatment by the Foreign Office – urged them not to. Under Spears's influence, Camille Chamoun telegraphed the Lebanese government, advising against a move to Paris, on the grounds that the French could not be trusted to act in good faith on their home turf. It would be best, he said, to negotiate with them either in Beirut or in London.

An embarrassing situation then arose. Riad el-Solh, who had no wish to offend his friend Spears, hesitated for a week, but finally decided that it would be best to follow the British government's advice and go to Paris. This would save time and would allow the Syrians and Lebanese to deal directly with the French prime minister and foreign minister, rather than with their subordinates in London or in Beirut. Spears was deeply offended, and immediately fired off a letter of complaint to President Bishara al-Khoury, which only made matters worse, because it was much resented by the delegates.

On 28 February 1946, the Lebanese delegation left for Paris, where Riad el-Solh immediately set to work reactivating his old political and journalistic contacts. Through the Lebanese Communist leader, Nicola Shawi, he got in touch with members of the French Communist Party. They assured him that their party's policy was to prevent French troops from being used in colonial adventures.

When, on 1 March, French and British military experts began talks on the evacuation of their troops, it soon emerged that, whereas the British were prepared to pull out within a few months, the French demanded more than a year – until April 1947. British troops, they argued, could simply march south to Palestine, whereas French troops had to be evacuated by sea. Shipping would be required, which was then very scarce. Many of the Lebanese immediately assumed that the French were playing for time to secure guarantees for the 'privileged position' they had long sought. The Beirut and Damascus governments were understandably worried that, if British troops were to withdraw first, they would find themselves alone with the French, as they had been in 1920 – and that their governments would once again be put in danger. They therefore demanded a *simultaneous* evacuation by Britain and France.

Unlike the situation in London, where the British government had paid the bills of the Levant delegations, in Paris the Lebanese received little attention and were not the guests of the French government (although a lone car was put at their disposal). In contrast to the national discipline they had so admired in London, the delegates found that morale was low in Paris after the hardships and humiliations of the German occupation, and that trade on the black market was ubiquitous.

The delegation's initial contacts at the Quai d'Orsay were hardly satisfactory, as Georges Bidault merely repeated that the French military authorities had 'decided' not to complete the evacuation before 1 April 1947. The Lebanese retorted that, whatever the military situation might be, they had come to discuss the political situation, which would not admit any such delay. Their anxiety was heightened when they learned that, throughout their talks, the *Délégation Générale* in Beirut was sending a stream of telegrams to Paris, invoking new pretexts for delay. After still more meetings it emerged that whereas Georges Bidault was prepared to be flexible about the date for the French troops to leave, Count Ostrorog and his advisers – especially General Beynet, who had hurried to Paris from Beirut – were adamantly opposed to any such 'hasty withdrawal'.

When no progress was made, the presidents of Syria and Lebanon met on 10 March 1946, and resolved that if the French refused to budge, they would instruct the Lebanese delegation in Paris to leave at once for New York, to put their case to the Security Council at its next session on 21 March.

To break the deadlock, Riad el-Solh in Paris then devised a plot – part political comedy, part ruthless manoeuvre – to embarrass the hardline Ostrorog, whose intransigence had become the major obstacle to an agreement. The plot was carefully rehearsed with other members of the Lebanese delegation, before it was put into effect at a dinner given for them by Georges Bidault. Once the guests had risen from the table, Hamid Frangieh, Lebanon's Christian foreign minister, approached Count Ostrorog with a wide smile. 'I hope, Monsieur le Comte,' he said, 'that in spite of our differences, France will not forget her traditional role in my country, especially her historical and cultural mission towards the Christians of Lebanon.'

'*Quelle joie!*' the count cried excitedly. 'This is what I have been waiting to hear. Rest assured, Your Excellency, France will do everything in its power to defend the Christians of Lebanon. There is no doubt whatsoever about that!'

Riad el-Solh had been lurking unseen behind Ostrorog's back. On hearing these words, he reacted with feigned fury. 'What did I hear you say, Monsieur le Comte? France will defend the Christians of Lebanon? What am I doing in this place then?'

Taken aback, Ostrorog sought to make excuses, but Riad el-Solh had already turned his back on him, declaring, 'This is intolerable! I am leaving at once and will return to Beirut tomorrow!' In a display of high drama, Riad strode out of the hall, leaving alarm and confusion behind him.

Bidault wanted to know what had happened. When Frangieh related the incident to him, Bidault exclaimed: 'I am the head of the French delegation, not Count Ostrorog. I alone can speak for France. Please tell Monsieur Solh that I wish to call on him at his hotel tomorrow morning to present my regrets.' The next day, Bidault visited Riad to inform him that Ostrorog was no longer a member of the French delegation and had been sent back to Beirut. He begged the Lebanese to resume negotiations in an atmosphere of friendship and mutual trust.[16]

Negotiations resumed on 17 March and were concluded on the 23rd with an exchange of letters between Georges Bidault and Hamid Frangieh. The French agreed that their forces would withdraw from Lebanon before 31 August, with the exception of 30 officers and 300 technicians, who would see to the transfer of munitions and other equipment, and leave before 31 December 1946. Riad el-Solh and Yusuf Salem returned to Lebanon via Egypt on 30 March and were given a huge welcome there. They came by road, and were fêted in proud succession at Tyre, Sidon and in the Muslim quarter of Beirut. Hamid Frangieh was in Rome and followed them some days later.

Upon arrival, Riad el-Solh at once started to plan his return to power. He took the line that Lebanon could no longer afford to be entrusted to his cousin, Sami el-Solh, whom he considered too volatile, or indeed to any prime minister other than himself. The principal opposition to him came from Henri Pharaon, who commanded considerable support in the Chamber. Pharaon, who had close family and political ties to Bishara al-Khoury, was – unlike him – totally opposed to what he considered Riad's pro-Muslim and pro-Arab League policies.

For their part, both Riad el-Solh and Yusuf Salem feared that Pharaon's attitude would lead to a revival of dreaded sectarianism.

---

[16] Salem, *Khamsun sana ma' al-nas*, pp. 255–8, quoted by Hilal el-Solh in *Tarikh rajul wa qadiyya*, part III, chapter 2.

Since Lebanon was now independent, they believed it was necessary to get rid of confessionalism, once and for all, in order to build a stable state. President Bishara al-Khoury, however, was anxious to keep Sami el-Solh in office for a little while longer. He wanted Riad to conduct the 1947 elections, and feared that if he were to take office at once, he might not be able to remain there until then.

Sami el-Solh let it be known that he would ask for the confidence of the Chamber on 18 May, but when two of his ministers, Ahmad al-As'ad and Sa'di Munla, resigned, it precipitated his own departure. The president then invited Sa'di Munla to form a government, when it became clear that Henri Pharaon's opposition would make it difficult for Riad el-Solh to obtain the necessary majority. Riad continued his feud with Pharaon, attempting to weaken him by urging the president to dissolve Pierre Gemayel's paramilitary *Phalanges* movement, which was giving Pharaon its muscular, if not quasi-military, support.

It was not until 14 December 1946 that a tactical, if wary, rapprochement between Riad el-Solh, Henri Pharaon and 'Abd al-Hamid Karami finally made it possible for Bishara al-Khoury to ask Riad el-Solh to form a new government – which he did that same day. Two weeks later, on 31 December, the last French soldier left Lebanese territory. Riad recorded the event in his diary.

> *31 December 1946,*
> *At 3 p.m. today, a French military aircraft took off, carrying the last foreign soldier from our country. Half an hour later, I conveyed the news to the Chamber. It was a solemn moment. I was proud and moved when I announced: 'The evacuation has been completed.'*
> *My hand shook as I held the text of my speech and my voice trembled with emotion. I could hardly pronounce words which I had been rehearsing all my life.*
> *'Evacuation!' That sweet word which we called for in our demonstrations, which our martyrs cried as they fell under the bullets of the occupiers . . .*
> *In that instant, my mind raced over the whole epic from beginning to end. It was the history of a quarter of a century of occupation, or rather of long centuries of struggle against imperialism. We wept for freedom, but we only truly deserved it once we had shed blood for it.*

> *I remembered the day we revised the Constitution*
> *to annul the articles which restricted our independence.*
> *I thought of Rashaya, where, by locking us up, the French*
> *silenced our feeble voices, only to hear the far more*
> *powerful voice of the country. I remembered the day*
> *that we went to the Security Council, and how we then*
> *mastered our nerves to go to Paris.*
> *I would have wished our martyred companions to*
> *have been with me here today. I see the ghost of my father,*
> *happy and smiling. I am filled with joy at being lucky*
> *enough to be alive on this day.*[17]

Not wishing to seem petty, the Lebanese government awarded Count Ostrorog the decoration of Grand Officer of the Order of the Cedar. He left Beirut shortly afterwards to take up his appointment as French minister in Dublin, where it was believed he could do less harm.

[17] Extract from Riad el-Solh's diary, published in *Akhbar al-Yom*, 11 January 1947.

23 MASTER OF THE LOCAL SCENE

On 14 December 1946, Riad returned to power as prime minister of Lebanon, a position he was to hold without interruption for the next four years and two months. Having mastered the game of local politics, he remained the dominant figure on the Lebanese political scene for the whole of that period. Until his resignation on 14 February 1951, he was unassailable, displaying great skill in outmanoeuvring his enemies, while nurturing his alliance with President Bishara al-Khoury, the essential precondition for his continuance in power.

The pre-eminence of Riad el-Solh among Muslim politicians and that of Bishara al-Khoury among Christian ones – and their close-knit partnership – were striking features of Lebanese politics in 1947–48. To foreign observers, Riad el-Solh was the nearest Lebanon had come to producing a statesman of international stature. He was – and remains to this day – the hero of independence, the leader who rid his country of foreign military occupation, and who did so before major Arab states like Egypt and Iraq, let alone countries like Jordan, the Gulf shaykhdoms, Aden and south Arabia, Libya and French North Africa. Their liberation was not to come until much later. In one or two cases, it even remains incomplete to this day.

Professor Walid Khalidi, the eminent Palestinian historian – whose sister, Sulafa, married into the prominent Beirut political family of the Salams – was in a position to observe Riad el-Solh at that time. 'The years 1947–48', he wrote,

> saw Riad Bey at the height of his powers in the full bloom of his flamboyant personality. With Bishara al-Khoury, he dominated the Lebanese scene and was the other pillar of the Lebanese arch. The National Pact derived its validity

56 – Riad el-Solh aged 56, in 1950, as prime minister
of Lebanon.

in Muslim eyes from his personal imprimatur. On this account, Maronites held him in awe.

As a young man I was fascinated by him: his appearance, his body language, and his mannerisms. He was of medium height, burly and portly, conveying weight but not obesity. He had a white complexion, bovine eyes, pudgy rubber-like cheeks, graying hair, an impish smile, and an ever-present tarbush at a rakish angle with dangling tassels, and a voice loud and commanding, gruff but not coarse.

He was a powerful orator. His Arabic was less than perfect. He was more of a demagogue than a Cicero; a wit and master of repartee, very brisk on his feet. He exuded health, energy and confidence. In charm, gravitas and charisma, he easily overshadowed his Sunni 'peers' – 'Abd al-Hamid Karami, Sami el-Solh, 'Abdallah al-Yafi, Sa'ib Salam, Sa'di Munla, Hussein 'Uwayni. His prestige and reputation were solidly built on the foundation of his opposition to the French throughout the 1920s and 1930s.[1]

On his return to power, Riad's overriding priority was to lay solid foundations for the fledgling Lebanese state, which had so recently become free. When he first became prime minister in 1943, his aim had been to wrest Lebanon's independence from France, but in 1947, state-building became his major preoccupation. He was determined – in the words of his ministerial statement – to 'create a homeland'.

This was no easy task, because, as usual, Riad el-Solh was up against Lebanon's sectarianism. Divisive French policies had resulted in the creation of a bear pit of conflicting identities. While Riad enjoyed enormous support among Muslims, many hardline Christians viewed him with reserve, imagining that his devotion to Lebanon was a sham, and that he harboured an ambition to merge the country into a wider Arab entity, in which they would be swamped by a Muslim majority. To soothe such fears, Riad el-Solh went out of his way to take on a 'Lebanese' persona, positioning himself as the most ardent defender of Lebanon's new borders. Indeed, he felt he had to go so far in this

---

[1] Letter to the author from Professor Walid Khalidi.

direction, that many of his friends and admirers in the region began to rue what they suspected was his fading commitment to the goals of Arab nationalism.

Bishara al-Khoury's ambitions

There was no doubt that President Bishara al-Khoury shared Riad el-Solh's ambition to build a strong and stable state in Lebanon, so as to create that shared sense of citizenship which French policies had long denied it. But his immediate priorities were not the same as Riad's. The president brought Riad el-Solh back to power in December 1946 for one primary purpose: to conduct elections in the spring of 1947 – elections which, for Bishara al-Khoury personally, were of the utmost importance. Although his six-year term of office was due to end in 1949, he was determined to win a second term. He dreamed of continuing in power, and of eliminating his old rival, Emile Eddé, from the political scene entirely. But, as it stood, the Constitution did not allow a president a second term of office. Bishara al-Khoury, therefore, needed an obedient Chamber, which would agree to amend the Constitution before his current mandate ended. He knew that Riad el-Solh was the only Muslim prime minister who would be able to secure the election of the sort of Chamber he needed.

In his choice of cabinet colleagues, Riad was therefore forced to pay more attention to satisfying Bishara al-Khoury's desire to win the forthcoming elections, than to his own personal requirement of choosing good and capable men to help build the state. But he had also to be sure that the men he excluded from his cabinet would not be capable of forming a coalition powerful enough to put the outcome of the elections in doubt. Hence, the government he formed in December 1946 was a coalition which brought together key figures from all communities – friends as well as foes. It was described, not without irony, as a 'government of giants'.

In putting it together, Riad el-Solh had to struggle to satisfy a host of proud egos and individual ambitions; to neutralise endemic rivalries between parties, sects and regions; to conciliate the various currents in the Chamber; and to deal with the real or supposed interventions of foreign powers. In spite of his own personal prestige and undoubted political skills, Riad found himself forced to make extensive concessions to his opponents and to distance himself from some of his most loyal supporters. He was obliged to play the game in conformity with a political system which he knew was deeply flawed and which he disliked intensely. At that moment in Lebanese politics, confessionalism was rampant and unreformed; clan leaders, country grandees and city notables jousted for power – and the spoils of power – oblivious to the gathering storm in the region around them.

Riad el-Solh could not, for example, afford to exclude from his cabinet his principal opponent, the Greek Catholic magnate, Henri Pharaon, to whom he gave the Foreign Ministry. Pharaon had served as foreign minister once before, in 1945, when, at the time of the creation of the Arab League, he had managed to water down the already modest proposals of the Alexandria Protocol, so as to prevent any hint of pan-Arab encroachment on Lebanon's independence. As well as being of considerable electoral weight, Pharaon was socially ostentatious, and a leading racehorse owner. His considerable power rested in part on his large fortune, extrovert personality and wide-ranging contacts. But it also rested on the backing of Kamal Jumblatt's Druze clan in Mount Lebanon and on Pierre Gemayel's *Phalanges libanaises* in Beirut, the paramilitary organisation that had come to control the Christian 'street'. Like Henri Pharaon himself, these groups had been hostile to Riad el-Solh's previous government.

In sum, the new government was dominated by two strong individuals: Riad el-Solh and Henri Pharaon. Although they did not trust each other, they decided to patch up their relations in the interest of winning this election. The French welcomed Pharaon's appointment. They had never forgotten the concern he had shown for *their* interests in the critical period of May–June 1945, when their wanton bombardment of Damascus had sparked such strong anti-French feeling in Lebanon.

To give further satisfaction to Christian opinion, Riad created a new portfolio to deal with overseas Lebanese, which he also entrusted to Pharaon. The extensive Lebanese diaspora in both North and South America, like the Lebanese community in West Africa, did not like the idea of Lebanon retreating into the orbit of Arab politics. It wanted it to be open to the world. This diaspora disposed of considerable financial assets, which would come into play during elections.

In a further concession, Riad appointed three of Pharaon's allies to cabinet posts: the Druze leader Kamal Jumblatt was made minister of national economy and of agriculture, and was also given the Ministry of Social Affairs, newly created to fight poverty and reduce unemployment; 'Abdallah al-Yafi, a pro-French Sunni lawyer, unpopular among his fellow Muslims, was made minister of justice; while the Shi'i squire Sabri Hamadi was given the sensitive post of minister of interior.

Sabri Hamadi was head of the most prominent Shi'i family of the Biqa', which claimed 60,000 loyalists. He had been speaker of parliament in 1943 and 1944, and had always been pandered to by the French and, later, by the Lebanese authorities, because of his nuisance value in the remote north Biqa' region. His appointment as minister of interior made him, in effect, the deputy prime minister. Riad thus broke with Lebanese tradition by having two Muslims at the head of the government – himself and Hamadi, a Sunni and a Shi'i.

President Bishara al-Khoury had wanted Riad to fill his cabinet with Destour Party members, but Riad would not agree to do so. The president's party in Mount Lebanon had been worn down by the exercise of power, and was tarnished by its many abuses. Several of the men on Bishara's list were already discredited. Had they found their way into the cabinet, they would have aroused formidable opposition at the polls, and this would have been foolishly self-defeating. Riad, therefore, limited himself to three Destour members: the Maronite Camille Chamoun as minister of finance; the Druze Emir Majid Arslan, as minister of defence and health; and the Maronite Dr Elias Khoury as minister of education. Dr Khoury was the son-in-law of Dr Ba'qlini, the president's personal physician. He could be counted on to keep Bishara informed of Riad's every move.

Camille Chamoun, an able and ambitious lawyer from the Maronite stronghold of Dayr al-Qamar, was a Destour man only in name, since he thought it would help him achieve his ambition of one day replacing Bishara al-Khoury as president of the Republic. After the completion of his mission as Lebanese minister in London, he had returned to Lebanon with enhanced prestige. His appointment as a cabinet minister may even have been a friendly gesture to Britain, since the French considered him Britain's spy in the cabinet. As for Bishara al-Khoury, he knew that Chamoun and Pharaon were potential rivals for the presidency in his own Christian camp, and he was determined to weaken them both if he could.

Riad managed the quite considerable feat of bringing the two rival Druze chieftains, Kamal Jumblatt and the Emir Majid Arslan, together in the same cabinet. Although intelligent and ambitious, Jumblatt, then only 29, was private and rather shy. He was still under the powerful influence of his mother, the Sitt Nazira Jumblatt, formidable matriarch of the clan. Arslan, a striking figure, with his outsize and carefully waxed moustache, was the hero of Bshamoun, and could not be passed over lightly.

All these men jockeyed for position. Camille Chamoun immediately joined forces with Kamal Jumblatt in attacking the administration, which he accused of corruption, and thus, indirectly, attacked the president himself. However, in seeking to promote his own political fortunes, he made the arrogant mistake of neglecting to enlist adequate Muslim support. Henri Pharaon avoided this pitfall by closely associating himself with the ex-Prime Minister 'Abd al-Hamid Karami, but together they committed a tactical blunder. In an effort to intimidate Karami's opponents in Tripoli – the Muqaddam clan – they played up the nationalist soldier, Fawzi al-Qawuqji, who arrived in Tripoli on 5 March 1947 to a hero's welcome.

Qawuqji enjoyed a great popular following as an intrepid fighter against imperialism. He was a veteran of the revolution against the French in Syria in 1925, of the Arab rebellion in Palestine in 1936, and of Rashid 'Ali's 1941 uprising against the British in Iraq (when he suffered a face wound during a British air raid). He had then escaped to Germany, where he spent the latter part of the war and married a German wife. After the war, he managed to pull off another daring feat, and escape from Russian-occupied East Germany, fleeing to Paris and then to Lebanon (via an airfield in Palestine where the British nearly arrested him). Unfortunately, the rowdy celebrations of welcome for him in Tripoli soon turned into a running gun battle between the supporters of the Karamis and the Muqaddams. Fourteen people were killed and many others badly injured. This ugly showdown dealt a massive blow to 'Abd al-Hamid Karami's political prospects.

In the event, whereas Mount Lebanon supplied five cabinet ministers out of a total of nine, not a single minister was chosen from North Lebanon. Hamid Frangieh, Riad's old friend, had seemed certain to represent North Lebanon in the cabinet, but he had damaged his chances by breaking with 'Abd al-Hamid Karami (with whom he had been on a joint list in 1943), and drawing close to his rivals, the Muqaddams. Henri Pharaon, for his part, who had allied himself to Karami, was adamantly opposed to Frangieh's entry into the government. Rather than having to choose between two rival North Lebanon lists, Riad appointed no one from that region. His personal authority allowed him to get away with such a controversial decision.

The cohesion of Riad el-Solh's cabinet rested, not on any shared principles or goals, but on the far stronger bond of its members' personal interest in the outcome of the elections. Riad knew it, and it was therefore with some disdain that, on 21 December 1946, he listened to criticisms in the Chamber of his ministerial statement. He was certain he would get unanimous approval nevertheless, because he was conducting an election on which so many political and financial careers depended.

The flawed 1947 elections

The elections dominated Lebanon's internal political scene for much of 1947, overshadowing more crucial regional developments, such as Britain's decision in February, following the breakdown of the London Conference on Palestine, to refer the problem to the United Nations. Riad threw himself wholeheartedly into the elections, which he described as a 'plebiscite for the regime'. Polling took place in two rounds, on 25 May and 1 June. Seventeen deputies out of fifty-five came from Mount Lebanon. These were not all men of the first rank, but Riad had made an effort to satisfy almost everyone there, in order to pay homage to the Mountain region which Christians considered the bastion of Lebanon's independent existence.

The extraordinary thing was that just one week before the first round, Riad found himself in electoral peril. He was put at the mercy of his hereditary antagonist, the Shi'i chieftain Ahmad al-As'ad – so-called 'Lord of Taybeh'. As jealous master of South Lebanon, Ahmad al-As'ad refused to include Riad el-Solh on his list, and wished to force him onto an opposition list with little electoral weight, led by the 'Usayran family. For a nervous moment it even looked as if Riad might face defeat at the elections, despite having the whole machinery of government at his command.

To flaunt his power, As'ad liked to make a habit of travelling about South Lebanon – between Sidon and Tyre, and in and out of lesser towns and villages – at the head of his armed retainers, without government gendarmes daring to intervene. In the week or two before the election, Riad invited him to Beirut no fewer than a dozen times, threatening and cajoling him. He attempted to win him over by promising him a diplomatic post for the Emir Khaled Shihab, the Sunni candidate on As'ad's list, if the latter were to step down in Riad's favour. But Ahmad al-As'ad adamantly refused to give way. He was determined to boost his prestige among his followers by scoring a success against Riad el-Solh. For a whole week, the prime minister was at the mercy of this Shi'i warlord and his ragtag private army.

A few days before the election, Ahmad al-As'ad assembled some 40,000 people at his village of Taybeh, and there, in the midst of a delirious crowd, he deigned to receive the head of the Lebanese gendarmerie, whom President Bishara al-Khoury had sent to attempt a final mediation. The mediation was successful, but brought little joy to the president or the prime minister. The next day, a triumphant As'ad came to the Presidency in Beirut to agree terms. He would take Riad el-Solh on his list, he declared, but without any of his friends. Riad had no option but to accept. The incident illustrated the power which traditional clan leaders still exercised in Lebanon's peculiar version of democracy.

The composition of Riad el-Solh's cabinet came as a severe shock to Emile Eddé. It was clear that Bishara al-Khoury had politically outdistanced him by his alliance with Riad. Eddé did his best to fight back, but to no avail. When Monsignor Ignatius Mubarak, Maronite bishop of Beirut and a fervent Christian nationalist, came out in Eddé's favour, Bishara al-Khoury resorted to all legal and extra-legal means to quash his rival. He deployed large numbers of gendarmes in Mount Lebanon to overwhelm Eddé's supporters and, when it came to the actual poll in the spring of 1947, he did not hesitate to resort to vote-rigging at the polling stations.[2]

Out of a total of fifty-five seats, forty-seven were won by pro-government parties. Emile Eddé and his group were defeated. Pharaon and Chamoun retained their seats, but returned to the Chamber shorn of many of their supporters. Once he had been outmanoeuvred in Tripoli, 'Abd al-Hamid Karami declined to stand at all. Chamoun succeeded in excluding the president's controversial brother, 'Sultan' Salim al-Khoury, from the official Destour list in Mount Lebanon, but he was

---

[2] MAE, Nantes, Fonds Beyrouth (Amb.), série 199A4, carton 20, Armand de Chayla, Ministre de France, à Georges Bidault, Ministre des Affaires Etrangères, 21 May 1947.

unable to prevent him from forming a second list – and from winning a seat. Such disunity in the Destour ranks was largely responsible for the irregularities which marred the elections in Mount Lebanon, and which led to the resignation of Kamal Jumblatt, and to the insistence of Chamoun on the establishment of a Committee of Enquiry.

Largely eliminated from parliament, the opposition accused the government of establishing false electoral rolls, of putting their own men in charge of polling stations, and of falsifying returns. Government pressure had indeed been rife, together with the free use of money by prospective candidates to buy off their opponents. Unsuccessful candidates tried to force the government to annul the elections and hold a fresh poll, but Bishara al-Khoury and Riad el-Solh would have none of it.

When Riad el-Solh first became prime minister in October 1943, he had promised to reform the complicated Electoral Law, based on the list system. But he never managed to do so, perhaps because the struggle against the French had left him with little time or energy for anything else. But in 1947, rather than proceed with this long-delayed electoral reform, he and the government actually took full advantage of the law to produce the compliant Chamber that President Bishara al-Khoury wanted – to the extent of deciding who its members would be even before the elections had taken place! Stung by accusations of electoral fraud, Riad resigned immediately after the elections. But the president called on him to form a new government. In his *Memoirs*, Bishara al-Khoury later admitted that there had been irregularities, with some officials removing the names of absent electors from the rolls, and stuffing the ballot boxes with more votes than there were electors. 'This was illegal and did us harm, and we could have done without it', he ruefully confessed in retrospect.[3]

In any event, the result of these flawed elections did yield what the president wanted. On 9 April 1948, forty-six deputies signed a petition in favour of amending the Constitution to enable Bishara al-Khoury to stand a second time. On 21 April, the Chamber adopted the constitutional amendment. And, on 27 May, at a special session of the Chamber, the forty-six deputies present re-elected the president unanimously for a second term. Nine deputies stayed away, including Chamoun, Pharaon and Jumblatt. The part played by Riad el-Solh in

[3] Al-Khoury, *Haqa'iq lubnaniya*, vol. III, p. 30.

these proceedings was of the utmost importance. He knew only too well that he was committing a politically grave mistake, but he had got used to working with Bishara al-Khoury and did not want to upset their long-standing relationship. Michel Chiha tried hard to persuade Bishara, his brother-in-law, not to go through with his bid for a second presidential term, since public opinion would naturally condemn it. But the president would not be dissuaded.

Thus, Bishara al-Khoury got what he wanted from the 1947 elections and Riad el-Solh's pre-eminence was confirmed. He was able to preside over four successive ministries during the next four years, which, because of his personal supremacy, were, in effect, 'one-man' governments.

The controversy over the TAPLINE terminal

Throughout 1947, Riad el-Solh was much preoccupied with a prolonged and acrimonious dispute with Syria over the location of an oil terminal.[4] Towards the end of 1946, Aramco had begun consultations with Arab governments over the plan of TAPLINE (the Trans-Arabian Pipeline Company) to build a 1,000-mile pipeline from the Persian Gulf to the Mediterranean.

The Syrians would not allow the pipeline to pass through their territory unless the terminal was built on the Syrian coast at Latakia. The Lebanese were furious at this decision, since they feared that Syrian stubbornness would cause Aramco to look elsewhere and lay the pipeline through Jordan and Palestine instead. The Syrians then softened their position, suggesting a point on the Syrian-Lebanese border near Tripoli, but this was rejected by American engineers. When Beirut pointed out that it made no sense to build a new port, since there were several already-equipped ports in Lebanon, the Syrians finally consented that the terminal be located in Lebanon.

They then raised the question of transit fees, which they insisted should be paid to them in gold. They also wanted Aramco to supply Syria with 400,000 tons of oil at a preferential rate – the same benefit that Aramco had given 'Abd al-'Aziz ibn Sa'ud when he granted the

---

[4] For this account of the Syro-Lebanese disputes over the TAPLINE project and the monetary agreement with France, I am particularly grateful to Youssef Chaitani, *Post-Colonial Syria and Lebanon*, chapters 3 and 4.

company a concession in his kingdom. Aramco pointed out that there was a substantial difference between an oil concession and a transit agreement, but it was prepared to go some way to satisfying Syrian demands, while pressing the government to ratify the agreement with all possible speed so that work could begin. In Lebanon, political and economic circles began to worry that Syrian delays would cause the whole TAPLINE project to collapse. Even Ibn Sa'ud was irritated by Syrian foot-dragging, as he made clear to his friend, President Quwatli.

When the Americans threatened to abandon the project altogether, Riad el-Solh shuttled back and forth between the different parties throughout July and August, in an attempt to seek to align Syrian demands with Aramco's interests. His efforts finally bore fruit. At the end of August, Syria and Aramco signed an agreement, followed in September by an amended Lebanese-Aramco agreement, which took into account the concessions that Syria had secured. By December 1947, the only remaining obstacle was Syrian ratification of the agreement. But this then ran into serious trouble. The storm of anti-American feeling, aroused by US support for the partition of Palestine, made it impossible for the Syrian government to proceed with the project.

This was by no means the only quarrel to sour the climate between Beirut and Damascus. An even more fundamental issue was their relations with France. Once Lebanon's independence had been won, and once Riad el-Solh had focused his attention on state-building, he decided to make it up with the former mandatory power. Having beaten the French in November 1943, routed their local friends like Emile Eddé and forced their troops out of the country, he saw no need to antagonise them any further. On the contrary, he felt that Lebanon now needed Western allies, and France could certainly be one of them. Since it had emerged weakened from the Second World War, it was less able to impose its will on the Arabs, and this made it more attractive in Riad's eyes. Unlike the Syrians – who were still raw from French brutality – he now made friendly gestures towards Paris. His natural Francophilia came to the surface, and he was determined to resolve all remaining problems with the French in a conciliatory spirit. Good relations with France were, after all, a prerequisite for internal peace in Lebanon, seeing that there were so many Lebanese who remained staunchly pro-French. The Syrians, however, could not share this attitude. Their relations with Paris were still marked by profound hostility and suspicion because of what they had experienced at French hands – especially the bombardment and burning of Damascus, with great loss of life and property.

Riad's friendlier approach was much appreciated by France's new minister in Lebanon, Monsieur Armand de Chayla, a career diplomat who had been sent to Beirut once France had given official recognition to Lebanon's sovereign independence on 8 July 1946. He at once set a very different tone from that of the overbearing high commissioners and *délégués généraux* of the past. In a report to Paris on Riad el-Solh's new government, de Chayla wrote:

> *I need not describe the deputy of South Lebanon whose strong personality is as well known in Paris as it is here. For more than twenty-five years he has been the champion of Arab nationalism. He is an exceptional and courageous agitator . . . But he does not harbour that personal spite which would have made him a petty adversary. In order to have a good laugh, he often brings up his past skirmishes with the Sûreté Générale and, in recalling such experiences, he often slips in a word of friendship for today's France, which is all the more striking – and the more evidently sincere – since it usually follows a reminder by him that he was a diehard enemy of the Mandate. He likes to claim that he is a friend of men of the Left, and has retained strong memories of his contacts with pre-war [French] leaders of the Socialist and Communist parties, declaring that he still counts on them for support.*
>
> *Behind this agreeable façade, what are Riad el-Solh's long-term objectives? This Sunni personage is certainly neither xenophobic nor fanatical. But he has retained from his religion and his race prodigious qualities of dissimulation and patience . . . Whatever he may say, his dream cannot be contained within the boundaries of Lebanon. His policy of Lebanese independence is only what he considers necessary at this stage. His stature is too great for his ambition not to extend, one way or another, to the vast project of Arab unity.[5]*

---

[5] MAE, Nantes, Fonds Beyrouth (Amb.), série 199A4, carton 20, Armand de Chayla, Ministre de France, à Léon Blum, Premier Ministre et Ministre des Affaires Etrangères, 26 December 1946.

In spite of Riad's newly cordial relations with France, there were still some areas of considerable tension, mostly to do with unfinished business with the Mandate. Of these, the most important was the economic matter of a French guarantee against the devaluation of the franc-holdings, which constituted the cover for the Lebanese and Syrian currencies. The French argued blithely that their obligations under the 1944 financial agreement had already been fulfilled by a payment they had made, some time before, in connection with an earlier devaluation of the franc. But the Syrian and Lebanese governments rejected this argument. In their view, it amounted to a unilateral withdrawal from the agreement on the part of the French, leaving their currencies and their economies vulnerable to harmful fluctuations, as in the past. In order to reopen negotiations, the new Lebanese Foreign Minister Hamid Frangieh – who had replaced Henri Pharaon in a cabinet reshuffle in June 1947 – left for Paris in September.

Although no final agreement was reached by the end of that year, the French showed themselves prepared to guarantee a large part of the currency cover, and to make the balance available either in the form of French exports or in foreign currencies – but which would not include the dollar. The Lebanese thought this a reasonable enough offer, but the Syrians, still mistrustful of the French, were not inclined to accept it. This difference of opinion heightened tensions once again between Beirut and Damascus, exacerbating the already existing disputes over customs duties and tariffs, and over economic policy more generally. Syria continued to favour protectionism for its agriculture and industry, while Lebanon preferred free trade, believing this was the best way to keep a lid on prices in a country suffering acutely from runaway post-war inflation. Indeed, the major preoccupation of both governments was fighting the high cost of living, which each tended to blame on the other.

In Lebanon, the public clamoured for a reduction in the price of bread, and politicians for a revision of the Syro-Lebanese grain agreement. Lebanese nationalists considered the economic union with Syria unnatural and artificial, established by the French to serve their own interests and those of Syria. The Syrians, however, felt that the whole of their country, including Damascus, had been reduced to a mere customs clearing area, subordinate to Beirut. Influential Syrian merchants demanded that their leaders take a tough line with Lebanon, while speeding up the development of Syria's own port at Latakia.

Beirut was a source of some envy for the Syrians, whose own infrastructure of ports, hotels, airports and railways was still wanting. Travellers were happy to break their journey in Beirut, where they were well and comfortably received, on their way from Europe to Iraq, Iran or India. But nothing connected Beirut to Damascus, save for a poorly maintained road, built in the 1860s, and a narrow-gauge railway better suited for the transport of coal and stone than passengers. In an attempt to resolve differences with Syria, Riad el-Solh spent much time and effort shuttling between ministerial meetings in Damascus and Beirut, as well as Shtaura, a village in the Biqa' valley located halfway between the two capitals. But differences persisted, with hostile feelings on both sides whipped up by the press in both countries.

Negotiations with the French, which had been proceeding since October 1947, were brought to a head by a further devaluation of the franc, and by a time limit of 31 January 1948, imposed by Paris for the Syrian and Lebanese governments to reply to its proposals. Riad sought the advice of leading businessmen and bankers. Their consensus was that a separation of the two currencies – the Syrian from the Lebanese lira – would not be fatal, and need not destroy the Syro-Lebanese customs union. So Riad el-Solh accepted the French proposals, while Syria rejected them. His decision was welcomed by Christians, and would have been rejected by Muslims but for his own convincing advocacy.[6] Riad believed that his decision was the right one, whereas Khaled al-'Azm, Syria's finance minister, was equally convinced that Riad had made a grave economic and political error.

On 6 February 1948, Lebanon's Foreign Minister Hamid Frangieh signed a monetary agreement in Paris with his French counterpart, Georges Bidault. The Syrians were outraged. In Damascus, the agreement was seen as a betrayal of the Arab nationalist cause. Riad was accused of backtracking on his famous pledge that Lebanon would never serve as a fiefdom for colonialism or as a conduit for foreign influence to Syria. The Syrian daily, al-Qabas, edited by Najib al-Rayyes, Riad's old Arab nationalist comrade-in-arms, thundered: 'We had expected that France would do everything it could against our country, but we were very much surprised that, in Lebanon, a government headed by such a man as Riad el-Solh should be party to this conspiracy'.[7]

---

[6] Beirut Political Summary, January 1948 (FO 371/68489).
[7] Al-Qabas, Damascus, 4 February 1948.

Such attacks were particularly painful to Riad, who had devoted his whole life to the Arab nationalist cause, and to Syrian-Lebanese entente in particular. The nationalists in power in Damascus had been his closest political associates for decades. He was now angered by what he saw as their unfair attempt to mix patriotism with economics. The Syrians called on Lebanon to renounce the agreement with France, or risk separation from Syria. Riad el-Solh replied to such stinging Syrian accusations with overblown Arabic hyperbole. 'May my tongue be cut out if I say anything that is not in friendship to the Syrians, and may my hand be cut off if I sign an agreement that infringes on the sovereignty of either Lebanon or Syria'.[8]

By this time, however, the dispute had gone well beyond economic issues and had affected every aspect of Lebanon's relationship with Syria. The Syrian decision to break away from the franc area was welcomed by pro-French newspapers in Beirut because, in their view, it meant that Lebanon was finally parting company with Syria, which is what they had always desired. The Syrian currency, which had hitherto been backed by the French franc, was therefore left without support.

In February, the Syrians stated their intention of establishing a new and independent currency. As a result, all business was brought to a standstill in Lebanon as Lebanese besieged the banks, vainly trying to change their Syrian notes. The border was closed for over two weeks, from 2 to 19 February, to the passage of goods and currency. This caused an immediate scarcity of food in Lebanon – especially of vegetables, which traditionally came from Syria – and prices rose by 50 per cent in a few days.

There was a real danger of a breach of relations between the two sister countries. Ibn Sa'ud sent urgent messages to both presidents, urging them to guard against such an outcome. Riad el-Solh called for arbitration by the Arab League. He said he would accept its verdict, whatever it might be, and would resign if it found against him. Negotiations, chaired by the League's Secretary-General 'Azzam Pasha, took place in Cairo and Beirut, and, after a lot of acrimony, a number of short-term agreements were reached in February and March 1948 – until the whole of this unhappy dispute was submerged by the catastrophe in Palestine.

---

[8] *Al-Nahar*, Beirut, 6 February 1948.

Riad el-Solh's relations with Britain

Riad el-Solh admired Britain, and, like many Arabs of his generation, he tended to overestimate its strength and cunning. Such attribution of extraordinary powers to the British was not altogether surprising, since, for many decades – indeed, for all of Riad's adult life – Britain had been the dominant power in the Middle East, actively present in every part of the region. The British had military bases and exercised hegemony in Iraq, Egypt, Palestine, Aden, South Arabia, in the Persian Gulf, in Cyprus and many other places. There was an Arab joke that if a man quarrelled with his wife, the British would know about it. Although a few Arab nationalists had turned to the Germans in the Second World War because of their disgust at Britain's policy in Arab Palestine, it was no great surprise to most Arabs that Britain did manage to triumph over Hitler in the end. Between the two world wars, most Syrians probably would have preferred to live under a British Mandate than a French one. This was because Britain, unlike France, tended to give the Arabs some margin in the management of their own local affairs – on condition that they were compliant in strategic and foreign affairs. Nuri al-Sa'id, for example, Britain's man in Iraq, enjoyed considerable independence and consideration under Britain's protective umbrella.

But Palestine was the glaring exception. It was the region where Britain was seen to have utterly betrayed the Arabs. Riad el-Solh, for one, could never comprehend how Britain had come to put its signature to the Balfour Declaration – the source of all ills, from his point of view.[9] Nevertheless – events in Palestine apart – Riad el-Solh had, by the end of the Second World War, become pro-British, in great part due to his friendship with General Sir Edward Spears, and to his gratitude for the extraordinary support this eccentric, strong-minded Briton had given him in the struggle for independence from the French. Riad knew that without Spears's physical presence in Beirut – and without his remarkable courage and political skills – Lebanon's independence would have been far harder to achieve, if it had been achieved at all. What Riad did not realise was that Spears was the exception rather than the rule among British officials, and that he was regarded as a dangerous maverick by powerful men in Britain, who kept calling for his head – and ultimately got it.

[9] Interview with Alia el-Solh, Paris, February 2006.

Riad's visit to war-battered, but tough-spirited London immediately after the end of the war, when he attended the first meeting of the UN General Assembly, had a profound effect on him. He was charmed by the courteous reception he received from Sir Alexander Cadogan, Britain's UN delegate, as well as by the devoted attentions of Spears, who took him round the House of Commons and invited him to dine at his club.

By 1947 – and no doubt primed by British ambassadors and other envoys whom he met – Riad el-Solh was fully alert to the possibility of a Communist takeover in Greece and Turkey, and of a Soviet thrust through Iran and Iraq towards the Mediterranean. He had been very close to the Lebanese Communist Party in the 1930s, when he befriended its leaders, like Nicola Shawi, and sought to win them over to his nationalist cause. He had been one of the very first Arab politicians to grasp that the workers' struggle for better pay and conditions from French concessionary companies was an integral part of the political struggle for independence. As late as 1945 – when he was in Paris negotiating the evacuation of French troops – Shawi introduced him to France's Communist leaders in a bid to help him sway public opinion there.

But Riad's sympathy for the Communists did not outlast this period. Once he became prime minister, he began to consider the party as a disruptive force. On 18 November 1947, for example, when demonstrators at Zahleh, a Lebanese town on the edge of the Biqa' valley, attacked a grain depot in protest at the shortage of wheat, Riad called in the army. Troops fired on the crowd, killing three people and wounding several others. In the Chamber, Riad defended himself by denouncing the Communists for having fomented the disturbances in the first place, and sent the Emir Farid Chehab – a French-trained police officer who had spent time in London studying British police methods – to report on Communist activities in the Biqa' region. Riad was evidently not reassured by what he learned because, as he told the British Minister in Beirut William Houstoun-Boswall, he decided to take strong measures against the party. Early in 1948, the Communist Party headquarters was closed down, together with the Society for the Promotion of Relations between Lebanon and the USSR, and the Communist-run Union of Syndicates, headed by Mustafa al-'Ariss – who was considered an instigator of frequent strikes.[10] In taking these

---

[10] Beirut Political Summary, March 1948 (FO 371/68489).

uncharacteristically repressive measures, Riad el-Solh had clearly come under the influence of the cold-war climate of the time.

Overshadowing his many other preoccupations – which included the stalemate over the TAPLINE project, the dispute with Syria over the monetary agreement with France, and growing hostility between Christians and Muslims in Lebanon itself – was the rapidly escalating crisis in Palestine. By late 1947, both the United States and the Soviet Union had come out in favour of its partition between Arabs and European Jews. Ironically enough, Britain now seemed the only friend among the Great Powers to whom the Arabs could turn in their hour of need. This was because Britain's actual weakness had been well concealed in the Arab world by its continued presence in the region, and by the regular visits of impressive British warships, such as the aircraft carrier HMS *Ocean* to Beirut and other Mediterranean ports. The wedding of Princess Elizabeth in 1947 attracted world attention and further boosted Britain's prestige. Such demonstrations of British pomp and ceremony led the Arabs to believe that Britain was still in a position to impose the 'just settlement' in Palestine for which they longed.

24 THE UNWANTED WAR

It was Riad el-Solh's misfortune that 1947 – his first year as prime minister of independent Lebanon – was also the year in which the Arabs woke up to the brutal reality of Zionist power in Palestine. Scarcely had Lebanon and Syria thrown off French rule than they were confronted with the emergence of a Jewish state, which had been actively and systematically in the making for decades – if not, indeed, since 1897, the year Theodor Herzl convened the World Jewish Congress in Basle, Switzerland, with the declared objective of creating a homeland for the Jews, although its location then had by no means been decided.

There was a glaring contrast between Riad el-Solh's political successes at home and his powerlessness in the Palestinian arena. He himself was all too aware of this discrepancy. Having been involved in Palestinian affairs since the early 1920s, he shared the anguish of the Palestine Arabs. Hopelessly split by internal feuding, and confronted by the far superior and combined power of Britain and the Zionists, they were being steadily dispossessed of their country. There was little that Arab leaders – even of Riad el-Solh's ability – could do about it.

By 1947, Riad was aware – perhaps more so than most Arabs – that there was now in Palestine a well-organised European Jewish community of over 600,000 people, with its own institutions and armed force, for which room would probably have to be found, one way or another, within the boundaries of historical Arab Palestine. But Arab opinion was so inflamed against these Jewish newcomers – and so ill-informed about what they had actually managed to achieve – that it utterly rejected any notion that they should demand a political entity of their own. Arabs held the view that Palestine had to remain an Arab state.

From the 1920s onwards, Riad el-Solh tried repeatedly to explore the possibility of some sort of pragmatic political deal with

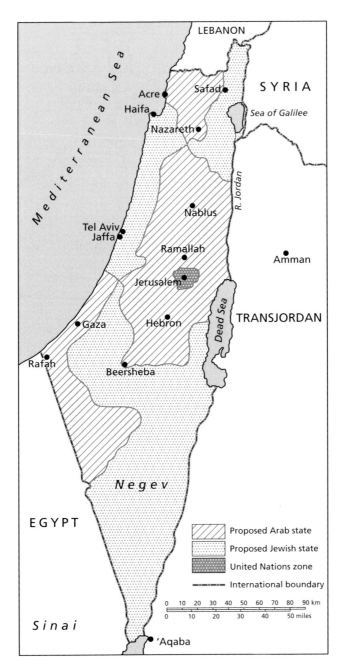

LEBANON

SYRIA

Mediterranean Sea

Acre

Safad

Haifa

Sea of Galilee

Nazareth

R. Jordan

Nablus

Tel Aviv
Jaffa

Ramallah

Amman

Jerusalem

Dead Sea

Hebron

TRANSJORDAN

Gaza

Rafah

Beersheba

Negev

EGYPT

	Proposed Arab state
	Proposed Jewish state
	United Nations zone
	International boundary

0 10 20 30 40 50 60 70 80 90 km
0   10   20   30   40   50 miles

Sinai

'Aqaba

5 – The UN 1947 partition plan for Palestine

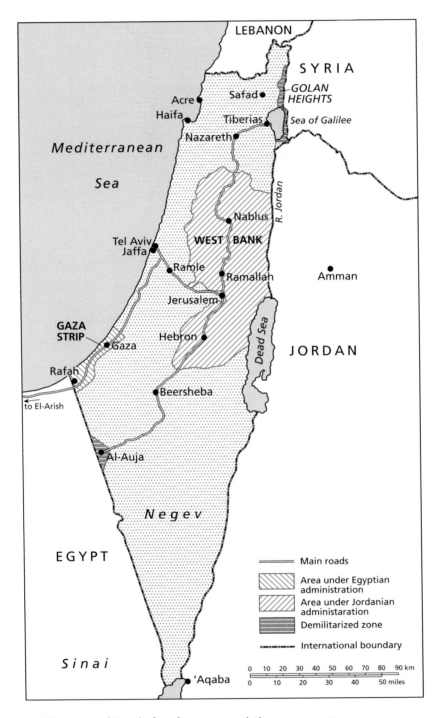

6 – The State of Israel after the 1949 armistice agreements

the Zionists. But by the mid-1930s, he had come to realise that Zionist ambitions were too great to be reconciled with whatever the Arabs might be prepared to concede. And by the 1940s, he was too immersed in his own country's struggle for independence from the French to be able to devote much time to the unfolding drama in neighbouring Palestine. In any event, he was painfully aware that Lebanon's own resources were far too puny to affect the outcome one way or the other.

In 1945, when he was in Paris negotiating the final agreement for the evacuation of French troops, he heard that the former Mufti of Jerusalem, the Hajj Amin al-Husayni, was living not far from the French capital. Having spent much of the war in Germany – and having earned opprobrium for his alliance with Hitler – the Mufti had somehow managed to make his way to France. The French were holding him, together with four members of his family, in a château outside Paris, under something like house arrest. It was there that Riad el-Solh found him. Riad had parted political company with the Mufti when the latter threw in his lot with the Nazis, but since they had been friends for decades – and had fought, though in different ways, for the same cause of Arab liberation – he retained some personal sympathy for him. The Mufti, Riad noted in his diary that day, remained as brave and nationalistic as ever. He had spoken in moving tones of the regard Lebanon had shown him in the past. But the imposing château where he was being held was 'only a cage, as the Mufti was a prisoner there'.[1] Riad could do nothing for him. He had enough problems of his own with the French.

It seemed at the time as if all Arabs were battling with constraints and injustices imposed on them by outside powers. Independent Lebanon in 1947 was a fragile entity, much like Syria was across the mountains. Both countries had problems of internal security, and their mutual relations were severely strained by a multitude of political and economic disputes. Neither country had armed services to speak of, save for a few gendarmes and the remnants of the *Troupes Spéciales* – amounting, in each country, to some 2,000 men, armed with nothing but the useless bits and pieces of military gear that the French had left behind. There was no money to replenish the arsenal. The Lebanese army disposed of little more than miscellaneous small arms, and still had to depend for its transport largely on the horse!

---

[1] Extract from Riad el-Solh's diary, published in the Egyptian daily, *Akhbar al-Yom*, 30 March 1946.

Lawlessness in the countryside was widespread, due to the prevalent carriage of personal firearms, to the power of local warlords and to bandits roaming the countryside, who constituted a law unto themselves. The road between Beirut and Damascus was often unsafe at night. Hashish was grown on a large scale in the Biqa' valley, and was something of an open scandal, since travellers to Damascus could actually spy the hashish fields from the road. The gendarmes could do little about it, because corruption was rife in their own ranks, and because of the determining political influence of the larger landowners. To clean things up, Riad el-Solh appointed the Emir Farid Chehab as head of the *Sûreté Générale*, replacing Edouard Abu Jawdi, who was generally considered inefficient and dishonest. But the task of restoring law and order was immense.

Syria's situation was, if anything, even more calamitous. Not only did the government have to wrestle with the usual problems of unsafe roads, banditry and feuding clans in the tribal interior, but it had also to subdue those regions of the country where the French had deliberately incited separatism. In the 'Alawi mountains, for example, the French had encouraged a local folk leader, Sulayman al-Murshid, to rebel against the National Bloc in Damascus. An illiterate charlatan who had proclaimed himself divine, Murshid founded a politico-religious cult which attracted tens of thousands of followers among the untutored inhabitants of the 'Alawi villages. Government troops were sent to bring him in. He was seized after a gun battle and hanged in the main square of Damascus in November 1946. A year later, the government had again to send troops to put down a revolt in the Jabal Druze, where the powerful Atrash clan was threatening to secede to Jordan.

In both Syria and Lebanon, the nationalists had inherited from the French feeble, unstable and impoverished countries, profoundly fractured on sectarian and regional lines, and with no effective institutions in place. They were a colossal headache to govern. Exhausted by their long and costly struggle against the Mandate, the nationalist leaders were ill-prepared for such a task. It was hardly surprising that when war broke out in Palestine, neither country found itself able to do much about it.

Egypt, the most important of the Arab countries, was itself still engaged in the struggle to rid itself of the remnants of British rule, in particular the large British garrison camped along the Suez Canal. Egypt wanted sovereignty over Sudan and the withdrawal of British troops from the Canal, but Britain would concede neither demand. Iraq was under similar constraints. Britain had retained airbases there and control over its foreign policy. When Rashid 'Ali tried to break free in 1941, Britain had crushed his movement, handing a semblance of power to the Regent 'Abd al-Ilah and Nuri al-Sa'id, who were content thereafter to govern under British protection and be guided by Britain in all matters of foreign policy. In Saudi Arabia, Ibn Sa'ud had not suffered the actual indignity of British military occupation, but he was certainly made fully aware of what British interests were – and of where British strong points around his desert kingdom lay – which he was careful not to challenge. In Transjordan, the Emir 'Abdallah was the nominal ruler, but effective power was in the hands of Sir Alec Kirkbride, the long-serving British minister in Amman, and of Sir John Glubb (or 'Glubb Pasha', as he liked to be called), commander of the British-officered Arab Legion. In any event, 'Abdallah himself had been in contact with the Zionists since 1921, and had been in their pay for years.

The Palestine Arabs were worse off than any of the others in that there was never even a pretence on the part of Britain of wishing to help them achieve independence. It was the Zionists, not the Arabs, who were to get a homeland with British support. When the Arabs rebelled in 1936–39 against the flood of Jewish immigrants, they were smashed by the British army, and their political and military leaders killed or deported. They never fully recovered from this defeat at the hands of a major imperial power.

There was, in sum, a fundamental dissimilarity between the mandatory experience of the Zionists in Palestine and of the Arabs in the Levant states. Committed to its pledge in the Balfour Declaration, Britain supported the Zionist national project for a quarter of a century, creating the conditions for large-scale Jewish immigration and effective state-building. France, in contrast, did everything it could to stifle the Arab national movement from the moment it took control in Syria and Lebanon. The Jews emerged as winners from the mandatory experience, while the Arabs staggered out as losers.

By the end of the Second World War, European Jews in Palestine were close to having achieved the main elements of a state. The *Histadrut*, founded in 1920, was much more than a trades union for the Jewish working class, since it was involved in a score of varied state-building activities, such as a bank, public works companies, the distribution of the *kibbutzim*'s agricultural products, medical insurance for immigrants, housing, education, culture, newspapers and much else besides. The head of the *Histadrut*, David Ben-Gurion, had in 1935 taken over the top job at the Jewish Agency, which was a well-honed government in all but name, divided into a considerable number of departments, responsible for political, financial, immigration, settlement, security and other affairs. Ben-Gurion was the supreme leader, but he was assisted by many others of exceptional ability, including Moshe Shertok (later Sharett) and Golda Meyerson (later Meir).

The Jewish community could boast of an array of political parties engaged in vigorous debate; a well-endowed Jewish National Fund, founded in 1901 to finance the buying of Palestinian land and the settlement of Jewish immigrants; and a wide-ranging diplomatic and intelligence service, which had acquired detailed knowledge of the surrounding Arab countries, as a result of the work of many loyal local Jews, as well as paid Arab informers. It also had an extensive scientific and industrial base and several distinguished centres of learning, such as the Weizmann Institute of Science and the Hebrew University on Mount Scopus, which were well-established research and teaching institutions. Above all, it had a clandestine army, the *Haganah*, built up underground from the 1920s onwards with British help, which was to benefit after the Second World War from an influx of battle-hardened Jewish fighters, who had served in Allied armies. The Jewish community in Palestine had a further extremely valuable asset. This was the political and financial support of tens of thousands of wealthy, committed and influential friends overseas, notably in the United States.

In addition to all this, the Zionists were driven by a single-minded and overpowering impulse. Hitler's genocide of millions of European Jews had bred in those who survived an unquenchable determination that the Jewish people should never again have to suffer such a fate. It had become an article of faith that only a state of their own could provide the protection the Jews required. Ben-Gurion was convinced that a trial of strength with the Arabs would be necessary to bring to birth such a state, in as much of historical Palestine as could be cleared of its Arab inhabitants. He had been preparing for a military showdown since the mid-1930s. At a celebrated meeting at the Biltmore Hotel in New York in 1942, he even made a claim for a

Jewish state in the *whole* of mandatory Palestine. In the event, he had to settle for less.

Thus the Zionists had the single-minded and able leadership, the organisation, the resources, the trained manpower – and the pressing motivation. The Arabs had few of these assets. Arab opinion detested what was happening in Palestine, but the means and organisation to do something about it were lacking. The contest between the Zionists and the Arabs was profoundly unequal, as has been amply documented in recent years by several historians of note. Prominent among them are the Palestinian scholars Walid Khalidi and Nur Masalha, and the Israeli scholars Simha Flapan, Benny Morris, Avi Shlaim and Ilan Pappé, whose important works have revolutionised thinking about Zionist policies before, during and after the 1948 war – discrediting and dispelling the romantic and fraudulent Zionist myth, that an Israeli 'David' fought and miraculously triumphed over an Arab 'Goliath' in the shape of the combined might of five Arab armies.

In addition to their many political, economic and logistical handicaps, the Arabs suffered from the fatal disease of factionalism, from which they have still not been cured. Bitterly divided by feuds, rivalries and conflicting ambitions, they were as concerned to fight each other as to fight the Zionists. Even when confronted with a threat that endangered them all, they found themselves incapable of working together. They were thus unable to protect Arab Palestine from the Zionist onslaught which, following the Arab defeat and the emergence of the State of Israel, led to a prolonged period of Arab turbulence, to which Riad el-Solh himself was eventually to fall victim.

King Abdallah's Syrian ambitions

The most serious of the many inter-Arab quarrels was that between the Hashemites and their enemies. This bitter quarrel, dating back to the 1920s, acquired an acute importance in the late 1940s, when the Arabs were confronted with what to do about Palestine. As they awoke in panic in late 1947 to the imminence of the Zionist threat, their will to put up a joint fight had already been fatally sapped by profound mutual suspicions. This may have been the single most important reason why they were unable to save Arab Palestine. It has even been argued (not so outlandishly) that the 1948 war was primarily an inter-Arab struggle – even an Arab civil war – and only secondarily a war against the European Jews who were taking over Palestine.[2]

The origin of the inter-Arab conflict may be traced back to the disappointment which the Sharif Husayn of Mecca suffered after the First World War at the hands of the British. He had hoped that his Arab Revolt against the Ottoman Turks, which had been encouraged and financed by the British in order to bring down the Ottoman Empire, would lead to the creation of an independent Arab kingdom with himself at its head. He was convinced that the British had made him such a promise – and perhaps they had – only to retract it. But when it became clear after the First World War that Britain and France had no intention of leaving a region where they had considerable economic and strategic interests, the Sharif and his sons sought to devise a compact to salvage what they could from the imperial designs of the Great Powers.

They hoped that 'Ali, the Sharif's eldest son, would succeed his father as king of the Hijaz; that 'Abdallah, the second son, would become king of Iraq; and that Faysal, the third son, would become king of Syria. This family plan collapsed, however, when Faysal was ejected from Syria by the French in 1920, and when the Sharif Husayn himself, along with his son 'Ali, were chased out of the Hijaz a few years later by 'Abd al-Aziz al-Sa'ud.[3] Faysal alone was given a new lease of life by the British, who, at the Peace Conference in Paris, put him forward as their candidate for the throne of Iraq. He was duly crowned king in Baghdad in 1921.

'Abdallah never forgave his younger brother for accepting the Iraqi throne, for which he himself had been destined. As a consolation prize, the British set him up as emir of Transjordan in Amman, but this impoverished backwater hardly satisfied him. He continued to harbour an obsessive conviction that Faysal's lost Syrian kingdom should be his. This was the origin of his long and persistent campaign for a 'Greater Syria' – or, rather, for the unification under his own crown of the four countries of Syria, Lebanon, Transjordan and Palestine.

---

[2] Henry Laurens, the great French historian of Palestine, has called his chapter leading up to the 1948 war 'La Guerre civile palestinienne'; Henry Laurens, *La Question de Palestine*, vol. III, 1947–1967, *L'Accomplissement des prophéties*, Paris 2007. See also Joshua Landis, 'Syria in the 1948 Palestine War: Fighting King Abdallah's Greater Syria Plan', in Eugene Rogan and Avi Shlaim (eds), *The War for Palestine: Rewriting the History of 1948*, Cambridge 2001, pp. 178–205.

[3] See Sir Alec Kirkbride, *A Crackle of Thorns*, London 1956; Seale, *The Struggle for Syria*, chapter 1.

Faysal, in turn, could not easily forget having been king of that venerable and ancient Arab capital, Damascus, from which the French had so unceremoniously expelled him. His twenty-month rule there provided the justification for the Fertile Crescent unity plan, which was later taken up and promoted by the pro-British Iraqi statesman, Nuri al-Sa'id. There were thus in the region two powerful rival currents of thwarted Hashemite ambition – one flowing from Amman, the other from Baghdad.

Nuri al-Sa'id's Fertile Crescent plan and 'Abdallah's Greater Syria were both given their first formal outing during the Second World War. Of the two, Nuri's plan was the more ambitious. It was his significant achievement to manage to give substance – in the form of an official document – to the nebulous aspirations for a union of Arab states in the Fertile Crescent, which had been floating around for several years. The fall of France early in the war encouraged him to think that Britain would now support the Arabs in realising their national goals, a view he put to Richard Casey, the British minister of state for the Middle East, whom he met in Cairo early in 1942. Casey asked for Nuri's proposal in writing. The result was the famous 'Note on the Arab cause with particular reference to Palestine, and suggestions for a permanent settlement', which was presented to Casey and confidentially circulated in other interested quarters.[4]

Nuri proposed a two-stage plan: first, the union in one state of Syria, Lebanon, Palestine and Transjordan, with semi-autonomy under international guarantees for the Jewish minority in Palestine, as well as safeguards for the Christians of Lebanon. Second, once this 'Greater Syria' had been formed, it would unite with Iraq in a Fertile Crescent association, which other Arab states could also join if they so wished, to form a still wider grouping. 'Abdallah's vision was more limited. His view of Arab unity was the reunification under his leadership of the four territories of 'Greater Syria'. The problem of what to do with the Palestine Jews could, he believed, be solved by granting them administrative autonomy; if the unity of all four regions could not be immediately realised, a start should be made by uniting Syria and Transjordan, with provisions for the later adherence of Palestine and Lebanon to form a union on the model of the United States of America or the Swiss Confederation. The heart of 'Abdallah's proposals – and

---

[4] Nuri al-Sa'id, *Istiqlal al-'Arab wa wahdatahum*, Baghdad 1943.

their only practical feature – was the immediate merger of Transjordan and Syria. This was the plan he fervently believed in and which he put forward, with minor variants, in speeches, official memoranda and private communications to Syrian politicians, and in instructions to his representatives at the grand debate on Arab unity, to which Egypt's Prime Minister Nahhas Pasha invited the Arab states in 1944, and which resulted in the Arab League Charter of 1945.[5]

Having secured nominal independence – if not real freedom – from Britain on 28 March 1946, the Emir 'Abdallah proclaimed himself king of the Hashemite Kingdom of Transjordan (later 'Jordan'). He then set about promoting more actively his long-cherished expansionist ambitions. The notion of 'Greater Syria' was declared a primary principle of his foreign policy. He would let no occasion pass without pressing his case: 'There is neither a great nor a little Syria', he told the Egyptian newspaper *al-Ahram*.[6] 'There is only a single country bounded to the west by the sea, to the north by Turkey, to the east by Iraq and to the south by the Hijaz – which constitutes Syria'. Needless to say, such declarations and unilateral *démarches* met with unrelieved hostility from Cairo, Beirut, Damascus and Riyadh. On a visit to Damascus in December 1946, Ibn Sa'ud's adviser, Shaykh Yusuf Yasin, told the British chargé d'affaires that 'if King 'Abdallah persisted in his scheme for a Greater Syria, the Arab League might find itself obliged to expel Jordan'.[7]

'Abdallah was no more successful with his Hashemite neighbour, Iraq. Throughout 1945 and 1946, he discussed at some length with his nephew, the Iraqi Regent 'Abd al-Ilah, the merits of a union between Iraq and Transjordan. 'Abdallah's proposal was that he himself should accede for life to the joint thrones of the two countries, the succession passing at his death, not to his own heirs, but to the young King Faysal. Another proposal was that 'Abd al-Ilah should become king of Transjordan and Palestine and 'Abdallah king of Iraq for life, the succession once again passing to Faysal at his death. Both plans were stillborn. They met with an outcry from what was now a thoroughly republican Syria – as well as from Lebanon's Christians, who saw in them a step towards the Greater Syria project which had always

[5] See Jordanian White Paper, *al-Kitab al-urduni al-abyad: al-watha'iq al-qawmiyya fil wahda al-suriyya al-tabi'iyya*, Amman 1947.
[6] *Al-Ahram*, Cairo, 31 August 1946.
[7] Syria and Lebanon Weekly Political Summary, for week ending 17 December 1946 (FO 371/62119).

enraged and alarmed them. Saudi Arabia was viscerally opposed to any extension of Hashemite power – as was, to a lesser extent, Egypt. As for Arab nationalists everywhere, they were deeply suspicious of 'Abdallah's overly strong ties to Britain and of his suspected dealings with the Zionists.

On 4 August 1947, 'Abdallah sought to bring matters to a head by calling a meeting in Amman of an 'All Syria Congress' to discuss his union plans, on the model of the General Syrian Congress of 1920 that had, more than two decades earlier, elected his brother Faysal to rule as king of Greater Syria. Arab leaders expressed surprise and indignation at 'Abdallah's unseemly persistence. His cause was not served by the general belief that he was driven to seek the Syrian throne not for patriotic reasons, but by obsessive personal ambition alone. To checkmate him, every Arab capital concerned decided to reaffirm its attachment to the Arab League Charter, with its built-in guarantee of the independence of each member state.

President Shukri al-Quwatli of Syria was the most adamant of the Arab leaders in his opposition to 'Abdallah. Much like Riad el-Solh in Lebanon, he had spent his entire inheritance, suffered exile and prison and, indeed, devoted his whole life in order to secure Syria's independence, first from Turkey, and then from France. It had been a hard-fought fight, culminating in the French bombardment of Damascus in 1945. He had no wish to see his country's independence endangered by 'Abdallah's expansionist ambitions, in which he saw Britain's imperial hand and the blessing of the Zionists. He sought to eliminate Hashemite influence in Syria by shutting down Jordan's consulate in Damascus, policing the borders and arresting the more vociferous of the Greater Syria agitators.

Thus, in both Syria and Lebanon, the *ideals* of Arab unity were forced to give way to a more pragmatic particularist sentiment. Just as Lebanon's splintered population – and, in particular, the Christians' fear of being 'swamped' by Muslims – had forced Riad el-Solh to focus on narrow Lebanese goals, putting off to some distant horizon his Arab nationalist aspirations, so Shukri al-Quwatli, the other committed and lifelong nationalist, found himself in the uncomfortable position of having to defend purely Syrian interests against 'Abdallah's deeply suspect and threatening inroads.

As the Arab states drifted into war with the Zionists – a war which they did not have the means to wage – Quwatli was possessed by the fear that if 'Abdallah did seize portions of Palestine, he might then strike northwards to Damascus to fulfil his Greater Syria dream. The threat posed by 'Abdallah to Syria's territorial integrity and independence seemed immediate to many Arab leaders. Indeed, one further reason why many were so utterly opposed to the very idea of the partition of Palestine was because of the fear that 'Abdallah might seize the Arab half of it as a springboard for his further conquests.

It was against this threat that Quwatli tried to conclude a defensive pact with Egypt and Saudi Arabia. He was concerned by the treaty which 'Abdallah had signed with Turkey in 1947, in which he had shown himself ready to renounce the Arab claim to Alexandretta, if Turkey were to support his Greater Syria plan. That very same year, 'Abdallah also signed a treaty of 'Brotherhood and Alliance' with British-controlled Iraq, which Quwatli also read as a threat to Syria's strategic position.

The challenge of partition

Whatever their pressing domestic preoccupations – and they were legion – Arab leaders were confronted in 1947 with a situation in Palestine which they could not ignore. In February, Britain had decided to hand the problem over to the United Nations, whereupon a special UN commission – UNSCOP – was set up to investigate the situation on the ground. Although the Arabs were hostile to UNSCOP, Riad el-Solh nevertheless arranged for the Commission to visit Lebanon in July and meet Arab representatives there. Then came a political bombshell, when, on 8 September, UNSCOP issued a report recommending the partition of Palestine into two states, Arab and Jewish, but on terms even more favourable to the Zionists than those of 1937.

Meeting in Beirut later that month, the Arab League Political Committee even considered economic sanctions against Britain and the United States, but Riad el-Solh, who chaired the meeting, managed to persuade the irate Committee not to proceed with them. Riad was convinced that, since the Arabs could do little to stem the Zionist tide, their best bet was to try to bring Britain over to their side. He assumed – as so many others did at the time – that if things deteriorated any further in Palestine, Britain would be compelled to intervene and impose a settlement. Had not Britain's 1939 White Paper promised a unitary state in Palestine? Had it not proposed to limit Jewish immigration and land purchase and provide for the establishment of a government with an Arab majority?

With hindsight, it is easy to see why the Arabs miscalculated so hugely. They had no way of knowing that Britain's traumatic withdrawal from India in 1947 – and the tragic chaos and horrific intercommunal killing that followed the partition of *that* country – had already robbed Palestine of almost all of its importance in British strategic planning. Protecting the sea route to India was no longer the overriding preoccupation that it had been for nearly two centuries. Moreover, Jewish terrorist attacks against the British in Palestine – designed to stampede the British out of the country and leave the field open to the Zionists – had resulted in a popular revulsion against the Palestine Mandate in British public opinion. Between August 1945 and September 1947, Jewish terrorists killed 338 British officials, both military and civilian, both inside and outside Palestine. The number of Jews killed by the British in this same period was 44 – a 'ratio of casualties between insurgents and an imperial power . . . unique in the annals of rebellion', according to the historian Walid Khalidi, who noted the remarkable 'pampering' by Britain of guilty Zionist criminals.[8]

Then, as now, the Arabs failed to comprehend Britain's behaviour. They imagined that this mighty imperial power would eventually put down the ungrateful Zionists, who were killing its own troops and officials, much as it had brutally put down any number of Arab revolts. They did not realise how much Britain had been weakened by the war and how dependent it had become on the United States. In any event, British policy in Palestine had been hijacked by the American presidential candidate, Harry Truman, who, in a bid to attract the already influential American Jewish vote, had promised that, if elected to the White House, he would send 100,000 displaced European Jews to Palestine – thus reversing Britain's policy of restricting Jewish immigration to 15,000 a year. During the Mandate – and especially in its last, post-war years – Britain had been unable to control the flood of illegal Jewish immigrants to Palestine, estimated to total 120,000.[9]

---

[8] Walid Khalidi, 'Illegal Jewish Immigration to Palestine under the British Mandate', in *Journal of Palestine Studies*, 35(4) (summer 2006), p. 66, quoting Nicholas Bethell, *The Palestine Triangle*, London 1979, p. 397.
[9] Khalidi, 'Illegal Jewish Immigration', p. 64.

When, in September 1947, Britain announced that it was terminating the Mandate and withdrawing from Palestine by midnight on 14 May 1948, the Arabs could scarcely believe their ears. With its military bases and its political influence throughout their region, they imagined Britain to be still all-powerful, and continued to rely on it for a 'just settlement' – an illusion which they were to retain to the very end. They were later to transfer these same desperate hopes to the United States, only to suffer an even sharper disillusion in our own time.

A strident wake-up call came on 27 November 1947, when the UN General Assembly, meeting in Paris, voted by a two-thirds majority to partition Palestine. The plan, which had the active support of both the United States and the Soviet Union, gave the Jews over 50 per cent of the country, although they constituted by then only one-third of the population, and legally owned only 7 per cent of the land. The Jews were jubilant, and the Arabs outraged. Beirut closed down as students took to the streets in angry protest. Bombs went off in the Jewish quarter, near the American Legation, and at the headquarters of the Communist Party, since the Soviet Union was considered highly culpable in the mess. Stone-throwers damaged the TAPLINE offices in both Beirut and Damascus. British and American schools in Iraq were vandalised. In Palestine, the Arab Higher Committee called for a three-day general strike.

Jews and Arabs skirmished in Jerusalem, while, in December, Jewish terrorists of the Stern Gang and the Irgun attacked Arab quarters, exploding booby-trapped cars and trucks, and setting off a cycle of mutual violence. During the month of December 1947 alone, 208 Arabs, 204 Jews and 17 British were killed.[10]

The UN plan brought to a head the divisions between the Hashemites and their Arab opponents – Egypt, Saudi Arabia and Syria. In Lebanon, Riad el-Solh attempted to keep on reasonable terms with both camps, although he could not help leaning more towards his friends, the kings of Egypt and of Saudi Arabia, and the president of Syria. Riad suspected that 'Abdallah had been in touch with the Zionists for years, but he had no way of knowing that in November 1947 – and after more than twenty years of secret contacts – 'Abdallah had reached a clear and explicit agreement with the Zionists to divide

---

[10] Laurens, *La Question de Palestine*, vol. III, p. 47.

Palestine between themselves. Golda Meyerson (later Meir), then the acting head of the Jewish Agency's Political Department – its diplomatic and espionage department – had paid 'Abdallah a secret visit and 'returned home with what amounted to a non-aggression pact'.[11]

Britain, which closely monitored 'Abdallah's foreign dealings, was well aware of what was going on. Even though the proposed division of Palestine undermined the policies of its own 1939 White Paper, Britain was not unhappy with it. The Foreign Office may have imagined that, by helping Jordan acquire the Arab-designated half of Palestine, it would somehow set a limit to the borders of the proposed Jewish state and preserve Britain's position in the region. Some officials in London, as well as Glubb Pasha, the British commander of the Arab Legion in Jordan, saw 'Abdallah's Greater Syria as a possible fortress protecting British strategic interests in the Middle East. As Glubb explained to the British government, 'It is not fanciful to imagine the Arab Legion as the nucleus of the Army of a Greater Syria in the future'.[12] Some officials believed that it was actually in Britain's interest to create a territorial continuity between Transjordan and Gaza, thus cutting off any future Jewish state from the Red Sea. In any event, few could foretell that the convenient plan to divide Palestine 'peacefully' between Jordan and the Zionists would come to be imperilled by the (ineffectual) military agitations of the Arab League.

In Lebanon, the Chamber of Deputies responded to the crisis on 5 December by deciding to levy a tax on luxury goods. It was felt that money was even more important than men to the defence of Palestine. Ministers and deputies agreed to contribute a month's salary to a Palestine Fund. By the end of December, the Fund had collected the princely sums of 120,000 Lebanese pounds (about £15,000 sterling) in Beirut and 29,000 Lebanese pounds (about £2,000 sterling) in Tripoli. It was also decided to prohibit further demonstrations and strikes. Nineteen Palestinian Jewish students, who were studying at the American University of Beirut at the time, were asked to leave the country for their own safety.

---

[11] Avi Shlaim, *The Politics of Partition: King Abdallah, The Zionists and Palestine, 1921–1951*, Oxford 1990, pp. 99–100. This is an abridged version of Shlaim's classic work, *Collusion Across the Jordan*.

[12] General J. B. Glubb, 'A Note on the Future of the Arab Legion', quoted in Maan Abu Nawar, *The Struggle for Independence, 1939–1947: A History of the Hashemite Kingdom of Jordan*, Reading 2001, p. 305.

A week after the UN vote on partition, Riad el-Solh – accompanied by the former Mufti, the Hajj Amin al-Husayni, who had arrived unexpectedly in Beirut in October – left for Cairo to attend a meeting of Arab prime ministers. The meeting condemned the UN partition plan and pledged to keep Palestine united and Arab. But this was mere empty rhetoric for public consumption. No Arab leader had the means to come to the defence of the Palestine Arabs. There was no Arab 'master plan' for fighting the Jews, but this could not be admitted, since the Arab public, unlike its anxious and impotent political leaders, was ravaged by war fever.

Brigadier Gilbert Clayton, Britain's director of military intelligence in Egypt (who had been Allenby's chief political officer and knew the Arab world well), called on Riad el-Solh in Cairo on 11 December and 'found him very depressed about the situation'. Fighting in Palestine, Riad told him, was inevitable because the Arabs could not accept partition. Opinion was so inflamed that it would be impossible to prevent volunteers rushing to help the Palestine Arabs. Any government that tried to stop them would be immediately overthrown. 'I formed the impression', Clayton reported to London, 'that he would like to see a way out of the dangers of the situation, but felt the matter had got out of his control'. Riad el-Solh, he added, had said nothing about Arab plans after the termination of the Mandate – indeed, there was nothing to say.[13]

As a sop to public opinion – and to absolve themselves of an impossible military task – Arab leaders decided actively to encourage Arab irregulars to enter Palestine and fight the Zionists. A recruiting station was, for example, opened in Beirut for volunteers. In this, Lebanon was by no means the exception. All Arab leaders of the time preferred to leave the fighting to intrepid volunteers – and to the Palestinians themselves – rather than risk committing their own feeble armies to battle. The idea was to try to wear down Jewish forces by guerrilla operations. Like Riad el-Solh in Lebanon, Shukri al-Quwatli knew that the Syrian army was useless as an effective fighting force. Its two thousand or so ill-trained soldiers lacked ammunition, armour or supplies. The country was virtually bankrupt after the French departure and could not afford expensive arms purchases abroad. In any event, there was hardly anyone then in Syria who knew how

---

13 Cairo to Foreign Office, 11 December 1947 (FO 371/61580).

to go about obtaining such things, as the species of 'arms merchants' only came into being with the later *coups d'état*. Quwatli's reasonable concern was to protect his misnamed 'army' from utter defeat in Palestine, which he feared would then leave his country exposed to attack. Other Arab governments were frightened of military defeat too, since it would have doomed them in the eyes of their subjects and risked their downfall.

The Arab irregulars

Two Arab volunteer forces took shape in late 1947 and early 1948, known respectively as the *jaysh al-inqadh* (the army of rescue) and the *jaysh al-jihad al-muqaddas* (the holy war army). The first force – which Western diplomats and commentators referred to as the Arab Liberation Army (ALA) – was created by the Arab League and was commanded in the field by the veteran guerrilla fighter Fawzi al-Qawuqji. The second was a more private initiative of the Hajj Amin al-Husayni, who refused to hand control of his supporters to Qawuqji. He insisted that Palestine did not need a volunteer army and that all the money raised for it – from the Arab League or from private donations – should be channelled directly through him. The commander of his men in central Palestine was his cousin, 'Abd al-Qadir al-Husayni, while Hasan Salameh led the Hajj Amin's irregulars in the coastal region of Palestine. Relations between the ALA and the Mufti's irregulars were therefore marked, inevitably but disastrously, by some considerable hostility.

The ALA had been formed on the recommendation of General Isma'il Safwat, a former Iraqi chief of staff, whom the Arab League in Cairo had appointed at the head of a Technical Committee to assess the situation in Palestine. This Technical Committee was eventually renamed the Military Committee and moved to Damascus. A Palestine Committee, chaired by Syria's Prime Minister Jamil Mardam, was appointed to take overall charge of the situation. Mardam then appointed another Iraqi general, Taha al-Hashimi – a former prime minister of Iraq, who had chosen exile in Syria after the overthrow of Rashid 'Ali – as overall chief or inspector-general of the ALA.

Brave volunteers poured in – Syrians, Iraqis, Jordanians and Egyptians. They were Muslims and Christians; Arabs and Kurds; Circassians and Assyrians – some 3,500 courageous men in all. They were given a rifle, a few hundred rounds of ammunition and three days of rudimentary training at a Syrian army camp at Qatana, near Damascus, before being sent into Palestine, with no further equipment and with hardly any supplies. Jamil Mardam and his Political Committee may have hoped that, in addition to fighting the Zionists, they would nip in the bud 'Abdallah's expansionist ambitions. With this cynical end in mind, many of these hapless but well-intentioned volunteers were sent to the areas that 'Abdallah was planning to annex.

'Abdallah, of course, had no liking for these irregular forces. If there was to be an Arab force at all, he insisted, it had to be under his leadership. He was perfectly aware that Syria's support for the ALA was also meant to scuttle his own hopes of annexing the Arab part of Palestine to his kingdom. He therefore started arming his own supporters there. On 5 March, Qawuqji was invited to Amman, where he and King 'Abdallah agreed on their common opposition to the Mufti and his followers. Meanwhile, local Palestinian 'militias' of startled and poorly armed farmers, dispersed in their villages and with little coordination between them, were left to face the centralised Zionist command alone. They were very soon disastrously overwhelmed.

Riad el-Solh's appeal to Britain

Riad was clear-headed about the catastrophic situation in which the Arabs found themselves. The Arab governments had no viable military option: their regular armies were too weak to send into Palestine to fight the Jews. In any event, technically they could not do so before Britain withdrew on 14 May, because of the risk of clashing with British forces, something they all wanted to avoid. Small bands of volunteers were already slipping across the border. They might just about serve to defuse some popular anger, but they could not even begin to take on the far better armed and trained Zionists. They might even make the Arab situation yet more perilous, by handing the Jews a perfect pretext to attack.

Pondering these gloomy conclusions, Riad searched with growing anxiety for a way out of the impasse. The solution he came up with was a bold one. Because he was then on cordial terms with the British – and because he liked to think that he knew how *they* thought – he decided to make a final attempt to get Britain to halt Palestine's slide into the abyss. The plan he devised was to offer Britain a global deal with the Arabs – an 'overall settlement', as he called it – which would consolidate British influence throughout the region by forging nothing less than a defensive alliance between Britain and the Arab states. It would even include an Arab commitment to fight Communism – which Riad el-Solh knew had by then become a major Western preoccupation. Britain would, in return, have to resolve to Arab satisfaction the two problems of Palestine and Egypt. In Palestine, a just settlement was needed which would contain the Zionists and protect Arab rights, while in Egypt, Britain would have to agree voluntarily to evacuate the Suez Canal Zone, so as to open the way for a new era of cooperation and friendship.

On every possible occasion – in the months between the UN Partition Plan vote of November 1947 and the end of the Mandate at midnight on 14 May 1948 – Riad el-Solh put his proposal for such an 'overall settlement' to every senior British official he had occasion to meet, as well as to Arab leaders. Such an overall understanding, he urged, was clearly in the interest of both the British and the Arabs. Arab leaders, he was relieved to find, were on the whole 'well-disposed' to his views. He was greatly encouraged when, on his return to Lebanon from Cairo, William Houstoun-Boswall, the British minister in Beirut, told him that he had been instructed by the Foreign Office to say that 'his ideas in general coincided with those of His Majesty's Government'.[14]

Riad was led to feel that he was making serious headway. But London made no move. In January and February 1948, in renewed talks with Houstoun-Boswall in Beirut and with Gilbert Clayton in Cairo, Riad reverted repeatedly to his plan. He told Houstoun-Boswall that he wanted 'frank and discreet discussions' between Britain and the Arab states, in which each side would state its requirements. Such discussions, he maintained, would facilitate an understanding between Britain and Egypt.[15] It was his firm intention, he said, to work on his Arab colleagues to persuade them of the merits of his plan. When Iraq was swept by huge and violent demonstrations in protest against the Anglo-Iraqi 'Portsmouth Treaty' of 15 January 1948 – signed by Salih Jabr, who had replaced Nuri al-Sa'id as prime minister in March

---

[14] Beirut Political Summary, December 1947 (FO 371/68489).
[15] Beirut to Foreign Office, 6 February 1948 (FO 371/68384).

1947 – Riad was quick to tell Houstoun-Boswall that the difficulty could have been avoided if the treaty had been signed under the cover of a general Anglo-Arab understanding.[16] Instead, the Iraqi Regent had to abandon the treaty, and the Jabr government fell on 27 January.

A few days later – in the wings of an Arab League Council meeting in Cairo held from 7 to 24 February, devoted almost entirely to Palestine – Riad again took up the subject with Brigadier Clayton. 'He began talking of the importance of HMG arriving at a general Arab settlement', Clayton reported.

> But he said it was no use attempting anything until the Egyptian question was settled. He kept repeating this and emphasized that it was most important in the eyes of Arab countries. It should, if possible, be settled before we finally withdraw from Palestine. It could be settled if we got over the evacuation difficulty. He attributed events in Iraq to personal feeling against Salih Jabr, but even more to the Palestine and Egyptian questions.[17]

In March, Houstoun-Boswall kept reminding London, somewhat desperately now, that he had 'for several months been reporting the efforts of the Lebanese Prime Minister to make possible a sound understanding between HMG and the Arab States'. But, once again, London did not respond. In early April, Houstoun-Boswall was reporting that Riad el-Solh had gone so far as to offer Britain specific military facilities within the context of an overall defence agreement. Such facilities 'would flow naturally from a general understanding', Riad had said. The Arabs, he explained, shared British objectives in resisting Soviet aggression. If Russia were to attack Iran or Iraq, he would be prepared to allow British troops to land in Lebanon. But, he added, the Arabs had a further objective: it was the liquidation of the outstanding differences between themselves and the West, notably over Palestine and Egypt. 'It was important for HMG to appreciate that national pride among the Arabs was now a fact', he insisted.

What Riad el-Solh had failed to grasp was that, seen from London, the dye was already cast. It was far too late to give attention

---

[16] Beirut Political Summary, February 1948 (FO 371/68489).
[17] Beirut to Foreign Office, 27 March 1948 (FO 371/68385).

to his ambitious plan. An enfeebled Britain was leaving Palestine; the Zionists were to have their state; and the Arabs would have to make do with whatever they could hold on to. The best outcome, British officials had already decided – and especially those who had not served in the Arab world and had no knowledge of what was actually taking place on the ground – was a division of Palestine between 'Abdallah and the Zionists.

In the meantime, Arab leaders continued to live in a fantasy world. Meeting in Beirut from 16 to 21 March, the Arab League's Political Committee instructed Arab delegates at the UN – then in session at Lake Success, near New York – that the Arabs were prepared to maintain security in Palestine if Zionist terrorists were deported, the *Haganah* dissolved and Jewish immigration prohibited!

The pre-war clashes

By the end of March 1948, the *Haganah* had 22,000 men and women under arms, out of a Jewish population of about 645,000, of whom 284,000 (or 44 per cent) were of military age. Arab forces numbered 12,000, including volunteers from other countries, out of a Palestinian population of 1,357,000.[18] But this Palestinian population included women, who played no military role, and many children. It was also largely rural and poorly educated. Urban middle-class Palestinians, with some money or contacts, had for several months been moving abroad, largely to Lebanon, or sending their families ahead for safety after the series of murderous attacks on civilians by the Stern Gang and the Irgun.

The Zionist objective was to attack enemy bases and lines of supply, destroy Arab villages and expel their inhabitants, while taking control of as much territory as possible. The plan was to wage total war, so as to break the will of the Palestine Arabs and of the neighbour-ing Arab states. In the view of Israeli Galilli, the *Haganah* commander, the borders of the Partition Plan were meaningless. Force alone would determine the borders of the future Jewish state.

On 5 April 1948, 'Abd al-Qadir al-Husayni, commander of the *jaysh al-jihad*, came to Damascus to plead for help. He begged Quwatli

---

[18] Cairo to Foreign Office, 16 February 1948 (FO 371/68384).

and the Military Committee for arms and artillery. If the Zionists broke through to Jerusalem, Palestinian resistance would collapse, he warned. But Quwatli was unable to help at this eleventh hour. The Hajj Amin had, after all, from the very start, refused to cooperate with Qawuqji and the ALA. And it was now too late. 'Abd al-Qadir al-Husayni stormed out of the meeting, shaking with fury. Only four days later he was killed defending a small hilltop town at the gates of Jerusalem.[19]

April was a terrible month for the Arabs. On 9 April, Irgun and Stern Gang terrorists fell on Dayr Yasin, a small Arab village west of Jerusalem. Firing indiscriminately, they massacred some 245 men, women and children. In the account by the Oxford historian Avi Shlaim,

> some of the villagers were driven in a lorry through the streets of Jerusalem in a 'victory parade' before they were taken back to the village and shot against the wall. News of the massacre spread like a whirlwind through the land, striking terror into Arab hearts. More than any other single event, it was responsible for breaking the spirit of the civilian population and setting in motion the mass exodus of Arabs from Palestine.[20]

On 13 April, the *Haganah* strike force, the *Palmach*, seized Safed in Galilee. Dozens of young Palestinian prisoners were massacred – no doubt in cold-blooded revenge for those Jews who had been slaughtered at Safed, almost two decades earlier, in 1929. Several other Arab villages were seized, pillaged and destroyed, and their population put to flight. While the Arab League Political Committee was sitting in Cairo that April, news arrived of the fall of Haifa to Zionist forces. The meeting broke up in confusion. There had been British collusion in the collapse of Haifa, since the Arabs were given only a few hours' warning of Britain's decision to withdraw from the town. Jaffa was to fall shortly afterwards. Hundreds of thousands of distraught, destitute and panic-stricken refugees fled and began pouring across the borders of Palestine into neighbouring countries. In Lebanon, there were

---

[19] Landis, 'Syria in the 1948 Palestine War', quoting Walid Khalidi (ed.), 'Selected Documents on the 1948 Palestine War', in *Journal of Palestine Studies*, 27(3) (1998), p. 75.

[20] Shlaim, *The Politics of Partition*, p. 136.

20,000 by the end of April; then, within weeks, 60,000; then 85,000; then 140,000. In Jordan and Syria, and eventually in Gaza, there were many, many more.

The *Haganah* denied responsibility for the massacre at Dayr Yassin. But, as the Israeli scholar Ilan Pappé has so thoroughly demonstrated in *The Ethnic Cleansing of Palestine*, Ben-Gurion and a small group of his colleagues had devised a plan, known as Plan Dalet, for the systematic expulsion of Palestinians from vast areas of the country – a programme of 'ethnic cleansing' far wider and only somewhat less brutal than that which had been visited on Dayr Yassin. Long and meticulous planning had gone into recruiting a network of Arab collaborators who had helped in compiling the chilling 'village files' – that is to say, a detailed registry of all Arab villages in Palestine: their topographic location, access roads, quality of land, water springs, main sources of income, religious affiliation, names of village headmen and of shop owners, average landholding per family, the age of individual men and many more such details, as well as the number of guards, if any (most villages had none), and the quantity and quality of arms at the disposal of each village. Special focus was put on people who were alleged to have killed Jews in the 1936–39 uprising, or who were thought to be associated with the Mufti. Informers helped establish a list of such 'wanted' men.[21]

In March 1948, each commander of the twelve *Haganah* brigades received a list of villages in his zone that had to be occupied, burned to the ground and the inhabitants expelled, with the dates when this should take place. These were clear-cut operational orders. Mines were placed in the rubble to prevent the inhabitants from returning. When Jewish troops occupied a village, the men were lined up and the 'wanted' persons identified. They were often shot on the spot. This was the plan, Pappé writes, according to which the 1948 war was fought. Houses were looted and many prisoners of military age executed. Refugees were thrown onto the roads with no more than what they could carry.

Over the next six decades and more, Israel has sought to annihilate all forms of Palestinian resistance, and to abort any move towards Palestinian statehood, perhaps because it knows that the

---

[21] Ilan Pappé, *The Ethnic Cleansing of Palestine*, Oxford 2006; and an article by Pappé on the same subject, 'The 1948 Ethnic Cleansing of Palestine', in *Journal of Palestine Studies*, 36(1) (autumn 2006), pp. 6–20.

immense crimes committed at its birth cannot be forgotten or easily forgiven.

Arab armies join the fight

The massacres and mass expulsions opened Arab eyes to the superior power of the Zionists and to the shamefully inadequate preparations of their own leaders, who were accused in the press – then a great deal freer than it is today – of being pitifully stupid, tools in the hands of others, or of having sacrificed Palestine on the altar of their own ambitions. It became painfully obvious that Arab irregulars were hopelessly inadequate to deal with the highly trained forces of the *Haganah*. With war fever now at its peak, there was a universal call for the intervention of regular Arab armies. Yet, UN Security Council Resolution 46 of 17 April, which had imposed a total embargo on the delivery of weapons to the Middle East, hit the Arabs hard. The Zionists, on the other hand, continued to receive arms and equipment clandestinely from the Soviet bloc and from France.

In a state of some panic, the Arab League Political Committee met in Damascus on 9 May, to attempt to draw up a plan for military operations. It was proposed that, in the north, the Syrian and Lebanese armies, reinforced by the ALA, would march on Haifa; that the Egyptian army in the south would march on Jaffa; and that the Jordanian and Iraqi armies would drive to a point on the Mediterranean north of Tel Aviv, thus cutting Jewish-held territory in two. But a lack of means and a host of petty squabbles quickly threw doubt on the possibility of such coordinated action. Arab leaders were faced with a dilemma: the British had urged them not to intervene before 15 May – and indeed they decided not to – but they knew that, in the meantime, the Jews would seize vital strategic points in Arab areas.

As they dithered, it was Riad el-Solh who, by dashing about the region, took the initiative in an attempt to forge some sort of Arab unity of purpose. In early May, he persuaded the Iraqi Regent 'Abd al-Ilah to accompany him to Cairo, in a bid to secure the intervention of the Egyptian army. There was a widely held Arab illusion that Egypt would be able to defend Palestine. But King Farouk, too, was deeply suspicious of 'Abdallah's scheming. And he wanted nothing to do with Arab irregulars, whether led by the Mufti or by Qawuqji. But, after much discussion and still with considerable reluctance, he agreed to take part in the war – only four days before the end of the British Mandate and the official beginning of hostilities on 15 May.

It was also Riad el-Solh who, on 6 May, accompanied Jamil Mardam to Riyadh to secure Ibn Sa'ud's agreement to the decisions of the Political Committee. And it was again at Riad's instigation that the Lebanese and Syrian Presidents Bishara al-Khoury and Shukri al-Quwatli met King 'Abdallah of Jordan at Dar'a, on the Syrian-Jordanian border, on 20 May, to put a final touch to their temporary (and exceedingly limited) cooperation. Riad's apparent success in coordinating the various Arab plans for armed intervention greatly enhanced his prestige among Muslims in Lebanon and throughout the Arab world. The war in Palestine had come to be seen as an existential jihad.

Following Arab reverses on the ground in late April and early May, and the virtual disintegration of the ALA, opinion began turning to King 'Abdallah, in the hope that he and his Arab Legion could provide some hope of salvation. Pragmatic as ever, Riad el-Solh was prepared to give the king the benefit of the doubt. 'Abdallah's contacts with the Zionists were widely suspected, but no one knew the actual extent of his collusion. Certainly, no one was aware of his secret agreement to divide up Palestine between himself and the Jews. 'Abdallah was then in some difficulty: he needed to continue to make some belligerent noises to prove to the Arabs that he was no traitor; at the same time, he needed to keep telling the Jews, by secret messages, that he had no intention of attacking them. In fact, he had explicitly agreed not to. This doublespeak on his part was to provide the Zionists – when it suited them – with the pretext to seize territory in areas he hoped to annex, as well as to engage the Arab Legion in combat on several occasions, notably around Latrun for control of the road to Jerusalem, which was vital to the Zionist command.

The proclamation of the State of Israel

At 4 p.m. local time on 14 May 1948, and just before the beginning of the Shabbat on the 15th, the State of Israel was proclaimed by David Ben-Gurion in Tel Aviv. The United States recognised his provisional government as the de facto authority of the new state, but the Soviet

Union trumped this announcement by giving Israel de jure recognition, as well as the immediate establishment of diplomatic relations.

The Egyptian army crossed the border into Palestine on 15 May and, after difficult progress, reached Isdud, 32 kilometres from Tel Aviv. A second column, consisting mainly of members of the Muslim Brothers and some Egyptian regular soldiers, travelled through the Negev and entered Hebron on 20 May, but could go no further for lack of supplies. The Iraqis tried to cross the river Jordan near its junction with the Yarmuk, but were held before the Jewish settlement of Gesher. After a council of war between King 'Abdallah and the Iraqi Regent, the Iraqis entered the West Bank over the Allenby Bridge, reaching Nablus on 21 May and Tulkaram on the 23rd. By the end of May, they were a mere 11 kilometres from the Mediterranean. Israeli forces then attacked them from the north in the sector of Jenin, where fierce battles took place in early June.

'Abdallah's Arab Legion entered Palestine officially on 15 May, with orders not to cross the partition lines – to the great anger of its Arab officers. But it only had ammunition for three weeks, and was outraged when the Egyptians confiscated an arms shipment in Egyptian waters that was on its way to Jordan. The Legion's object was to occupy central Palestine from Jericho to Ramallah, leaving the Iraqis to hold the north. The Legion also took control of the heights near Jerusalem, including control of the Jaffa–Jerusalem road near Latrun.

Some 2,000 Arab fighters had assembled to defend Jerusalem. They were members of village militias, policemen, a contingent of Syrian Muslim Brothers led by Mustafa al-Siba'i, as well as members of the ALA and the al-jihad al-muqaddas, all poorly armed and with no overall command. Nevertheless, they managed to repulse repeated Israeli assaults on the Old City in mid-May, losing the Shaykh Jarra quarter only. When the Old City was threatened with encirclement, King 'Abdallah and Glubb, with the greatest reluctance, finally came to the aid of the defenders, knowing full well that this would risk open war with Israel. On 19 May, a 300-man Arab Legion column broke the encirclement and retook Shaykh Jarra, winning 'Abdallah accolades as the saviour of Jerusalem. After fierce fighting, some 800 inhabitants of the Jewish quarter of the Old City were allowed to leave, and another 350 of military age taken as prisoners to Jordan.

The enraged Israelis suspected that the Legion's intervention was dictated by London in order to thwart the expansionist territorial ambitions of the Jewish state. Repeated Israeli attacks in brigade strength, intended to break the Legion's control of the road to Jerusalem, were repulsed with heavy losses. Micky Marcus, the overall Israeli commander on this front, was killed in error by a Jewish sentry who did not understand English. Marcus was a Jewish American officer who had rushed to Israel to join in the fighting, and had achieved the rank of general – the first to do so in the new Israeli army.

Count Bernadotte's failed mediations

With Palestine slipping deeper into uncontrollable violence, Trygve Lie, the Norwegian secretary-general of the United Nations, decided to appoint a mediator in a bid to halt the killing. His choice fell on Count Folke Bernadotte, a grandson of the king of Sweden and a high official of the Swedish Red Cross. On 29 May, the Security Council voted for a four-week ceasefire and instructed the mediator, assisted by a team of military observers, to see to its implementation. A truce came into effect on 11 June and gradually took hold, though with many murderous violations.

Both sides sought to strengthen their positions, but whereas the Arabs – plagued as usual by disunity, by a lack of funds and by a lack of suppliers willing to breach the embargo – did little or nothing to re-equip their forces, Israel seized the opportunity to arm its forces and reorganise them into bigger units. The *Haganah* had long anticipated war with the Arabs and had embarked, from 1945 onwards, on a large-scale effort to buy weapons and bring in men who knew how to use them. The truce gave a fresh impetus to these efforts. Through several front companies – and with the cooperation of certain Latin American countries where the Zionists had established contacts – arms and equipment were purchased from America's War Assets Administration, which, after the Second World War, was disposing of surplus US military equipment. These weapons, which included three B17 Flying Fortresses, were then transferred clandestinely to Palestine.[22] In June, Israeli planes bombed the Syrian front line, as well as Damascus, where, ironically enough, they managed to hit and destroy the house of the US

---

[22] See Ricky-Dale Calhoun, 'Arming David: The Haganah's Illegal Arms Procurement Network in the United States, 1945–49', in *Journal of Palestine Studies*, 36(4) (summer 2007), pp. 22–32.

air attaché. Czechoslovakia – with Moscow's blessing – was another major source of weapons, as was France. Unlike the Arabs, who were short of funds, Israel could call on large contributions, in the hard currency of scarce dollars, from its loyal American supporters.

Bernadotte's inspectors were too few and too scattered to monitor the flow of weapons, or to check the numerous violations of the truce. Israel continued to empty Arab villages, and kill or expel their inhabitants. It adamantly refused to allow any refugees to return. Any who attempted to do so were shot on sight. Indeed, an Israeli committee under Yosef Weitz had been set up at the end of May to direct the expulsion of the Arab population, seen as a heaven-sent opportunity to resolve the 'Arab question', once and for all.

Determined to torpedo Bernadotte's efforts, Israel launched attacks on several fronts. Operation Dekel was designed to destroy Qawuqji's forces in western Galilee. Nazareth fell on 16 July, forcing the ALA to flee north in disorder. Operation Dani, under the command of Ygal Allon and Yitzak Rabin, was intended to clear the Arab towns of al-Lud and Ramla, and assault Latrun. Large numbers of refugees were forced onto the roads in intense heat, causing the death of many children and old people. The Arab Legion's failure to intervene brought some of its Arab officers close to mutiny and earned 'Abdallah his first accusation of treason.

Having failed to secure the demilitarisation of Jerusalem, or even an outline of a political settlement acceptable to both sides, Bernadotte recalled his observers. He then went to the UN at Lake Success on 12 July to seek an unlimited truce, which he intended to come into effect on 18 July. Israel, backed by the Soviet Union, was quick to accept it, but the Arabs demanded a withdrawal to the lines of 29 May. Meeting in the Lebanese town of Aley on 17 July, the Arab League Council was torn between its perilous military situation and an Arab public, largely unaware of the impending catastrophe, which demanded immediate military action. This was a time when Arab leaders still feared the reactions of their people, which they could not yet crush with impunity.

The Lebanese front

Riad el-Solh was prime minister of a country, some of whose inhabitants were reluctant to go to war against the Zionists. Some Christians even saw them as potential allies against the Arab world's Muslim majority.[23] Monsignor Ignatius Mubarak, the Maronite Archbishop of Mount Lebanon, had been indiscreet enough to write to UNSCOP, the UN special committee on Palestine, recommending the establishment of a 'Christian National Home' in Lebanon at the same time as a 'Jewish National Home' in Palestine! In late 1947, he had gone so far as to challenge the Lebanese government by issuing a pamphlet inciting the armed services to insubordination and the population to civil disobedience. The Vatican (no doubt under some pressure from the Lebanese government) ordered him to leave Lebanon in April 1948. Two months later, Monsignor Antun 'Arida, the 85-year-old Maronite Patriarch, who shared Mubarak's views, was also relieved of his functions.

Emile Eddé, the disappointed pro-French presidential candidate – who bore both Bishara al-Khoury and Riad el-Solh enormous grudges – was also known to be working for a 'Christian National Home', side by side with that of the Jews. He was rash enough to raise the possibility of a Christian revolt in Beirut if Israel entered South Lebanon. Three members of his group visited Amman in December 1947, arousing intense suspicions in the nationalist press. Unlike these other Christians, Bishara al-Khoury's attitude on this matter was above reproach. He worked throughout the war in close coordination with Riad el-Solh. There is no doubt, however, that Lebanon's options in 1948 were severely restricted by the active hostility of a part of the Maronite community to any war in Palestine.[24] This was an added burden that Riad el-Solh had to bear.

The British minister in Beirut, William Houstoun-Boswall, warned London of the danger of communal strife if Lebanon were sucked into the war. Riad el-Solh's government, he wrote, could not rely on sincere cooperation from the Maronite clergy. 'The danger inherent in the Palestinian commitment is that if the very weak and futile Lebanese forces were to suffer defeat (which can be taken as a foregone conclusion if they were ever engaged in earnest) serious communal troubles must be expected, which the government would be unable to control'.[25]

---

[23] For the war on the Lebanese front, I have relied on Matthew Hughes, 'Lebanon and the 1948 War', in *Journal of Palestine Studies*, 34(2) (winter 2005), pp. 1–18.
[24] Ibid., pp. 2–3.
[25] Beirut to Foreign Office, 26 June 1948 (FO 371/68495).

Commanded by the Emir Fu'ad Chehab, the Lebanese army was far from ready when war broke out on 15 May, as it was still engaged in the difficult task of converting the remnants of the *Troupes Spéciales* into a fighting force. There was much sorting out to be done, as the *Troupes* had been recruited in both Lebanon and Syria, mainly from minority backgrounds, and most of its Syrian officers had gone home to join the Syrian army once the French had departed. In any event, Lebanon's four infantry battalions, each of about five hundred men, were heavily involved in anti-bandit operations, and were more of a police force than an army. Shortage of funds – and the crippling Western arms embargo – made it impossible for Lebanon to acquire new weapons and equipment to replace the outdated materiel discarded by the French, even if it did have the funds available, which it did not. When Riad el-Solh and Fu'ad Chehab asked the British for artillery and aircraft, they were turned down. The Zionist high command knew that it had little to fear in Galilee, as the Lebanese army would be unable to attack Jewish border settlements.

'What is certain', Matthew Hughes wrote in his account of the war on the Lebanese front, 'is that the confessional and inchoate nature of the army, combined with a weak order-of-battle, hampered effective military operations'. Lebanon's role in the war was extremely modest, confined to the passive role of containing Jewish troops along the border. This somewhat satisfied the Muslims' wish for intervention, while causing little resentment among the Christians, who opposed any excursion of the army outside Lebanon's borders. On 15 May 1948, instead of striking down the coast from Ras al-Naqura to Acre – as it had been tasked to do, and where it was meant to combine with the Syrian, Iraqi and Jordanian armies to detach the Galilee and threaten Israel with strategic envelopment – the Lebanese army simply dug in on its side of the border. Riad el-Solh had wanted the army to launch an offensive,[26] but Chehab felt it was best to restrict Lebanon's role to one of mere defence of its own borders.

The Zionists, however, were not passive when it came to Lebanon. A few days before 15 May, Jewish commandos damaged the river bridge over the Litani, and on the 23rd, blew up Ahmad al-As'ad's house at Taybeh, which naturally enraged him and his Shi'i followers

---

[26] Arif al-Arif, II, *al-Nakba*, Beirut 1956; Sadiq al-Shari', *Hurubna ma'a Isra'il*, Amman 1997.

in South Lebanon, who pressed the government to hit back. On the 28th, Jewish patrols set fire to two of Lebanon's antique armoured cars near the border, while aircraft bombed the border villages of Bint Jbail and Tibnin. These cross-border raids forced Chehab to respond, if only to maintain Lebanon's standing in the Arab League. The result was an engagement with the Zionists at the village of Malikiyya on 5–6 June, when Lebanese forces were assisted by 250 men of the ALA, including a battalion commanded by Lieutenant Colonel Adib al-Shishakli, later to become strongman and president of Syria, a position he was to gain by military *coup d'état*. By this time, the ALA had been largely redeployed from the Jerusalem-Jaffa-Nablus area to Galilee, through Syria.[27]

Malikiyya was a village some 700 metres across the Lebanese border into Palestine. It was to change hands a number of times during this period. The Israelis captured it on 13–14 May, but were forced out a couple of days later by Shishakli's battalion. It was then retaken by the Israelis on 28–29 May, with an attack from the rear through Lebanese territory. On 5 June, however, a battalion of the Lebanese army managed to push the Israelis out of Malikiyya, and also entered the neighbouring village of Qadas. Eight Israeli and two Lebanese soldiers were killed. The Lebanese force did not, however, attack the nearby Jewish border settlement of Ramot Naftali, nor make any attempt to link up with Syrian forces.

To celebrate the victory at Malikiyya, the Lebanese held a victory parade at Bint Jbail on 9 June, attended by President Bishara al-Khoury, Prime Minister Riad el-Solh, Defence Minister Majid Arslan and the Army Commander-in-Chief Fu'ad Chehab. Lebanese soldiers were paraded, medals distributed and photographs taken. Fawzi al-Qawuqji was awarded the Medal of the Cedar for the ALA's part in the battle. The Lebanese army then handed Malikiyya and Qadas over to the ALA and returned to its side of the border. Matthew Hughes concluded that 'by 9 June, the war for the Lebanese army, which had begun on 5 June, was over'.[28]

The fight against Israel in Galilee now passed back to the ALA, which, without proper equipment or training, was soon routed in a series of *Haganah* offensives between April and November 1948.

---

[27] Hughes, 'Lebanon and the 1948 War', pp. 5–6.
[28] Ibid., p. 10.

Indeed, in June 1948, the Arab League *reduced* the size of the ALA, in order to ensure that every man had a rifle! In July, it cut it in half because it could not afford to pay all its men.[29] 'Lacking food, basic field equipment and shelter, and suffering from diseases such as diphtheria, the men of the ALA were now beginning to desert en masse, firing off their weapons, and harassing visiting officials'.[30]

Qawuqji was well aware of the suspicions and mutual hostility that had prevented any coordinated Arab military action and had starved the ALA of political and material support. 'Each Arab state feared its so-called sister', he was to write in his memoirs; 'each coveted the territory of its sister, and conspired with others against its sister'.[31]

Snapshot of Riad el-Solh during the war

The Palestinian historian Walid Khalidi had occasion to call on Riad el-Solh at home in June 1948, during the truce in the Palestine War. He wanted to convey to the prime minister a secret offer, made by a British Royal Air Force pilot, to help Lebanon in the war. (In fact, angered by Jewish terrorist attacks against British targets, several British soldiers had volunteered to fight for the Arabs.) Sa'ib Salam, who was Khalidi's relative by marriage, advised him to put the offer to Riad in person. Salam then called Riad to arrange the interview, which was set for eight o'clock one morning. The following is Professor Khalidi's account of the meeting:

> *Riad Bey and his family lived in a rented flat above some shops in the middle of the main Basta road [the Muslim quarter of Beirut], opposite a mosque. A short dingy flight of steps led from the street to the entrance, which itself opened on to a simple windowless hall in traditional style, with shut doors leading to rooms on the two sides and at the farther end. The furniture was sparse, mostly chairs*

---

[29] Ibid., p. 11.
[30] Ibid., p. 12.
[31] Fawzi al-Qawuqji, *Filastin fi Mudhakkarat Fawzi al-Qawuqji*, 2 vols, ed. Khayriyya Qasimiyya, Beirut 1975, vol. II, pp. 135–6. See also Laila Parsons, 'Soldiering for Arab Nationalism: Fawzi al-Qawuqji in Palestine', in *Journal of Palestine Studies*, 36(4) (summer 2007), pp. 33–48.

*with straw seats lined against the wall. There were a score
of men, qabadai-like, some in long Damascene qumbaz,
laughing and loudly exchanging remarks with Riad Bey
himself who, still in his dressing gown, was being shaved
by a barber. He acknowledged me and gestured me to a
seat. Presently, he stood up and led me into one of the
side rooms, a bedroom. After shutting the door, he said
that Sa'ib Bey had explained to him what the matter was
about. The only trouble was that Lebanon had no air
force! He thought for a while and then said, 'Syria has an
air force. What I will do is give you a card to Jamil Bey
[prime minister of Syria Jamil Mardam]. You can explain
things to him and introduce your Englishman to him.' He
then produced a visiting card and scribbled on it: 'Please
let the bearer and his companion pass. They are on official
business,' followed by his signature. Handing me the card,
he said: 'Show this at the frontier and they will let you
through.' After shaking my hand and patting me on the
back, he wished me luck and sent me off.[32]*

The Syrian role in the war

The Syrian army played a limited role in the war. It is estimated that it managed to field a total of 2,500 men – 1,000 deployed inside Palestine and 1,500 on the Syrian side of the border. Six days after the official start of hostilities on 15 May, the Syrians attacked into Palestine, but were repulsed at the village of Samakh and at the Degania A and B *kibbutzim* just south of Lake Tiberias, when 300 Syrian soldiers were killed or wounded, largely by Israeli artillery and machine-gunners. Following this heavy loss of life, Defence Minister Ahmad al-Sharabati resigned and Prime Minister Jamil Mardam took over the defence portfolio.

President Quwatli dismissed the Chief of Staff General 'Abdallah 'Atfi, and replaced him with the tough-talking Colonel Husni al-Za'im, head of the gendarmerie – a decision he would come to rue. Under Za'im's command, Syrian forces were able to occupy a thin strip of

---

[32] Letter to the author from Walid al-Khalidi.

Palestinian land running the length of the border, as well as three small enclaves within Palestine in the northern, central and southern regions of the 1923 border. Following the 1949 armistice between Syria and Israel, these enclaves became demilitarised zones. The tussle over who was to control them was later to trigger the 1967 war, and they remain contested areas to this day.

Riad el-Solh was to claim that Lebanese and Syrian forces were instrumental in keeping 15,000 Jewish troops tied down in the north of Palestine, thus facilitating the task of the Egyptians in the south and the Arab Legion in the centre. But, in fact, the passivity of the Lebanese army, the incompetence of the ALA and the limited operations of the Syrian forces, provided the Israelis with a considerable strategic asset. Since the Arabs lacked the essential ability to coordinate militarily, Israel was able to deal with one Arab front at a time, switching forces at critical moments to achieve local superiority.

The endgame

On returning to the region in early September, Count Bernadotte set his sights on the fate of the refugees and the internationalisation of Jerusalem. In order to establish a principle, he wanted Israel to allow back 250,000–300,000 Palestinians, mainly to Haifa and Jaffa, as well as to abandon the Negev in exchange for the Galilee. But Israel wanted both the Negev *and* the Galilee, and utterly refused to allow back even a single refugee. Bernadotte became the target of a vicious Israeli press campaign, in which he was accused of being pro-Arab, anti-Semitic and an agent of British imperialism. On 17 September, he was assassinated in Jerusalem by a team of Stern Gang killers, which included Nathan Yalin-Mor, Yitzak Shamir (a future Israeli prime minister) and Israel Eldad.

By October, the Israeli army numbered 90,000. Well equipped and under a unified command, it was now able to field large units. The combined field forces of the Arabs never exceeded 20,000–25,000, and were woefully dispersed and indifferently led. Fearing that the UN might seek to impose a territorial settlement and a return of refugees, Israel now went on the offensive. On 14 October – the day the Security Council was to debate the murdered Bernadotte's proposals – Israel launched Operation Yoav against Egypt, which, after heavy fighting, opened the way to the Negev. By 21 October, Israel had captured the Negev capital of B'ir al-Sab'i, forcing some 200,000 refugees to flee to the Gaza Strip. Jordan did nothing to relieve the pressure on Egypt, causing relations between them to fall to a new low.

Arab impotence was further revealed when, on 29 October, Israel launched Operation Hiran, with the mission to destroy the remaining Arab forces and reach the Lebanese border. Israel seized all of the Galilee territory which had been allotted to the Arabs by the UN in 1947, and tens of thousands of Palestinians in Galilee were forced into exile at gunpoint. There was hardly any fighting, since the seizure was a walkover. The *Palestine Post* noted that 500 square miles of territory were taken by Israel with a loss of only ten men. Keeping up their momentum, Israeli forces then crossed into Lebanon and occupied fourteen Lebanese villages, emptying them of their inhabitants. Ben-Gurion stopped their advance at the Litani river, despite strong requests from the Northern Front's chief of operations to allow him twelve hours more to reach Beirut. The Israeli occupation of parts of South Lebanon continued into 1949, and was used as a bargaining counter in the armistice talks. When these were concluded on 23 March 1949, hostilities between Lebanon and Israel came to an end.[33]

Operations Yoav and Hiran resulted in the flight of between 200,000 and 230,000 Arabs.[34] On 22 December, Israel launched Operation Horev against Egypt's remaining strong points at Gaza, Rafah and Al-Auja, and then, crossing into Sinai, at Abu Ageila, El-Arish and Falluja. When Britain put its troops on alert, invoking its obligation to defend Egyptian territory under the 1936 Anglo-Egyptian Treaty, and sent six reconnaissance Spitfires to monitor the battlefield, Israel shot them down. Israeli attacks and counter-attacks continued until March 1949, when a final operation in the south took its forces to the Red Sea and to what would become Eilat, thus bringing the war to an end.

Israel lost a little more than 6,000 dead. Arab forces, both regular and irregular, lost 3,700 men, including over a thousand Egyptians. Palestinian losses amounted to 13,000 dead, although the great majority of these were non-combatants.[35]

Israel was not only superior on the battlefield. As far as intelligence was concerned, it had already penetrated several Arab countries,

---

[33] Hughes, 'Lebanon and the 1948 War', p. 13.
[34] Laurens, *La Question de Palestine*, vol. III, p. 175.
[35] Ibid., p. 194.

and had a thorough knowledge of their internal situation. Avi Shlaim has described how the Arab Section of the Jewish Agency's Political Department established an extensive espionage network in the Arab world, directed by fluent Arabic speakers such as Yaacov Shimoni and Elias Sasson. Born in Damascus in 1902, brought up among Arabs, Sasson was head of the Arab Section from 1937 to 1948, during which time he was able to make contact with hundreds of Palestinian, Transjordanian, Syrian, Lebanese, Iraqi and Egyptian public figures, some of whom he had first met as a student in Beirut or as a member of the Arab Club in Damascus. One of his paid agents was Muhammad al-'Unsi, who rose to be Jordan's minister of interior and deputy prime minister, and who, in Shlaim's words, 'supplied the Jewish Agency with valuable information about Jordanian, Palestinian and inter-Arab affairs over a period of fifteen years'.[36] Another paid Israeli agent with high-level contacts, not only in the Arab world, but also in Geneva and New York, was 'Umar Dajani, a Palestinian Arab from a well-known family. Dajani had two Israeli controllers, Sasson and Yaacov Shimoni.[37]

Yet another Zionist expert on the Arab world was Yehoshua Palmon. Having spent the Second World War as a secret agent in Syria, he was to become one of the *Haganah*'s ablest intelligence officers and Ben-Gurion's adviser on Arab affairs.[38] These spymasters and their agents played skilfully on Arab rivalries and sectarian differences. Arab leaders, in contrast, had only the vaguest notion of Zionist capabilities, war plans or ultimate intentions.

Riad el-Solh's last efforts in the war

Well into the war, Riad el-Solh was still hoping against hope that Britain could be persuaded to save Palestine – or at least a substantial part of it – for the Arabs. Early in June, he approached Houstoun-Boswall again, this time with the suggestion that he travel to London for an urgent meeting with Foreign Secretary Ernest Bevin. Houstoun-Boswall passed on the message, with his own positive recommendation. Riad el-Solh, he advised, was astute and well-disposed, and could be useful

---

[36] Shlaim, *The Politics of Partition*, pp. 67–8.
[37] Ibid., pp. 85–6.
[38] Ibid., p. 131.

to the British. But, under considerable American and Zionist pressure, Bevin could not afford to take the risk. 'I greatly appreciate [Riad el-Solh's] friendly and cooperative attitude', he wrote back, 'and, had the circumstances been different, would have welcomed his suggestion for an immediate visit to London. Unfortunately, the critical situation in Palestine makes it impossible for me to invite him to visit me at present because his visit would be misrepresented both here and in the United States'.[39]

Riad was deeply disappointed. He had finally to admit that his ambitious plan for an 'overall settlement' between Britain and the Arabs was a non-starter. Further shocks were to follow. He was very disturbed when Count Bernadotte was murdered in Jerusalem on 17 September, seeing it as further proof of Israel's terrorist policy. He had had a meeting with the affable Bernadotte in Beirut the day before his killing.

Meanwhile, Lebanon, like other Arab states, was swamped by a flood of destitute Palestinian refugees. Altogether, some 750,000 Palestinians had fled or were driven out of their homeland. In September, the British, in a token gesture, sent Lebanon 2,500 tents from their military stores in the Suez Canal Zone. Five hundred tents were erected in Tyre, to accommodate more than 5,000 refugees from Bint Jbail and the Galilee.

Riad el-Solh spent much of October and November 1948 in Paris, attending the meetings of the UN General Assembly, where he hoped to rally support for the Arab cause. It proved a brutal lesson in power politics. The United States and the Soviet Union both supported Israel, while the Arabs found themselves entirely alone. On 5 October, Riad had a meeting with the American Secretary of State George Marshall, but it yielded no result. Yet Riad was determined to contest the loss of Palestine. The greater the Jewish success – even if they were to occupy the whole of Palestine – the stronger would be the Arab determination to resist, he told a British diplomat.

Armistices were concluded between Israel and its Arab neighbours at the beginning of 1949, and frontiers agreed. Israel secured more than three-quarters of historical Palestine. Egypt took under its administration a strip of land, flooded with refugees, stretching along the southern coast from Gaza to the Egyptian border. What was left

---

[39] Beirut to Foreign Office, 4 June 1948 (FO 371/68386).

of Palestine was annexed by King 'Abdallah. Jerusalem was divided between Jordan and Israel, although the division was never clearly or widely recognised.

Riad was forced to admit the Arabs' catastrophic defeat. There was nothing now but to try to save whatever could be saved from what had been Arab Palestine. Contemplating the wreckage of a country he had known so well, an idea took root at the back of his mind that a 'one-room government' – if necessary in exile, on the analogy of allied governments in London during the Second World War – might now, as a last resort, provide a focal point for Arab resistance. It was an analogy he was often to recall in conversation with foreign diplomats.[40] From Paris, he sent a message to Lebanon that was published in the Beirut press on 11 November. He was ready to resign, he declared, and lead a 'new campaign' against the Zionists.

40 Beirut to Foreign Office, 21 September 1948 (FO 371/68376).

25 THE CHALLENGE FROM THE REVOLUTIONARIES

It is hard to overestimate the calamitous impact on the Arabs of the emergence of Israel in 1948. Arab armies were defeated. Arab guerrillas were routed. The stuffing was knocked out of Arab governments. Arab states were exposed as hollow shells; Arab leaders as incompetents or traitors. Arab nationalism itself was discredited. The newly created Arab League, meant to signal a will for closer cooperation and greater unity, was revealed to be an ineffectual talking shop, unable to bridge the chasm of inter-Arab quarrels, and woefully incapable of conducting joint military operations.

An ancient Arab society – Palestine – was shattered. Some 450 Arab villages were razed to the ground. Numerous cities were cruelly emptied of their inhabitants. Three-quarters of a million people, stripped of everything they owned, were driven out at gunpoint. They had to flee for their lives, to a life of great suffering and humiliating destitution across the borders. Their new host countries, themselves poor and unstable, only recently independent or still struggling to become free, were ill-prepared to receive them, and were hugely – and durably – upset by their influx. Tiny and overcrowded Lebanon, in particular, anxiously concerned to maintain a confessional balance between Christians and Muslims, viewed the sudden arrival of the mostly Muslim Palestinian refugees with the greatest alarm. It desperately wanted them to return home – although they no longer had any home to return to – or at least move on somewhere else.

Geopolitically, too, the impact was dire. Palestine, which had been the land-bridge between Arab Asia and Arab Africa, was torn out of the Arab map. An aggressive and expansionist foreign power, planted in the very heart of their region, had brutally managed to subdue the Arabs. The shock to the Arab military and political system was immense. A vast tremor – something that became a social and ideological earthquake – convulsed the region, generating in its wake violent disturbances over the following months, years and decades. Coups, assassinations, wars, massacres, population transfers; an extended Israeli occupation of Arab territory; the rise of violent resistance movements to it; the contagion to states beyond Israel's immediate proximity, like Iraq and Iran; the arousal of militant Islam, which held the West (and especially Britain and the United States) responsible for the shocking fate of the Palestinians; the resort to terrorism, that weapon of the desperate, the oppressed and the enraged, which the Zionists had been the first to use – all this stemmed from the creation of the State of Israel. The Arab-Israeli conflict, with its accompaniment of immense human misery, has continued to hold the region – and the world – hostage to this very day.

In 1948–49, Arab opinion suffered a collapse of morale, a profound humiliation, together with a sense of acute vulnerability. Further Israeli aggression was expected and feared. The conviction took root that the Arabs had been betrayed by their own leaders, as well as by outside powers. Imperialism had left through the door, only to return by the window. Taken together, these feelings bred in many Arabs an overwhelming sense of injustice, but also an explosive sense of rage. Such was the ground from which revolutionaries sprang.

One such revolutionary was Antun Sa'ada.

The PPS without Sa'ada

On 2 March 1947, a day after his forty-fifth birthday, Antun Sa'ada, the charismatic founder of the *Parti populaire syrien*, returned to the Middle East to rapturous hero worship from his followers. He flew in to Beirut from Latin America, via Cairo. Although he had been absent from the Middle East for nine eventful years, he had not been forgotten, either by his disciples or by his enemies. He was welcomed with the sort of veneration usually reserved for gurus rather than for political leaders. This was not entirely surprising, since Sa'ada had none of the qualities usually associated with successful politicians: he had no guile, no pragmatism, no ability to appraise a situation realistically; no spirit of compromise, and no down-to-earth practical sense. Rather, he was an impassioned and dogmatic ideologue, in the obsessive grip of an idea largely of his own making. This doctrinaire conviction was allied to an authoritarian temperament, to a boundless confidence in his personal mission as leader. He was disparaging of lesser mortals, and had an extraordinary gift for invective and for mesmerising speechmaking. These attributes accounted, no doubt, for his remarkable appeal, but they also added up to his fatal weaknesses.

Sa'ada founded his party in Lebanon in 1934. He built up a paramilitary wing on Fascistic lines, very much in accordance with the general spirit of the times.[1] His movement, which won adherents in neighbouring countries too, was soon identified by the authorities as a worrying threat to public order. This earned him and his principal associates short spells in jail in Lebanon in 1935, 1936 and 1937. Faced yet again in 1938 with the threat of arrest because of his flirtation with Nazi Germany, he decided to leave Beirut precipitately, and make his way to Latin America. There he had friends, family and followers in both Argentina and Brazil.

His guiding principle – his lodestar – was a mystical vision of a unique pan-Syrian people, forged over the millennia by Syria's unique geographical environment. He defined this as a great sweep of territory, extending from the Taurus mountains in the north to the Sinai peninsula in the south, from the Mediterranean in the west to the desert in the east. This doctrine set him at odds with almost everyone else in the region – with pan-Arabists like Riad el-Solh, as well as with all those who believed in Arab unity; with narrow Lebanese nationalists like the Maronite clergy, and with Pierre Gemayel's *Phalanges libanaises*; with Communist internationalists; and, indeed, with the whole post-First World War state structure. Sa'ada wanted to redraw the map of the Levant, to merge Syria, Lebanon, Jordan, Palestine and even the island of Cyprus, into a single 'Syrian' polity, an ambitious plan that could not but arouse the hostility of all the various state authorities concerned.

One should add that, although of Greek Orthodox background, Sa'ada was a confirmed secularist. He wanted to sweep Lebanon's confessional obsessions into the dustbin of history – which, indeed, was the most attractive part of his programme. Moreover, his idealised 'pan-Syrian state' had nothing to do with King 'Abdallah's 'Greater Syrian project', although there was clearly some territorial overlap

---

[1] See chapter 14 of this book for the history of the PPS from its creation in 1934 to the outbreak of the Second World War.

between the two concepts. Whereas 'Abdallah dreamed of restoring his own monarchy, as well as Hashemite fortunes, by acceding to the throne of Damascus, Sa'ada, like some ancient mariner, was under the spell of a fictitious realm, an idealised geopolitical unity. What he and 'Abdallah had in common, perhaps, was the obsession with which they pursued their respective and far-fetched goals.

Such was the Antun Sa'ada who flew in to Beirut on 2 March 1947 to reclaim his party. While he had spent the war in Latin America in some safety and comfort, his followers in Lebanon – led by Ni'mat Thabit, his earliest and most devoted disciple – had had a hard time. They were arrested for being pro-German in 1940, only to be let out again by the Vichy regime. But when the British and the Free French marched into Syria and Lebanon in 1941, defeating Vichy forces, PPS activists were hunted down and rearrested. Some seventy important party members – including Ni'mat Thabit himself – were locked up in harsh conditions, both in the Lebanese prison of Mieh-Mieh and in the fort at Rashaya.

Having managed to evade arrest and spend a year on the run, As'ad al-Ashqar – number three in the party after Ni'mat Thabit – gave himself up in 1942 to Commandant Auboire, an officer of France's intelligence service, the *Services Spéciaux*. To the Commandant, Ashqar said that he had studied in French schools, that his family had demonstrated more than once its attachment to France, and that his own sentiments were visibly pro-French. He also asked Patriarch Antoine 'Arida to intervene on his behalf. On 22 December 1942, Monsieur Gautier, director of the *Sûreté Générale*, summoned him from Mieh-Mieh for a private talk. A second confidential meeting took place on 9 January 1943. But nothing much came of these contacts, even though Ashqar followed them up with several letters to Gautier, pleading for the party to be recognised as an ally of France.

In one of these letters, Ashqar argued that 'The principle of the Unity of the Syrian Nation is a doctrine, an ideal, rather than an immediate objective [of our party]. Lebanon's independence is a political principle to be implemented at once and which should be extended into the future until a merger [with Syria, Jordan, etc.] can take place'. In turn, Ni'mat Thabit, the head of the party, sent a letter on 8 June 1943 to Ambassador Helleu, the *délégué général*, following the restoration of constitutional life in the Levant states. 'For the past eight years,' he wrote,

*we have veered from periods of collaboration with France
to periods of rejection . . . Whenever we were free, we
rendered services to France and to our country . . . We
know that you are now preoccupied with a most important
question – the question of Lebanon. As we are the Parti
Populaire Syrien, you may well ask whether we can limit
ourselves to the Lebanese arena. I want to underline here
that my comrades and myself are, more than ever, faithful
to Lebanese independence. Our Syrian ideal remains an
ideal. But for it to be realised it would be necessary for one
civilisation to replace another . . . Lebanon and Syria are
not at present at the level at which they could form a single
state, or a single social community . . . We therefore pray
you to solve our problem, and to believe that we are a party
of young people of value, and that these young people wish
to side with France in its mission in the Levant.*[2]

But the French continued to hesitate. They were heartily committed to
the territorial integrity of Lebanon, and were well aware that, whatever its leaders might say, the PPS wanted to attach Lebanon to Syria.
French doubts were confirmed at the parliamentary elections of August
1943, when nine out of the ten members of the PPS's Higher Council
gave their backing from prison to Bishara al-Khoury's constitutional
list, rather than to that of the pro-French Emile Eddé. The party was
evidently trying to work all sides. For example, while engaging in talks
with the French, it never broke off relations with the British. The PPS
was desperate to secure the release of its leading members and re-
launch its party activities. It was therefore prepared to give whatever
undertaking was necessary to meet these ends. The spectacular Allied
campaigns, and the loss of all hope in an Axis victory, contributed to
forcing the party to change its line – together, of course, with the hardships that its members had suffered, the discussions that its leaders
had had in detention, and the approaches they had made to both the
French and the British.

In the event, the British outwitted the French by seizing the
initiative to release PPS members and rally them to their cause. They

---

[2] MAE, Fonds Beyrouth, série B, carton 5, dossier 61, Sûreté aux Armées, Beirut,
19 June 1944.

were released in 1944 by Camille Chamoun, the Anglophile minister of interior, after an intense campaign of lobbying on their behalf. The French were convinced Chamoun was a British agent, and that he had released PPS members at the instigation of the Spears Mission, 'whose wish to combat Communism won out over any other consideration'.[3] Riad el-Solh later accused Chamoun of freeing PPS activists without proper consultation with him, and conveniently, at a time when he was away in the Hijaz on a visit to Ibn Sa'ud.

Wadad Nasif and Clodagh Thabit

Antun Sa'ada had the benefit of many influential friends. He enjoyed, at different times of his life, relationships with two well-educated and enterprising women, Wadad Nasif, born of an Irish mother and a Lebanese father, and her young cousin, Clodagh Thabit. Both good-looking and spirited, these two women created a considerable stir in Lebanese society at the time. Wadad Nasif was Sa'ada's lover in 1934, when he first launched his movement. As a young woman, she had studied painting in Italy, where she spent some years with her mother and sister, before contracting a brief loveless marriage to one of her cousins in 1926. She soon decided, however, to resume the free life she had previously enjoyed, settling in the Druze village of Mukhtara, in a house belonging to Sitt Nazira Jumblatt, the matriarch of this powerful Druze clan. But the two strong-willed women eventually quarrelled, and Wadad left Mukhtara, to take up residence at the New Royal Hotel in Beirut (an establishment which has since disappeared). It may have been at about this time that she was introduced to Antun Sa'ada by her cousin Ni'mat Thabit, Clodagh's brother.

The relationship between Wadad Nasif and Antun Sa'ada is thought to have lasted about two years, until 1936, when the authorities clamped down on his clandestine movement. Wadad urged him to escape to Palestine with her, but they were stopped by a police patrol. Sa'ada was arrested, but she was set free. Her detractors – especially the female members of the party – accused her of having betrayed him. At any rate, the incident was enough to cause the lovers to part.

---

3 MAE, Fonds Beyrouth, série B, carton 5, dossier 61, Général Paul Beynet, Délégué Général et Plénipotentiaire de France au Levant à M. René Massigli, Commissaire aux Affaires Etrangères, Alger., Beirut, 28 June 1944.

Ni'mat and Clodagh Thabit were the children of Constantin Thabit, correspondent of *The Times* in Beirut, believed by the French to have been an agent of British intelligence. Their mother was Eva Chakkur, maternal aunt of Wadad Nassif. Wadad and Eva were very attached to each other, and had shared a house in the village of Ayn Zhalta, where the Chakkurs were landowning Christian notables.

Through her father Constantin's connections with the British in the early 1940s, as well as by way of her relative Camille Chamoun's interventions, Clodagh did manage to secure the release of PPS party activists in 1944 and the rehabilitation of the party. As early as 1941, Major Musgrave, a British liaison officer with the French *Sûreté Générale*, began talks with Ni'mat Thabit through the intermediary of his sister Clodagh and of Camille Chamoun. Clodagh also managed to protect Sa'ada on his return to Lebanon in 1947.

It was this network of friends – Wadad Nassif in the 1930s, then Ni'mat and Clodagh Thabit, and Camille Chamoun a decade later – that was to be of such great help to Antun Sa'ada. It was instrumental, in the 1940s, in giving the PPS a new lease of life.[4] Always suspicious of British intrigues, French intelligence kept a watchful eye on these relationships. In March 1944, it reported that General Spears and his wife had attended a lunch near Sidon with Monsieur and Madame Camille Chamoun, Madame Clodagh Thabit, and a Druze *qadi*, Milhim Hamdan, whose son, 'Adil Hamdan, was a hunting companion of General Spears. Madame Clodagh Thabit, the report said, 'est une jolie femme assez répandue dans les milieux où l'on "s'amuse"' (a pretty woman who gets about in circles where people like to have fun). 'She is said to be intriguing with the British to get them to accept the backing of the PPS as a counter-weight to the pro-French *Phalanges*'.[5]

On his release from jail, Ni'mat Thabit, chairman of the party's Higher Council, at once set about adapting the party to the new circumstances of Lebanon's independence. His brainwave was to issue a tract in February 1944, announcing that the PPS had dropped the word 'Syrian' from its name and would henceforth be known simply as the *Parti populaire*. He let it be known that the party had decided to work within a purely Lebanese framework, leaving until later the task

---

[4] MAE, Fonds Beyrouth, série B, carton 5, dossier 61, Sûreté Générale, Beirut, 10 November 1940.
[5] MAE, Fonds Beyrouth, série B, carton 5, dossier 61, Sûreté aux Armées, 31 March 1944.

of bringing Syria, Palestine and Transjordan into the fold. This was to become known in the party as the 'policy of stages'.[6]

The party resumed its activities simultaneously in Damascus and Beirut on 1 March 1944, the day of its leader's birthday. In Damascus, some fifty party members, mainly teachers and students, both Muslim and Christian, met for tea at the house of one of their number to hear a message from Ni'mat Thabit. 'You might ask what is our attitude towards the present government in Lebanon,' he declared.

> *I would answer that the elements that form that*
> *government are today the only forces able to paralyse*
> *the reactionary movement in the country, and put an*
> *end to the criminal manoeuvres, which nearly foiled the*
> *preparations you made for the decisive battle.*
>
> > *You might also ask about the attitude of the Allies*
> *towards you. This is my answer: The friendship of the*
> *Allied Powers, for which we worked for so long – and*
> *which our enemies, through their self-serving propaganda*
> *sought to prevent – has now been consolidated, thanks to*
> *our direct contacts with the Allied authorities. They now*
> *recognise our good intentions towards them, together with*
> *our attachment to the interests and rights of our country.*
> *We can say that we are now embarked on a stage of*
> *collaboration with the Allies which will continue and be*
> *permanently reinforced.*[7]

On 2 May 1944, the leadership of the party held a meeting at which it decided to lend its support to Riad el-Solh's government, on condition that he protect it from arrest by the British and French authorities. The next day, As'ad al-Ashqar and Ma'mun Ayass called on the prime minister to inform him of their decision. The party, they told him, had 3,000 members, but was short of weapons. Gratified by the party's attitude towards him, Riad el-Solh (according to French intelligence) promised to provide them with what they needed.[8] The line the party took in its

---

[6] MAE, Fonds Beyrouth, série B, carton 5, dossier 61, Sûreté aux Armées, 29 February 1944.

[7] MAE, Fonds Beyrouth, série B, carton 5, dossier 61, Délégation de Syrie, Damascus, 2 March 1944.

[8] MAE, Fonds Beyrouth, série B, carton 5, dossier 61, Sûreté des Armées, 6 May 1944.

propaganda was that Lebanon had been forced to abandon the isolationist policy of Lebanese nationalists, and was drawing closer to the Arabs. Nature dictated that Lebanon would be compelled to unite with its neighbours, in order to create a strong and viable 'Syrian' state.[9]

The Communist Party was outraged by Chamoun's decision to allow the PPS to re-emerge, and clamoured for it to be banned. Some 300 Communist Party activists, led by the party's leaders – Farajallah al-Hilu, Nicola Shawi, Tanius Diab, Mustafa al-'Ariss and Hasan Quraytem – held a meeting at the offices of *Sawt al-Sha'b* (The Voice of the People), the party organ, on 26 June to plan their campaign against the PPS. Antoine Thabit, fellow-traveller and head of the Anti-Fascist and Anti-Nazi League, sent a strongly worded telegram of denunciation to the prime minister:

> *At this decisive hour, when the world observes the struggle of free peoples against Fascism, and when Allied soldiers are shedding their blood to obliterate the Fascist and Nazi threat, the Minister of Interior of the Lebanese Government has allowed the PPS to rise from the dead, a party which was created by Fascism and whose leaders were and remain agents of Hitler in our country, enemies of our national cause, enemies of the democratic and constitutional regime, enemies of our Lebanese territorial integrity, and enemies of the pan-Arab idea.*
>
> *The Anti-Fascist and Anti-Nazi league protests energetically against this measure and asks that it be annulled, together with the protection which the Minister of Interior gives to the slaves of Fascism in this country.*[10]

Riad el-Solh's relations with the PPS blew hot and cold. Since his minister of interior had authorised their release, party members could not afford to be too hostile to him, although some rumblings and demonstrations at the base of the party caused Riad to have to summon Ni'mat Thabit, Ma'mun Ayass and As'ad al-Ashqar, and ask them to suspend their party meetings. The following month, however, and as if to make up for this, he contrived for them to arrange a PPS ceremony in

[9] MAE, Fonds Beyrouth, série B, carton 5, dossier 61, Sûreté aux Armées, 16 May 1944.
[10] MAE, Fonds Beyrouth, série B, carton 5, dossier 61, 27 June 1944.

his favour at Dhur Shwayr, to demonstrate that his government had the approval of the largely Christian inhabitants. The mayor of the village, 'Adil Mujais Hubaiqa, was given 5,000 Lebanese lira by the Ministry of Interior to put out flags and decorations for the occasion. Riad attended the ceremony, accompanied by the Emir Majid Arslan.[11]

That same month, a delegation of top party members called on Riad el-Solh to pledge their loyalty to his government, and to plead for the return of Antun Sa'ada to Lebanon. Their agitation was to prove ultimately successful.

The return of the leader

When Antun Sa'ada flew in to Beirut on 2 March 1947, he was welcomed by large numbers of rapturous supporters, which included delegations that had come from as far as Syria, Jordan and Palestine. He was driven at once to the house of one of his followers in the suburb of Ghobayri, where, from the balcony, he harangued the vast crowd gathered to hear him:

> O National Socialists!
> This is the happiest day of my life. I return among you after nine years of absence to join the flourishing groups that represent a nation that refuses to die.
> After fifteen years of stubborn struggle without precedent in the world, we are here today, a living nation, free and victorious; a nation which has triumphed over the will of foreigners, who wanted it to remain torn apart and divided into enemy communities and religions, although they all believed in one God.
> Like a new religion, united and unifying, our doctrine has come to raise up this nation towards the same sky and towards immortality.
> Our flags fly alone today. No flags of a foreign occupier fly beside them. And if our flags fly alone, the merit lies with your teachings, with your faith, with your action and your united struggle.

---

[11] MAE, Fonds Beyrouth, série B, carton 5, dossier 61, Sûreté aux Armées, 30 August 1944.

> *The independence which we now have is not the*
> *last stage on the road of life. It is only the step with which*
> *this great nation started out.*

Sa'ada paid homage to the fighting spirit of his followers, reminding his listeners that the only martyr to die fighting the French was a member of his party, killed at Bshamoun in November 1943. Lebanon's independence had released its people from jail, he declared, only to confine them in 'a state created by foreigners and surrounded by walls', which was aimed at preventing them from merging their destiny with that of the rest of the Syrian nation.

On 5 March 1947, Pierre Gemayel, the leader of the *Phalanges libanaises*, responded combatively to Sa'ada in the columns of his newspaper, *al-Amal*:

> *Between Lebanon and 'geographic Syria' one must choose.*
> *The Lebanese have chosen.*
> *Between Lebanese nationalism and 'socialist*
> *geographic-Syrian nationalism' no confusion or*
> *honourable compromise is possible.*
> *Mr Sa'ada freely takes up a position against the*
> *Lebanese Nation. The Nation must react. It will react. The*
> *State, the Government, the defenders of the Nation must*
> *also do their duty.*
> *Mr Sa'ada and his colleagues must certainly have*
> *weighed the implications of their actions: they must now*
> *assume responsibility for the consequences.*
> *No subtlety of language, no Byzantine discourse,*
> *can change matters anymore.*
> *Those whom the Lebanese know under the name*
> *of the 'Populaires' do not believe in the Lebanese Nation.*
> *They struggle against the Lebanese Nation. It is no longer*
> *a matter of freedom of opinion or belief: it is a matter of*
> *a crime against the State and the Nation. There can be no*
> *freedom for crime.*

On 6 March, Foreign Minister Hamid Frangieh declared in the Chamber: 'This man [Antun Sa'ada] has learned nothing. He has lost sight of the fact that the present regime stems from the National Pact of 1943, and that Lebanon is an entity that cannot be tampered with. No one will be allowed to tamper with it!' At the same session, Riad el-Solh himself spoke up:

> *Mr Sa'ada has been asked to present himself to the Sûreté Générale to explain his remarks. He has not done so, but has instead disappeared. This, in itself, is a charge against him. He will have to explain himself sooner or later.*
> *Rest assured that we will not hesitate to crush anyone who dares take action against the 1943 Pact and the independence of Lebanon.*

Sa'ada's speech was published on 5 March in the PPS organ, *Sada al-Nahda*, on the same day as Gemayel's riposte in *al-Amal*. The French-language newspapers did not reprint the speech, but launched their attack on Sa'ada on the 7th. The escalating press campaign compelled the government to intervene against 'a group which was dividing the country and annihilating its identity'. On 12 March, the PPS newspaper, *Sada al-Nahda*, was suspended. The Communist *Sawt al-Sha'b*, which had attacked Sa'ada with particular virulence, was suspended for nine days also.[12]

On 13 March, the *Procureur* (Prosecutor) of the Republic issued a warrant for Antun Sa'ada's arrest, following his failure to respond to a summons by the director of the *Sûreté Générale*. It seemed as if the government intended to react vigorously to the threat he posed to Lebanon's sovereignty and territorial integrity – highly sensitive and controversial issues in the charged climate of the time, when King 'Abdallah of Jordan and the regent in Iraq were both raring to redraw the map of the Levant.

But to general surprise, Antun Sa'ada was not arrested. He was known to be living comfortably in Madame Clodagh Thabit's villa near Beirut.[13] The correspondent of the Agence France Presse was able to interview him, followed by the correspondent of the Damascus newspaper, *al-Qabas*. 'What do you think of the measures the government has taken against you?' the *al-Qabas* journalist asked him. 'I declare',

---

12 MAE, Fonds Beyrouth, série B, carton 5, dossier 61, Note de l'attaché militaire à la Légation de France à Beyrouth, 18 April 1947.
13 MAE, Fonds Beyrouth (Amb.), carton 48, Légation de France, Note pour Monsieur le Ministre, Beirut, 25 March 1947.

Sa'ada replied, 'that they are not justified and smack of despotism. I repeat that my speech contained no attacks against the Lebanese regime, and that I have taken no action that would require such measures. Freedom of opinion and freedom of speech are two fundamental freedoms. Any government that seeks to stifle them is acting contrary to democratic principles'.

Yet, to many, it seemed as if the government did not dare arrest him. 'How much longer will the spy Sa'ada remain at liberty?' the Communist organ, *Sawt al-Sha'b*, demanded. Some thought that the British – or Anglophile members of the cabinet like Camille Chamoun – were protecting him, because they considered that the PPS might check the Communist threat to the country. Others believed that he was being given immunity because various politicians hoped to rally the party's 8,000 members to their side at the forthcoming elections. Others still thought that Syria had applied pressure on Lebanon in Sa'ada's favour, since his programme accorded with some Syrian ambitions. The French were certain that the British were intriguing to prevent Sa'ada's arrest. Sa'ada himself left Clodagh Thabit's villa after some weeks for the village of Bshamoun, where he was said to be under the 'protection' of the Emir Majid Arslan. After all, there were many Druze among the membership of the PPS.

Sa'ada restates his doctrine

On his return to Lebanon, one of Sa'ada's first acts was to dismiss his Higher Council and suspend the membership of Ni'mat Thabit, As'ad al-Ashqar, Mu'min Ayass, Georges 'Abd al-Masih and other pillars of the party, who – at considerable sacrifice to themselves – had kept the movement alive during his own long absence. By dismissing them in this brusque way, he no doubt wished to assert his full control over the party once more and to demonstrate his unchallenged personal authority. But his motive was also to express his intense disagreement with the concessions and compromises that these men had had to make in his absence. His return, therefore, immediately destroyed the conciliatory steps they had taken.

Sa'ada wasted no time in declaring that he intended to implement his party's programme to the full and as soon as possible, with the 'construction of natural Syria from the Taurus to al-'Arish'. Lebanon, he declared, had no particular vocation for independence, since its existence was no more than an artificial vestige of the 1860 massacres and the interwar mandatory period. The aim of his party was to impose, by all possible means, a Greater Syrian secular state, which would be concerned with neither the Sunni majority nor the Christian minority. In Beirut that same year, 1947, he published the principles of his party in a book entitled *Kitab al-ta'alim al-suriyya al-qawmiyya al-ijtima'iyya* (The Syrian Book of Nationalist and Social Teachings). A characteristic passage read: 'The Syrian *umma* is the unity of the Syrian people, born out of a lengthy history going back to prehistoric times'.[14]

As the region sank into the turmoil of the Palestine conflict, Sa'ada continued openly to defy the Lebanese police who had instructions to arrest him. His followers threatened to kidnap the chief of police if he persisted in seeking to obey the government's instructions. As a result, Sa'ada remained at liberty, and barely under surveillance. The French ambassador reported to Paris that he had even asked for an audience at the ambassador's summer residence at Aley, 'which of course I could not grant him'.[15] And, as the Arabs staggered to defeat, Sa'ada, in a series of fiery articles, cast doubt on Arabism, calling it 'a doctrine that has failed', and claiming that it 'was responsible for the defeat of Arab armies in Palestine'.[16]

Sa'ada did not bother to remain discreetly in Beirut, but travelled openly and freely about Syria. In November 1948, the French consul general in Aleppo reported that he was seen spending a few days at Baron's Hotel, a historic landmark of the city, where he received numerous visitors, gave interviews and attended receptions in his honour, before planning to proceed to Latakia on a tour of inspection of party branches. The Arabs, Sa'ada told the press, should accept the fait accompli of a division of Palestine with Israel. In the context of the times, this was a highly incendiary remark. For some, it confirmed Sa'ada's British connection. The French, for example, were convinced that Sa'ada owed his freedom of movement and of expression to the British. Was not Kamal Khawli, the head of his party branch in Aleppo,

---

[14] Antun Sa'ada, *Kitab al-ta'alim al-suriyya al-qawmiyya al-ijtima'iyya*, Beirut 1947, p. 17.

[15] MAE, Fonds Beyrouth (Amb.), série B, carton 48, Situation politique, Beirut, 13 August 1948.

[16] Labib Zuwiya Yamak, *The Syrian Social Nationalist Party: An Ideological Analysis*, Cambridge 1966, p. 65.

employed as a press officer at the British consulate?[17] It seems more probable, however, that Sa'ada was merely taking advantage of the government's weakness under the impact of the Palestine defeat.

It needs to be remembered that Sa'ada was operating at a time of great disturbance – not least in men's minds. Israel's violent emergence had redrawn the map. 'Abdallah's political and territorial ambitions, and his annexation of what was left of Arab Palestine, had once more revived the nervous debate over Greater Syria. Arab regimes were weak and discredited. The blow inflicted on Arab nationalism, as well as the petty squabbles of Arab leaders themselves, had created a sense that everything was now up for grabs. Sa'ada seems to have felt that the historic moment had come for the creation of his Greater Syrian nation.

In Beirut, Riad el-Solh watched these escalating developments with some gloom. There was much about Sa'ada that he did not like, since Riad was by instinct a democrat, believing in political pluralism. Sa'ada's instincts, on the other hand, were unapologetically authoritarian. In negotiation, Sa'ada would remain rigid and uncompromising, whereas Riad would try to understand the other person's point of view in order to reach a compromise. Sa'ada's open disparagement of Lebanon's independence – which he dismissed as nothing but an artificial and temporary phenomenon – upset Riad, as it belittled his own achievement of having won Lebanon's freedom from the French. Sa'ada's mystical and confused pan-Syrianism had upstaged and even hijacked Riad's own lifelong ideal of Syrian unity. Bu whereas Riad had always viewed Syrian unity as a stepping-stone to greater Arab unity, Sa'ada made it his ultimate and *non-Arab* destination. The ideological chasm between the two men was unbridgeable. There were other areas too where Sa'ada came perilously close to robbing Riad el-Solh of his most cherished ideals. Sa'ada preached the end of confessionalism and the creation of a Greater Syrian nation, built not on religion or ethnicity, but on a sense of common citizenship. This was a goal Riad, too, had set himself for Lebanon. But he had so far been unable to achieve it. In the meantime, Sa'ada's own provocative statements, as well as the unchecked muscle-flexing of his followers, began to pose a threat to the physical security of the Lebanese state.

[17] MAE, Fonds Beyrouth (Amb.), série B, carton 48, M. Charles Clair, Consul-Général de France à Alep, à M. Jean Serres, Ministre de France en Syrie, Alep, 26 November 1948.

The violent entry of a second revolutionary

Such was the situation when another revolutionary burst upon the scene. Syria's chief of staff, Colonel Husni al-Za'im, seized power in Damascus on 30 March 1949, dealing a devastating blow to the existing parliamentary order by this brutal intrusion of the army into politics – Syria's first. President Shukri al-Quwatli, the veteran nationalist and father of independence, was arrested unceremoniously in hospital where he was receiving treatment for a gastric ulcer and a heart complaint. In Beirut, Riad el-Solh and Bishara al-Khoury viewed these dramatic developments with the greatest anger and distaste. It was now evident that Za'im represented an even greater threat to Lebanon's fragile independence than had Antun Sa'ada's PPS.

Seen from Beirut, it was ominous that Husni al-Za'im was assisted, in planning and carrying out his coup, by two rising figures on the Syrian political scene, Lieutenant Colonel Adib al-Shishakli and Akram al-Hawrani, both known for their links with the PPS. Shishakli was the Syrian officer who, early in the 1948 war, had captured the village of Malikiyya just across the border into Palestine – a village subsequently retaken by the Israelis. Hawrani was a populist leader from Hama, who had mobilised the peasantry to make war on the landowners of the central Syrian plain. Their closeness to Za'im had quickly heightened the threat that he posed. When Antun Sa'ada then visited Damascus and was hailed by the new military dictator, the danger to Lebanon became acute.

Little was known about Za'im, save that he was a rough, ener-getic and fast-talking personality. President Quwatli had promoted him to chief of staff after the early defeats of the Syrian army in the Palestine War. Za'im had managed to perform reasonably well, consid-ering the inadequate resources in men and equipment available to him. Of Kurdish minority background, he had initially been recruited and trained in the French *Troupes Spéciales*, like so many other men from Syria's various minorities. Indeed, the French may have seen Za'im's coup as a chance to recover some of their lost influence in Syria, and defeat President Quwatli, who had fought them and their influence for so long. It was indeed remarkable that the French ambassador took to paying this strongman daily visits.

It soon emerged, however, that Za'im had had a chequered past. Like many men in the *Troupes* during the Second World War, he had had to adapt to rapid and abrupt changes in French political authority – from the pre-war Mandate, to Vichy, to General de Gaulle – switching allegiance often and seamlessly. In 1941, the Vichy authorities instructed him to raise a band of guerrilla fighters with which to harass the Allies, whose invasion of Syria was expected at any moment. He was given a large sum of money, and prisons were thrown open to allow him to recruit common criminals into his force. But instead of fighting the Allies, Za'im pocketed the cash and took to crime instead. He used his bunch of desperados to extort money from landowners and merchants in and around Damascus. He even staged a fake execution of one such landowner, 'Umar Qawadri, to get him to stump up. When the British and the Free French defeated Vichy and took control, Za'im was arrested, tried and sentenced to ten years in jail.

Irrepressible as ever, he pestered the Free French for clemency, and managed to get himself released from prison and placed instead under house arrest in Lebanon. He was eventually let back into Syria. There, posing as a victim of the changing fortunes of war, he managed to get his sentence reviewed.

Not everyone among the French was happy with this turn of events. In 1944, Colonel Oliva-Roget, General Beynet's representative in Damascus, wrote to the judicial authorities of the French Army of the Levant, urging them not to give Za'im a pardon or reinstate him in the *Troupes*. Any such move, Oliva-Roget warned, would expose the French to charges of weakness and incompetence, and would endanger those officers in the *Troupes* who had agreed to testify against Za'im. These would now be exposed to his revenge.[18] But Oliva-Roget's prescient warnings went unheeded. Za'im recovered his rank, and soon gave a sinister demonstration of his power by staging his military *coup d'état* of March 1949.

The fall of the old regime

Za'im and his fellow officers, of course, thought themselves possessed of legitimate grievances against the government. It had neglected to

---

[18] MAE, Nantes, Fonds Beyrouth, série B, carton 5, le Colonel Oliva-Roget, représentant en Syrie le Général d'Armée, Délégué Général et Plénipotentiaire de la France au Levant, à Monsieur le Commissaire du Gouvernement auprès du 2e Tribunal Militaire du Q. G. des Troupes du Levant, Damascus, 31 August 1944.

re-equip the army, and had proved unprepared to face the Zionist challenge. No doubt Syria's courageous and well-meaning National Bloc, which had waged the bloody interwar battle for independence from the French, when people like Za'im had been in French service and pay, was not in the best shape to assume the burden of government. Between August 1943 and 1947, it had to labour against terrible odds. The French refused to relinquish power before extracting from the Syrian government a treaty to secure their economic, strategic and cultural interests. The contest was only resolved by a bloody trial of strength.

The National Bloc suffered a further blow with the death, on 20 June 1947, of Sa'dallah al-Jabiri – the uncle of Riad el-Solh's wife, Fayza – who was a brave Bloc leader, and one of the few men whose reputation and authority had survived the trials of the preceding years. Sa'dallah's death weakened the Bloc, but it strengthened President Quwatli's position, since Sa'dallah had persistently opposed Quwatli's wish to amend the Constitution, so as to allow himself to stand for re-election for a second five-year presidential term – an ambition much like that of Bishara al-Khoury in Lebanon. Elections were held in Syria in July 1947, following which the government did, indeed, table a bill amending the Constitution, which led to Quwatli's re-election in April 1948. The extension was believed by some to have blocked a movement of political and social reform in the country when this would still have been possible by peaceful means. It may have contributed to the overthrow of Syria's parliamentary system a year later.

In the meantime, the Bloc had split into two: a National Party, *al-hizb al-watani*, with Damascus as its stronghold, where men like Quwatli himself, Jamil Mardam, Faris al-Khuri, Lutfi al-Haffar and Sabri al-'Asali each had a personal following; and a People's Party, *hizb al-sha'b*, based in Aleppo and led by such men as Rushdi Kikhia, Nazim al-Qudsi and Mustafa Barmada. The People's Party primarily represented business interests in northern Syria, which had traditional links with Iraq. However, it also won the support of the influential landed family of the Atasis, whose fief was Homs, and who were opposed to the monopoly rule of Damascus politicians.

President Shukri al-Quwatli, who had been too trusting of his associates and appointees – like Husni al-Za'im, most spectacularly – governed a country that was being eroded at the base by price inflation, crop failures due to drought, and rumblings of discontent from emerging labour unions. Exhausted veteran politicians, their energies already spent in the decades-long battle with the French; untried institutions; and a young, ill-trained and ill-equipped army – all were soon to suffer the trauma of the Palestine War. This, then, was the context for Husni al-Zaim's coup of March 1949.[19]

Za'im's rebellion was no isolated phenomenon. It was the symptom of a general disturbance in the region caused by the Arab defeat. Aftershocks were to follow thick and fast over the following years. In Egypt, Prime Minister Nuqrashi Pasha was murdered by a member of the Muslim Brotherhood in December 1948. A guerrilla war was waged against the British garrisons in the Canal Zone. King 'Abdallah of Jordan was revealed as a traitor to the Arab cause, and lost any hope of realising his Greater Syrian project. He fell to an assassin's bullet in 1951. In Cairo in January 1952, an explosion of nationalist anger – triggered by Britain's brutal siege of an Egyptian police barracks at Ismailia, in which forty-one policemen were killed and another seventy-two wounded – released an explosion of killing and destruction, which came to be known as 'Black Saturday'. The mob's chosen targets – among them Shepheard's Hotel, Barclays Bank and the British Turf Club – symbolised the hated alliance between foreigners and Egyptian pashas.

Enraged by their government's lack of preparation for the war in Palestine, Gamal Abd al-Nasser's 'Free Officers' seized power that summer, deposing King Farouk. In 1954, they reached an agreement with Britain for the withdrawal of its troops. But in 1956, Britain, France and Israel invaded Egypt, in an attempt to break Nasser's independent government and his nationalisation of the Suez Canal Company, only to be compelled by the United States to withdraw ignominiously. Anthony Eden, Britain's prime minister at the time, was forced from office, and British prestige in the region suffered a blow from which it never recovered. The Hashemite regime in Iraq managed to hang on until 1958, when the monarchy was overthrown, the royal family butchered and Britain's man there, Nuri al-Sa'id, lynched by the mob.

---

[19] For a more extensive account of these events, see Seale, *The Struggle for Syria*, pp. 24–100.

Husni al-Za'im and Antun Sa'ada

Za'im's putsch in Damascus in March 1949 seems to have spurred Sa'ada to think of seizing power in Lebanon, perhaps as a first step towards his pan-Syrian union. Many Lebanese opposition politicians had traditionally sought support in Damascus against their own government, and Sa'ada now made the mistake of taking the same road. He was received by the Syrian dictator and discussed plans for a coup in Lebanon. Each hoped that he could put the other to use: Za'im saw in Sa'ada an instrument for bringing down Riad el-Solh, who was not only an ally of Quwatli, but whom the paranoid Za'im also suspected of despising him and personally wishing to bring about his downfall. He presented Sa'ada with a silver pistol as a token of friendship. Sa'ada, in turn, may have seen in Za'im a temporary vehicle with which to realise his own ambition, to be discarded when the time came to take over the whole of Syria.

The Lebanese government hesitated for three long weeks – from 30 March to 23 April – before recognising Za'im's government. Bishara al-Khoury and Riad el-Solh were outraged that this jumped-up military dictator had dared to lock up Shukri al-Quwatli. He was now receiving members of the Lebanese opposition and was evidently hostile to the Lebanese state. Za'im, in turn, was annoyed at being cold-shouldered and so obviously regarded with disdain. On 4 April, he even accused Riad el-Solh of inspiring attacks on him in the Lebanese press, and on the 14th, he sent a message to President Bishara al-Khoury, accusing Riad of actually plotting to kill him, in association with Ahmad Charabati, the mild and well-mannered former Syrian defence minister, who had taken refuge in Beirut. Za'im, in petty retaliation for his baseless accusations, forbade the export of Syrian meat to Lebanon, thereby driving up the price on the Lebanese market, together with that of butter, milk, oil, fruit and vegetables. It looked as if Syria and Lebanon were once again headed for a serious confrontation.

Za'im's coup had implications well beyond Lebanon. It put Syria back in play in the regional power struggle between the Hashemites in Jordan and Iraq, and their opponents in Egypt and Saudi Arabia. Everyone wanted to know to which side the upstart Colonel would tilt. Za'im began by looking to Iraq for support – even proposing the immediate conclusion of a military agreement with Baghdad – in the belief that this might strengthen his hand in Syria's armistice talks with Israel. But Nuri al-Sa'id – much like Riad el-Solh – considered Za'im a dangerous adventurer, who had thrown open the door to violent army takeovers in the Middle East, which, miserably enough, of course, he had. Nuri was, therefore, not inclined to rush into any partnership with him.

The irritable and no doubt unstable Za'im was deeply offended by this. He veered abruptly away from Iraq and towards Egypt. After paying a secret visit on 21 April to King Farouk's estate at Inshas, he succumbed to the king's flattery. Farouk was as lavish and open-handed as Nuri al-Sa'id had been careful and circumspect. Za'im impulsively declared that he adored everything Egyptian. He reassured the king about his peaceful intentions towards Lebanon, and his total opposition to all Hashemite projects. Arm in arm, the king and the colonel toured the royal plantations together, before an Egyptian Spitfire escort started Za'im on his return flight to Damascus.

He seemed a changed man after this heady brush with royalty, and this brief glimpse of the gravitas and grandeur of the Egyptian state. He withdrew his accusations against Riad el-Solh, soon receiving several official Lebanese envoys – Foreign Minister Hamid Frangieh; Muhammad 'Ali Hamadi, the head of the Foreign Ministry's Arab department; and the Emir Farid Chehab, director of the *Sûreté*. Within a few days of the visit, Egypt, Saudi Arabia and Lebanon recognised his regime, and, on 24 April, forced to conceal his visceral distaste, Riad el-Solh travelled to Damascus to meet the colonel. The encounter was not cordial, but it was correct. Warning his host against becoming implicated in the intrigues of the Lebanese opposition, Riad stressed the need for Syria to respect Lebanon's territorial and political independence. He also secured a promise that Shukri al-Quwatli would be allowed to leave his prison in Damascus for exile in Cairo with his family. During this visit, Za'im let fly against King 'Abdallah and Nuri al-Sa'id, denouncing their twin projects of 'Greater Syria' and of 'Fertile Crescent'. Indeed, he soon closed Syria's border with Jordan and massed troops against Iraq.

Syria and Lebanon were now back on talking terms. On 26 April, Hasan Jabara, the head of the Syrian delegation to the Higher Council of Common Interests, came to Beirut for negotiations. These resulted in trade returning to normal. Damascus authorised the export to Lebanon of 20,000 head of cattle, as well as many agricultural products.

But these thawing relations suffered a severe blow in mid-May, when a Syrian hit team crossed the border clandestinely into Lebanon, and assassinated a Lebanese citizen of Syrian origin, Kamil Husayn al-Yusuf, at his home near Hasbaya, claiming that he had been sending intelligence to the Israelis. His killers were Syrian army soldiers, under the command of Captain Akram Tabbara. Lebanese gendarmes were tipped off and managed to arrest the group. The Syrians immediately demanded that Tabbara and his men be returned to them. When Lebanon refused to extradite them, Syria closed the border. The dispute became a personal trial of strength between Husni al-Za'im and his boorish Prime Minister Muhsin al-Barazi on the one hand, and, on the other, Bishara al-Khoury and Riad el-Solh.

Egypt and Saudi Arabia attempted to mediate. They recognised Lebanon's right to put Tabbara and his men on trial, but called on it nevertheless to hand them over to Syria, if only in the interest of good relations. In his memoirs, the Emir 'Adil Arslan, who was then a member of the Syrian government, alleged that Kamil Husayn al-Yusuf – whom he described as the 'murdered spy' – had once given Za'im a bribe of 50,000 Syrian pounds from Zionist funds, when Za'im was in command of the Syrian front in 1948. Za'im, he said, had had al-Yusef murdered in order to bury this guilty secret.[20] In early June, Tabbara and his men were returned to Syria to stand trial there, but were quickly released. As a result of their extradition, trade between Syria and Lebanon returned once more to normal.

If Za'im had indeed taken a Zionist bribe during the war, which is more than probable, then it must be seen not only as an example of his own avarice, but as further evidence of Israel's deep penetration of its Arab neighbours. Shortly after seizing power, Za'im secretly offered Israel full peace, with an immediate exchange of ambassadors, normal economic relations and the settlement in Syria of 300,000 Palestinian refugees. In exchange, he wanted Israel to agree to moving the Syrian border to the middle of the Sea of Galilee. But Ben-Gurion did not consider the price worth paying. He considered, no doubt, that armistice

---

[20] Al-Amir 'Adil Arslan, *Mudhakkarat al-amir 'Adil Arslan*, 3 vols, Beirut 1983, vol. II, pp. 831–43, 877. Arslan quotes as his source a statement by the Syrian Golan princely tribal chief, the Emir Fa'ur al-Fa'ur. For Bishara al-Khoury's account of the crisis, see his memoirs, *Haqa'iq lubnaniyya*, vol. III, pp. 222–5. This paragraph is drawn from Beydoun, 'Riad el-Solh et les élections législatives de 1943', p. 452, n. 176. For the impact of the affair on economic relations between Syria and Lebanon, see Youssef Chaitani, *Post-Colonial Syria and Lebanon*, pp. 134, 137–8.

agreements – which did not involve making any concessions to the Arabs or giving up an inch of territory – met Israel's essential needs of recognition and security far better than Za'im's extraordinary offer.[21]

The first ominous clashes

It was at just this moment that Antun Sa'ada's quarrel with Lebanon took a nasty turn. It began, almost by accident, with a clash between the PPS and the *Phalanges libanaises* in the Beirut suburb of Jummayza, where the PPS had their printing works. Hostility between the two movements had been building up over the previous three months, and feelings on both sides were dangerously overheated. Jummayza was a *Phalangist* fief, but it was there that the PPS provocatively chose, in early June 1949, to hold a meeting at which Antun Sa'ada delivered a fighting speech, in which he did not neglect to aim several broadsides at the *Phalanges*.

A day or two later, on the night of 9–10 June, the *Phalanges*, in turn, held a meeting at Jummayza, very close to the café where the PPS had held theirs, and a mere stone's throw from the works where the PPS printed its journal, *al-Jil al-Jadid*. The *Phalanges* had just ended their meeting, when Antun Sa'ada came out of the printing works and drove off in his car, to fervent cries from his followers of 'Long live the Leader!' The *Phalangists* responded with cries of 'Long live Lebanon!' and 'Long live Pierre Gemayel!' As the Beirut press later reported, some PPS members then fired shots at the *Phalangists*, who fired back. In the general firefight that followed, seven PPS men were hit and wounded, and fell to the ground. Others barricaded themselves into the printing works. This was then attacked and set on fire. When the police arrived, flames could be seen rising from the building. In the meantime, the *Phalangists* had managed to take prisoner eighteen PPS members, whom they then handed over to the police.[22]

An investigation into the incident began at 11 p.m. that very night and continued through the next day. It was conducted by the general prosecutor of the Appeal Court in person, assisted by the director-general of the Ministry of Interior, the director of the *Sûreté*

---

[21] For a full account of Za'im's dealings with Israel, see Itamar Rabinovich, *The Road not Taken: Early Arab-Israeli Negotiations*, Oxford 1991.
[22] *Le Jour*, 11 June 1949.

Générale and the commander of the gendarmerie. Within twenty-four hours, 150 members of the PPS were arrested in Beirut and surrounding districts, and a further 100 the next day. Fifty members of the *Phalanges* were also arrested.[23] Explosives and weapons, including two machine guns, were found by the police at the printing works, while firearms and grenades were discovered at the homes of PPS party members in Beirut and its suburbs, together with incriminating documents suggesting, the police said, that the party had been conspiring, not only against the *Phalanges*, but against the state itself. The party was outlawed, but Sa'ada himself escaped arrest. He was suspected to be hiding in the house of one of his party members in the Beirut area.[24]

The assault on the state

The crisis then escalated into something a great deal more serious than a shoot-out between rival paramilitary youth movements. A series of armed attacks now launched by the PPS were at once seen as an attempt to overthrow the government. From the earliest days of his movement, Antun Sa'ada had given great attention to what he called 'military matters'. His uniformed squads – who liked to march, salute and parade in their uniforms – were the backbone of his party. They were the instrument with which he attracted angry young men and, more importantly, intimidated his opponents. Colonel Za'im in Damascus, showing his true colours as an anti-democrat and a military adventurer, immediately offered Sa'ada arms and men, if he would undertake to overthrow Riad el-Solh's government. Sa'ada accepted the arms – which Za'im had shamelessly taken from the gun-racks of the Syrian gendarmerie – but refused the men, not wishing to give Za'im the opportunity to dictate terms to him in Lebanon. But the assault he soon launched against the Lebanese state was woefully inept. As a military tactician, he was revealed to be utterly incompetent.

The assault started with a series of uncoordinated attacks against Lebanese gendarmerie posts near the Syrian frontier and in the mountains near Beirut. On the night of 2–3 July, a band of armed PPS members gathered at the Lebanese village of Mtain. Their mission was to attack the

---

[23] Beirut to Foreign Office, 11 June 1949 (FO 371/75320).
[24] Beirut to Foreign Office, 11 and 22 June 1949 (FO 371/75320); Légation de France, Beirut, 13 June 1947.

local gendarmerie post. Later that night, another band was sent to attack the post at Harat Hraik. Although not particularly lethal, these attacks served to alert the commander of the Lebanese gendarmerie that this was something more serious than the usual banditry that was common in those parts. All police and gendarmerie posts were immediately put on alert. They were, therefore, not taken by surprise when Sa'ada struck again with far larger numbers on the night of 4–5 July.

That night, over a hundred party members assembled in Damascus, and were transported by buses to a point about 10 kilometres from the Lebanese border. There, Antun Sa'ada and his military aide, Asaf Karam, awaited them. Sa'ada then delivered a fighting speech and distributed arms and ammunition to each man. One group headed for Rashaya, while another took the road for the village of Mashghara.

A little before midnight, the first group, brandishing rifles and machine guns, was halted by a gendarmerie patrol. Shooting broke out which lasted for nearly an hour, before the PPS men managed to drive off, heading back to Syria in their vehicles, but leaving a trail of blood behind them. An assistant driver of one of the buses, a Syrian named 'Abd al-Salam Ma'kuk, was arrested. This group had apparently intended to seize the fort at Rashaya. It was led by the Emir Zayd Hasan al-Atrash, a Druze member of the PPS, and was mainly composed of Syrian Druze and Palestinians.

The second group, which was about sixty strong, managed to reach its destination of Mashghara undetected. Asaf Karam and his men dispersed in nearby caves and in an abandoned mill, where they rested for a while, before surrounding and attacking the gendarmerie post at midnight. Two gendarmes sustained bullet wounds. A Lebanese army unit then raced to the aid of the post, routed the attackers and chased them to a nearby village, where, in a fierce firefight, Asaf Karam was killed. His companions all surrendered.

At dawn on 5 July, the gendarmes learned that a suspicious-looking car had been seen on a bridge over the Litani river. The road leading to the bridge was immediately closed and the vehicle stopped and searched. It was found to contain three Syrians and two Lebanese, in possession of 5,000 tracts by Antun Sa'ada, in which he declared war on the Lebanese government from the 'Headquarters of the First Popular Social Revolution'.[25] Later that day, two of the men who had

---

[25] *Le Jour*, 6 July 1949.

attacked the post at Mtain gave themselves up and made confessions, implicating other party members.

Fully alert by this time to the danger posed by the PPS, Captain Tawfiq Chamoun, commander of the gendarmerie for the Aley region, learned that large numbers of armed men were camped in the woods at Sarhamul. Going forwards, he saw that they were more numerous than he had expected. He returned to his command post and called for reinforcements. An army unit arrived and prepared to engage. Captain Chamoun went forwards with it, but when he paused to observe the rebels through his binoculars, he was shot through the head and died instantly.

The PPS band was eventually surrounded and surrendered to the army. The untimely death of the young army captain aroused great emotion throughout the country, especially, but not exclusively, in the Maronite community to which he belonged. By 7 July, some 900 members and sympathisers of Antun Sa'ada's party had been arrested. As the prisons could not hold them all, an army barracks on the outskirts of Beirut was turned into a detention centre. In a statement to the press, Gabriel Murr, the deputy prime minister and minister of interior, announced that the party had attempted to seize power by a military *coup d'état*, in order to carry out its project of a Greater Syria.[26]

Meanwhile, phone lines between Beirut and Damascus were extremely busy – between the gendarmerie and army commands on both sides of the border, and, more significantly, between the office of the Lebanese prime minister and the Syrian Presidency. No one was ever to know exactly what Riad el-Solh said to Husni al-Za'im, but he may have threatened him. According to Hanna Ghusn, owner of *al-Diyar* – a paper which often reflected the government's views – Riad el-Solh told Za'im that Lebanon would attack Syria, with military assistance from both Iraq and Turkey, unless Za'im withdrew his backing for the PPS.[27] Others said that Riad 'bought' Antun Sa'ada from the notoriously greedy Za'im for a large sum of money. Za'im's Prime Minister Muhsin al-Barazi – who was known to detest

---

[26] *Le Jour*, 7 July 1949.

[27] A statement made by Hanna Ghosn at a private party given at Bayt Meri, on 9 July 1949, by Alexandre Riachi, president of the Lebanese Press Syndicate, on the occasion of the Riachi daughter's birthday. Among the guests were Husni al-Barazi, Camille Chamoun, Alfred Thabit, Sa'di Munla and several journalists; Fonds Beyrouth (Amb.), série 199A4, carton 20, 11 July 1949.

Sa'ada – was believed to have helped persuade the colonel to hand him over to the Lebanese. Za'im also received calls from Cairo and Riyadh, urging him to cooperate with the Lebanese authorities. For his part, Riad el-Solh later told Houstoun-Boswall, the British minister in Beirut, that Za'im had financed and armed the PPS. But when he realised that his behaviour might drive the Lebanese government into the arms of the Hashemites, he had quickly abandoned the party and handed over its leader, although well aware that Sa'ada would be executed.[28]

Within hours of the intense phone calls between Damascus and Beirut, the Syrian authorities started rounding up those PPS members in their own country. They managed to lay their hands on the Emir Hasan al-Atrash, who had led the abortive attack on Rashaya, and promised Lebanon that they would hand him over for trial. Sa'ada's long-suffering wife, Juliette Mir, and her three daughters – the youngest only a few months old at the time – were seized in a suburb of Latakia, at the house of a PPS member. Several Lebanese security officers went over to Damascus, where they helped in the arrest of some thirty Syrian and Lebanese PPS members in Latakia, Tartus, Safita, Banias and Jableh. These were brought to Beirut and locked up.

Meanwhile, in Damascus, the duplicitous Za'im invited Sa'ada to the presidential palace, where, after being courteously received, he was overpowered and taken under guard, in the night of 6–7 July, to the Lebanese border, where he was handed over to the Emir Farid Chehab, director-general of Lebanon's *Sûreté Générale* – on 'condition' that he be killed on the journey to Beirut. These were Za'im's specific terms. Sa'ada was to be shot, while 'attempting escape',[29] no doubt to protect the colonel from the charge of betrayal, and to conceal the detailed secrets of Za'im's actual dealings with him.

President Bishara al-Khoury relates in his memoirs that he was woken that night by a phone call at 2.30 in the morning. It was Riad el-Solh, informing him of Antun Sa'ada's extradition from Syria and his arrest by the Lebanese authorities. The president was amazed because, like most people, he assumed that Za'im would use Sa'ada for an attack on Lebanon, and would not give him up quite so lightly. Bishara al-Khoury dressed hurriedly and went to collect Riad on the way to the

---

[28] British Commonwealth Relations Office, Outward Telegram, 25 July 1949 (FO 371/75320).
[29] Beirut to Foreign Office, 7 July 1949 (FO 371/75320).

office. It was only then that Riad el-Solh told him that the Emir Farid Chehab had phoned to convey Za'im's terms – namely to kill Sa'ada en route. Riad told the president that he had instructed Chehab to ignore these instructions, and to bring the PPS leader to Beirut instead, and lock him up in a military barracks.

The president and the prime minister then sat down to discuss what should be done. The army commander, the Emir Fu'ad Chehab, was called in to give his views. Bishara al-Khoury was concerned that the unstable Za'im might react violently once he learned that Sa'ada had not, after all, been killed in the manner that he had demanded. So, at 5 a.m., Shaykh Bishara rang the presidential palace in Damascus to explain. But there was no answer. Finally, at 6 a.m., Husni al-Za'im himself picked up the phone. After thanking him for his support for Lebanon, Bishara al-Khoury told him that Sa'ada would shortly be put on trial before a military court for treason, in accordance with the country's law. 'That's fine,' Za'im said abruptly, ending the conversation – to the astonishment and relief of the Lebanese officials.[30]

A little while later that morning, the Lebanese cabinet met in extraordinary session and decided, no doubt mistakenly, to try Sa'ada in accordance with the state of emergency, which had been declared on 14 May 1948, at the official start of the Palestine War. A complete blackout was ordered on the affair. Charges against Sa'ada were hastily drawn up and the military court went into session at 1 p.m. The president of the court, Major Anwar Karam, was assisted by Captain Semrani, Lieutenant Ahdab, Judge Gabriel Bassila, as well as by the General Prosecutor Yusuf Sherbel, and his deputy, Michel Talhameh. Sa'ada's defence lawyer, Emile Lahoud, requested a forty-eight-hour delay in which to study the case, but this was refused. He therefore stepped down, and was replaced by Lieutenant Elias Rizqallah.

The trial was held behind closed doors. It was attended only by the minister of defence and a number of senior officers. The road outside the court room – rue Fouad 1er – was closed to traffic. The press was not allowed in, except during a short suspension of the proceedings around 5 p.m. Sa'ada sat in the dock, calm but evidently exhausted and dejected.

The charges were then read out. Antun Khalil Sa'ada was accused of attempting to seize power and overthrow the regime by

---

[30] Al-Khoury, *Haqa'iq lubnaniyya*, vol. II, pp. 240–1.

armed force; of attacking gendarmerie posts as well as army posts, officers and other ranks; of killing Captain Tawfiq Chamoun and attempting to kill other agents of the security forces. Sa'ada then spoke for two hours in his own defence. He explained the political philosophy of his movement at some length. He recalled the harassment his members had suffered since the incident at Jummayza, to which his members had had no alternative but to respond. He denied that he was the author of the tracts calling for revolution. Seven witnesses were called – Syrians, Palestinians and Lebanese. They all confirmed that Sa'ada had distributed arms to his members and called on them to rise against the government. The general prosecutor demanded the death penalty.

At 8 p.m. on 7 July, the military court sentenced Sa'ada to death in accordance with Article 79 of the Military Code of Justice. The file was passed to the Amnesty Commission, which confirmed the sentence. After hearing the defence of the condemned man, and before taking the decision on Sa'ada's fate, the president called a meeting attended by Riad el-Solh and the Emir Farid Chehab, as well as by Habib Abi Chahla and Gabriel al-Murr, notables of Sa'ada's own Greek Orthodox community. According to a note by the Emir Farid Chehab, Riad el-Solh expressed the opinion that he disliked executions. President Khoury said nothing. But the two Greek Orthodox notables were adamant that Sa'ada should be executed. No doubt they considered him a dangerous upstart, who posed a threat to their dominant position in their community. This aspect of the circumstances of Sa'ada's execution remained unknown for more than half a century, and was only revealed on the publication of the Emir Farid Chehab's reports in 2006.[31]

President Bishara al-Khoury then signed the decree authorising the sentence to be carried out. At 3 a.m. on 8 July, a Greek Orthodox priest spent some moments alone with Sa'ada, who asked for a cup of coffee and a cigarette, while he drew up his will and testament. At 3.30 a.m. he was taken by soldiers to the place of execution in the barracks. His eyes were bound and his hands tied behind his back. In accordance with army regulations, he was made to kneel and was tied to a stake. At 3.40 a.m., an officer gave the order to fire. Less than twenty-four hours had passed between Sa'ada's arrest and his execution.[32]

[31] Ahmad Asfahani (ed.), *Antun Sa'ada wa'l hizb al-suri al-ijtima'i: fi 'awraq al-'amir Farid Chehab, al-mudir al-'amm lil 'amn al-'amm al-lubnani*, Beirut 2006.
[32] Beirut to Foreign Office, 8 July 1949 (FO 371/75320).

Jacques Barre, the Agence France Presse correspondent in Beirut, cabled Paris on 8 July with news of Sa'ada's death. 'Known as the "Führer" by his followers', he wrote, 'he was a curious figure who had sought to place himself among the ranks of the great dictators'. On 9 July, Lebanon Radio announced a reward of 10,000 Lebanese lira – a fortune at the time – for information leading to the arrest of Georges 'Abd al-Massih, one of Sa'ada's earliest and most devoted followers, who now succeeded him as the head of the party. He had led the rebel group in the Sarhamoul woods that killed Captain Tawfiq Chamoun. The police were also looking for As'ad al-Ashqar, and several other party members.

Also on 9 July, Ghassan Tuéni, editor-in-chief of the Beirut daily *al-Nahar*, published a bombshell of an article, under the head-line, 'Sa'ada, the martyred criminal'. It was to land him in jail for three months. Tuéni had been a member of the PPS in the past, and had clearly retained some sympathy for it. In his article, he denounced what was indeed an over-hasty execution of Sa'ada.

'The authorities', Tuéni wrote,

> have managed to lay their hands on Antun Sa'ada, to interrogate him, try him, condemn him to death, confirm the sentence and execute him – all with such speed as to plunge the world into consternation. The event has outstripped the understanding of the public. No one has been able to grasp the motives for such speed, and the drama has borne down on the Lebanese with all its weight. Even those who disapproved of Sa'ada's doctrine could not restrain themselves from exclaiming: This is monstrous!
>
> The public does not know whether Antun Sa'ada was executed or assassinated, whether it was a trial or a plot . . . Sa'ada was accused of launching an insurrection and armed attacks against the security forces, of having incited sabotage and assassination. Accusations of this sort can be made against a gang leader . . . But Anton Sa'ada did not spark a revolt for the sake of a revolt, nor did he incite his followers to attack, rebel, and commit crimes for the pleasure of attacking, rebelling and killing. No! Anton Sa'ada was a man with a doctrine, the bearer of a message, the leader of an organised political party. But the Court chose to ignore that.

If the authorities were determined to rid themselves of this man as quickly as possible, for fear that he would bring the sky down on their heads, we say to them that they have thus, by their own hand, forged a giant greater than Antun Sa'ada in strength and grandeur. They have made him a martyr, not only in the eyes of his followers, but also in those of many others who, at bottom, did not wish him any other ending.[33]

Sixty-eight members of the PPS stood trial on 16 July 1949 before the Lebanese military court. They were accused of taking part in the attacks on the gendarmerie posts at Harat Hraik, Mtain, Sarhamoul and Mashghara. Twelve were sentenced to death and fifty-three to terms of imprisonment with hard labour, varying from three years to life. Six of the twelve under sentence of death were executed on 21 July;[34] the other six had their sentences commuted to life imprisonment. Another 800 party members were in custody awaiting trial. Georges 'Abd al-Massih, who was considered Sa'ada's most dangerous associate, remained at large.[35]

On 17 July, and only a day after the trial, Riad el-Solh was received in Damascus with full honours by Husni al-Za'im, who had by this time promoted himself to the rank of marshal! A week before Riad's visit, on 8 July, Syria and Lebanon signed a financial and trade agreement. The long-running quarrel between the two countries was patched up. On returning to Beirut, Riad el-Solh confided to Bishara al-Khoury that he had had to hold back his tears on entering the now much-degraded and alien presidential palace, where his dear friend and ardent fellow nationalist Shukri al-Quwatli had only recently presided.[36]

At the same time, the Lebanese government made a move at rounding up members of the *Phalanges libanaises*. There were thirteen arrests – out of a membership which some said was over 20,000. The movement was dissolved, its offices closed and its weapons confiscated.

---

[33] MAE, Fonds Beyrouth (Amb.), série B, carton 48, translated from the Arabic by the Information Department of the Légation de France, Beirut, 11 July 1949.

[34] 'Abbas 'Abd al-Ra'uf Hammad, Sunni Palestinian; Muhammad Ibrahim Shalabi, Sunni Palestinian; Muhammad Ahmad al-Zu'bi, Sunni Syrian; 'Abd al-Hafiz 'Alami, Lebanese Shi'a; Ma'ruf Muhammad Muwaffaq, Lebanese Druze; and Adib Sam'an Jada', Greek Catholic Palestinian.

[35] *The Times*, London, 18 July 1949.

[36] Al-Khoury, *Haqa'iq lubnaniyya*, p. 218.

The Muslim paramilitary movement, *al-Najjada*, was also dissolved. As a result of these measures, the *Phalanges* and the *Najjada* both took the significant, far-reaching decision to transform themselves into political parties.

The outcome of the Sa'ada affair

Why did Bishara al-Khoury and Riad el-Solh decide to do away with Antun Sa'ada so swiftly? The obvious answer is that they considered that he posed a real threat to Lebanon – especially in view of his alliance with the dangerous, untrustworthy Husni al-Za'im. After the Palestine defeat, violent revolution was in the air, with Za'im himself showing the way. Sa'ada had taken up arms against the state, and had led an armed insurrection. He had attacked gendarmerie posts. There had been casualties. Men had been killed. The Lebanese president and prime minister were convinced that Za'im had plotted with Sa'ada to do away with both of them, which he no doubt had. Za'im had supplied Sa'ada with new automatic weapons, which had recently been given to him by France. It was thought that Sa'ada's plan had been to occupy the Biqa' valley, then Hasbaya, Rashaya and South Lebanon, and finally encircle the capital, thus attaching Lebanon to Syria in fulfilment of his geopolitical doctrine.

Unfortunately for himself, Sa'ada was not a man who could be reasoned with. He was an ideologue, whose cast of mind ruled out any possibility of compromise. He was guilty, above all, of the double crime of attacking not just Lebanese nationalism, but Arab nationalism as well, thereby uniting against himself a wide range of impassioned and dearly held opinions. Seen from Beirut, he was a highly dangerous demagogue and revolutionary, who simply had to be eliminated. Bishara al-Khoury and Riad el-Solh were both much concerned at the possible contagion of such revolutionary ideas to Lebanon's own security forces. They needed to quash – and quickly –any temptation that Lebanese army officers might have had to follow in the footsteps of their Syrian counterparts.

Camille Chamoun – by now a bitter opponent of Bishara al-Khoury, who aspired to win the presidency for himself – was concerned to show that Sa'ada had been executed for far baser motives than these. He told a private gathering of politicians and journalists on

9 July[37] – the day after Sa'ada's execution – that the PPS leader had been tried in camera and executed immediately, in order to conceal his connection with Salim and Khalil al-Khoury, the corrupt brother and son of President Bishara al-Khoury. Sa'ada had been seen at Salim's table and at the house of Khalil, Chamoun claimed. At the 1947 elections, Salim had relied on PPS support in order to win a seat he could not have hoped for otherwise. The famous printing works at Jummayza had been bought by Salim al-Khoury for the PPS, and now served to print his own newspaper, *Nida' al-Watan*. As for the economic agreement with Syria, Chamoun said that it had been signed immediately after Sa'ada's execution, mainly to protect the economic interests of Fu'ad al-Khoury, another of the president's brothers, who was known as the 'cement king' of Lebanon. It was not clear, however, whether any of Chamoun's bald accusations were founded on anything other than political hostility.

What was certain was that Sa'ada was a dangerously unknown quantity. Was he in league with King 'Abdallah, as many Arabs believed? How seriously had he plotted with Husni al-Za'im? Were any other revolutionaries involved in his planning? On his return to Lebanon on 2 March 1947, Sa'ada had flown in from Cairo on the plane with Fawzi al-Qawuqji, the veteran guerrilla leader. Later that same year, Qawuqji was appointed field commander of the ill-fated Arab Liberation Army, which, starved of weapons and supplies, was to turn Qawuqji into the bitterest of all revolutionaries.

Taha al-Hashimi – the former Iraqi prime minister whom Jamil Mardam had appointed to direct the ALA – later claimed in his memoirs that Qawuqji had plotted with members of the PPS, as well as with King 'Abdallah himself, to overthrow the two regimes of Bishara al-Khoury in Beirut and Shukri al-Quwatli in Damascus. ALA leaders had apparently reported to Hashimi that Qawuqji's plan was to march his men into Lebanon, where, with PPS assistance, he intended to topple the government. He then planned to take Syria, and ultimately unite Syria and Lebanon with Jordan and Iraq, to King 'Abdallah's benefit.[38] With all these revolutionary threats in the air, it was hardly surprising that Sa'ada was cut down in a hurried way, victim both of his own delusions and of the dangerous disturbance of the times.

---

[37] At the same private party at Bayt Meri, mentioned in note 27, given by Alexandre Riachi; Fonds Beyrouth (Amb.), série 199A4, carton 20, 11 July 1949.

[38] Taha al-Hashimi, *Mudhakkirat Taha al-Hashimi*, 2 vols, ed. Khaldun Sati' al-Husari, Beirut 1978, vol. II, p. 234.

On 14 August 1949, four and a half months after seizing power, Husni al-Za'im was himself overthrown by another Syrian army colonel, Sami al-Hinnawi. One of the putschists, Fadlallah Abu Mansur, shot his way into the presidential palace, and, finding Za'im in pyjamas in the hall there, struck him on the face. Significantly enough, he charged him with the crime of betraying Antun Sa'ada. Za'im was bundled into an armoured car and, together with his Prime Minister Muhsin al-Barazi, was taken out and shot. Farouk's Egypt heard the news of Za'im's overthrow with considerable consternation. The court even went into mourning for three days. King 'Abdallah and Nuri al-Sa'id, however, sent hearty congratulations, as well as emissaries, to the new colonel in Syria. In Damascus, the People's Party, which was overtly favourable to Iraq, was asked to form a government. Close relations between Syria and Iraq now suddenly seemed a distinct possibility – until a third Syrian colonel, Adib al-Shishakli, overthrew Hinnawi on 19 December, and moved to restore Syria to the pro-Egyptian camp. Shishakli managed to remain in power until 1954.

In spite of the trials of its members and their numerous arrests, the PPS continued to exist in the shadows, by the iron virtue of its discipline and organisation. From his hiding place, Georges 'Abd al-Massih rallied the faithful and vowed to avenge the fallen leader. Riad el-Solh was known to be particularly targeted. He was widely seen as the one who had 'persuaded' Za'im to hand over Sa'ada. But there was another reason too: Riad was the Lebanese leader who best represented the Lebanese nationalism of the National Pact, and one of the most prominent Arab nationalists of his generation. On both these grounds, he was a sworn enemy of the Syrian nationalists.

Nevertheless, Habib Abi Shahla, one of Riad's former cabinet colleagues, invited 'Isam al-Mahayri, a Syrian PPS leader, to lunch at Shtaura, a village in the Biqa' valley on the main road to Damascus, in a bid to effect a reconciliation between Riad el-Solh and the party. But when Mahayri discovered, on arrival, that Riad himself was to be present, he categorically refused to stay for lunch. He returned to Damascus, saying he was in no position to take such an initiative on behalf of his party.[39]

---

[39] See item 62/2F, in the private papers of the Emir Farid Chehab, Lebanon's director-general of national security, in the Middle East archive of St Antony's College, Oxford.

On 9 March 1950, Riad el-Solh was the target in Beirut of an assassination attempt. He had just stepped out of his car on the rue Verdun, in the late afternoon, to attend a reception given for him by the Ghalayini family, when a man hidden behind a palm tree fired three shots at him at close range. Showing considerable courage, Riad turned on his assailant and tried to catch him. But the man ran off, firing several more shots. Three children were hit, as well as a man who was standing close by. Two of the children died on their way to hospital. A bullet went through the sleeve of Riad's jacket without wounding him, although he later complained of a sharp pain in his elbow. The prime minister's bodyguard, 'Abd al-'Aziz 'Arab, shot at the assailant's legs, bringing him to the ground. His attacker was found to be Tawfiq Hamdan, a 23-year-old Druze, and a member of the outlawed PPS. He was a cousin of one of the party members executed the previous July, following their abortive coup. His motive may have been simply one of family revenge. Riad el-Solh pretended to remain calm, and managed to attend the reception, as well as all his other engagements that evening.

The attempted murder aroused great indignation in the country. The whole opposition – with the sole exception of the Druze leader Kamal Jumblatt – hastened to congratulate Riad el-Solh on his escape. Crowds of his supporters, and deputations from all over the country, called at the *salamlik* of his house in order to congratulate him in the flesh. In parliament on 13 March, he was warmly applauded and speeches were made by numerous deputies, both government and opposition. Kamal Jumblatt, however, struck a discordant note. 'Unlike all the friends and enemies of the Government', he declared, 'I did not visit Mr. Riad el-Solh and I have not congratulated him, and I shall not congratulate him, until I am sure that he will not seek to take advantage, for his own ends, of this unsuccessful attempt on his life. I'm only sorry for his daughters'.[40] This ugly last remark caused Riad el-Solh finally to lose his temper. 'My daughters', he retorted furiously, 'were brought up with pride and honour, not in the lap of the imperialists!' This was a deliberately wounding reference to the affair which Jumblatt's mother, the Sitt Nazira, was believed to have conducted with a French high commissioner. Cut to the quick, Jumblatt stormed

---

[40] William Houstoun-Boswall, Beirut, to Foreign Office, 20 March 1950 (FO 371/82268).

out of the Chamber, declaring that he would only return there at the head of bayonets! 'Where are the bayonets?' Riad enquired with his usual wry humour, when Jumblatt was seen to resume his seat the next day.[41] At any rate, Riad ensured that the man who had attempted to kill him was pardoned.

Some years later, a monument was allowed to be erected to the memory of Antun Sa'ada at his village of al-Arzal, in the region of Dhur al-Shwayr.

[41] Interview with Alia el-Solh, Monte Carlo, 4–5 October 2004.

26 MURDER IN AMMAN

Of all the Arab leaders, Riad el-Solh was by far the most active in seeking to win support for joint Arab military action during the Palestine War. But his efforts proved unsuccessful. At the start, he believed that Arab interests might still be protected. But he found himself unable to overcome the profound hostility and suspicion which divided one Arab state from another. As a result, Israel was able to defeat the Arabs only too easily, thus setting in motion a process of popular revolt throughout the region. Kings, presidents, pashas, beys and other representatives of the old ruling order were discredited, while revolutionary forces arose from far lower down the social scale. Syria led the way with a rash of violent army coups, which toppled the veteran nationalists and tossed the country back and forth between the Hashemites and their enemies. Revolt stirred not only among impecunious soldiers from the country-side, but also among Damascus school-teachers like Michel 'Aflaq and Salah al-Din al-Bitar, the two founders of the Ba'th Party – the party of 'Arab rebirth'. In Egypt, a year or two later, the devastating experience of defeat was to inspire Gamal 'Abd al-Nasser and his 'Free Officers' to bring down King Farouk's tottering regime.

Across the region, there was dismay at the proven incompetence or weakness of Arab rulers, and great bitterness at the way the Great Powers had rushed to establish and then recognise the Jewish state. When the Korean War broke out in 1950, Arab opinion simply refused to understand why the UN Security Council should consider Communist aggression a threat to world peace, but not Zionist aggression in Palestine. There was outrage in Lebanon when a Lebanese civilian aircraft was shot down by an Israeli fighter on a flight from Jerusalem to Beirut – without so much as eliciting a word of protest from any Western capital.

57 – Riad el-Solh aged 57, in 1951, with three of his five daughters (from right to left, Alia, Lamia and Mona), shortly before his death.

Throughout this turmoil, Riad sought, with increasing desperation, to salvage something from the wreckage of Arab pride and strength. He had no army of his own to throw into battle, but, by exhortation and personal diplomacy, he tried hard to rally the Arabs for a last push on the Palestine front, with the aim of recovering some part of what had been so spectacularly taken away.

The Iraqi option

In August 1948, Riad el-Solh paid a visit to Amman for talks with King 'Abdallah. He wanted to find out exactly why the Arab Legion – which had been hailed as the best and strongest of Arab armies, and on which he himself had placed such hopes – had managed to perform so poorly. Jordan, he knew, had simply refused to implement the Arab League invasion plan. Had the British held it back? Was Glubb Pasha to blame? The Arab Legion had never sought to engage the *Haganah*, except when it was itself attacked by Jewish forces in and around Jerusalem. Jordan had totally disregarded what was happening on other Arab fronts and had acted abysmally, if as yet inexplicably, as far as Riad could tell. 'Abdallah's sole concern seemed to be to seize what he could of Arab Palestine in order to annex it to his kingdom.

Riad suspected that 'Abdallah had had occasional contact with the Zionists over the years, like many others – himself included; but he had no notion of the extent to which, in pursuit of his personal ambitions, the Jordanian ruler had departed from any sort of Arab consensus and abandoned any sense of loyalty to his fellow Arabs. Riad could not have known that 'Abdallah and the Zionists had been in intimate contact since 1921; that they had concluded a secret agreement to partition Palestine between them; and that 'Abdallah had even benefited over the years from substantial Jewish subsidies. Any reader of Avi Shlaim's definitive account of the Zionists' relations with 'Abdallah and with other prominent Arabs will notice with what regularity the phrase 'money changed hands' occurs.[1]

In going to Amman, Riad el-Solh's optimistic plan was to persuade the king to merge his Arab Legion with the as yet undefeated

---

[1] Shlaim, *The Politics of Partition*, pp. 424–5. For more detail, see the longer version of this work by Shlaim, *Collusion Across the Jordan.*

Iraqi army, so that they could resume the fight together. He believed that Jordan and Iraq combined might still be able to save the day. If they could not defeat Israel, they might at least manage to contain it, and even recapture the territory lost after the June truce. That was the project which occupied his mind and that was the proposal he put to the king. But his mission was doomed even before he set out. His attempt to mobilise Iraq for action against Israel – as well as his frenetic efforts to mobilise Arab League members for the fight – were wholly unwelcome to 'Abdallah and, of course, to his Israeli friends. It posed a direct threat to their common objective of partitioning Palestine between them.

After his depressing talks with King 'Abdallah in Amman, Riad sent a memorandum by special messenger to the Iraqi Prime Minister Muzahim al-Pachachi, entitled 'The present state of the Arab world and its peoples'. It was his pessimistic assessment of the situation.[2] It is worth quoting at length because it is a document which throws light on Riad's thinking, both during and immediately after the Palestine War. King 'Abdallah and the Israelis lost no time in acquiring a copy.

Riad el-Solh's memorandum

'His Majesty King 'Abdallah asked to meet me, and repeated this request', Riad wrote.

> *He wanted the meeting to take place before the celebration*
> *of the 'Id. I considered it my duty to accept his invitation.*
> *I left for Amman on Wednesday, 4 August [1948].*
> *He received me for a long time, with only Tawfiq Abu*
> *al-Huda, prime minister of Transjordan, present. As is*
> *his habit, he showed both reasonableness and courtesy at*
> *the meeting. We spoke of the shortcomings of the Arab*
> *attitude towards Transjordan, and the unfulfilled promises*
> *regarding funds to recruit men to fight alongside the*
> *Jordanian army and to purchase weapons. At the meeting,*

---

2 The memorandum is reproduced in 'Abd al-Rahman Mahmud al-Huss, *Riad el-Solh*, Beirut 1951, pp. 18–29. It was not made public at the time, but was published in 1951, after Riad's murder. Muzahim al-Pachachi served as Iraqi prime minister from June 1948 to January 1949.

he asked for my help in the transportation [to Jordan] of weapons, which he had bought.

He complained bitterly of the confiscation by Egypt, on ships in Egyptian territorial waters, of munitions which had been on their way to him. I replied that I was among those who had taken the decision to remit these sums to him – on two main conditions: that the British suspend their subsidy to him, as had already been announced, and that he continued to fight. I told him that these two conditions had not been met, but that I was nevertheless prepared to help him with the Arab League, if he were prepared to resume hostilities.

I added that frankness had become necessary, since the king's reputation had been tarnished by the cessation of hostilities. I reminded him that at the meeting at Aley, held before that of the Security Council, the representatives of Transjordan had made clear that Transjordan could not reject the decision of the Security Council, even if all the Arab States were to reject it.

I told His Majesty that, if he could not resume hostilities or remove his British officers, it would be better to say so frankly to the Arab countries. This would be more honourable, and would be more in conformity with our interests, than to remain in a state of uncertainty. The Arab States would then be in a position to make their assessment of the balance of power, taking Transjordan's withdrawal into account. If they wished to resume hostilities, they would do so on that basis. But, if the situation remained as it was, and if we found ourselves once again in a situation lacking in sincerity, His Majesty's responsibility would be dangerously greater. I insisted to His Majesty that his reply should be clear and definitive, leaving no room for doubt or misinterpretation.

The king replied that he could not resume hostilities unless the Arab Nation gathered all its forces together and threw them into the battle. And he could not remove the British officers from his army. His argument for not resuming the fight was that he did not have enough weapons and munitions, and that his army was not well trained. Concerning the British officers, he listed several arguments: the first was that he had detected in them no sign of disloyalty; that he could not change horses in mid-course; and finally that he did not have in his army Arab officers able to replace the British officers.

There was a fourth argument, which the king mentioned, and which was of special significance. He wished to protect the military spirit which had always been present in his armed forces. To dismiss the British officers, under the pressure of discontent with them or criticism of them, would break this spirit. He did not want the Transjordanian army to become like the Iraqi army, which interfered in political matters. His Majesty remarked that if the army were to rebel today against its British officers, it could rebel tomorrow against the King himself . . .

I then asked His Majesty whether he could not entrust his army to the Iraqi army, so that the latter could take it in hand as if it were part of its own force. He replied that Sumu al-wasi (His Majesty the Regent) had already made such a proposal, but that he himself did not think it could be done, for a number of reasons. After leaving Transjordan, I learned that he was considering the suggestion, but I did not think that it could be put into effect.

After meeting with His Majesty, I left with the firm conviction that Transjordan would not resume hostilities, and would not take part in a war, even if the Arab States decided to wage one. In truth, I did not feel that the King was acting out of choice, but rather under constraint. I did not feel that it was normal or logical that a man, who had achieved great popularity in the Arab countries in the last few weeks, would willingly subvert his own reputation.

In view of the situation in Transjordan, the Arab Governments must now devise a new policy, review their forces and their plans, while taking this reality into account . . . If the Arab Nation is betrayed by its leaders in not resuming hostilities, what I fear most of all is that it will succumb to the defeatism and lack of confidence, which already afflict the Palestinian people . . .

There is no lack of arguments for resuming hostilities: the Jews provide them daily by violating the truce. It is very probable that we will soon be surprised by an event which will endanger Jerusalem itself. I feel I must warn you straight away of this possibility . . .

It is obvious that the first thing to be done in view of an early resumption of hostilities is to fill the vacuum created by the withdrawal of Transjordan from the battlefield, because of the political pressures on that country.

This time, the fighting did not stop out of fear of Security Council sanctions, as one might have supposed, or because of Jewish armament, but because Transjordan declared – even before the Security Council's decision – that it could not continue the fight for lack of weapons. (I do not believe that the restitution of the weapons confiscated by Egypt will induce Transjordan to resume the fight.)

The Iraqi command has declared that if the Transjordan army withdraws, it too would withdraw its forces. This report has worried the Egyptian government, which sent His Excellency 'Azzam Pasha [the secretary-general of the Arab League] to attempt to retrieve the situation . . .

Egypt has been profoundly affected by these events. You yourself are well placed to know all that Egypt has done for Palestine, both in war and in peace. You are also aware of the precious place it occupies in the struggle, as well as in all pan-Arab affairs, and the role played by His Majesty, the King of Egypt in these matters . . .

Having described the position of Transjordan and the military situation in Palestine, and also the situation of the Arab Nation, I repeat once again that war cannot be avoided – either to retake from the Jews what they seized in the second phase of the battle, or to prepare for the future, to be stronger and more united. The enthusiasm of the Iraqi government and people to pursue the struggle is a great source of comfort to all Arabs.

I believe Iraq has a well-constructed plan to secure its goals. We would like to be informed of it, so

that everyone may know what to do thereafter. We must
unify the command since the reason we were prevented
from doing so no longer exists (that is to say, doubts
over Transjordan's intentions). The forces and the plans
should be put under the command of a single chief, who
could then proceed in accordance with the decisions of the
leadership, in order to ensure victory for the Arabs.

Allow me to say to you that the key to the
situation is now in Iraq, whereas before the war it was
in Transjordan, then in Egypt, when it accepted the first
truce during the meeting of the Political Committee in
Amman. I believe that, initially, we should exchange ideas
and opinions with Iraq, before broaching the subject with
Egypt. Then we could meet to discuss it. I do not think
that it would be necessary, before that, to convene the
Political Committee.

As for the vacuum created by Transjordan, it is up
to Iraq to fill it, for several reasons. First of all, because of
the special ties which link the two monarchies, which allow
the one easily to take the place of the other. In any event,
the military situation is such that the route from Iraq to
Palestine passes through Transjordan, which for Iraq
would remain the place for supplies and communications.

It would be necessary, however, for
Transjordanian troops to hold their positions – and defend
them – even if they wished to withdraw from the battle.
That was, in fact, King 'Abdallah's intention. After he
asked for arms, he was told that he would not need them
since he did not wish to resume hostilities. But he answered
that he needed them to defend himself, because the Jews
might advance, seize a strong point, and penetrate into
Transjordan itself.

Iraq will not feel comfortable to resume the
fight unless it fills the vacuum (left by Transjordan) with
troops under its command and that of the Arab League,
composed of Palestinian and Jordanian fighters – as
happened at Jenin. Iraq should not worry unduly since
its army is best placed to fight. It seems to me that all
this must be done with great caution, and in a spirit of

friendship and fraternity, because it is very difficult for military and non-military elements to cohabit. In view of your wisdom, I feel sure that you will be able to bring this about.

This is all I wanted to tell you after my meeting with His Majesty, King 'Abdallah. This is a subject on which depends not only the destiny of Palestine, but of all the Arabs. I wanted to let you have my views on this question, under the seal of secrecy.

In writing these lines to you, I am glad that Iraq has, at its head, a man who gives importance to these questions. I look forward to your swift reply so that each government may take suitable decisions and measures.

May God crown your actions with success, for the good of the Arab Nation. Peace be upon you.

Troubles on the home front

Riad el-Solh's worries about Palestine were compounded by the serious problems he faced at home in Lebanon. His partnership with President Bishara al-Khoury, which had lasted for over five years, had begun to break down in the immediate aftermath of the Palestine War. It became increasingly bad-tempered, even hostile, with the result that Riad began losing control of the machinery of government, before losing office altogether in February 1951.

His partnership with Shaykh Bishara had been launched in 1943, when they had together devised the National Pact. This was a set of unwritten principles for Christian–Muslim power-sharing, and was intended to shape Lebanon's internal and Arab policies. Shaykh Bishara had been elected president – trouncing his rival, the pro-French Emile Eddé – and had immediately called on Riad el-Solh to form a government. Together, they had fought the battle for independence against France, of which the dramatic high point was the November 1943 crisis. Their partnership had worked well, perhaps because Riad el-Solh was so dominant a partner, and had managed to set the pace and to build on an already towering reputation on the Arab scene. But it could not have remained agreeable for a president to be so overshadowed by a prime minister, and resentment inevitably built up.

Bishara al-Khoury was always conscious that keeping Riad el-Solh at the head of the government throughout a six-year mandate would be problematic. After all, some alternation of power was necessary from time to time, since there were other Sunni candidates who aspired to the premiership. Riad accepted this, even if not entirely happily. He was well aware that the president had the constitutional power to replace him at any time. But what damaged their relationship was Riad's sense that Bishara al-Khoury had not played him fair. For Riad had worked hard to ensure the renewal of the president's mandate. Indeed, he had even used up much of his own popularity in the process, and incurred the enmity of those other Maronite leaders who themselves aspired to the presidency. But once Bishara al-Khoury found himself assured of a second six-year term, he had immediately sought to satisfy other Sunni hopefuls – at Riad's expense.

Moreover, the severe tensions generated by the Palestine War had begun to erode the principles of the National Pact and to revive confessional loyalties. Muslims – with Riad el-Solh at their head – would have liked Lebanon to play a more robust role in support of Arab Palestine. Many Christians, however, did not feel that their country's small force should be deployed beyond its borders. In a way their reserve was justified, since Lebanon's army was little more than a gendarmerie, used mainly for internal security purposes, and mostly failing even at that. As a result, in the Arab League and in other high-profile Arab political circles, Riad el-Solh found it humiliating to be prime minister of so divided a country, especially one that had played so little part in the war.

Changes were beginning to take place on the Lebanese scene, especially within the two big parliamentary blocs – Bishara al-Khoury's Destour Bloc and Emile Eddé's National Bloc, both of which had long dominated Lebanon's political life. These multi-confessional groupings had traditionally managed to bring together men from different religious backgrounds, in tactical alliances around a leader. But the pressure of events made these blocs break up into mere confessional parties. Faced with a revival of sectarianism, Riad el-Solh's dream of creating a unitary state to which all citizens would owe allegiance – rather than a hateful patchwork of feuding religious communities – began to seem more distant than ever.

Meanwhile, attacks on the government's record became increasingly virulent from several prominent politicians, especially the

Maronite Camille Chamoun and the Druze Kamal Jumblatt, who criticised the mismanagement of public affairs and the delays in implementing overdue reforms. They denounced as wholly illegitimate the 'rigged' 1947 elections and the unconstitutional renewal of Bishara al-Khoury's presidential mandate. In addition, there was harsh criticism of the over-hasty execution of the PPS leader, Antun Sa'ada – an execution that opponents now described as a political assassination. All these pressures contributed to the estrangement of Riad el-Solh and Bishara al-Khoury. The two men, who had once been such close friends and supportive colleagues, now became antagonists.

The quarrel with Salim al-Khoury

A further reason they fell out – and it may have been one of the main reasons – lay in Bishara's unwillingness or inability to control his younger brother, Salim al-Khoury, who was universally and derisively nicknamed the 'Sultan'. To Riad and to many others, the president's tolerance of his brother's myriad abuses suggested that Shaykh Bishara had even fallen under his influence. Riad el-Solh's increasingly angry clashes with Salim al-Khoury finally affected his relationship with the president.

Salim al-Khoury's commercial and political power had become so considerable, and his interference in the affairs of the state so blatant, that at times he seemed more powerful than the government itself. He ran what was, in effect, a protection racket, which was to blame for the most rampant abuse. Every day brought new and breathtaking evidence of corruption in high places. In 1950, for example, two cases attracted particular attention. These were the cases of Basil Trad, director-general of the Ministry of National Economy, and of Muhammad Zuain, director-general of the Ministry of Agriculture. Although both men were universally valued as outstanding civil servants, they now refused to go to their offices, and even resigned in revulsion at Salim al-Khoury's pressure on them to employ men in their ministries who served no useful purpose whatsoever. Trad complained that, upon being appointed director-general, he was startled to discover that there were no fewer than seventy officials at his ministry for whom there was no actual work at all, and who only ever turned up there in order to draw their salaries! But he found himself unable to fire them, because they enjoyed brazen protection from higher up. Zuain, in turn, took the decision to keep away from *his* ministry for exactly the same reasons.

These cases were symptomatic of the malaise and disquiet pervading the senior ranks of the civil service. Salim al-Khoury's protégés were everywhere – in departments of government, in parliament, in the cabinet itself. In addition, and more ominously, he even had a great number of 'protected persons' who held tactical positions in the security forces. One of these was the chief of police himself, Nasser Bey Ra'd.

An incident in June 1950 involving Nasser Ra'd threatened to degenerate into an open fight – even an armed clash – between Riad el-Solh's supporters and those of Salim al-Khoury. The trouble started when Riad el-Solh, in his capacity as minister of interior (which he was, in addition to being prime minister), sent for Police Chief Ra'd, and asked him to explain why he had interrogated Sa'id Freyha, the renowned editor of *al-Sayyad* (who was also Riad's close personal friend) about an article Freyha had published on 1 June. Riad el-Solh was not at all satisfied with Nasser Ra'd's reply, and told him that before interrogating a journalist – a task that should normally be performed by a judge of the special press tribunal – Ra'd should have consulted the minister of interior. Friendship apart, Riad's instinct was to seek to protect newspapers from excessive censorship, even those newspapers opposed to him.

To indicate his displeasure, he told the chief of police to take one month's leave. A decree was issued appointing 'Izzat Bey Khorshid, then director of protocol at the Ministry of Foreign Affairs (who had been a police official) to serve as acting police chief in Ra'd's absence. But so incensed was Salim al-Khoury at this 'punishment' of his protégé, that he threatened to bring his Maronite partisans to demonstrate against the prime minister. In response, Riad el-Solh threatened to bring *his* Sunni supporters onto the streets. Fearing that the two sides might come to blows, the president eventually succeeded in persuading his brother to call off this showdown. Large numbers of Salim's supporters did, in fact, come down from the mountains and assemble outside his residence at Furn al-Shabbak, on the outskirts of Beirut. But since Riad's supporters did not come out to challenge them, they dispersed without incident.

The crisis, however, was far from resolved. Salim al-Khoury demanded the immediate reinstatement of his protégé, Nasser Ra'd. He even urged his brother to dismiss Riad el-Solh and to appoint another prime minister. He made several attempts to precipitate a cabinet crisis by pressing various ministers to resign, and was enraged when two key figures, Philippe Takla and the Emir Majid Arslan, refused to do so. The bitter hatred which Riad el-Solh and Salim al-Khoury now felt for each other put the president in a very difficult position. He did not want a total breach with Riad, nor did he wish to offend his now powerful brother. He needed his support at the next elections, especially in Mount Lebanon, where Salim wielded considerable influence.[3]

There was a further twist to the affair. Before Nasser Ra'd was allowed to resume his duties, Riad made sure that a decree was issued containing a clause to the effect that the police would in future fall under the direct responsibility of the prime minister, and not of the minister of interior. This caused a further rumpus because Anis Saleh, director-general of the Ministry of Interior, was one of Salim al-Khoury's 'men', whereas Nazem 'Akkari, director-general of the prime minister's office, was Riad el-Solh's protégé.

When Nasser Ra'd failed to show up at his office, the president telephoned to order him to return to his post at once, fearing that if he did not, Riad el-Solh would dismiss him altogether. Tactlessly, Nasser Ra'd replied that Salim al-Khoury was not prepared to accept the new decree. Another decree was therefore issued by Bishara al-Khoury, cancelling the earlier one, but sending Ra'd home for another month's leave of absence.

Faced with this stalemate, the two contestants decided to bury the hatchet, marking a pause in their protracted struggle. Nasser Ra'd resumed his duties on 2 September, and made sure that Sa'id Freyha, the offending editor, was severely punished. He was sentenced to three months in prison and a fine of 200 Lebanese lira. His paper was suspended for six months. The writer of the article was sentenced to one month in jail and a fine of 100 Lebanese lira.

What was important, however, was not so much the verdict, but the effect of this miserable episode on the cohesion of the team at the summit of the state, and on relations between the personalities involved. The incident certainly did not enhance the regime's reputation with the public, which followed the whole affair with cynical disgust. Riad el-Solh's prestige was eroded by this petty scandal. Some newspapers even clamoured that he should quit office.[4]

---

[3] Beirut Political Summaries, June and July 1950 (FO 371/82266).
[4] Beirut Political Summary, September 1950 (FO 371/82266).

The breach with Syria

The confrontation with Salim al-Khoury was not the least of Riad el-Solh's problems. He had been deeply disturbed by the military coups in Damascus, which overthrew his veteran nationalist friends. He suspected the coups were the fruit of conspiracies to make the Arabs submit to Israel. He was not reassured when, following Colonel Adib al-Shishakli's overthrow of Colonel Sami al-Hinnawi, Khaled al-'Azm became prime minister on 27 December 1949. Riad disliked both 'Azm and his family (which he had once narrowly escaped marrying into), and this dislike was mutual. 'Azm had never joined the National Bloc or shared in its struggle against the French occupation. Rather, he had had good relations with the French and had even served as prime minister in 1941 under Vichy. He was extremely rich and well educated, but, measured by a nationalist yardstick, he cut a poor figure.

Riad el-Solh was fond of saying that ties between Syria and Lebanon had been forged by God, and were sustained by each and every heart in the two countries. But this did not seem to prevent economic relations between them from deteriorating badly. Syrian merchants wanted 'Azm's government to impose a protectionist policy on Lebanon, or, if that failed, to sever economic relations with it altogether. The Lebanese, in turn, had their own grievances. To put pressure on Lebanon, Syria was forever threatening to halt grain deliveries, while selling its grain to Turkey and Saudi Arabia. Moreover, to free itself from dependence on Beirut, Syria had invited several foreign companies to bid for the development of the Mediterranean seaport at Latakia. 'Azm had himself laid the cornerstone of the port development on 14 February 1950. Syria was also developing its railway network and its irrigation system, and was generally putting up barriers to the import of goods from Lebanon.

Late in February, 'Azm chaired a meeting of Syrian businessmen and industrials which, after two days of deliberation, adopted a recommendation that Syria should either establish complete monetary, customs and economic union with Lebanon or enforce complete and immediate separation. A Syrian ultimatum along these lines reached Beirut a few days later. Lebanon was given until 20 March to respond. Riad el-Solh personally was pained by these strong-arm tactics – which he had never had to suffer from the courtly-mannered and diplomatic Shukri al-Quwatli – and the Lebanese press, in turn, condemned them strongly. Nevertheless, the Lebanese government replied reasonably enough on 10 March to the Syrian ultimatum, explaining that, in view of the conflicting interests of the two countries, the principle of complete economic unity was hardly acceptable. But it hoped that outstanding differences could be resolved in a friendly manner.

Utterly disregarding Lebanon's flexible approach, on 13 March the arrogant Khalid al-'Azm unilaterally dissolved the Customs Union between the two countries. This brutal action came as an unpleasant surprise, not only to the Lebanese public, but also to officials in the Lebanese administration. The latter did what they could to maintain a dignified attitude, while avoiding any measures which might further aggravate the quarrel. But Syria's uncompromising move had further ramifications. Syrian police and customs posts were erected on the border, and the travel of Syrians to Lebanon was prohibited without special permit. A Syrian infantry battalion was deployed on the Damascus–Beirut road, and another on the frontier north of Tripoli. The movement of goods between the two countries ground to a standstill. Lebanon found itself forced hastily to set up its own customs administration.[5]

In the middle of this crisis, Riad el-Solh had to head to Egypt for a meeting of the Arab League Political Committee. At a tea given in his honour by the Lebanese colony in Cairo, he was asked about the dispute with Syria. He declared: 'I refuse to describe as a breakdown a disagreement which, I hope, will soon be ended: the interests of both countries require it . . . We must mend matters. The Syrians are experiencing difficult times. We are obliged to come to their aid because they are our brothers, in good times and in bad'.[6] But there was no denying his extreme antipathy for the brutish military regimes that now controlled Damascus, and for Khaled al-'Azm, who was complicit with them. On 13 May, he told a French diplomat in Cairo that if President Quwatli did not return to power soon, Syria would sink into anarchy, which would be extremely damaging for the whole Arab world.[7]

---

[5] For a detailed account of the dispute, see Chaitani, *Post-Colonial Syria and Lebanon*, pp. 145–58; also British Legation, Beirut, to Foreign Office, Lebanon Political Summary, March 1950 (FO 371/82266).

[6] MAE, Nantes, Fonds Beyrouth (Amb.), série 199A4, carton 20, M. Charles Lucet, Chargé d'affaires, à M. Robert Schuman, Ministre des Affaires Etrangères, Cairo, 4 April 1950.

[7] MAE, Nantes, Fonds Beyrouth (Amb.), série 199A4, carton 20, M. Maurice Couve de Murville, Ambassadeur de France en Egypte, à Son Excellence M. Robert Schuman, Ministre des Affaires Etrangères, Cairo, 16 May 1950.

In October, Riad el-Solh called on Quwatli, his friend and fellow nationalist, who was then in exile in Egypt with his family. Riad had flown there with his wife to enrol two of their daughters, Alia and Mona, at the English Girls' College, in Alexandria. On his return to Beirut, he found that allegations had appeared in the Syrian press that he had been scheming in Egypt to overthrow the Syrian regime. Akram al-Hawrani repeated these allegations in the Syrian parliament in a bitter personal attack against Riad el-Solh.[8] Such were some of Riad's problems when the whole region was suddenly shaken up by evidence of King 'Abdallah's overly intimate relations with Israel.

King 'Abdallah's 'diplomacy'

Riad el-Solh's outrage at King 'Abdallah's behaviour reached a peak of vehemence and fury when, in March 1950, documents published in the Egyptian press exposed 'Abdallah's secret cooperation with Israel, even during the most critical moments of the war. The source of the documents was Lieutenant Colonel 'Abdallah al-Tal, an officer in Glubb Pasha's Arab Legion, who had defected from Jordan the previous January and sought asylum in Egypt. An Arab nationalist of strong views, Tal was sickened by 'Abdallah's secret diplomacy, by the extreme concessions he had made to Israel, and by Glubb Pasha's decision to ban the Arab Legion from engaging Zionist forces.

Tal had distinguished himself in the Palestine War on at least three occasions. On 4 May 1948, he had mounted an attack on the Zionist settlement of Kfar Etzion, but Glubb had ordered him to return to base. To force Glubb's hand, Tal had resorted to a ruse. He secretly ordered a subordinate to provoke a clash with Kfar Etzion and then to appeal to Glubb for help on the false pretext that an Arab Legion unit had been caught in a Zionist ambush. As he predicted, Glubb ordered reinforcements to be rushed to the rescue. On 12 May, Tal personally led the column which crushed the settlement, inflicted heavy casualties and took 350 prisoners to Amman.[9]

The second occasion occurred on 12 August, when Tal, together with other nationalist officers, blew up a pumping station near Latrun

---

[8] Lebanon Political Summary, October 1950 (FO 371/82266).
[9] Avi Shlaim, *The Politics of Partition*, p. 168.

that was providing water to the Jewish community in Jerusalem. Their aim was to subvert the growing cooperation they suspected was taking place between Tel Aviv and Amman. The third occasion was in October, when Tal, in order to help the Egyptians, launched an attack on Israeli troops in the Jerusalem area. His object was to force the Israelis to divert some of their forces from the Negev – where they had broken through the Egyptian front – to Jerusalem. But King 'Abdallah wanted neither to help the Egyptians nor to provoke the Israelis. Although he dared not admit it, he was totally opposed to Tal's personal and patriotic initiatives.

Perhaps in order to muzzle Tal, King 'Abdallah then made the surprising decision of entrusting him with the task of negotiating a ceasefire with Israel in Jerusalem. The king's real objective was to arrive at a far-reaching territorial compromise with Israel, although this, too, he could not admit to his representatives.[10] On 30 November, Tal and his Israeli opposite number, Lieutenant Colonel Moshe Dayan, signed a formal agreement for 'an absolute and sincere cease-fire' covering the entire Jerusalem area.[11]

The armistice talks between Israel and Egypt, which opened at Rhodes on 13 January 1949, then gave King 'Abdallah the impetus to get down to the real business of peacemaking. He invited Dayan and Elias Sasson to his winter palace in Shuneh, where he conveyed to them his sincere desire for peace talks. He declared he had no use for the Arab League, that he was determined to act alone, and that the fate of Palestine should be a matter for bilateral discussion between Israel and Transjordan.[12] At another meeting at Shuneh some weeks later, Walter Eytan, an Israeli diplomat who was present, noted that 'Abdallah al-Tal 'maintained an attitude of utter cynicism throughout the proceedings, though he helped actively to get the agreement concluded. He seems to be wholly disillusioned – about the Arabs, about the British, and about everything else – and speaks about the King, even in the King's presence, in a way which can only be described as contemptuous'.[13] This was the meeting at which, on 23 March, King 'Abdallah agreed, under Israeli pressure, to surrender a strip of territory in central Palestine, 5 kilometres deep and 60 kilometres long, cutting the inhabitants of

[10] Ibid., pp. 253–62.
[11] Ibid., p. 254.
[12] Ibid., pp. 271, 279.
[13] Ibid., p. 300.

Tulkaram and Qalqilya off from their lands, and expelling 15,000 Palestinians from their homes.

This crime seems to have been the psychological turning point which drove the by now disgusted Tal to defect.[14] The context for his decision was mounting popular anger at the king's policy of accommodating Israel. 'Abdallah al-Tal was later angrily to describe the rage experienced by Palestinians, who watched as their motherland disappeared before their very eyes, with Arab rulers serving it up, piece by piece, into the mouths of wolves.

Just before his defection, and perhaps still hoping to secure his loyalty, the king appointed Tal to the Special Committee called for by the armistice agreement with Israel. Dayan reported back to Ben-Gurion that the Jordanian officer was now very bitter indeed. The Jews alone, he had said to him, had benefited from the agreements which had so far been concluded.[15] Once 'Abdallah al-Tal had defected to Egypt, the prospect of any agreement in the Special Committee disappeared completely.

In spite of the king's pleas and pathetic sacrifices, Ben-Gurion was not prepared to recognise 'Abdallah's annexation of Arab Palestine, nor to make the slightest concession to him in the interest of peace. In fact, he was not at all persuaded that peace was in Israel's best interests. In view of Israel's strength and the Arabs' weakness, Ben-Gurion even toyed with the idea of seizing the entire Sinai Peninsula to the Suez Canal, and the entire West Bank up to the Jordan River. Peace with Jordan, he mused, might hamper such a tempting expansion.

Having failed to draw the Israelis into a full-blown peace agreement, King 'Abdallah, in February 1950, came up with the alternative idea of a five-year non-aggression pact with the new Jewish state. But to add to his growing discomfiture, the Israelis decided to leak the plan. On 1 March, the *New York Times* carried a front-page report that the Israeli government was considering a Jordanian proposal for such a pact. But negotiations ended inconclusively, and nothing came of 'Abdallah's efforts. To his great disappointment, he had to make do with the status quo of the armistice agreement. The Israelis handed him £10,000 as a consolation prize.[16]

Such was the situation when the Egyptian newspaper, *Akhbar al-Yom,* published 'Abdallah al-Tal's documents detailing the king's

[14] Ibid., pp. 310–11.
[15] Ibid., p. 336.
[16] Ibid., p. 392.

711 / Murder in Amman

dealings with Israel. One document was allegedly the full text of the peace treaty with Israel which 'Abdallah had been seeking to conclude. A French translation appeared in the Beirut newspaper, *Le Soir*. In interviews with the Egyptian press, 'Abdallah al-Tal denounced both King 'Abdallah and Glubb Pasha in violent terms. He derided the king as a lackey of the British and the Zionists, and a traitor to the Arab cause, and Glubb as the instrument of British imperial domination over Transjordan. Glubb, he claimed, had colluded with the Zionists to prevent the establishment of a Palestinian state. Tal called for the Arab League to send a court of enquiry to Amman to investigate the treachery of the Jordanian authorities and of the Arab Legion.[17]

Almost all Lebanon's Arabic-language papers joined in a bitter press campaign against the king. They gave prominence to Colonel Tal's reported statement that King 'Abdallah should abdicate in favour of his son; that the Anglo-Jordanian Treaty should be abrogated and the British subsidy ended; that the Constitution should be revised and the administration of Jordan put in the hands of 'Liberal' elements.[18] Several Lebanese newspapers quoted the Egyptian newspaper, *al-Misri*, as saying, 'Amputate this corrupt organ from the body of the Arab nation'.

Riad el-Solh was in Cairo in March 1950 for a meeting of the Arab League Council. In view of the outcry against Jordan, its absence from the meeting was hardly surprising. As head of the Lebanese delegation, Riad el-Solh proposed a motion referring Jordan's failure to attend to the League's Political Committee. Accordingly, the Committee – composed for the occasion of the heads of delegations – met on 27 March and resolved unanimously 'that the Palestine question was the concern of all the States represented in the Arab League, and that peace negotiations undertaken by any one of the States of the League, in isolation from the others, was a violation of the League's constitution and should entail the expulsion of the offending State from the League'.[19]

Riad el-Solh let fly at Jordan at the tea which the Lebanese colony in Cairo gave in his honour on 31 March.

The truth obliges me to say that the Arab League has suffered a major setback: it was not able to surmount all the difficulties it faced, notably over Palestine. But the

---

[17] Ibid., pp. 150, 386.
[18] Beirut to Foreign Office, 23 March 1950 (FO 371/82708).
[19] British Middle East Office, Cairo, to Foreign Office, 28 March 1950 (FO 1018/71).

League, as an organization, must survive, because it is
essential to all the Arab states.

One of these states, however, is actually negotiating
with our common enemy. You have read, as I have, the
text of an agreement which is due to be concluded between
the two countries. You are aware of the danger it poses to
the League and to all the Arab states: you will have noticed
that at the head of the accord figures the establishment of
commercial exchanges between the two countries and the
creation of Haifa as a free port [for Jordan's use].

We are all convinced that it is in our interest to
maintain the economic blockade of Israel. Unfortunately,
owing to the fault of one Arab country, Zionist goods will
flood our markets.[20]

Riad also referred to the attempt on his life, as well as to the question
of the independence and unity of Lebanon, which he described as 'a
country where Christians and Muslims live in perfect accord'. This,
however, was more an expression of wishful thinking, than a realistic
description of his now troubled relations with President Bishara al-
Khoury and his wider Maronite community.

Riad was in Egypt again in May, for a meeting of the Arab
League's Political Committee, when, at the opening session, he surprised the other delegates by the virulence of his diatribe against King
'Abdallah. Jordan, he declared, should be expelled immediately from
the League, without further discussion.[21] In Amman, as can be imagined, Riad el-Solh was now regarded as an enemy of the Kingdom.

Riad el-Solh resigns as prime minister

It was widely expected that Riad would resign on his return from the
Arab League meeting in Cairo. As Lebanese elections were due to take

---

[20] MAE, Nantes, Fonds Beyrouth (Amb.), série 199A4, carton 20, M. Charles Lucet,
Chargé d'affaires, à M. Robert Schuman, Ministre des Affaires Etrangères, Cairo,
4 April 1950.
[21] MAE, Nantes, Fonds Beyrouth (Amb.), série 199A4, carton 20, M. Maurice Couve
de Murville, Ambassadeur de France en Egypte, à Son Excellence M. Robert
Schuman, Ministre des Affaires Etrangères, Cairo, 16 May 1950.

place in April, President Bishara al-Khoury had made it known that he wished to appoint a government of technocrats to conduct them. Indeed, as his relationship with Riad had by now become execrable, he had for months been pondering how to get rid of him. Riad, for his part, had lost all respect for the president, mainly because of the behaviour of 'Sultan' Salim, Bishara al-Khoury's younger brother, whom the president seemed unable or unwilling to hold in check. Riad was particularly incensed by the fact that Salim al-Khoury had managed to tighten his grip on both the security and administrative departments of the government, thus giving himself tremendous, unelected power.

Another relevant factor was Lebanon's relations with Syria. In Damascus, the military dictator, Colonel Adib al-Shishakli, viewed Riad el-Solh with apprehension, and accused him of conspiring to restore the civilian, democratically elected Shukri al-Quwatli to power. To conciliate the colonel, who was known to have close connections with the PPS, Bishara al-Khoury decided to remove Riad from office as soon as possible. Fear of the PPS was very much on his mind: the president was concerned that the late Antun Sa'ada's party – which was allowed to operate openly in Syria – might even attempt to strike at him. Riad's open attacks on Bishara al-Khoury in several newspapers – and his refusal to attend the president's traditional *'Id al-Fitr* banquet – were interpreted in Lebanese political circles as a declaration of war.

Lurking beneath the surface of these quarrels was an element of confessional strife which seemed in danger of being fanned into flame at any moment, particularly as Lebanon was wrestling with the problem of how to deal with the influx of 150,000 Palestinian refugees. Adding to the government's problems was a sharp rise in the price of bread and other foodstuffs, which had aroused the anger of the population. It was at this moment of great anxiety and simmering upheaval that Bishara al-Khoury announced that he intended to appoint Husayn al-'Uwayni at the head of a 'neutral' three-man government to conduct the forthcoming elections. Riad had little choice but to give way. He resigned on 13 February 1951.[22]

Among the candidates who hoped to replace him as prime minister after the elections were 'Abdallah al-Yafi, Sami el-Solh, Sa'ib Salam and Sa'di Munla. But many expected Riad to let the others make the running and then come through with a burst of speed at the

---

[22] Lebanon Political Summaries, January and February 1951 (FO 1018/80).

finishing post. However, in view of the breakdown of his relations with the president, he decided to bide his time, fully intending to return to power later on.

Riad's last journey

In May 1951, three months after Riad el-Solh's resignation, King 'Abdallah paid a visit to Beirut and expressed a wish to meet him. Outraged at evidence of the king's collusion with Israel and the passivity of the Arab Legion in the 1948 war, Riad took the decision not see him. Indeed, to avoid 'Abdallah, Riad el-Solh left Beirut and went south to the village of Tamra. A week or two later, the king sent Riad a message inviting him to Amman. Once again, Riad declined, on the pretext that urgent matters kept him in Beirut.

That is where things stood at the end of June, when the king – speaking in Turkish, no doubt to avoid being overheard by phone-tappers – finally managed to reach Riad el-Solh on the telephone. With great insistence, he renewed his invitation: he needed, he said, to consult Riad about 'a very important matter'. It was this plea that induced a reluctant Riad to board an Air Liban plane for the short flight to Amman on Friday, 13 July 1951. He must have hoped against hope that a contrite 'Abdallah had had a change of heart, and now wished to rejoin the Arab camp, one way or another.

Riad el-Solh was accompanied on the journey by his personal physician, Dr Nasib Barbir; by his bodyguard, 'Abd al-'Aziz 'Arab, a former police officer; and by two journalists – Muhammad Shuqayr, editor of *al-Nida'*, and Bishara Marun, owner-editor of *al-Ruwwad*. Riad did not like flying. Shuqayr noticed that, whenever the plane encountered turbulence, he became agitated and would not allow the other members of his party to leave their seats. He loosened his tie, removed his shoes and seemed to be breathing with some difficulty. 'What can King 'Abdallah possibly want from me?' he kept exclaiming.[23]

Riad was met at Mafraq military airbase near Amman by Samir Rifa'i, Jordan's prime minister, Finance Minister Suleiman Nabulsi,

---

[23] Salim al-Lawzi, 'Limaza qatalu al-za'im?', in *al-Hawadess*, no. 837 (24 November 1972).

and Farhan Shbeilat, Jordan's ambassador to London. He was driven to the Basman palace, where the king was waiting to bid him welcome. He was then taken to the Philadelphia Hotel, the best in Amman at the time, before returning later to the palace for dinner. The meal passed off amicably enough, during which Riad and the king engaged in a poetry joust, in ancient Arab tradition. After dinner, they met privately for about an hour. Riad seemed relaxed after the meeting, but would say nothing about what had transpired. Three further private meetings took place between Saturday morning and Sunday evening.

On the Saturday, Riad lunched at the Lebanese embassy, and on the Sunday he was the guest at a reception at the Saudi embassy. He telephoned his wife that evening to say: 'We will meet tomorrow and you will hear things which will make you happy. I will bring news which will fill the heart of every Arab with happiness and pride'. His wife, who had not wanted Riad to go to Amman, took this to mean that King 'Abdallah had agreed to take up the fight against Israel, once again.[24]

Muhammad Shuqayr went to Riad's room at the Philadelphia Hotel on Sunday evening and found him in pyjamas and wearing a nightcap. He very much wanted Riad to tell him what the king had had to say. Before replying, Riad made him swear on the Qur'an that he would not publish a word of what he was about to learn.

'I insisted that you come to Amman,' the king had said,

> although I am well aware that you do not like me, and have often attacked me. May God forgive you! But I need a man like you for the matter which is on my mind. Of all the Arab personalities, you alone have the qualities of a leader, not just in your own country but abroad as well. You enjoy the trust of everyone.
>
> I was thinking of what would become of Jordan after my departure. You know the situation of my son, Talal [who was receiving treatment for mental illness]. You know, too, that his brother, Nayef, is good for nothing. My grandson, Husayn, whom I love, is still too young. I'm worried that my kingdom will fall victim to the ambitions of its neighbours.

---

[24] Interview with Alia el-Solh, Paris, February 2006.

> *That is why I thought of forming some kind of*
> *union between Jordan and Iraq, which my nephew, 'Abd*
> *al-Ilah, would head after my death. In this way, I would*
> *protect the throne of Jordan and take a step towards*
> *realizing my father's dream. I have chosen you to convince*
> *the Arabs of this project.*[25]

On Monday, 16 July, before starting on the return journey to Beirut, Riad el-Solh and his party lunched at the Amman Club at the invitation of the proprietor, himself of Lebanese origin. The French minister to Jordan, Monsieur J. Dumargay was seated next to Riad at the table. 'He seemed preoccupied throughout the lunch', Dumargay reported to Paris. 'He told me how much he regretted not having left Amman in the morning, instead of accepting the invitation to lunch'.[26] Once the meal was over, Riad paid a last visit to the palace to bid goodbye to the king, and then returned to the Philadelphia Hotel to collect his companions, before heading for the airport. He had wanted to return to Beirut by road, but the king had insisted that he go by air and had chartered a plane for him.

That afternoon, Riad left his room and made his way down to the hotel lobby, where the Jordanians were waiting to see him off. Suddenly, a man rushed forwards to greet him. Riad took off his sunglasses, stepped back and held out his hand. 'Do you know who that was?' he asked, when the man had gone. But no one seemed able to identify him. The party then set off for the airport in two cars. Riad sat in the back seat of the first car, with Dr Barbir at his side. Baqir Bey, an aide-de-camp from the Royal Court, sat in front, next to the driver. No other escort was provided. The two journalists, Shuqayr and Marun, travelled in the second car with Riad's bodyguard, 'Abd al-'Aziz 'Arab.

At about 3.45 p.m., when their convoy had reached the level crossing near Amman railway station, a Hudson travelling at high speed surged out of a side road, quickly overtook the second car and began closing in on the first car. This immediately aroused 'Abd al-'Aziz 'Arab's suspicions. He told the driver to give chase. But before he could

---

[25] Eyewitness account of Muhammad Shuqayr (Choucair), Amman to Foreign Office, 17 July 1951 (FO 371/91434).

[26] MAE, Nantes, Fonds Beyrouth (Amb.), série 199A4, carton 20, M. J. Dumargay, Ministre de France en Jordanie, à Son Excellence Monsieur le Ministre des Affaires Etrangères, Amman, 17 July 1951.

intervene, the Hudson had managed to draw level with the first car on a stretch of open road. Shuqayr and his comrades saw a hand holding a revolver reach out of the Hudson and take aim at Riad el-Solh's car. Half a dozen shots rang out. Riad's car was brought to a standstill, while the Hudson drove off at high speed. Shuqayr and Marun leapt out of their car to see what had happened to Riad and Dr Barbir, while 'Abd al-'Aziz 'Arab, now joined by Baqir Bey, set off in pursuit of the Hudson. Dr Barbir's wounds were not serious, but Riad had been shot through the heart. He must have turned to face his assailant. They were rushed to the Italian Hospital in Amman, but Riad was already dead when they arrived there. He was 57 years old.

Meanwhile, a police car near the airfield had joined 'Abd al-'Aziz 'Arab and Baqir Bey in their pursuit of the Hudson. As they were about to catch up with it, three men jumped out and ran off in different directions. Shots were exchanged. One of the men was killed outright; another turned his gun on himself; and the third, the driver of the Hudson, managed to escape – although there were later unconfirmed reports that he had been captured. 'Abd al-'Aziz 'Arab suffered a superficial leg wound from a stray bullet.

The three assailants were later named by the police as Michel Gabriel al-Dik, a Christian Lebanese from Tripoli, who was killed in the exchange of fire. He was the man who had shaken hands with Riad at the hotel, no doubt to identify him to the other conspirators; Muhammad 'Abd al-Latif al-Salahi, a Muslim from Haifa, who was captured, taken to hospital and interrogated, but died shortly afterwards; and the driver of the Hudson, Wadi' Nikola Spiro (or Isbiridon), a Christian Jordanian of Lebanese origin, who by all accounts was still at large. All three were members of Antun Sa'ada's PPS.

According to a former member of the PPS,[27] the order to kill Riad el-Solh had come directly from Georges 'Abd al-Massih, a fanatical follower of Antun Sa'ada, who, having assumed the presidency of the PPS after Sa'ada's execution, had vowed to avenge him. It was widely believed that the killers could not have acted without his personal instructions. Senior members of the party had then sought to rein in Abd al-Massih. He was told that the party could not tolerate further crimes.

---

[27] Telephone interview by the author with Muhammad al-Ba'albaki, head of the Lebanese Press Association and a former member of the PPS, Beirut, 13 January 2009.

But – to carry the story forwards a few years – this did not deter 'Abd al-Massih from ordering the murder of Colonel Adnan Malki in 1955. Malki, a leading Ba'thist officer in the Syrian army, was shot and killed by a sergeant in Syria's military police, who was a member of the PPS.[28] With backing from the Communists, the Ba'th in Syria was engaged at the time in a bitter struggle for power with the PPS. The Ba'th had the backing of the Communists, while the PPS was alleged to have covert support from the Western Powers, and from the United States in particular. In the wake of Malki's murder, the PPS was outlawed; large numbers of its members were arrested; and its sympathisers were purged from the Syrian army and administration. The party was accused of plotting with a foreign power to overthrow the government. To save what it could from the wreckage, the party expelled Georges 'Abd al-Massih, on suspicion of being a British agent.

Alia el-Solh's premonition

Two of Riad el-Solh's five daughters, Alia and Mona, spent the year 1950–51 at the English Girls' College at Alexandria, where they shared a dormitory with Salma Mardam, daughter of the prominent Syrian politician, Jamil Mardam. As Alia hero-worshipped her father, she was anxious to learn English so that she could be his secretary. Mona left for Lebanon at the end of the school year, but Alia stayed on to sit the matriculation examination.

After the attempt on Riad el-Solh's life in March 1950 – and the widely known fact that the PPS had vowed to get him – it was not surprising that she often had nightmares, in which she imagined him being shot. On the night of 15 July 1951, she dreamt that she saw a banner headline across the whole front page of the Egyptian daily *al-Ahram*, which read, 'Riad el-Solh killed'. She woke in panic and in the morning telephoned Robert Khlat, the Lebanese consul in Alexandra, begging him to take her out of school. 'You're trying to avoid sitting your exam this afternoon,' he scolded. But he came to the school to reassure her. He told her that Riad was in Amman on an official visit.

---

[28] For a detailed account of the Malki affair, see Seale, *The Struggle for Syria*, pp. 238–46.

After lunch the next day, Alia went to her room and fell into a deep sleep, only to wake up screaming at 3.45 p.m. The premonition of her father's death was overwhelming. Again the consul was summoned. To cheer her up, he took her for a drive and then returned her to the school, where she went back to bed and slept.

The following morning, 17 July, she woke at six to perform the dawn prayer. But she had barely unfolded her prayer mat than the tall figure of Miss Bloxham entered the dorm.

'He's dead, isn't he?' Alia screamed.

'Get dressed at once and come down to the hall.'

The consul was there with swollen eyes. She threw herself into his arms. Everyone cried. Riad el-Solh had been murdered at 3.45 p.m. on 16 July.

A plane was sent from Beirut to bring Alia home. Mustafa and 'Ali Amin, two barons of the Egyptian press, had learned of the assassination the previous evening. They sent a young reporter, Muhammad Hassanain Haykal, to accompany her on the plane. He tried to take a picture of her, but the camera slipped and fell to the ground. She sat next to the consul, while Haykal occupied a seat across the aisle. He opened *al-Ahram*. She glanced across and saw the headline: 'Riad el-Solh killed in Amman'. It was the exact headline she had seen in her nightmare, with the addition of the words 'in Amman'. She arrived home at the same time as her father's coffin.

Who killed Riad el-Solh?

Riad el-Solh's corpse lay in state all night in the Royal Diwan in Amman. King 'Abdallah made a long speech in praise of the dead man. The body, accompanied by the Emir Nayef, the king's son, was flown to Beirut in a special plane on the morning of 17 July. The emir returned to Amman immediately by the same aircraft. A special Jordanian Committee was formed to investigate the crime, composed of the general prosecutor, the attorney-general and the chief of police.[29]

So perished one of the great figures of the Arab world. Riad el-Solh was not only a leader of the Arab nationalist movement from its earliest days, and the prime architect of Lebanon's independence,

[29] Amman to Foreign Office, 18 July 1951 (FO 371/91434).

but he was also admired and respected as a statesman by friend and foe alike.

At first sight, his murder seemed a straightforward case of revenge killing. The PPS had managed to avenge their dead leader, as they had so often vowed to do. But several unusual aspects of the case aroused suspicion that there was more to it than that. Dumargay, the French minister in Amman, was astonished that Riad el-Solh had not been given police protection for his journey to the airport. King 'Abdallah himself never moved anywhere without an escort of two armoured cars. Samir Rifa'i had flown out of Amman under heavy protection that very same afternoon, an hour or so before Riad's plane was due to take off. But the security force which had protected him was withdrawn when Riad el-Solh took the same route shortly afterwards. The argument that Riad's visit did not justify an exceptional police presence because it was private did not hold up. The king was well aware that Riad's life was in danger, and in any event, his visit *was* official, since he had come to Amman at the king's own behest.

It was widely known in diplomatic circles – and well known to the Jordanian police – that the PPS was deeply implanted in Jordan in many walks of life. Dumargay reported to Paris that King 'Abdallah regularly provided asylum in Jordan to opponents of neighbouring Arab regimes – and especially to members of the PPS, whom he hoped to draw into his Hashemite orbit. Antun Sa'ada's dream of a pan-Syrian nation bore a marked resemblance to the king's own 'Greater Syria' ambitions.

According to Dumargay, one of the killers, Muhammad 'Abd al-Latif al-Salahi, was thought to be a member of the Jordanian secret police, as well as a member of the PPS. Indeed, M. T. Walker, the first secretary and consul at the British embassy in Amman, confirmed to the Foreign Office that Salahi was a 'sergeant in the Political Intelligence Section of the Arab Legion Headquarters'. He added, however, that 'The Legion are trying to avoid publicity on this point'.[30]

The French minister's conclusion was that the Jordanian authorities were guilty of extraordinary negligence, if not of actual criminal behaviour. This charge, in his view, had also to be laid at the door of Glubb Pasha, since the Jordanian police was incorporated into the Arab Legion, of which he was the commander. Even if King

---

[30] Amman to Foreign Office, 17 July 1951 (FO 371/91434).

'Abdallah had not actually plotted Riad el-Solh's murder, his government had, nevertheless, to be considered directly responsible.

Conspiracy theories abounded. Riad's daughter, Alia, believed that Jordan's Prime Minister Samir Rifa'i had planned the assassination and had flown out of Amman on the day in order to be abroad at the time of the killing. As the king's confidant, he was thoroughly involved in 'Abdallah's dealings with Israel, and was known to be totally opposed to Riad el-Solh's nationalist ideas. Alia was also convinced that the driver of her father's car was an Arab Legion officer, who had been instructed to slow down so as to allow the Hudson to come alongside.[31] There were widespread, if unconfirmed, rumours that Wadi' Nikola Spiro had made his escape into an Arab Legion camp, from which the British had spirited him away to Latin America – via Israel. This was certainly the belief of one of Riad's grandsons, Riad al-As'ad, which he expressed on an Al Jazeera television programme on 1 July 2005. He argued that, whereas the PPS had evidently killed Riad el-Solh, the crime had a dimension which extended far beyond Lebanon. 'In my view', he stated bluntly, 'British intelligence participated in the murder'.

In any event, there was something distinctly fishy about 'Abdallah's repeated appeals to Riad to come to Amman, as there was about his attempt to enlist his help in bringing about a Jordanian-Iraqi union. The king knew that Riad el-Solh had been anxious to merge the Iraqi and Jordanian armies so as to enable the Arabs to resume the fight against Israel in 1948–49. He might, therefore, have reckoned that Riad would be attracted by the plea that he should take the lead in canvassing for an Iraqi-Jordanian union. But 'Abdallah's proposal was evidently bogus. A union between Jordan and Iraq was the very last thing that 'Abdallah actually wanted *at that time* – or that his Israeli friends would have tolerated.

A union with Iraq had indeed been one of 'Abdallah's projects in the early 1940s, but by 1951, it had been overtaken by events. Far from wanting to bring Iraqi forces back into Palestine, 'Abdallah and the Israelis wanted them removed as far as possible from the battlefield.[32] With Israel's encouragement, 'Abdallah had even managed to get the Iraqis to evacuate the pocket of Palestinian territory they had

---

[31] Interview with Alia el-Solh, Paris, February 2005.
[32] Shlaim, *The Politics of Partition*, p. 280.

held on to and return home.[33] Israel was adamantly opposed to any further Iraqi involvement in the war,[34] and 'Abdallah himself had long considered the Iraqi army a dangerously radical force.[35] Ben-Gurion described Iraq as Israel's 'most despicable enemy among the Arab peoples'.[36] The very last thing the Israeli leader wanted was any linkage between his docile little Jordan and a still strong and defiant Iraq.

Far from seeking union with Iraq at that time, 'Abdallah too considered it to be his enemy, on a par with Egypt.[37] In sum, whereas Riad el-Solh wanted to bring Iraq back into the battle, Israel and Jordan wanted all Arab troops out; whereas Riad wanted to continue the confrontation with Israel, 'Abdallah fervently wanted to put a total end to it. What he sought above all else was to conclude a full-blown peace treaty with Israel, without interference from any other Arab state, so that he could annex what was left of Arab Palestine and resume his lucrative 'special relationship' with the Zionists.[38] Indeed, he was ready to defy the entire Arab world on this score.[39] As for the Western Powers, all they cared about was to stabilise the situation in the Middle East after the war. With war raging on the Korean peninsula, their main preoccupation was to protect their interests in the Arab world and to seek to contain Communism.

Such was the background to Riad el-Solh's visit to Amman. It was evident that, far from wishing to befriend him and take him into his confidence, 'Abdallah loathed and feared him. Far from wanting to seek Riad's help to bring about a Jordanian-Iraqi union, 'Abdallah wanted him done away with. He bore Riad a venomous grudge for having publicly denounced him as a traitor and for having demanded Jordan's expulsion from the League. He was threatened by Riad because the latter's campaign to get the Arabs to persist in their boycott of Israel, and be ready to resume war, could easily have sabotaged 'Abdallah's own secret accommodation with Israel.

The evidence suggests that King 'Abdallah's plea to Riad el-Solh to come to Jordan was nothing but a trap. If 'Abdallah did not actually plot Riad's murder, then he must at least be considered an

---

[33] Ibid., p. 314.
[34] Ibid., p. 352.
[35] Ibid., p. 289.
[36] Ibid., p. 376.
[37] Ibid., p. 364.
[38] Ibid., p. 331.
[39] Ibid., p. 416.

accessory in allowing it to take place in his country. The members of the PPS may have been the executioners, yes, but it was 'Abdallah – and almost certainly Glubb Pasha too – who provided the means and the opportunity for the crime actually to be committed.

On Friday, 20 July 1951, four days after Riad el-Solh's killing, King 'Abdallah was himself assassinated at the entrance to the al-Aqsa mosque in the Old City of Jerusalem. His killer was Mustafa Shukri 'Usho, a tailor, who had taken part in attacks against the British and the Zionists in Palestine during the Arab rebellion of the 1930s. It later emerged that 'Abdallah had come to pray in Jerusalem that Friday because he was due to have yet another secret meeting there with the Israelis on the following day. His concern remained – to the very last – to protect his intimate relations with Israel.[40]

Two months earlier, on 17 May, Sir Alec Kirkbride – Britain's long-term representative in Jordan, who knew the country and its intrigues better than any other Englishman – had reported to the Foreign Office that the Iraq government had received information, 'from a reliable source', that 'Abdallah al-Tal was in Damascus, and was plotting with the connivance of the Syrian *Deuxième Bureau* to assassinate both King 'Abdallah and Glubb Pasha. Kirkbride added that Tal had long feared assassination by the Jordan authorities.[41]

Ten persons were accused of conspiring to kill King 'Abdallah. In a long dispatch to the Foreign Office on 24 September 1951 – written once their trial had taken place and sentence had been passed – Ambassador Kirkbride concluded that 'informed opinion places the conception and the planning of the murder as a free-lance operation on Abdallah Tell [al-Tal]'. The Mufti's cousin, Musa Husayni, was also involved in the conspiracy, but, in Kirkbride's opinion, the Mufti 'would never have lent himself to such a clumsy plot, nor would he have used his somewhat stupid cousin, whom he personally disliked and distrusted, as the principal agent in its execution'.[42]

King 'Abdallah's assassination caused turmoil in Jordan. Inevitably, it distracted the attention of the authorities from the investigation into Riad el-Solh's killing. It seems that few serious enquiries were made. The curious uncertainty over what happened to 'the third man' – Wadi' Nikola Spiro, the driver of the Hudson – was never

---

[40] Ibid., p. 417.
[41] Sir A. Kirkbride, Amman, to Foreign Office, 17 May 1950 (FO 371/82775).
[42] Sir A. Kirkbride to Mr Younger, 24 September 1951 (FO 371/91839).

cleared up, at least not in any public fashion. An examination of the British archives reveals little about him. A dispatch on 18 December 1951 to the British Legation in Beirut from the British Legation in Amman reads as follows:

> *To complete the record you may like to know that Spiro Wadi' Nikola, one of the three men who assassinated Riad Bey Solh last July (he was the driver of the car and escaped) was tried in Amman in absentia on November 17th. The Court was specially set up under Ordinance No. 88 of 1951 (which was also the basis of authority of the Court which condemned King Abdullah's murderers).*
> *Spiro Wadi' Nikola was found guilty and sentenced to death in accordance with Article 322/1 of the Jordan Criminal Law No.8 of 1951. (This differed from the sentences on King Abdullah's murderers which, since the crime was committed in Palestine, was based on the Palestine Criminal Code of 1936, Articles 214/23 and 24.)[43]*

This dispatch was followed on 31 December by a handwritten internal Foreign Office memo of half a dozen lines, by a certain Ian (or Imn) Hunter, which reads as follows:

> *Please see now EL 1016/53 about the trial on 17 November under this Ordinance of the last of Riad el-Solh's murderers. If our representations have had effect, the court should now be dissolved. If we ask the Jordan government about it again they may take offence, but if we let it go it may appear that we were not serious in the first place. We had best consult Mr. Walker [the First Secretary in Amman] first.[44]*

The file EL 1016/53 appears to have been removed from the archives, as indeed were other documents concerning the case. At any rate, this author and his researcher failed to find them. We can deduce from these exchanges, however, that Wadi' Nikola Spiro, 'the last of Riad el-Solh's

---

[43] Amman to Foreign Office, 18 December 1951 (FO 371/91434).
[44] Internal Foreign Office memo by Ian(?) Hunter, 31 December 1951 (FO 371/91839).

murderers', managed to escape – whether with British complicity or not is unknown. Why the British were concerned that the Court, which tried Spiro in absentia, be swiftly dissolved remains unexplained.[45]

Then, and to the present, the British authorities decided to withhold all information in their possession about the case. Whatever their involvement might have been, or whatever knowledge they may have had of the escape of Wadi' Nikola Spiro, or of the other circumstances of Riad el-Solh's death, remains to this day a carefully guarded secret.

A possible Israeli connection

Was there an Israeli hand in Riad el-Solh's murder? The possibility cannot be ruled out, especially since Israel had planned to kill him eighteen months earlier in the winter of 1949. The Israeli Foreign Ministry, headed at the time by Moshe Sharett, certainly wanted him dead. It judged him to be 'the most extreme and dangerous' of the Arab leaders, since he had played a prominent part in pressing the Arab League to intervene in Palestine and had pleaded the Arab case at the United Nations. Orders were accordingly sent to an Israeli undercover agent in Beirut, Ya'acov Cohen, to carry out the assassination by blowing up Riad el-Solh's car as Riad drove from his home to parliament. The plot was revealed by Yosef Argaman, in *Milchemet Ha' Tzlalim: 25 parshiot modi'in uvitachon be-israel* (The Shadow War: Twenty-Five Intelligence and Security Cases in Israel), published in Hebrew by Israel's Ministry of Defence in 2007.

Ya'acov Cohen, the man chosen for the job, was a member of an Israeli cell of Arabic speakers in Beirut. Born in Jerusalem of Iranian

---

[45] The author's repeated requests to the Foreign and Commonwealth Office, under the Freedom of Information Act, to release documents relating to Riad el-Solh's murder have met with a firm refusal. Mr. Michael Kerr of the FCO's Information Management Group wrote to the author on 11 April 2008, to say that the documents he requested were covered by Section 23 of the Freedom of Information Act. 'This exemption', he explained, 'covers information supplied by, or relating to, bodies dealing with security matters and applies to all records regardless of their age. Section 23 is an absolute exemption and there is therefore no public interest test to apply'. Mr Kerr added, 'I acknowledge the importance of your forthcoming work and have taken into consideration the passage of time since the events of 1951. However, after reviewing this particular case and consulting appropriately, we uphold our decision to retain the relevant information under Section 23 of the Act'.

parentage, he was a veteran secret agent, who had worked undercover for Israel in several Arab countries, including Syria, Lebanon and Egypt. He was widely known in Israeli intelligence circles by his nick-name of Ya'akuba. In an interview with him before his death in 2003, Argaman was able to learn the details of this particular operation.

Having studied Riad's movements, Cohen told Argaman, he had noted that Riad was very poorly protected. His car would some-times be accompanied by two motorcyclists, while, at other times, two bodyguards would sit with him inside the car itself. Riad's journey from home to parliament took seven minutes. The trouble was that this short time span left little space to plant and detonate the explosives needed to blow up Riad's car. Cohen's handlers in Tel Aviv responded with the suggestion that the cell fill the carcass of a dead dog with explosives, and throw it in the path of Riad's car. But even so, how were they to prime the dog, put it in place and detonate it in the short time they had available? The mechanism they possessed, of British wartime manufacture, required a longer time span of between ten and fifteen minutes.

But Cohen's handlers in Tel Aviv had by now grown impatient. In a change of plan, they ordered him to find a suitable place where a light aircraft, flying low, could drop the quicker-acting 'equipment' that the cell required. As it so happened, Beirut's future airport was then under construction at Khaldeh, just outside the city. Runways were being levelled during the day, but at night the site was deserted. Making preparations to guide the plane in with lights, the cell waited for a signal from Israel.

For some reason, Tel Aviv delayed giving the word. Cohen therefore decided to act on his own, since the original order to him to kill Riad el-Solh had been firm, and required 'no further confirmation'. His plan was to fill a bag with explosives, wait for Riad's car to slow down at a crossroads, leap towards it, stick the bag on it, detonate the charge and then run for his life in the few seconds before the explosion. But when members of the cell informed Israel of Cohen's alternative plan, strict orders were issued to cancel the operation. It was consid-ered too foolhardy.

Against such a background, it is plausible to speculate that Israel, alarmed at Riad el-Solh's efforts to rally the Arabs after their defeat, may have decided in 1951 to make another attempt to eliminate him. But rather than use, and risk, an undercover Israeli agent for the task, members of Antun Sa'ada's party, led by Georges 'Abd al-Massih, were raring to do it – possibly with the complicity of King 'Abdallah, and of Glubb Pasha as well. Some murky conspiracy of this sort may perhaps explain the refusal, on 'security' grounds, of the Information Management Group of the Foreign and Commonwealth Office to release documents regarding the case. They might, if opened, finally reveal the truth of who was involved in the murder.[46]

The aftermath of Riad el-Solh's murder

The news of Riad el-Solh's murder broke in Beirut at a few minutes to eight on the evening of 16 July, when it was broadcast by the Beirut wireless station. Almost immediately, crowds from his quarter of the Basta poured out in anger and grief. Bands of demonstrators roamed the streets, overturning motor vehicles and breaking windows in their unleashed fury. The police could only watch, until armoured cars were called in to patrol the streets.[47]

Riad el-Solh was buried the next day. As the funeral cortège made its way to the mosque, vast crowds, close to half a million people – the like of which, according to the press, had never been seen before – lined the roads, windows, balconies and rooftops, to pay tribute to the man whose name, more than any other, was associated with Lebanon's independence. The authorities ordained three days of national mourning. All the papers carried eulogies of Riad, and even his bitterest enemies praised his strong personality, his great qualities as a statesman and the outstanding role he had played, not only in Lebanon, but in the whole of the Levant.

In the entourage of President Bishara al-Khoury, the reaction was more subdued. 'One may suppose', the French Minister Armand de Chayla commented,

that Shaykh Bishara al-Khoury feels a certain relief at being rid of a man with whom he had quarrelled when

[46] Yosef Argaman, *Milchemet Ha' Tzlalim: 25 parshiot modi'in uvitachon be-israel*, Tel Aviv 2007, pp. 209–14. See also a dispatch from Haifa on the same subject by Firas al-Khatib in the Beirut newspaper *al-Akhbar*, on 12 February 2008.
[47] Amman to Foreign Office, 18 December 1951 (FO 371/91434); Chapman Andrews, Beirut, to Foreign Office, 16 July 1951 (FO 371/91434).

he was Prime Minister, and who would no doubt have
been even more dangerous as leader of the opposition.
The second reaction is certainly one of fear. The murder
of Riad el-Solh proves that the PPS has not disarmed and
is determined to avenge the death of its leader, Antun
Sa'ada – for which it holds Husni al-Za'im, Riad el-Solh
and . . . Bishara al-Khoury responsible.[48]

In Damascus, the Syrian Chamber of Deputies, at its session of 17 July, observed one minute's silence as a tribute to Riad el-Solh, but the PPS deputy 'Isam Mahayri, and Akram al-Hawrani, leader of the Arab Socialist Party – who had been a PPS member and was still a sympathiser – callously walked out.[49] A few days after the funeral, Chapman Andrews, the British minister in Beirut, called on Bishara al-Khoury at his private residence. The murders of Riad el-Solh and King 'Abdallah, the president said, were evidence of the dangerous state of tension and instability in the Middle East. The very foundations of stability were being rocked, he said.[50]

The first anniversary of Riad el-Solh's death was commemorated in Beirut on 16 July 1952 by a ceremony at the mausoleum, which had been erected to his memory in a Beirut suburb. Flowers were placed on his tomb. In the afternoon, more than 10,000 people gathered at the municipal stadium to hear a dozen speakers extol Riad's political genius and ardent Arab patriotism, with the grandiloquence to which the Arabic language often lends itself. Shops closed and drivers stopped their cars for ten minutes throughout the country. President Bishara al-Khoury and his high-handed brothers would no doubt have preferred to play down the event, but they did not dare make their views known, as they would have caused deep offence and anger in Lebanon's Muslim community.

Several Arab countries sent representatives – but, tellingly, none came from Jordan. More than twenty figures from the National Bloc came from Syria – but none representing the hostile Colonel Adib al-Shishakli's regime. From Iraq, Riad el-Solh's old friend Nuri

---

[48] MAE, Nantes, Fonds Beyrouth (Amb.), série 199A4, carton 20, M. Armand de Chayla, Ministre de France au Liban, à Son Excellence M. Robert Schuman, 18 July 1951.
[49] British Legation, Damascus, to Foreign Office, 23 July 1951 (FO 371/91434).
[50] Chapman Andrews, Beirut, to Foreign Office, 23 July 1951 (FO 371/91434).

al-Sa'id led a delegation of a dozen dignitaries, which included Jamil Midfa'i, the president of the Senate. The most prominent Egyptian present was Muhammad Salaheddin Pasha, who had served as foreign minister in the Wafdist cabinet. His speech contained bitter references to the foreign presence in Arab countries, which caused the audience to explode with wild cheers. It was felt, as he spoke, that Egypt, then engaged in a struggle to remove British troops from the country, was clearly being drawn into the Arab nationalist orbit. The British minister in Beirut had warned the Lebanese organisers of the meeting not to allow attacks to be made on Britain, but no one was able or willing to silence Salaheddin Pasha. From Morocco, still under French control, came Riad's friend, 'Alal al-Fasi, head of the *Istiqlal* Party, who, in addition to reciting a poem celebrating Riad el-Solh's many qualities, made a passionate declaration of faith in Arab unity. To indicate his displeasure at al-Fasi's presence, the French minister stayed away from the ceremony. European colonialism may have been by now on the defensive, but it was still far from being completely defeated.[51]

The overthrow of Bishara al-Khoury

In the end, Bishara al-Khoury never managed to serve out his controversial second term as president. In June 1952, an opposition movement, calling itself the Socialist National Front (SNF), took shape under the impulse of nine deputies led by Kamal Jumblatt, head of the Progressive Socialist Party. It included Camille Chamoun's National Liberals, Emile Eddé's National Bloc, the Armenian Hentchak Party – and the *Parti populaire syrien* of the late Antun Sa'ada. It had the generous support of Emile Bustani, a self-made multimillionaire, and of other prominent businessmen. The new Front waged open war on the regime. It denounced its abuses – particularly those of the president's brothers and sons – and called for the eradication of favouritism and corruption; for an end to sectarianism; and for radical reform of the way Lebanon was governed. Bishara al-Khoury attempted to crush the revolt by muzzling the opposition press. Twelve newspapers were suspended and their editors put on trial for attacking the head of state. But all to no avail.

---

[51] MAE, Nantes, Fonds Beyrouth (Amb.), série 199A4, carton 20, M. Georges Balay, Ministre de France au Liban, à Son Excellence Monsieur Robert Schuman, Ministre des Affaires Etrangères, Beirut, 25 July 1952.

On 17 May 1952, the SNF held a mass rally at Dayr al-Qamar, Chamoun's home town, which was attended by 50,000 people. Speaker after speaker threatened to rise in rebellion against the government if the president did not resign. On 23 July, Pierre Gemayel's *Phalanges* movement lent muscular support to the Front by coming out in favour of the opposition. When the Front called a general strike on 11 September to force the president from office, all activity came to a standstill in the major cities. An increasingly desperate Bishara al-Khoury ordered the Emir Fu'ad Chehab, the army commander, to break the strike, but the cautious Chehab wisely refused to get involved. Bishara al-Khoury was compelled to resign on 18 September, and the Front's candidate, Camille Chamoun, was elected president in his place, by a near-unanimous vote.

On 21 April 1953, the Beirut Municipal Council decided to erect a bronze statue of Riad el-Solh in the city centre. A budget of 65,000 Lebanese lira was earmarked for the project. The artist Léon Mouradof produced a model, which was approved by a four-man committee, composed of 'Adil el-Solh, William Hawi, Dr Fawzi Da'uq, and Dr Bishara Dahhan. A square in the city, known formerly as the Place 'Assour, was renamed Place Riad el-Solh.[52]

---

[52] MAE-Nantes, Fonds Beyrouth (Amb.), série B, carton 20, numéro 421, cabinet politique.

AFTERWORD

Because he had always considered himself to be an Arab – rather than a Lebanese – Riad el-Solh was always going to be something of an anomaly on Lebanon's political scene. His vision embraced the whole region and was never confined to the narrow politics of one small country on the eastern Mediterranean seaboard, where he just happened to have been born. He was never merely a local politician, and his prestige rested on his deliberate internationalism. He became such a familiar figure in so many world capitals that Western chancelleries scurried to chart his every move.

As a lifelong advocate of Arab independence, he ranged far and wide across the Arab world and beyond. Although he was forced, at different times and for different reasons, to focus more narrowly on Lebanese affairs, his instincts and loyalties remained pan-Arab. Such was his reputation, and such were his interests, friendships and the range of his political action.

Although he dominated the Lebanese scene for decades, he was never wholly at ease in Lebanese politics. He detested the very basis on which the country's system had been built by the French – that is to say, confessionalism. He was adamant in his belief that confessionalism was the very opposite of freedom. For to take refuge in one's sectarian identity was, for Riad el-Solh, to build a barricade around oneself and against one's neighbour. He used to say, with no little exasperation, that he dearly wished he might never again have to hear the loaded words 'Christian' or 'Muslim'. He much preferred 'citizen' – and ideally, 'Arab citizen'. Confessionalism, he believed, ultimately led to rampant corruption. Anyone acquiring any influence, however slight, would soon be compelled to help out his co-religionaries. And this would be done irrespective of their honesty, merit or ability: get them out of prison, say, or place them in a government job, or seek to circumvent the law in one way or another on their behalf. Confessionalism, in Riad's view, had injected nothing but poison into Lebanon's public life.

'The age of confessionalism has passed in Europe', he would declare. 'Modern nations are built on the basis of nationalism, of independence, of competence. What importance can there be if this or that job is occupied by this or that category of persons? If all the officials of the state were to belong to a single community, I would be the first to accept it.'[1]

To both Muslims and Christians he preached compromise, tolerance and mutual sacrifice for the greater good. He urged them to bury their differences and join forces in the defence of their common homeland. Prophetically, he predicted that sectarian strife, if left unchecked, would lead to civil war, as indeed it did during the terrible years of 1975–90. Even today, Lebanon continues to be haunted by the grim possibility of yet another round of confessional bloodletting.

Riad el-Solh was a Sunni Muslim, yet never in a sectarian sense. He did not believe in the exclusion or repudiation of other sects or religions. He always sought to place himself in his political life above Lebanon's confessional strife. Because his own family roots were in South Lebanon, he had acquired a complex knowledge of and natural sympathy for the Shi'is, who historically had been neglected and deprived in his lifetime and before. Since his death, however, this community has risen to occupy a powerful place in Lebanon's political life. This is due to many factors, including Shi'i resistance to Israel's repeated assaults, invasions and long occupation of the South, and, more recently, because of the significant political, military and financial backing of the Iranian and Syrian regimes.

Riad also had a fraternal entente with Christians of all denominations – as well as a good understanding of Christianity – perhaps because he was raised in cosmopolitan Istanbul and Beirut by an enlightened family, and was sent to Jesuit mission schools. No prominent Muslim politician of his generation had a greater sensitivity for the anxieties of Eastern Christians in their nervous cohabita-

---

[1] Extempore speech in honour of Hanna Ghusn, editor of *al-Diyar*, delivered at a tea given by Sa'id Freyha, owner of *al-Sayyad*, MAE, Nantes, Fonds Beyrouth (Amb.), série 199A4, carton 20, *al-Diyar*, 15 April 1946.

tion with the Arab world's religious majority. None understood better that Lebanon's Christians needed constant reassurance, if they were expected ever to embrace the cause of Arab nationalism.

Although Riad grew to loathe and fear Zionism, which he considered to be an extension of the European colonialism against which he had fought so hard, he had no personal animus against Jews, and was certainly no anti-Semite. During a brief moment in the Second World War, he may have thought that Germany might be able to help the Arabs throw off British and French colonial rule, but he was horrified by Nazi racist theories and rejected them utterly. He had real sympathy for the horrors that Jews had had to suffer in Nazi-dominated Europe. He therefore was able to understand the mindset of Zionism's founding fathers in their stubborn determination to create a Jewish state at any cost.

Indeed, he made repeated attempts over the years to reach an agreement with the Zionists, even proposing to rally Arab support for a Jewish canton in a wider Arab entity. But by the late 1930s, he had already come to realise that massive Jewish immigration, the steady purchase of Palestinian land, the revival of the Hebrew language, and the strong support of wealthy Europeans and Americans, had made the Jewish presence in Palestine an imposing reality that could no longer be wished away. Zionist ambitions proved far greater than Riad el-Solh – or indeed any other Arab politician – could ever have imagined or willingly conceded.

This small community of less than a million people, most of them the remnants of persecuted European Jewry, managed to transform itself into the strongest military power in the Middle East, trouncing all the Arab states, which were weakened by their chronically bitter infighting. With the complicity of Britain and of 'Abdallah of Jordan, it captured much of Palestine, killing, dispossessing and expelling three-quarters of a million Palestinians in the process. For Riad el-Solh, the shock of this catastrophe was terrible indeed. Its ripple effects were literally to kill him.

Riad's enemy throughout his life was Western colonialism – and especially French colonialism – which he fought not only in Syria and Lebanon, but in North Africa too. He was in solidarity with a large number of anti-colonial freedom fighters – with 'Alal al-Fasi, the leader of the Moroccan *Istiqlal* (and the author of a classic work on *The Independence Movements in Arab North*

Africa²); with Algeria's Musalli al-Hajj; with Tunisia's Habib Bourguiba; with Bashir al-Sa'dawi of Libya; with Tarif bin al-Afriqi of Eritrea. He conducted a lively correspondence with some of them over many years. But although he fought European colonialism all his life, Riad was far from being a xenophobe. He loved Paris, the French language, French culture and France's great revolutionary inheritance. His tragedy was that scarcely had he and his fellow Arabs managed to throw off French rule in the Levant, than they were confronted with the threatening emergence of Israel in the heart of their region.

Riad el-Solh had great qualities – courage, charm, shrewdness, a quick wit, pragmatism and a great deal of patience – but at heart he was an idealist, a visionary, a fighter for freedom, rather than a conventional politician. There was something of the inspirational teacher about him. He wanted to free the Arabs from foreign control, and then show them how best to live their political freedom. Lebanon, he was fond of saying, was the best 'laboratory' – a word he liked the ring of – in which such a lesson could be learned.

The opening to the world afforded by the Mediterranean; the physical protection provided by the Mountain; the long tradition of emigration which had seen so many million Lebanese go abroad, while nevertheless retaining close links with their home country – all these, Riad believed, helped make Lebanon more suited for democracy than other Arab countries. This was the grand ideal he wished to live by. The other side of the coin was that he had little time and less inclination for the humdrum and bureaucratic work of government administration. He could hardly bring himself to open a ministry file; budgets bored him – his own as much as the state's. Although he had inherited a considerable fortune, he spent it all on political causes. Not concerned with possessions or with worldly ostentation – unlike some of today's avaricious Arab rulers – he was content to live modestly in a shabby rented flat. He never managed to buy a house. He was in crippling debt for almost all of his life, and died penniless. This was a hugely appealing characteristic, which set him apart from most other Arab politicians of his time – with the exception of his dear friend Shukri al-Quwatli, Syria's leading nationalist figure and first president, who also bankrupted himself for his country's political cause.

---

² Translated from the Arabic (*al-Harakat al-istiqlaliyah fi al-Maghrib al-'Arabi*) by Hazem Zaki Nuseibeh, Washington, DC 1954.

Riad el-Solh's contribution to Arab political life was highly important, in five particular areas. First and foremost, he fought unstintingly for Arab independence – from the Turks, from the French and from the Zionists. His greatest single achievement was against the French, thus securing his place in history as the main architect of Lebanon's independence. Second, he was a fervent believer in Arab unity – or, at a bare minimum, in Arab solidarity – as the only way the Arabs could hope to achieve self-respect and compel others to respect them. On this score, he was sadly defeated by the petty and deep-rooted rivalries between the various Arab leaders, and by Lebanon's own rivalries and its splintered society.

Third, he was a democrat. His instinct was always to seek a consensus and to let others have their say. He truly came alive in parliament, where he loved the cut and thrust of debate, at which he so visibly excelled. He also liked and believed in a free press. In 1943, on first becoming prime minister, he declared that 'since we have come to power under a democratic regime, it is our duty to ensure the freedom of the press . . . We are well aware that a free press means that we will have to give an account of ourselves. But, even more than praise and encouragement, we need to be told where we go wrong'.

In his attachment to democracy, Riad was profoundly influenced by what he had experienced in Istanbul in his early manhood, witnessing the stormy sessions of the Ottoman parliament during the last years of the Empire. He was also influenced by his stay in Europe, particularly in Switzerland, where different ethnic groups, speaking different languages, lived together in freedom and harmony. Could not this admirable Swiss model, he often wondered aloud, be replicated in Lebanon, itself made up of a mosaic of religions and national identities?

Fourth, he believed passionately in Christian–Muslim reconciliation and entente, as the indispensable basis for Lebanese citizenship and statehood. More than anyone else, he laid the basis for such an understanding with the National Pact of 1943, which remains to this day the foundation stone of Lebanon's political society. As well as being an ardent Arab nationalist, he was converted in mid-career to the cause of Lebanon's independence within its enlarged frontiers, as a necessary first step to its integration into the Arab world. As early as the 1930s, Riad had grasped that, for Lebanon to achieve its independence from France and play its full part in the Arab world to which it belonged, an understanding had to be found between the rival aspirations, ideologies and identities of Christians and Muslims. To both he preached the need for concession, for compromise. Unfortunately, his message was not always heard as clearly as he would have liked. 'I came to power to build a State', he was to say wistfully before he was killed, 'but they prevented me from doing so'.

Fifth, Riad was a fervent advocate of a relationship of trust between Lebanon and Syria, two sister states which, whatever their many disagreements, were destined by nature, history and a thousand intimate ties of kinship and mutual dependence, to live and work together. He was determined that Lebanon would not allow a foreign power hostile to Syria to establish a dominant position in Beirut; nor that Lebanon would provide a base for subversive operations against its Syrian neighbour.

If he were alive today, he would undoubtedly agree that much remains to be done on all five counts. The task of today's Arab generation must surely be to advance boldly along the road he pioneered.

Riad el-Solh loved the sea. He missed the stunning view he had once enjoyed from his mother's house on the Beirut seafront at Ayn al-Mraysa. His wife, Fayza, thought to build him a house close to the shore on a stretch of land on the coast near Beirut. It attracted her because of its unspoiled view of the sea, and also because of an old mosque, the outline of which he particularly liked. Today, the area is built up and densely inhabited, but in those days there was nothing there but dunes. She bought the plot and began slowly to build the house, financing the work by selling off pieces of land she had inherited near Aleppo. It was still unfinished when Riad died. He was destined never to live in it.

On the first anniversary of his death, in July 1952, King 'Abd al-'Aziz al-Sa'ud decided to complete the building in memory of Riad el-Solh, and gave instructions to build the house on a far bigger scale than Fayza had planned. When completed, it became more of a family compound than a single residence. All five of Riad's daughters and their children lived there at one time or another. Riad el-Solh and Ibn Sa'ud liked each other and respected each other's qualities. It was no accident that one of Riad's daughters, Mona, married one of the king's sons, Talal.

After Riad el-Solh's death, his widow remained in mourning garb for the rest of her life. But she continued to keep open house for his friends and followers until her own death on 13 April 1970, aged only 56. She had remained private and reserved all her life. When she died, her daughters discovered, hidden in her cupboard, pretty organdie table-settings for two, which she had made, but which she had never been able to use. The orphaned girl who so wanted a husband who would dine alone with her, who would be around to hold her hand or take her to the cinema, hardly got what she had hoped for. Riad el-Solh had been far more wedded to the Arab cause than he could ever have been to any one person.[3]

---

[3] Interview with Alia el-Solh, Monte Carlo, 4–5 October 2004.

CHRONOLOGY

1810: Ahmad Pasha, Riad el-Solh's grandfather, is born in Sidon.

1839: Sultan Abdülmecid I introduces the *Tanzimat* (reforms or reorganisation of Ottoman institutions).

1848: Louis-Napoleon Bonaparte is elected president of the French Republic.

1852: Louis-Napoleon Bonaparte assumes the title of Napoleon III.

1855: The Emir 'Abd al-Qadir al-Jaza'iri, a great revolutionary Algerian prince, settles with his family in Damascus, after having fought the French, been imprisoned and sent into exile.

1856: The Imperial Rescript of 18 February, known as the Hatt-i Humayan, gives full equality to all Ottoman subjects, irrespective of their religion.

Sultan Abdülmecid I extends the *Tanzimat*.

1860: A savage war between Maronites and Druze in the Lebanese mountains leads to great loss of life, and to the flight of thousands of mainly Christian refugees. The slaughter spreads to the Christian quarters of Damascus.

1861: Following the massacre of Christians in the Lebanese mountains, the European Powers obtain from the Sublime Porte a privileged status for Mount Lebanon. It becomes an autonomous province, a *mutasarrifiyya*, under an Ottoman Catholic (but non-Lebanese) governor, assisted by an Administrative Council, representing the six main religious communities of the Mountain.

(or possibly 1863): Rida el-Solh, Riad's father, is born.

1863: The first carriage road is completed between Beirut and Damascus.

1866: The Syrian Protestant College (later to become the American University of Beirut) is established.

1869: The Suez Canal – Ferdinand de Lesseps's dream of a waterway linking the Red Sea to the Mediterranean – is formally inaugurated in the presence of the Empress Eugénie of France, and of numerous European princes, statesmen, admirals, ambassadors and other dignitaries.

1876: Sultan Abdülhamit II, 34th Sultan of the Ottoman dynasty, comes to the throne at the age of 33.

1877: Sultan Abdülhamit agrees to adopt a Constitution and convenes parliament on 18 March.

1877–78: Russia inflicts a devastating defeat on Ottoman armies.

1878: Following the Ottoman defeat by Russia, the Sultan ends the brief constitutional experiment, dissolves parliament and consolidates his personal rule.

1878–82: In four years, the Ottoman Empire loses Serbia, Montenegro, Romania, Bosnia and Herzegovina, Cyprus, Tunisia and Egypt.

1880: Rida el-Solh, aged 19, is appointed 'first scribe' in a government office in Latakia. This marks the beginning of his twenty-eight-year career as a provincial administrator in the Ottoman service.

1883: The Emir 'Abd al-Qadir al-Jaza'iri dies in Damascus.

1884: Midhat Pasha, a former grand vezir and an enlightened Ottoman provincial governor, is murdered in prison in Ta'if, very probably on orders of the Sultan.

1887–88: The Sublime Porte makes Beirut the capital of a new vilayet, carved out of geographical Syria.

1894: On 17 August, Riad el-Solh is born in Beirut.

1895: Beirut and Damascus are linked by rail.

1898: The German emperor, Kaiser Wilhelm II, pays a month-long visit to the Ottoman Empire (and dines at the table of Ahmad Pasha in Sidon).

1900: On 2 May, the Sultan issues an imperial order for the building of the Hijaz Railway.

1902: Ahmad Pasha dies in Beirut.

Rida el-Solh is appointed *mutasarrif*, or governor, of a sanjaq. His last post in 1907 is *mutasarrif* of Preveza, an Albanian port in a European province of the Empire.

The first Young Turk Congress takes place in Paris.

1905: Riad is enrolled at the *Kulliyah al-'uthmaniyya al-islamiyya* (the Ottoman Islamic College, founded in Beirut in 1895 by Shaykh

Ahmad 'Abbas al-Azhari). He then moves on to the Lazarist school at 'Aintura, and then to the Jesuit college of Saint-Joseph.

1907: The Second Young Turk Congress takes place in Paris.

1908: On 23 July, the Young Turks of the Committee of Union and Progress (CUP) rise in revolt against the Sultan in the name of parliament and Constitution.

Rida el-Solh is elected to the *Meclis-i Mebusan*, the Ottoman parliament in Istanbul.

The Solh family arrives in Istanbul a few weeks after the revolt. Rida el-Solh takes his seat in the reconvened parliament, which holds its first session on 17 December.

1909: On 12–13 April, a monarchical counter-coup takes place against the CUP, but on 25 April it is defeated. The Sultan surrenders and is deposed. On 27 April he and his household are taken by special train to Salonica, where he is interned.

On 14 November, five Arab students in Paris found the secret Young Arab Society, *al-jam'iyya al-'arabiyya al-fatat*, with the goal of Arab autonomy within the Ottoman Empire.

Another secret society, *al-qahtaniyya*, is founded in Istanbul by 'Aziz al-Masri, an Egyptian officer of Circassian origin.

1910: Riad, aged 16, enrols at the Istanbul Law School, *Mekteb-i Hükük*.

1911: Italy wages war against Tripolitania, the last Arab African *vilaya* of the Ottoman Empire.

1912: In October, the Balkan wars begin, when first Montenegro, then Bulgaria, Serbia and Greece, declare war on the Ottoman Empire.

On 8 November, the Greeks seize Salonica, the home base of the CUP, thus inflicting a severe psychological blow.

Towards the end of the year, a political party, the Ottoman Administrative Decentralisation Party (*hizb al-lamarkaziyya al-'idariyya al-'uthmani*) is founded in Cairo, with the full knowledge of the Ottoman government.

1913: In January, a Beirut Reform Society is formed by Christian and Muslim notables, representing every denomination in the city. It is dissolved by the Ottoman vali shortly afterwards.

On 23 January, CUP officers invade the Sublime Porte, kill the minister of war and force the Sultan to appoint a new cabinet, with Mahmud Shawkat Pasha as grand vezir. This marks the emergence of Enver,

Jamal and Talaat as the powerful CUP triumvirate that will govern the Empire until its collapse in the First World War.

On 18 June, a General Arab Congress holds its first meeting in Paris, attended by delegates from every Arab province, as well as by émigrés from Europe and the Americas.

In October, another secret society, *al-ahd* (the Covenant), the military counterpart of *al-fatat*, is founded in Istanbul by 'Aziz al-Masri, who had founded *al-qahtaniyya*.

The Solh family leaves Istanbul for Beirut.

1914: On 14 February, Rida el-Solh retires on a pension from Ottoman government service.

In August, war breaks out between the European Powers.

On 29 October, the Ottoman Empire enters the war on the side of the Triple Alliance of Germany, Austro-Hungary and Italy.

On 1 October, the Sublime Porte abolishes the Capitulations, the commercial and other privileges extended to European Powers and their local clients, which for the Ottomans are the hated expression of Western domination.

In December, Jamal Pasha, minister of the navy, is sent to Damascus as vali at the head of the 100,000-strong 4th Ottoman army.

1915: In February, Jamal Pasha launches an unsuccessful attack against the Suez Canal.

In February, British and French ships attack the Dardanelles and troops are landed at Gallipoli in April.

1915–16: Jamal Pasha rounds up hundreds of prominent Arabs, sends many of them to the gallows in Beirut and Damascus, and deports a great many more to remote parts of Anatolia.

The Sharif Husayn of Mecca and Sir Henry McMahon, British high commissioner in Cairo, exchange a number of letters, which lay the foundations for the Arab Revolt. The Sharif and his sons declare war on Turkey.

1916: In January, the British and French operation in the Dardanelles is abandoned in the face of stiff Turkish resistance.

1916: On 5 June, the Sharif and his sons attack Turkish garrisons at Jeddah, Mecca and Ta'if.

1916–18: Rida and Riad el-Solh escape the gallows but are exiled to Smyrna (Izmir), where they spend the last two years of the war.

1917: On 9 November, the British and Egyptian press publish the text of the Balfour Declaration, whereby Britain pledges its 'best endeavours' to facilitate the 'establishment in Palestine of a National Home for the Jewish people'.

On 11 December, General Sir Edmund Allenby enters Jerusalem on foot two days after its capture from the Turks.

1918: On 23 September, Haifa falls.

Early on 1 October, Arab and Allied troops enter Damascus as Ottoman forces flee northwards.

On 3 October, the Emir Faysal enters Damascus to a delirious welcome.

On 8 October, Beirut falls.

On 23 October, Aleppo falls.

On 30 October, an armistice between the Ottoman Empire and the Allies is signed on board a British warship.

On 31 October, hostilities cease.

Riad el-Solh and Hajj Amin al-Husayni meet in Damascus during the rule of the Emir Faysal.

1918–19: Towards the end of 1918, Riad el-Solh, aged 24, is sent to govern Sidon, his family's home town in South Lebanon. But he is forced to give up his post when General Henri Gouraud arrives in Lebanon in 1919, at the head of a French army.

Faysal has meetings in London with Lord Balfour and with the Zionist leader Dr Chaim Weizmann. He submits a memorandum about Arab aspirations to the Peace Conference at Versailles. But he gradually comes to understand that Britain, France and the Zionists all have ambitions in geographical Syria, which greatly restrict Arab claims.

1919: On 25 March, the Supreme Council of the victorious powers adopts President Wilson's proposal to send a commission of enquiry to Syria 'to elucidate the state of opinion'. France and Britain decline to take part. Led by two Americans, Dr Henry C. King and Charles R. Crane, the Commission spends more than two months that summer in Syria and Palestine.

On 28 April, the Peace Conference decides to place the former Arab provinces of the Ottoman Empire under European Mandates.

In July, a General Syrian Conference meets in Damascus to lobby the King–Crane Commission and to demand 'complete political independence for Syria'.

On 28 August, the King–Crane Commission's report recommends 'that the unity of Syria be preserved in accordance with the earnest petition of the great majority of the people of Syria'; that 'it would be better if [Lebanon] were a constituent member of the [Syrian] state, rather than entirely independent of it'; and that the Zionist claim to Palestine, 'based on an occupation of two thousand years ago, can hardly be seriously considered'. But when President Wilson suffers a stroke in October 1919, the report is shelved.

1920: On 8 March, the General Syrian Congress reconvenes in Damascus. It proclaims the independence of Syria 'in its natural boundaries'; rejects the project of a national home for the Jews in Palestine; and elects the Emir Faysal King of Syria.

Meeting in San Remo on 24–25 April, the Supreme Allied Council decides to give France the Mandate over Syria and Lebanon, and Britain the Mandate over Iraq and Palestine.

In July, Riad el-Solh, aged 25, persuades seven members of Lebanon's Administrative Council to 'defect' from the French and come over to Faysal's side. The French arrest the 'defectors' and send them into exile. Riad flees to Damascus.

On 24 July, a small Syrian force is crushed at Maysalun, some 30 kilometres from Damascus, by a vastly superior French army. Yusuf al-'Azma, Syria's brave defence minister, is killed.

On 25 July, French troops enter Damascus. Faysal leaves the city by special train for Palestine. He is followed on a second train by Riad el-Solh and some seventy other nationalists.

On 9 August, a French court in Damascus sentences Riad and a score of others to death in absentia for their support of Faysal's regime.

On 1 September, General Gouraud proclaims the creation of *l'Etat du Grand Liban* (Greater Lebanon) within expanded frontiers. Over the next couple of years, Syria is carved up into a number of statelets and autonomous districts.

On 29 October, another court in Beirut sentences Riad to five years in jail and a fine of 1,400,000 French francs for attempting to mobilise members of Lebanon's Administrative Council against the French.

1920–25: The French army loses 6,722 men in Syria, either killed or listed missing, and incurs military expenditure of 2,500 million francs.

1921: In March, at a conference in Cairo, Winston Churchill, then colonial secretary, devises a policy of creating Arab client states, run by local leaders and policed by native armies, which can be counted on to protect British interests. The Emir Faysal is installed on the throne of Iraq in June.

Sir Herbert Samuel, British high commissioner in Palestine, appoints Hajj Amin al-Husayni, aged 24, to the office of Grand Mufti of Jerusalem.

On 25 July, Riad attends the founding meeting in Geneva of the Syro-Palestinian Congress. The brainchild of Prince Michel Lutfallah, it is the first organised manifestation of Arab protest against the Mandates.

In November, Riad travels to London to offer his services to Musa Kadhim al-Husayni, a former Palestinian mayor of Jerusalem, in his talks, conducted under British auspices, with the Zionist leader Dr Chaim Weizmann. On 7 November, Riad meets Dr Weizmann to see whether Zionist influence can be mobilised to prevent the ratification of the League of Nations Mandates over Syria and Lebanon.

1922: In March, Riad and other leading Arabs hold further talks with Zionists in Cairo, but these contacts come to nothing.

1924: King (formerly Sharif) Husayn of the Hijaz is driven out of Mecca, Medina and Jiddah by the forces of Ibn Sa'ud, the rising leader of the Arabian Peninsula. The Hijaz as a whole is brought under Ibn Sa'ud's rule.

Early in the year, as Riad el-Solh waits in Palestine for the French to allow him back into Lebanon, he has another meeting with Dr Weizmann in Jerusalem. Throughout the 1920s, and well into the 1930s, Riad seeks a formula for Arab-Zionist coexistence, but Zionist ambitions are too great for him or any Arab to accept.

1925–26: An insurrection against the French – known as the Great Syrian Revolution – breaks out in the Jabal Druze and spreads to Damascus and beyond.

1925: On 8 April, Lord Balfour visits Damascus and is given a hostile reception.

A People's Party, led by Dr 'Abd al-Rahman al-Shahbandar, holds a founding rally in Damascus, attended by over a thousand people.

In July, a Druze tribal force, led by Sultan al-Atrash, ambushes and routs a French column of 3,000 men under General Roger Michaud, capturing 2,000 rifles.

On 23 August, Sultan al-Atrash issues a call for an uprising in Damascus. 'To Arms! Oh sons of the glorious Arabs'.

Shahbandar joins the revolt and, on 24 August, a combined force of Druze and other tribesmen march on Damascus. They are put to flight by a French cavalry charge.

On 9 September, Shahbandar in the Jabal Druze proclaims a general Syrian rebellion and the formation of a National Government. Insurgents enter Damascus on 18 October and set fire to the 'Azm palace.

On 18–20 October, High Commissioner Maurice Sarrail orders the bombardment of Damascus. Entire quarters are flattened and about 1,500 people are killed.

1925–26: After a spell in rebel-held territory, Riad el-Solh heads for Geneva, where he joins the Emir Shakib Arslan and Ihsan al-Jabiri in the reactivated Permanent Delegation of the Syro-Palestinian Congress. Together, they lobby the League of Nations on behalf of the Syrian cause.

A new high commissioner, Henry de Jouvenel, takes up his post in Beirut in December 1925 and gives the rebels a pledge that they will escape execution if they surrender by 6 January 1926. But fierce fighting continues throughout that year, with the French resorting to mass executions, house demolitions and other collective punishments. By 1927, the last of the insurgents are driven across the border into Transjordan. The Revolution collapses.

1926: Under Henry de Jouvenel's eight-month tenure as French high commissioner, a new Constitution for Lebanon is adopted on 23 May. It provides for an elected president and an elected Representative Council, but it is a far cry from the real independence the nationalists demand. It entrenches sectarianism in Lebanon's public life by stipulating that ministerial portfolios and public sector jobs are to be filled on an 'equitable' confessional basis.

On a visit to Beirut, Riad is arrested by the French and, by a decree dated 27 June, is confined to the citadel on the island of Arwad, off the Syrian coast. He manages to escape and rejoins the Delegation at Geneva.

1927: Riad el-Solh throws himself into frenetic activity for the Syrian cause in Paris, Geneva, Brussels and Beirut. Rather than seeking to defeat the French by force of arms, he becomes the advocate of a more pragmatic nationalist strategy, which is bent on persuading French opinion of the folly of French policy.

On 27 October, nationalists from different Syrian cities assemble in Beirut for the first Congress of the Syrian National Bloc, *al-kutla al-wataniyya*. By 1928, it becomes the leading political formation in Syria. Riad el-Solh joins later as an associate member.

1928: Lebanese nationalists create a forum in Beirut known as the Conference of the Coast, with the goal of securing the return to Syria of the 'disputed territories', which the French had added to Mount Lebanon in order to create *le Grand Liban*.

On 20 May, Riad el-Solh returns to Lebanon – and to his father's house in Sidon – after the new French High Commissioner Henri Ponsot (who replaced de Jouvenel in the summer of 1926) agrees to allow him back into the country.

On 20 June, Riad el-Solh makes a triumphal entry into Damascus in a convoy of several hundred cars. He is honoured over the following weeks by a number of grand receptions.

On 23 September, the Zionists press their claim to the Wailing Wall in Jerusalem by setting up a screen to separate men from women. This contravenes a ruling by the Muslim *waqf* authorities that nothing must be done which might be seen as creating a synagogue. Hajj Amin produces an Ottoman ruling of 1912, which bars Jews from bringing any objects to the wall.

1929: In August, violent clashes between Jews and Arabs lead to mutual killings in Jerusalem, but also in Hebron, Safed and Haifa. All remaining illusions that European Jews and Arabs can cohabit peacefully in Palestine are dispelled.

Aged 35, Riad el-Solh wins an international reputation as a scourge of the French and the British presence in the Levant, and as an eloquent advocate of Arab liberation.

In November, Riad sets off for another triumphal visit to Syria, this time to Aleppo. He has become, by now, one of the most prominent Muslim political figures in Lebanon and Syria.

1930: Riad comes to realise that lobbying the League of Nations is a futile exercise. He decides to leave Geneva for Beirut.

Riad el-Solh marries Fayza al-Jabiri, the orphaned daughter of the late Nafi' Pasha al-Jabiri of Aleppo. She is 17 and was to bear him five daughters.

On 30 June, the Anglo-Iraqi Treaty provides for a fifteen-year alliance between the two countries, assigns two airbases to the RAF, and guarantees Britain's military and transport facilities in times of war.

In July, Antun Sa'ada, aged 26, returns to the Near East after some years in Brazil and Germany.

1930s: The rise of Fascism in Europe has a disturbing impact on opinion in the Levant states, which has already been unnerved by the defeat of the Palestinian rebellion of 1936–39, as well as France's failure to ratify the 1936 treaties, and the restoration of the hated Mandates. Noisy youth movements spring up in imitation of their Fascist European counterparts.

1931: Hajj Amin and Riad el-Solh conceive the idea of convening a major pan-Islamic conference to focus Muslim attention on Palestine, where Jewish immigration is creating an explosive situation.

On 7 December, the General Islamic Conference opens in Jerusalem and remains in session for ten days.

1933: Riad opens a law office, but politics and his active support for the incipient trades union movement leave him little time to practise.

In January, Hitler's rise to power is welcomed by many Arabs, who hope that Germany will provide a counterweight to Britain and France.

On 6 March, the Drivers' Solidarity Association calls a general strike, which is observed by 8,000 drivers in Lebanon and Syria. Militancy spreads throughout the working classes. Cooks and waiters, silk weavers and woodworkers, fishermen and bank clerks, lawyers, doctors and pharmacists all start to organise themselves in the early 1930s.

In September, King Faysal of Iraq dies in Switzerland, dealing a blow to nationalist hopes of convening a pan-Arab conference in Baghdad.

Rashid 'Ali al-Gaylani becomes prime minister of Iraq. His task is to oversee the transition to King Ghazi.

1934: In February, Charles Corm, a Lebanese intellectual, launches a publishing house, *Editions de la Revue Phénicienne*, to promote the notion that Lebanon's identity owes much to its roots in the seafaring Phoenicians of 3000 BC. The Phoenician idea is contested by those who believe that the centre of Lebanon's identity lies in the Mountain, rather than the Mediterranean, and that the legacy of thirteen centuries of Islam cannot be ignored.

On 21 November, Sa'ada's party – the *hizb al-qawmi al-suri*, more widely known as the *Parti populaire syrien* or PPS – is secretly constituted, but comes to the attention of the authorities a year later, in November 1935.

1934–36: David Ben-Gurion decides to enter into discussions with a number of leading Arabs to press the case for a Jewish state in Palestine and Transjordan. By 1934, the Jewish community in Palestine numbers about 400,000. Ben-Gurion holds a series of talks with Musa al-'Alami, Riad el-Solh, 'Awni 'Abd al-Hadi, the Emir Shakib Arslan, Ihsan al-Jabiri and George Antonius.

1935: On 15 April, the French High Commissioner comte Damien de Martel orders the closure of the drivers' union office and deports Riad to Qamishli, in the far north-west of Syria, where he is placed under house arrest.

On 30 June, after a storm of protest, de Martel relents and orders Riad to be brought back to Beirut.

'Izz al-Din al-Qassam, a devout Syrian who had fought the French, flees to Haifa, where he gathers a band of followers to fight the Zionists, the British and their Arab collaborators. On 21 November he is killed in a gun battle with the police. His funeral is the occasion for a huge political demonstration.

On 21 November, Ibrahim Hananu, uncontested leader of Syria's National Bloc, dies. He had been an active leader of the Great Syrian Revolution of 1925–26. Riad el-Solh leads a large Lebanese group at his funeral.

On 5 November, Sa'ada is arrested with ten of his colleagues and is sentenced in January 1936 to six months in jail and a small fine. He is arrested a second time in 1936.

1936: On 10 January – forty days after Hananu's death – massive street demonstrations take place in Syria, followed by a general strike.

In Palestine, an Arab strike lasting 176 days escalates into an armed insurgency, which 20,000 British troops crush with great brutality. Up to one thousand Arabs are killed, as well as thirty-seven Britons and sixty-nine Jews.

On 20 January, the pro-French Emile Eddé is elected president of the Lebanese Republic, defeating Bishara al-Khoury.

On 28 February – the fortieth day of the Syrian general strike – the nationalists organise massive demonstrations. Many rioters are killed by French live fire.

On 1 March, faced with the crisis, High Commissioner comte Damien de Martel gives an undertaking to restore constitutional life. He authorises a Syrian delegation to travel to Paris to negotiate a treaty.

On 10 March, leading Muslims from Lebanon's coastal cities hold a conference in Beirut – the 'Conference of the Coast' – to demand the return to Syria of Beirut, Tripoli and Sidon, as well as the four *cazas* which had been attached to Lebanon in 1920 – the so-called 'disputed territories'. Riad el-Solh does not attend the conference. He no longer thinks that dismantling Greater Lebanon is a credible objective.

Riad's cousin, Kadhim el-Solh, shocks the Conference by declaring that calling for the dismantling of Lebanon does a disservice to the Arab nationalist cause. A wiser course, he argues, is to persuade Maronites to join Muslims in the struggle for Lebanese independence. Kadhim el-Solh's views are published in *al-Nahar* in March, and then as a pamphlet in April 1937.

On 12 March, Riad el-Solh arrives in Paris ahead of the Syrian delegation, which he is to advise in treaty negotiations with the French. He has a meeting with Nahum Goldman, founder and president of the World Jewish Congress.

The Popular Front – a left-wing coalition of Radical Socialists, Socialists and Communists – wins the French general elections. On 4 June, the Socialist leader Léon Blum forms a government and, on 7–8 June, reaches a historic agreement with employers and unions – the so-called Matignon Accords – which changes the life of the working classes.

On 26 August, the Anglo-Egyptian Treaty establishes a 'perpetual alliance' between the two countries, and makes temporary provision for the stationing of British forces in Egypt for the defence of the Suez Canal.

On 9 September, a twenty-five-year Franco-Syrian treaty of 'friendship and alliance' is initialled at the French Foreign Ministry. It is hailed as a great triumph for the National Bloc, and for Riad el-Solh himself.

On 29 September, the Syrian delegation returns home to a tumultuous welcome.

On 29 October, Iraq's constitutional life is shattered by General Bakr Sidqi's military *coup d'état*.

On 21 December, the National Bloc leader Hashim al-Atasi is elected president of the Syrian Republic.

The Peel Commission arrives in Palestine to 'investigate causes of unrest.'

1936–37: Sa'ada's movement is challenged in Lebanon by the *Phalanges libanaises*, a Christian youth movement, and by the *Najjada*, its Muslim counterpart.

1937: In January, Lebanon's President Emile Eddé appoints Khayr al-Din Ahdab as prime minister – the first Muslim to hold so high a post.

On 7 March, Sa'ada is arrested a third time, but is freed two months later.

On 21 June, having lost his majority in the Senate, Léon Blum resigns. He returns to power some eight months later on 13 March 1938, only to leave office for good within less than a month. The collapse of the Popular Front dooms the Syrian Treaty and gives heart to all those who wish to perpetuate the Mandate.

On 7 July, the Peel Commission's report is published, concluding that the Palestine Mandate is unworkable and recommending that the country be divided into an Arab state, a Jewish state and a small British mandatory zone.

Violence erupts again in Palestine, with persistent reports of arms trafficking and the formation of armed bands in the countryside.

On 8 September, nearly 400 delegates from across the Arab world attend the opening session of a conference dedicated to the Palestine cause in the Syrian village of Bludan. This marks the high point of pan-Arab concern for Palestine. Riad el-Solh leads a large group of Sunni Lebanese politicians.

At the October elections, Riad el-Solh stands for parliament, but withdraws on the eve of the poll, when the French make clear that they will rig the vote to keep him out.

On the night of 13–14 October, Hajj Amin al-Husayni escapes from the *Haram* where he had been hiding and, disguised as a Beduin, escapes by fishing boat up the coast to Lebanon. To British annoyance, the French let him stay, although he moves on, in October 1939, to Baghdad.

On 29 October, the first session of the new Lebanese parliament takes place. Prime Minister Khayr al-Din Ahdab tenders his resignation, but President Emile Eddé asks him to form another government.

Sa'ada petitions the French high commissioner for a Syro-Lebanese union.

On 10 September, the Bludan conference passes a unanimous resolution declaring Palestine an integral part of the Arab homeland.

In November (and again in August 1938), Syria's Prime Minister Jamil Mardam goes twice to Paris, in a desperate bid to save the Franco-Syrian Treaty. He makes further concessions to France.

On 18 November, President Emile Eddé issues a decree declaring illegal all the paramilitary youth movements.

1937–39: Violence in Palestine erupts more fiercely than ever in October 1937, as armed bands attack British troops and Jewish settlements. The fighting degenerates into a murderous inter-Palestinian blood feud. Britain responds with a ferocious campaign of counter-terror. The uprising and its repression destroy the Palestinian economy. More than 5,000 Arabs are killed and another 14,000 wounded. While the Arabs are ruthlessly put down, the *Haganah* grows, with British help, into a substantial Jewish underground army of 15,000 men and women.

1937–41: Several German officials and propaganda agents visit the Levant and attempt to stir up anti-British and anti-French feeling.

1938: Threatened again with arrest, Sa'ada leaves Lebanon for Cyprus, Berlin, Rome and Brazil, from where, in 1939, he issues a call to his party members to stage an insurrection in Lebanon.

On 3 July, France and Turkey reach an agreement on the future of the sanjaq of Alexandretta.

On 5 July, Turkish troops enter the sanjaq of Alexandretta, with the blessing of the French, to supervise the plebiscite. The electoral rolls are made to show a Turkish majority. The sanjaq is integrated into Turkey and is renamed Hatay. Some 20,000 refugees flee to Syria and Lebanon.

On 14 December, French Foreign Minister George Bonnet tells the National Assembly that the French government no longer intends to ask parliament to ratify the Syrian Treaty.

1939: On 18 February, under attack from enraged public opinion, Syrian Prime Minister Jamil Mardam resigns.

In March, the government of the National Bloc, the *kutla al-wataniyya*, falls from office, sealing the fate of the abortive Franco-Syrian Treaty of 1936.

On 3 April, King Ghazi of Iraq dies in a car accident. His uncle, the Emir 'Abd al-Ilah, becomes regent.

On 17 May, the British government publishes a White Paper which appears to deal a serious blow to Zionist ambitions by declaring that it is 'not part of [British] policy that Palestine should become a Jewish state'. But the White Paper's proposals bear little connection to the facts on the ground.

On 7 July, President Hashim al-Atasi of Syria withdraws from public life.

On 25 August, General Maxime Weygand, a former French high commissioner in Beirut, is brought out of retirement to assume command of French forces in the eastern Mediterranean. His task is to rebuild the Army of the Levant. He arrives in Beirut on 30 August.

On 1 September, Germany attacks Poland and war is declared.

On 3 October, a French Military Tribunal passes sentences on forty-two PPS members; the sentences range from one to twenty years. Sa'ada's closest associate, Ni'mat Thabit, is given ten years.

1940: A wave of nationalist protest in Iraq sweeps from power the pro-British Prime Minister Nuri al-Sa'id and carries Rashid 'Ali to the premiership. He calls for a revision of the Anglo-Iraqi Treaty.

On 10 May, Hitler launches his *Blitzkrieg* against Belgium and France. Within days, the war is lost.

On 16 June, Marshal Philippe Pétain becomes prime minister of France and concludes an armistice with Germany.

On 18 June, General Charles de Gaulle broadcasts over the BBC from London his call to the French people to continue the fight against Nazi Germany, under his leadership.

In June, Italy enters the war on the side of Germany, threatening the British position in the Mediterranean, the Middle East and East Africa.

On 3 July, the Royal Navy attacks the French fleet at Mers el-Kebir, killing 1,500 sailors and sinking or damaging several French ships. This prompts Vichy France to break off relations with Britain.

On 6 July, Dr 'Abd al-Rahman al-Shahbandar, a key figure in the Great Syrian Revolution of 1925–26, is assassinated in Damascus, causing disarray in the nationalist camp.

General de Gaulle sends General Georges Catroux to the Middle East to defend French interests. Catroux arrives in disguise in Cairo on 27 September. His ambitious plan is to topple the Vichy administration in Syria and Lebanon, and bring the territories over to de Gaulle by means of an armed coup.

In December, General Henri-Fernand Dentz, commander-in-chief of French forces in the Levant, is appointed high commissioner by Vichy.

1941: On 31 January, Rashid 'Ali is forced to resign, under pressure from the regent and the British.

In February, the nationalists call a general strike in Damascus. It spreads to other Syrian cities and then to Lebanon.

On 25 March, General Delhomme, the French military commander, proclaims a 'state of siege'. Many nationalists are arrested and threatened with deportation.

On 1 April, just two days before Rashid 'Ali's coup in Baghdad, General de Gaulle and Major-General Edward Spears, head of the British Mission to the Free French, land in Cairo.

On 1 April, the Iraqi army surrounds the royal palace in Baghdad. The regent manages to escape.

On 2 April, General Dentz appoints Khalid al-'Azm – a prominent politician and businessman opposed to the National Bloc – as head of the Syrian government and minister of interior.

On 3 April, backed by four generals known as the 'Golden Square', Rashid 'Ali seizes power in Iraq. He moves Iraqi forces to confront the British RAF base at Habbaniya.

On instructions from Winston Churchill, the British give Rashid 'Ali an ultimatum: Iraqi forces must withdraw from Habbaniya by 2 May or face attack. Once the ultimatum expires, British aircraft bomb Iraqi troops. A ground attack lifts the siege of the base.

On 18 April, France withdraws from the League of Nations – the body which in 1919 had entrusted it with the Mandates over Syria and Lebanon.

On 9 May, the first German aircraft lands in Damascus en route for Iraq. In all, about a hundred German aircraft pass through Syria in May and June.

On 18 May, an Anglo-Arab column, named Habforce, crosses 500 miles of desert from Palestine and reaches Habbaniya. Another column travels from Transjordan.

On 30 May, Baghdad falls and the regent is restored to power. A pro-British government under Nuri al-Sa'id is formed. Rashid 'Ali flees to Iran and then to Germany.

On 27 May, on orders from Churchill, Wavell presents London with the outline for 'Operation Exporter' – an attack on Syria and Lebanon to defeat and expel Vichy forces. A battle plan is drawn up by General Henry 'Jumbo' Wilson.

In June, Oliver Lyttelton, president of the Board of Trade, is appointed British minister of state for the Middle East.

On 8 June, Allied troops cross the border into Syria and Lebanon and meet stiff resistance from General Dentz's forces. On the same day, General Catroux issues a proclamation promising the Levant states independence and sovereignty. The hard-fought campaign lasts five weeks.

On 14 July, an armistice is signed at Acre, bringing the war to an end.

On 14 July, Riad's cousin, Kadhim el-Solh, submits a memorandum to the Iraqi Prime Minister Jamil al-Madfa'i – for him to pass on to the British – in which the demands of the Levant nationalists for independence and free elections are spelled out.

On 20 July, a furious de Gaulle arrives in Cairo, intent on challenging the terms of the armistice.

On 25 July, de Gaulle and Oliver Lyttelton, the British minister of state in the Middle East, reach an agreement on the division of authority in the Levant territories between the British and the Free French.

On 9 September, Winston Churchill declares in the House of Commons that 'We have no ambitions in Syria . . . We do not seek to replace or supplant France . . . We are only in Syria in order to win the war'.

On 27 September, General Catroux issues a manifesto of Syrian independence which leaves all effective power in French hands. He nominates as prime minister the notoriously servile Shaykh Taj al-Din al-Hasani.

On 20 December, Riad el-Solh circulates a memorandum to the main diplomatic missions in the Levant in which he declares that Catroux's proclamation contradicts the promise of independence made by Catroux himself, and reiterated by de Gaulle and Churchill.

Ahmad Da'uq resigns as prime minister of Lebanon and is replaced by Riad's cousin, Sami el-Solh, president of the Criminal Court.

By the end of the year, the once passionately pro-French General Spears has become thoroughly disillusioned with his former hero, General de Gaulle, and bitterly anti-French.

1941–43: Britain's Foreign Secretary Anthony Eden expresses cautious support for Arab unity in two statements – one at the Mansion House in London on 29 May 1941, the other in the House of Commons on 24 February 1943. But Eden is concerned not to offend the French or endanger cooperation with de Gaulle.

1942: In March, Spears returns to Beirut from London, with wider powers and a new title. He has been knighted and is now known as General Sir Edward Spears. He makes clear that he no longer recognises the French Mandate.

In early summer, Riad el-Solh's relations with the Spears Mission start to blossom.

To cope with a wheat crisis, General Spears devises a scheme to collect wheat directly from growers against payment in cash. The scheme is administered by the *Office des céréales panifiables* (Wheat Office), established in May.

On 11 August, General de Gaulle arrives in Lebanon 'to take men and affairs in hand . . . and demonstrate the predominance of France'. He sets off on a regal progress through the Levant states, but his pronouncements alienate nationalist opinion – and strain Churchill's patience to breaking point. When the British Foreign Office backs de Gaulle in stressing the continued validity of the Mandate, Spears – in cooperation with Riad el-Solh – resolves to force the French out of Syria and Lebanon for good.

1942–43: Political uncertainty in Lebanon is compounded by the grim economic situation. Spears blames it on the French and their local stooges.

1943: As the German threat to the Middle East eases, Eden is less concerned to conciliate Arab opinion. He takes the view that it is better to keep the Mandate system in place.

On 17 January, Syria's President Shaykh Taj al-Din al-Hasani, a tool of French policy, dies. The nationalists shed no tears.

On 24 January, the French National Committee in Algiers gives General Catroux the green light to restore constitutional life in the Levant states.

On 18 March, Catroux issues decrees restoring the Lebanese Constitution, providing for general elections, and for the election of the president of the Republic by a new Chamber of Deputies. The elections are to be conducted by a non-political provisional authority, under Dr Ayyub Thabit.

On 17 June, Thabit issues two decrees: one includes overseas (mainly Christian) Lebanese in the count of Lebanon's population, the other increases the number of deputies from forty-two to fifty-four. Of the twelve new deputies, ten are Christian and only two Muslim.

On 19 June, Muslim leaders meet to demand that the French cancel Thabit's decrees. Failing that, they threaten to boycott the elections.

Spears proposes a 6:5 ratio between Christian and Muslim deputies, a formula which wins wide approval and results in thirty seats for the Christians and twenty-five for the Muslims in the new Chamber.

On 21 July, Jean Helleu – who replaced Catroux as delegate general of the Fighting French in the Levant – promulgates a decree replacing the unpopular Dr Thabit with Butros Trad, a Paris-educated lawyer, as head of state. It is announced that elections will be held on 29 August and 5 September, followed by presidential elections on 19 September.

In early August, Riad el-Solh decides to contest the one Sunni Muslim seat in South Lebanon. A 'unified list' is formed of Riad el-Solh, Ahmad al-As'ad and 'Adil 'Usayran, which wins more than three-quarters of the votes cast in South Lebanon. Other Muslim leaders also do well, changing the sectarian balance of power in Lebanese politics.

In August, Riad el-Solh is elected to the Lebanese parliament.

On 19 September, Riad el-Solh and Bishara al-Khoury, leader of the Destour Party, meet for a historic tête-à-tête in the Lebanese mountain town of Aley. They reach a gentleman's agreement to the effect that, if Bishara al-Khoury is elected president, he will appoint Riad el-Solh prime minister. They agree to share power, with the aim of making a bid for independence from France.

On 21 September, the Lebanese parliament elects Bishara al-Khoury president of the Republic. The next day, he appoints Riad el-Solh prime minister. Their accord – fleshed out by Riad el-Solh in his first statement to parliament – comes to be known as the National Pact, al-mithaq al-watani. The Sunnis give up all idea of dismantling Greater Lebanon, while the Christians acknowledge that Lebanon is essentially an Arab country.

On 25 September, Riad el-Solh forms his first government, with himself as prime minister and finance minister.

On 7 October, Riad makes his ministerial statement to parliament. 'We want true independence', he declares. 'We want total national sovereignty'. His key phrase – 'Lebanon is a country with an Arab face, which draws from Western civilisation what is good and useful' – sums up the National Pact's ground-breaking compromise between Christians and Muslims, and is greeted with loud cheers. Riad wins an overwhelming vote of confidence. Riad announces plans to amend the Constitution to remove articles incompatible with true independence. The Arabic language is to be the only official language. He proposes to take over the management of the so-called *Intérêts Communs*, in agreement with Syria.

On 22 October, Jean Helleu, the delegate general, writes to President Bishara al-Khoury to say that France will not accept Riad el-Solh's constitutional amendments. He claims that the Mandate continues to exist in law. Riad asks for Helleu's letter to be withdrawn.

On 5 November, the French embassy hands the Beirut press corps a toughly worded communiqué from the French National Committee in Algiers: no amendments to the Constitution can be made without the explicit consent of France.

On 8 November, the Lebanese parliament passes the constitutional amendments by an almost unanimous vote.

Before dawn on 11 November, President Bishara al-Khoury, Prime Minister Riad el-Solh and other ministers are arrested at their homes. The Tripoli leader 'Abd al-Hamid Karami is also seized. They are incarcerated in the fortress at Rashaya.

At 8 a.m. on 11 November, Jean Helleu broadcasts a statement in which he declares that the time has come to put an end to Riad el-Solh's 'dictatorial regime'. He annuls the constitutional amendments and places executive power in the hands of the pro-French Emile Eddé, named head of state and head of government.

On 12 November, a 'provisional government' is established in the mountain village of Bshamoun by Deputy Premier Habib Abu Shahla and Defence Minister Majid Arslan, who had both escaped arrest. Thirty-three deputies manage to make their way to the house of Sa'ib Salam, a prominent Sunni leader in Beirut, where they give the 'provisional government' a vote of confidence. A 'National Committee' is formed to organise passive resistance. Demonstrators are killed in clashes with French troops.

On 12 November, General Sir Edward Spears sends Helleu an official letter of protest, expressing his outrage at the delegate general's actions.

On 12 November, Roger Makins, a member of the British liaison office with the French in Algiers, is told by General de Gaulle that the Mandate cannot legally be terminated during the war.

On 13 November, the *Phalanges libanaises* and the Muslim *al-Najjada* bring their members onto the street in defiance of the French. The Phalanges leader Pierre Gemayel is arrested. Many clashes are reported in different parts of Lebanon.

On 16 November, General Catroux arrives in Beirut from Algiers, with instructions to reinforce Emile Eddé and evict Riad el-Solh from office. In mid-November, a French force attacks the village of Bshamoun, but is repelled.

On 18 November, Catroux has separate and secret meetings with President Bishara al-Khoury and Riad el-Solh, who are brought from Rashaya to Beirut to meet him. As a result of these talks, Catroux is convinced that there can be no solution to the crisis without the return to power of the two men.

On 19 November, Richard Casey, British minister of state for the Middle East, hands Catroux an ultimatum at Spears's house. If Helleu is not replaced and the detainees freed by 10 a.m. on 22 November, Britain will declare martial law and British troops will release the president and the detained ministers.

On Sunday night, 21 November, the BBC broadcasts news of the imminent release of the arrested ministers, sparking an explosion of joy throughout Lebanon.

On the morning of 22 November, the prisoners are released and head for Beirut, where they are welcomed by a vast cheering crowd. Early that day, Emile Eddé escapes in a French van for an unknown destination.

On 24 November, Catroux pays on official visit to the *Sérail*, where he confirms that Helleu's decrees have been annulled. The situation reverts to what it had been on 10 November.

On 7 December, Foreign Secretary Anthony Eden chairs a meeting of top British officials in Cairo. He is displeased by Spears's actions. Peoples under mandate, he says, should not be permitted to terminate mandatory arrangements without agreement with the mandatory power. Eden wants Spears to help the French save face.

On 16 December, General Catroux returns to Beirut from Algiers, with instructions from General de Gaulle to compel the Syrian and Lebanese governments to sign a treaty, which would restore France's pre-eminent position in the Levant. Assisted by Yves Chataigneau, the *délégué général*, Catroux enters into negotiations with the Syrian and Lebanese governments.

On 22 December, an agreement is reached on the transfer of the *Intérêts Communs* to the Levant states.

1944: On 3 January, the December agreement is followed by the transfer of the customs administration and the tobacco monopoly, but the transfer is largely a fiction as French officials remain in place.

In January, Riad el-Solh – accompanied by Foreign Minister Salim Takla and by Musa Mubarak, President Bishara al-Khoury's *chef de cabinet* – sets out on a tour of Arab capitals. This provides him with a refresher course on Arab rivalries and antagonisms.

In March, Riad el-Solh's government presents its first budget to parliament. No financial provision is made for a national army.

On 1 March, the *Parti populaire syrien* (*al-hizb al-qawmi al-suri*) is allowed to resume its activities in Damascus and Beirut.

On 10 March, General Paul Beynet arrives to take over from Chataigneau. There are rumours of French plots to unseat Riad el-Solh.

On 2 May, the *Parti populaire syrien* decides to lend its support to Riad el-Solh's government.

On 23 August, the liberation of Paris from the Germans is announced on the BBC and is celebrated by the French in the Levant.

On 24 August, René Massigli, de Gaulle's commissioner for foreign affairs, sends a stiff note to Anthony Eden, complaining of British encroachments on France's 'pre-eminent position' in the Levant. Eden rejects the charge, but expresses support for the conclusion of treaties between France and the Levant states – in total contradiction with what Spears has recommended.

At the end of August, Anthony Eden decides to put an end to Spears's career in the Levant. On 1 September, he sends Spears a letter which amounts to a dismissal.

From 25 September to 7 October, Arab delegates meet at Alexandria to prepare for the founding conference of the League of Arab States. Riad el-Solh heads the Lebanese delegation.

General Beynet precipitates a crisis with the Lebanese government by sending a note to President Bishara al-Khoury. He claims that, by ruling out the possibility of a treaty with France, the Alexandria Protocol has invalidated the declaration of Lebanese and Syrian independence made by General Catroux in 1941. The British protest. The Lebanese ask for Beynet's note to be withdrawn. Riad makes an impassioned statement in parliament: 'We shall hold on to our independence and defend it whatever the cost'.

On 7 October, seven Arab states sign the Alexandria Protocol.

On 8 December, Spears replies to Eden with a robust defence of his policies and actions. He is made an honorary citizen by both Syria and Lebanon. His departure from the Levant marks the end of an era.

In mid-December, President Bishara al-Khoury falls in the street and breaks an arm. He suffers a nervous breakdown and goes to Palestine for treatment.

1945: On 9 January, Riad el-Solh resigns the premiership. The French rejoice at the departure of both Spears and Riad.

In early January, French tanks move to Damascus. Colonel Oliva-Roget, the French *délégué*, sends a threatening note to the Syrian government, breaking off negotiations over the transfer of the *Troupes spéciales*. French colonial troops embark for Beirut.

On 22 March, the League of Arab States is created in Cairo, initially with six members: Egypt, Iraq, Transjordan (renamed Jordan in 1946), Lebanon, Saudi Arabia and Syria.

On 30 April, Duff Cooper, the British ambassador in Paris, warns de Gaulle of the danger to public security if French reinforcements arrive in Beirut when Franco-Syrian negotiations are about to take place.

On 5 May, Yemen joins the League of Arab States.

On 8 May, General Beynet reveals the tough terms for the proposed treaties with Syria and Lebanon. The two governments refuse to negotiate on this basis and condemn French troop landings. Violent demonstrations break out in Damascus.

On 29–31 May, French artillery and tanks bombard prominent targets in Damascus, including the Citadel and the parliament building, causing much destruction and loss of life.

On 31 May, Anthony Eden announces in the House of Commons that Prime Minister Winston Churchill has sent General de Gaulle a message, informing him that British troops will intervene to prevent further bloodshed, and asking him to order French troops to cease fire and withdraw to their barracks.

On 1 June, a British armoured column enters Damascus. Britain assumes military control until the Syrian government can resume its normal functions.

Following the bombardment of Damascus, the French agree under international pressure to proceed with the transfer of the *Troupes spéciales*. This takes place over the following months.

1946: In January, London is the venue for the first meeting of the newly created United Nations Organisation. Riad el-Solh flies to the UK to advise the Lebanese delegation, led by Foreign Minister Hamid Frangieh.

On 4 February, the Lebanese and Syrian delegations send a letter to the UN secretary-general, complaining about the presence of French and British troops on their territory, and demanding their complete and simultaneous withdrawal.

On 14 February, the Security Council examines the Syrian and Lebanese complaint. On the 15th, the heads of the two delegations put their case to the Council.

On 28 February, the Lebanese delegation leaves for Paris to resume negotiations with the French. It learns, however, that the French military authorities do not intend to complete the evacuation of their troops from Lebanon before 1 April 1947.

The presidents of Syria and Lebanon meet and resolve that, if the French refuse to budge, they will instruct their delegations to travel to New York to put their case to the Security Council at its next session on 21 March.

On 17 March, Franco-Lebanese negotiations are resumed in Paris, after Riad el-Solh manages to outwit the hardline Count Stanislas Ostrorog, secretary-general of the French *Délégation Générale* in Beirut. Ostrorog had come to Paris for the negotiations, but is sent back to Beirut by Foreign Minister Georges Bidault.

On 23 March, in an exchange of letters between Georges Bidault and Hamid Frangieh, the French agree to withdraw their troops by 31 December 1946.

On 28 March, the Emir 'Abdallah secures nominal independence from Britain and proclaims himself king of the Hashemite Kingdom of Transjordan (later Jordan). He then sets about promoting his long-held ambition of creating a 'Greater Syria' under his rule.

On 14 December, Riad el-Solh resumes the premiership.

On 21 December, Riad el-Solh makes his ministerial statement to the Lebanese parliament.

On 31 December, the last French soldier flies out of Beirut.

1946–1951: Riad el-Solh serves as prime minister from 14 December 1946 to 14 February 1951, a period of four years and two months.

1947: On 2 March, Antun Sa'ada, the charismatic founder of the *Parti populaire syrien,* returns to the Middle East from Latin America, and harangues a vast crowd of supporters.

On 5 March, Pierre Gemayel, leader of the *Phalanges libanaises,* denounces Sa'ada violently in his party newspaper.

On 13 March, Lebanon's public prosecutor issues a warrant for Sa'ada's arrest. But Sa'ada remains at large and defies the Lebanese police to arrest him.

Lebanese general elections take place in two rounds – on 25 May and 1 June. Out of a total of fifty-five seats, forty-seven are won by pro-government parties. The opposition accuses the government of falsifying the returns. Stung by accusations of electoral fraud, Riad el-Solh resigns, but President Bishara al-Khoury calls on him to form a new government.

On 20 June, the National Bloc in Syria suffers a blow with the death of Sa'dallah al-Jabiri, one of its most prominent members. The Bloc has, in the meantime, split into a National Party and a People's Party.

On 4 August, King 'Abdallah calls an 'All Syria Congress' in Amman – on the model of the General Syrian Congress of 1920 – to discuss his union plans. His ambitions arouse the hostility of other Arab leaders, especially President Shukri al-Quwatli of Syria.

In September, Britain announces that it is terminating the Palestine Mandate and will withdraw from the country by midnight on 14 May 1948.

On 29 November, the UN General Assembly, meeting in Paris, votes by a two-thirds majority to partition Palestine between Arabs and Jews. The Jews are awarded 50 per cent of the country, although they are only one-third of the population and legally own only 7 per cent of the land. The Jews are jubilant, the Arabs outraged.

In December, Jewish terrorists of the Stern Gang and the Irgun attack Arab quarters of Jerusalem, setting off a cycle of mutual violence.

1947–48: In late 1947 and early 1948, two Arab volunteer forces take shape – the Arab Liberation Army, commanded by Fawzi al-Qawuqji, and the Holy War Army, a private initiative of Hajj Amin al-Husayni, commanded by his cousin, 'Abd al-Qadir al-Husayni.

In the months between the UN Partition Plan vote of November 1947 and the end of the Palestine Mandate on 14 May 1948, Riad el-Solh makes repeated proposals to the British for an 'overall settlement'. But Britain fails to respond positively. Seen from London, an enfeebled Britain is leaving Palestine; the Zionists are to have their state; and the Arabs will have to make do with whatever they can hold on to.

1948: On 6 February, Lebanon's Foreign Minister Hamid Frangieh signs a monetary agreement in Paris. It provides for a French guarantee against the devaluation of the franc-holdings, which constitute the cover for the Lebanese currency. Syria refuses to sign a similar agreement, leading to the separation of the Syrian and Lebanese currencies, and to a serious breach between the two countries.

In March, commanders of twelve *Haganah* brigades are given lists of Palestinian villages, which they are ordered to burn to the ground and expel their inhabitants.

On 9 April, Irgun and Stern Gang terrorists massacre 245 Arab men, women and children at the village of Dayr Yassin.

On 9 April, forty-six deputies sign a petition in favour of amending the Constitution to allow Bishara al-Khoury to stand a second time. The amendment is adopted on 21 April, and on 27 May Khoury is re-elected.

On 17 April, UN Security Council Resolution 46 imposes a total embargo on arms deliveries to the Middle East. The Arabs are hard hit, while the Zionists continue to receive weapons clandestinely from the Soviet bloc and France.

On 9 May, the Arab League Political Committee meets in Damascus to draw up a plan for military operations. Riad el-Solh attempts to rally Arab leaders for war.

On 14 May, David Ben-Gurion proclaims the creation of the State of Israel in Tel Aviv.

On 15 May, the Egyptian army crosses the border into Palestine and reaches Isdud, 32 kilometres from Tel Aviv.

On 15 May, Jordan's Arab Legion enters Palestine, but does not cross the partition lines.

On 21 May, Iraqi forces enter the West Bank over the Allenby Bridge and reach Nablus, and Tulkarem on the 23rd.

On 29 May, the UN Security Council votes for a four-week ceasefire and instructs Count Folke Bernadotte to see to its implementation. But Israel continues to empty Arab villages, and kill or expel their inhabitants.

In May–June, the village of Malikiyya is fought over by Zionist and Lebanese forces, and changes hands several times.

In August, Riad el-Solh pays a visit to Amman to find out from King 'Abdallah why the Arab Legion has performed so poorly in the Palestine War. Did the British hold it back? Was Glubb Pasha to blame? Riad has no notion of the extent to which the Jordanian ruler has departed from the Arab consensus in his secret dealings with the Zionists. After his talks with the king, Riad el-Solh sends a gloomy memorandum, entitled 'The present state of the Arab world and its peoples', to the Iraqi Prime Minister Muzahim al-Pachachi, in which he appeals for an Iraqi intervention in the war. 'Allow me to say to you that the key to the situation is now in Iraq'.

On 17 September, Count Bernadotte is assassinated in Jerusalem by the Stern Gang.

1948–49: A series of operations by Israeli forces between October 1948 and March 1949 result in the overall defeat of the Arabs and the capture by Israel of much territory. Arab states are swamped by 750,000 Palestinian refugees. Arab opinion suffers a collapse of morale and a profound humiliation as a result of the defeat in Palestine.

1949: On 13 January, armistice talks open at Rhodes between Israel and Egypt. At armistice agreements concluded early in the year, Israel secures more than three-quarters of historical Palestine. Riad is forced to recognise the Arabs' catastrophic defeat.

On 30 March, Colonel Husni al-Za'im seizes power in Damascus, overthrowing the parliamentary regime of the veteran nationalists. President Quwatli is arrested in hospital. Za'im's coup spurs Sa'ada into thinking of seizing power in Lebanon. On a visit to Damascus, he discusses plans for a coup with Za'im.

On 21 April, Za'im pays a secret visit to King Farouk of Egypt and succumbs to the king's flattery.

On 23 April, the Lebanese government recognises Za'im's government, after a three-week hesitation.

On 24 April, Riad el-Solh, concealing his distaste at the brutal intrusion of the Syrian army in politics, travels to Damascus for a meeting with Colonel Za'im.

In mid-May, a Syrian army team crosses clandestinely into Lebanon and murders Kamil Husayn al-Yusuf, a Lebanese citizen of Syrian origin. Al-Yusuf is suspected of being an Israeli spy, who had allegedly given Za'im a large bribe from Zionist funds, when the latter was in command of the Syrian front in 1948.

On the night of 9–10 June, Phalangists and supporters of Anton Sa'ada clash in the Beirut suburb of Jummayza. The PPS printing works is set on fire. Large numbers of Sa'ada's party are arrested in the following days.

On the night of 2–3 July, armed PPS men attack Lebanese gendarmerie posts. By 7 July, some 900 members of the party have been arrested, allegedly for attempting to seize power by military coup, in order to carry out Sa'ada's Greater Syria project.

Za'im lures Sa'ada to the presidential palace in Damascus. He is overpowered and handed over to the Lebanese authorities, on condition that he be killed on the journey to Beirut.

Sa'ada is tried in camera before a Lebanese military court and, on 7 July, sentenced to death. He is executed at dawn the next day.

On 16 July, sixty-eight PPS members stand trial before a military court. Six are executed. Another 800 are in custody awaiting trial.

On 17 July, Riad el-Solh is received with full honours in Damascus.

On 14 August, four and half months after seizing power, Husni al-Za'im is himself overthrown by another Syrian army colonel, Sami al-Hinnawi. Za'im and his prime minister are shot.

On 27 December, in Syria, Colonel Adib al-Shishakli overthrows Colonel Sami al-Hinnawi and appoints Khalid al-'Azm prime minister.

1950: On 14 February, Khalid al-'Azm lays the cornerstone for the development of Syria's Mediterranean port of Latakia.

On 9 March, Riad el-Solh is the target of an assassination attempt in Beirut by a young member of the PPS.

On 13 March, Khalid al-'Azm dissolves the Syrian-Lebanese Customs Union.

In March, documents supplied by Lieutenant Colonel Abdallah al-Tal are published in the Egyptian press, exposing King 'Abdallah's secret cooperation with Israel. One document is allegedly the full text of a proposed peace treaty. Lebanon's Arabic-language newspapers join in a bitter campaign against the king.

On a visit to Cairo in March to attend the Arab League Political Committee, Riad el-Solh proposes a motion referring Jordan to the Committee for failing to attend the meeting. The Committee proposes to expel Jordan from the League, for its peace negotiations with Israel.

On a visit to Cairo in May for another meeting of the Arab League Political Committee, Riad makes a violent attack on King 'Abdallah. On the same visit, he tells a French diplomat that Syria will sink into anarchy if President Shukri al-Quwatli is not soon returned to power.

Riad el-Solh's prestige is eroded by his conflict with Bishara al-Khoury's younger brother, Salim al-Khoury, nicknamed the 'Sultan'.

1951: Riad's mother, Nazira Muftizada, dies in Beirut.

On 13 February, Riad el-Solh resigns as prime minister.

In May, on a visit to Beirut, King 'Abdallah expresses the wish to meet Riad el-Solh, but the latter declines. In a later telephone conversation, 'Abdallah urges Riad to come to Amman to discuss 'a very important matter'.

On 13 July, Riad el-Solh flies to Amman, accompanied by his doctor, a single bodyguard and two journalists.

On the afternoon of 16 July, after several sessions with King 'Abdallah, Riad sets off by car for the airport for his return flight to Beirut. His car is intercepted by three members of Antun Sa'ada's party, the *hizb al-qawmi al-suri*, and he is shot dead.

On 17 July, Riad's body is flown to Beirut for burial. Close to half a million people line the streets to pay tribute to him.

On 20 July, four days after Riad el-Solh's murder, King 'Abdallah is himself assassinated in Jerusalem, at the entrance to al-Aqsa mosque.

1952: On 16 July, the first anniversary of Riad el-Solh's death is commemorated in Beirut at a ceremony at the Mausoleum erected in his memory.

On 18 September, a general strike forces President Bishara al-Khoury from office. Camille Chamoun is elected president in his place.

1953: On 21 April, the Beirut Municipal Council erects a statue of Riad el-Solh in the city centre.

2007: Yosef Argaman's *The Shadow War* is published by Israel's Ministry of Defence. The author relates the testimony of an Israeli secret agent in Beirut, Ya'acov Cohen, who claims that he had orders to kill Riad el-Solh in 1949, because Israel judged him to be the most dangerous of the Arab leaders. This testimony raises the possibility that Israel had a hand in Riad's murder in 1951.

BIBLIOGRAPHY

Anouar Abd el-Malek, *Anthologie de la littérature arabe contemporaine*, 2 vols, Paris 1965, vol. II.

Ibrahim Abu Shakra, *al-Hajj Amin al-Husayni munthu wiladatihi hatta thawrat 1936*, Latakia 1998.

Feroz Ahmad, *The Young Turks*, Oxford 1969.

Adnan A. Aïta, *Le Conflit d'Alexandrette et la Société des Nations*, doctoral thesis no. 464, Law Faculty, University of Geneva, Damascus n.d.

Fouad Ajami, *The Vanished Imam: Musa al-Sadr and the Shia of Lebanon*, London 1986.

Maurice Albord, *L'Armée française et les états du Levant 1936–1946*, Paris 2000.

Denise Ammoun, *Histoire du Liban contemporain 1860–1943*, Paris 1997.

Meropi Anastassiadou, *Salonique, 1830–1912: Une ville ottomane à l'âge des réformes*, Leiden 1997.

A. M. Andrew and S. Kanya-Forstner, 'The French Colonial Party and French Colonial War Aims, 1914–1918', in *The Historical Journal*, 17(1) (1974), pp. 79–106.

George Antonius, *The Arab Awakening*, London, 1951.

Gérald Arboit, *Aux Sources de la politique arabe de la France: Le Second Empire au Machrek*, Paris 2000.

Yosef Argaman, *Milchemet Ha' Tzlalim: 25 parshiot modi'in uvitachon be-israel*, Tel Aviv 2007.

Arif al-Arif, II, *al-Nakba*, Beirut 1956.

Jean-Luc Arnaud, *Damas: Urbanisme et architecture, 1860–1925*, Paris 2006.

Al-Amir 'Adil Arslan, *Mudhakkarat al-amir 'Adil Arslan*, 3 vols, Beirut, 1983.

Ahmad Asfahani (ed.), *Antun Sa'ada wa'l hizb al-suri al-ijtima'i: fi 'awraq al-'amir Farid Chehab, al-mudir al-'amm lil 'amn al-'amm al-lubnani*, Beirut 2006.

Khaled al-'Azm, *Mudhakkarat*, 3 vols, Beirut 1973.

Uri Bar Joseph, *The Best of Enemies: Israel and Jordan in the War of 1948*, London 1987.

Dimitri Baramki, *Phoenicia and the Phoenicians*, Beirut 1961.

Muhammad Jamil Bayhum, *Lubnan baina mushriq wa mughrib, 1920–1969*, Beirut 1969.

David Ben-Gurion, *My Talks with Arab Leaders*, New York 1972.

Folke Bernadotte, *To Jerusalem*, London 1951.

Serge Bernstein, *Léon Blum*, Paris 2006.

Nicholas Bethell, *The Palestine Triangle*, London 1979.

Ahmad Beydoun, *Identité confessionelle et temps social chez les historiens libanais contemporains*, Beirut 1984.

    Le Liban, itinéraires dans une guerre incivile, Paris 1993.

    'Extrème méditerranée: Le libanisme contemporain à l'épreuve de la mer', in Elias Khoury and Ahmad Beydoun, *La Méditerranée libanaise*, Paris 2000.

    'Riad el-Solh et les élections législatives de 1943', in Gérard D. Khoury (ed.), *Sélim Takla, 1895–1945: Une contribution à l'indépendance du Liban*, Paris and Beirut 2004.

Edwin Black, *The Transfer Agreement. The Dramatic Story of the Pact between the Third Reich and Jewish Palestine*, New York 1984 (new edn Cambridge, MA 1999).

Fouad L. Boustany, *Introduction à l'histoire politique du Liban moderne*, Paris 1991.

Hamit Bozarslan, *Histoire de la Turquie contemporaine*, Paris 2004, 2007.

Marwan R. Buheiry (ed.), *Intellectual Life in the Arab East, 1890–1939*, Beirut 1981.

    Beirut's Role in the Political Economy of the French Mandate 1919–1939, Oxford n.d.

Sir Reader Bullard, *Britain and the Middle East: From Earliest Times to 1952*, London 1951.

S. Tufan Buzpinar, 'The Question of Citizenship of the Algerian Immigrants in Syria, 1847–1900', in Moshe Ma'oz *et al.* (eds), *Modern Syria: From Ottoman Rule to Pivotal Role in the Middle East*, Brighton 1999.

Ricky-Dale Calhoun, 'Arming David: The Haganah's Illegal Arms Procurement Network in the United States, 1945–49', in *Journal of Palestine Studies*, 36(4) (summer 2007), pp. 22–32.

Neil Caplan, *Futile Diplomacy*, 2 vols, *Early Arab-Zionist Negotiation Attempts 1913–1931*, London 1983–86, vol. I.

Gabriel Carbillet, *Au Djebel Druze*, Paris 1929.

Richard Casey, *Personal Experience, 1939–1946*, London 1962.

General Georges Catroux, *Dans la bataille de méditerranée*, Paris 1949.

    Deux Missions en Moyen-Orient, 1919–1922, Paris 1958.

Youssef Chaitani, *Post-Colonial Syria and Lebanon*, London 2007.

Tamara Chalabi, *The Shi'is of Jabal 'Amil and the New Lebanon: Community and Nation State, 1918–1943*, London 2006.

Joseph G. Chami, *The Book of Syria: Photos from Syrian Life*, Damascus 2005.

Dominique Chevalier, 'Lyon et la Syrie en 1919', *Revue historique*, 224(2) (1960), pp. 275–320.

    La Société du Mont Liban à l'époque de la Révolution Industrielle en Europe, Paris 1971.

Michel Chiha, *Le Liban d'aujourd'hui*, Beirut 1942.

Youssef M. Choueiri (ed.), *State and Society in Syria and Lebanon*, Exeter 1993.

William L. Cleveland, *Islam Against the West: Shakib Arslan and the Campaign for Islamic Nationalism*, London and Austin, TX 1985.

Vincent Cloarec, *La France et la question de Syrie, 1914–1918*, Paris 1988.

W. B. Cohen, 'The Colonial Policy of the Popular Front', in *French Historical Studies*, 7 (spring 1972).

Charles Corm, 'Méditations nationalistes', in *La Revue phénicienne*, no. 3 (September 1919). (The four numbers of *La Revue phénicienne* were reproduced in a single volume by Dar al-Nahar, Beirut 1996.)

George Corm, *Le Liban contemporain*, Paris 2005.

Jacques Couland, *Le Mouvement syndical au Liban 1919–1946*, Paris 1970.

Inès-Leila Dakhli, *Les Intellectuels syro-libanais dans la première moitié du XXe siècle (1908–1940)*, doctoral thesis, Université Aix-Marseille I 2003.

Raphael Danziger, *'Abd al-Qadir and the Algerians*, New York 1977.

Muhammad 'Izzat Darwaza, *Mudhakkarat*, 2 vols, Beirut 1993.

C. Ernest Dawn, *From Ottomanism to Arabism: Essays on the Origins of Arab Nationalism*, Chicago 1973.

General de Gaulle, *Mémoires de guerre: Le salut, 1944–1946*, Paris 1959.

Djemel Pasha (Jamal Pasha), *Memories of a Turkish Statesman, 1913–1919*, New York 1922.

Air Vice-Marshal A. G. Dudgeon, *Hidden Victory: The Battle of Habbaniya*, London 1941.

Carla Eddé, 'La Mobilisation "populaire" à Beyrouth à l'époque du Mandat: Le cas des boycotts des trams et de l'électricité', in Méouchy (ed.), *France, Syrie et Liban*.

Henri Eddé, *Le Liban d'où je viens*, Paris 1997.

William A. Eddy, *FDR Meets Ibn Saud*, New York 1954.

Laura Zittrain Eisenberg, *My Enemy's Enemy: Lebanon in Early Zionist Imagination 1900–1948*, Detroit 1994.

Marcel Emerit, 'La Crise syrienne et l'expansion économique française en 1860', in *Revue historique*, 207 (janvier–mars 1952), pp. 211–32.

John P. Entelis, *Pluralism and Party Transformation in Lebanon: al-Kata'ib 1936–1970*, Leiden 1974.

Bruno Etienne, *Abdelkader*, Paris 1994.

Muhammad 'Ali Farhat (ed.), *Ahl al-Solh*, Beirut 1891.

'Alal al-Fasi, *The Independence Movements in Arab North Africa*, trans. Hazem Zaki Nuseibeh, Washington, DC 1954.

Leila Tarazi Fawaz, *An Occasion for War: Civil Conflict in Lebanon and Damascus in 1860*, London 1994.

Kais Firro, *Inventing Lebanon: Nationalism and the State under the Mandate*, London 2003.

Antoine Fleury, 'Le Mouvement national arabe à Genève durant l'entre-deux-guerres', in *Relations internationales*, 19 (autumn 1979), pp. 329–54.

William Fortescue, *The Third Republic in France, 1870–1940*, London and New York 2000.

Pierre Fournié, 'Le Mandat à l'épreuve des passions françaises: L'affaire Sarrail (1925)', in Méouchy (ed.), *France, Syrie et Liban*.
　and Jean-Louis Riccioli, *La France et le Proche-Orient, 1916–1946*, Paris 1996.
Geoffrey Furlonge, *Palestine Is My Country: The Story of Musa Alami*, London 1969.
A. B. Gaunson, *The Anglo-French Clash in Lebanon and Syria 1940–45*, New York 1987.
Amine Gemayel, *Peace and Unity*, Gerrards Cross 1984.
Irene L. Gendzier, *Notes from the Minefield: United States Intervention in Lebanon and the Middle East, 1945–1958*, Oxford 1999.
François Georgeon, *Abdülhamid II*, Paris 2003.
Martin Gilbert, *Churchill and the Jews*, New York 2007.
Ahmad Qassem Goudah (ed.), *al-Makramiyyat*, Cairo n.d.
Basil C. Gounaris, 'Thessaloniki, 1830–1912: History, Economy and Society', in Henri Gouraud, *Mauritanie Adrar*, Paris 1945.
Yusuf al-Hakim, *Suriyya wal 'ahd al faysali*, Beirut 1966.
Hasan 'Ali Hallaq (ed.), *Mudhakkarat Salim 'Ali Salam 1868–1938*, Beirut 1982.
Taha al-Hashimi, *Mudhakkirat Taha al-Hashimi, 1942–1955*, 2 vols, Beirut 1978.
I. K. Hassiotis (ed.), *Thessaloniki: History and Culture*, Athens 1997.
Amer Bader Hassoun, *The Book of Syria: Photos from Syrian Life*, Damascus 2005.
Akram al-Hawrani, *Mudhakkarat Akram al-Hawrani*, Cairo 2000.
Joseph Heller, *The Stern Gang: Ideology, Politics and Terror, 1940–1949*, London 1995.
Werner Otto von Hentig, *Mein Leben. Ein Dienstreise*, Göttingen 1962.
David Hirst, *The Gun and the Olive Branch: The Roots of Violence in the Middle East*, London 1977 (rev. and expanded edn, New York 2003).
Philip K. Hitti, *The Origins of the Druze People and Religion, with Extracts from their Sacred Writings*, New York 1928.
　Lebanon in History, London 1957.
Frederic C. Hof, *Galilee Divided: The Israeli-Lebanon Frontier, 1916–1984*, Boulder, CO and London 1985.
　Beyond the Boundary: Lebanon, Israel and the Challenge of Change, Washington, DC 2000.
A. H. Hourani, *Syria and Lebanon: A Political Essay*, Oxford 1946.
　Minorities in the Arab World, London 1947.
Albert Hourani, *A Vision of History*, Beirut 1961.
　Arabic Thought in the Liberal Age, 1798–1939, Oxford 1962.
　'Lebanon from Feudalism to Modern State', in *Middle Eastern* Studies (April 1966), pp. 142–8.
　'Ideologies of the Mountain and the City', in Roger Owen (ed.), *Essays on the Crisis in Lebanon*, London 1976.
　The Emergence of the Modern Middle East, London 1981.
　'From Jabal 'Amil to Persia', in *Bulletin of the School of Oriental and African Studies*, 49 (1986), pp. 133–40.

A History of the Arab Peoples, London 1991.

Political Society in Lebanon: A Historical Introduction, Oxford 1986.

Philip S. Khoury and Mary C. Wilson (eds), *The Modern Middle East*, London 1993.

Michael C. Hudson, *The Precarious Republic: Political Modernization in Lebanon*, New York 1968.

Matthew Hughes, 'Lebanon and the 1948 War', in *Journal of Palestine Studies*, 34(2) (winter 2005), pp. 1–18.

J. C. Hurewitz, *The Struggle for Palestine*, New York 1950.

Diplomacy in the Near and Middle East, 2 vols, Princeton 1956, vol. II.

Amin al-Husayni, *Mudhakkarat al-hajj Amin al-Husayni*, Damascus 1999.

Sati al-Husri, *Yawm Maysalun*, Beirut 1964.

'Abd al-Rahman Mahmud al-Huss, *Riad el-Solh*, Beirut 1951.

P. Huvelin, *Que vaut la Syrie?* Paris 1921.

Zahida Darwiche Jabbour (ed.), *Les Villes cosmopolites arabes 1870–1930: Beyrouth, Alexandrie, Alep*, Beirut 2004.

M. Jaber, *Pouvoir et société au Jabal Amel de 1749 à 1920 dans la conscience des chroniques chiites et dans un essai d'interprétation*, Paris 1978.

Richard L. Jasse, 'Great Britain and Abdullah's Plan to Partition Palestine: A "Natural Sorting Out"', in *Middle Eastern Studies*, 22(4) (1986), pp. 505–21.

Basim al-Jisr, *Mithaq 1943, limadha kana wa limadha saqat?* Beirut 1978 (2nd edn 1997).

Michael Johnson, *Class and Client in Beirut: The Sunni Muslim Community and the Lebanese State, 1840–1985*, London 1986.

Jordanian White Paper, *al-Kitab al-urduni al-abyad: al-watha'iq al-qawmiyya fil wahda al-suriyya al-tabi'iyya*, Amman 1947.

M. Jouplain (alias for Bulus Nujaym), *La Question du Liban: Étude d'histoire diplomatique et de droit international*, Paris 1908 (2nd edn Lebanon 1961).

Rana Kabbani, *Imperial Fictions*, London 1986 (new edn London 2008).

Aykut Kansu, *Politics in Post-Revolutionary Turkey 1908–1913*, Leiden 2000.

Samir Kassir, *Histoire de Beyrouth*, Paris 2003.

Asher Kaufman, *Reviving Phoenicia: The Search for Identity in Lebanon*, London 2004.

Hasan Kayalı, *Arabs and Young Turks: Ottomanism, Arabism and Islamism in the Ottoman Empire, 1908–1913*, Berkeley 1997.

Ian Kershaw, *Fateful Choices: Ten Decisions that Changed the World, 1940–41*, London 2007.

Samir Khalaf, *Heart of Beirut: Reclaiming the Bourj*, London 2006.

Rashid Khalidi, "'Abd al-Ghani al-'Uraisi and *al-Mufid*: The Press and Arab Nationalism before 1914', in Buheiry (ed.), *Intellectual Life in the Arab East*.

'Ottomanism and Arabism', in Khalidi *et al.* (eds), *The Origins of Arab Nationalism*.

Lisa Anderson, Muhammad Muslih and Reeva S. Simon (eds), *The Origins of Arab Nationalism*, New York 1991.

Walid Khalidi, *From Haven to Conquest*, Beirut 1971.
  Conflict and Violence in Lebanon: Confrontation in the Middle East, Cambridge, MA 1979.
  (ed.), 'Selected Documents on the 1948 Palestine War', in *Journal of Palestine Studies*, 27(3) (1998), pp. 60–105.
  'Illegal Jewish Immigration to Palestine under the British Mandate', in *Journal of Palestine Studies*, issue 140, 35(4) (summer 2006), pp. 63–8.
Bishara al-Khoury, *Haqa'iq Lubnaniyya*, 3 vols, Beirut 1960.
Gérard D. Khoury, *La France et l'Orient arabe: Naissance du Liban moderne 1914–1920*, Paris 1993 (new edn 2009, with a preface by Henry Laurens).
  (ed.), *Sélim Takla, 1895–1945: Une contribution à l'indépendance du Liban*, Paris and Beirut 2004.
  Une Tutelle coloniale: Le mandat français en Syrie et au Liban. Écrits politiques de Robert de Caix, Paris 2006.
  (ed.), *États et sociétés de l'Orient arabe: En quête d'avenir (1945–2005)*, Paris 2007.
Philip S. Khoury, 'Factionalism Among Syrian Nationalists During the French Mandate', in *International Journal of Middle Eastern Studies*, 13 (1981), pp. 411–69.
  Syria and the French Mandate: The Politics of Arab Nationalism 1920–1945, London and Princeton 1987.
  'Syrian Urban Politics in Transition', in Hourani, Khoury and Wilson (eds), *The Modern Middle East*.
Faris al-Khuri, *Awraq Faris al-Khuri*, ed. Colette Khuri, 2 vols, Damascus 1989, 1997.
John King, ''Abd al-Qadir and Arab Nationalism', in John Spagnolo (ed.), *Problems of the Modern Middle East in Historical Perspective: Essays in Honour of Albert Hourani*, Reading 1992.
Sir Alec Kirkbride, *A Crackle of Thorns*, London 1956.
  From the Wings: Amman Memoirs, 1947–1951, London 1976.
Jean Lacouture, Ghassan Tuéni and Gérard D. Khoury, *Un Siècle pour rien: Le Moyen-Orient arabe de l'empire ottoman à l'empire américain*, Paris 2002.
Henri Lammens, *La Syrie: Précis historique*, 2 vols, Beirut 1921.
Joshua Landis, 'Syria in the 1948 Palestine War: Fighting King Abdallah's Greater Syria Plan', in Rogan and Shlaim (eds), *Rewriting the Palestine War*, pp. 178–205.
Henry Laurens, *L'Orient arabe: Arabisme et islamisme de 1798 à 1945*, Paris 1993.
  La Question de Palestine, 3 vols, vol. I, *1799–1922, L'Invention de la Terre Sainte*, vol. II, *1922–1947, Une Mission sacrée de civilisation*, vol. III, *1947–1967, L'Accomplissement des prophéties*, Paris 1999, 2002, 2007.
Hugh Leach, 'Lawrence's Strategy and Tactics in the Arab Revolt', in *Journal of the Royal Society for Asian Affairs*, 36(3) (November 2006), pp. 337–41.

Wm. Roger Lewis, *The British Empire in the Middle East, 1945–1951*, Oxford 1984.

Ends of British Imperialism: The Scramble for Empire, Suez and Decolonization. Collected Essays, London 2007.

Stephen Hemsley Longrigg, *Syria and Lebanon under French Mandate*, Oxford 1958.

Pierre-Jean Luizard, *La Vie de l'Ayatollah Mahdî al-Khâlisi*, Paris 2005.

Comment est né l'Irak moderne, Paris 2009.

Nasri Maalouf, 'Riad el-Solh doit être avec Béchara el-Khoury', in Khoury (ed.), *Sélim Takla*.

Callum A. MacDonald, 'Radio Bari, Italian Wireless Propaganda in the Middle East and British Countermeasures, 1934–38', in *Middle Eastern Studies*, 13(2) (1977), pp. 195–207.

Compton Mackenzie, *Eastern Epic*, London 1951.

A. Mahafzah, 'La France et le mouvement nationaliste arabe de 1914 à 1950', in *Relations internationales*, 19 (autumn 1979), pp. 295–312.

Ussama Makdisi, *The Culture of Sectarianism: Community, History, and Violence in Nineteenth-Century Ottoman Lebanon*, Berkeley 2000.

Chibli Mallat, *Shi'i Thought from the South of Lebanon*, Oxford 1988.

Neville Mandel, *The Arabs and Zionism before World War I*, Berkeley 1976.

Moshe Ma'oz, Joseph Ginat and Onn Winckler (eds), *Modern Syria: From Ottoman Rule to Pivotal Role in the Middle East*, Brighton 1999.

Farouk Mardam-Bey and Elias Sanbar, *Etre Arabe*, Paris 2001.

Salma Mardam Bey, *Syria's Quest for Independence 1939–1945*, Reading 1994.

John Marlowe, *The Seat of Pilate: An Account of the Palestine Mandate*, London 1959.

Louis Massignon, *Écrits mémorables: Textes établis, présentés et annotés sous la direction de Christian Jambet par François Angelier, François L'Yvonnet et Souad Ayada*, 2 vols, Paris 2009.

Philip Mattar, *The Mufti of Jerusalem: Al-Hajj Amin al-Husayni and the Palestine National Movement*, New York 1988.

Mark Mazower, *Salonica, City of Ghosts: Christians, Muslims and Jews*, London 2004.

Nadine Méouchy (ed.), *France, Syrie et Liban, 1918–1946: Les ambiguïtés et les dynamiques de la relation mandataire*, Damascus 2002.

'Le Pacte national 1943–1946: Les ambiguïtés d'un temps politique d'exception', in Khoury (ed.), *Sélim Takla*.

and Peter Sluglett, *The British and French Mandates in Comparative Perspectives*, Leiden 2004.

Franck Mermier, *Le Livre et la ville: Beyrouth et l'édition arabe*, Paris 2005.

Sabrina Mervin, *Un Réformisme chiite: Ulémas et lettrés du Jabal 'Amil de la fin de l'empire ottoman à l'indépendance du Liban*, Paris 2000.

Antoine Nasri Messarra, *Le Modèle politique libanais et sa survie*, Beirut 1983.

André Miquel, *L'Islam et sa civilisation*, Paris 1991.

Jean-David Mizrahi, 'La France et sa politique de mandat en Syrie et au Liban, 1920–1939,' in Méouchy (ed.), *France, Syrie et Liban*.

Andrew Mollo, *The Armed Forces of World War II*, London 1981.

Elizabeth Monroe, *Britain's Moment in the Middle East, 1914–71*, new rev. 2nd edn London 1981.

Marie-Renée Mouton, 'Le Congrès syro-palestinien de Genève (1921)', in *Relations internationales*, 19 (autumn 1979), pp. 313–28.

Muçafir, *Notes sur la Jeune Turquie*, Paris 1911.

Sa'id Murad, *al-Haraka al-wahdawiya fi lubnan bayn al-harbayn al-'alamiyatayn 1914–1946*, Beirut 1986.

Muhammad Muslih, 'The Rise of Local Nationalism in the Arab East', in Khalidi *et al.* (eds), *The Origins of Arab Nationalism*.

Sir Lewis Namier, *Vanished Supremacies*, London 1962.

Jacques Nantet, *Pierre Gemayel*, Paris 1986.

Albertos Nar, 'Social Organization and Activity of the Jewish Community in Thessaloniki', in Hassiotis (ed.), *Thessaloniki*.

Nasser-Eddin Nashashibi, *Jerusalem's Other Voices, Ragheb Nashashibi and Moderation in Palestinian Politics, 1920–1948*, Exeter 1990.

Maan Abu Nawar, *The Struggle for Independence, 1939–1947: A History of the Hashemite Kingdom of Jordan*, Reading 2001.

James Nicholson, 'The Hejaz Railway', in *Journal of the Society for Asian Affairs*, 37(3) (November 2006), pp. 320–36.

Francis R. Nicosia, *The Third Reich and the Palestine Question*, Austin, TX 1985.

W. Ochsenwald, *The Hijaz Railway*, Charlottesville, VA, 1980.

Irfan Orga, *Portrait of a Turkish Family*, London 1950.

Zuheir Osseiran, *Zuheir Osseiran yatazakar al-mu'amarat w'al inkilabat fi duna al-arab*, Beirut 1998.

Roger Owen (ed.), *Essays on the Crisis in Lebanon*, London 1976.

Ilan Pappé, *The Making of the Arab-Israeli Conflict, 1947–1951*, London 1994.

A *History of Modern Palestine: One Land, Two Peoples*, Cambridge 2004.

The Ethnic Cleansing of Palestine, Oxford 2006.

'The 1948 Ethnic Cleansing of Palestine', in *Journal of Palestine Studies*, issue 141, 36(1) (autumn 2006), pp. 6–20.

Laila Parsons, 'Soldiering for Arab Nationalism: Fawzi al-Qawuqji in Palestine', in *Journal of Palestine Studies*, issue 144, 36(4) (summer 2007), pp. 33–48.

Maurice Pearlman, *Mufti of Jerusalem: The Story of Haj Amin al-Husseini*, London 1947.

Elizabeth Picard, *Liban, état de discord: Des fondations aux guerres fratricides*, Paris 1988.

Lebanon: A Shattered Country, London 2002.

Nadine Picaudou, *La Déchirure libanaise*, Paris 1989.

La Décennie qui ébranla le Moyen-Orient 1914–1923, Paris 1992.

'La Question libanaise ou les ambiguïtés fondamentales', in Khoury (ed.), *Sélim Takla*.

Y. Porath, *The Emergence of the Palestinian-Arab National Movement, 1918–1929*, London 1974.

Michael Provence, 'An Investigation into the Local Origins of the Great Revolt', in Méouchy (ed.), *France, Syrie et Liban.*

The Great Syrian Revolt and the Rise of Arab Nationalism, Austin, TX 2005.

Khayriyya Qasimiyya, *al-Hukuma al-'Arabiyya fi Dimashq bayna 1918–1920*, Beirut 1971.

(ed.), *Filastin fi mudhakkarat al-Qawuqji*, Beirut 1975.

(ed.), *al-Ra'il al-'arabi al-awwal. Hayat wa awraq Nabih wa 'Adil al-'Azma*, London 1991.

Edmond Rabbath, *L'Evolution politique de la Syrie sous mandat*, Paris 1928.

La Formation historique du Liban politique et constitutionnel, Beirut 1973 (new edn 1986).

'L'Insurrection syrienne de 1925–1927', in *Revue historique* 267 (1982), pp. 405–47.

Itamar Rabinovich, *The Road not Taken: Early Arab-Israeli Negotiations*, Oxford 1991.

Rudolf Rahn, *Rubeloses Leben*, Düsseldorf 1949.

Sir William Mitchell Ramsay, *The Intermixture of Races in Asia Minor: Some of its Causes and Effects*, Proceedings of the British Academy, vol. 7, London 1917.

Andrew Rathmell, *Secret War in the Middle East: The Covert Struggle for Syria, 1949–1961*, London 1995.

André Raymond (ed.), *La Syrie d'aujourd'hui*, Paris 1980.

'La Syrie du royaume arabe à l'indépendance', in Raymond (ed.), *La Syrie d'aujourd'hui.*

Graham Robb, *The Discovery of France*, London 2007.

Eugene Rogan (ed.), *Village, Steppe and State*, London, 1994.

and Avi Shlaim (eds), *Rewriting the Palestine War: 1948 and the History of the Arab-Israeli Conflict*, Cambridge 2001.

Pierre Rondot, *Les Institutions politiques du Liban*, Paris 1947.

'L'Expérience du mandat français en Syrie et au Liban (1918–1945)', in *Revue de droit international public*, 3–4 (1948), pp. 387–409.

Aviel Roshwald, *Estranged Bedfellows: Britain and France in the Middle East during the Second World War*, Oxford 1990.

Stephen Roskill, *Hankey, Man of Secrets*, 3 vols, London 1972.

Antun Sa'ada, *Nushu' al-umam*, 1 vol., Beirut 1938.

Kitab al-Ta'alim al-suriyya al-qawmiyya al-ijtima'iyya, 4th edn Beirut 1947.

The Principles of the Syrian Social Nationalist Party by The Leader, n.p. n.d.

Muhammad Jaber Safa, *Ta'rikh Jabal 'Amil*, Beirut n.d.

Nuri al-Sa'id, *Istiqlal al-'Arab wa wahdatahum*, Baghdad 1943.

Nawaf Salam, *La Condition libanaise: Communautés, citoyen, état*, Beirut 1998.

(ed.), *Options for Lebanon*, London 2004.

Salim 'Ali Salam, *Mudhakkarat, 1868–1938*, Beirut 1982.

Yusuf Salem, *Khamsun sana ma' al-nas*, 2nd edn Beirut 1998.

Kamal S. Salibi, *The Modern History of Lebanon*, London 1965.
'The Lebanese Identity', in *The Journal of Contemporary History*, 6(1) (1971), pp. 76–86.
Beirut under the Young Turks as Depicted in the Political Memoirs of Salim Ali Salam, Beirut 1974.
A House of Many Mansions: The History of Lebanon Reconsidered, London 1988.
Lebanon and the Middle Eastern Question, Oxford 1988.
Elias Sanbar, *Figures du Palestinien*, Paris 2004.
General M. Sarrail, *Mon Commandement en Orient, 1916–1918*, Paris 1920.
Yusuf al-Sawda, *Fi Sabil al-Istiqlal*, Beirut 1967.
Yazid Sayigh, *Armed Struggle and the Search of State: The Palestine National Movement, 1949–1993*, Oxford 1997.
Linda Schatkowski-Schilcher, *Families in Politics: Damascus Factions and Estates of the 18th and 19th Centuries*, Stuttgart 1985.
Marius Schattner, *Histoire de la droite israélienne de Jabotinsky à Shamir*, Brussels 1991.
Joseph Schechtman, *The Mufti and the Führer: The Rise and Fall of Haj Amin al-Husseini*, New York 1965.
Kirsten E. Schulze, *Israel's Covert Diplomacy in Lebanon*, London 1998.
Patrick Seale, *The Struggle for Syria: A Study of Post-War Arab Politics 1945–1958*, Oxford 1965 (new edn London and Yale 1986).
Asad of Syria: The Struggle for the Middle East, Berkeley 1989.
Jacques Séguin, *Le Liban Sud: Espace périphérique, espace convoité*, Paris 1989.
Philippe Séguin, *Louis Napoléon le Grand*, Paris 1990.
Samir Seikaly, 'Damascene Intellectual Life in the Opening Years of the 20th Century: Muhammad Kurd 'Ali and the Muqtabas', in Buheiry (ed.), *Intellectual Life in the Arab East*.
'Shukri al-'Asali: A Case Study of a Political Activist', in Khalidi *et al.* (eds), *The Origins of Arab Nationalism*.
Avraham Sela, 'Transjordan, Israel and the 1948 War: Myth, Historiography and Reality', in *Middle Eastern Studies*, 28(4) (1992), pp. 623–88.
Noureddine Séoudi, *La Formation de l'Orient arabe contemporain 1916–1939: Au miroir de la Revue des Deux Mondes*, Paris 2004.
Robert Wilson Seton-Watson, *The Rise of Nationality in the Balkans*, London 1917.
'Abd al-Rahman al-Shahbandar, *al-Thawra al-wataniyya*, Damascus 1933.
Fatima Qaddura al-Shami (ed.), *'Arif Bek al-Na'mani, watha'iq hawla al-'alaqat al-lubnaniyya al-suriyya al-firansiyya*, Beirut 1999.
Sadiq al-Shari', *Hurubna ma'a Isra'il*, Amman 1997.
James Vincent Sheean, *Personal History*, New York 1935.
Avi Shlaim, 'Husni Za'im and the Plan to Resettle Palestinian Refugees', in *Journal of Palestine Studies*, 15(4) (1986), pp. 68–80.
Collusion Across the Jordan: King Abdallah, the Zionist Movement, and the Partition of Palestine, Oxford 1988.

The Politics of Partition: King Abdullah, the Zionists and Palestine 1921–1951, Oxford 1990.

The Iron Wall: Israel and the Arab World, London 2000.

Elizabeth Sirriyeh, *Sufi Visionary of Ottoman Damascus: 'Abd al-Ghani al-Nabulsi, 1641–1731*, London 2005.

Peter Sluglett, 'Will the Real Nationalists Stand up? The Political Activities of the Notables of Aleppo, 1918–1946', in Méouchy (ed.), *France, Syrie et Liban*.

Britain in Iraq: Contriving King and Country, New York 2007.

Adil el-Solh, *Sutur min al-risala: tarikh haraka istiqlaliyya qamat fi al-mashriq al-'arabi sanat 1877*, Beirut 1966.

Alia el-Solh, *'Indama dakhalu al-tarikh*, Beirut 1959.

Hilal el-Solh, *Tarikh rajul wa qadiyya 1894–1951*, Beirut 1994.

Raghid el-Solh, *Lebanon and Arabism: National Identity and State Formation*, London 2004.

'Sélim Takla et la création de la Ligue arabe', in Khoury (ed.), *Sélim Takla*.

Sami el-Solh, *Ahtakimu ila al-tarikh*, Beirut 1970.

Lubnan, al-'abath al-siasi wa'l-masir al-majhul, Beirut 2000.

Major-General Sir Edward Spears, *Assignment to Catastrophe: The Fall of France, June 1940*, Melbourne 1954.

Fulfilment of a Mission: Syria and Lebanon 1941–1944, London 1977.

Michael W. Suleiman, *Political Parties in Lebanon: The Challenge of a Fragmented Political Culture*, New York 1967.

Christopher Sykes, *Crossroads to Israel*, London 1965.

Ahmad Tarabein, 'Abd al-Hamid al-Zahrawi: The Career and Thought of an Arab Nationalist', in Khalidi *et al.* (eds), *The Origins of Arab Nationalism*.

Mohammad A. Tarbush, *The Role of the Military in Politics: A Case Study of Iraq to 1941*, London 1982.

Eliezer Tauber, *The Formation of Modern Syria and Lebanon*, London 1995.

Shabtai Teveth, *Ben Gurion and the Palestinian Arabs*, Oxford 1985.

Igor Timofeev, *Kamal Joumblatt et le destin tragique du Liban*, Beirut 2000.

Fawwaz Trabulsi, *A History of Modern Lebanon*, London 2007.

Charles Tripp, *A History of Iraq*, Cambridge 2000.

Ghassan Tuéni, *Une Guerre pour les autres*, Paris 1985 (3rd edn 2006).

(ed.), *Le Livre de l'indépendance*, Beirut 2002.

and Farès Sassine (eds), *El Bourj: Place de la Liberté et Porte du Levant*, 3rd edn Beirut 2003.

Henri de Wailly, *Syrie 1941: La guerre ocultée, Vichystes contre Gaullistes*, Paris 2006.

Keith David Waterpaugh, *Being Modern in the Middle East: Revolution, Nationalism, Colonialism and the Arab Middle Class*, Princeton 2006.

N. Weinstock, *Le Sionisme contre Israel*, Paris 1969.

Maxime Weygand, *Mémoires*, 3 vols, *Rappelé au Service*, vol. III Paris 1950.

Ann Williams, *Britain and France in the Middle East and North Africa 1914–1967*, London 1968.

E. L. Woodward and Roham Butler (eds), *Documents on British Foreign Policy, 1919–39*, series 1, vol. 4, London 1952.

Labib Zuwiya Yamak, *The Syrian Social Nationalist Party: An Ideological Analysis*, Cambridge 1966.

Yusuf Yazbek, *Awraq Lubnaniyya*, 3 vols, Beirut, 1955, 1956, 1957.

Meir Zamir, 'Emile Eddé and the Territorial Integrity of Lebanon', in *Middle Eastern Studies* 14(2) (May 1978), pp. 232–5.

The Formation of Modern Lebanon, New York, 1988.

Lebanon's Quest: The Road to Statehood 1926–1939, London 1997.

'An Intimate Alliance: The Joint Struggle of General Edward Spears and Riad al-Sulh to Oust France from Lebanon, 1942–1944', in *Middle Eastern Studies*, 41(6) (November 2005), pp. 811–32.

'Ali Zayn, *Min awraqi*, Beirut n.d.

Zeine N. Zeine, *Arab-Turkish Relations and the Emergence of Arab Nationalism*, Beirut 1958.

The Emergence of Arab Nationalism, Beirut 1966.

Nicolas Ziadé, 'Beyrouth, des années soixante du XIXe siècle à 1908', in Jabbour (ed.), *Les Villes cosmopolites arabes*.

Hanna Ziadeh, *Sectarianism and Intercommunal Nation-Building in Lebanon*, London 2006.

Eyal Zisser, *Lebanon: The Challenge of Independence*, London 2000.

Erik J. Zurcher, *Turkey: A Modern History*, London 1993.

INDEX

Bold page numbers refer to maps and photographs